PUCCINI

Series edited by Stanley Sadie

THE MASTER MUSICIANS

Titles Available in Paperback

Berlioz · Hugh Macdonald

Brahms · Malcolm MacDonald

Britten · Michael Kennedy

Bruckner · Derek Watson

Chopin · Jim Samson

Grieg · John Horton

Handel · Donald Burrows

Liszt · Derek Watson

Mahler · Michael Kennedy

Mendelssohn · Philip Radcliffe

Monteverdi · Denis Arnold

Purcell · J. A. Westrup

Rachmaninoff · Geoffrey Norris

Schoenberg · Malcolm McDonald

Schubert · John Reed

Sibelius · Robert Layton

Richard Strauss · Michael Kennedy

Tchaikovsky · Edward Garden

Vaughan Williams · James Day

Verdi · Julian Budden

Vivaldi · Michael Talbot

Titles Available in Hardcover

Bach · Malcolm Boyd

Beethoven · Barry Cooper

Chopin · Jim Samson

Elgar · Robert Anderson

Handel · Donald Burrows

Musorgsky · David Brown

Puccini · Julian Budden

Schumann · Eric Frederick Jensen

Schütz · Basil Smallman

Richard Strauss · Michael Kennedy

Stravinsky · Paul Griffiths

Titles in Preparation

Bartók · Malcolm Gillies

Dvořák · Jan Smaczny

Tchaikovsky · R. John Wiley

THE MASTER MUSICIANS

PUCCINI

His Life and Works

Julian Budden

OXFORD

UNIVERSITY PRESS

2 0 0 2

OXFORD

UNIVERSITY PRESS

Oxford   New York
Auckland   Bangkok   Buenos Aires
Cape Town   Chennai   Dar es Salaam   Delhi   Hong Kong   Istanbul
Karachi   Kolkata   Kuala Lumpur   Madrid   Melbourne   Mexico City   Mumbai
Nairobi   São Paulo   Singapore   Shanghai   Taipei   Tokyo   Toronto

Library of Congress Cataloging-in-Publication Data
Budden, Julian.
Puccini / Julian Budden.
p. cm. — (The master musicians)
"List of Works" : p.
Includes bibliographical references (p.) and index.
ISBN 0-19-816468-8
1. Puccini, Giacomo, 1858–1924.
2. Composers—Italian—Biography.
I. Title.
II. Master musicians series.
ML410.P89 B83 2002
782.1'092—dc21   [B]   2002020155

Series designed by Carla Bolte

1 3 5 7 9 8 6 4 2

Printed in the United States of America
on acid-free paper

Contents

Preface

I HAS TAKEN MORE THAN A HUNDRED YEARS FOR PUCCINI TO BE admitted to the ranks of the Master Musicians Series. At the time of the series's foundation the English musical establishment held opera at a discount (had not Sir Hubert Parry declared that lovers of the genre possessed the lowest taste of all those who considered themselves musical?). Therefore inclusion was limited to opera composers who had distinguished themselves in other fields, Wagner alone, as the self-proclaimed heir of Beethoven, being excepted; hence the belated recognition of Verdi, Bellini, and, most notably, Rossini.

A milestone in the revaluation of Puccini was Mosco Carner's classic study *Puccini: A Critical Biography* (1958, 3rd edition 1993.) High on the list of its successors stand William Ashbrook's *The Operas of Puccini* (1968, reprinted 1985); Dieter Schickling's meticulously researched *Giacomo Puccini: Biographie* (1989), which, as well as bringing fresh information to light, corrects numerous errors and assumptions to be found in earlier biographies of the composer, due partly to the unreliable memories of those who knew him, partly to his frequent failure to date his letters; and Michele Girardi's detailed and penetrating *Giacomo Puccini: l'arte internazionale di un musicista italiano* (1995, Eng. 2000). To these must be added the publications of the Istituto di Studi Pucciniani, directed by the composer's granddaughter Dr Simonetta Puccini, and of the recently founded Centro Studi Giacomo Puccini, Lucca, to say nothing of various articles by distinguished scholars in the standard periodicals, many of which have furnished material for the present overview.

In discussing the operas I have opted for a narrative technique as the simplest way of illustrating Puccini's way of adapting his musical ideas to the needs of the drama in hand. I have also dwelt briefly on a number of the subjects which occupied him for some time before being laid aside, since they can often be shown to have had a bearing on the works that he completed. In this way I hope to fill out the picture of a composer whose music has spoken directly to the public since the day it was written, and does so still.

Acknowledgments

For help in preparing this book my thanks go to Gabriele Dotto, who granted me unlimited access to the archives of that Casa Ricordi; to Mrs Teresa Melen for permitting me to consult the autographs of Puccini's letters to her grandmother, Sybil Seligman, still available only in the English translation made by her own father, Vincent Seligman; to various Puccini scholars, such as Debra Burton-Wrobel, Helen Greenwald, and Roger Parker, and to my colleagues at the Centro Studi Giacomo Puccini, Lucca, especially Gabriella Biagi Ravenni for her tireless assistance and encouragement; Dieter Schickling, for directing me to unexplored regions of the composer's life and works; and Michele Girardi, whose insights into the music of Puccini and its relation to that of his contemporaries provided me with a wealth of ideas, and do still.

Julian Budden
Florence and London, 2002

Key to Sigla

ARP   G. Adami: *Il romanzo della vita di Giacomo Puccini* (Milan, 1944)

BPP   *Biblioteca Passerini Landi, Piacenza*

CP   E. Gara (ed.): *Carteggi pucciniani*

FPL   *Fondazione Puccini, Lucca*

FGP   A. Fraccaroli: *La vita di Giacomo Puccini* (Milan, 1925)

GGP   M. Girardi: *Giacomo Puccini: l'arte internazionale di un musicista italiano* (Venice, 1995)

GPE   G. Puccini: *Epistolario,* ed. G. Adami (Milan, 1928)

MP   G. R. Marek: *Puccini* (New York, 1951; London, 1952)

MPI   G. Marotti and F. Pagni: *Giacomo Puccini intimo* (Florence, 1926, repr. 1942)

PAF   V. Seligman: *Puccini among Friends* (London, 1938)

PCB   M. Carner: *Puccini: A Critical Biography* (London, 3rd ed. 1992)

PCE   A. Marchetti: *Puccini com'era* (Milan, 1973)

PGP   C. Paladini: *Giacomo Puccini* (Florence, 1961)

PLI   G. Pintorno (ed.): *Puccini: 276 lettere inedite* (Montecatini, 1974)

PRS   S. Puccini (ed.): *Giacomo Puccini: lettere a Riccardo Schnabl* (Milan, 1981)

QP   S. Puccini (ed.): *Quaderni pucciniani* (Milan, 1982–)

SGP   D. Schickling: *Giacomo Puccini: Biographie* (Stuttgart, 1989)

CHAPTER 1

Early Life at Lucca

'AND YOU, MY BELOVED BROTHERS, WHOSE HEARTS RESPOND to the call of Christian charity, would do well to spare a thought for a mother, now in her eighties, for a bereaved and lonely widow, for *six daughters* of tender years, for a *young lad*, sole survivor and inheritor of the art of harmony which his forebears so abundantly reaped, and which he will one day be able to revive.'[1] With these words Giovanni Pacini, together with Mercadante one of the two foremost living composers of his generation, wound up his funeral oration on Michele Puccini, organist of Lucca Cathedral and director of the city's musical institute, on 18 February 1864. His injunction was duly heeded. Not only was Albina Puccini accorded a modest pension, sufficient to provide for a young family that would soon be increased by another son; the functions performed by the deceased were transferred to her brother, Fortunato Magi, until such time as 'Signor Giacomo' should be able to discharge them himself. Born on 22 December 1858, Signor Giacomo was just over five years old.

Musical dynasties, common enough in the seventeenth and eighteenth centuries, were exceptional in the nineteenth. That the system should have survived at Lucca is mainly due to the city's unusual position and circumstances. Situated on the banks of the Serchio, where the river debouches from the Apuan Alps into a broad, fertile plain

---

[1] G. Pacini: *Discorso in Morte di Michele Puccini* (Lucca, 1865), 9–10.

before threading its way through wooded hills to the sea at Viareggio, it first emerged as a Roman fort, the remains of which can be seen to this day. During the Middle Ages 'The Most Serene Republic of Lucca' disputed the hegemony of Tuscany with Pisa and Florence; and though it eventually lost ground to its rivals, it continued to thrive as an industrial city, internationally famous for its silks and textiles. The massive ramparts, constructed in the late sixteenth century and never breached in anger, helped to keep the local institutions free from outside contagion.

For centuries Lucca had boasted a strong tradition of sacred music. Of the many fine romanesque churches that throng its labyrinthine network of narrow streets, several possessed their own seminary of voices and instruments: the Metropolitan San Martino, graced from 1467 to 1486 by the presence as musical instructor ('magisculus') of the Carmelite monk John Hothby; San Michele al Foro, massive in white marble; San Frediano with its spectacular west-front mosaic. During the eighteenth century Lucca gave to the world two composers of note: Francesco Geminiani and Luigi Boccherini, both born into the profession. But from 1739 the overwhelming presence was that of the Puccini family. That year Giacomo (1712–81), the first of the line, came from the mountain village of Celle to be appointed organist of San Martino and director of the municipal Cappella Palatina. As a youth he had studied at Bologna with the famous Padre Martini, with whom he kept up a life-long correspondence. His son Antonio (1747–1832), grandson Domenico (1772–1815), and great-grandson Michele (1813–64) likewise matriculated at Bologna, the last two continuing their studies at Naples. Among them Domenico achieved more than local fame. His opera *Quinto Fabio* was performed to general acclaim in Livorno in 1810 with Maria Marcolini, Rossini's first Tancredi, in the title role, and as late as 1850 his portrait appeared in an album published by Breitkopf & Härtel alongside those of Bach, Handel, and Beethoven. But the hopes expressed by the *Corriere mediterraneo* that he would assume the mantle of Cimarosa were dashed by his sudden death at 42—from poison, some said, due to his liberal politics. His son Michele devoted himself mainly to church music. If his compositions lack the creative spark, he was sufficiently eminent as a teacher to rate a mention in Arthur Pougin's supplement to Fétis's *Biographie universelle des musiciens* (1865).

In 1849 the republic of Lucca, a duchy since the Napoleonic wars successively under French and Austrian suzerainty, became absorbed into the state of Tuscany. In the meantime its musical institutions had suffered a certain decline. Gone since 1799 were the triennial Feste delle Tasche, held during the local elections, with their orgy of pageant-like oratorios. In 1842 the various music schools were amalgamated into the present Institute, housed in an ancient monastery in the Via Elisa under the directorship of Giovanni Pacini. Composer of some 90 operas, friend and one-time colleague of Rossini, detested by Bellini and held in low esteem by Verdi, Pacini had settled at nearby Pescia, whence he exercised a powerful influence on musical education in the region. In the years that followed he handed over more and more of his teaching to Michele Puccini, who in 1862 became the institute's official director. Like all such establishments it was funded by the municipality, as was the Cappella Comunale, successor to the Cappella Palatina, which played for the more important yearly functions and whose members gave six concerts a year as the Società Orchestrale Boccherini directed by the city's leading violin teacher, Augusto Michelangeli. In 1867 Pacini died, leaving his name to the institute that he had brought into being.

Inevitably the city's cultural life was overshadowed by that of Florence, temporary capital of the new united Italy during the late 1860s. Yet, considering the size of the population, it remained remarkably rich. The principal events of the year, including the schools' prize-giving, were grouped round the Festa della Santa Croce, held on 14 September, on the eve of which a wooden crucifix of medieval origin is still carried in a solemn procession headed by the bishop from the cathedral to the church of San Frediano, to be returned the following day. Services covering a period of some ten days required the composition of two sets of vespers, a mass and a 'grand motet' (*motettone*) for soloists, double choir, and double orchestra. Not only were 'sopranisti' hired from the Sistine Chapel; the annual opera season at the Teatro del Giglio was planned to coincide with the festivities, so that the guest artists could take part in it. During the 1830s and 40s under the tolerant régime of

Duke Carlo Ludovico, the disorder of whose private life was matched only by his munificence towards the arts, Lucca's municipal theatre had enjoyed a period of genuine glory. Its seasons were managed by 'the Napoleon of impresarios', Alessandro Lanari, and visiting stars included Maria Malibran. But the Tuscan annexation had put an end to all that: no more novelties, merely an unremitting diet of stale repertory fare. Two operas a year were the rule. However, a further two were usually mounted during Carnival time at the Teatro Pantera, run by an association of the local nobility; while the Teatro Goldoni, founded for the performance of spoken drama, would often start its post-Easter season with a couple of comic operas or operettas. In no case did expenses run to the engagement of front-rank singers. The orchestra was, of course, recruited locally, with results that left much to be desired. A performance in 1877 of *Guglielmo Tell* moved a critic to remark that the opera was unrecognizable as Rossini's. Puccini's claim, as reported by most of his biographers, to have seen his first opera at Pisa in 1876 is refuted by a recently discovered letter in which he recalls having admired Mercadante's *La Vestale* 'while a student in Lucca'[2] (it was given at the Pantera in 1874); but the Pisan *Aida* may well have been the first opera that he saw decently mounted and performed.

It was quite otherwise with spoken drama. Here, it seems, Lucca enjoyed a certain pre-eminence in the peninsula with a constant succession of touring companies under an actor-manager of distinction. The fare ranged from Goldoni and Alfieri to the latest offerings of Dumas (*père et fils*), Octave Feuillet, and Sardou, not to mention Dal Testa and Giacosa. In 1876 we hear of a 'seconda donna' who in Ludovico Muratore's *Virginia* was 'more and more applauded, and deservedly, because she combines charm and elegance with beauty of expression and a fine stage presence'.[3] Her name was Eleonora Duse. All this must surely have contributed to Puccini's theatrical flair, his extraordinary ability to conceive his music in terms of realistic action and gesture and even to envisage the operatic possibilities of a play when performed in a language of which he understood not a word.

[2] Letter to Avv. G. De Napoli, 9 April 1910, in the possession of the Associazione Civica S. Mercadante, Altamura.

[3] *La Provincia di Lucca*, 13 March 1876.

At the time of Michele's death in 1864 the family were housed in the Via del Poggio, near the church of San Michele. Albina, eighteen years younger than her husband, was a capable manager, able to keep up their middle-class status with two servants, and moreover a woman of rare determination. Not that the infant Giacomo showed much aptitude for the role that she hoped would one day be thrust upon him. By all accounts, including his own, he was an idle young scamp, the despair of his uncle, Fortunato Magi, who was training him as a chorister and giving him elementary lessons on the keyboard. Whenever he sang out of tune Magi would kick him sharply on the shin, with the result that for the rest of his life Puccini was unable to hear a lapse of pitch without imaginary twinges of pain. Fortunately for him, Magi resigned his position at the Istituto Pacini in 1872 after a fierce dispute with the local authorities and moved to Sarzana to take up a similar post. A gifted composer with a fine orchestral imagination, an efficient conductor, and a first class teacher, much respected by his pupils, Magi had an uncommon talent for making enemies; hence, it would seem, successive moves from Sarzana to Ferrara, La Spezia, and finally Venice, as director of the Liceo Musicale Benedetto Marcello (where his pupils included Alberto Franchetti, soon to be numbered among the leading lights of his generation). But Magi's character seems not to have softened. A laudatory review of his direction of Massenet's *Le roi de Lehore* in 1879 contains dark references to 'the envious, the impotent and the malevolent', which tell their own story. He died in 1882 aged 43, not, however, before relenting towards his nephew sufficiently to provide him with a testimonial for the Milan Conservatory.

As a schoolboy Giacomo was first admitted to the church seminary of San Michele, from which he passed at the age of eight to that of the cathedral, as befitted one destined for an organist's career. Unfortunately for him, the seminary's musical traditions had been recently curtailed by the archbishop in favour of an austere, almost medieval scholasticism. No wonder that the boy proved a recalcitrant learner: 'He comes into class', ran one of his reports, 'merely to wear out the seat of his trousers. He pays not the slightest attention to anything, and continually pretends to play on his desk as though it were a piano. He never reads.'[4] He

---

[4] From D. Del Fiorentino: *Immortal Bohemian*, 9–10.

took five years instead of the usual four to scrape through the curriculum, impeded by a deep antipathy to mathematics—a trait later to be held against him by his musical detractors. His general schooling finished in 1874, he became a full-time student at the Istituto Pacini, whose junior classes he had frequented for the past two years. By now the desk-drumming fingers had acquired sufficient skill for him to deputize as organist at various parishes in the neighbourhood, notably the summer resort of Mutigliano, where he would scandalize the faithful by weaving operatic hits into his voluntaries. He played the piano for popular entertainments at the Café Caselli in Lucca's main street, the Via Filungo, and also, it is rumoured, like the young Brahms, in less reputable establishments. It was in 1874 that he took on a pupil, Carlo Della Nina, a tailor's son from the nearby village of Porcari. The tuition, which lasted four years, was unlikely to have been systematic; for teaching was no more Puccini's métier than it was Verdi's. But it allowed him to provide the lad with voluntaries that he could pass off as his own. Less to his credit is the story, confirmed by Puccini himself, of his banding together with some friends to filch pipes from the decrepit organ of the Benedictine Sisters in order to buy Tuscan cigars. Clearly, the smoking habit that persisted throughout his life had been contracted early.

Since his departure from Lucca, Magi's functions at the Istituto Pacini had been divided between two of his colleagues. Carlo Marsili succeeded him as director, while Carlo Angeloni took over his harmony and counterpoint classes, so becoming Puccini's first teacher of composition. Five years older than Magi and, like him, a pupil of Michele Puccini, Angeloni was a far less colourful figure, whether as man or musician. Two of his operas had been given with some success at the Teatro Pantera; but there is no hint of the theatrical in his sacred works, which are at least respectable. The counterpoint is strict and unadventurous, the melodic writing bland with chromatic touches, much in the style of Teodulo Mabellini, organist of Florence Cathedral and presiding genius of the region, who frequently came to Lucca to direct his own masses. The honours heaped upon Angeloni after his death in 1901 prompted a few caustic comments from the Puccini family about the city that had failed to erect an adequate monument to Boccherini. But there is no reason to doubt Giacomo's sincerity when he wrote to Toscanini urging him to perform a *Stabat mater* by his old teacher at the Paris International Exhibition of 1898 ('Believe me, Angeloni is a truly and thoroughly distinguished composer of church music.')[5] Certainly he proved a congenial professor, under whom Giacomo made steady progress. Already in his first year Puccini's name appeared among the various prize-winners of the institute—below, however, that of his friend and fellow-pupil Carlo Carignani, for whom an outstanding career as a pianist was confidently predicted (in fact he would be remembered merely as the arranger of Puccini's vocal scores). A document of 1875 attests that 'over the past year Signor Puccini Giacomo has distinguished himself in the organ school and is thus genuinely worthy of the Primo Premio Lucca del Palazzo Comunale on this day of September'.[6]

So far nothing of the future composer. Yet it is to this year that his earliest known composition has been ascribed: a song for mezzo-soprano and piano to an anonymous love poem entitled 'A te'. Clearly a student work, Puccini thought sufficiently well of it to present the autograph to the institute in 1901. Three distinct melodic ideas couched in the faintly cloying idiom of Angeloni bear witness to a certain fluency of invention: a plain 16-bar period by way of piano introduction; a long vocal paragraph in ternary design; and a lighter concluding section (*più mosso*), which features a progress from subdominant start to tonic close. In a short coda the accompaniment changes from chordal pulsations to tremolando, bringing an increase of tension. The operatic composer *in posse*? It is a little early to say. It was the following year that saw the event, already alluded to, which turned Puccini's thoughts in that direction. For the Quaresima season of 1876 the Teatro Nuovo, Pisa, decided to mount an 'opera mostro' in the grand style. The choice lay between Meyerbeer's *Gli Ugonotti* and Verdi's *Aida* and finally fell on the latter. The management of the newly opened railway from Lucca announced a special train to carry ticket-holders to the theatre and another at two o'clock in the morning to take them home. The first of these was cancelled after the opening night; but Puccini was not to be baulked of his attendance. Together with Carignani and another friend, the painter and sculptor Zizzania, he made the nineteen-mile

[5] CP 181, p. 158.
[6] G. Musco: *Musica e teatro di Giacomo Puccini*, i, 42.

journey by way of Monte Pisano on foot. The evening's experience proved decisive for his career. From then on, he later told his friends, his sights were firmly set on the theatre. Many years would pass, however, before the seed sown by *Aida* would have a chance to ripen. Meanwhile we may note a few months later the completion of Puccini's first composition to which a definite date can be assigned: a *Preludio a orchestra* inscribed by him 'August 8 1876', and possibly intended for the annual September concert of works by students of the institute, though there is no record of its having been performed there or anywhere else. The autograph, recently presented by a private owner to the Comune di Lucca (missing, however, a single page) shows a fairly short piece based on the polarity of two ideas in E minor and major, respectively: the first a murmur of tremolando strings with woodwind embroidery, shifting in its tonality, the second a periodic theme, wide-spanned and assertive. The concluding measures offer two features of marginal interest: a couple of bars of 4/4 within the prevailing triple pulse, foreshadowing that flexibility of rhythm that will characterize the mature composer, and a striking, Tchaikovskian cadence with a bass in contrary motion to the preceding melodic figuration.[7]

For the autumn of 1877 the city of Lucca planned a prestigious Esposizione Provinciale with exhibits in every branch of the arts and sciences. Its musical contribution was to be a piece for voices and orchestra with tenor or bass soloist and an opening prelude or overture. For this a competition was announced in January, the winner to receive 200 lire, the runner-up half that amount. All entries were to be written 'clearly and intelligibly' and submitted anonymously. Puccini offered a setting of a patriotic poem, 'I figli d'Italia bella', only to have it returned to sender with the recommendation to study more and to improve his handwriting. In the event no prize seems to have been awarded; nor has Puccini's ode ever come to light.

Had the adjudicators been aware of the composer's identity they might have examined the manuscript more carefully. For in the meantime Puccini had suddenly begun to attract attention with a motet, *Plaudite populi* for baritone solo, mixed chorus, and orchestra, first given

---

[7] The piece was given its first performance on 6 October 1999, at the church of San Frediano by the Orchestra of La Scala, Milan, conducted by Riccardo Muti.

at a student concert on 29 April and repeated at the church of San Paolino, the city's patron saint, on 11 July, the eve of the appropriate feast day. 'Hearing this music', observed the critic of *La provincia di Lucca*, 'we are reminded of an old proverb, "Cats' children catch mice".' In fact Giacomo Puccini represents the fifth musical generation of his family; he has before him excellent examples to imitate and could become a composer of considerable skill, since he shows a suitable aptitude for his art'. There follow the usual exhortations to study classical models and so prove himself worthy of his forefathers. The praise was not misplaced. Set to a commonplace Latin text in the saint's honour, the motet shows little sign of individuality, but it is fluently and confidently written in ternary form, the baritone having the entire central section to himself. Only a tiny phrase featuring the dip of a seventh, several times repeated, hints at the Puccini to come.

The chance to follow up his first triumph came exactly a year later. The occasion was a performance again at the church of San Paolino of a composite mass written by pupils of the Istituto Musicale Pacini. Neither the 'Sinfonia' by Pietro Giusti nor the Kyrie and Gloria of Carlo Guerini aroused much critical interest. But then came Puccini's motet ('which we heard last year and whose manifold beauties we duly noted')[8] and a Credo ('newly composed, showing real invention and a fine orchestral sense; there are some original ideas, and the "Incarnatus et crucifixus" does not sound like the work of a beginner, but rather of an experienced composer'). The Sanctus and Agnus Dei by the once so promising Carignani were judged merely 'melodious' and 'effective'. Reviewing the performance in *Il Moccolino*, Dr Nicolao Cerù, Albina's cousin by marriage, recalled the adage about cats and mice, which had doubtless become a catchphrase in the family. The only other composition that has been tentatively assigned to 1878 is a setting for tenor and bass (whether soloists or chorus is not specified) with organ or harmonium of the Passiontide hymn *Vexilla regis prodeunt*. Commissioned by a music-loving chemist from Bagni di Lucca (another scene of the young Puccini's moonlighting activities), it is a straightforward, naïf piece with moments of Italianate sweetness but little else. His payment, the chemist's son tells us, was 10 lire (about 50p) and one of the

---

[8] Unsourced quotations in this chapter are from *La provincia di Lucca*.

special cakes for which Bagni di Lucca was famous. It is certainly not worth more.

Over the next two years we hear little of the budding maestro, now entering his twenties. There are references to his accompanying visiting singers at their benefit concerts 'with his usual skill'. In 1879 he is credited with a 'Valzer' written for the town band but as yet untraced. A concert given during Holy Week 1880 included pieces by, among others, 'I carissimi maestri Puccini Giacomo e Puccini Michele' (*père*), but what they were is not recorded. Once again it was the Feast of San Paolino that brought the revelation: a *Messa a quattro voci* entirely composed by Puccini as his passing-out piece for the Pacini Institute. Not all the music was unfamiliar. The Credo was the one written two years earlier; and the performance included the motet, inserted after the Gloria. This time the praise was unstinted. Originality, melodic charm, grandeur of conception and structure, strict adherence to the 'philosophy' of the text—all these attributes were found in the latest offering. The reviewer of the *Provincia di Lucca* had only two reservations: the Sanctus was too short (a frequent complaint in those days), and the 'Cum sancto spiritu'—'un fugone coi baffi' (a grand fugue with moustaches, or, as we might say, 'with knobs on') was over-ingenious for liturgical use.

For three quarters of a century the existence of this mass was known only to scholars, until in 1951, the priest Dante Del Fiorentino (who in his youth as curate at Torre del Lago had known Puccini and had since emigrated to America) made an edition of the music, which was published under the erroneous title of *Messa di gloria,* since when it has enjoyed numerous performances and more than one commercial recording. Laid out for tenor and baritone soloists, mixed chorus, and full orchestra, its stylistic patchwork reflects the dilemma that affected Italy's church music during the late nineteenth century. At a time when sacred and secular styles were moving ever further apart, her composers had long been content to incorporate theatrical elements alongside the time-honoured contrapuntal procedures deemed proper to a liturgical work. By the 1860s, under the influence of foreign models, they felt the need to aspire to a loftier, more consistently devotional manner without renouncing their national heritage of spontaneous melody or, in some cases, of operatic immediacy. The problem lay in the lack of a common

Ex. 1.1

denominator. There were no choral festivals in Italy comparable to those of the Lower Rhine in Germany and the Three Choirs in England, which fostered a long line of cantatas and oratorios from Spohr and Mendelssohn to Gounod, Saint-Saëns, and Dvořák, nourished at the roots by Bach and Handel yet capable of absorbing modern techniques akin to those of the symphony and the tone-poem. Certainly Italy had her masses and oratorios composed anew for the yearly feast days; but unlike those of the north they were not commercially profitable and rarely spread outside the city for which they were written, with the result that each composer went very much his own way. The situation is aptly illustrated by that strange coat of many colours, the *Messa per Rossini* of 1869, to which at Verdi's suggestion 13 of the country's leading composers, himself included, contributed a movement by way of homage to the Grand Old Man of Italian music, recently deceased. No two pieces are written alike. Solutions vary from the naïf to the sophisticated, from scholastic rigour to almost improvisatory freedom, from chamber-like intimacy to grand, ceremonial gesture. Not until the first notes of Verdi's 'Libera me' does the air become charged with electricity. Amid such a gallimaufry, Puccini's mass cuts a not ignoble figure. The invention is fresh, if not always distinguished, the part-writing skilful: above all the composer is totally in command of his material. The opening Kyrie is a ternary structure based on two ideas, major and minor, the first of which has a seductive sweetness that Puccini will put to more than liturgical use in his second opera, *Edgar* (Ex. 1.1). Each is furnished with its own imitation point, both deftly woven into a peaceful, delicately scored coda. The main theme of the Gloria has all the naiveté of a nursery-rhyme, enlivened, however, by an extension of the final phrase into one of those successions of parallel unresolved chords, subtly varied with each repetition, that will become a personal hallmark.

There is breadth and nobility in the 'Laudamus te'; while a still clearer glimpse of the future is offered by the 'Gratias agimus', a lyrical tenor solo introduced by an orchestral motif that exerts a strong sub-dominant pull with each recurrence. The independence of the orchestral part, scored throughout with rare imagination, allows an element of dialogue in the central episode; and the concluding phrase of the main period is emphasized by a doubling of the outer parts—a device soon to be regarded as a Puccinian mannerism, though he was not the first to employ it. Most remarkable of all is the manner in which the melody itself comes to rest in the dominant key with a perfect sense of finality—a scheme to be epitomized in Prince Calaf's 'Nessun dorma', far in the future. Less distinguished is the 'Qui tollis', a somewhat jovial melody announced by the basses and later taken up by full chorus over a tramping accompaniment. A homophonic 'Quoniam' coloured by touches of modal harmony and punctated by fanfares prepares for the 'Cum sancto spiritu', a *tour de force* of polyphony in which all the standard devices of canon, imitation, augmentation, diminution, pedal point, and stretto are used with a freedom that raises it far above the level of a school exercise. As a crowning stroke of ingenuity, the opening strain of the Gloria is re-introduced as a countermelody to the fugue subject, slightly altered so as to accommodate it. The same theme, thundered out in full choral and orchestral panoply, will take charge of the conclusion, so rounding off a massive structure which, if not an expression of deep religious feeling, is at least a remarkable flexing of musical muscles.

A similar strength of architecture marks the Credo, composed two years earlier. Here the prevailing mood is sombre, though charged at the outset with a sense of energy—note the wide sweep of the unison melody and the propulsive thrust of the orchestral syncopations in the fourth bar (Ex. 1.2). This is the main thematic nucleus of the movement, within which both the 'Incarnatus' and the 'Crucifixus' form consecutive episodes, the first a tenor solo above murmuring chorus, the second a dark, sepulchral melody for basses that rises and falls with a weary insistence beneath plangent harmonies. Unusually, the minor mode is preserved throughout the 'Et resurrexit', conceived as a long

Ex. 1.2

build-up with imitative entries leading to a full-blooded reprise of Ex. 1.2 ('Et in spiritum sanctum')—not, one feels, a particularly comforting faith. There is a tranquil oasis in the 'Et unam sanctam catholicam', after which the syncopations of Ex. 1.2 raise their menacing heads, this time to dissolve into a graceful, pastoral melody with a typically Puccinian downward gradient over a bass of purling semiquavers. It is as though the composer envisaged the life of the world to come in terms of the rural retreat to which in later years he loved to retire. But this too will be whipped up to an emphatic conclusion.

The Sanctus is indeed perfunctory; and a few bars of 'Hosanna' are sufficient to wind up the Benedictus, a suave baritone cantilena, which will furnish a phrase for the minuet in Act II of *Manon Lescaut*. Destined for the same opera, where it is rechristened 'madrigale', is the entire Agnus Dei, here laid out for tenor and baritone soloists with choral refrain (Ex. 1.3). So familiar is the melody in its later context that it may seem to jar in a sacred work (for an Agnus Dei of similarly intimate character, however, see an undated *Mass in G* by Angeloni held at the Istituto Boccherini). At all events it was highly praised at the time, and to the unprejudiced ear the caressing triplets at the words 'Dona nobis pacem', echoed by the orchestra in the final bars, may seem a suitably haunting *envoi*.

With this mass Puccini had by the standards of Lucca proved himself

Ex. 1.3

fully worthy of his ancestors. Its technical mastery is indeed striking, particularly in the care given to the orchestra, whether in the accompaniments or in the interstices between vocal paragraphs. Here was a composer who had already learned, in Verdi's words, to move notes around to his own purposes. Yet for one who aspired to an international career his training still lacked what might be called the symphonic dimension; and this was not to be had within the walls of his native city.

To an earlier generation it would not have seemed important. The decline of instrumental music in Italy during the early nineteenth century was a by-word throughout Europe, and accepted without demur by Italians themselves. If the basic skills continued to be taught at the conservatories, it was purely as an academic discipline.

By the mid-century, however, the more far-seeing spirits had begun to realize that without an infusion of instrumental techniques learned from the north, Italian opera was heading for sterility. With this in mind, Abramo Basevi, a doctor from Livorno, founded the Società del Quartetto Florence, which gave regular performances of the German classics during the 1850s accompanied by analytical programme notes. In 1863 Milan followed suit with its own Società del Quartetto, Giulio Ricordi acting as its secretary. The society published its own journal, in which Boito preached the gospel of Mozart, Beethoven, and Mendelssohn—strictly with a view to the enrichment of Italian opera. From the Villa d'Este outside Rome, where he spent several months of each year, Liszt promoted a similar activity with the aid of Baron von Keudell and his own pupil, Sgambati. Slowly the symphony concert began to take shape under the pioneering batons of Carlo Pedrotti in Turin and

Giusppe Martucci in Naples. At first single movements were the rule, interspersed with overtures and an assortment of 'lollipops' (Boccherini's popular minuet played by full strings and Mozart's 'Rondo alla Turca' scored for full orchestra with 'Turkish' percussion were steady favourites). By 1873 Turin had progressed as far as a complete Beethoven symphony. Faccio's concerts in Milan, on the other hand, continued for years to be burdened with a superabundance of overtures. As for the concerts given by the Società Orchestrale Boccherini of Lucca, these would hardly do credit to a Sunday afternoon bandstand. Throughout the 1870s the fare never varied: an overture by Auber or Rossini to begin with; a couple of vocal solos from well-known operas, usually with piano accompaniment; a handful of short pieces by local composers with titles such as 'Elegy', 'Religious Melody' or 'Triumphal March': at least one 'divertimento' on themes from *La sonnambula, Linda di Chamounix,* or some such repertory work with the director, Augusto Michelangeli, as concertante soloist; and the evening would end with a set of Strauss waltzes. Mendelssohn's Violin Concerto, rashly introduced in 1874, was greeted by an empty hall. The first complete symphony to be heard in Lucca was Haydn's 'Farewell' in 1882—as if a work of such length could be tolerated only if it involved an element of spectacle. When four of the society's members presented a movement from one of Haydn's string quartets, they were taken to task for sitting in a group and playing as though to each other instead of coming to the front of stage and performing towards the audience!

But the conservatories were already changing with the times. In 1870 a parliamentary bill had been passed reforming the curriculum so as to give greater prominence to the teaching of instrumental music. In Milan the trend had already begun under the directorship of Lauro Rossi, who not only published an up-to-date manual on harmony and orchestration but also initiated the revival of Italy's Renaissance heritage. His progressive policies were maintained and developed by his successors, Alberto Mazzucato and Stefano Ronchetti Monteviti. In 1873 the teaching staff had a valuable acquisition in Antonio Bazzini, an internationally renowned violinist much admired by Schumann, who at the age of 46 had renounced the career of virtuoso to devote himself to composition and the promotion of chamber music (he was one of the first Italians to form his own permanent string quartet). Cultural capital of the new Italy, visited by all the star performers of Europe, Milan was the obvious destination for a young man of Puccini's talents, as it had been for Verdi nearly half a century before.

Accordingly, Albina applied to the Lucca city council on behalf of her son for an appropriate grant; but, though repeated over the next two years and supported in 1882 by an application from Giacomo himself, her request was refused. Early biographers have hinted that Puccini had already disqualified himself by his love of irreverent pranking. A more likely explanation is that by this time the council did not dispose of the necessary funds. Not only had the 1870s been a time of international recession, but, ever since the formation of the Italian state, an increasing financial burden had fallen upon local authorities, resulting in the temporary closure of many theatres throughout the peninsula. With his *Messa a quattro voci* of 1872, first performed not at the church of San Paolino but at the cathedral itself, Catalani had caused an even greater stir than Puccini, and at a considerably younger age. But there is no evidence that the city council subsidized his move first to Paris, then to Milan, though the local papers proudly reported his subsequent triumphs. Should Puccini rise to similar heights, the authorities were doubtless ready to bask in his reflected glory; but they saw no reason to help him up the ladder, especially since he had renounced all thought of becoming their cathedral organist and director of the Istituto Pacini.

Fortunately Albina had a further shot in her locker. In his funeral speech for her late husband Pacini had spoken of 'two noblewomen who have already expresserd the wish to extend a beneficent hand towards the education of two young daughters of him who now reposes in a better world'. It was therefore to them that the widow turned for help. The Duchessa Carafa suggested that she apply directly to Queen Margherita for one of the royal bursaries available to musicians born of needy families. Her request was supported by the Marchesa Pallavicini, herself a lady-in-waiting to the queen; and the money was duly forthcoming. True, it did not amount to much—a mere 1200 lire. But Dr Cerù came to the family's aid with an additional subsidy, so that the completion of Giacomo's musical education was now assured.

CHAPTER 2

The Student at Milan

'To-day Milan is without doubt the first musical city in Italy.' Not a proclamation but rather a simple statement of fact thrown out in the course of a review by a correspondent of the *Gazzetta musicale di Milano*. It was not an exaggeration. No other centre could offer such a wide range of musical fare combined with so high a standard of performance. Puccini's arrival there could hardly have been better timed. The city was fast pulling out of the economic recession of the 1870s that had resulted in many a bankruptcy throughout Europe and more than a few suicides in Vienna. A massive International Exhibition was being planned for 1881 and with it a grand concert hall (never, alas, completed). New ideas in politics, literature and the arts were in the air. No wonder the young provincial from Lucca felt exhilarated. 'How beautiful Milan is, and what youthfulness!'—so he concluded one of his earliest letters home.[1] Pride of place, as always, belonged to the Teatro alla Scala, which presented much the same appearance as it does today. The houses that had obstructed the view of its façade had been cleared away, making room for the present piazza complete with memorial to Leonardo da Vinci and linked to the more spacious Piazza del Duomo by the Galleria Vittorio Emanuele, then regarded as a marvel of modern engineering. Each year the theatre commanded an array of star singers, stage artists of the highest distinc-

[1] PCE 1, p. 15.

tion and an orchestra 110 strong under the direction of Italy's ablest conductor, Franco Faccio. Of its annual seasons only one was regular: the Carnevale-Quaresima, which ran from Boxing Day to Holy Week and offered five or six operas distributed among a double cast of principals. Here grandeur was the order of the day. Of the 60 performances given during the winter months of 1879–80 *Aida* accounts for 23, *La Gioconda* (heard for the first time in Milan in its definitive form) for 14; the rest of the tally was made up by *Lucia di Lammermoor*, *Rigoletto*, and Gounod's *Faust* (an honorary Italian opera since 1863). Shorter evenings were filled out with the spectacular ballet *Excelsior*, the first of several similar confections with choreography by Leopoldo Manzotti and music by Romualdo Marenco, two names that have long since passed into near-oblivion. Over the next three years the same pattern was maintained. The lodestars of 1880–1 were Ponchielli's exotic *Il figliuolo prodigo* with its Assyrian bacchanal and the newly revised *Simon Boccanegra*. Lesser offerings included an Italian version of *Der Freischütz* with the spoken dialogue 'musicked' by Faccio and the part of Ännchen adapted for contralto. The season of 1881–2 opened with *Guglielmo Tell* followed by *Gli Ugonotti;* but the principal efforts were directed towards the prestigious novelty, Massenet's *Erodiade*, commissioned by the Casa Ricordi, though first given the previous year at Brussels to the French text to which it had been composed. In the event it may not have measured up to the expectations aroused three years earlier by the same composer's *Le roi de Lehore*; but its influence on Puccini's generation is all too apparent. The soaring strain doubled by cellos and violins in octaves with its melting half-close that introduces Salome's air 'Il est doux, il est bon' could have been taken from any opera by Mascagni, Giordano, or even Puccini himself (Ex. 2.1).

The principal items of the following year were Halévy's *L'ebrea* and *Dejanice* (a more licentious *Gioconda* with an Aegean setting) by Puccini's fellow-Luccan Alfredo Catalani, whom he had several times visited during his first year at Milan and found 'most kind'[2] (sad to say, their cordial relationship would not last). 'In general, it doesn't send people into raptures', Puccini observed, 'but artistically speaking it's a fine piece,

[2] PGP, 31.

Ex. 2.1

Massenet: *Hérodiadè*

and if they do it again I shall go back there.'[3] *Dejanice* would likewise leave its mark on the younger composer.

Milan's second lyric theatre was the Dal Verme, a huge edifice situated between the Arena and the Castello in the modern quarter facetiously known as the Milanese 'Ring'. Originally an all-purpose wooden theatre, the nobleman whose name it bears had had it rebuilt in 1872 in the latest style with only two tiers of boxes (as against La Scala's six), a large amphitheatre gallery, and a raked auditorium which allowed every stallholder a clear view of the stage. Its seasons were longer than those of La Scala, with which they frequently overlapped, and the turnover of works was more rapid, though standards of performance were inevitably lower. Mostly the Dal Verme dealt in repertory pieces; but it had more than one novelty to its credit. Ponchielli's revised *I promessi sposi*, given in the theatre's inaugural year, rescued its author from sixteen years of provincial drudgery. In 1877 the première of *Preciosa* launched Antonio Smareglia on his operatic career. It was the Dal Verme, too, that introduced the Milanese public to Bizet's *Carmen*—'a very fine opera indeed', noted Puccini,[4] who had attended the third performance. Elsewhere opera seasons of varying length sprouted like mushrooms, and at no time more prolifically than in 1881, the year of the Exhibition. Milan's leading prose theatre, the Manzoni, offered Thomas' *Mignon*, *Crispino e la comare* by the brothers Ricci, *Rigoletto*, and Emilio Usiglio's comedy *La notte in prigione*. At the Castelli there

[3] Ibid., 33
[4] PCE 2, p. 19.

was Gomes's *Il Guarany*, a grand-opera hit of 1870, *Guglielmo Tell, Semiramide* and *La favorita*. The Dal Verme's *cartello* included *Carmen, Gli Ugonotti, La forza del destino, Faust*, and Auteri's *Stella*, while a brief summer season at La Scala presented *Don Giovanni* and, as its *pièce de résistance* (at Verdi's suggestion), Boito's *Mefistofele*, not heard in Milan since its disastrous première of 1868. An operetta company paraded an assortment of Offenbach, Lecocq, Suppé, and Johann Strauss at the Teatro Fossati; and the Santa Radegonda would find room for Paisiello's *Il barbiere di Siviglia* amongst a host of lighter entertainments. 'Not bad, eh?', was Puccini's summing up.[5]

Meanwhile instrumental music was making steady, if belated strides in the Lombard capital. Its oldest concert-giving organization was the Società del Quartetto, whose mainstay was Bazzini's string quartet with local artists added as required; but it also offered hospitality to distinguished visitors such as Sarasate, Joachim, and Anton Rubinstein, not to mention the adolescent prodigy Ferruccio Busoni. Nor were its activities confined to chamber music. From 1872 Faccio put the orchestra of La Scala at its disposal, until their success at the Paris Exhibition of 1878 led to the formation of the Società dell'Orchestra del Teatro alla Scala, which gave an average of six concerts a year after the closure of the Carnevale-Quaresima season. For these, however, sights were lowered. Each concert was divided into two parts, both beginning and ending with a well-known overture. In between there was nothing more substantial than a suite (e.g., Bizet's *L'Arlésienne*), a Liszt Hungarian Rhapsody or, at most, Beethoven's Septet with the string parts increased to full orchestral strength. One searches in vain for a complete symphony. Virtuosity was what drew an audience. Paganini's *Moto perpetuo* played by massed violins would be sure of a 'bis!'; Beethoven's 'Eroica' would merely empty the hall.

For those in search of genuine symphonic fare there were only the Concerti Popolari given during the winter months by pupils of the Conservatory, following an initiative launched by Alberto Mazzucato in 1877. As with the Victorian 'Monday Pops', the title was euphemistic, for the programmes made no concessions to popular taste. Brahms's First Symphony, Mendelssohn's 'Scotch' or Beethoven's Fifth

[5] PCE 6, p. 29.

would feature alongside a Mozart concerto or a Dvořák tone-poem, and on one occasion Tchaikovsky's fantasy-overture *Romeo and Juliet*, then regarded as the height of daring modernism. True, the concerts were often diluted by chamber items; but at least when Schubert's Octet was given at a Concerto Popolare it was performed by eight players only—much to the disapproval of a critic, who would have preferred a doubling up of the string parts and the whole work directed from the podium.

Far more surprising is it to come across such items as the Prelude to *Die Meistersinger* or the *Siegfried Idyll*. For if there is one name conspicuous by its absence from the Milanese scene it is that of Richard Wagner. Not that it was unknown in Italy. The theories propounded in *Oper und Drama* had been a matter for discussion since the 1850s, if only at second or third hand, since the book had yet to be translated into Italian. Indeed, 'music of the future' had become a catchphrase that had even reached Lucca. Of Wagner the composer nothing was known until the first Italian performance of *Lohengrin* at Bologna in 1871. Its effect was to divide Italy's musical world into two camps. Many who had dreaded an avant-garde monstrosity were surprised to find the music so accessible—understandably, since it had been written before its author had formulated his more radical theories. Others maintained an entrenched opposition from the start. For them Wagner remained the German enemy, the operatic equivalent of General Radetzky who had so ruthlessly put down the uprising of 1848. National honour demanded that he be resisted at all costs. No-one was more zealous in the anti-Wagnerian cause than Giulio Ricordi, already the driving force behind the firm of which his frequently ailing father, Tito, was the titular head. A man of uncompromising views, a witty controversialist, a skilled diplomat and even a modest composer of songs and operettas under the pseudonym of J. Burgmein, 'Sör Giuli' (as he was known to his Milanese intimates) was destined to play an important role in Italy's musical life and in Puccini's in particular. His god was Verdi, and his chief ambition to bring about a collaboration between the Grand Old Man and his own friend, the former iconoclast Arrigo Boito. Not only were his years of patient angling successful; in the meantime he had won a far greater share of Verdi's confidence than his father or grandfather had ever enjoyed. Few photographs of Milan's musical events are without the trim little figure with the wing collar and spade-shaped beard who seems to be surveying the scene with an air of faintly amused proprietorship.

Ricordi's opposition to Wagner was, no doubt, fuelled by the fact that the rights to his operas had been acquired by the rival firm of Francesco Lucca. Clearly, however, it rested on artistic conviction, since after the widow Lucca sold him her entire establishment in 1888 his attitude never changed. In the year of Verdi's death he infuriated Wagnerians throughout the peninsula by withholding the Meister's operas out of respect for the deceased.

During the 1870s a torrent of articles denouncing Wagner and all his works poured from Ricordi's house magazine, the *Gazzetta musicale di Milano,* at Giulio's instigation. But by 1880 the Wagnerian tide was proving difficult to stem. For Puccini's entire generation from Catalani to Mascagni his operas possessed a deep and abiding fascination, far greater than that of mere forbidden fruit. 'Wagner's kind of music', Catalani wrote, 'may certainly not be the one that should prevail in the manner that he himself would wish, but it is undoubtedly that which speaks most directly to us; therefore we should rejoice every time we hear that the music of the great German has triumphed.'[6] For Mascagni Wagner was simply 'the *Papa* of all *composers*, present and future'.[7] His name would haunt Puccini's early career like a hidden motif.

He had a notable sympathiser in Antonio Bazzini. A musician of European horizons and a close friend of Hans von Bülow, Bazzini had been the first to introduce Wagner's music into the concerts of the Società del Quartetto. As a composer his forte was instrumental music (his only opera, *Turanda,* had failed disastrously at La Scala in 1867), and his output includes several string quartets of decent workmanship, none of which, alas, has weathered the years as hardily as his violin lollipop *La ronde des lutins.* Resident for many years in Paris, Bazzini's idols were Gounod and Saint-Saëns, whose influence is evident in his contribution to the *Messa per Rossini.* Happily, it was to Bazzini's tuition that Puccini was assigned during his first two years at the conservatory. Although

[6] Letter to S. Stampa quoted without date, M. Zurletti: *Catalani* (Turin, 1982), 45.

[7] Letter to V. Gianfranceschi, 8 April 1887, in P. Mascagni: *Epistolario,* ed. R. Iovino, M. Morini, and A. Paloscia, i (Lucca,1996), no. 85, p. 72.

strictly speaking he was over the required age limit, his admission had been easy. 'Tell my dear teacher Angeloni', he wrote to Albina, 'that the examination was a pushover ('sciocchezza'), because they made me fill out a bass line unfigured and very easy; then they made me develop a melody in D major which didn't strike me as very happy' (and he quoted the first four bars, which as the wife and sister of professional musicians she would have been able to read); 'all right, it went almost too well.'[8] In fact he was awarded first place among the applicants and passed directly into the senior class.

From now on a series of letters home lifts the curtain for the first time on Puccini's character and personality. Especially racy and high-spirited are those to his youngest sister Ramelde, with whom he had developed a special bond that included his brother Michele, all three set faintly apart from their more strait-laced elders. Here we notice his eye for detail, whether describing the latest fashions in women's hats or, much later, the workings of a new bicycle model to her husband. The letters to Albina, whom, like all her brood, he addressed with the polite 'Lei', are more serious in tone, never failing to assure the anxious mother that he was getting enough to eat and not spending too much money ('I went to hear *L'étoile du nord* with Donadia and Auber's *Fra Diavolo* with the famous tenor Naudin. *L'étoile* cost me a few pence ('bigei') in the gallery and *Fra Diavolo* nothing at all, because Frances-coni, who used to be the manager at Lucca, gave me a free ticket.')[9] Sometimes a note of defensiveness creeps in—even of contrition (' . . . if I've often made you angry, it isn't because I don't love you but because I've been a beast and a scoundrel, I admit it myself').[10] Within a month of his arrival he gives an account of his daily routine:

> In the morning I get up at 8.30. When I have a lesson I go to it. If I have no lesson I practise the piano a little. A little does me, but I do need to practise. I shall now buy an excellent method by Angeleri, one of those in which everyone can teach themselves perfectly well. To continue: at half past ten I have breakfast, then I go out. At one o'clock I come home and do some work for Bazzini for a couple of hours; then from three to five

[8] CP I, p. I.
[9] PGP, 30–1.
[10] Ibid., 33.

it's back to the piano to read through a bit of classical music. Actually I'd like to take out a subscription for scores, but this costs quite a few pence. At present I'm going through Boito's *Mefistofele*, which Favara, a friend of mine from Palermo, has lent me. At five o'clock I go and take a frugal meal (but a lot of that frugality!) and have some minestrone alla milanese, which, to tell the truth, is very good. I have three platefuls, then something else to fill up with; a small hunk of cheese . . . and half a litre of wine. Then I smoke a cigar and go off to the Galleria to take a walk up and down, as usual. I stay there until nine o'clock and return home dead tired. Back home I do a bit of counterpoint, but I don't play, because at night one isn't allowed to. After that I climb into bed and read seven or eight pages of a novel. Such is my life.[11]

Throughout his student years his official residence was with his cousin by marriage, Carlo Biagini, whom the law required to act 'in loco parentis', since Giacomo was not yet 25. But in the meantime he moved successively to other addresses, always with an eye to saving costs. For though he was by no means as hard up as his future Bohemians, money was tight, and his letters home drop frequent hints that a little more would not be unwelcome. Albina did what she could; she sent him clothes and, at his special request, a jar of good Luccan olive oil in which to cook his beans. But she had a household to run and the dowries for three of her daughters, Tomaide, Nitteti, and Ramelde, to provide for. By April 1881 she felt the need for a more reliable account of her son's progress and prospects than he himself was likely to give her. She therefore wrote a hopeful letter to Bazzini, who replied at length:

Your son Giacomo is doing well and making progress in his principal study of composition. He has been somewhat neglectful of his subsidiary studies (piano, aesthetics, dramatic theory etc.) despite repeated urgings from me, and for this there are penalties to be paid. I know that these are not serious matters; but he really must convince himself (and I have told him so) that the Academic Council *does not make deals* and that *all the courses must be followed.*

I cannot therefore at present let you have the letter for which you ask

[11] CP 2, pp. 2–3.

me, but I hope I shall be able to do so later on and still in time for the purpose you have in mind.

I think that if he applies himself seriously he may be able next year to leave the conservatory with honour. As for finding him immediately after-wards the means of making enough money in his profession, I can make no promises, dear Madam, because I would merely be telling you a lie. . . . It is not in my power to grant a lucrative position to a pupil, however gifted and deserving he may be. The competition in Milan is enormous. Certainly he may be sure of a recommendation from me, wherever possible. In the meantime he must make useful contacts; and I think this will not be difficult, since he has a pleasant way with him and a likeable personality.

But above all he must work diligently and keep to the rules of discipline.[12]

How many ambitious mothers have received just such a letter from their son's tutor! Doubtless its substance was communicated to Gia-como. That he took much notice of it may be doubted; for he was not one to apply himself to topics in which he had no interest. He made no secret of being bored to death by aesthetics. His notebooks on the subject, which he presented to the Istituto Boccherini at Lucca, are full of marginal scribblings: 'Ouch!! Oh God!! Help for God's sake!! I can't stand it!!! It's too much!!! I'm dying!!!' and so on. Puccini was never an intellectual.

During his first year in Milan the harvest of composition is meagre. All that can be assigned with near-certainty to that period is a string quartet in D, written (so he told his mother) for Bazzini, of which only the opening Allegro can be said to have survived in its original form. While containing no hint of the mature composer, it at least bears witness to a fluent technique and a decent command of the medium. Launched by a 'Mannheim rocket' on the viola, it proceeds through sequences and imitation-points to a smooth contrasted theme in the orthodox manner, followed by development and reprise. There are mo-ments, too, which raise it above the level of a mere exercise: a com-bination of first subject with elements of the second subject-group to form a new theme at the start of the development; the long preparation

[12] Letter to Albina Puccini, 17 April 1881, in C. Sartori: 'Quisquilie pucciniane e intuizioni bazziniane', *NRMI*, viii (1974), 370.

for the reprise involving a steady increase of chromatic dissonance; and a surprise turn to F major for the recapitulated second subject—the only point at which the music breaks out of the circle of related keys. There is even a note of Haydnesque impudence at the final cadence. Mendelssohn, however, would seem to be the chief model; and if, on the debit side, the texture is somewhat unvaried, this is understandable in a composer accustomed to think mainly in terms of top-line melody. A four-handed piano arrangement of the final movement, a 'Scherzo', made by Giacomo's brother Michele exists in the Puccini museum at Celle. Like so many of Puccini's early compositions, it would be put to operatic use, as will be seen. Possibly to the same period belongs a string quartet movement in A minor also entitled 'Scherzo'—a quirky little piece that suggests an acquaintance with the ballet music from Verdi's revised *Macbeth*. This too would find a place on the stage.

The following year Puccini's studies took a new turn. In November 1881 the conservatory's director Stefano Ronchetti-Monteviti had died, and his place was taken by Bazzini, whose teaching activity accordingly ceased. His pupil, therefore, passed under the tutelage of Amilcare Ponchielli. On the face of it this might seem a retrograde step. Although younger than Bazzini by nearly a generation, Ponchielli was by comparison a provincial, who had never ventured outside his country's borders. Born in a village near Cremona in 1834, he passed with honours through the Milan Conservatory and at the age of 22 scored a modest success at Cremona's Teatro della Concordia with an operatic version of Manzoni's famous novel *I promessi sposi*. Thereafter ill-luck aggravated by a shy, retiring disposition, condemned him, in Verdi's phrase, to 'sixteen years hard labour' as a local bandmaster. He competed in 1868 for the professorship of counterpoint and fugue at his old conservatory. The panel judged him the winner; but due to pressure from the 'progressives' of the Società del Quartetto the post went to the runner-up, Franco Faccio. However, the monumental fiasco that year of Boito's *Mefistofele*, the failure of Faccio's *Amleto* at its revival in 1870, causing its composer henceforth to devote himself exclusively to conducting, and finally Milanese alarm at the threat of a Wagnerian invasion posed by the triumph of *Lohengrin* at Bologna in 1871 all combined to turn the tide in Ponchielli's favour. *I promessi sposi*, revised to fresh verses by the 'scapigliato' (for which read 'progressive') poet Emilio Praga, was mounted at the Teatro Dal Verme before a delighted audience. Verdi, admittedly, was among the doubters, remarking that though Ponchielli was clearly a good musician the old and new passages in his score did not marry and that both were behind their respective times. Giulio Ricordi, on the other hand, who had bought the rights, was convinced that, given careful grooming, here was a winner. His hopes were amply fulfilled four years later by the instant success of *La Gioconda*, written to a libretto by Boito. By the time it returned to La Scala in 1880 in its definitive form, *La Gioconda* had established itself as a modern classic and its composer as a person of consequence, over whose ability even Verdi no longer had reservations. Not surprisingly, therefore, in 1881 the institution which had shut its doors in his face thirteen years before now welcomed him as a senior professor of composition along with Bazzini. Despite a wholly traditionalist approach—indeed, perhaps because of it—Ponchielli was clearly an admirable teacher and much beloved by his pupils, to whom he was always ready to lend a helping hand, however little he liked their music. With Puccini's style he was frankly out of sympathy, 'since he follows in the footsteps of Wagner, Massenet etc.', so he claimed to have confided to Verdi.[13] Yet it was to Ponchielli's good offices that Puccini owed the start of his operatic career. Not only that. Certain of the teacher's traits would find an abiding echo in the works of the pupil: the ability to evoke an ambience with a few instrumental brush-strokes; the occasional integration of a recurring motif within the melody of a closed number; and, in particular, the winding-up of an important scene by means of an orchestral peroration based on its most memorable theme—a device first used to general critical acclaim by Ponchielli in the definitive finale to Act III of *La gioconda* and by Puccini in one opera after another. Both composers, it may be added, shared a sense of fun that expressed itself in doggerel verse.

It was to his new teacher, too, that Puccini owed, if indirectly, the company of a fellow-student of similar promise. The son of a baker from Livorno, Pietro Mascagni had determined on a musical career in the teeth of parental opposition. His latest work was a cantata, *In filanda*, couched in that gentle, idyllic style to which he would return time and again in the intervals of bombast. Submitted to the Concorso

---

[13] Letter to his wife, undated, in F. Abbiati, *Giuseppe Verdi* (Milan, 1959), iv, 26.

dell'Esposizione di Milano in 1881, it had won high praise from the jurors; and Ponchielli advised the young man to apply for admission to the Milan Conservatory. Like Puccini before him, he passed the entrance examination without difficulty and was enrolled as a student in May 1882. The experience was not a happy one. Accustomed to being a big fish in a small pool, Mascagni found the discipline of a student's life in Milan intolerable. To relieve the tedium he indulged in extramural pursuits—deputizing as a double bass player at the Teatro Dal Verme, teaching the piano to amateurs, writing songs under the anagram 'Pigmeo Scartani', since conservatory students were strictly forbidden to publish their works while *in statu pupillari*. The result was missed lessons and poor examination results. After two years Mascagni decided that he could no longer bear it and left without a word to the authorities to join an operetta troupe as conductor. Characteristically, he regretted his decision and tried for re-admission to the conservatory if only to be allowed to take the final exam. But this time not even Ponchielli's benevolence could help him.

Throughout his stay in Milan he shared rooms with Puccini. Despite their different temperaments—Mascagni quick-tempered and irrepressible, Puccini shy and easy-going—a cordial friendship developed between them, which outlasted their student days. When Mascagni, down on his luck, applied for the post of municipal music-master at the obscure Adriatic township of Cerignola, a 'certificate' from Puccini 'moved me almost to tears'.[14] True, an unguarded remark about his colleague's work thrown out at one of those press interviews to which Mascagni was much given would sometimes arouse Puccini's suspicions. Otherwise they remained on as good terms as their respective wives would allow. Throughout his life Mascagni made enemies without number; but Puccini was never one of them.

Evidently their musical tastes were alike. Both were devout Wagnerians and would pool their meagre resources to buy a score of *Parsifal*. Mascagni shared his companion's approval of Catalani's *Dejanice*. As for Gounod's *Redemption*: 'I sat through it religiously and religiously lost all patience with it. . . . All those long recitatives, mostly on one note, all

[14] Letter to V. Gianfranceschi, 22 March, 1887, *Epistolario*, no. 87, p. 70.

those little phrases that never develop into a melody!' Thus Mascagni.[15] And Puccini, more succinctly: 'Yesterday evening I went to *Redemption* (an oratorio by Gounod) which bored me a good deal.'[16] Years later both composers would summon up remembrance of mutual assistance in dodging creditors, of 'no go areas' marked in red on a map where unpaid tradesmen might be lying in wait, of a single shared receptacle which served both as a cooking-bowl and a wash-basin—all strictly *à la Bohème* and doubtless exaggerated. At all events the yoke of academe lay easier on Puccini than on his fellow-student, even if, as he later declared, he sometimes saved himself trouble by presenting to Ponchielli the fugues that he had written for Bazzini.

His chief composition of 1882 is the *Preludio sinfonico* in A major, which was performed at a students' concert on 15 July. At the time it aroused little enthusiasm. 'The Prelude seems to me rather long', wrote Filippo Filippi, doyen of Milanese music critics, in *La perseveranza*, 'consisting as it does entirely of an adagio, which begins with woodwind chords that bring to mind Wagner's "Cigno gentil"; then comes a violin melody with some effective crescendos, but it is not easy to make sense of the way the phrases develop, and the young composer is inclined, as the saying is, to beat about the bush.' Here Filippi puts his finger on the main weakness of the *Preludio* and also on its source of inspiration. Puccini's Wagnerian predilections are confirmed that year by a jotting in one of his exercise books, which shows him succumbing to the temptation of writing his own obituary: 'This great musician was born in Lucca in the year . . . and can rightly be called a worthy successor to the famous Boccherini. He was handsome and extremely clever and in the field of Italian art possessed a power which echoed that of Wagner from beyond the Alps.' At the time Italy's favourite Wagner opera was *Lohengrin*. The limpid, radiant A major to which the *Preludio* continually returns, the rhetorical climax returning three quarters of the way through, the hushed evanescent close—all evoke the prelude to Wagner's medieval drama. Nor is Filippi's puzzlement over the phrase-structure hard to account for. Altogether there are four variants of the

[15] Letter to A. Soffredini, 4 April 1883, *Epistolario*, no. 55, p. 44.
[16] PGP, 33.

main theme, but no sense of purpose in their succession. Rather it seems as though the composer had difficulty in choosing between them. Not until the fourth statement does the melody begin to generate new ideas, notably a languorous waltz-like tune, by which time the listener might be forgiven for having allowed his attention to wander.

On the other hand, as an essay in rich harmonies and shifting orchestral colours the piece possesses genuine interest (not for nothing had Puccini's reading that year included Berlioz's celebrated treatise on instrumentation). There is even a premonition of the mature master where at the subject's third reprise an unexpected pull towards the subdominant is driven home by a splash of trumpet tone.

Certainly the *Preludio* was not a wasted exercise: for snatches of it would be recycled into Puccini's second opera, *Edgar*, though not in the work's final form. Sketches exist for a song, 'Ah, se potesse', whose autograph, now missing, is said to be inscribed 'Lucca, 15.7.1882' (but was Puccini absent from the performance of his *Preludio sinfonico*?). One document, however, stands out like a beacon: a letter written in December of that year to Dr Cerù (by now sole provider of the funds necessary for his maintenance at the conservatory, since Queen Margherita's grant had already expired), in which we find the passage: 'Tell Michele' [his brother] 'to seek out Cappelletti Medarse and ask him whether he has yet found anything for that little libretto he's promised me. I would need it soon, for I could then get ready to do something.'[17] Clearly Puccini was in no doubt about his vocation.

His three-year course at the conservatory would finish in midsummer 1883. In January the anxious mother wrote to Ponchielli a letter similar to the one she had sent to Bazzini, to receive a similar, if slightly more encouraging reply. Puccini was one of his best pupils; Ponchielli was happy with him and would be still happier if he showed a little more assiduity, 'because when he wants to he does well'. He would have no difficulty in getting his diploma at the end of the scholastic year, though, to be frank, another year at the conservatory would not do him any harm. Once his studies had been completed (and only then) Ponchielli would do his best to help him find employment. In the

[17] PCE 8, p. 31.

meantime he should pursue his studies beyond the mere curriculum and 'write . . . write . . . and pour out ('buttar giù') music'.[18] This last injunction was surely wasted, since all his life Puccini was as parsimonious with notes as Berlioz. Nor was it mere indolence, but rather a reluctance to commit to paper any idea of whose value he was not convinced. The few compositions that survive from his final year at the conservatory would all serve as material for future operas. An *Adagietto* for orchestra, of which only the first part exists, would furnish the theme of the heroine's aria 'Addio, mio dolce amor' in Act III of *Edgar*. Four songs quarried from Antonio Ghislanzoni's *Melodie per canto* would likewise be drawn upon. *Melanconia* was composed in two versions, one for baritone and piano, the other for voice and string orchestra. The manuscripts of both have disappeared, though not before being seen by Karl Gustav Fellerer, who quotes the incipit and the inscribed date, 19 June 1881.[19] The first of these surely gives the lie to the second, since the opening gesture is altogether too bold for a first-year student. Here we note for the first time Puccini's fondness for the 'soft dissonance' that results from the piling-up of thirds while avoiding any note that produces a semitonal clash.[20] The whole phrase will be transferred to the love duet in *Le Villi* with a characteristic improvement in the distribution of bass notes and the addition of a cluster of semiquavers at the end—this too a Puccinian 'tic', which will form a central idea in the opera itself (see Ex. 3.4, below).

Salve regina for voice and organ (or harmonium), whose text bears no more relation to the office hymn than does Walter Scott's 'Ave Maria', has also been falsely assigned to an earlier period, namely the years at Lucca. But since Ghislanzoni's poem did not appear before 1881 this is impossible. Moreover, the fluent keyboard writing, the Massenet-like grace and harmonic shading and a certain effortless freedom of design within the strophic ground-plan again point to a more advanced stage in his career. A caressing cadential phrase cannot fail to bring to mind the Intermezzo from *Cavalleria rusticana*: clearly the lyricism of

[18] Letter to Albina Puccini, 8 Jan 1883, in L. Marchetti: *Puccini nelle immagini*, pls. 24, 25.

[19] K.G. Fellerer, *Giacomo Puccini*, 20.

[20] See N. Christen: *Giacomo Puccini: analytische Untersuchungen*, 87ff.

the 'giovane scuola' is not far off. The entire 'romanza' would be elaborated into the communal 'preghiera' from *Le Villi* (see Ex. 3.2a, below).

Ad una morta exists complete only in a copyist's manuscript signed by Puccini and dated 'Milan 27 July 1883'. The autograph is confined to two substantial sketches for baritone and piano and a page of orchestration, from which the design emerges of a standard minor-major romanza, fragments of whose opening theme would be recycled into Roberto's romanza in the definitive version of *Le Villi*. The 'maggiore' unfolds a broad, soothing melody for which Puccini had already found a wordless context (see Ex. 3.2d, below). Even so, its first phrase would reappear, harmonically enhanced, in the last act of *Manon Lescaut*. A discarded chord sequence in one of the sketches carries the annotation 'alla Wagner'. The model, however, remains obscure.

The pick of the bunch is *Storiella d'amore*, dated 8 June 1883, the first work of Puccini to find a publisher. Laid out in two ample strophes of ternary design, it tells of the seduction of Dante's Paolo and Francesca by their reading of a book, though without any hint of the tragedy to come. Hence a fleet, conversational discourse in the manner of Mimì's future 'Sola mi fo il pranzo da me stessa'. In each strophe the reprise is expanded by five bars of plunging declamation in the relative minor ('Eco alla voce mia'), the only point at which the voice takes undisputed command of an otherwise self-sufficient piano part. The passage is sufficiently striking for Puccini to quote it in Act III of *Edgar*. A further feature of interest lies in the distribution of the melody within the accompaniment, varying between top, middle, and bottom line. Here, surely, is a clue to Puccini's later habit, often regarded as a mannerism, of doubling the outer parts of a chordal sequence in defiance of academic rules. But left-hand melodies without a bass are a commonplace of nineteenth-century piano music; and Puccini was not the first opera composer to reinforce them at a higher pitch (see Elisabeth's 'Prince, si le roi veut se rendre à ma prière' from *Don Carlos*). Admittedly, for the older composer this was exceptional. For Puccini it was a normal weapon in his expressive armoury. But there is nothing slipshod about it. When a separate fundamental is required it is always there.

Evident in these Ghislanzoni settings is an unusual concern for expressive and dynamic nuance, almost as if the composer intended each to be acted as well as sung—a foretaste of that integration of word, note, and gesture which is as fundamental to Puccini's conception of opera as it is to Wagner's.

As midsummer approached there was much trepidation amongst the Puccini clan. Dr Cerù was all for sending a special recommendation from the Istituto Pacini on his young cousin's behalf, much to the latter's irritation ('You people at Lucca have got recommendations on the brain; damn whoever invented them! . . . You just don't know what kind of people Ponchielli and Bazzini are. They would send you packing with a vengeance!').[21] But there was no need for concern. Puccini graduated with honours, receiving 163 points out of 200 and so qualifying for a copper medal. Two compositions mark the occasion. The first, *Mentia l'avviso*, is a 'scena ed aria' for tenor and piano to a text by Felice Romani that had doubtless been set for decades before by students in their final year. Taken from his *melodramma serio, Il solitario delle Asturie*, written for Carlo Coccia in 1838 and re-set by several other composers including Mercadante, it is sung by a renegade Spanish count who has come at night to a lonely valley for an assignation with the ghost of his supposedly dead daughter and (as he wrongly thinks) evil genius. On the 'scena' Puccini imposes a tighter, more organic unity than would ever have occurred to Mercadante. The 24-bar introduction for piano opens with a pregnant gesture that furnishes the rhythmic scaffolding of everything that follows. The vocal setting falls into two sections, each rounded off by a modified reprise of the introduction. The first ('Mentia l'avviso') begins as conventional recitative, part conversational, part declamatory, shading into a moment of arioso. The second ('Tu cui nomar non oso') is more energetic, tremolandos giving way to galloping triplets in the accompaniment, while the voice mounts to a sustained B flat, but the opening motif returns like an obsession. The final note of the cadence is withheld as the singer imagines that he hears a groan; but it was merely the wind and waves, whereupon a hushed transition to the major prepares for the aria ('É la notte che mi reca'), in which the listener will recognize an early version of Des Grieux's 'Donna non vidi mai' from *Manon Lescaut* (see Ex. 5.4).

Of a very different order is the *Capriccio sinfonico*, his passing-out

[21] CP 4, pp. 4–5.

piece for the conservatory. Performed at the annual students' concert on 14 July it at once alerted the critics to a new voice in Italian music. Filippi of *La perseveranza* shed all his reservations of the previous year. 'In Puccini', he wrote, 'we have a decisive and rare musical temperament and one which is especially symphonic. There is unity of style, personality, character. In his *Capriccio sinfonico* there is a good deal that more experienced composers . . . have not succeeded in doing. . . . There are no uncertainties or gropings in the young author. . . . The ideas are clear, strong, effective and sustained with much truth.'

This insistence on the piece's symphonic qualities has always raised a smile among Puccini's biographers—a sign, they say, of how little the term meant to Italian musicians of the time. Certainly there is no trace here of classical symphonic form. But Carner's description of the *Capriccio* as a mere sequence of themes 'loosely strung together like beads on a string'[22] and interspersed with ineffectual attempts at development does it less than justice. Each of its ideas has a well-defined function in a coherent musical discourse laid out in a ternary plan with a scherzo-like central episode. Two contrasted gestures, one massively scored and heavy with appoggiaturas, the other lighter and more luminous, both extended sequentially, epitomize an emotional conflict that will not be resolved until the end of the composition. A profound melancholy pervades the main subject of the Andante (Ex. 2.2a), relieved by a major-key consequent (Ex. 2.2b) which, after a few valedictory references to the movement's opening gesture, subsides into a prolonged half-close. Both themes have sufficient character for Puccini to recall them in the funeral music of *Edgar*, Act III.

The idea that launches the ensuing Allegro is all too familiar from the start of *La bohème* (see Ex. 6.1a). but how astonishlingly bold it must have seemed in 1883: 24 bars over an inverted dominant seventh posed by an abrupt rhythmic 'fidget' (did Puccini know Liszt's E flat piano concerto?) resolving into 14 bars of tonic, the pattern repeated in the subdominant key! As in the opera, its function is essentially preparatory. The point of arrival is a dance-like theme (Ex. 2.2c) whose initial hemiola will be turned to good purpose later. This in turn generates a lively succession of related ideas, underpinned by recurrences of the rhythmic

---

[22] PCB, 332.

Ex. 2.2a

Andante moderato

p con espressione

Ex. 2.2b

pp

Ex. 2.2c

Allegro vivace
sostenuto   a tempo

Ex. 2.2d

pp

gesture that opened the section. A protracted cadential design effectively balances the long opening stretch. So back to the Andante. But this is no ordinary reprise: it begins directly with Ex. 2.2a interspersed with rhythmic recollections of the Allegro, then works up through sequences of increasing dissonance to a brutal climax like a question mark. There is a dramatic pause, after which Ex. 2.2b steals in with an enhanced warmth which counterpoints of Ex. 2.2a are powerless to stifle; and the movement culminates in a broad, calm melody (Ex. 2.2d), which is nothing less than a transformation of Ex. 2.2c, facilitated by the hemiola already noted. So what had been a playful interlude takes on a serene nobility. This is surely prophetic; for one of Puccini's great strengths as a music dramatist is his ability to distil different emotional properties from the same motif according to pace, dynamic, scoring, and, above all, context. Evidently he felt that in its final form this melody deserved a text and the aid of a human voice; so he turned it into the major-key conclusion of his romanza *Ad una morta*.

Certainly the piece is not free of bombast, as might be expected from a young composer concerned to demonstrate his mastery of a modern orchestra (note the Tchaikovsky-like flourishes on flute and piccolo in the reprise of the Andante). What remains striking is the sense of proportion and the logical working-out of the ideas. None of this was lost on Filippi, who stressed the music's structural coherence and ingenuity. It was on the strength of its reception that *La musica popolare* printed *Storiella d'amore* in its issue of 4 October. The following year Faccio included the *Capriccio sinfonico* in a concert given at the International Exhibition at Turin, placing it between Beethoven's Symphony no. 1 and the March from *Tannhäuser*. The orchestral score was never published during Puccini's lifetime; but the firm of Lucca brought out an arrangement of it for piano duet. Indeed, the proprietress, the redoubtable Giovannina, suggested commissioning from Puccini a symphony in four movements. But nothing came of this; for in the meantime the composer had embarked on a project that would lead him in quite another direction.

Le Villi

'IN NO OTHER COUNTRY IN THE WORLD', WROTE THE ROMAN critic Francesco D'Arcais in 1879, 'does the publisher possess the power and authority that he does in Italy.'[1] This was true. Indeed, an understanding of that power and the internecine warfare between rival firms that resulted from it is as necessary to explain the operatic scene of Puccini's day as is a knowledge of the Spanish civil war of 1519 to explain the events of *Il trovatore*.

The state of affairs had come about gradually, beginning with the steady growth during the first half of the century of Giovanni Ricordi's empire. By the time of his death in 1853 he had acquired a monopoly of Italy's leading composers from Rossini to Verdi, to whom he had been able to extend a measure of copyright. But already in 1841 he faced a rival in Francesco Lucca, a former copyist in his establishment, who had in the meantime spent several months in Leipzig studying up-to-date German techniques. It was he who introduced to Italy the octavo vocal score, so much more suited to the domestic upright piano than the oblong format that Ricordi continued to turn out. Lucca was also the first to use the treble or 'violin' clef for all the upper voices. But his most far-reaching innovation was to pioneer a system whereby composers offered their works directly to a publisher, who would himself place them at a suitable theatre, so relieving the author of tedious

---

[1] F. D'Arcais: 'L'industria musicale in Italia', *Nuova antologia* (May–June 1879), 134.

dealings with the management. By 1870 this had become the general rule. The advent of the professional conductor meant that composers were no longer expected to direct their own rehearsals; but if this source of income was denied to them, they were amply compensated by a generous percentage of all subsequent hire-fees.

Under the lackadaisical direction of Tito Ricordi the older firm lost a certain amount of ground, though it still held the stronger hand in native talent. Lucca meanwhile had been quick to sign up foreign composers whose works had begun to flood the peninsula during the 1860s—Meyerbeer, Gounod, Thomas—and finally, by a stroke of far-seeing genius, Wagner. However, during the following decade the balance was soon redressed. The death of its proprietor in 1872 left the Casa Lucca in the hands of his widow Giovannina, an energetic businesswoman with a heart as large as her frame, who lavished a maternal care on the firm's protégés from the dissipated Petrella to the frail, consumptive Catalani. But she found more than a match in Tito's son Giulio. The gloves were now off. Every new opera would be launched with a barrage of publicity from its publisher's house magazine, to receive a douche of cold water from that of the rival firm. If Giovannina Lucca could ensure the temporary success of Gobatti's *I Goti* at Bologna in 1873, we may be sure that Giulio Ricordi had a hand in the quashing of *Lohengrin* at La Scala that same year.

Clearly, then, for an aspirant to operatic fame it was more important to interest a publisher than an impresario. Following the example of his fellow-townsman Catalani, Puccini first looked to the widow Lucca; hence the frequent references to her in his letters home. Not that he was unduly sanguine: 'As regards the theatre there's nothing to hope for from La Lucca because Ricordi has everything in his clutches and she's in competition with him.'[2] Nonetheless, after the success of the *Capriccio sinfonico*, of which Giovannina had bought the rights, he decided to approach her personally 'so as to fix something up and at least be given some hope for the future'.[3] But evidently the lady herself was in no hurry, since every time Puccini called on her she was 'not at home'. Nor were Ponchielli's attempts to interest the Casa Ricordi on

[2] PCE 2, p. 16.

[3] PCE 18, pp. 36–7.

his pupil's behalf any more successful. Doubtless Sor Giulio hesitated to favour a young composer whose sympathies were confessedly Wagnerian.

In the event it was neither Ricordi nor Lucca who would provide Puccini with his operatic launching-pad. The firm of Sonzogno had been in existence since the beginning of the century; but it was the founder's grandson Edoardo who in 1874 first entered the musical field. No musician himself, but merely a shrewd man of business, he employed Amintore Galli, future teacher of composition at the Milan Conservatory, as his artistic adviser. By this time Ricordi and Lucca had between them cornered the market both in native opera and prestigious imports from abroad. Sonzogno therefore turned his attention to the one area which had remained unexploited, namely French *opéra comique* from Auber and Boieldieu onwards. Here fortune dealt him a trump card in *Carmen*. Introduced at a minor theatre in Naples in 1880, it lost no time in circulating throughout the peninsula, rousing audiences to enthusiasm, and with good reason. For ten years grand opera (or 'opera ballo', as it was called) had hung like a millstone round the neck of Italian composers, whose works, according to the critic Girolamo Biaggi, too often drove out of the theatre in the second act all who had not fallen fast asleep in the first. To these Bizet's masterpiece offered the perfect antidote: theatrical immediacy achieved with a light touch and a nod towards that vogue for realism, initiated by the literature of Giovanni Verga and Luigi Capuana, which would find its musical expression ten years later in *Cavalleria rusticana*.

About this time Sonzogno, already proprietor of the periodical *Il secolo*, decided to challenge Ricordi's weekly *Gazzetta musicale di Milano* with two monthly publications of his own: *Il teatro illustrato*, advertised as 'the richest theatrical journal in existence', and the already mentioned *La musica popolare*, which not only reported on local events but contained articles on music theory and, like the *Gazzetta*, printed a composition, new or old. It was in the first of these that in April 1883 readers were informed of 'a competition open to young musicians of Italian nationality for an opera in one act on an *idyllic, serious,* or *comic* subject with a prize of 2000 lire following a performance in a Milan theatre at the journal's expense'. The panel of judges would consist of three professors from the conservatory—Ponchielli, Dominiceti, and

Galli—together with Pietro Platania, organist of Milan Cathedral, and the conductor Faccio, who would select for performance the two best operas submitted. The public would be allowed to choose the winner. Entries were to be submitted before the end of the year and the panel's decision made known by the following March. With three more months of studentship ahead of him Puccini decided to compete.

In its concluding paragraph the announcement had laid particular stress on the choice of a good libretto, 'both as regards subject matter and versification . . . since it is desirable in a theatrical work that there should be no discrepancy between the qualities of music and text'. It was the ever-helpful Ponchielli who found his student a worthy librettist in the young poet and jounalist Ferdinando Fontana, already active in the operatic field. Nearly nine years Puccini's senior, Fontana was a late offshoot of that iconoclastic movement in literature and the arts known as the 'scapigliatura' which flourished in Milan during the 1860s with the novelist Giuseppe Rovani as its high priest and Arrigo Boito its chief propagandist. Like all such movements it soon developed internal divisions. While Boito held to a high aesthetic plane, many of Rovani's followers, socially committed, moved towards the new 'realism' of the 1870s, among them Felice Cameroni, who first introduced the works of Zola to Italy. By 1880 most of the leading figures of the original 'scapigliatura'—Rovani, the poet Emilio Praga, the painter Tranquillo Cremona—were dead. Boito had become a respected figure of the establishment, already at work on an *Otello* for Italy's Grand Old Man. Fontana remained with Cameroni and Cleto Arrighi (originator of the movement's title) to keep the radical torch alight. But if in politics he was a partisan of the extreme left, whose involvement in the disturbances of 1898 would earn him a lifetime's exile in Switzerland, in matters operatic Fontana was very much the heir of Boito. His ideals are expounded in a polemical tract, *In teatro*, published in 1884. Its thesis is that in its present form the theatre is dead; that historical drama, whether musical or spoken, falsifies the events it relates, and that those works which are supposed to have fired the Risorgimento can be compared to men who hide in cellars when the fighting begins, to emerge crying 'Freedom!' when it is all over. The public's growing taste for symphonic music would eventually transform conventional opera into a 'poema sinfonico scenico', of which each act would form a movement and in which scenery, costumes, libretto, and singers would function like individual instruments within an orchestra. Thus the libretto should no more be given to the spectator to read than a part for oboe or clarinet; instead he should be provided with a 'poem', which should fill in the outlines of the plot in language worthy of the subject. It was as cloudy and unrealistic a theory as any propounded by the young Boito; but it would have a certain bearing on the author's first collaboration with Puccini.

A meeting between them was arranged at Ponchielli's country house at Lecco on the shores of Lake Como; and happily the young men took to each other at once. In view of Puccini's straitened circumstances Fontana agreed to lower his fee provided that the composer would make good the balance in the event of his winning the contest. Moreover, he had a subject ready to hand, taken, as usual with the 'scapigliati', from a near-contemporary French source: *Les Willis*, a short story by Alphonse Karr, journalist and friend of Alfred de Musset. Its basis is the Central European legend recounted by Heine in his *Deutschland II: Elementärgeister* (1834) about the ghosts of jilted maidens who dance nightly in the forests; and woe betide the faithless lover who encounters them, for he must join in the dance until he falls dead. The classic version is Théophile Gautier's scenario for Adolphe Adam's ballet *Giselle* (1846): village maiden, courted by the already affianced son of the local prince, goes mad and dies of grief on discovering his identity. The betrayer, visiting her grave by night, is surprised by the ghostly troupe, whose queen orders that he be danced to death by his victim. But Giselle's love sustains him to the end, while his fiancée understands and forgives.

Karr's treatment is both more realistic and more gruesome. His setting is a village community in the Black Forest ruled by the head forester, Wilhelm Wulf. The story begins with the betrothal at a dance of his daughter Anna with the young villager Heinrich, with whom she has long been in love. Soon afterwards Heinrich is summoned to Mainz to the bedside of a sick uncle. Before leaving he hangs a wreath of flowers outside Anna's window as a pledge of his constancy. However, the sight of his favourite brother's son restores the old man to health. Heinrich agrees to prolong his stay, the more willingly since he has begun to take to his new surroundings. What is more, his uncle has a beautiful daughter who will one day inherit his wealth; and Heinrich soon yields to his family's pressure to marry her. Anna's brother Konrad arrives on the day of their wedding and bitterly insults the bridegroom. A duel is fought, from which Konrad returns home mortally wounded. Anna pines and dies. Only Wilhelm is left to invoke God's vengeance on 'the murderer of my two children'.

A year has passed. Heinrich's uncle has at last died leaving him the richest man in Mainz. To please his wife, now expecting their first child, Heinrich has bought a castle not far from his native village. One night he returns from hunting later than usual. As darkness falls he hears distant voices singing melodies that recall the village dances of his past. Drawn by their sound, he finds himself in a clearing surrounded by dancing maidens of unearthly beauty, one of whom bears the face and form of Anna. She holds out her arms to him and they begin to dance. . . .

Next morning his body is found in the glade.

In digesting the story for a one-act opera Fontana concentrated the action on two moments: Heinrich's departure for Mainz and his return to the forest, to be danced to death. Konrad is eliminated and Heinrich re-christened, more singably, Roberto. A more radical alteration turned the rich uncle into an aunt whose death has occurred before the rise of the curtain, so that Roberto has merely to go to Mainz to collect his inheritance. While there he falls under the spell of a local 'siren', on whom he spends all his newly acquired wealth, returning home penniless and remorseful. But his repentance is unavailing. He tries to pray, but cannot. Anna-turned-Willi is as bent on vengeance as Catalani's Elda (later Loreley).

'With the success of his *Capriccio sinfonico* still fresh in my memory', Fontana recalled, 'I thought the young composer would need a fantastic subject, and I sketched out to him the scheme of *Le Villi*.'[4] He was not far wrong. 'It is a good little subject', Puccini wrote to his mother. ' . . . It will mean working quite a lot in the symphonic descriptive genre, and that appeals to me a good deal since I think I can succeed in it.'[5] The libretto was ready by mid-September, and Puccini returned

---

[4] Ibid., 37n.

[5] CP 6, p. 6.

to Lucca to begin the composition. Time was short, and he was a slow worker. No documents exist to chart the opera's progress. Somehow it was finished within the prescribed deadline and consigned to the panel at the last possible moment. A fair copy was out of the question.

There followed three months of anxious waiting. At the beginning of April the judges announced their findings. Out of 28 entries five were deemed worthy of mention. The two selected for performance were Luigi Mapelli's *Anna e Gualberto* and Guglielmo Zuelli's *La fata del Nord*. Both would be given on 4 May at the Teatro Manzoni; and since both received equal applause the prize was divided between them. Of *Le Villi* not a word.

At first sight this seems puzzling. Although the entries were submitted anonymously, two of the jury—Ponchielli and Faccio—must have been familiar with Puccini's handwriting. He had already attracted attention as a composer of promise; nor had he made any secret of his intention to compete. On the other hand, a clause in the original notice specified that the score should be clearly 'intelligible'. The autograph of *Le Villi* starts neatly enough but soon degenerates into an untidy scrawl with blotches and corrections. Several of the pages are in the hand of a later copyist, evidently replacing the originals. Five judges, all fully employed in other fields, had three months in which to examine individually twenty-eight scores and then deliberate together on their findings. Is it surprising that they should have refused to waste time on a barely legible manuscript? Puccini had been despondent from the start. 'The result of the competition will be known at the end of the month', he wrote to Albina, 'but I've little hope.'[6] Doubtless Ponchielli had hinted as much.

Fontana, however, was not prepared to give up the battle as lost. One of his acquaintances was the influential, if eccentric journalist Marco Sala (among his less savoury diversions was the teaching of improper songs to prim young Englishwomen, who would perform them without understanding a word of what they were singing). It was at Sala's home that Fontana arranged a meeting at which Puccini would play his score to a select gathering that included Boito, Catalani, and Giovannina Lucca. All declared themselves in Puccini's favour and

[6] PCE 29, p. 44.

against the verdict of the jury. Fontana himself undertook to raise a subscription towards a performance of *Le Villi* at the Teatro Dal Verme. Boito headed the list of subscribers with a gift of 50 lire—a ninth of the estimated cost. The performance took place as part of a triple bill on 31 May 1884 under the conductor Alfredo Panizza with Rosina Caponetti (Anna), Antonio D'Andrade (Roberto), and Erminio Pelz (Guglielmo Wulf). Among the double basses was Mascagni, who at Puccini's invitation left his post to join the composer in his box. The reception exceeded all expectations. Each number was warmly applauded, in particular 'La tregenda', the second movement of the Intermezzo or 'Parte sinfonica', which earned a double encore. Puccini himself was called to the footlights 18 times, so he told his mother in a telegram. The three scheduled performances were increased to four, at the end of which the impresario presented the composer with a laurel wreath.

No less flattering were the notices. 'Never can we remember having seen a budding maestro as heartily acclaimed as was Puccini at the Teatro Dal Verme' (*La musica popolare*); and the writer went on to praise the self-assurance, the boldness, the individuality of a work in which the influences of Bizet, Thomas, Massé, and the like were all confidently assimilated. Antonio Gramola (*Il corriere della sera*): 'The virtues we encounter in *Le Villi* reveal in Puccini an imagination singularly inclined to melody. In his music there is freshness of fantasy, there are phrases that touch the heart because they must have come from the heart, and there is craftsmanship so elegant and refined that from time to time we seem to have before us not a young student but a Bizet or a Massenet. . . . In short we believe that in Puccini we may have the composer for whom Italy has been waiting for a long time'—a sentiment echoed in almost identical words by Marco Sala in *L'Italia* and by the critic of *La Lombardia*. As for the most eminent of them all, Filippi (*La perseveranza*): 'Puccini to the stars! . . . Poor competition panel, that threw the opera into a corner like a rag!' But doubtless remembering the *Capriccio sinfonico* he felt bound to add: 'Puccini is by nature essentially a symphonist, and by exaggerating the symphonic element he often overloads the pedestal to the detriment of the statue.' Evidently this judgment penetrated the sacred walls of Sant Agata. 'I've heard the musician Puccini very well spoken of', Verdi wrote to a friend. 'He follows modern trends, which is natural, but he keeps steadily to melody, which is neither ancient nor modern. However, it seems that the symphonic element predominates in him! No harm in that. Only here you have to tread carefully. Opera is opera and symphony is symphony, and I don't think it's a good thing to put a symphonic piece into an opera merely for the pleasure of making the orchestra dance.'[7] Such is the only first-hand account we have of Verdi's reaction to Puccini's music—of which he had not yet heard a note! But that he was prepared to give *Le Villi* the benefit of every possible doubt appears from a letter of his former pupil Emanuele Muzio to Giulio Ricordi: ' . . . I congratulate you, because Verdi wrote to me a few weeks back that you've at last found what you've been looking for for thirty years, a true maestro—one Puccini who, it seems, possesses qualities out of the ordinary.'[8]

Indeed, Ricordi had been swift to pounce. The day after the final performance he invited composer and poet to his villa on Lake Como to discuss future plans. In the meantime he bought the world rights of *Le Villi* and commissioned a full-length successor from its authors. An announcement to that effect was splashed on the front page of the *Gazzetta musicale di Milano* of 8 June, where the opera is named *Le Willis*, so misleading Puccini's biographers into the belief that this was the title under which it was first presented to the public, though the printed libretto clearly indicates otherwise. To enable him to compose the new work in relative comfort Ricordi granted Puccini a monthly stipend of 200 lire for two years. It was not a princely sum—just twice what he had received for his maintenance as a student; but at least he could now liquidate his outstanding debts.

So began an association that would last until the publisher's death in 1912. Giulio Ricordi would become the father that Puccini had lost in infancy, always ready to find him suitable librettists and to smooth out any difficulties that might (and frequently did) arise between them. Nor was he less prodigal with fatherly advice, artistic or moral. His imme-

---

[7] Letter to O. Arrivabene, 10 June 1884; in A. Alberti: *Verdi intimo* (Verona, 1931), 311–15.

[8] Letter to G. Ricordi quoted without date in F. Abbiati, *Guiseppe Verdi* (Milan, 1959), iv, 248.

diate concern was that *Le Villi* should be enlarged into two acts, the better to circulate. Puccini meanwhile returned home for a well-earned rest.

Here tragedy awaited him. Albina had for some time been ailing, unable to keep her food down and growing weaker by the day. Doctors had diagnosed a liver complaint and prescribed rest and relaxation. But on 17 July Albina died, aged 54. She had never ceased to exert herself on Giacomo's behalf. While the outcome of the Concorso Sonzogno was awaited she had written again to Ponchielli asking him to find employment for her son (though whether Puccini ever delivered the letter seems doubtful). Hearing of the success of *Le Villi* she had sent a cordial letter to Fontana, which touched the poet deeply. 'I am always thinking of *her*', Puccini wrote to Ramelde later that summer, 'and to-night I even dreamed about her. So today I'm feeling sadder than usual. No matter what triumphs my art may bring me, I shall have little happiness without my dear mother. Take what comfort you can and try to summon up more courage than I have so far been able to do.'[9]

'Work is the only balm for great sorrow.'[10] Such was Fontana's advice; and over the next few months the revision of *Le Villi* proceeded apace. First a cavatina was added for Anna ('Se come voi piccina') to be inserted after the opening chorus. Next the slow movement of the Intermezzo ('L'abbandono') was rewritten so as to allow for a chorus of mourners who would pass behind a gauze veil bearing Anna's body. What now became the second act was expanded by a dramatic 'scena' for Roberto, while Anna's solo, her one aria in the original version, in which she throws in her lover's face all his former protestation of eternal constancy, became a duet for them both. In the 'scena' Fontana proclaimed himself still more explicitly the descendant of Boito. Already in the original score his Villi, as yet unseen, had echoed Mefistofele's exhortation to Faust on the Brocken ('Cammina! Cammina! Cammina!'). Now the siren of Mainz was to be compared to a 'lombrico'—a worm that feeds on the dead, and evidently a term so recherché that

[9] CP 14, p. 14.
[10] PCE 75, p. 82.

Fontana himself was uncertain how it should be stressed. He later re-placed it with the more prosaic 'verme', this too an image that obsessed Boito as late as Iago's Credo. The concluding Totentanz was enriched by a chorus of invisible demons, male and female, which delighted Giulio Ricordi beyond measure, so Fontana reported. Finally the opera's subheading was changed from 'Legend in one act and two parts' to 'Opera ballo in two acts'. Puccini worked on the score at the home of his by now married sister Ramelde at San Martino in Colle, a few miles outside Lucca, which from henceforward became his base during his visits to his native city. By 21 November everything was in fair copy and ready for dispatch.

Meanwhile on 19 October the *Gazzetta musicale di Milano* had pub-lished a two-page biography of the composer accompanied by a head-and-shoulders portrait. Like all his early photographs it shows a thin, solemn face, lips slightly parted beneath a thin moustache, large eyes, and a crop of dark curls. The prose is Fontana's and characteristically fanciful. 'This extremely young maestro from Lucca is 172 years old; yes, 172, because he is the latest bloom on a tree that was planted in 1712. He absorbed music with his mother's milk, showed remarkable aptitude from the start'—and so on. Among various inaccuracies a men-tion of Ponchielli as Puccini's only teacher at the conservatory elicited a mild protest from Bazzini, and Fontana duly corrected the error in the following issue.

In December Puccini enjoyed a further bonus with the publication by the firm of Pigna of three minuets for string quartet both in their original form and in an arrangement for piano duet. 'Very pretty little pieces', remarked *La musica popolare*, 'full of good taste and refinement, . . . marked by that elegance and fluency that makes his music so agree-able.' Each has a smooth, even gait of quavers and semiquavers; each is in the key of A major with a trio in the subdominant; and each bears a dedication to a citizen of Lucca: Her Royal Highness Vittoria Au-gusta, Principessa di Capua; Professore Augusto Michelangeli; and Carlo Carignani. Therein surely lies the clue to their similarity. All three could be seen as Puccini's homage to the city's most illustrious son, Luigi Boccherini, whose Minuet from the Quintet in A, played by full strings, had long been a staple of the local orchestral repertory under Miche-langeli's direction. Later Ricordi would re-issue the first and third of the set; not, however, the second, whose opening strain, transformed into a brisk allegro, had by this time furnished the start of *Manon Lescaut.*

Le Villi in its new form opened the Carnival season of 1884-5 at the Teatro Regio, Turin, on 26 December, with an undistinguished cast and conductor. Poet and composer were both present. Neither was impressed with the staging or the performance. Puccini himself received only four curtain calls. Far more importance attached to a revival at La Scala on 24 January 1885. The conductor was Franco Faccio and the cast included Romilda Pantaleoni, soon to create Verdi's Desdemona. In the event she alone proved equal to the occasion; but the public responded favourably and the opera ran for thirteen nights. Among the critics Filippi (in *La perseveranza*) confirmed his positive judgment of the previous year. In its original version, he observed, *Le Villi* seemed not so much an opera in the accepted sense, but rather a symphonic cantata adapted for the stage; and so, essentially, it remained even in its more amplified form. But Filippi found no harm in that. 'One spent a delightful hour and a half with music that is good, thoughtful, and stands on its own feet without the prop of vulgar sensationalism; and this indicates in the writer not only a rare talent but an even rarer artistic conscience.' This and other complimentary reviews were duly printed in the *Gazzetta musicale di Milano* together with a preface by Giulio Ricordi himself, which mixed praise with words of warning against the 'Wagnerian poison' that was corrupting native talent. 'Let Puccini remember that he is Italian, and let him feel no shame on that account; and let him prove it by allowing free rein to his fertile imagination. He will reap the glory of it; and it will be Italian glory.' That month the first vocal score of *Le Villi* was printed with a dedication to its benefactors, Arrigo Boito and Marco Sala. But its composition was not yet at an end. Some time during the Milan performances Puccini added to Roberto's 'scena drammatica' the romanza 'Torna ai felici dì'. This would appear in the opera's second edition, issued in May 1885. Three years later a third edition would be brought out in which the final duet for Anna and Roberto was extended by eight bars; and finally in 1892 no fewer than 98 bars were excised from Roberto's 'scena' (including the reference to the 'verme') and replaced by eight. Such would be the opera's definitive form.

Not everyone shared Filippi's and Ricordi's enthusiasm. A performance at Naples in the spring of 1888 would be drowned by whistles and boos. Many singers were critical. Teresa Stolz, Verdi's first Aida on Italian soil, complained of too much descriptive music which swamped the voices, particularly the tenor in Act II, and found the dances all too reminiscent of Bizet. Clara Novello, now married and retired, saw in Puccini merely an imitator of Wagner, the score all harmony and no melody. Nonetheless in the years that followed *Le Villi* achieved a respectable circulation at home and abroad. In 1892 Gustav Mahler conducted a performance at Hamburg. Five years afterwards it reached England, where it was given in Manchester by the Carl Rosa Opera Company in a translation by Percy Pinkerton as *The Witch Dancers*. As late as 1916 Puccini considered reviving it as part of a double-bill with *Il tabarro*, in which case he would have done well to revise the score according to Verdi's practice, since not all the music is characteristic or even fully effective.

The prelude, however, offers a fine sample of musical and dramatic economy. Here we can salute one of those hushed, pregnant openings that will characterize many an opera of the 'giovane scuola'. This presents us straight away with the pivot of the drama: Roberto's foresworn oath. An extended melody in his first duet with Anna derived from the song 'Melanconia' (see Ex. 3.4), it is here hinted at in sequentially repeated fragments: first, the opening chordal gesture (*x*), then, superimposed on it, the semiquaver cluster (*y*) that concluded the initial strain and which will later carry Roberto's faintly blasphemous 'Ah! dubitar di Dio', to be answered by a caressing phrase, 'ma no, dell'amor mio non dubitar!' that emphasizes the vow with grace-notes in the French manner (Ex. 3.1). An interrupted cadence introduces two ideas in a new key, both from the Act I 'preghiera' ('Angiol di Dio'), in turn based on the romanza 'Salve regina'. The first of these (Ex. 3.2a) has

Ex. 3.1

Andante mosso

Ex. 3.2a

Ex. 3.2b

suggested to more than one commentator a recall of the 'Abendmahl-Motiv' from *Parsifal*, though it is merely the romanza's opening phrase curtailed for sequential purposes. The second (Ex. 3.2b) carries the unmistakeable Puccinian fingerprint of a falling fifth. A threefold repetition of Ex. 3.1 brings the piece to a close on a note of dramatic irony.

By comparison the 'coro d'introduzione' ('Evviva i fidanzati!') is fairly commonplace; but it presents a procedure that will become habitual with Puccini for opening a busy scene: two contrasted ideas, one in sharply pointed rhythm, the other smoother and more lyrical with, in this case, a cursive bass line as opposed to the former's tonic pedal. But their working out is as yet rather clumsy. When the chorus gossip about Roberto's inheritance to a resumption of the second theme in notes of double value, the impetus sags, and is not revived until the final reprise. The dance that follows ('Gira! Gira!') is simply the Scherzo in A minor for string quartet, re-scored, amplified by an episode in which Guglielmo proves that he can still cut a caper with the best of them, and sealed off with a major-key coda *in diminuendo*—a stock device for emptying the stage. An abundance of hemiolas throughout brings to mind the Kermesse waltz from Gounod's *Faust*.

On a far higher level is Anna's cavatina with its two strophes lightly varied in the manner of Aida's 'O patria mia'. But here the design is more elaborate, since this is also an action-piece, during which Anna plucks a nosegay of forget-me-nots, which she then addresses. Hence a 25-bar orchestral proemium of rare delicacy, its modally inflected harmonies poined up by glinting piccolo and glockenspiel together with harp, cymbals, and a cascade of semiquaver triplets on violins. Here, too, Puccini 'plants' those leaps of a fourth or fifth that will recur charged with menace in Act II (clearly an inspired afterthought, since Anna had no cavatina in the original version). Ten bars of arioso beginning on a seventh chord ('Se come voi piccina') prepare for the main melodic period ('Allor dirgli vorrei') which for the first time establishes the home key, rises effortlessly to a climax, and falls away to a protracted cadential phrase beneath the words 'Non ti scordar di me!' (Ex. 3.3). Here the mature Puccini is prefigured: the purely diatonic line with no chromatic inflections, the rhythmic freedom and supple articulation; the wealth of appoggiaturas and suspensions, so prolonged as to seem added notes—which in the later operas is exactly what they will become. There is a climactic orchestral peroration as Anna goes to place the

Ex. 3.3

flowers in Roberto's travelling bag. A lively interrupted cadence marks his sudden appearance ('Ah! ti ho colta!').

The first part of their duet (Ex. 3.4) is a dialogue with constant recurrences of the opening gesture, always approached from a dominant direction, so giving the sense of a doubt that refuses to be dispelled: for Anna has dreamed that she died waiting in vain for her lover's return. Roberto's reply ('Tu dell'infanzia mia') launches what is in effect a 'clinching' cabaletta, Anna repeating his music note for note, the voices finally joining in unison. The period concludes with the two cardinal motifs of Ex. 3.4 (marked *x* and *y*) both given a subdominant tilt which Ex. 3.1 at once corrects—a neat illustration of doubt allayed by assurance. But to make the latter double sure there is a further extension to the dominant followed by an emphatic assertion of the home key. How could Roberto break his vow after that?

During the 1880s the central 'pezzo concertato' was still *de rigueur*. In expanding his *Salve regina* for the purpose, Puccini developed some

Ex. 3.4

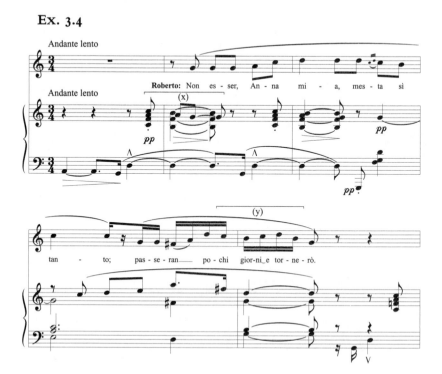

of the material into a species of 'hurry' music with choral intervention, as the villagers prepare to speed Roberto on his way. But first the young man asks a blessing from his father-in-law to be. All kneel while Guglielmo declaims the arpeggiated opening phrase of *Salve regina*, extended by a bar's anacrusis to accommodate Fontana's text ('Angiol di Dio'). The three soloists then unite in what had been the melodic substance of both the introduction and the second verse of the Ghislanzoni romanza, to which Ex. 3.2b now forms a pendant, its rising sequences laid out in a rudimentary canon. The chorus enter with Ex. 3.2a sustained by basses, propelling the music to a broad climax that dwindles into a pianissimo close. Throughout the ensemble the skills learnt at Lucca enabled Puccini to exploit to the full the limited resources offered by a theatrical chorus. Twelve bars of mutual salutation in fast tempo culminate in a full-blooded orchestral peroration *à la* Ponchielli, reaching back not to the 'pezzo concertato' but to the duet of Roberto's oath ('Tu dell'infanzia mia'). For that is what the opera is about.

From the outset Fontana had prefaced each of the two movements that make up the Intermezzo ('Parte sinfonica') by a snatch of poetry, recounting respectively Anna's death and the legend of the Willis. In modern performances both are assigned to a narrator, although Fontana made it clear to Puccini that he intended them merely to be read by the audience—doubtless a sample of that 'poem' which was to be given to them in place of the printed libretto. But Fontana, alas, was no poet, and the lines are embarrassingly banal.

The first movement ('L'abbandono') explores an elegiac world of grief and pity in a language that recalls the orchestral Prelude of 1882 with its meandering triplets, its gravitational pull towards the subdominant and an occasional splash of trumpet melody. Three ideas are linked so as to form a continuous cantilena of more than Bellinian length, to which a characteristic dwelling on the softer discords gives a yearning insistence. One example will suffice (Ex. 3.5). This is the real Puccini, to be echoed forty years later in Liù's 'Tanto amor segreto.' Four bars of chromatic murk suggest Anna's coffin being lowered into the earth, after which strings and chorus murmur their final benediction.

'La tregenda', a miniature 'Walkürenritt', has been roughly handled by biographers, who, like Teresa Stolz, consider it too much indebted

Ex. 3.5

to Bizet. Yet the harmonic style is very much Puccini's own (note again the subdominant tilt within the first eight bars). André Gauthier, one of its few defenders, is not far wrong in discerning a likeness to Mendelssohn.[11] For, as in many a Mendelssohn scherzo, there is no strict reprise. The ideas are deployed, juxtaposed, united, dissolved (developed is too strong a word—'ringing the changes' would be a more appropriate metaphor) so as to hold the listener's attention. If they are not especially striking in themselves, they have an *élan* that is highly theatrical. A mere gesture of syncopated octaves will suffice to recall 'La tregenda' at later points in the opera.

In Guglielmo's 'preludio e scena' convention prevails. Horns in thirds trace a chromatically descending line over lower strings, depicting both the desolate winter landscape and Guglielmo's sorrow. Anger rears its head in a triplet figure given out by full orchestra. Surely, Guglielmo cries, such guilt cannot remain unavenged. Ex. 3.4 (*x*) with its familiar woodwind scoring recalls Roberto's broken vow. From these three elements, varied and enriched, Puccini builds an effective 'scena', only to relapse in Gugliemo's cantabile ('Anima santa della figlia mia') into a mechanical regularity of phrase-length. Nor does the music follow the sense of the text. Guglielmo, like Monteverdi's Arianna and Verdi's Fiesco, inveighs against Heaven's negligence, then retracts the thought in a moment of contrition. But nothing of this is reflected in the bland harmonies and vocal line of what is no more than a competent piece of lyrical writing for the baritone voice.

No sooner has Guglielmo re-entered his house than the air becomes charged with menace. Fragments of the 'tregenda' are thrown out, punctuated by wisps of chromatic scales and the distant voices of the Willis (clearly Puccini's studies of *Der Freischütz*, attested by his notebooks, had not been in vain). Roberto arrives distraught, feeling himself pursued not by the Willis but by the 'viper' of remorse. His nostalgic romanza ('Torna ai felici dì') has rightly been likened by Carner to Admeto's 'Mio bianco amor' from Catalani's *Dejanice*. But Puccini has nothing to lose by the comparison. Catalani's is a large-scale, straggling design of regular periods ending with the traditional major-key resolution. Puccini's is more concentrated and at the same time freer and more varied in its articulation, cutting short the steady march of the opening strain with a triplet figure derived from *Ad una morta* and turned to expressive account as the piece proceeds. No less imaginative is the scoring with its four-octave gap between piccolo and double bass and its cor anglais countermelody, transferred to violins in octaves by way of an instrumental peroration. As usual Puccini enriches the orchestration for the second strophe.

The 'scena' resumes. 'Perhaps she still lives', Roberto muses; but a minor-key distortion of Ex. 3.5 refutes the notion (a Wagnerian device for giving the audience information over and above the sung text). About to knock at Guglielmo's door, Roberto is overcome by a wave of horror, pithily conveyed by the orchestra. His 'O sommo Iddio' is set to Ex. 3.2b, which here takes on a quality of desperation as the musical fabric becomes increasingly undermined by chromatically slithering cellos and bassoons. Unable to continue, he bursts into imprecations against the 'vile cortigiana' of Mainz.

From here to the end there is no new material. Anna appears to a recall of Ex. 3.5 and launches the duetto finale with Ex. 3.4 to the same words as before with sinister tremolandos on cellos to point up their altered significance. The vocal line too is rendered more emphatic by a vehement downward swoop that brings to mind Gioconda's 'Suicidio!' Again the music of 'L'abbandono' takes over as the duet proceeds. After the final cadence the Willis appear and surround the pair, their voices joined by an invisible chorus of male spirits. To the strains of 'La tregenda', now reinforced by two cornets, they cry 'Gira! balza!', cruelly echoing the words of the village dance of Act I. Roberto breaks away and hurls himself at Guglielmo's door, but is dragged away to die at Anna's feet pleading for mercy. 'You are mine!', she replies, and vanishes. Amid choral cries of 'Hosanna!' the curtain falls. The last words spoken by Guglielmo as he surveys Roberto's corpse ('God is just!') remain unset.

In 1895, with Mascagni still riding the crest of *Cavalleria rusticana*, Puccini wrote bitterly to Carlo Clausetti of the Casa Ricordi: '*Le Villi* initiated the type which is nowadays called "mascagnano", and nobody gives me the credit.'[12] This was not quite true. According to a letter of Catalani to his friend, the critic Giuseppe Depanis, 'In Hamburg they found *Cavalleria* to be a derivation from *Le Villi*'. In the same letter we read:

> At a supper given by Franchetti in Milan there was some talk about Tuscan composers; it seems that some held up Puccini, others Mascagni as the founder of a school. Then Franchetti entered the conversation and said that, since it really did seem as though a Tuscan school was being formed, the merit belongs neither to Puccini nor Mascagni but to Catalani. . . . That's what Franchetti said . . . and it pleased me very much because . . . I wouldn't have had the courage to say it myself.[13]

So who was in the right? From one point of view Catalani certainly. He was four years older than Puccini and had been subjected to the same formative influences at Lucca and Milan. Like Puccini he loved Wagner's music; and he had learned his French lessons even more thoroughly than his fellow-townsman, having spent half a year in Paris. All his operas beginning with *Elda* (1880) contain anticipations of Puccini: the elastic vocal line combining sustained notes with flurries of semiquavers, the rich harmonies, and, above all, that pervasive melancholy often referred to as 'mestizia toscana'. But to the end his style remained basically eclectic, its elements never coalescing into a strong personal synthesis. His music, despite its many beauties and a refinement of thought at which his contemporaries (apart from Smareglia) never aimed, inevitably made less of an impact than theirs.

Le Villi in its turn did indeed affirm the 'stile mascagnano' and far

---

[12] CP 127, p. 117.

[13] A. Catalani, *Lettere*, ed. C. Gatti (Milan, 1946), 151–2.

more powerfully than anything by Catalani, but only in certain numbers. Elsewhere it too has its share of imperfectly assimilated influences. But there is a still more cogent reason why it would yield pride of place to *Cavalleria rusticana*. Unlike Mascagni's opera it is not so much a drama as a story. There is no cut and thrust of emotional dialectic to keep audiences on the edge of their seats. Not only is its successor all of a piece; from the moment we hear Turiddu's offstage serenade in the prelude, we apprehend a tension between the characters such as is entirely absent from *Le Villi*, where there is no-one to react to Guglielmo's grief or Roberto's remorse; which is why *Cavalleria rusticana* made history and *Le Villi* did not. As always, the winner is not who does it first but who does it best. In this case it was not Puccini.

CHAPTER 4

Edgar

IN COMMISSIONING ANOTHER OPERA FROM PUCCINI AND FON-
tana Ricordi was clearly determined that no time should be lost. 'Set
all your imagination in an eruption for the new libretto to be given to
Puccini', he told the poet, who was still at work on the additions to
Le Villi. 'If I insist on this, it's because one must strike while the iron
is hot *et frapper l'imagination du public.*'[1] Fontana had already suggested
to Puccini the subject of Alfred de Musset's 'poème dramatique', *La
coupe et les lèvres;* but if Puccini decided against it, he would offer it to
Zuelli. Puccini, however, made no demur; so the plan went ahead.

Fontana's choice of author is not surprising, for had not that arch-
scapigliato, Emilio Praga, been described by Cameroni as 'the Musset
of our generation'? And if the play was never intended for stage performance, this too could be seen as a recommendation by one who
held that Shakespeare is best enjoyed in an armchair. The hero, Frank,
is a Tyrolean peasant, half Faust, half Manfred, who despises his fellow-
men and sets out on a voyage of self-discovery, having first burned
down his home and cursed his father's memory. He encounters the
young girl Deidemia, his neighbour's daughter, who gives him a bou-
quet of eglantine. With her, Frank muses, he might have been happy;
but now it is too late. The knight Stranio passes by on horseback,
carrying on his saddle the fair courtesan Monna Belcolore. Rudely he

[1] PCE 88, p. 95.

orders Frank out of the way; they fight, and Stranio is killed. Belcolore at once attaches herself to the victor. With her help Frank accumulates vast wealth and spends his nights in dissipation. Yet despite his apparent contentment Belcolore senses that he is about to leave her—as indeed he does, to join a passing soldier on his way to the wars. Soon news of Frank's military exploits spreads far and wide; but Belcolore is determined to seek him out and win him back ('C'est un diable incarné que cette femme-là!' murmurs a lieutenant). Reported killed in a duel, Frank attends his own funeral in the guise of a monk. He interrupts the eulogies of an officer to recall his previous misdeeds and so rouses the bystanders to curse his memory. They tear open the coffin, only to find in it an empty suit of armour. Frank orders the crowd away and places the officer under arrest. He reassumes his disguise as Belcolore appears in deep mourning. She succumbs, however, to his offer of untold riches and jewellery and agrees to embrace him, though he tells her that he is hideous and diseased. Once again he reveals the empty suit of armour and his own identity, and drives her away with a dagger. After two hundred lines of philosophical reflection Frank decides to return to his native village and to Deidemia, who has waited for him for fifteen years. All appears set fair for their wedding, but Deidemia feels threatened by an unseen presence. As Frank goes to investigate, Belcolore enters and stabs Deidemia to the heart. The cup is thus dashed from his lips.

With the revisions to *Le Villi* behind him, Fontana set to work on the libretto in the spring of 1885. His first task was to concentrate the sprawling narrative within a narrower framework of time and place. Accordingly he transferred the action to Flanders in 1302, the year in which the Flemings routed the French at the Battle of Courtray—a fitting occasion for the hero's deeds of valour, and one which would lend itself to a symphonic intermezzo leading without a break into the funeral scene. For the distribution of characters *Carmen* offered a suitable precedent, with Micaela as the model for Deidemia, re-named first Taroé, then Fidelia, and Carmen herself for Belcolore, now Tigrana. The protagonist, a medieval Don José, from Abgar became Edgar— strangely, since neither name is specifically Flemish or easy for an Italian to articulate in two syllables. As in Bizet's masterpiece the baritone had to be found outside the literary source. Fontana therefore invented a brother for Fidelia who, originally Efrem, would inherit the name of the play's hero, Frank, and would combine the three functions of Stranio, the soldier who recruits the by now penitent sinner and the officer who pronounces his funeral oration. The canvas was further filled out by Fidelia and Frank's father Gualtiero as a comprimario bass.

The plot had then to be re-worked so as to allow the principals to participate in as much of the action as possible. A new pedigree was devised for Tigrana, who became an orphan of Moorish origin brought up in Gualtiero's house as his foster-daughter. Frank is in love with her; but already in Act I she has set her sights on Edgar. At first repelled by her advances, it is the villagers' hostility to her that prompts him to burn down his house and carry her off, after having wounded Frank in a duel. In the funeral scene it was necessary to avoid two revelations of the empty suit of armour, each followed by Edgar's unmasking. Fidelia was therefore introduced to defend the hero's memory against the attacks of the false monk. This she does so eloquently that the crowd are for the moment appeased. It is left to Tigrana, bribed by the offer of jewels, to denounce him as a traitor to his country and so detonate the wrath of the bystanders. In the third and final act Frank would return home with Edgar; both he and Gualtiero would be present at the final débâcle.

All this was submitted to Puccini with the aid of graphic diagrams 'à la Berlioz' illustrating the shape of each of the three acts—a typical 'scapigliato' ploy that must have meant as little to Puccini as it does to the modern reader. Act II caused Fontana the most difficulty. Where to find an aria for Tigrana? How to avoid two duets between her and Edgar? The first problem was solved by giving Tigrana a brindisi with chorus of revellers; the second by turning the 'temptation duet' into a trio with the participation of Frank. The by now over-long second act was split into two, the 'symphonic intermezzo' eventually dropped, and Tigrana given another aria in the new Act III. The libretto was complete and in Puccini's hands by May, and a performance the following year confidently predicted. In the event nearly four years would pass before *Edgar* saw the stage.

Various circumstances contributed to the delay. Since his mother's death Puccini had become head of the family. His sisters were by now

married off except for Iginia, who had taken the veil. There remained
Michele, a likeable young scapegrace, for whom a musical career had
also been decided upon, though he possessed not a tithe of his brother's
aptitude. Already in March 1884 Giacomo had found him employment
with the Milanese publisher Pigna, pending his entrance examination
for the conservatory—which, however, he missed due to illness.
Through Bazzini's intervention he was allowed to sit for it again and
so begin his course of study in November. His story is soon told. Over
the next three years he made desultory progress under the tutelage of
Michele Saladino (Mascagni's teacher), assisted by subventions from the
ever-provident Dr Cerù and from Puccini himself. But in 1888 he left
the conservatory without a diploma and, like many of his fellow-
countrymen, emigrated to Argentina. Letters to Ramelde and Giacomo
dwell on the amenities of Buenos Aires, and above all on the honours
paid to him as brother to the composer of *Le Villi*, heard there in 1886.
After a few months spent in private tuition he was offered a post as
teacher of piano and Italian at a school in the town of Jujuy, situated
in a remote part of the Andes. His new salary was more than satisfactory,
and there was excellent hunting in the neighbourhood, but also a certain drawback, 'Feminine virtue here is quite incredible; the girls want
husbands and the married women never give way, and so? One has to
make do with some coloured girl, Indian or servant, for the sake of
one's bodily health'.[2] If only he had kept to that rule! In no time he
was involved in an intrigue with the wife of an influential friend. A
duel was reported, the husband wounded in the shoulder and Michele
hounded out of the town. He returned for a while to Buenos Aires,
then decided to try his fortune in Rio de Janeiro. Here he fell victim
to an epidemic of yellow fever and died in an isolation ward on 12
March 1891. 'How utterly heartbeaking!' Puccini wrote to Ramelde
on receiving the news:

> I don't think I felt such sorrow even when our poor mother died, and that
> was fearful enough. . . . I too long for death; what have I to do with this
> world? . . . I can get no peace; night-time is terrible for me. . . . God knows

[2] Letter to N. Cerù, 20 May 1890, in PCE 139, p. 152.

what consternation you must all be feeling, but not so great as mine; I'm completely finished, this has been the final straw for me and I don't believe that in this case time will prove the usual healer.[3]

And to his brother-in-law: 'If God exists, He is very cruel.'[4]

Meanwhile Puccini himself had become entangled in a relationship no less adulterous than his brother's. How and when he first came to know Elvira Gemignani (née Bonturi), wife of a Luccan commercial traveller, has never been established. Elvira was younger than her lover by over a year and already the mother of two children when her name first surfaces in a letter from Puccini to Fontana of January 1886. When the composer left for Milan in June she followed him, giving out to friends and relations that she was going to Palermo. On 22 December their child was born, to be christened Antonio Ferdinando Maria. Elvira obtained an official separation from her husband which allowed her custody of their six-year-old daughter Fosca, while the son Renato remained in his father's care. Not until Gemignani's death in 1904 were Elvira and Giacomo able to marry.

It was not a peaceful union. Like his brother Puccini had a roving eye. Women were as necessary to him as they were to Wagner, even if he never made the same demands upon them. That such extra-marital relationships filled him with a sense of guilt, which he then visited on the heroines of his operas, is unlikely. The Italian society of his day was strongly male-orientated. A husband's peccadillos were venial and the matrimonial horns a universal joke. Relevant here is a letter written to Puccini shortly after the première of Le Villi by an unnamed 'old friend' from Milan. After much sententious advice to work hard, not to rest on his laurels, and to avoid running into debt comes a more specific warning:

Keep clear of women, who, with rare exceptions, are the plague of society; treat them as playthings, to be thrown away into a corner once you have done with them; use them as a physical necessity, nothing more. As you know, I speak from experience. . . . One last word of advice. Take care not to fall in love if you can possibly avoid doing so, since that will lead you

[3] Ibid. 145, p. 159.
[4] Ibid. 144, p. 156.

into the grave of matrimony, which ninety-nine times out of a hundred hampers, cuts short and ruins a young man's career, especially one such as yours, who need absolute freedom and independence. But if by any chance you should fall into the net, for goodness sake marry a woman whom you love, who is beautiful, 'simpatica', well-educated, and kind, because if you don't, heaven help you![5]

In her youth Elvira was certainly beautiful—tall, dark-eyed, full-figured with regular features and a Roman nose—and Puccini was no less certainly in love with her. Her decision to leave her husband testifies to considerable courage, since the scandal of their liaison bore far more heavily on her than on Puccini. She was also reasonably well-educated. But 'simpatica' in the full sense of that untranslatable word, she was not. Unable to share Puccini's love of rural solitude or to enjoy the company of his hunting and card-playing friends, let alone to enter into his creative world ('You never mention the word "art" without a sneer', he once complained to her), she was no more qualified to be a composer's wife than Minna Wagner. Whether, given a greater degree of understanding on her part, Puccini would ever have made a model husband may be doubted. But there can be no question that by her incessant suspicions, whether well-founded or not, Elvira drove him more and more to take refuge in what he liked to call his 'little gardens'[6] (i.e., amorous escapades). As the years brought him poise and presence, while Elvira's looks declined into sullen heaviness, her jealousy took the most extravagant forms. She would sprinkle his trouser pockets with bromide in the hope of curbing his sexual drive, and even follow him in disguise. Yet only once, after a particularly grim tragedy, did he seriously think of leaving her. But that is to anticipate.

Inevitably the liaison took its toll of the new opera. In May 1886 Puccini was obliged to beg Ricordi for an extension of his monthly stipend which was due to end in June, giving as his reason the extreme difficulty of the opera and the fact that he had a brother to help maintain at the conservatory. Aware or not of the true situation, Ricordi obliged. No-one was more helpful to the young couple than Fontana, himself similarly involved with another man's wife. Prodigal with advice re-

[5] Ibid. 56, p. 70.
[6] MP, 92.

garding their departure from Lucca when Elvira's pregnancy was becoming too advanced to escape notice, he it was who found them suitable lodgings at Monza, where Elvira could give birth to their son in relative seclusion—all this in the teeth of opposition from his partner Palmira, who had evidently taken against the two runaways from the start. However, they could not afford to remain in Monza for long. By March 1887 they were both back in Lucca as guests of Ramelde and her husband, much to the annoyance of Gemignani, who considered it unfitting that his wife should come to a town where so many of her relations were living.

Whether for this reason or out of sheer economic necessity she and Giacomo decided to live apart for a while. Elvira took Antonio and Fosca to stay with her mother and sister in Florence. Puccini moved between Milan and the neighbourhood of Fontana's country residence at Caprino Bergamasco, where they could work together on *Edgar*. In a letter of October 1887 to Luigi Mancinelli, who he hoped might conduct a performance in Madrid, he announced that the opera was already finished and would have been scheduled for the Carnival season in Rome, had it not been displaced by the work of a local composer.[7] This was probably optimistic, for in fact the score was not ready for performance until the autumn of 1888. Conflicting dates on the autograph suggest that parts of it had been radically re-worked in the meantime.

Throughout this period Puccini continued to attend revivals of *Le Villi* at cities that were hearing it for the first time; hence the visits to Bologna, Trieste (whence he returned post-haste to catch a performance of Verdi's *Otello*), and Naples, where the afore-mentioned fiasco earned him a 'protest banquet' given in his honour by friends at Lucca. Of special interest is the listing of 'Puccini Giacoma and Fontano (*sic!*)' among the guests to the Bayreuth Festival of 1888.[8] Of the two works performed *Parsifal* would remain a special favourite with Puccini. *Die Meistersinger* would have its Italian première at La Scala on 26 December 1889, Puccini having travelled to Bayreuth with the conductor Faccio at his publisher's expense to advise on suitable cuts. On this occasion,

[7] CP 26, p. 25.
[8] SGP, 74.

however, he and Fontana appear to have paid their own way; for some months later we find the poet dunning Puccini for his share of the financial outlay.

Also to this year belongs a 'mattinata' contributed by Puccini to the short-lived 'periodico-artistico-musicale' *Paganini*, founded in Genoa by the violinist Camillo Sivori in memory of his famous teacher. The same issue contains Catalani's piano piece *A sera*, which became the basis of the Prelude to Act III of *La Wally*. Puccini's *Sole e amore* would likewise be put to operatic use as the quartet that ends Act III of *La bohème* (see Ex. 6.15). The text, for which no author is given, is for once in prose; but it faintly suggests a paraphrase of a sonnet by Giosuè Carducci entitled 'Mattinata', in which the sun is likened to a lover who comes tapping at a young girl's window. As a typical joke Puccini's autograph carries a final reprise of the opening strain to the words 'Il primo di marzo dell'ottant'otto', presumably the date of completion. For the published version this was changed to 'Al *Paganini* G. Puccini'. One of his freshest melodic inspirations, Puccini was surely right in thinking the manuscript worthy to be given as a 60th birthday present 'to my dearest friend F. P. Tosti, this first germ of *Bohème*, Milan, 1st April 1906'. One hopes that the music master to the English royal family and composer of fashionable drawing-room songs felt suitably flattered. With *Edgar* still uncompleted Puccini announced in a laconic postcard to Ramelde (recently the mother of a daughter, Albina) that he was working on a third opera; but what it was remains a mystery.

At long last *Edgar* was scheduled for the Carnevale-Quaresima season 1888–9, at La Scala with an outstanding cast under the direction of Franco Faccio: in the title role Gregorio Gabrielesco, famous for his performances of *La Gioconda* and a worthy substitute for the Tamagno on whom Puccini had set his hopes; as Fidelia Aurelia Cataneo, Italy's first Isolde; as Tigrana Romilda Pantaleoni, creator of Verdi's Desdemona. Rehearsals began towards the end of March and proceeded slowly, 'because of the difficulty of the music', so Catalani reported,[9] himself anxious to attend a performance. Ricordi stocked his *Gazzetta musicale di Milano* with many a 'puff-preliminary'; and all seemed set fair for a triumph that would throw that of *Le Villi* into the shade.

[9] A. Catalani, *Lettere*, ed. C. Gatti (Milan, 1946), 96.

It was not to be. The première on 21 April was received not un-kindly by the leading critics. They noted the technical advance on the music of *Le Villi;* they singled out certain moments for special praise; but they did not disguise the fact that the public had been cool. That there were harsher judgments—among them that of *La Lombardia,* whose critic accused the composer of 'great sins against art, lack of faith, conviction, and well-defined ideals'—is evident from Ricordi's summing-up the following week. Characteristically he tried to make the best of the situation, pointing out that hostility is preferable to indifference. Puccini wrote a cordial letter to Faccio thanking him and his cast for their immense trouble. But neither he nor his publisher was under any illusion. The opera had failed and something would have to be done about it. After three performances *Edgar* was taken off and composer and librettist called by Ricordi to a conference with a view to making changes. How little progress was made becomes clear from one of Ricordi's long, cautionary letters to his protégé:

> That interminable discussion of nearly five hours!! . . . Your good Fontana has shown himself an eloquent orator but a cavilling one. More of a philosopher-lawyer than a poet, his subtleties are admirable but they do not convince. . . . He holds to the same ideas as before . . . and I honour him for it. Yet after all it is the imagination and personality of the musician that are everything. It is the musician who colours the work, who presents it to the public. Without him it is a nullity. . . .

> The upshot of my long letter is this: that before you lay hands on *Edgar* in order to re-touch it, it is necessary that I talk to you in private.[10]

To tell Puccini, perhaps, that Fontana was not the librettist for him?

For the present, however, their collaboration continued. That sum-mer they both travelled to Cernobbio on Lake Como to work on the revisions together with Carlo Carignani, whose task it was to arrange the vocal score (to be dedicated to J. Burgmein, alias Giulio Ricordi). 'Do you realize,' Catalani wrote indignantly to Depanis, 'that Verdi himself has acted as a go-between . . . to persuade the Corti brothers to put on *Edgar* again next year, and that Verdi himself begged Pantaleoni

[10] MP, 76–7.

to take on the part of Tigrana once more?'[11] The revival, however, was cancelled owing to the illness of the leading tenor. *Edgar* was not heard again until 5 September 1891, when it formed the main attraction of Lucca's annual season at the Teatro del Giglio, running for 13 nights before a wildly enthusiastic audience with Eugenio Durot in the title role and Emma Zilli, Verdi's future Alice, a particularly evil Tigrana. The Florentine critic Eugenio Checchi ('Tom') stressed the music's originality, adding, 'nor would I approve the sacrifice of Act IV, which some have advised'. Yet sacrifice it Puccini did, and with Ricordi's and Fontana's full approval. The new three-act version was to have been launched at the Teatro Real, Madrid, under Mancinelli, again with Durot as Edgar, Eva Tetrazzini, sister of the more famous Luisa, as Fidelia and Giuseppina Pasqua, soon to create Verdi's Mistress Quickly, as Tigrana, so enabling Puccini to revert to his original idea of a mezzo-soprano villainess. Durot's indisposition, however, forced a postponement, perhaps fortunately, since Ricordi and Puccini succeeded in having him replaced by the great Tamagno. In the meantime *Edgar* in three acts made its début at Ferrara on 28 January 1892, where it was conducted by Carignani and reasonably well received despite a mediocre cast. The Madrid performance, for which Puccini made certain modifications to the scoring, took place on 19 March and was to all appearances successful. Four of the numbers were encored; and the widowed Queen Maria Cristina invited Puccini to the royal box to offer her congratulations. Six days earlier a revival at Turin under Vittorio Vanzo, who had conducted the opera at Lucca, earned the absent composer a benevolent, if guarded notice from Depanis, who spoke of 'a power, colour and vitality not often found in today's composers', and indeed its reception was sufficiently favourable for the three scheduled performances to be extended to six. A second vocal score in three acts was published later that year.

But Puccini had still not finished with *Edgar*. As late as 1901 he considered cutting the second act altogether and restoring the fourth with various alterations. Nothing came of this, however. The definitive edition, prepared for a performance at Buenos Aires in 1905 conducted by Leopoldo Mugnone with Giovanni Zenatello in the name part

---

[11] Catalani, op. cit., 100.

merely shortens the three-act version of 1892. As usual Puccini travelled there for the occasion. '*Edgar* last night only so-so', he reported. 'It is warmed-up soup. I've always said so. What is needed is a subject that throbs with life and is believable—not trash.'[12] A vocal score sent to his English friend Sybil Seligman is plastered with marginal jibes, while the title is thus defaced: E Dio ti Gu A Rdi da quest'opera! ('And God preserve you from this opera!').

Edgar is the least performed of Puccini's stage works and the only one never to have been translated. But if it remains a theatrical failure, it lies very much on the high road of his development both as musician and dramatist and therefore deserves attention. Effectively it passed through four versions, of which the first, presented only at La Scala, Milan, is irrecoverable. We can, however, take two bearings on it. One is from the libretto printed for the Milan première. As usual with Fontana, this is an elaborate affair, preceded by a Sapphic ode that points the moral of the story and furnished with a detailed historical note on the Battle of Courtray. It includes three choruses that were expunged from the first printed vocal score, though one of them, occurring near the beginning of Act II, would be restored for the definitive version of 1905, presumably with different music. A further total of 85 lines, many of them from Edgar's duets with Tigrana (Act II) and Fidelia (Act IV), were later excised. On the other hand, the finale to Act II was shorter in the first than in the second version, Edgar's resolve to join the army being followed by a single chorus led by himself with no interventions from Frank and no concluding malediction from Tigrana. Another source of information is a letter of Giulio Ricordi published in the *Gazzetta musicale di Milano* in reply to a correspondent who claimed not to have noticed any difference between the first printed score and the version that he had heard in 1889. From it we learn that 'the physiognomy of the concertato that precedes the close of Act I has been completely changed so as to render it swifter and more natural. . . . The third act contains no changes' (in fact, the autograph shows that there were a few); 'the fourth has several, and they are very important; the opening scene is quite different, the love duet is differently developed, the scene of "the battle of the flowers" discarded, so that

[12] MP, 79.

the finale takes on a completely different aspect'.[13] And that is as far as we can proceed.

Our knowledge of *Edgar* must begin with Ricordi's first printed vocal score of 1890, corresponding to the version given at Lucca in 1891 and never heard again. Unfortunately, the autograph full score and orchestral material are missing for Act IV, which Puccini later suppressed, and Act II, which he wrote out afresh for Buenos Aires; so that neither the second version nor the third (Ferrara, Turin, Madrid, 1892) can be given complete without re-orchestration. Consideration of the opera will therefore be concentrated on the definitive edition of 1905 with passing references to the discarded material.

There is no prelude. The curtain rises immediately on a village square with church and inn, before which Edgar lies asleep. The orchestra evokes a rural dawn with repetitions of a four-note arpeggiated motif and the same orchestral palette that had served for the introduction to Anna's romanza in *Le Villi*. The Angelus bell tolls; a distant chorus salutes the break of day, underpinned throughout by the orchestra's opening discourse. Oboes and clarinets, faintly suggesting piffero and zampogna, prepare for Fidelia's aubade ('O fior del giorno'), a simple diatonic melody of two varied strophes over recalls of the four-note motif, now worked into a 6/4 rhythm. Like most of Puccini's best-known heroines Fidelia is heard before she is seen—a theatrical device possibly copied from Bellini's *I Puritani*, where it occurs in all three acts. Not until the mid-point of her solo does she appear in the square, as she goes to wake Edgar. Their amiable exchanges proceed over a pattern of pulsating seconds on woodwind pairs, embellished by the occasional melodic bloom—a typically Puccinian solution for what in an earlier age would have been set as recitative, and quite new for its time. Fidelia plucks a sprig of almond blossom, kisses it, and throws it to Edgar. Her brief aria ('Già il mandorlo vicino') points still more to the Puccini of the future. Purely diatonic in contour, its melody rests on unresolved dissonances that move in a subdominant direction (Ex. 4.1). A choral reprise of the aubade rounds off a scene which would provide an excellent start to a pastoral opera in the tradition of *La sonnambula*

---

[13] *Gazzetta musicale di Milano*, xlv, no. 6, p. 91.

Ex. 4.1

or *Linda di Chamounix*, but which fatally compromises Musset's dramatic premise. The mainsprings of his hero's actions are boredom and misanthropy; only when they have been purged by the burning of his house can he bring himself to look kindly on Deidemia. In the opera he is already half in love with her (with such idyllic music how could it be otherwise?). All the harder to accept is his subsequent behaviour.

Enter Tigrana. Her visiting card (Ex. 4.2), scored in the manner of the 'fate' motif from *Carmen*, spawns related flourishes, any of which will be sufficient to recall her presence later in the drama. As with the Scarpia to come, Puccini does not need the minor key to connote villainy. When Edgar returns, gazing tenderly at the sprig of almond blossom that he still holds, she mocks his new taste for 'the honey of pastoral love' to a cheeky motif on clarinet and strings recalling Verdi's Abigaille. As an organ prelude sounds from within the church, she reminds him of quite other desires that he once entertained. Here Puccini again shows his ability to distil different meanings from the same

Ex. 4.2

material; for the music that underlies Tigrana's sensual probings is that
of the 'Kyrie' from the Mass of 1880 (Ex. 1.1). Unable to silence her
('Demonio, taci'), Edgar takes refuge in his house. With a burst of
sardonic laughter Tigrana launches into a stage song (' "Tu il cor mi
strazi . . . Io muoio" '), a heartless ditty about a lamb that protests pit-
eously against a devouring vulture. In the definitive version she gets no
further than the noisily scored, modally inflected ritornello (marked
'allegro satanico') before Frank appears, furious at her neglect of him.
Their dialogue—he anguished, she contemptuous—is twice punctuated
by a cluster of Wagnerian dissonances which could be called the Leitmotiv of Frank's despair (Ex. 4.3). Exit Tigrana, leaving Frank to a
conventional 'footlight' aria ('Questo amor, vergogna mia') whose
model, as to key and ternary design, would appear to be Leila's 'Comme
autrefois, dans la nuit sombre' from Bizet's *Les pêcheurs de perles*, already
circulating in the peninsula in the wake of *Carmen*. The opening strains
of both are similar, each concluding with a cadential figure which in
Puccini's case recurs throughout the piece like a sorrowful obsession.
Here, within a framework of chaste lyricism, Puccini has created a personality, simple and steady, in contrast to the volatile Edgar.

The scene is now set for a 'sommossa', that staple ingredient of
grand opera from Meyerbeer's *Le prophète* onwards. The villagers
assemble in church for the Mass (Ex. 1.1 in its original, devotional
character, sung as a hymn exalting the meek). Tigrana, seated without, takes up her song about the lamb and the vulture. The crowd
pour out of the church in high indignation; but Tigrana is quite una-
bashed. She taunts them with a sneering melody ('Sia per voi

Ex. 4.3

l'orazion') whose wide intervals follow a descending graph with a 'ri-tenuto' in alternate bars. The villagers react with angry chromatic mutterings, fragments of which persist as Tigrana resumes her melody, now decorated with upward scales. Its conclusion is interrupted by cries of 'Vattene! . . . Cortigiana!' that soon coalesce into a unison theme of no great distinction ('D'ogni sozzura simbolo'). As they hurl themselves on the villainess Edgar appears and inexplicably takes her side. He threatens the crowd with his dagger, curses his father's house and re-enters it to set it alight. All exclaim in horror as smoke and sparks issue from the windows. Edgar reappears holding the crowd at bay with a flaming brand. To Tigrana's motif (Ex. 4.2—'Tigrana, vi-eni') he embraces her and prepares to lead her away 'for ever'; but his path is barred by Frank. As they defy one another the theme of Frank's despair (Ex. 4.3) growls on violas and cellos between sustaining lower woodwind and horns. A duel is about to be fought, when Gualtiero hurries in with Fidelia and bids the combatants lay down their arms. With all the principals present for the first time an old-style pezzo con-certato of confrontation follows. Puccini rises to the occasion with a widely arched theme—a bass melody doubled by Edgar at pitch and Fidelia at the octave above, and thus a genuine innovation—that gen-erates a suitably massive ensemble (Ex. 4.4). Rapid scales on voices and orchestra reinforce the energy, and there is even a major-key comple-ment to bring the piece to a stirring conclusion. Action is resumed to various designs of 'hurry' music. The crowd try vainly to disarm Edgar and Frank; they fight and Frank is wounded (again Ex. 4.3). With a supreme effort he rises and makes to strike his adversary, but his dagger

Ex. 4.4

is snatched by Gualtiero. As Edgar and Tigrana make their escape, Frank and the crowd hurl their imprecations ('Maledizion!'). Edgar's house finally collapses (it has taken an unconscionable time a-burning); and to a Ponchiellian peroration based on the concertato theme (Ex. 4.4) the curtain falls.

The original setting of this entire *scène-à-faire* as published in Ricordi's first vocal score shows Puccini aiming for 'grand opera' at its most sensational, still the prevailing genre in Italy. By reducing the big set pieces, lightening the orchestration and adjusting certain melodic details, he removed much of the bombast, speeded up the action and made the music easier to perform. But he also created inconsistencies of pacing during which it is difficult to maintain the required tension, as at least one recent recording has shown. Above all, Edgar's behaviour becomes even more capricious and unmotivated than before.

Of the four acts of Musset's drama selected for musical setting the second was to prove the least tractable. It opens with a monologue for the hero as he contemplates the vast wealth he has accumulated with Belcolore's help. All that life has to offer is his, including a beautiful mistress. Only when she insists on telling him the story of her life does he begin to realize that outside the bedroom Belcolore is rather a bore; hence his decision to leave her and join the army. But praise of gold, however suited to Beethoven's Rocco, is poor material for a romantic hero. Fontana therefore presents an Edgar already surfeited with debauchery and thinking nostalgically of his first love. Puccini sets the scene with a cheerful melody in which, as in the opening of *Le Villi* and of many an opera to come, a strongly accented idea is balanced by a smoother continuation. This frames a distant chorus of revellers ('Splendida notte, notte gioconda'), whose text is present in the libretto of 1889, though its original setting has vanished. Certainly it cannot

Ex. 4.5

have been like the impressionistic version of 1905 with its unresolved dissonances and tonal ambiguity, features that bespeak a strictly post-*Butterfly* idiom (Ex. 4.5).

Edgar comes in from the banqueting hall 'with a bored and weary air', reflected in a recall of the concertato theme (Ex. 4.4), now melancholy on solo clarinet. 'Orgy, glassy-eyed chimera, whose fiery breath inflames the senses.' Violas and cellos underline the words with a chromatic pattern of seventh inversions that for the moment obliterates all sense of key—a daring stroke for 1889. But before Edgar has finished his invective the theme of the almond blossom (Ex. 4.1) reveals the direction of his unexpressed thoughts. He apostrophizes Tigrana in an arioso ('Non più dai tuoi sguardi ammaliato sarà il mio cor!'; Ex. 4.6), based on an ostinato of alternating chords, soon to be a Puccinian device for winding up the emotional temperature. It will be quoted almost literally in *La fanciulla del West*, where Dick Johnson resigns himself to the prospect of a lynching.

The climax is reached with a bold modulation, as Edgar accuses himself of a 'cowardly terror' of the morrow. Again Ex. 4.1 brings back memories of Fidelia, so leading into the aria 'O soave vision', again in French ternary form. In the main section the influence of Massenet is patent (even the words bring to mind 'Vision fugitive' from *Hérodiade*). More characteristic is the central episode, in which Edgar contemplates the abyss into which he has fallen, the altered note (E natural) a Puccinian device for stamping an otherwise unremarkable motif on the memory so as to make it instantly recognizable at moments of recall (Ex. 4.7). Throughout the entire solo, revised and improved in succes-

Ex. 4.6

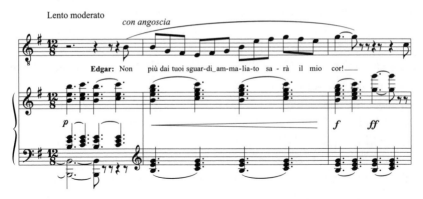

sive versions, Puccini's touch never falters. But from this point on problems arise which, far from being resolved, become aggravated with each
attempted solution.

In 1889 a chorus of revellers irrupted upon the scene to the opening
music of the act ('Evviva! Evviva! Le coppe colmate') with Tigrana at
their head; she led them in a brindisi in polonaise rhythm ('La coppa
è simbol della vita'), whose opening strain has already been briefly
hinted at in her scene with Frank in the preceding act. Shortened in
1892, it vanished in 1905, and with it the decision of the 'cortigiani'
to settle to a game of cards, since in the final version the chorus is
banished to the wings throughout the act.

Ex. 4.7

However, this does not prevent the three scores converging for the start of Tigrana's duet with Edgar. She reminds him of those desires that she alone enabled him to fulfil, the recollection strengthened by the 'Kyrie' theme, now in sensual guise. The pace increases as Edgar puts up an agitated resistance, then subsides for Tigrana to exert all her powers of seduction.

Here in 1892 there was a radical change of plan. Originally Tigrana had continued her blandishments in a lilting 6/8 andante, embellished by the kind of vocal pirouettes that had served Gioconda for her deception of Barnaba in Ponchielli's final scene. When these failed, she summoned to her aid fragments associated with her Leitmotiv (Ex. 4.2), so reducing Edgar to helplessness. But the suppression of the fourth act had deprived the score of what Puccini rightly considered to be one of his finest inspirations: a lyrical theme of unusual cut sung by Fidelia who, convinced of her imminent death, begs Gualtiero and the village maidens to adorn her with the bridal veil ('Un'ora al men a te rapir'). Clearly this was far too good a tune to lose. Accordingly, Puccini inserted it as a concluding 'cabaletta' to the Act II duet, replacing the original material. Begun by Tigrana (Ex. 4.8a), it is resumed by the two voices as a joint soliloquy, each singing different words. In all this the musical gain is offset by a dramatic loss. Not only is the tug-of-war slackened. Removed from its original context, shorn of the delicate accompanimental details, the melody becomes depersonalized, even though its one bitter compo-

Ex. 4.8a

Ex. 4.8b

nent—the dip of a major seventh over dissonant harmony (Ex. 4.8b)—
is confined to Edgar. Otherwise it could have served for the most
conventional of love duets. Unlike its predecessor of 1889 it comes to
a full close, followed by an orchestral coda based not on anything
that has gone before but on a senseless anticipation of the music
which in 1905 will conclude the act.

A distant side-drum is heard, followed by a fanfare of trumpets which
from now on will stand as an ideogram for military valour (Ex. 4.9).
From here on the score was drastically reduced in successive editions.
In that of 1890 Ex. 4.9 mounted sequentially to a fortissimo as a column
of soldiers entered the stage, then formed an orchestral background to
a general chorus in the Franco-Italian military style ('Colla fronte lieta
e altera'). A conversational theme then developed in martial rhythm, as
Edgar beckoned to the captain and offered him a glass of wine, fully
intending to enlist. The captain lowered his visor to reveal—Frank!
Tutti explosion of his despairing Ex. 4.3 for the moment of recognition;
then concertato. For this Puccini had recourse to his *Preludio sinfonico*
of 1882, starting with the main theme's first variant, now an 'allegro
deciso', as a unison gesture for the three principals: Edgar crushed and
ashamed, Tigrana triumphant, Frank observing the 'serpent of remorse'
already about to accomplish his former rival's redemption. Thence, after
more breast-beating on Edgar's part, punctuated by muted distortions
of Ex. 4.9, to an old-style 'largo concertato' based on the *Preludio* theme
in its final form, the principals voicing different sentiments from the
footlights while the chorus comment in the background—all within a
lyrical serenity which seals the reconciliation between Frank and Edgar,
and which the angry mutterings of Tigrana are powerless to disturb.
The action moved forward, Edgar grabbing a sword, Tigrana begging
Frank 'if ever he loved her' (Ex. 4.3) not to take Edgar from her . . .
or else! So to what Puccini referred to as 'the Flemish hymn' ('Della

Ex. 4.9

Fiandra alla gloria') which in the first version of 1889 it may have been, though its irregular phrases and minor-key orientation hardly suit it to the purpose. In the score of 1890 it expanded into a huge stretta, launched by Edgar and followed by a long orchestral march-out which swelled and darkened in preparation for a vehement imprecation from Tigrana, parading the full vocal extension of a 'donna di forza', to bring down the curtain.

For the age that had tasted *Cavalleria rusticana* this was all too long and slow-moving. Therefore in 1892 Puccini eliminated the 'serpent of remorse'. After his duet with Tigrana Edgar roused himself from passivity with a new recitative ('No, all'infamia Iddio mi toglierà'), so that when Frank entered with the soldiery, his face no longer covered by a visor, their rapprochement was immediate; therefore no 'largo concertato'. The 'stretta' was shortened by more than half with all suggestions of a Flemish hymn removed; and in the play-out a mere blast of her original Ex. 4.2 on trombones sufficed to indicate Tigrana's continuing presence. Her malignant 'declamato' remained as before.

Still more ruthless are the revisions of 1905. Frank now enters without out his men. At first hostile, he accepts his former rival's apologies, their duel having cured him of an 'abject, unworthy love'; and at Edgar's resolve to join him in battle the two men embrace. Their exchanges, conducted mostly over the conversational music that originally followed the chorus 'Colla fronte lieta e altera', sound almost comically offhand. Only Tigrana is allowed a moment of pathos. Where she begs Frank not to take Edgar from her, Ex. 4.3—originally Frank's despair, now hers—is wound up to a fresh pitch of anguish. Tigrana, it seems, like Gomes's Fosca and Catalani's Dejanice, from *femme fatale* has become simply a woman in love; so out goes her concluding 'declamato'. Instead the act finishes with a reprise of the coda to her duet with Edgar, now speeded up into march time—a transformation as bathetic as any of Liszt's—and sung in unison by the male principals ('Or la patria sacra in cor ci sta'). An invisible chorus takes it up in rudimentary canon, Tigrana adding to the final phrase a line of menace wholly at variance with the reach-me-down heroics of the music. 'This finale', Puccini wrote in Sybil's score, 'is the most horrible thing that has ever been written.' One can see what he meant.

The prelude that opens Act III is a miniature tone-poem symbolizing the conflict in Edgar's soul and its resolution. Evil desires are recollected by Ex. 4.7 rising from murky depths. It fades into silence as a new idea begins to take shape over a restless murmuring bass, bursting into full flower on violins and oboes with a widely spaced accompaniment of woodwind chords and rippling harp (Ex. 4.10). But Ex. 4.7, scotched, not killed, returns 'straziante con forza', its countermelody extended canonically. Once more it is overcome by Ex. 4.10 scored with the utmost simplicity, as it will be when sung by Fidelia, so leaving us in no doubt that she, like Wagner's Elisabeth, will be the hero's redeemer. In short, a gem of which, for some unknown reason, the first night audience was deprived.

The scene, a military esplanade near Courtray with catafalque centre-stage, is set for a grand choral tableau, whose basis is a flowing orchestral design in 12/8 rhythm suggestive of a chorale prelude and interwoven with minor-key fragments of the fanfare motto. A funeral cortège approaches from the distance chanting a 'Requiem', the chorus augmented by trebles. The texture thickens and elaborates as a company of soldiers enters with Frank at its head, bearing the figure of a knight in armour, which is then laid in the catafalque. By now the onlookers have been joined by Fidelia and Gualtiero. From this point on Puccini helps himself liberally to his *Capriccio sinfonico* of 1883. 'Del Signor la pupilla veglia nell'ombre eterne' sing the trebles to the mournful Ex. 2.2a, doubling its bass melody at the octave above. A few bars later Ex. 2.2b, sung pianissimo by the full adult choir, brings a note of consolation ('Entra nel cielo il buon che cade'), the boys contributing a shrill 'Ora pro eo' and Fidelia a lyrical aside that floats down over an octave and a half ('Non basta il pianto al dolor mio, O Edgar, mio solo amor!'). The two quotations are then juxtaposed, extended rhetorically and finally combined to the advantage of the second, exactly as in the *Capriccio*—even down to the inclusion of rhythmic derivatives of the

Ex. 4.10

Allegro's opening theme, not to be heard again until the start of *La bohème*! In this way the 'ghost' programme of the orchestral piece takes on flesh and blood.

A recall of the rustic introduction to the Act I aubade brings forward Fidelia to pay her own tribute to the 'deceased'. Her solo ('Addio, mio dolce amor') is marked in Sybil Seligman's score 'This is good'—and rightly. Here Fidelia speaks the future language of Mimì over harmonies of a Schumannesque sensibility. The piece culminates in the redemptive Ex. 4.10 ('Edgar la tua memoria sarà il mio pensier'), which the chorus take up to similar sentiments. A recall of the 'valour' motif (Ex. 4.9) on muted trumpets is answered by a general benediction from twelve monks, whose monotonous chants have punctuated the previous ensemble. Frank mounts the catafalque to begin his funeral oration. He has not gone far with it when he is interrupted by a solitary monk, his face covered by a cowl, who insists on denigrating the hero's memory. The soldiers bid him be silent; and Frank proceeds with his eulogy to the strains of Ex. 4.9, whose triplet rhythm allows Puccini to draw on further material from the *Capriccio*, this time from the Allegro without disturbing the continuity. For the monk persists. He calls on some of the bystanders from Edgar's native village as witnesses to his past misdeeds and, with the aid of a few lurid details of his own invention, works up the crowd to a passion of fury against the man they had previously honoured. 'Let his body be fed to the ravens!', they cry in lusty unison as they hurl themselves to the catafalque; but Fidelia's voice restrains them ('Non più! fermate!'). An oboe recalls the almond blossom (Ex. 4.1) over tremolando strings; and an arioso follows ('D'ogni dolor questo è il più grande dolor') full of delicate fioriture and backed by an orchestral palette of shifting colours with harp and cor anglais prominent. A few bars of solo cello introduce Fidelia's second aria ('Nel villaggio d'Edgar') with its characteristic lyrical sweep (it too was marked 'good' in Sybil Seligman's copy). The opening strain derives from an *Adagietto* for orchestra, probably dating from 1882. That its continuation should recall one of the false monk's accusations ('È vero che ferì? . . . Che con Tigrana, la cortigiana, allor fuggì?')[14] is entirely apt. For Fidelia is not rebutting the charge, but re-interpreting it in the

[14] GGP, 66.

light of her own tenderness. Edgar, she insists, was true at heart; his sins were those of hot-blooded youth, and he has atoned for them. She will have his body taken home and buried in the village graveyard. She bids the soldiers kneel before their dead captain and enters the nearby church with her father. The crowd disperses to an orchestral reprise of 'Nel villaggio d'Edgar' re-worked into a broader triple rhythm, finally transformed into the redemptive Ex. 4.10 and sealed by peaceful echoes of the fanfare.

Enter Tigrana in deep mourning ('Voglio passar!') to that same snatch of the discarded brindisi music that was heard in Act I. A bouncing theme in 2/4, prefiguring the fussy activity of Goro in *Madama Butterfly*, suggests that we are in for a scene of comedy—by no means foreign to the tradition of grand opera (see Bertrand's temptation of Raimbaud in *Robert le Diable* and the Anabaptists' recruitment of the disguised Oberthal in *Le prophète*). But in 1889 Romilda Pantaleoni had to be accommodated with a 'gran scena ed aria' worthy of her status as a principal. The autograph shows that it was a late insertion: a flurry of restless figuration interspersed with declamatory pauses and culminating in the villainous Ex. 4.2, a driving allegro in the minor key ('A se scuoter della morte') and a major-key complement in lilting Massenet-like 6/8 ('Vo' d'ogni labbro il riso'), in which Tigrana mused that, if she cannot bask in the hero's reflected glory, she can at least take comfort from the thought that she herself is still alive. To this the reminiscence of 'Sia per voi l'orazion' (Act I) formed a suitable epilogue.

As a show-piece for a 'donna di forza' it evidently succeeded, since Ricordi included it in his first printed edition. Presumably the intention was to explore the psychology of the villainess: but in fact neither music nor text tells us anything about her that we do not already know. Dramatically it offered one advantage: it allowed the 'Monk' plausible time to reveal his true identity to Frank, so that from then on they could act in collusion. By 1892 it had been dropped, to be re-instated only once that same year by Emma Zilli in a revival of the three-act version at Brescia.

The buffo motif is resumed for a terzetto during which Tigrana's feigned grief is observed sardonically by the men. Her temptation, like its Meyerbeerian precedents, is cast in rondo form. For its main theme Puccini found a simple, insinuating melody, its harmonies slightly thickened for the 1905 revision, which fits the situation perfectly as conceived by Fontana and Puccini (not, however, by the more serious-minded Musset). Parodistic melismata point up the men's outrageous flattery; while a quotation from *Storiella d'amore* helps to lend emphasis to their offer of jewels. Tigrana's motif (Ex. 4.2), rising from the depths together with its associated gestures, indicates the surge of avarice that will induce her to denounce Edgar as a traitor to his country. A prolonged flourish of offstage trumpets combined with a pattern from the terzetto brings back the soldiers and the townsfolk (unlike Verdi, Puccini always allows plenty of time for his crowds to assemble). Tigrana is asked by the 'Monk' whether Edgar betrayed his country for gold. Over 23 bars low clarinets insist in various rhythms on a major second, until she finally answers, 'Yes!' Once more the chorus's anger is unleashed. To the same music as before they rush to the coffin, tear it open and find only an empty suit of armour—'because Edgar *lives*', cries the 'Monk' ('a lie!', Puccini to Sybil), for the first time revealing his face. He turns on Tigrana with a soft, savage 'declamato'. If the words, 'O lebbra, sozzura del mondo' are a jumble of 'scapigliatura' decadence, the music speaks with Puccini's voice. This is the language that will characterize Des Grieux (*Manon Lescaut*) in moments of high tension. Interspersed with gestures of increasing violence, it will provide the act's conclusion—the abject humiliation of Tigrana, the retirement of the crowd in a state of confusion, the departure of Edgar and Frank.

So at least in the four-act version. From 1892 onward the music remained the same; but in the meantime Fidelia and Gualtiero have come out of the church. The lovers embrace. Tigrana steals up to Fidelia and stabs her to the heart. 'Orrore!', exclaim the crowd ('How right they are!', Puccini to Sybil). The murderess is dragged off to execution. Curtain.

Bewildered by the violent conclusion of Frederick Cowan's *Signa*, similarly curtailed at Covent Garden in 1894, Bernard Shaw remarked, 'I can understand that Ancona, in stabbing Madame de Nuovina, may have yielded to an irresistible impulse to finish the opera and go home.'[15] He could have said much the same of Tigrana; but here the impulse was Puccini's.

---

[15] *Shaw's Music*, ed. Dan H. Laurence (London, 1981), iii, 267

Certainly it was a drastic solution; and one can understand why in 1901 Puccini seriously thought of restoring the fourth act and cutting out the second, which is the least successful. In the meantime he had already recovered the prelude to the act, which from 1892 until the definitive score of 1905 was placed at the beginning of the opera, if in a reduced form. It opens with the dawn music extended and elaborated. As the music subsides onto a long pedal, Tigrana's Ex. 4.2 raises its menacing head—an unwelcome recollection that isolated gestures try to shake off. Thence to the prelude's main theme (Ex. 4.8a), that of Fidelia's 'Un'ora al men' in the four-act version, Edgar's and Tigrana's 'Dal labbro mio' in the subsequent revisions. Now Puccini's habit of preparing the audience for his most striking melodic ideas has been much commented on, not always favourably. Why not let the listener be taken by surprise by the fully fledged version in its proper dramatic context? A possible answer is that he had already seen the procedure yield dividends in the case of an opera now totally forgotten but highly popular in his youth. This was Filippo Marchetti's *Ruy Blas* (1869), which owed its fortunes to a single number, the duet 'O dolce voluttà!', tantalizing fragments of which are fed to the audience well in advance of the full statement.

A central episode (expunged together with reprise from the 1892 score) exploits the contrasting motif (Ex. 4.8b), its dip of a seventh charged with all the connotations of extreme sorrow. It returns by way of a coda wound up to a climax, then subsides into a quiet epilogue returning to the dawn motif.

As a preface to the fourth act the piece works well enough. It re-establishes the ambience of Edgar's native village (all too easily lost sight of during the events that followed his self-imposed exile); it reminds us of the baleful presence of Tigrana; and its main theme is suited to convey the mood of longing that precedes the prodigal's return. As a generic proemium to the opera it will not do at all. To begin and end a self-contained prelude with the music that opens the first scene is, to say the least, pleonastic, while the main idea no longer has the importance in the three-act version that it had in the original. The only advantage that the version of 1892 has to offer is that it exists in Puccini's own orchestration.

The discarded fourth act is far from negligible, its slow narrative pace allowing the music to expand and develop. The scene in which Fidelia awakes from a brief slumber to recount her dream of Edgar to the sorrowing Gualtiero and a group of village girls exploits both elements of Ex. 4.8 to moving effect, interweaving them with reminiscences of the *Preludio* and the *Capriccio sinfonico*. Her thoughts are interrupted by Edgar's Ex. 4.7, sounding pianissimo high in the orchestra and proceeding through a crescendo to the redemptive Ex. 4.10, hardly disturbed by a snatch of Tigrana's motif, as Frank and Edgar burst on the scene with a crowd of villagers at their heels. The centrepiece of the act is an extended love-duet ('Sia benedetto il giorno in cui sei nata, o mio tesor!'), whose model is surely Verdi's 'Già nella notte densa' (*Otello*). Both duets summon up remembrance of things past, each articulated in a succession of melodic paragraphs within a consistent rhythm and tempo (4/4 in Verdi's case, 3/4 in Puccini's); and just as the placid surface is disturbed by Otello's recollection of 'hair-breadth 'scapes i' th' imminent deadly breach', so Edgar's disgust at his former excesses is reflected in fierce accents and eddies of orchestral figuration. In the penultimate movement Puccini's mature harmonic style emerges fully formed with a pattern of widely spaced dissonances from which all traces of harshness have been removed (Ex. 4.11). So here was another gem from the original score worth recovering, this time in Act III of *Tosca*, where it is far more beautifully elaborated. The final tableau recalls that of *Carmen*: a joyous chorus without ('The Battle of the Flowers', evidently a Flemish 'Nuts in May'), a death within. For the orchestral peroration Puccini turned to the act's most memorable tune— Ex. 4.8a, of course.

In its original form *Edgar* was a late outcrop in the 'grand opera' tradition. But in 1889 the tradition's days were numbered; even Franchetti's monumental *Cristoforo Colombo* (1892) would scarcely outlive the quatercentenary for which it was written. 'Verismo' was knocking at the door, to be welcomed with open arms in 1890 in *Cavalleria rusticana*. For *Edgar* to circulate it was as necessary to slim it down as it was for Catalani's *Elda* to be reduced and tightened into *Loreley*.

But every operatic genre has laws of its own, and you cannot reduce the long reach of a grand opera without diminishing it in more senses than one. Even Verdi's four-act *Don Carlos* suffers in this respect. In the less experienced hands of Catalani and Puccini the proportions are

Ex. 4.11

damaged; the action jerks and sputters where it should move forward smoothly. All that Puccini achieved by his successive revisions of *Edgar* was to deprive Tigrana of her prima donna status and to strain ever further the credibility of a plot rendered incoherent from the start by the elimination of Musset's long philosophical reflections.

However, if the opera as a stage work is beyond redemption, its musical strengths are considerable. In it Puccini not only formed a personal language that is strong, supple, and wide-ranging, he also succeeded, as none of his Italian contemporaries would ever do, in using motifs both as principles of musical organization and as a means of complementing a text in Wagner's manner, not merely plastering it with redundant labels. Musically the Puccini of *Edgar* is far ahead of the Mascagni of *Cavalleria rusticana*. But the subject was against him. Years later he told Marotti, 'In setting the libretto of *Edgar*, with all due respect to the memory of my friend Fontana, I made a blunder. It was more my fault than his.'[16] Not entirely, perhaps; for however flexible in matters of versification, when it came to dramatic structure Fontana proved adamant. The truth is that for Puccini the 'scapigliatura' of Fontana was a false trail. The time had come for him to change direction once and for all.

[16] MPI, 157–8.

CHAPTER 5

Manon Lescaut

A FTER THE SEMI-FIASCO OF *EDGAR* PUCCINI'S POSITION WAS TO all appearances perilous. At a meeting of Ricordi's shareholders a majority was in favour of dropping the composer from the firm's roster. But this was to reckon without Giulio's tenacity, who not only proposed to renew his protégé's stipend, but declared that he would resign from the board if his motion was not carried (a somewhat empty threat since he himself held the bulk of the shares). Needless to say, his counsels prevailed.

Meanwhile, having completed the revision to *Edgar* in preparation for the first published vocal score, Puccini returned to Milan to address the problem of his next opera. While still at Cernobbio Fontana had suggested to him Sardou's *Tosca*, seen by both of them in Turin and Milan with Sarah Bernhardt in the title role. Accordingly, Puccini had written to Ricordi asking him to obtain the author's permission for a musical setting, 'since in this *Tosca* I can see the drama that I need; its proportions aren't excessive, nor is it a spectacular show, nor does it call for a superabundance of music',[1]—a clear indication, this, of the composer's concern to evade the dead hand of 'grand opera'. Fontana had already made preliminary approaches to Sardou, which Ricordi duly followed up. On 18 June 1889 the periodical *Il mondo artistico* announced that of two further operas to be commissioned from Puccini

[1] CP 31, p. 32.

by the Casa Ricordi the subject of one would be derived from Sardou's *Tosca* with Fontana as librettist.

This was premature. The playwright was not easily persuaded to offer his work to a composer of unestablished reputation (in 1870 he had refused his *Patrie* to Faccio after Verdi had turned it down); and, since negotiations threatened to prolong themselves indefinitely, Ricordi put forward another idea: a libretto by the Italian poet and dramatist Giuseppe Giacosa based on an original subject set in Russia. Thereafter events assumed a pattern that would become all too familiar. Puccini was at first sufficiently enthusiastic for Ricordi to arrange for delivery of the text by November; but by mid-July he had gone into reverse. In an apologetic letter to the publisher he confessed that the more he thought about 'that Russia' the more it terrified him. By all means let the contract with Giacosa stand, provided that the delivery date was postponed to the following year. Surely he could find something 'more poetic, more likeable, less gloomy, and rather nobler in conception'. He himself would discuss the matter personally with the poet 'on my return from Germany'.[2]

The German visit was once again to Bayreuth, where Puccini had been sent with the conductor Faccio for the Festival production of *Die Meistersinger*, which Ricordi, as Wagner's Italian proprietor since 1888, was preparing, if reluctantly, to mount at La Scala during the forthcoming Carnival season. According to his son Tito, who had seen the opera in London, 'it is beautiful, but terribly, mortally long!! . . . The public is interested but also bored! . . . The cuts made in Vienna are few and insufficient; our public, however Wagnerian it may be, will not tolerate this'. Would Puccini therefore please advise on further cuts. 'Affectionately, our Königlischerbuckdruckereistempelmaschinenstaupfeditor, Giulio Ricordi.'[3] Catalani, who would have given his eyeteeth for a visit to Bayreuth, all expenses paid, was outraged at this plan, and wrote to Depanis that the scissors put to work on Wagner would merely cut the threads of publicity that Ricordi was weaving around his favourite protégé. 'Joking apart', he continued, 'I think that Puccini, with an unheard of irresponsibility, has taken on a task that will do him real

[2] GPE 30, pp. 78–9.
[3] MP, 78.

harm.'[4] But this was the voice of envy. Certainly the shortened *Meistersinger* would be poorly attended, but no-one blamed Puccini for that. In the meantime he himself had benefited immensely from his second experience of Bayreuth, where he also attended a *Parsifal* conducted by Hermann Levi and, very possibly, a *Tristan und Isolde*.[5] A Wagnerian presence can be readily discerned behind his next opera, which would also prove his first unqualified triumph.

Even before leaving for Germany, Puccini had already decided on the subject. As early as 1885 Fontana had dangled before him Prévost's classic novel, *L'histoire du Chevalier Des Grieux et de Manon Lescaut*, first in its original form, then in a dramatic adaptation, hoping that its 'blend of tragedy and elegance' might catch his imagination—without, of course distracting him from his work on *Edgar*.[6] Evidently he had sown a seed that now burst into full flower. In vain Ricordi pointed to the universal success of Massenet's *Manon* (1884), the rights to which he had failed to obtain from the publisher Hartmann. 'A woman like Manon can have more than one lover', was Puccini's alleged reply.[7]

Prévost's novel, first published in 1731 as part of the fictional autobiography *Mémoires et aventures d'un homme de qualité* and subsequently reprinted on its own, is a product of 'the age of sensibility' with tendrils that reach forward into the next two centuries. Described by A. J. Symons as 'the most perfect story ever written, just as *Madame Bovary* is the most perfect novel ever created', it presents the first in a line of *femmes fatales*, who, without any especially vicious propensities, bring moral and even physical ruin on the men that love them, turning them from decent members of society into outlaws and criminals. Merimée's Carmen and Wedekind's Lulu are among her descendants. Dumas's Marguerite is a near relation, as she herself is the first to recognize; no wonder, therefore, that Prévost's *Histoire* was her favourite reading as she waited for death in Armand's absence.

The glamorization of Manon was the work of the Romantic age. Only then did it become possible to elevate her amoral charm into an

[4] A. Catalani, *Lettere*, ed. C. Gatti (Milan, 1946), 100–1.
[5] SGP, 83.
[6] QP, iv, 10–11.
[7] D. Del Fiorentino: *Immortal Bohemian*, 70.

aspect of the 'eternal feminine', mysterious and irresistible (significantly, Musset's line from his poem *Namouna*, 'Manon! Sphinx étonnant! Véritable sirène!', is quoted verbatim in Act IV of Massenet's opera, while its musical setting figures prominently in the prelude to Act I). But the ladies of easy virtue who had hitherto won acceptance on the nineteenth-century stage, from Hugo's Marion Delorme to Dumas's Marguerite, had all been capable of moral decision. Not so Prévost's Manon, which may explain why in her first operatic incarnation her character is effectively bowdlerized. Apart from the heroine's deportation and death in the Louisiana desert, Scribe's libretto for Auber's *Manon Lescaut* (1856) has little in common with the novel. His Manon is flighty, rash and provocative; but even when trapped in a compromising situation her fidelity to Des Grieux remains unshaken. Her worst failing is a disinclination to work for her living, as any honest *petite bourgeoise* should. This was one way of making her story palatable to frequenters of the Opéra Comique; but it would not suffice to ensure the opera a place in the repertory. Only Manon's 'laughing song' ('C'est l'histoire amoureuse'), admired by Charles Dickens amongst others, would stay the course as a show-piece for coloratura soubrette.

It was left to Bizet's *Carmen* to open the doors to the real Manon. Here for the first time on the operatic stage we find feminine amorality in action. From there to Massenet's opera of 1884 was but a short step, accomplished with far less violence to the original than in *Carmen*. The libretto by Henri Meilhac and Philippe Gille encapsulates the essence of Prévost, shirking only the grosser incidents. The two poles of Manon's existence—cupidity and love for the Chevalier—are planted right from the start; nor can we ever be certain which will get the upper hand. Even as she dies in her lover's arms on the way to Le Havre she sees a star in the night sky 'like a diamond'. And are not diamonds a girl's best friend?

In short the libretto milks Prévost's story of its most theatrical situations, adapting them so as to keep all the principals in view for as much of the opera as possible and at the same time to allow for the traditional ensembles. To improve on it would not be easy. However much Puccini and his librettists would try to vary the general scheme, their Act I would remain firmly anchored to Massenet's. In both operas Des Grieux steals Manon from under the nose of an elderly *roué* with

Lescaut (her cousin in Massenet, her brother in Prévost and Puccini) in the offing. In the novel the elopement is a private affair, with no-one to oppose it except a deaf servant of Manon.

Ricordi's objections to a new *Manon* written within less than a decade of Massenet's is therefore understandable. That Puccini remained inflexible in his determination to challenge the Frenchman at least argues a new-found confidence after the uncertainties of *Edgar*. Inevitably the path to an acceptable solution would mean a long haul.

Indeed the genesis of Puccini's third opera is a story well-nigh impossible to unravel, distorted as it is by the unreliable and often divergent testimony of those involved in it. By his own account, given many years later to Giuseppe Adami, the first author to be approached was Marco Praga (son of the 'scapigliato' poet Emilio), then on the threshold of fame with his play *La moglie ideale* written for Eleonora Duse. Somewhat taken aback, since he had never written an opera text, he allowed himself to be persuaded, but on one condition: that the versification be entrusted to a poet of his choice. The name of Domenico Oliva was suggested: and Puccini was agreeable.

All this Praga places in the spring of 1890. But the contract between him and Oliva and the Casa Ricordi is clearly dated July 1889. The meeting must therefore have taken place soon after the composer's return from Cernobbio, where he had been working on the revisions to *Edgar*. From the same letter in which Puccini rejected Giacosa's Russian subject we learn that the libretto of *Manon Lescaut* was to be delivered in August. Praga goes on to record a session of the three collaborators where it was read aloud in the presence of Ricordi and the song-writer Paolo Tosti. All professed themselves delighted, none more so than Puccini.

But from then on our peace was at an end. The approval of my plot, enthusiasm for Oliva's verses, the full agreement of Giulio Ricordi, Paolo Tosti's admiring comments all melted away one after the other in the face of Puccini's later misgivings. The more he meditated on my plan and its division into acts, the less he liked it. . . . He wanted a third act of a completely different colour, such as he had vaguely in his head. I dug my heels in. He was just as obstinate. Signor Giulio, while trying to reconcile our points of view, took Puccini's side. So that finally, tired of sessions and arguments, I announced that I would retire in good order and leave Oliva as umpire of the situation, free to write and re-write according to the whims and desires of the composer.[8]

Precise dates are lacking; but since it was in September 1889 that Tosti came to Milan from London for the publication of a set of his songs by the Casa Ricordi, we may conjecture that the first consultation with the librettists over the completed text of *Manon Lescaut* took place about that time. But Puccini was in no hurry to begin work on it. Not until January 1890 did he inform his brother in Buenos Aires that 'I'm working on *Manon!*', adding enigmatically, 'and after that I shall do *Budda*'.[9]

Nor is that all. In February he promised to send Michele not only scores of *Le Villi* and *Edgar* but also '*Crisantemi*, a composition for string quartet which was performed by Campanari with great success at the Brescia Conservatory. I wrote it in a single night for the death of Amedeo of Savoia.'[10] A discourse on two elegiac themes, both later put to use in *Manon Lescaut*, *Crisantemi* is a distillation of 'mestizia toscana', which even the envious Catalani confessed to finding 'very beautiful'.[11] Set out in a simple ABA design, its two melodies neatly balance one another, the first restless with Tristanesque chromatic inflections, the second (Ex. 5.1) tranquil and poised over a tonic pedal, its poignancy enhanced at its repetition by a doubling at the octave of first violin and cello. A command of structure, a sure sense of the quartet medium, fluent part-writing enhanced by unobtrusive touches of imitation all bespeak the fully fledged craftsman.

But soon Puccini's standing as the white hope of Italian opera was further threatened. On 17 May at the Teatro Costanzi, Rome, came the bombshell of Mascagni's *Cavalleria rusticana*, submitted for the same Concorso Sonzogno which had thrown out *Le Villi* six years earlier. Now the man of the moment was Mascagni. Drawn from a story-

[8] ARP, 87–9.

[9] CP 34, p. 35.

[10] CP 36, p. 37. Leandro Campanari was a pupil of Bazzini, who formed his own string quartet in 1887.

[11] Catalani, op. cit., 152.

Ex. 5.1

Andante mesto

p con molta espressione   *pp*3

turned-play by Giovanni Verga, his one-act vignette of Sicilian peasant life with its wealth of fresh, if not always distinguished melody, its raw emotion, and simple, unencumbered action was everywhere hailed as marking the re-birth of Italian opera after decades of progressive stagnation. Critics and historians would see in it the first affirmation of operatic 'verismo', reflecting a movement which had already established itself in literature with the works of Verga himself, Luigi Capuana, and Federico De Roberto. This is true only up to a point. For Verga's characters life is all too real. Not for them the careless rapture of Mascagni's Alfio, worthily rendered by the opera's English translator: 'Ho, the jolly life, boys/Free from care and strife, boys!' Nor would they have recognized themselves in the peasants who return from the fields carolling happily, abandon themselves to religious fervour in the Easter Hymn and echo Turiddu's paean to 'foaming wine'. These are still the country folk of *La sonnambula* and *Linda di Chamounix*. In a word, reality is repeatedly sacrificed to the picturesque, as at times in *Carmen*, from which Mascagni's opera can claim a direct line of descent. Its real strength lies in the precipitation of forces that had been brewing in Italian opera during the previous decade: a retreat from formalism, grandeur, and historical spectacle, and with it the release of an emotional charge—part naturalistic, part hyper-Romantic—that the traditional operatic forms had held in check. In *Cavalleria rusticana* these forms are not abolished but frequently dissolved from within by interruptions and changes of time-signature that hasten the assimilation of a set number to its surrounding tissue, so maintaining a dynamic continuity approximating to that of a spoken play. The one-act format worked to Mascagni's advantage in more ways than one. It prevented him from lapsing into the formless rhapsodizing characteristic of the 'giovane scuola', Puccini alone excepted; and it proved once and for all that large forces and a drawn-out action were not essential to the success of a lyric drama. Above all, the score speaks with a sustained self-confidence: hence its extraordinary impact.

Puccini in no way grudged Mascagni his triumph. The first telegram of congratulation received by the victorious composer came from his former fellow-student, as he himself recalled with pride. 'Have you seen what a success Mascagni has had?', Giacomo wrote to his sister Tomaide. 'He was here yesterday—I had him to dinner.'[12] Whatever Puccini's shortcomings, envy was not one of them.

But his own situation was far from happy. Dr Cerù was demanding the return of the money he had provided for his cousin's subsistence at the conservatory together with the accumulated interest; and *Manon Lescaut* was running aground. 'The libretto is driving me to despair', he told Tomaide in the afore-mentioned letter, 'and I've had to get it redone. Even now you can no longer find a poet who can do you something decent.'

Presumably it was at this point that Praga decided to bow out. His original scheme, he tells us, was: Act I, the meeting of Manon and Des Grieux at Amiens; Act II, the young lovers in their miserable apartment 'under the interested protection of Lescaut, his bragging immorality, wicked pranks, and perfidious counsel'; Act III, Manon living in luxury as a kept woman, the arrival of Des Grieux, their attempted theft and flight, only to be surprised and arrested; Act IV, Manon's death in the Louisiana desert. Once Praga had withdrawn:

> Oliva followed Puccini's advice. . . . The second act disappeared. The act at Le Havre was born with the roll-call of the prostitutes and the embarcation. But not even then did matters proceed smoothly. At every moment Puccini wanted changes and transformations; and in the end Oliva had had enough. He came to see me and declared that he would go no further, and so he in his turn retired from the enterprise.[13]

Not so. Oliva remained in harness until the end, if latterly at a distance. Nor did the second act disappear as soon as Praga implies. A letter from Oliva to Puccini of mid-October makes it clear that the embarcation

[12] CP 40, p. 45
[13] GPE, 72–3.

at Le Havre was added as a second scene to the existing Act III. In handing over the text he had a few pertinent comments to make. What worried him especially was the failed attack on the convoy of prostitutes led by Lescaut. 'For what purpose should a shameless rascal like him, a cynic, drag himself all the way to Le Havre? To bring together Manon and Des Grieux? What do either of them matter to him?'[14]

Here Oliva touches on a delicate problem. In the novel Lescaut's role, though important, is fairly marginal. He it is who first leads Des Grieux into vice, introducing him to a gang of card-sharpers and providing him with a loaded pistol that shoots a prison guard. Thereafter he vanishes in a Mafia-style killing. At no point is he in league with his sister's seducers. But his status as an operatic principal requires him to impinge on the action wherever possible. In Prévost it is Des Grieux who plans the attack on the convoy, only to see his hired accomplices melt away. The transference of this episode to Lescaut is borrowed shamelessly from Massenet.

By now it is clear that another hand was at work on the libretto. Adami tells us whose: 'At that time there was to be found hanging about the Casa Ricordi a plump young man, rather short of stature, with a quiff of black hair that dangled over his forehead like a question mark. That quiff questioned its owner's future. Did it lie in poetry or music? He couldn't make up his mind either way.'[15] Unfortunately more than one question mark hangs over the brow of Ruggero Leoncavallo. For details of his early life musical encyclopedias have hitherto relied on an unfinished autobiographical sketch in the possession of the Casa Editrice Sanzogno. Recent research has shown this document to be an extraordinary tangle of fact and fiction that has yet to be fully unravelled. Certainly he studied at the Naples Conservatory. Certainly he moved to Bologna in 1877, but not to study literature at the university, where his claim to have graduated is utterly specious. Rather it was to place his opera *Chatterton* at one of the city's lesser theatres. For years Bologna had prided itself on its forward-looking policy. It had reclaimed Boito's *Mefistofele* after its débâcle at La Scala, launched Stefano Gobatti's *I Goti*, unaccountably hailed as Italy's prime

---

[14] QP, ii, 213.

[15] G. Adami: *Giulio Ricordi e i suoi musicisti italiani*, 116–17.

specimen of 'the music of the future', and, above all, housed the first Wagner performances in the peninsula. Like most of his generation, Leoncavallo was an ardent Wagnerian and even claimed to have had personal encouragement from the Meister (a likely story!).

Tommaso Chatterton was scheduled for the autumn season of 1877 at the Teatro del Corso; but the failure of Gounod's *Faust*, the opening event, necessitated its replacement by a repertory piece. It is not true, as the sketch claims, that the impresario absconded with the material. On the contrary, he announced the opera for the following spring season. But by December Leoncavallo's funds had run out and he was forced to return to his father's house at Potenza. His presence in Paris during the 1880s is attested by letters to the Bolognese publisher Zanichelli. Here his experience as coach and accompanist in the suburban music-halls would be put to fruitful use in his opera *Zazà* (1900). But all the while he was planning a *magnum opus*: a trilogy set in the Florence of the Renaissance, words and music by himself, with the significant title *Crepusculum* ('Twilight'). In due course his professional activities brought him into contact with the baritone Victor Maurel, to whom he read the the libretto of *I Medici*, the only component of the trilogy to be completed. Maurel was impressed. He persuaded the author to move to Milan, where he would introduce him to the all-powerful Giulio Ricordi. There Leoncavallo arrived in the spring of 1889 in time to witness the semi-fiasco of *Edgar* and to make its composer's acquaintance.

The following year he was summoned to Ricordi's office. He found Puccini with tears in his eyes and a notebook in front of him containing the libretto of *Manon Lescaut*. 'Look here', said Signor Giulio, 'you who have such an aptitude for composing librettos . . . should make this personal sacrifice to help a *confrère*.' 'In composing librettos', Leoncavallo continues, 'I have always been in the habit of first jotting down a plan of the subject and then setting out the scenes, writing almost the entire dialogue in prose. . . . Thus for *Manon* I jotted down a detailed scheme, and I might well have completed all the rest if I hadn't had to think of my *Medici*.' Leoncavallo's account is heavily slanted against Ricordi; witness his ridiculous statement that the publisher had foisted the subject on Puccini merely to spite Massenet for having sold to Sonzogno the rights to his own *Manon* 'which for six years had been making a triumphal progress throughout Europe'.[16] But the mention of six years at least makes it possible to place Leoncavallo's intervention in 1890 and not, as has been so often assumed (by Adami among others), in 1889. Not that we can arrive at precise dates. Puccini spent the summer and autumn of 1890 with his 'family' at Vacallo, just across the Swiss border. That Leoncavallo was close at hand in August is clear from a letter addressed to both composers by Ricordi, inviting them each to contribute an easy piece for piano duet to the firm's *Practical School for Sightreading* ('the invitation carries no remuneration with it; however, the publisher has whispered in my ear that for you two he would make a unique exception, giving you a little, yes, a modest compensation').[17] But of progress on *Manon Lescaut* we hear nothing until a letter from Ricordi of 23 October enclosing for Puccini's approval a scheme worked out with Leoncavallo for Act II, set in Des Grieux's Paris apartment, together with modifications to Act IV. If acceptable it would be passed on to Oliva, and so it was. In mid-November Puccini replied to a jokey letter from Signor Giulio in similar terms: 'His Majesty the Doge of Vacallo is well and at work. . . . My mistress Manon has grown and seems to be in good health. No further news from my prime minister Oliva; I await the second and fourth acts.'[18] Note here the beginning of a standing joke. From now on Puccini would be for Ricordi 'the Doge'. Both parties continued to use the formal 'Lei' or 'Ella' in their letters to each other.

But when Oliva's versification of Leoncavallo's second act arrived, Puccini found it not at all to his liking, as he explained in an undated letter to Ricordi.[19] It was lengthy, rhetorical, and convoluted where the sketch had been so clear. References to Geronte and Lescaut, a quartet, a supper party, 'asides', and 'comedy' suggest an action based on Prévost's episode in which a shabbily dressed Des Grieux presents himself to G. M., the first of Manon's elderly admirers, as her cruelly orphaned cousin, lately arrived from the provinces. And comedy it certainly is. During an intimate supper *à quatre* he holds forth about the miserable

[16] R. Leoncavallo, *Appunti vari delle autobiografici*, 60–2.
[17] MP, 115.
[18] PLI 2, p. 36.
[19] GPE 29, pp. 76–8.

life he leads with his friends, for one of whom he invents a story that strangely resembles his own, much to the amusement of Manon and Lescaut. Hence, no doubt, the 'asides'; and hence too a multi-faceted irony that would naturally appeal to the future composer of *Pagliacci*.

All to no purpose, however, since Puccini was unable to come to terms with Oliva's verses. But still he ploughed on. By January 1891 Act I was completed in full score and would undergo no changes of importance until after the première. Sufficient progress was made on the remaining acts (the second alone excepted) for Ricordi to count on a première during the next Carnival season. But as usual domestic problems were slowing down the proceedings. At the end of March Elvira left Milan to stay with relatives in Florence, taking Fosca with her. Tonio in the meantime was sent to Tomaide in Lucca. There Puccini himself arrived at the beginning of May to make arrangements for the production of the four-act *Edgar* during the September season at the Teatro del Giglio. He was joined by Elvira for a few days; but their stay at a little village on the outskirts was cut short by the landlady's discovery that they were not married ('She said you were a very nice lady', Puccini wrote to Elvira after she had returned to Florence, ' "but I am a respectable widow and cannot have" etc. etc.').[20]

During the weeks that followed the composer wrote constantly to Elvira, sometimes in terms of embarrassing intimacy, at others woundedly rebutting rumours of his own misconduct. Happily the problem of a domicile was soon solved. One week in June the painter Ferruccio Pagni, who lived by the Lake of Massaciuccoli not far from Viareggio, happened to see a carriage pass by with two men inside. 'The younger, plumper one', said his companion, 'do you know who he is?' 'No.' 'It's Puccini, author of *Le Villi* that we went to hear at the "Verdi", Pisa last winter.' An introduction was duly effected and a life-long friendship struck up between Pagni and the celebrity who would be his neighbour for the foreseeable future. For Puccini had rented rooms in the rudimentary tower-house of one Venanzio Barsuglio, where Elvira would shortly join him. 'You'll find it enchanting here', Pagni assured him; 'the lake is so beautiful. And if you have a passion for hunting, with a permit from the Marchese Ginori you'll be able to

[20] MP, 88

enjoy yourself"[21]—always an important consideration for Puccini, and the source of many a colourful anecdote thereafter.

Following the triumph of *Edgar* at Lucca in September, the rest of the year was largely taken up with that opera's revision into three acts for the projected performance in Madrid. Not until January 1892 is there any further mention of *Manon Lescaut*, by which time yet another librettist was in harness, an author destined to play a vital role not only in Puccini's output but in that of the entire 'giovane scuola'.

Born at Castell'Arquato near Piacenza in 1857, Luigi Illica first made his name as a journalist before embarking on a theatrical career with a collection of witty sketches entitled *Intermezzi drammatici*, for which he was saluted as 'a modern Aristophanes'. During the 1880s he formed associations with the leading literary figures of his day, notably Giacosa, his future partner in the operas of Puccini. In 1883 he collaborated with Fontana in a play in Milanese dialect, *I Narbonnerie de la Tour;* and it would seem that in proposing *Tosca* as a subject for Puccini Fontana had Illica in mind as a co-author.

In the meantime Illica had ventured into the world of opera with Smareglia's violent melodrama *Il vassallo di Szegeth* (1889). The following year found him at work on *La Wally* for Catalani and *Cristoforo Colombo* for Franchetti, the first a near-'veristic' picture of life among the peasants of the Tyrol, the second a grandiose historical canvas. Here already is an indication of Illica's versatility as a librettist. All literary threads, past and present, would be gathered into his hands, from symbolism (Mascagni's *Iris*) to the spy story (Giordano's *Fedora*); from *commedia dell'arte* (Mascagni's *Le maschere*) to pre-Raphaelite romanticism (the same composer's *Isabeau*). He was one of the first to break down the traditional Italian metres into irregular lines of free verse which Giacosa might jokingly describe as 'illicasillabi' but which were perfectly suited to the Massenet-influenced style of the 'giovane scuola'. Personally he was hot-headed and quarrelsome (a duel had cost him part of an ear), yet he was not one to bear a grudge, and his relations with Puccini remained cordial for many years after they had ceased to collaborate.

By the time he was called to the rescue of *Manon Lescaut* Illica was

[21] MPI, 18–19.

already part of the Ricordi circle. But again the dates are only approx-
imate. He himself recalled how

> one day Puccini came to my house very worried. He said he'd been too
> long at work on a libretto of *Manon* written by Oliva and Praga, but that
> he didn't like it and therefore couldn't find any inspiration. He added that
> Ricordi had obtained for him the right to make an operatic version of
> Sardou's *Tosca* and suggested that I do the libretto. He had the outline sent
> to me since I didn't yet know the play. I formed a very bad impression of
> it—so much so that I strongly advised him against it. . . . I went to Ricordi
> and told him that I thought the subject of *Manon*, which I much liked, was
> altogether more suited to Puccini's temperament. By dint of much argument
> hither and thither I managed to beat him down. He gave in on one con-
> dition, that I should re-do the *Manon* libretto because, as it stood, it *just
> didn't work.*

Through the good offices of his friend Giacosa the necessary permission
was obtained from the original authors, 'and that is how I came to
remake the libretto of *Manon*'.[22] No mention, be it noted, of Leoncavallo, which strengthens the impression that his intervention, however
brief, was strictly unofficial and kept secret from the other collaborators.

The first mention of Illica in connection with Puccini occurs in the
Gazzetta musicale di Milano of 13 December 1891: 'The firm of G.
Ricordi has acquired from Victorien Sardou the right to make an operatic version of *La Tosca*. Maestro Giacomo Puccini, having finished
his commitments with that firm, has been given by them a new assignment to write two further operas, one of which will be *La Tosca* to
a libretto by Luigi Illica.' A note from Ricordi dated two days later and
inviting Illica to dinner with Puccini and himself makes it clear that
Tosca was still the subject of discussion ('. . . *post prandium toscabimus*').[23]
Of *Manon Lescaut* nothing until the new year—which, broadly speaking, tallies with Illica's own account.

The first weeks of 1892 found poet and composer engaged with
other commitments: Illica with Catalani's *La Wally*, due to open at La
Scala on 20 January, Puccini with the first performance of the three-

---

[22] 'Confessioni di un librettista italiano', *La tribuna* (13 November 1908).
[23] BPP.

act *Edgar* at Ferrara. A still longer absence followed, this time at Madrid, where Puccini was required to assist with the long-delayed Spanish première of the same opera. From there he wrote nostalgic letters to Elvira, professing a profound dislike of the city and all its inhabitants, of whose language he understood not a word. 'Nonetheless, there are types here capable of raising one's trousers. But I am Topisio [Mousie], your faithful Topisio'[24]—words unlikely to reassure the distant beloved, but all too frequent in Puccini's correspondence with her.

To Queen Maria Cristina he claimed nearly to have finished *Manon Lescaut*—an exaggeration, of course; but the wheels had certainly been turning. Illica's first concern was with the second act, which he had drafted anew, merely keeping in a scene between Manon and Lescaut which Puccini had already set to music. 'In this second act', Puccini wrote to Ricordi, 'there are two scenes of real musical importance— the scene of the *seductions*, when Manon has on one side Geronte, who tries to tempt her with descriptions of the grand life, and on the other Lescaut, who advises and persuades her with the examples of the Fillons, Ninons, Marions, Madelons—and even Maintenants' (joke), 'and the last scene, that of the *game*, a scene which I think powerful and original by virtue of two such contrasted personalities, and one which clearly lends itself to music.'[25] But what that game was is likely to remain a mystery; for by August the entire act had disappeared, much to the detriment of the dramatic continuity.

Over the same period the embarcation scene was gradually hammered into shape, still for a while regarded as part 2 of Act II. Ricordi was all for a musical transition 'lowering the curtain but continuing the music which, it seems to me, ought to describe the consequences of the turmoil of the arrest, then change little by little into a mood of sadness and become dark in colour at the beginning of the second scene, night, etc. etc'.[26] Puccini's response would be the intermezzo, 'The Journey to Le Havre', dated 5 June 1892, its mood sombre from the start, which made far better sense once the embarcation scene had been hived off into a separate act.

[24] MP, 101.
[25] CP 68, p. 70.
[26] MP, 117.

Meanwhile Illica turned his attention to what follows. He replaced Oliva's dialogue between Lescaut and the prison guard

> with a very rapid scene between Lescaut and Des Grieux to keep the public up to date with events. . . . Lescaut has prepared a surprise attack . . . and while he's carrying this out there's the duet at the window . . . which will be broken into by a cheerful voice singing a little ditty of the time; it's the lamplighter who goes round putting out the lights. Once he has gone the duet continues, and Des Grieux convinces Manon that her freedom is assured. Manon believes him, but just then a shot rings out, there's a shout of pain and Lescaut's voice crying out sorrowfully, 'The game is over!', cut short by a death rattle. Their friends come flying across the stage, while from within the guards call, 'To arms!' Des Grieux, in despair, wants to return to the attack, but Manon cries out to him to make his escape; he's hauled away by the fugitives, while the square is invaded by an inquisitive populace and immediately afterwards by soldiers dragging in the prostitutes.

For the roll-call Illica had a still more ambitious plan. Originally it was to have been an isolated passage between two ensembles, each forming part of a conventional concertato at the footlights. Illica proposed making it the basis of the concertato itself, a single movement based on 'a steady hammer-blow . . . short, sharp, growing in volume, of names called out by the soldiery (basses), while the populace (tenors) murmur'. Of the courtesans half would be cheerful, the other half sad. 'The last name is Manon's; and with Manon's name the concertato comes to an end.'[27]

Puccini was only half-convinced. He wanted a stronger lyrical idea than the roll-call for the basis of the concertato. He suggested instead Des Grieux's *cri de coeur* to the ship's captain, during which Manon could have a number of asides, while the populace and prostitutes could comment variously.[28] He also wanted a convincing reply from the captain to Des Grieux's plea: and here it was that Giulio Ricordi came to the rescue with his one contribution to the definitive text: 'Ah! popolar le Americhe / giovinotto, desiate? / Ebbene . . . ebben, sia pure . . . / Via,

[27] CP 69, p. 71.
[28] CP 70, p. 72.

mozzo, v'affrettate!'[29] Des Grieux as midshipman is certainly a novel idea.

Illica was still not satisfied; once again he foresaw the danger of a conventional operatic concertato with everybody motionless. He therefore returned to the roll-call as the basis of the ensemble, but this time surmounted by a long, sad plaint from Manon, 'a surge of true melody', beneath which the soldiers murmur. Des Grieux, overcome by emotion, would be reduced to silence; not until he heard Manon's name called would he implore the captain to take pity on him.[30]

By now the definitive solution was already in sight, a finale of rare originality and one with far-reaching consequences for operatic dramaturgy. Throughout the nineteenth century the concertato in which time stands still and action ceases had been a fixture in Italian opera, avoidable only in the rarest of cases (*Rigoletto* for one). It was the architectural pinnacle of the score, the moment at which within a non-symphonic tradition a composer could display his purely musical skills. Illica's roll-call, on the other hand, conveys the passage of time as inexorably as the ticking of a clock. The result has all the verisimilitude of a spoken play, while projecting the situation with an immediacy only possible to an opera.

The final details were worked out at a conference held at the Casa Ricordi in late June. Manon's lament would be re-inforced towards the end by Des Grieux, the roll-call given to a single voice, Manon's name interspersed with those of the other female prisoners, with Lescaut still alive to explain his sister's history to the more sympathetic bystanders. The act in Des Grieux's Paris apartment was scrapped, so that the action proceeds directly from Amiens to Geronte's town house where Manon is installed in luxury. It remained to reach an amicable agreement with Oliva over the attribution of the libretto. Through the good offices of Giacosa this was achieved with the decision to publish the text anonymously. Only when on the eve of the première the *Corriere della sera* announced that the author was in fact Luigi Illica did Oliva think it necessary to protest in a letter to the editor. The libretto, he maintained,

[29] RC.
[30] CP 70, p. 73.

was essentially his, but distorted by modifications on which Puccini had insisted, but of which he himself heartily disapproved; that was why he was unwilling for it to be published under his name. 'I will add, however, that I accept full responsibility for the last act, which has been preserved just as I had conceived and written it.'[31]

To complete the composition Puccini returned without Elvira to his Swiss retreat at Vacallo. Once more Leoncavallo would be his neighbour, having by now savoured the triumph of *Pagliacci* at the Teatro Dal Verme under Toscanini, in token of which he hung outside his door a banner showing the figure of a clown. To this Puccini responded with another daubed with a large hand ('manone'), so punning on the title of his own opera. Leoncavallo even provided him with four lines for Des Grieux preceding Manon's arrest, of which two would remain in the final text. In the meantime Puccini himself had supplied the words for an aside for Manon during her duet with Lescaut earlier in the same act. These too would be included with modifications in the libretto.

In the weeks that followed Ricordi continued to bombard his protégé with advice, above all exhorting him to brevity ('It is only Wagner who is permitted to exceed all bounds with words devoid of common sense and ultra-Gothic notes').[32] However, by mid-November the opera was complete, and Puccini free to go to Hamburg for the German première of *Le Villi* under Mahler's direction. A breathless letter to Cesare Blanc of the Casa Ricordi records his impressions: 'the orchestra excellent, the singers reasonably good—*the woman devil-a-bit*' (this in Milanese patois). 'Hellish cold—the Germans bears—Don't understand a word. Much miming. And a French of my own invention. That's about it.'[33] Had he understood German he would doubtless have been gratified by the reviews, all of which hailed him as Mascagni's creditor for the language of *Cavalleria rusticana*.

Puccini returned to Milan by way of Vienna, calling *en route* on Baron Angelo Eisner, Ricordi's unofficial agent in the Austrian capital. Here a letter reached him from Ricordi allaying his doubts as to the

[31] M. Morini: 'Nuovi documenti sulla nascita di *Manon Lescaut*', 96.
[32] MP, 118–19.
[33] CP 78, p. 76.

new opera's title. To change it would be absurd. There was no way of avoiding comparison with Massenet's work—Ricordi had warned him of this from the start. However, to *Manon, tout court*, as the opera had figured in practically all the related correspondence, was now added the surname *Lescaut*. The opera was at last re-divided into its present four acts and the libretto published without an attribution, though essentially the work of Domenico Oliva and Luigi Illica.

As La Scala would be taken up with preparations for Verdi's *Falstaff*, understandably regarded as the year's most important event, Ricordi had decided to place *Manon Lescaut* at the Teatro Regio, Turin. If not star-studded, the cast was a strong one: in the name part Cesira Ferrani ('You will be an ideal Manon', Puccini wrote to her, 'as regards appearance, talent, and voice');[34] as Des Grieux Giuseppe Cremonini, soon to prove a noted Puccinian tenor at home and abroad until his untimely death in 1903; Achille Moro as Lescaut and Alessandro Polonini in the 'basso brillante' role of Geronte de Revoir. The conductor was Alessandro Pomè, a decent professional, no more.

The première on 1 February 1893 was widely attended. 'The élite of Italy, and especially Milan, were represented; and there were numerous foreigners'—so reported the *Gazzetta piemontese*. Mascagni had come with a group of friends to give his former fellow-student moral support. For the only time in Puccini's career press and public were of one mind. He and the artists received more than 30 curtain-calls. Each of the critics found something in the opera that accorded with his own predilections. For Alfredo Colombani of the *Corriere della sera*, author of a study of Beethoven's symphonies, '*Manon Lescaut* could be called an opera of classical character. The music has all the developmental style of the great symphonies, without on that account rejecting the need for dramatic expression—or indeed what is generally termed "italianità". Puccini is truly an Italian genius.' For Berta of *La gazzetta del popolo*, the opera's virtue lay in its reckless profusion of ideas deployed with contrapuntal skill, exquisite scoring and taste, and only limited development. 'In this *Manon*', he concluded, 'Puccini stands revealed for what he is: one of the strongest, if not *the* strongest of the young Italian opera composers'. The final word may be left with Giuseppe

[34] CP 74, p. 74.

Depanis, writing ten days later in the same journal: 'Puccini's inspiration stands out for its remarkable clarity, an enviable gift which those who mistake obscurity for profundity affect to despise. His temperament is robust and passionate, teaming with vitality, and his music reflects this. . . . Amid so much that is hysterical, Byzantine, and decadent, this is healthy music.' No mean tribute from the champion of Catalani! Puccini himself received a signed photograph from Verdi that he would treasure to the end of his life.

Over the next year *Manon Lescaut* pursued a triumphal course throughout the Peninsula, with excursions to Hamburg and the Italian theatres of Buenos Aires and the Austrian Trieste. Meanwhile October saw the long-awaited Milanese debut of Massenet's *Manon* at the Teatro Carcano, given in the Italian translation of Zanardini and considerably shortened, with no Cour-la-Reine scene, no ballet, no trio of mocking females, and with all the 'mélodrame' converted into recitative. Despite its favourable reception Illica was sure that Puccini's opera had nothing to lose by comparison with it. Nonetheless he proposed an alteration to the finale of Act I designed to render more plausible Lescaut's apparent change of allegiance in the act that follows. So it was that the last of Puccini's footlight concertati fell to the scissors and was replaced by a brief exchange between Lescaut and Geronte with no heavier backing than a chorus of ribald students. The new finale was tried out at Naples in January 1894 and has remained standard ever since.

In his dealings with the major European theatres Ricordi pressed home his advantage by linking the hire of *Manon Lescaut* with that of *Falstaff*, allowing a substantial discount to managements that placed them in the same season. That this could prove counterproductive was shown by the reaction of the London critics when both operas were mounted at Covent Garden in 1894. *Falstaff* was duly hailed as a masterpiece, *Manon Lescaut* deplored as having been forced by a publisher on boards that still reverberated to the success of *Cavalleria rusticana* and its stable mate. A lone voice was raised in its defence. 'In *Cavalleria* and *Pagliacci*', wrote Bernard Shaw in *The World*, 'I can find nothing but Donizettian opera rationalised, condensed, filled in, and thoroughly brought up to date; but in *Manon Lescaut* the domain of Italian opera is enlarged by an annexation of German territory.' He noted in the first act 'genuine symphonic modification, development, and occasionally combination of the thematic material, all in a dramatic way, but also in a musically homogeneous way, so that the act is really a single movement with episodes instead of being a movement of separate numbers, linked together, to conform to the modern fashion, by substituting interrupted cadences for full closes and parading a leitmotif occasionally'. He praised the harmonic sophistication of the 'giovane scuola' that enabled them to turn out 'vigorous, imposing and even enthralling operas without a bar that is their own in the sense in which 'Casta diva' is Bellini's own; but Puccini, at least shows no signs of atrophy of the melodic faculty: he breaks out into catchy melodies quite in the vein of Verdi: for example, "Tra voi belle", in the first act of *Manon*, has all the charm of the tunes beloved by the old operatic guard. On that and other accounts, Puccini looks to me more like the heir of Verdi than any of his rivals.'[35] He was right.

'*Manon*', Puccini used to say in after years, 'is the only one of my operas that has never caused me any worry.'[36] Nonetheless he continued to tinker with it almost to the end of his life. Evidently he remained uneasy about the gap in the action between Acts I and II: hence an undated letter to Illica proposing an intermediate act for which he would make room by shortenings elsewhere.

> It should be a picture all love, youth, and springtime. The scene in an orchard garden crowded with small trees in bloom almost down to the footlights—a floor of green *pelouse* [grass] with garden walks and a few seats. A scene of depth, since the blossoming trees should lose themselves in infinity. A vision, therefore, of *freshness* and *an excess of bloom*. Manon and Des Grieux—happy lovers—lavishing caresses on one another, playing like two children in love.

This last was surely prompted by Prévost's vignette of the runaways at Saint-Denis on the way to Paris; but the setting is a patent borrowing from Part 2 of Zola's distinctly operatic novel *La faute de l'Abbé Mouret*, on which Puccini had set his heart as early as 1895, with *La bohème* already on the stocks. Zola, however, claimed to have granted the rights to Massenet (in fact, it was Alfred Bruneau who would treat the subject

[35] *Shaw's Music*, ed. Dan H. Laurence (London, 1981), iii, 216–17.
[36] ARP, 92.

in 1907, but only with incidental music). But this was a scene that Puccini was reluctant to forgo: the difficulty was how to get out of it. 'We must at all costs steer clear of Massenet', he continued. 'That's where you come in! Here we need the Illican brainwave! Not an abduction, because there's almost that in Act I. I don't really know what we can find.'[37] He rarely did: nor in this case did Illica. The plan was therefore abandoned.

Another problem was the last act, a scene strictly *à deux* and virtually devoid of action. To escape the threat of *longueur* Puccini made a number of successive tucks in the score, even dropping Manon's aria ('Sola, perduta, abbandonata') for the penultimate edition of 1909. To Toscanini belongs the credit for persuading him to restore it with trifling modifications for a revival at La Scala, Milan, at the end of 1922, repeated on the occasion of the opera's thirtieth anniversary on 1 February the following year. The next day Puccini wrote to the conductor:

> You have given me the greatest satisfaction of my life. *Manon* as rendered by you goes far beyond what I imagined in those distant days. You performed this music of mine with a poetry, a 'souplesse', a sense of passion that will never be equalled. Yesterday evening I really felt all your greatness of soul and your affection for your old friend and comrade-in-arms. . . . Thank you from the bottom of my heart![38]

One further document remains of interest. Ever since the mid-1850s the Casa Ricordi had been in the habit of printing for each of Verdi's operas a 'disposizione scenica' (production manual) based on the so-called 'mises-en-scènes' issued for the spectacular stagings of the Paris Opéra, in which every move, gesture, and grouping is prescribed with the help of diagrams. *Manon Lescaut* is the only work of Puccini to have been granted that privilege. Thereafter, as the ritual element in opera declined, such aids to production were thought unnecessary (though the Casa Sonzogno continued to publish them). The manual for *Manon Lescaut*, while overburdened with supernumeraries, serves at several points to focus the action more sharply than the instructions given in the vocal score and thus merits the attention of the modern producer.

[37] CP 52, p. 54 (misdated)
[38] CP 855, p. 537.

In describing Act I as a single movement with episodes, Shaw was, of course, exaggerating. Puccini's basis here is a motivic discourse such as opens Catalani's *La Wally*, but far richer in components, harmonically more sophisticated (for there was no question of renouncing the conquests of *Edgar*), and laid out in large contrasted 'areas', each dominated by a uniform rhythmic pulse, and each marked by a tonal centre, more or less defined. So much is evident from the start. There is no prelude; instead, a thumbnail orchestral exposition of the opening material, during which the curtain rises on a public square peopled by a crowd in holiday mood. The main theme (Ex. 5.2) is derived from the second of the three minuets of 1884, the original eight bars teased out into a period of eleven, speeded up, and brilliantly scored. A significant alteration, too, is the conversion of the first two notes of each phrase into a 'snap' (*x*), which will generate many a 'chirrup' throughout the scene. For this is a fine spring evening in which the presence of swallows might be expected (at least by an Italian), and indeed they are later mentioned in the text ('Van le rondini a vol'). Two episodes provide a smooth complement to the sharply accented figuration of Ex. 5.2, each with built-in sequence, the first swinging over descending sevenths, the second couched in the subdominant.

Edmondo's entry with a group of friends (sopranos and tenors) provides an excursus into the relative minor. The melodic burden of his song to the evening ('Ave, sera gentile') is carried by the orchestra, Edmondo engaging with it here and there in a line studded with many a falling fifth and interspersed with mockery from his companions. The madrigal, 'half comic, half sentimental' is taken up by the chorus in expansive sequences with a characteristic subdominant bias, reflecting a faint melancholy that rises to the surface in a 'resolving' theme sung by eight sopranos ('Vaga per l'aura un'onda di profumi'), pitched in the

Ex. 5.2

same key as the second episode and taking in the same sequence, now underpinned by a tonic pedal.

This ambivalence of mood ('Fra le spemi lottano e le melanconie') invades the whole canvas with further shifts towards the flat side of the key beneath the insistent swallow chirrups. Des Grieux enters to a descending line of cellos and bassoons—not, as might be expected, a personal Leitmotiv, but merely a 'madrigalism' portraying his leisurely gait. Invited by Edmondo to join the students in quest of amorous adventure, he has nothing to say. Can he have been crossed in love? Des Grieux disclaims all knowledge of the tender passion. No-one believes him for a moment. As all protest to patterns of Ex. 5.2, the tonal bias is reversed, and a shortened version of the cello descent prepares for the centrepiece of this first scene, Des Grieux's aria 'Tra voi, belle, brune e bionde',[39] jokingly addressed to the girls that surround him. Is there no-one hiding amongst them, dark or fair, who will be his for evermore? Notable here is the skill with which Puccini has integrated a formal number into the freer discourse that precedes and follows it. Not only does it preserve the 3/4 pulse, the opening phrase (Ex. 5.3a) centres on the same arpeggio notes as Ex. 5.2, now gathered into a nucleus (x) that will function as a cohesive agent for much of the score. The episodic theme (Ex. 5.3b) will be heard again in a very different context.

The girls react indignantly.[40] But soon the holiday atmosphere resumes with a huge paragraph proceeding from a recall of Edmondo's 'madrigale' to a full-blooded reprise of the first episode ('É splendente e irruente') embellished with a soprano descant. A post-horn sounds in the distance, announcing the arrival of the coach from Arras. As all turn to watch, the orchestra seals off with a noisy re-statement of the act's opening theme. This is the 'area' that lends itself most readily to the type of abstract formal analysis that certain commentators have tried to impose

---

[39] For the aria's transposition from F sharp (autograph) to F (vocal scores) see J. Budden, 'Puccini's Transpositions'. SP; 7h The published orchestral score allows for a performance in either key.

[40] The autograph contains four cancelled bars during which Des Grieux 'detains a girl from the chorus and pairs off with her'. This certainly accords with Edmondo's 'Guardate compagni, di lui nessun si lagni!', as well as with the snatch of rococo melody. In the production manual, however, Des Grieux 'takes a book from his pocket and strolls away reading it', so that the girls' 'Ma bravo!' is now sarcastic.

Ex. 5.3a

Poco meno
con grazia

Des Grieux: Tra voi, bel - le, bru-ne_e bion - de si nas-con-de gio-vi-net - ta va-ga_e vez - zo - sa,

Ex. 5.3b

Più mosso ma poco
p

Des Grieux: Pa-le-sa - te mi_il de - sti - no e_il di– [vi-no]

on Wagner's music dramas (indeed there is an element here of Alfred Lorenz's 'bow-form'). From this point on the action takes increasing charge of the musical structure.

The tonality switches to B flat and the pulse broadens into 9/8 as all turn to admire the new arrivals ('Discendono, vediam!'). The harmonic rhythm slackens almost to a standstill, partly to accommodate the stage action—Geronte helping Manon to alight, Lescaut obsequiously fussing round the old gentleman, the landlord of the inn running up with his servants—partly to plant in the listener's mind anticipatory fragments of what will be the most important motif of the opera (Ex. 5.5), henceforth associated with Manon herself and therefore a genuine Leitmotiv. Dramatically this makes perfect sense, since she is the cynosure for all present. The carriage is driven into the courtyard, the crowd disperses, the students settle down to drink and play cards, Lescaut enters the inn with Geronte, signalling to Manon to wait for him outside, Des Grieux remains frozen, unable to take his eyes off her—all this to an interlude recalling Ex. 5.2 and finding room for a sly theme depicting the watchful Edmondo, aware of what is about to happen.

Here Puccini faces a problem relatively new to Italian opera: how to portray the burgeoning of young love. In the works of his predecessors hero and heroine are normally in love before curtain-rise and have only to remind one another of the fact. Verdi's *Don Carlos* may be accounted an exception, but that is a French opera; moreover, the singers' expression of feeling is restrained by court etiquette. With no-one to guide him, Puccini's solution is remarkably neat. Des Grieux's first words ('Cortese damigella, il priego mio accettate') are backed by one of the happiest of the composer's early inspirations, the melodic centrepiece of his student 'scena' *Mentia l'avviso* (Ex. 5.4) played by muted strings with a thread of low flutes.[41] Manon replies with her motif (Ex. 5.5) in its definitive form, a simple cadential phrase with a cursive bass line and a characteristic Puccinian avoidance of the dominant seventh. By making the two ideas complementary to one another Puccini creates an instinctive rapport between his singers. As the dialogue proceeds, we may note a touch of Tristanesque chromaticism where Manon mentions the convent for which she is destined. Des Grieux counters with a passionate effusion of diatonic lyricism ('E in voi l'aprile nel volto si palesa e fiorisce! O gentile, qual fato vi fa guerra?'). Manon laments her situation in a lightly scored ostinato that comes to rest on widely spaced, dream-like chords punctuated by the occasional harp arpeggio, over which the voices alternate in free recitative. No sooner has Des Grieux told her his name than Lescaut's voice from the balcony of the inn ('Manon!') pulls them up short. To patterns of 'hurry' music they separate, but not before Manon has promised to return under cover of darkness.

Ex. 5.4

<hr />

[41] In the autograph and first edition the opening phrase is sung by Des Grieux to the words 'Deh! Se buona voi siete siccome siete bella/mi dite il vostro nome, cortese damigella'. The text was altered to its present form so as to leave the tenor's first line blank and allow the orchestra to initiate the thought that will then take hold of him—a truly Verdian refinement!

Ex. 5.5

Alone (as he thinks) Des Grieux launches into his most important aria ('Donna non vidi mai'), a compound of Exx.5.4 and 5.5 with special emphasis on the latter—a 'caro nome' for the singer. The higher key of B flat, the tonal centre of the 'area', allows full scope to the tenor's ardour; while the instrumental texture, lined with harp throughout, is both rich and sensitive. Especially happy is the flutter of sextuplets on muted violins divisi that follows the first recurrence of Ex. 5.5, like a breath of enchantment. Having reached his final cadence, Des Grieux remains in a state of ecstasy, but not for long. During his encounter with Manon subdued fragments of Ex. 5.2 have been spliced into the discourse, indicating the eavesdropping of Edmondo and his friends, the swallow-twitters suggestive of knowing winks. They now creep up behind him to more material from Ex. 5.2, leading to a fortissimo explosion like a slap on the back. Their congratulations ('La tua ventura ci rassicura') are wasted, however, since Des Grieux has left in dudgeon.

So to the third 'area', an action-scene of rare complexity marked 'Scherzo' in the autograph for no better reason than that its thematic basis is the scherzo-finale of the string quartet in D written for Bazzini in 1881, with its characteristic hemiola (Ex. 5.6). Here Puccini employs the kaleidoscopic technique foreshadowed in the Allegro section of his *Capriccio sinfonico*, with its short melodic proliferations. Against a background of student flirtation Geronte and Lescaut come out of the inn, the first pompous, the second deferential. During their exchanges Edmondo, who has been paying court to one of the girls, slips behind a

Ex. 5.6

tree, the better to overhear their conversation. As Manon seems to be unhappy, Geronte will treat her and her brother to a lavish supper at the inn; then, struck by a sudden thought, he begs to be excused while he has a word with the landlord. As the stage darkens, Lescaut turns to watch a card-game. If only he could join in (of course, he has every intention of cheating)! The students make no difficulty; and Geronte, seeing him fully engaged in play, takes the landlord apart and unfolds his plan to abduct Manon. The scherzo rhythm yields an athematic gesture that will embody the old man's evil purpose (Ex. 5.7). The texture is reduced to a minimum to allow every detail of the scheme to emerge clearly: a carriage to be got ready to depart within the hour, the occupants to leave by a secret door, and a purse for the landlord's pains. But Geronte has reckoned without Edmondo, who has listened to every word. With all attention switched to the card game, the movement reaches its climax, Ex. 5.6, now in the major key, pealing forth in a noisy tutti re-inforced by a descending counter-line and violent syncopations.[42]

Order restored, Edmondo mutters an apostrophe to the 'powdered Pluto, whose Proserpine may not be as easily carried off as he thinks'. When Des Grieux arrives, he tells him what is afoot in a conversational oasis of 2/4. 'The post-boy's horn will sound' (a woodwind arpeggio figure faintly distorted). The chevalier's alarm re-awakens to the urgent 3/8, the accompaniment now sparse, as Edmondo proposes to help him forestall the *coup*, first giving whispered instructions to his friends to ply Lescaut with wine.

An orchestral montage provides a transition to the final 'area', whose

---

[42] The production book suggests 'fists banged on the table, coins, bets, etc. etc. During the first bars a scuffle breaks out. One of the players is seized by the others and dragged off into the wings'.

Ex. 5.7

centre-piece is the love duet. A recollection of the turmoil, infused with fragments of Manon's motif, is brought up short by the post-horn figure, beneath which Des Grieux's 'Donna non vidi mai' proceeds to unfold on cellos, horn, and bass clarinet. Manon's first words ('Vedi? Io son fedele alla parole mie') maintain a light, conversational style. But surely they ought not to meet again. With Des Grieux's protest ('O come gravi le vostre parole!') the 2/4 dissolves into triplet motion, and a new theme gradually takes shape in the orchestra, reaching its full definition on the flute following Manon's words 'Eppur lieta, assai lieta un tempo fui!', the movement settling down into a steady, 'amoroso' 6/8 (Ex. 5.8, an evolution to be echoed in *La rondine*, Act II). It is, of course, a typical love-duet *à la Massenet*, but for one particular: the dissonant up-beat (*x*), whose implications will be exploited later. Although it is Manon who is speaking, the melody is plainly Des Grieux's; so it is with his voice that the melody returns in full orchestral panoply, doubled by strings in unison ('Ah! Date all'onde del nuovo incanto il dolce labbro e il cor!'). Once again the orchestra has formulated a

Ex. 5.8

thought that the singer is not yet ready to express. In this way Puccini maintains the sense of growing emotional involvement established at the start of the previous *scène à deux*—certainly not the least valuable of his Wagnerian lessons.

A concluding phrase sung by both voices in unison is interrupted by Lescaut calling for more wine. To a resumption of the scherzo rhythm Des Grieux reveals to Manon Geronte's villainous plot. Edmondo hurries in to say that the coach is ready and that they must fly at once. After repeated urgings, to an orchestra that increases in pace, volume, harmonic and rhythmic dislocation, Manon's resistance is overcome. There is a protracted fortissimo cadential phrase whose last note converts into the tied up-beat (*x*) of Ex. 5.8, now thundered out as a Ponchiellian peroration as the lovers make their escape. The consequent switch from G flat major to G is a stroke of tonal drama, all the more impressive for having arisen from the implications of the theme itself.

At this point Puccini made the substantial change to his score recommended by Illica. Though unperformable today, since the autograph pages and orchestral material are lacking, the original version is of interest as an experiment in crowning a relatively organic act-structure within the conventions of a concertato finale. To reiterations of the sinister Ex. 5.7 Geronte comes out of the inn, claps Lescaut on the shoulder and reminds him of their supper engagement, observing with satisfaction that the sergeant has difficulty in rising to his feet. Harness bells jingle in the distance; and again the post-horn figure. Strange! A departure at this hour? Re-enter Edmondo and the students to break the news. The stage fills with a crowd of townsfolk, girls and children. So to a massive concertato based on the melody of 'Donna non vidi mai' expanded into a slow 3/2 (a neat way of summing up the triple pulse that has dominated so much of the act) with an accompaniment, choral and orchestral, split into every conceivable subdivision from crotchet triplets to simple semiquavers and semiquaver sextuplets. The curtain falls on a frozen tableau, Geronte and Lescaut breathing fire and slaughter, Edmondo and the populace convulsed with laughter.

In the revision of 1894 Puccini retained the build-up of Ex. 5.7, reducing it from 46 bars to 38 and simplifying the action. The climax is reached with a trumpet recall of the post-horn figure over an effectively paced exchange between Geronte and Lescaut. 'They have abducted . . . ' 'Whom?' 'Your sister.' 'A thousand, thousand bomb-shells!' But the mood soon relaxes. While Geronte is all for pursuit, Lescaut, now fully sobered, points out that it is too late. Manon's charms, he is delighted to see, have aroused a fatherly interest in the old gentleman. Des Grieux is but a student; and a student's purse will not hold out long. Manon does not take kindly to poverty and will be only too grateful for a rich man's protection. She will prove an excellent 'daughter'; and he himself will complete the family. The material here is new; but soon the melody of 'Tra voi belle', sung by Edmondo and the students to different words and delicately embellished, insinuates itself into the texture; and as Geronte and Lescaut enter the inn it is they who bring down the curtain with a burst of joyous laughter. Version 1 ends in B flat, the principal tonality of areas 2 and 4, version 2 in E—two keys that could not be further apart. So much for Puccini's concern for long-range tonal architecture! But there is a certain dramatic point in choosing a key related to the carefree A major of the opening.

Act II is looser, more episodic in design, much of it in the nature of a divertissement. Yet even at the outset Puccini adheres to the principle of thematic cohesion. For the main subject of the opening scene is an extended quotation from Des Grieux's first aria (Ex. 5.3b) scored in the French manner for flute and harp, twice stamped with a fantastic implication of bitonality, and at its recurrence underpinned by a typically Puccinian hemiola rhythm.

Installed in a luxurious apartment, Manon is in the hands of her hairdresser, issuing pettish instructions the while. Lescaut swaggers in and proceeds to give helpful advice as to her make-up, a Malatesta to Manon's Norina. He congratulates himself on having rescued his sister from the clutches of a penniless student, his reference to their 'humble abode' prompting a characteristic foretaste of an important number to come (see Ex. 5.9b). But Manon's reaction is agitated and barely coherent, Lescaut understands; she wants news of Des Grieux, the lover whom she sadly admits to having left without even a farewell kiss.

'In quelle trine morbide', in which she contrasts the chilly splendour of her present surroundings with the modest dwelling where she basked in Des Grieux's love, is an archetypal Puccini aria with two lyrical components, the first (Ex. 5.9a) a lingering descent over syncopated

Ex. 5.9a

Ex. 5.9b

pulsations, doubled at its recurrence by full strings extending over three octaves, the second (Ex. 5.9b) sequentially prolonged and coming to rest (like the future 'Che gelida manina') on the fifth note of the scale. A change of key from E flat to G flat points up the polarity of the text without impairing the sense of completeness achieved at the final cadence. To thematic recollections of Act I interspersed with the leaping figures that will characterize him throughout the act, Lescaut gives his sister news of her lover, with whom he is now as friendly as with Geronte. He has persuaded him . . . to forget her? No, to turn card-sharper so as to gain the money that will win her back. A formal duo movement, Lescaut complacent, Manon remorseful, sums up the situation somewhat conventionally with the four-note arpeggiated nucleus that surfaces from time to time throughout the opera. Her mood does not last long. A tonal wrench, and we are soon back with Ex. 5.3b in its new guise, tinkling on piccolo, flute, and harp with basses pizzicati, as Manon admires herself in the mirror.

Enter a group of 'musici' (i.e., castrati) to entertain her with one of Geronte's 'madrigals'. 'Su la vetta tu del monte' is simply the 'Agnus Dei' from the Mass of 1880 (Ex. 1.3), sung by a mezzo-soprano with a supporting quartet of sopranos and contraltos and adapted to a fatuous text in which Geronte and Manon figure as Arcadian shepherd and shepherdess. In its new context the music anticipates the affected wist-fulness of Giordano's 'O pastorelle, addio' (*Andrea Chénier*), the sighing triplets adding an element of 'mestizia toscana'.

Manon hands Lescaut a purse for the singers, which he promptly pockets, since why should art be insulted? The singers bow and withdraw, to be replaced by a string quartet, who seat themselves and proceed to tune their instruments. Very pretty, Manon thinks—but boring (and a chromatic slither on three flutes illustrates a discreet yawn). Geronte enters with a dancing master, while to the sound of tuning fifths Lescaut departs in search of Des Grieux.

The scene that follows makes abundant use of rococo figuration without ever descending into the pure period pastiche of Tchaikovsky's 'Il pastor fido' in *The Queen of Spades*. Rather it presents the world of Louis XV refracted through the 'art nouveau' of Puccini's own day, while recurrences of the four-note nucleus link the material with what has gone before. The dancing lesson is conducted to a minuet, for whose opening strain Puccini availed himself of a cadential figure (*x*) taken from the last of his three published in 1884, extending it into a long period with many a simpering gesture. Among the episodes one (Ex. 5.10) will qualify for a later reminiscence.

By now a number of guests have arrived with presents for their host's favourite. All watch admiringly the progress of the lesson, Geronte with undisguised concupiscence ('Voi mi fate spasimare, voi mi fate delirar!'). It is he who partners Manon, 'performing', says the production book, 'without caricature, superbly happy and proud'. But there is caricature in the music, which mounts through sycophantic cries of 'Mercury and Venus!' from the guests to a most unbaroque half-close, followed by a cadenza-like flourish on violins that plunges into three bars of hushed chromatic harmony as Geronte executes a sweeping bow. Manon counters with a pastoral of her own ('L'ora, o Tirsi, è vaga e bella'), again

Ex. 5.10

featuring the four-note arpeggio motif. Originally a solo, Puccini enriched it with an admiring chorus, eliminating seven bars during which the attentions of a young abbé became a little too pronounced. This, rather than the lateness of the hour, may explain why Geronte should call a halt to the proceedings ('Galanteria sta bene, ma obbliate che è tardi'). He proposes an evening stroll, Manon to join the company on a litter which he will order for her. As she gazes complacently at her mirror, soft thuds on timpani and the first two chords of her motif (Ex. 5.5) on low woodwind prepare an unexpected arrival—not, as she first thinks, the litter, but Des Grieux, pale and drawn. Their duet ('Tu . . . tu, amore'), beginning with quiet intensity, evolves in a swirl of emotional rhetoric that owes much to the Wagner of *Tristan* while preserving the Puccinian fingerprints—the falling line, the rising sequences, the frequent doubling of melody and bass (Ex. 5.11). Characteristic, too, is the broad diatonic strain that carries Manon's attempt at self-justification.

But it is the orchestra that sweeps the music to a desperate climax from which the singer falls away in unsupported wheedling ('Ah! Non lo negar! . . . Son forse della Manon d'un giorno meno piacente e bella?'). The sadness of Des Grieux's surrender ('O tentatrice!') is gradually transformed into a glow of happiness as the two voices join in a recall of 'Donna non vidi mai' interwoven with recollections of their previous love-duet (Ex. 5.8). Their reconciliation, reached through a whole-tone chord functioning as a sophisticated dominant, establishes a home-key of F to which they will return at the end, but not before an excursus to A flat has brought a note of heroic resolution, as Des Grieux looks to the future (Ex. 5.12). The theme is not entirely new. Its first strain has been anticipated as a cadential phrase in Manon's 'In quelle trine morbide' and before that as an orchestral link in Des Grieux's 'Donna non vidi mai'. What gives it a fresh significance here

Ex. 5.11

Allegro moderato con agitazione

Manon: Io vo glio_il tuo per - do - no... Ve - di? Son ric - ca...

Ex. 5.12

is the moving bass line, the added notes in the harmony, and the more energetic continuation. A climactic restatement sung by both voices in unison points forward to a similar moment in *Tosca*, where the lovers contemplate a no less illusory life of freedom and bliss. Thence the movement sinks back to the original key through chromatic sequences *à la* Tristan ending with the same hexatonic approach to the tonic. Across the trajectory of moods dramatic sense and musical design are thus perfectly co-ordinated.

The sudden appearance of Geronte launches what promises to be a fugato subject of rare energy sufficiently akin to the scherzo theme of Act I to accommodate two quotations from it together with the leaping figure associated with Lescaut in the scene that follows. Geronte, though furious, maintains an ironic dignity throughout. So *this* is why Manon has kept him and his friends waiting. *This* is how she repays the love he has lavished on her. For answer Manon picks up a hand mirror and holds it to his face ('Amore! Amore! Mio buon signore, ecco! Guardatevi!'). In the novel this ploy quashes the attentions of an elderly Italian prince to whom she has no thought of yielding. In the opera it amounts to a gesture of senseless, not to say cruel bravado. Puccini dispatches it with Geronte's villainous Ex. 5.7 converted into a tinkling ostinato of high woodwind, violins, violas, and triangle. Again Geronte masters his anger. In his 'O gentile cavaliere, o vaga signorina' we hear twice a ceremonious bow; but there is no mistaking the menace of his 'arrivederci e presto!'

Manon's hilarity at the old man's departure ('Ah, ah! . . . Liberi come l'aria!') is conveyed by the same music that had brought the stage coach to Amiens, the fragments of her personal motif, quickened into an *allegro deciso*, falling happily into place in their new context. Des Grieux does not share her mood. His only thought is to fly from the 'accursed roof' as soon as possible. A snatch of Ex. 5.10 from the dancing lesson indicates Manon's regret at having to leave behind such luxury ('Peccato! Tutti questi splendori! Tutti questi tesori!'). It is no more than an automatic reaction, uttered 'quasi involontariamente', but it prompts Des Grieux to an outburst of intense bitterness, beginning in the sombre baritone register, the melody doubled instrumentally throughout, violins adding a sharp edge to the tone by playing inremittently 'sul tasto'. Within an unrelieved minor tonality the music keeps returning obsessively to the same idea, once transposed into the higher D minor, as the singer reflects on the abyss of infamy into which his slavish devotion to Manon has plunged him (Ex. 5.13). He concludes with the two lines supplied by Leoncavallo ('Nell'oscuro futuro/dì, che farai di me?'), Manon replies in a simple 'declamato' ('Un'altra volta . . . ancora, deh, mi perdona!'), later to be expanded into a full lyrical period (see Ex. 5.15, below).

A breathless Lescaut bursts in and collapses onto a chair. So to the 'baruffa finale', 185 bars of rapid 6/8 crowned by a noisy 2/4 coda. The starting point is the 'fugato' theme, fortissimo on violins, now developed contrapuntally, but soon dispersed in a proliferation of secondary figures so deployed as to set in relief every detail of the action: Lescaut's barely articulate announcement that the city guards are on their way: his repeated urgings of the lovers to escape, first by this door, then by that; Des Grieux's imprecations; Manon's mindless panic, her inability to leave without helping herself to valuable trinkets—'a continuous scurrying hither and thither', as the production book has it. All the latest Puccinian counters of 'hurry' music are here—syncopations, displaced accents, leaps in vocal and orchestral lines—while the feeling of an *impasse* is conveyed by moments of ostinato and tonal stasis. Every recurrence of the 'fugato' motif seems to bring the danger closer. Tutti poundings of minor seventh harmony (identifiable as the 'Tristan chord'

Ex. 5.13

from the manner in which it is approached, though Wagner resolves it quite differently) bring in Geronte and the guards ('Nessun si muova!' from their sergeant). In her terror Manon lets her mantle slip so that all the stolen jewels spill out on to the floor. The guards seize her, to shouts of laughter from the old man. Des Grieux draws his sword on Geronte, but is disarmed by Lescaut ('Se vi arrestan, cavalier, chi potrà Manon salvar?'). The curtain falls on a distracted Des Grieux ('O mia Manon!') watched by Lescaut, says the production book, 'with a chuckle half-way between compassion and irony'.

The Intermezzo that begins Act III, subtitled 'The Imprisonment— the Journey to Le Havre', is prefaced by a quotation from the novel, in which the hero recalls his fruitless efforts on Manon's behalf and his determination to follow her, if need be, 'to the ends of the earth'. Yet, surprisingly, the themes of which it is compounded are mostly associated with Manon rather than Des Grieux. Twelve bars of solo strings establish the mood of helpless grief with a fragment of her Ex. 5.5 chromatically harmonized and surmounted by a drooping figure derived from an orchestral link in the Act II duet (Ex. 5.14). Wagnerian ruminations on solo cello and viola (see the opening of *Die Meistersinger*, Act III) prepare for a long lyrical paragraph which accounts for the rest of the Intermezzo. Essentially it is a free variation on the Act II duet, its themes woven into a seamless paragraph of 83 bars in which the harp is rarely silent. The opening strain is a lyrical flowering of Manon's remorse ('Un'altra volta . . . deh, mi perdona!'), bearing many a hallmark of the elegiac Puccini—the emphasis on the flattened leading-note, the line that descends over dissonances that resolve into one another, the doubling of melody across harmony (Ex. 5.15). It is an-

Ex. 5.14

Ex. 5.15

swered by Ex. 5.11 (Manon's self-defence), its attendant sequences worked up to a more powerful climax than before, in which the rhythmic definition is all but lost. As the music wanders into a remote key the heroic Ex. 5.12 steals in on harp and high woodwind shaded by tremolando violins, then passes through a whole-tone cloud to emerge in the home-key of B, the final chord fortified by a triad of muted trumpets. In a word, there is still hope.

From here on brightness falls from the score. The third act opens as a night scene with a dark-hued orchestral theme, surely inspired by the start of *Tristan*, Act III. What in Wagner is a gesture, fading away in a long ascent, is here extended into a period, three times stated, during which Des Grieux and Lescaut converse in low tones, the Chevalier in an agony of impatience. Lescaut has bribed one of the sentinels to effect Manon's escape from the barracks visible stage left. Her next duet with Des Grieux, which she sings from the window, evolves in three phases. The first is introduced by Des Grieux's Ex. 5.4 high up on muted strings after the time-honoured manner of musical reminiscence in mid-century 'melodramma', but with altered harmonies suggestive of longing. The subsequent dialogue takes up material from the latter part of the Intermezzo; and the phrase concludes with Manon's Ex. 5.5 in its original form ('Tua . . . fra poco . . . fra poco . . . tua').

The lamplighter, passing by to douse the lights (for dawn is breaking), causes the lovers to separate. His ditty ('E Kate rispose al re') is invented folk-music, its model is probably the steersman's song from *Tristan und Isolde*. Puccini has been careful to stamp it with two of his patents— the avoidance of the dominant seventh and the approach to the tonic note from the fourth above.

In the final phase of the duet Des Grieux puts all his strength of feeling into persuading Manon to do as he asks. For this Puccini avails himself of the second melody from *Crisantemi* (Ex. 5.1) extended by a coda that anticipates the theme of the concertato to come. The soothing recall of Ex. 5.12 that follows Manon's consent is broken off by the sound of a cannon-shot and distant cries of 'To arms!' In a word, Lescaut's plot has failed. An action scene allows time for guards and populace to assemble. Thence to one of the most original *pezzi concertati* ever devised: a perfectly formed structure, free of conventional grandeur, and one in which time never freezes for a moment. Throughout the texture remains transparent. The initial theme, with its flattened supertonic and leading note, forms an ideogram of quiet desolation; while the wide interstices between each phrase allow the behaviour of the individual prostitutes and the crowd's reaction to them to register with the audience. (Ex. 5.16). The period is repeated with minute elaborations that heighten its intensity; a middle section rises through steep progressions to a fortissimo for Manon's despairing cry 'Addio!', then returns through reminiscences of the Act I love-duet to the initial idea, whose final statement finds the lovers in sorrowful unison.

At a brusque command from the sergeant the prostitutes form up in line between two columns of marines and prepare to board the ship to

Ex. 5.16

Ex. 5.17

a lugubrious theme with a characteristic downward gradient and emphasis on the flattened leading-note (Ex. 5.17). This same melody will serve for Des Grieux's appeal to the captain to take him aboard, now converted from a subdued dirge to a passionate outcry with doubling 'sviolimata' ('Guardate, pazzo son'). The captain consents; and the curtain falls to a Ponchiellian peroration of Ex. 5.12.[43]

The setting of Act IV is an immense desert of bleak, rolling hills and a wide horizon beneath cloudy skies. For a scene of similar desolation the last act of *La Wally* offers the nearest precedent with its evocation of the snow-capped Mürzoll. But what in Catalani requires a slow build-up of detail Puccini achieves at a stroke with two unrelated minor chords spanned by a melodic leap of two octaves and scored for full orchestra. Strings (partly muted, partly tremolando), bunched horns and trumpets reflect the movement of the melodic line, trombones and harp emphasize the louder of the chords (Ex. 5.18). There is no mistaking the derivation from Ex. 5.5; and indeed fragments of the Manon motif are interspersed throughout the act in various permutations, from simple minor-key progressions to chromatic clusters in which the tonal focus is entirely blurred.

Enter Manon, supported by Des Grieux. Both are miserably clad and in a state of total exhaustion. The cause of their plight is to be found only in the novel. Arrived in New Orleans, Des Grieux and a reformed Manon lead exemplary lives together. It is only when they

---

[43] Here the production book has the lovers high on deck applauded by a wildly enthusiastic crowd. As the guards present arms below, a cannon shot is fired from the ship, smoke rises, and the curtain falls.

Ex. 5.18

decide to regularize their union that the local governor, having discovered that Manon is legally single, decides to marry her to his son, who has already been casting covetous eyes in her direction. Des Grieux challenges the young man to a duel and, as he thinks, kills him. Flight with Manon is therefore the only course open to him. None of this is mentioned in the libretto, which concentrates throughout on the lovers' agony.

Their opening exchanges are set against material from the first part of *Crisantemi* expanded and diversified in pace and scoring. Manon is at the end of her strength; a moment's rest, she insists, and she will recover; but a recollection of Ex. 5.18 contradicts her and she faints, whereupon Des Grieux launches the first lyrical period of the act ('Vedi, vedi, son io che piango'); it is Ex. 5.15 from the Intermezzo raised by a different continuation to new heights of eloquence. In barely coherent phrases with derivatives of Ex. 5.5 much in evidence he tries to bring Manon to her senses. She revives in time for a reprise of Des Grieux's Ex. 5.15; but it is not allowed a full close, for she now feels herself dying of thirst (Ex. 5.5 at its most unfocused). Her lover's helpless agony breaks forth in explosions of *Crisantemi* music. As Manon begs him to go in search of human habitation, Puccini throws out a new idea (Ex. 5.19), part weary, part consolatory, its brief span rendered memorable by the harmonization (the leading note in the first progression, the A natural in the second). About to leave, Des Grieux turns to look at Manon, so bringing a last recurrence of Ex. 5.12 on harp and muted strings; but the brutal succession of unrelated minor chords that follow the eighth bar precludes all hope.

Manon's lament ('Sola, perduta, abbandonata') is among the most

Ex. 5.19

original pages of the score. It opens as a long drawn-out ostinato the chief melodic element supplied by an oboe echoed at times by an off-stage flute (Ex. 5.20); and it is their material that spawns the singer's desperate outcry ('Ah non voglio morir, no, non voglio morir!'), which is as fundamental to the 'Stimmung' of the aria as Cavaradossi's 'E muoio disperato' will be to that of 'E lucevan le stelle'. In an *Allegro vivo* Manon, like Verdi's Princess Eboli, blames her fatal beauty for her present pass and in a state of delirium sees her past sins accusing her. Ex. 5.20 rounds off the aria with sufficient emphasis to give a hint of ternary design.[44]

With Des Grieux's return the soothing Ex. 5.19 and Ex. 5.1 from *Crisantemi* in its most extended form account for the rest of the act, interspersed with fragments of Manon's motif in a progressive state of chromatic dissolution. To a snatch of the minuet (Ex. 5.10), its wist-fulness enhanced by a discordant note in the second bar, Manon 'con voce debolissima' begs for her sins to be forgotten. The epilogue is pronounced by Ex. 5.18 now evoking both Des Grieux's helpless grief and the vast emptiness of the desert. Note that it is reached chromati-cally by the same whole-tone chord that has twice sealed the reconcil-iation of the lovers in Act II. As always, Puccini devoted the utmost care to his act-conclusions.

With *Manon Lescaut* Puccini's genius as a theatrical composer is finally

---

[44] An eight-bar postlude in which the same melody is treated canonically was expunged when the aria was re-instated in 1922.

Ex. 5.20

affirmed, and with it an ability to steer clear of pitfalls that would beset the majority of his Italian coevals. In a conception of opera that aspires to a realistic continuity within the act, the difficulty of avoiding a dilution of musical content in the interests of stage action is more easily surmounted on the limited scale of a *Cavalleria rusticana* or a *Pagliacci* than in a work which lasts the evening. For composers of Puccini's generation Wagner's system of *Leitmotiven* seemed to offer a way forward; but all were aware of the difficulty of reconciling it with a style that required the supremacy of the human voice. Franchetti's *Cristoforo Colombo* (1892), for all its use of recurring motifs, remains true to the 'grand opera' formula of the 1880s, since, as the critic Luigi Torchi would later put it, 'The need to understand Wagner *à la* Meyerbeer— that was the gift of Franchetti's fairy godmother'.[45] In Catalani's *La Wally* of the same year, a work of far greater imagination, the tight motivic organization of the first act is later relaxed into a succession of numbers embedded in fairly conventional 'scena' material. Only Puccini was able to profit by the Wagnerian lesson, reducing the Meister's procedure to his own terms. In none of his operas is Wagner's influence more apparent than in *Manon Lescaut,* whether in the well-nourished orchestral texture, the Tristanesque chromaticisms that portray the agony of the lovers, the emotional surge and swell of their love-music, or the interweaving of vocal and orchestral melody in the manner of *Die Meistersinger.*

But in judging the work as a whole there are other parameters to be taken into account. In dramatic continuity and characterization Puccini's treatment of the subject undeniably falls short of Massenet's. In the French opera, where Manon's cupidity is programmed from the outset, her subsequent defection appears quite logical. Puccini and his

---

[45] L. Torchi: 'Germania', *Rivista Musicale Italiana*, xx (1902), 410.

librettists evidently conceived her quite differently: a simple, innocent girl who yields to corruption only under the combined pressure of Lescaut and Geronte, much as Donizetti's Lucia succumbs to the successive urgings of Enrico and Raimondo. Paradoxically, therefore, Massenet's opera could afford more easily than Puccini's to dispense with an act set in the lovers' Paris apartment. Between the Manons of Act I and II of *Manon Lescaut* there is no psychological connection.

Then, too, musical characterization requires the composer to stand back from the individuals portrayed. By entering wholeheartedly into the feelings of Manon and Des Grieux Puccini ends by creating a generic pair of *innamorati* for whom the course of true love runs anything but smooth. The concentration of all the gaiety in the first half of the opera and all the gloom in the second is another inconvenience which Massenet manages to avoid. Finally, 18 minutes is distinctly long for an act in which nothing happens apart from the heroine's death.

But in richness of musical invention *Manon Lescaut* far outshines its Gallic predecessor. However little differentiated his lovers from one another in their musical language, the steady growth of their relationship from mutual sympathy to desperate passion is traced with a master hand. If his highly developed harmonic sense has led Puccini to pile on the agony too thickly (as Mosco Carner rightly observed, no other opera of his contains such an abundance of minor tonality), self-indulgence of this type is a youthful failing, a by-product of the intense vitality that permeates the entire opera. Here, too, we are made aware of Puccini's concern for the complete integration of note, word, and stage movement. The only trace of conventional routine is to be found in the solos of Acts I and II, all of which are prepared by a few bars of orchestra (twice a solo cello in free rhythm), presumably to allow the singer time to advance to the footlights. Two such passages are visible in the autograph of Act IV; but both have been scored out.

For years outside Italy *Manon Lescaut* had to compete with Massenet's masterpiece—mostly without success. But since World War II time has dealt more kindly with Puccini's heroine than with her more deftly limned predecessor. The French opera, for all its charm and delicacy, remains essentially a period piece. Puccini's speaks loud and clear to young lovers the world over.

CHAPTER 6

La bohème

FROM NOW ON PUCCINI'S FINANCIAL WORRIES WERE AT AN
end. The proceeds envisaged from the world-wide hire of *Manon
Lescaut* together with Ricordi's doubling of his 'retainer' enabled him
not only to pay off his existing debts but also to buy back the house
in which he was born (a mere family gesture, since he had no intention
of living there himself), just when his brother-in-law Franceschetti was
on the point of selling it. His standing in the profession was likewise
established beyond question. 'Now that Puccini has had his triumph
which no-one can diminish or take away from him', Catalani wrote to
Depanis, 'I beg you to use your influence . . . to get my latest opera
[*La Wally*] also performed soon at Turin.'[1] Not soon enough, however.
On 7 August 1893, during the Bayreuth Festival which for years he had
longed in vain to attend, Catalani died in Lucca of the consumption
that had been slowly killing him. Bazzini offered his teaching post at
the Milan Conservatory to Puccini, who predictably turned it down.
For the present he was a man of leisure, able to travel (usually at his
publisher's expense) to revivals of *Manon Lescaut* in Italy and abroad, to
spend the autumn months shooting in the woods around the Lake of
Massaciuccoli, and to compose just as he felt inclined. Among his prize
purchases of the time was a bicycle of the latest model; and

[1] Catalani, *Letter*, ed. C. Gatti (Milan, 1946), 153.

many are the tales related by his artist friends of Torre del Lago of his first attempts to ride it.

Even before the triumphal première of *Manon Lescaut* Ricordi had been stocking up on possible subjects for his protégé. As early as 1891, with an eye to the international success of *Cavalleria rusticana*, he had signed a contract with Verga for another libretto based on a story from his *Vita dei campi*, to be drawn up in collaboration with a fellow-author of the 'veristic' persuasion, Federico De Roberto. This was *La lupa*, which treated of a devouring *femme fatale* of the Sicilian countryside. *Tosca* was still on the cards with Illica as librettist; failing that a 'Greek idyll' or a 'fisherman's tale' (*pescatorio*), both Illica's suggestions, as the publisher reminded him in a letter of December 1892, adding that he had not the least desire to turn to anyone else.

The poet's reply was discouraging. 'Regarding Puccini I must confess to you that between him and me something . . . in the state of Denmark.' He went on:

> Puccini has confided to a friend of his that he could well do without my libretti . . . and, besides, *nobody* understands him because he longs for something . . . something . . . something . . . that . . .

> You will see that this 'something', expressed like that, is very difficult to interpret. It means that amid this darkness I should have to grope around to find out just what is this 'something' on which Puccini has set his heart, only to hear him answer 'I don't like it' [this in an imitation of the composer's Tuscan accent]; hence the risk of a libretto set to music . . . with the system of *Manon,* with lines in pidgin Italian

and a snatch of incoherent doggerel follows by way of illustration. But exactly what, Illica wanted to know, *did* Puccini like? He had already begun to blow cold over *Tosca*. Ever since the operas of Verdi and Boito modern theatre had required a literary text of decent quality wedded to music that expressed in depth the sentiments of the words. Only if Puccini was prepared to observe this rule would Illica resume their collaboration.[2]

Here he had put his finger on a problem that would affect all *fin de*

[2] CP 80, pp. 78–9.

siècle opera, especially in Italy, where till then a play had been one thing, a libretto another. In France only Scribe had been able to bestride both genres with equal mastery. Italian librettists from Romani to Ghislanzoni kept within the orbit of lyric drama. Somma had indeed written plays for Adelaide Ristori before setting to work on *Un ballo in maschera* and the abortive *Re Lear*; and precisely for that reason he needed Verdi to teach him the librettist's craft. With Boito all this would change. He too had a spoken play to his credit, *Le madri galanti*, written jointly with the poet Emilio Praga: and his aim from the start was to enlist the values of literary drama in the service of opera. His *Otello* was generally thought to have set a new standard in this respect even by those who found difficulty in coming to terms with Verdi's music for it. 'From now on', the writer Antonio Fogazzaro declared, 'it will not be possible to set to music absurd dramas and lamentable verses: the words will have to be worthy of being followed.'[3]

Time has taken its toll of Boito's literary reputation. Yet, being himself a musician with a strong intellectual bent, he had a sure grasp of a composer's requirements. He knew that the recent convergence of opera and spoken drama could never amount to more than an asymptote, since, as he remarked to Verdi, 'Our art lives by elements unknown to spoken tragedy.'[4] To librettists of Illica's generation, most of whom had begun their stage careers as playwrights, this was less evident; and it would form a lasting bone of contention between them and Puccini, who was more exacting in the matter than his contemporaries of the 'giovane scuola'. Only Leoncavallo adopted Wagner's solution: he wrote his own libretti.

For Puccini and Illica Ricordi decided on the recruitment of a third partner. Hitherto Giuseppe Giacosa had remained in the wings—an *éminence grise*, to be consulted on questions whether of art or copyright. Now he entered the lists as co-librettist. Born at Parella in 1847, he had made his name during the 1870s with a number of verse plays set in an idealized medieval past, turning to Zolaesque realism with *Tristi amori* (1887), a bourgeois tragedy that is still revived today. Subsequent plays, notably *Come le foglie* (1900), show the influence of Ibsen. One

[3] F. Abbiati, *Giuseppe Verdi* (Milan, 1959), iv, 312.

[4] *Carteggio Verdi-Boito*, ed. M. Medici and M. Conati (Parma, 1978), i, 2.

of the outstanding literary figures of the day, his enlistment in the service of Puccini was a major *coup* on Ricordi's part. Broadly speaking, his task would be to put Illica's dialogue into polished verse. Not the least of his qualities were tact and patience. Illica would recall how at their numerous sessions, while he himself would fly into tantrums and Puccini bite his fingernails to the quick, Giacosa with his domed head and patriarchal beard (hence his nickname 'the Buddha') would remain calm and poised throughout. Over the next ten years their labours would result in Puccini's three best-loved operas—*La bohème* (1896), *Tosca* (1900), and *Madama Butterfly* (1904). Significantly, when Giacosa died in 1906, Puccini's collaboration with Illica effectively came to an end.

A gap in Ricordi's correspondence with Illica between January and April prevents us from knowing exactly when the partnership was set up. But by the time their letters resume it is clear that the subject of Puccini's next opera had already been decided upon and its libretto was under way.

Henri Mürger's *Scènes de la vie de bohème*, a collection of short stories strung together on the slenderest of narrative threads, first made its appearance in the periodical *Le Corsair-Satan* edited by Gérard de Nerval during the last years of the Orleanist monarchy. The title is easily explained. Bohemia was traditionally the land of gypsies (appropriately, Balfe's opera *The Bohemian Girl*, 1845, was translated in Italy as *La zingara*); and the four young men who inhabit Mürger's pages are the gypsies of Parisian culture, artistic neophytes of more imagination than talent, who prefer a life of hardship with no thought for the morrow to the restraints of bourgeois society. All four are based on people known to the author: Rodolphe, poet, playwright, and journalist, his features 'lost in a beard the size of a forest, offset by a head as bald as a knee-cap, over which a few solitary strands of hair have been trained' (evidently a self-portrait); Marcel, the painter 'with the wide-brimmed hat recalling the ancient kings of France', forever submitting the same canvas under different titles to the Louvre only to have it rejected; Schaunard, musician, poet, and painter, 'whose magnificent aquiline nose could tell many a tale of gallantry'; and the most picturesque of all, Gustave Colline, of the 'large blue eyes set in a smooth face the colour of old ivory, the double chin surmounting a crooked cravat, the mouth that seemed to have been sketched by an amateur whose elbow had been jogged during the process, the thick, protruding lips covering a set of long, powerful teeth'. The prevailing tone is humorous. Even the Bohemians' mistresses are drawn without sentimentality: Schaunard's goose of a Phémie; Marcel's Musette, a singer, the darling of the Latin Quarter, with her fresh, youthful voice, not always perfectly in tune, and her availability to any man, rich or poor, who happened to take her fancy; and Rodolphe's Mimi, *petite*, blue-eyed, and lively'— but, we are told, 'at moments of boredom or bad temper, her delicate features could assume an almost savage brutality, wherein a physiognomist might have recognized the signs either of deep selfishness or an utter lack of sensibility'. Only two of the episodes strike a note of tragedy. 'Francine's Muff', presented almost apologetically with interventions *à la* Sterne from an imaginary reader, tells the story of the sculptor Jacques, cast off by an avaricious parent, and the pure-hearted seamstress Francine, doomed from the outset to die of consumption. Convinced even in her final moments that she will recover, her dying request is for a muff to keep her hands free of chilblains. In 'The Epilogue to the Loves of Rodolphe and Mimi', the latter returns on Christmas Eve starving and penniless to the Bohemians' garret. All four sacrifice their few belongings to buy her admission to the public hospital, where, due to a bureaucratic error, she dies in her lover's absence.

The fortunes of Mürger's subject began with his play *La vie de bohème*, written jointly with Théodore Barrière and first given at the Théâtre des Variétés in 1849. It is a popular piece interspersed, like Beaumarchais's *Le barbier de Séville*, with songs, some set to traditional airs, others newly composed by one M. J. Nargeot. Here the original 'scènes' are subjected to a stronger narrative structure with the aid of fresh episodes and even fresh characters, among them a young widow of means whom Rodolphe is under pressure to marry. Mimi, unequivocally the heroine, is softened by the attributes of Francine (eliminated together with Jacques for reasons of dramatic economy), much as Dumas's Marguerite would be idealized in the transition from novel to play. Nor is that the only link with *La dame aux camélias*. Rodolphe's rich uncle Durandin, a shadowy presence in one of the stories, is elevated into a counterpart to Dumas's Germont *père*, who persuades Rodolphe to give up Mimi for his own and the family's good, using the same arguments as Armand's father (he too does not believe that the girl is really ill). Not that there is any question of Mimi's returning to a life of sin which she has never known. Rodolphe's suspicions of her infidelity, caused by his discovery of his uncle's letters to her, are entirely unfounded. But she, like Marguerite Gauthier, dies on stage.

It is not a good play—indeed Rodolphe's curtain-line 'O ma jeunesse, c'est vous qu'on enterre!' is typical of its stagey banality; but it served to rekindle interest in the original 'scènes'. These Mürger published at greater length in book form in 1851. At once they became a minor classic of their genre with descendants that included George Du Maurier's *Trilby* and echoes that reached as far as Henry James's *The Ambassadors* and Somerset Maugham's *Of Human Bondage*. In 1872 came the first complete edition in Italian translated by Felice Cameroni, who claimed it as an implicit manifesto of the socially committed 'seconda scapigliatura' ('*La bohème* is destined to pass from the purely artistic field to social conflict. After thought comes action'[5]). But such was never Mürger's intention. Far from being underprivileged, his Bohemians are young men of the middle class sowing their wild oats. Their language, by turns slangy and bombastic, is that of students the world over, their poverty self-inflicted.

> Oh, ye impecunious, unpinnacled young inseparables of eighteen, nineteen, twenty, even twenty-five, who share each other's thoughts and purses, and wear each other's clothes, and swear each other's oaths and smoke each other's pipes and respect each other's lights o' love, and keep each other's secrets, and tell each other's jokes, and pawn each other's watches and merrymake together on the proceeds, and sit all night by each other's bedsides in sickness, and comfort each other in sorrow and disappointment with silent, manly sympathy—wait till you get to forty year!
> Wait even till each or either of you gets himself a little pinnacle of his own, be it ever so humble!
> Nay, wait till either or each of you gets himself a wife!

The words are Du Maurier's, but their sentiment that of Mürger's 1851 preface. For the mistresses there is an even easier way out, and one which they are only too ready to take when the opportunity arises. The

---

[5] A. Groos and R. Parker: *Giacomo Puccini: La bohème'*, 57.

only perfect love—that of Jacques and Francine—is sealed by the death of both parties, as is that of Trilby and Little Billee. Understandably, it was the novel, not the play, that Puccini would urge on his librettists.

By his own account, given years later to Arnaldo Fraccaroli, his enthusiasm for the subject dates from shortly after the première of *Manon Lescaut*. During his train journey from Turin to Milan for the first night of Verdi's *Falstaff* on 9 February he talked of it to his fellow-passengers, the lawyer Carlo Nasi and the journalist Berta. 'I will draft the scenes', said Nasi; 'and I will write the verses', added Berta[6]—obviously a joke, but one which suggests that the division of labour between Illica and Giacosa had already been settled.

But very soon there occurred a contretemps. The following month Puccini and Leoncavallo met in a café in the Galleria De Cristoferis, Milan, to discover that both were engaged on the same subject. At once Leoncavallo flew in a rage to his publisher, Sonzogno, who leaped into action with a cannonade of publicity. On 20 March *Il secolo* announced that 'the brilliant author of the much-loved *Pagliacci* will follow his next opera [*I Medici*] with another, *La bohème*, based on Mürger's novel of the same name. This opera, on which he has been working for several months, will be given next year, 1894.' Next day the news was repeated in *Il corriere della sera*, while *Il secolo* amplified its original announcement with a statement from the composer himself:

Maestro Leoncavallo wishes to make it known that he contracted for the new opera last December, and has since been working on the music. He had not announced the opera previously, only because he wished to retain an element of surprise. As proof of this, the distinguished artist Maurel can testify that at the time of his arrival in Milan for the rehearsals of *Falstaff* Maestro Leoncavallo told him he was writing the part of Schaunard for him, just as Signora Frandin can testify that four months ago the Maestro spoke to her about the role of Musetta, which was intended for her. Maestro Puccini, to whom Maestro Leoncavallo declared two days ago that he was writing *Bohème*, has admitted that not until his return from Turin a while back did he think of setting *La bohème* to music, and that he had spoken

[6] FGP, 83.

of it to Illica and Giacosa, who, according to him, have not yet finished the libretto. Maestro Leoncavallo's priority as regards this opera is thus indisputable.[7]

Nor did Puccini attempt to dispute it. In a letter signed by him but drafted by Illica, he merely brushed it aside, at the same time rebutting any suggestion of deliberately poaching on his colleague's territory:

> Maestro Leoncavallo's declaration to *Il secolo* yesterday must have made the public aware of my complete good faith; for it is clear that if Maestro Leoncavallo, to whom I have been tied by strong feelings of friendship, had confided to me earlier what he unexpectedly told me the other evening, I would not have thought of Mürger's *Bohème*.
>
> Now—for reasons easy to understand—it is too late for me to be as courteous to him as a friend and musician as I would like.
>
> Besides, what does it matter to Maestro Leoncavallo?
>
> Let him compose, and I will compose, and the public will judge for themselves. Precedence in art does not imply that one must interpret the same subject with the same intentions. I am merely concerned to make it known that for about two months, since the first production of *Manon Lescaut* in Turin, I have been working seriously on my idea and have made no secret of it to anybody.[8]

What neither composer knew was that they had a potential rival in Massenet, who had longed to make his own setting of the subject, especially since he had known personally several of the originals. It was his publisher Hartmann who dissuaded him.[9]

Meanwhile Ricordi had lost no time in telegraphing to Mürger's publishers in Paris in the hope of securing exclusive rights to the novel on his protégé's behalf. Two undated letters from Puccini to Illica help to chart the course of events. The first approves the poet's riposte to Leoncavallo in his name, adding that, given a favourable reply from Paris, they could mount a more savage attack. The second relays the

---

[7] A. Foletto: 'La guerra degli editori', programme book, Teatro Comunale di Bologna, 3 March 1990, pp. 23–47.

[8] CP 81, pp. 81–2.

[9] J. Massenet: *Mes souvenirs* (Paris, 1912), 166 ff.

disappointing news that, since Mürger had died intestate, the novel was in the public domain. Only the play was still in copyright—clearly of no interest to either composer, since an operatic version of it would steer dangerously close to *La traviata*. At most it would provide both libretti with a few minor details. 'Don't forget', Puccini continued, 'the gauntlet has been thrown down, the challenge taken up. Leoncavallo writes to me from Venice that *he* will have to wrestle with *two* colossi, you and Giacosa, and that he is now going off to study the ambience of the Quartier Latin.'[10] This suggests that the breach between the two composers was of short duration; indeed they would remain on speaking, even visiting terms. But for Puccini his rival would henceforth be 'Leonasino' ('lion-ass') or 'Leonbestia' ('lion-beast'). Not least among Leoncavallo's misfortunes was a surname that invited ridicule.

Illica had little need of urging, for by 22 March Giacosa had received from him a basic treatment, which he commended highly. Only the last act seemed to him as yet unsatisfactory, but doubtless they could work something out together; and he greatly looked forward to their collaboration. Illica's plan was essentially the one we know to-day, except that the present Act II (referred to in their correspondence as the 'Quartier Latin') formed the second scene of Act I, while between the act set at the Barrière d'Enfer and the final one in the Bohemians' garret there was another set in the courtyard of the Vie La Bruyère where Musetta is throwing an open-air party for her friends, her landlord having impounded her furniture as security for her unpaid debts. Here Mimì would elope with her last protector, the Visconte Paolo, before returning to die by Rodolfo's side. A further letter from Giacosa written a month later ('. . . a good idea, those self-descriptions of Rodolfo and Mimì'[11]) indicates that Illica had decided to lift the lovers' first encounter from the story of Jacques and Francine.

So much was the merest groundwork. Gradually the libretto took shape during the spring and early summer months of 1893 with speed and secrecy enjoined on all parties by the ever watchful Ricordi ('Leoncavallo may or may not do *La bohème*, but there's always the risk of

---

[10] CP 83, p. 83.

[11] CP 104, pp. 101–2 (misdated).

being forestalled . . . a word let slip inadvertently might give him some idea for the libretto, which would be a real disaster').[12] Ricordi himself, as is clear from another context, was well aware of the debt owed by *Pagliacci* to a closet drama by Catulle Mendès.

'It seems to me', he would write to Illica after the première, 'that this most beautiful *Bohème*, if not just a bit my own daughter, is at least to a small extent my godchild.'[13] He was not exaggerating. Every scene, whether in Illica's draft or Giacosa's versification, was channelled through him before being submitted to Puccini at a meeting of all four. The version that resulted was then copied out by Ricordi himself so as to serve as a working basis for the composer. With each delivery he waxed ever more enthusiastic. Here was novelty, 'verismo' in the best sense of the term; if Puccini could find the right musical colours the result would be a genuine work of art which would startle the world.

By 2 July, after Puccini's return from a revival of *Manon Lescaut* at Trento, Ricordi felt able to announce in his *Gazzetta musicale di Milano* that 'Giacosa and Illica have completed the libretto for the new opera being written by Giacomo Puccini'. So they might have done, but only after a fashion. Much revision awaited them; and it would be some time before a word of it would be set to music.

For next month the shooting season would begin at Torre del Lago ('Go easy, Puccini!', Ricordi admonished him. 'Let not your passion for birds seduce you away from music. Therefore, an eye on the gun-sight, but your thoughts on *Bohème!*'[14]). And indeed Puccini had already assured Illica from his country retreat that he was 'at grips with our types'.[15] But soon he was again on his travels. A performance of *Manon Lescaut* at Brescia on 29 August was followed on 3 September by the opera's première at his home town of Lucca, accompanied by lengthy festivities to which various friends—Illica, Ricordi, Mascagni, Carignani—were cordially invited. By now it was Giacosa who was dragging his feet. Despite persistent urgings from Ricordi he had failed to deliver his revised version of the 'Barriera' act ('From now on,' Ricordi wrote

[12] MP, 137–8.
[13] CP 157, p. 143.
[14] MP, 129.
[15] CP 90, pp. 87–8.

to him in exasperation, 'I shall talk not of sailors' promises but of poets' promises').[16] In reply Giacosa humbly explained that the French première of his *Tristi amori* had held him up, and then proceeded to dwell on the difficulties of libretto-writing ('not a work of art but a work of pedantry—meticulous, indispensable, and very fatiguing'). Nevertheless he promised to have the act ready in two days' time. His next letter began, 'I give up the enterprise. I will send you the little that seems to me presentable out of the vast amount that I've done, and I will lay down my arms, admitting my impotence.' Now it seems that the obstacle was the 'Quartier Latin', which he had written a hundred times to no avail. Yet from the letter's continuation it becomes clear that Giacosa was not so much throwing in his hand as issuing an ultimatum. If allowed enough time he would remain in harness. If not, Illica could easily finish the libretto on his own.[17]

Worse, however, was to come. From Hamburg, where the German première of *Manon Lescaut* was in preparation, Puccini wrote to Illica that he was becoming 'fed up' with the lack of news from Giacosa and Ricordi. On his return to Milan he looked forward to working 'if not on *Bohème*, on something else that we will come up with, eh?' Alarmed, Illica sent this card on to Ricordi with a covering letter: 'What? Is Puccini already tired of *Bohème*? The other day I had Elvira to lunch, and I heard from her—and it didn't surprise me—that Puccini has worked very . . . very . . . little.' After so much advance publicity to abandon the project would be a disaster for all concerned. 'Therefore, for pity's sake don't give in to Puccini!'[18]

Ricordi replied:

What you tell me displeases me a great deal, but I'm not surprised because I saw it coming. . . . As far as I am concerned, my conscience is easy. The subject was chosen by Puccini, and I didn't fail to point out to him the very great difficulties, both dramatic and musical, that he would be up against. You know quite well how worked up Puccini was, how he absolutely wanted that subject, and then the polemical exchanges with Leoncavallo. And now—if you'll pardon the expression—he does it in his pants

[16] RC.
[17] CP 91–2, pp. 88–90
[18] CP 94, p. 91.

when faced by the first difficulties. . . . However, I hope it is merely one of those hesitations common to composers, and very common with Puccini!—and that it will soon pass.[19]

Ricordi knew his man. After a hectic bout of promotional touring—from Hamburg to Bologna, then to Rome and back to Hamburg—the composer was available for further discussion. A note from Ricordi invites the partners to a 'Seduta Bohèmienne' on 21 November; while a New Year card from Giacosa to Illica asking for his copy of the 'Quartier Latin' indicates that the author of *Tristi amori* had once more resigned himself to the drudgery of libretto-writing.

The start of 1894, then, found *La bohème* once more on course. But it seems that the pressure of speed was now off. Possibly Leoncavallo had taken fright at the announcement that Puccini's libretto was complete. Equally the comparative failure of his own *I Medici* in November (though it would procure him a commission from the German Kaiser) had rendered the prospect of his competition less formidable. Then, too, there were a number of prestigious revivals of *Manon Lescaut* to be attended to: on 12 January at Naples, where Puccini had the satisfaction of hearing his new finale to Act I encored; at La Scala in February and at Pisa in March, for the first time under Toscanini, of whose direction he has unfortunately left us no impressions. On the other hand Artur Nikisch, who conducted the performance in Budapest, aroused his enthusiasm; indeed he would recommend him for the Neapolitan première of *La bohème*. It was Ricordi who vetoed the engagement of a foreigner.

From Budapest Puccini made a leisurely return via Vienna and Munich before setting out for London in May for Covent Garden's first *Manon Lescaut*, armed with letters from the Florentine pianist Giuseppe Buonamici to, amongst others, Alexander Mackenzie, Principal of the Royal Academy of Music, whom he found 'gentilissimo' ('For me London will always be a delightful memory', he wrote to Buonamici. 'What a country!'[20]).

During this period the librettists had been busy. By 25 March Ricordi was sufficiently confident of the outcome to announce Puccini's con-

[19] CP 93–5, pp. 91–3.
[20] PLI 10, p. 42.

tract for the opera together with further commissions from Leoncavallo (never implemented, hence a prolonged law-suit), Mascagni, and Franchetti. The last two would be, respectively, *Iris* and *Tosca* (temporarily relinquished by Puccini), both to texts by Illica. Meanwhile the act set in the courtyard had been jettisoned, evidently at Puccini's insistence. This was for Illica a serious matter; for with it Mimì's separation from Rodolfo—an essential aspect of the 'free love' that prevails among the Bohemians—had disappeared. 'We have a meeting in an attic between a seamstress and a journalist', he wrote to Ricordi. 'They love each other, they quarrel, then the seamstress dies. A sad story; but it is not *La bohème.* . . . Mürger's Mimì is more complex.'

This was certainly true. The text of the 'Courtyard act', recently discovered among Illica's papers and published by Arthur Groos and Roger Parker,[21] is to all appearances as vital to the dramatic continuity as the 'scene of the seductions' to that of *Manon Lescaut.* Puccini's objections to it can only be guessed. Most probably he was afraid that the wealth of action (a common failing in Illica's librettos) would inhibit the musical development.

In order to heal 'the enormous wound' inflicted on the libretto by the removal of the 'Courtyard act' Illica proposed beginning Act III (as it now for a while became) with Rodolfo alone, reminded of the absent Mimì by an autumn leaf floating through the window (a detail borrowed from 'Francine's Muff'). Rodolfo, he pointed out, had as yet no 'a solo'.[22] There would then be a chance of showing the Bohemians for the first time in a state of abject poverty. And would Ricordi please for once side with his long-suffering librettists instead of backing up Puccini at every move.[23] Ricordi evidently did so; for though Rodolfo's solo would become a duet with Marcello, the start of the act remains more or less as Illica had envisaged it.

During Puccini's absence in London there were urgent exchanges regarding the 'Quartier Latin' and the 'Barriera' between Ricordi and Illica, whose patience was now wearing thin—and no wonder, for,

---

[21] Groos and Parker, op. cit., 152 ff.

[22] In the terminology of the time an 'a solo' meant a soliloquy delivered from the footlights. Therefore Rodolfo's 'Che gelida manina', being addressed to Mimì, does not qualify as such.

[23] CP 101, pp. 99–100.

while still committed to *La bohème*, Puccini was temporarily set on another tack, and with his publisher's full approval.

Since Ricordi's contract of 1890 with Verga and De Roberto for a libretto based on *La lupa*, work on the project had been going on behind the scenes. Verga had decided to turn his 'novella' into a play, which he would evolve concurrently with his libretto for Puccini. In April 1893 he reported to De Roberto that Puccini had read the first draft with approval, merely asking for a few modifications. He wanted the part of Maricchia, the she-wolf's daughter and wife of her male victim Nanni, expanded and rendered more tender and pathetic. Whether Puccini was genuinely interested in the subject Verga doubted; and in any case there was plenty of time, since he was at present fully engaged on *La bohème*.

However, Verga did more than was required of him. By April 1894 he had produced an entirely new draft of his play, at which the composer's imagination seems to have taken fire. This he dispatched to De Roberto for versification, asking him to vary the metres 'as Puccini says. So as to keep him happy, now that he is in such a hurry to begin, you could send me the scenes one by one as you write them.' By the end of the month he could tell De Roberto that he, Puccini, and Ricordi were in perfect agreement as to how to proceed and that 'this time the project is seriously going ahead'.[24] A note of 10 June from Puccini to Illica about a 'trovata latina' for the 'Quartier Latin' (evidently Musetta's entrance with Alcindoro) ends with the words 'For the present I'm she-wolfing (lupeggio)'.[25]

That Ricordi should have given his blessing to *La lupa* at such a time may seem odd. However, his letters to Puccini show that he thought of it as a short work, roughly of the dimensions of *Pagliacci* or *Le Villi*; and he foresaw the need for cuts in the first act. In the meantime he authorized a visit of Puccini to Verga at Catania in order to absorb local colour; and he asked him to take photographs of the countryside and even to buy a peasant costume which might serve for the staging. Yet beneath all this a note of anxiety over *La bohème* can be heard. 'Don't fail to keep me informed about your work on *La lupa*, which I won't

[24] M. Sansone: 'Verga, Puccini and *La lupa*', 63–76.
[25] CP 105, p. 102.

call 'brothels' (*lupanari*) nor yet 'lupins'—but which at this moment I'm very keen to know—and in the meantime won't you give a nudge to *La bohème?*' And again, 'I'm very glad to hear that you're working. Illica tells me wonderful things of what he's heard of *La lupa*—Fine! For my part I'm thinking of what I've heard of *La bohème*—and I say, what a *pity* it isn't going ahead!'[26]

Puccini set out for Catania at the end of June, returning ten days later via Malta (where his camera caused him to be detained briefly by the police on suspicion of being a spy!) to Torre del Lago. From there he wrote an apologetic letter to his publisher:

> Since my consultations with Verga, instead of being stirred to enthusiasm over *La lupa*, I've been assailed by a thousand doubts, which have made me put off my decision to set it to music until after the production of the play. My reasons are the abundance of dialogue, carried to extremes in the libretto and the unpleasantness of the characters, without a single *luminous* figure that stands out. I had hoped that Verga would have made more of the character of Mara [Maricchia], but it was impossible given the layout of the plot. . . . My only regret is for the time lost, but I will make up for it by throwing myself heart and soul into *La bohème*.

As usual, he did not altogether close his options; but for those who could read the signs it was clear that Verga's subject was not for him. Marotti relates how his doubts were confirmed at a meeting on board ship with the Countess Blandine Gravina (née Bülow), who particularly disapproved of the dénouement—the murder of the protagonist during a Good Friday procession. In any case the composer who had failed with Fontana's 'tigress' was unlikely to succeed with Verga's 'she-wolf', a character more easily written about than represented (even in the play she loses some of her original force). Nevertheless, the time spent on *La lupa* had not been entirely wasted. According to Marotti it had supplied Puccini with Rodolfo's motto theme ('Nei cieli bigi')—not to mention ideas that would serve for *Tosca*, so Illica informs us; and, having heard some of the music, he is unlikely to be wrong.

On the subject of *La bohème* Puccini's letter continues, 'The second act—"Barriera"—pleases me little or not at all. All those rubbishy episodes that have nothing to do with the drama I find tedious. We need a different, more effective scene, whether dramatic or comic. Illica should be able to find valuable material in Mürger's work.' Meanwhile, he begged to be excused his change of front, 'which I would rather call *late perception;* but better late than never.'[27] Ricordi replied:

> No, I don't wonder at your decision, though it saddens me. . . . Nor do I see in you a firm resolve with regard to *Bohème,* since you throw out the second act [the 'Barriera']. So what is to be done? I will see Illica and talk to him straight away; let us hope something can be managed! Allow me, however, my dear Doge, to point out with my usual frankness that you have taken a long time to notice the excess of dialogue in *La lupa*—after you had begun to set it to music and after the newspapers had announced the imminent appearance of the opera, . . . Then your journey to Catania!! But in the end these are useless observations. What matters is that you should get down to work and go on without letting up and so regain at least some of the time lost. . . . For Elvira and Fosca we wish excellent health and a pleasant stay in the country; and for yourself a ticket for *Bohème Station* by the fastest train.[28]

First, however there was a threat of signal-failure. The idea of starting Act II from scratch was too much for the hard-pressed author, already at grips with a *Tosca* for Franchetti. 'I am writing to you in some perplexity,' Ricordi reported to his protégé

> having found Illica very annoyed with you. He has almost decided to have nothing further to do with *La bohème.* He complains of having wasted much time and effort only to find himself used, cast aside, taken up again and shoved away like a dog. Well, I need not labour the point. The conclusion was this: I succeeded in making Illica go back to work on the 'Quartier Latin'. But he insists that I tell you that he is going on with his work solely out of regard for me!! . . . He finds the 'Barriera' scene in its original form very good (and I agree with him). As you work on it we can see what needs to be done in the way of cuts or modifications.[29]

[27] CP 106, pp. 102–3.

[28] FPL; MP, 134–5.

[29] MP, 138–9.

Puccini was all injured innocence. At his last meeting with Illica they had been entirely agreed about the 'Quartier Latin' including the scene with Musetta 'which was my idea'. He himself still disliked the 'Barriera' because there was nothing in it that allowed for lyrical expansion. Why should he blindly accept the Gospel according to Illica?[30] Happily at a meeting of all three on 24 July, reluctantly and belatedly attended by the librettist, the 'perfect chord' hoped for by the publisher was struck. For the next two months all went merry as a marriage-bell. By the end of August Illica had completed a revised version of the whole opera, which he submitted to Puccini and Ricordi. Both were delighted with it, though foreseeing the need for further pruning, notably in the 'Quartier Latin' and 'Barriera'—for Puccini still the weakest act of the three ('Am I wrong? In that case so much the better!'). Doubtless Giacosa's versification could effect the necessary tautening. Nonetheless he insisted on throwing out a mountebank from the Café Momus together with certain 'freakish conceits' (*bizzarrie*) 'which Illica clings to like his own children (if he had any)'; also a number of details from the start of the 'Barriera'. No question but that the last act was indescribably moving.[31]

By now Puccini claimed to have 'practically finished' Act I, presumably in sketch form. But not even composition was allowed to curb his enjoyment of the social amenities of Torre del Lago, among them frequent games of 'scopo' and 'briscola' with his artist-friends in an old delapidated hut, the property of one Giovanni Gragnani, a cobbler by trade with a side-line in the sale of general provisions. That summer Gragnani emigrated to Brazil, whereupon Puccini and his cronies bought the premises to serve as headquarters for their newly founded 'Bohème Club'. Its membership extended far beyond the village to include old acquaintances from Lucca: Carlo Paladini, teacher of English and author of an unfinished biography of the composer; Alfredo Caselli, the Luccan Maecenas; the musicians Carlo Carignani and Alfredo Vandini, and, of course, Ramelde's husband, Raffaello Franceschini, his receding chin the butt of his brother-in-law's gibes. There was the poet

[30] CP 109, pp. 104–5.
[31] CP 118, p. 110.

Renato Fucini, a frequent guest of the Marchese Ginori-Lisci and therefore a useful contact, and, in an honorary capacity, Luigi Illica. The rules were suitably lax. Members were required to fare well and eat better; the treasurer was empowered to abscond with the funds; only wisdom, silence, and lawful games were prohibited (for details of their various pranks, see Marotti, *passim*). Clearly there was much of the perpetual schoolboy in his subject.

As the shooting season recommenced, Ricordi's fears as to the opera's progress revived—and with good reason. During September Puccini and the forester Giovanni Manfredi were arrested for poaching on the Marchese's estates. Their case was tried at the court of Bagni San Giuliano; but, given the celebrity of one of the defendants, the outcome was a foregone conclusion.

Meanwhile, with Ricordi's fair copy of the scenario in his hands, Puccini's grumbles began again. How could he be expected to resume work without Giacosa's verses? For Giacosa, heavily committed as always, was proving singularly elusive. Eventually Tito Ricordi, acting in his father's absence, had succeeded in tracking him down and persuading him to send the composer four or five lines a day, only to find later that the poet had taken umbrage on discovering changes in his text for Act I and was once more threatening to resign unless Puccini reverted to the original. Ricordi returned from the première of Verdi's French *Otello* at the Paris Opéra to find himself at a football ground with the libretto of *La bohème* doing duty for the ball. And all the while Puccini was dallying at Torre del Lago like Hannibal at Capua (and look what happened to him!). Not until the Holy Trinity 'P—G—I' could foregather in Milan was there any chance of finishing the libretto to everyone's satisfaction.[32]

Somehow Giacosa was pacified; Puccini quitted his country retreat on 20 November and the brakes on *La bohème* were again lifted. On 12 January 1895 Illica wrote to Ricordi: '*Bohème* is—as you might say— finished. And, what matters more, the Doge is pleased with it.'[33] His trouble now was with Franchetti over *Tosca*. Certainly it had promised well. During the rehearsals for the French *Otello* Franchetti and

---

[32] FPL.

[33] CP 120, p. 113.

Illica had gone to Paris for consultations with Sardou. The playwright had given the project his blessing, Franchetti being a composer of whom he had at least heard; and even the aged Verdi, who had been present at the reading of the libretto, declared that he would have been happy to set it himself. Yet in the months that followed Franchetti dragged his heels. He liked the general plan and the dialogue; it was the lyrical passages that defeated him. Ricordi's suggestion that these be handed over to another poet was angrily rejected by Illica. By the end of March it had been decided to offer Franchetti a new libretto in exchange for *Tosca*, thus leaving the field open once more to Puccini. (So much for Adami's story, retailed as gospel in all the standard biographies, that he had colluded with Ricordi in obtaining the subject by means of a dishonest trick.)

On 25 January 1895, so the autograph tells us, the scoring of *La bohème*, Act I, was begun. Puccini's letters of the time breathe confidence and high spirits, among them an outpouring of doggerel of almost Mozartian scurrility to his sister Ramelde. Meanwhile *Manon Lescaut* was speading throughout the world in ever-widening circles—to St. Petersburg, Moscow, Warsaw, and Odessa, not to mention various centres nearer at hand, only one of which merited the composer's presence. In March the opera was to be mounted at Livorno under the direction of an old friend, Pietro Mascagni, already on his way to becoming a conductor of note. But it was not to be. A few days before the première he telegraphed that, having failed to find a suitable deputy to take charge of his opera *Guglielmo Ratcliff* and with an untried baritone on his hands, he was unable to move from Milan ('Believe me, Giacomo, I am more grieved than you, forgive me!'). What irked Puccini far more was the absence of family and friends from Lucca—even Franceschini, whose fare he had offered to pay. Worse still, the brother-in-law of his widowed sister Nitteti now applied to him for a monthly subsidy on her behalf. 'Who do you people take me for, a Rothschild?'[34] Puccini exploded. The following year, however, he would comply with the request, if not over-generously.

His promotional travels for *Manon Lescaut* were not yet finished. On 3 May he and Elvira set out for Fiume (Rijeka), passing through Venice

[34] PCE 184, p. 198.

and Trieste, thence once more to Budapest, returning by way of Vienna ('Come back soon', Ricordi telegraphed, 'for *Bohème* is weeping'[35]). But on one count the publisher could take comfort. Barsuglia's house at Torre del Lago no longer being available to him, Puccini decided to look instead for a 'modest villa' not too far from Lucca, where he could devote himself exclusively to composition; but modest villas in that region were not easily come by; and in the end Puccini rented from Count Orsino Bartolini the Villa del Castellaccio near Pescia, moving in at the end of June.

While still in Milan he had managed to finish the present Act I on 8 June. The 'Quartier Latin', now turned into a separate act, carries 19 July as its date of completion (deferred to 23 July by a graffito on the walls of the villa). For the rest of the opera Giacosa remained the chief problem. Ricordi had obtained from him the 'Barriera', which he dispatched to Puccini with suggestions of his own for further cuts and a reprise of Musetta's waltz-song behind the scenes. The poet was again growling about the miseries of a librettist's craft. Puccini might do well to sweeten him with a small present; he might also think of paying a visit to Verdi at Montecatini. Whether Puccini did either is not recorded. But by mid-July he had begun the scoring of Act III, so he told Ricordi, at the same time sending cordial messages to Umberto Giordano, then busy with *Andrea Chénier*, another Illica libretto taken up and relinquished by Franchetti.

Act IV took longer to arrive, not being in Puccini's hands until the end of July; and it is perhaps significant that all future adjustments to the libretto were entrusted either to Illica or Ricordi—'*mender of other men's faults*', as Puccini called him.[36] As the composition of Act III ('Barriera') proceeded apace, Puccini's morale received a blow from a blast of publicity in the *Corriere della sera* on behalf of Leoncavallo. He unburdened himself in a long letter to Carlo Clausetti, Ricordi's branch-manager in Naples (see p. 284). Clausetti might at least prime the local journalist Russo with a list of the theatres that were clamouring for *La bohème;* and surely it was about time to be thinking of a suitable cast. Evidently he continued to press the matter with Ricordi, whose reply

[35] FPL.
[36] CP 128, p. 118.

was unequivocal. The Milanese press, he observed, was not worth any-one's attention. Verdi had always ignored it, and see where he was today! As for publicizing in advance the theatres that were vying for *La bohème*, Ricordi thought this impolitic. Who knew what influences might be brought to bear in order to block its performance?[37] Of a proposed cast not a word. Nor did Puccini mention that he had ob-tained from one of the firm's employees a full score of *Parsifal* (the publisher would not have been amused).

The orchestration of Act III was completed by 18 September with Carignani at hand to work on the vocal score. Act IV saw the elimi-nation one by one of three of Giacosa's episodes. The first to go was a mock-subversive speech by Schaunard with comments from his fellow-Bohemians, who end by denouncing him as an *agent provocateur* of the government.[38] A 'credo', also for Schaunard, consisting of a diatribe against the female sex, Puccini thought ill-suited to one who had availed himself of the favours of a maidservant to poison a parrot. He dismissed as mere padding an alternative version supplied by Illica. Yet if Schaun-ard were not to have a number to himself at some point, he might regularly be entrusted to a comprimario singer; and his role was too important for that. A possible solution was to give him a leading part in Giacosa's 'brindisi' in praise of water; but this, too, was proving difficult to set to music, the poet having compounded it of different verse-metres; so could Illica please render it more succinct and 'quar-tettistic'? Puccini reminded him that all this foolery was merely there for contrast, and the sooner they arrived at Mimì's death-scene the better. In the end the 'brindisi' joined the 'credo' on the scrap-heap, Illica patching up the gaps according to the composer's indications. Among further adjustments to the text are a few lines of verse sent by Ricordi and signed 'Carducci'(!).

Despite Puccini's habitual failure to date his letters, most of the mod-ifications can be assigned to the first fortnight of October. For it was after the cutting of the 'brindisi' that at Ricordi's suggestion he and Elvira set out for Florence to see a performance of Sardou's *Tosca* with Sarah Bernhardt in the title role. Afterwards he could report to Illica

---

[37] CP 130, pp. 129–30.
[38] See Groos and Parker, op. cit., 144–6.

that he had found it vastly inferior to his libretto ('In the Italian treatment the element of *poetic love* (lyrical) is there in abundance; in the French it is lacking'[39]). Nor did he care for Bernhardt. But he returned twice in order to soak himself in the atmosphere of the drama.

On 20 October Puccini left Pescia for his beloved Torre del Lago, this time with Ricordi's blessing, who saw the end of *La bohème* in sight; he merely hoped that Doge Nimrod would not devote too many hours to his web-footed prey. He had found more commodious lodgings than before in the house of Count Grottanelli, where at least he did not have to share a kitchen. Here, according to his biographers, on an evening in late November, while his friends were at a game of 'briscola' in the next room, he brought *La bohème* to its conclusion. As he played and sang to them the final bars, all fell a-weeping, the composer not excluded ('It was as though I had seen my own child die', he recalled to Fraccaroli). A day or two later they were joined by some of Puccini's old acquaintances from Lucca; and all celebrated the joyous event with a fancy-dress party. The fact remains, however, that the finishing touches were not applied until midnight, 10 December, according to the autograph, where the point at which Mimì dies is marked with a skull and crossbones. There is even a further sketch for Act IV dated two days afterwards. Already back in Milan, Puccini was evidently composing up to the last minute.

Meanwhile, he had contracted a debt of gratitude to the Marchese Ginori-Lisci, who had not only granted him a permit to shoot on his estates, but had put a hunting lodge at his permanent disposal. The Marchese shared many of Puccini's interests: music, field sports, and mechanical gadgetry (he is said to have been the first to import a motorcar into Italy). That year he had acquired the Scottish-built steam yacht, the *Queen Mary*, which he re-christened *Urania* and would presently launch under the Italian flag. To celebrate the occasion on 18 December Puccini had undertaken to set a poem by Renato Fucini. Behind schedule, as always, he begged the Marchese in the meantime to accept the dedication of *La bohème*, the first of his operas to be inscribed to someone outside the profession. He would send the ode, he said, within a few days. In fact it would not be ready until the following October.

[39] CP 143, p. 131.

Ricordi was now convinced that he had a masterpiece on his hands, one which would make the orchestra 'dissolve in tears'. Nor was he alone in that opinion. Edoardo Mascheroni, first conductor of *Falstaff*, to whom he had played the first two acts, 'jumped from his chair and burst into continuous cries of enthusiasm'. Giacosa, treated similarly to Act III, 'howled like a great bullock' at the scene between Mimì and Marcello. No longer did he complain of Puccini's tampering with his text. Having insisted in June that he would never again be trapped into writing librettos, he was already versifying Illica's *Tosca*. 'Dear Puccini', the publisher declared, 'if this time you have not succeeded in hitting the nail squarely on the head, I will give up my profession and sell salami.'[40]

The first question was, where to place the première. La Scala was ruled out, being then under the direct management of Edoardo Sonzogno, who made a point of excluding all his rival's operas from the *cartello*. Ricordi planned his campaign in four stages spanning the whole peninsula: Turin in the last week in January, Rome and Naples in early and late February, respectively, and Palermo in March. Puccini had misgivings about the order. He would have preferred that it begin in Rome or Naples, where Clausetti had organized a certain amount of advance publicity. To Turin he opposed the rule *non bis in idem* (referring to the première of *Manon Lescaut*): besides, the acoustics of the Teatro Regio were poor and the city itself too near Milan, where, presumably, Sonzogno's partisans would be out in force. But Ricordi held firm, knowing that in Piontelli he had an impresario on whom he could rely. Unfortunately, the long gestation of the opera and the uncertainty as to when it would be finished had put difficulties in the way of casting. From the start Ricordi had decided on a well-integrated company of intelligent artists rather than a galaxy of celebrities. To Puccini he pointed out that not even the great Tamagno had saved Leoncavallo's *I Medici* (a clear case of 'Physicians, heal yourselves!'), nor yet Fernando De Lucia Mascagni's *Silvano*, successor to *Guglielmo Ratcliff*. Aware, however, that De Lucia was the composer's ideal Rodolfo, Ricordi duly auditioned him, only to be told that he found Act III too difficult. In any case, his financial demands were excessive. The chief stumbling

[40] MP, 149–50.

block was Musetta. Where would they find a soprano with the necessary verve and temperament? Ricordi tried for Rosina Storchio, but she proved unavailable for the Turin première (she would, however, figure in the production in Rome which immediately followed). Finally there was the need to attract a suitable Schaunard. As late as November Ricordi hoped that Puccini might revert to the idea of a 'brindisi', or even the discarded 'programma elettorale'; and he held up the engraving of Act IV to accommodate it. But Puccini was happy with the act as it stood; anything further would be otiose. Nor would his first Schaunard disgrace him: Antonio Pini-Corsi, creator of Verdi's Ford—a famous comic baritone, for whom Ponchielli had written his witty monologue *Il parlatore eterno*. There was also a worthy Mimì in Cesira Ferrani, the first Manon.

Otherwise Puccini arrived in Turin on 5 January 1896, to face a relatively untried cast. Not that he was unduly discouraged. Camilla Pasini, his Musetta, he found excellent, well up to the level of Ferrani and Pini-Corsi; likewise Alessandro Polonini, who doubled Benoit and Alcindoro. But his chief enthusiasm was reserved for the young conductor. 'Toscanini! Extraordinary!', he wrote to Elvira, at the same time telling her not to think of coming to Turin—she would hardly see him. This, of course, did not prevent him from tormenting her, as was his wont, with tales of women who sought an appontment with him ('But be easy! I won't answer them!'[41]). Soon he had more serious problems on his mind. Evan Gorgo, the Rodolfo, had a good voice but was continually ailing; and though Puccini had lowered much of his part he doubted whether he would hold out. The real worry was Tieste Wilmant, the Marcello—a harsh voice ('and Marcello is such a kind creature!') and a total inability to act. From Milan Ricordi counselled patience. But when Illica arrived to direct the production and confirmed all Puccini's misgivings, near-panic set in at headquarters. On 22 January Ricordi dispatched four successive telegrams begging them not to tire the singers to no purpose and even offering to suspend the performance. Fortunately, this proved unnnecessary.

Nevertheless, the première on 1 February 1896—three years to the day after that of *Manon Lescaut*—proved something of an anticlimax. A

[41] MP, 154.

packed house, which included Mascagni, Franchetti, and Boito as well as three members of the royal family, awarded the composer no more than 15 curtain-calls distributed between the four acts. The more favourable notices were duly fielded by the firm's house magazine; but of these few were entirely free of reservations. They found the opera an advance on *Manon Lescaut*—'nobler, less brutal in its scoring, less given to overblown perorations' (*Il corriere della sera*), 'simple, logical, succinct' (*La sera*), 'Every scene matches the situations portrayed in the libretto, whether coquettish or moving' (*La tribuna*); but there were hints that Puccini's idiom was a trifle restricted ('He repeats himself too often', from the Genoese *Il secolo XIX*). On one point all were agreed: apart from Musetta's waltz-song, Act II was the weakest of the four. Nonetheless they were certain that *La bohème* would circulate.

Not so the local press. '*La bohème*, just as it left no impression on the minds of the listeners, will not leave much of a mark on the history of our lyric theatre, and it would be as well for the composer to regard it as a momentary aberration and boldly proceed along the path of art' (*La gazzetta piemontese*, today's *La Stampa*). 'The music of *Bohème* is in truth music made for immediate enjoyment. . . . In this judgment lies both praise and condemnation' (*La gazzetta di Torino*). 'We wonder whether amid the intoxicating wave of applause Puccini's conscience did not feel a sense of abdication. Has he not noticed that *La bohème* compromised a past hour that has brought him serious and lasting glory? . . . For this case let us say no more, but may he in future return to the great and arduous battles of art' (*La gazzetta del popolo*). The writer of this last was Berta. Perhaps his offer of three years earlier to write the libretto had been meant seriously after all.

According to Toscanini the critical reaction had been conditioned partly by his own performance six weeks earlier of the season's other novelty, *Il crepuscolo degli dei* (*Götterdämmerung*). His view was confirmed by the Florentine 'Tom' (Eugenio Checchi) of *Il farfulla*, who attended the second performance of Puccini's opera, by which time the tide of opinion was already on the turn. 'Both critics and public', he wrote:

> have undergone for over a month the difficult experience of Wagnerian music, and they needed all their strength to liberate themselves from this experience. But the public, which, according to the old saying, has more

sense than Voltaire, was able to detach itself from Wagnerian impressions to enter into the spirit of the Parisian *Bohème* . . . and to breathe—let us say frankly—an air more congenial to Italian lungs. The gentlemen of the press, however, . . . were unable to leave the world of German transcendentalism in order to hear music which expresses sweet sentiments of the soul and which speaks in exquisite melodies of the eternal passions of humanity. Between the two contestants I take the side of the public.

So, of course, did Ricordi. The sour comments of the Turin press left him completely unruffled. 'All this', he wrote to Illica, 'merely confirms me in my belief that [*La bohème*] is a new and daring work of art and therefore much argued about, and even little understood—that is, by the intellectuals, who can never be truly unbiased, while the public is moved and delighted.'[42] By the end of the season *La bohème* had run for 24 performances, all of them sold out.

Long before then Puccini had already left for Rome, where his opera was launched at the Teatro Argentina on 23 February under Edoardo Mascheroni with the Romanian tenor Giovanni Apostolu (Rodolfo), Angelica Pandolfini (Mimì), and Rosina Storchio ('a number one Musetta', as Ricordi called her). The second performance was attended by Queen Margherita; while at the third Puccini was nominated Commendatore of the Italian Kingdom, and a banquet was subsequently held in his honour.

Yet here too the press was cool, though nowhere hostile. Again the second act was found wanting by one and all. Similar criticisms awaited the Neapolitan performance on 14 March, where Puccini had the satisfaction of seeing Fernando De Lucia as the tenor lead. But the scant applause that followed the second curtain was still a matter of concern. From Torre del Lago, where he had permitted himself a brief vacation, Puccini wrote to his publisher:

> I agree with you, Tito [Ricordi] and Illica about the ineffective finale to the second act, but the remedy suggested [by Illica] doesn't seem to me what's needed. Scenically it would unfold better, but in my view those few words spoken by Alcindoro alone at the end of the act . . . would come like a douche of cold water. What's needed is something noisier and more

[42] CP 156, pp. 140–1.

general. And while we're about it I'd like to give a little more breathing space to the middle of the act.[43]

Both modifications would be made, but not until Ricordi's north-to-south campaign had run its course. Meanwhile Puccini expressed to Clausetti and Illica his delight at the success of Giordano's *Andrea Chénier* at La Scala on 28 March ('he's really a good lad, provided that he doesn't change!').[44] Later he would ask for a score of the opera.

The Palermo performance of *La bohème* took place on 24 April under Leopoldo Mugnone. Hero and heroine were Edoardo Garbin and Adelina Stehle, Verdi's original Fenton and Nannetta, the former having been expressly vetoed by Puccini for the Turin première. For once his judgment was at fault; for this time the opera's triumph was uncontested, only one critic venturing to suggest that Act II (again!), though much applauded, might please less after repeated hearings. Curtain calls totalled 45. Puccini returned to Torre del Lago by way of Florence, where he was able to catch a gala performance at the Teatro Pagliano with several of the Roman cast. In his absence the critics had been mildly captious; but, called to the stage 40 times, the composer could afford to ignore them. Already audiences at Naples were being treated to a parody, *Bohème in casa di Don Carlos*—a sure sign of the opera's popularity. In a word, Puccini's best-loved work had finally arrived.

Given the novelty of the subject, the authors decided to head the score and libretto with a certain amount of prefatory material, beginning with an extract from Mürger's preface of 1851, which describes the hand-to-mouth existence of the Bohemians and their special jargon—'the hell of rhetoric and the paradise of neologism', by which is meant a mixture of high-flown poetic diction and down-to-earth slang that reflects the world of half-humorous make-believe in which they exist (see Marcello's 'Rodolfo, io voglio dirti un mio pensier profondo: Ho un freddo cane!'). To this Giacosa and Illica add a footnote of their own, explaining that they have kept to the spirit rather than the letter of Mürger's original (indeed Act III is a pure invention of Illica's) and in particular

[43] CP 159, pp. 144–5.
[44] CP 160, p. 146.

how they amalgamated the figures of Mimì and Francine into an 'ideal' of young womanhood. In fact, their fanciful description of Mimì that precedes Act I is a direct quotation from the novel referring only to Francine. No moments of savagery there.

To open the act Puccini employs his technique of two contrasted ideas in an entirely new way. No longer embedded within a continuous orchestral discourse, as in *Manon Lescaut,* they stand out sharply from one another, outlining each of the two Bohemians present on stage. To Marcello, working with freezing fingers on his time-honoured canvas, goes a boisterous theme lifted with identical scoring from the *Capriccio sinfonico* of 1883, which, since he is their leading spirit, will come to connote the Bohemians in general (Ex. 6.1a)—a period of 39 bars teased out by internal repetition and followed by a snatch of unsupported declamation ('Questo Mar Rosso mi ammollisce e assidera!'). The harmonic stasis not only establishes an ample scale, but by beginning on a dominant progression sets in motion that thrust towards the subdominant inherent in so much of Puccini's writing. A parallel statement, moving in the same direction, brings the music to a point of repose for the second theme (Ex. 6.1b). Vocal, where its predecessor had been orchestral, it will serve as Rodolfo's *Leitmotif* throughout the opera. The rising major-key arpeggio is a well-known 'topos' of youthful idealism; while the dreamy harmonies over a tonic pedal (note the extraneous E natural in the harmony at the fifth bar, a typical Puccinian departure from the norm) illustrate the poet's fanciful contemplation of the smoking chimney-pots outside, compared to which their own smokeless hearth seems like a noble lord basking in idleness. The turn to the dominant in the second strain balances the reverse trend of Ex. 6.1a, at the same time suggesting that Rodolfo is more of an optimist than his companion. Here too Puccini has followed his favourite practice of hinting in advance at one of the opera's hit-numbers—in this case Rodolfo's 'Che gelida manina', in which Ex. 6.1b holds an important place. New for Puccini, though foreshadowed in the Act I 'scherzo' of *Manon Lescaut,* is the manner in which the melodic ball is tossed back and forth between voices and orchestra within a strict pulse. The chief influence here is surely Verdi's *Falstaff.*

Colline enters to a theme whose initial bars of heavy 2/4 within the prevailing 6/8 suggest both his clumsiness and mock-pomposity (Ex.

Ex. 6.1a

Ex. 6.1b

6.2). Its siting as a mere consequent of Ex. 6.1b can cause his appearance to pass unnoticed unless he follows the stage instructions requiring him to enter noisily and slam a pile of books on the table. But this conforms entirely to Puccini's naturalistic strategy. Rodolfo and Marcello are too busy attempting to light a fire with the pages of the poet's latest tragedy to pay the new arrival any heed. The ceremony is conducted over a 'soft dissonance' of two pairs of superimposed triads alternating in a characteristic ostinato, then dissolving in such a way as to suggest leaping flames. This is more than mere onomatopoeia: for triadic patterns

Ex. 6.2

play an important part in the *Bohème* style. A resumé of previous material rounds off the scene of general frustration.

At Schaunard's appearance with money and provisions the mood changes to one of high spirits. As the humorist of the group he rates a jaunty motif of his own, one which will accompany him throughout the opera wherever he stands out from his fellows (Ex. 6.3). Amplified by a kindred, more periodic theme sprinkled with Lescaut-like leaps it forms the basis of his story of the English lord and the troublesome parrot. Its conclusion is drawn out like the elastic of a catapult to launch the missile of the parrot's death ('like Socrates'). But such narrative refinements are lost on the Bohemians who have already laid the table for a feast. In a fit of annoyance Schaunard removes the comestibles and proposes instead a visit to the Quartier Latin; whereupon strings, woodwind, and harp outline a theme to be associated with the Café Momus (see Ex. 6.8a) The soft, seductive scoring tells us that this is no more than a distant idea—in other words, a typical Puccinian anticipation.

Schaunard's Ex. 6.3 rounds off his solemn proposal to drink at home and dine abroad. But its continuation is cut short by a knock on the door. The name of Benoit, the landlord, releases a flurry of Wagnerian distress music, dwindling to single instrumental strands as the friends hurriedly confer. Marcello takes charge. He welcomes Benoit with the utmost cordiality, bids him be seated, plies him with wine and, helped

Ex. 6.3

by his companions, flatters him into indiscreet confidences. Two leisurely themes set out in an ABA design trace the course of the conversation. The first, announced by orchestra, has a touch of the
berceuse, weaving melodic threads over an alternation of tonic and
dominant chords in Chopin's manner. Benoit's interventions wander off
into irregular phrases that end in duplets like question marks; for he has
not forgotten the object of his visit, namely the rent. Neither has Marcello, who, much to his companions' alarm, lays out the required sum
on the table. But first he has another matter to discuss—and here the
second theme ('Dica: quant'anni ha') takes over, hovering insinuatingly
round a related minor key. The subject is an amorous adventure of
Benoit at the Bal Mabil. The Bohemians pay tribute to his prowess in
terms that barely stop short of indecency ('Una quercia! . . . un can-
none! . . . '). The return of the first melody, sung by Marcello finds the
landlord well in his cups, the duplets now boastful, as he expatiates on
his sexual tastes—women with a bit of flesh on them, not massive or
moonfaced; and certainly not skinny, such as—his wife. But he gets no
further. The Bohemians rise in pretended indignation to the same music
that had expressed their genuine dismay at Benoit's knock. A fierce
denunciation from Marcello is taken up by the others, its martial se-
verity soon belied by leaping figures derived from Schaunard's narration.
A triumphant major-key cadence and a burst of laughter mark Benoit's
unceremonious ejection from the garret.

Again the Quartier Latin beckons (Ex. 6.8a in a still more alluring
garb of woodwind, soft trumpets, harp and pizzicato cellos, and basses).
To this a late insertion—Marcello's advice to Colline to have his beard
trimmed and Colline's consent to submit to the 'ridiculous outrage' of
a razor—offers an amusing pendant. To cries of 'Andiam!' Marcello,
Schaunard, and Colline prepare to leave. Rodolfo, with an article to
finish, remains behind, promising to join them later. A side-slip into a
new key ensures both continuity and contrast with Rodolfo's Ex. 6.1b
on solo violin over sustaining strings and occasional harp punctuation,
the entire melody underpinned by a dominant pedal. To this the still
longer subdominant pedal of Ex. 6.1a makes answer, the theme spilt
out in fragments as the three Bohemians make their way gingerly down
the darkened staircase, only Colline losing his foothold with a cry of
'Accidenti!' ('Damnation!'). It remains for solo clarinet to wipe the slate

clean with a few Schaunard 'leaps' capped by a full close on pizzicato cellos and basses.

So ends the first half of the act, entirely comic as the second half will be entirely serious. In order to accommodate the action of Part 1 Puccini has loosened the musical fabric in a way that he never attempted in *Manon Lescaut*, but without the slightest detriment to the overall structure. Both the Schaunard and Benoit episodes share a ternary plan. While the section as a whole begins with Ex. 6.1a followed by Ex. 6.1b, it ends with the same motifs in reverse order, more succinctly juxtaposed, so giving a hint of bilateral symmetry seen down a perspective of time.

In Part 2 motivic interplay gives way to lyrical expansion. Rodolfo settles down to work to an amiable flute melody that trails away into inconsequence as he succumbs to 'writer's block'. Again there is a knock at the door, then a woman's voice. As in *Edgar* and many a future opera the heroine is heard before she is seen. But our first impression of Mimì comes from the orchestra. Clarinets within a cocoon of strings outline what will become her personal motif throughout the opera (Ex. 6.4a), here extended and dovetailed into an agitated figure (Ex. 6.4b) swaying back and forth over a Wagnerian secondary seventh in the subdominant region to suggest weakness and laboured breathing. Here in a nutshell is the heroine, pinpointed in her two main attributes—naïf charm and failing health (note the shyness conveyed by the pause on the 'frozen sixth' (*x*)). There is no *coup de foudre*. The love of Mimì and Rodolfo will ripen over a sustained lyrical growth as slowly and inevitably as that of Manon and Des Grieux. To begin with their exchanges are tentative, punctuated by a short phrase that suggests an unfinished leave-taking. Only when Mimì, having reached the door, realizes that she has dropped her key, does the music knit into a continuous theme, conversational, but with a hint of urgency ('Oh! sventata, sventata!').

Clearly the situation called for a key-jump. In the autograph it is from G to A, a solution that Puccini later rejected, partly, no doubt, because it was too drastic—after all, suddenly to remember something left behind is not an uncommon occurrence—but also because he would reserve the identical juxtaposition for a far more important moment later on. As poet and seamstress search in the darkness for the key (soon found and pocketed by Rodolfo) the music slips downward from

Ex. 6.4a

Ex. 6.4b

its tonal moorings onto a single held dominant note. Cue for the opera's most famous number (Ex. 6.5).[45]

So popular has this aria become that it is easy to overlook its originality: a structure of three musically independent paragraphs which, with no attempt at tonal balance, achieve a completely rounded statement, together with a crescendo of ardour that forms a subtext to the words. The opening is all delicacy and tenderness, the vocal line surmounted by strands of flute descant (slightly more elaborate in the autograph than in the printed score) and a masterly use of the 'frozen sixth' (x), here suggestive of a subdued longing. The second phase ('Chi son? . . . Sono un poeta'), bold and confident, is introduced by a whole-tone chord which obfuscates the original tonality and so permits au-

[45] The original tonal progression brought the aria into C major. Since many tenors found the new key of D flat too high for comfort (and still do), Ricordi suggested an optional lowering by a semitone of the chromatically inflected gesture that precedes Mimì's 'Cerca!'—a stand-by which has remained in force ever since.

Ex. 6.5

tograph and printed score to converge. Its point of arrival is Rodolfo's motif (Ex. 6.1b) proceeding from divisi strings pianissimo ('In povertà mia lieta scialo da gran signore') to a full-throated climax on full orchestra. This in turn ushers in the concluding phase ('Talor del mio forziere'), a regular period of 16 bars extended to 18 by two of half-length, each functioning as a built-in rallentando (Ex. 6.6). The opening strain will from here on constitute a 'love' motif, and none the less convincingly for being practically identical with that which began the Benoit episode earlier on. There is no dramatic significance in the likeness; it is merely an element in the 'tinta' of *La bohème*, comparable to the four-note matrix already noted in *Manon Lescaut*. The melody is energized throughout by a careful disposition of bass notes, while a moving inner part sets the final bars in high relief.

To Rodolfo's eloquence Mimì's life story ('Mi chiamano Mimì') offers a complete contrast. Here too the form arises from the expression of character. It begins as a rondo, whose subject (Ex. 6.4a sung for the first time) is sited well to the flat side of the aria's main tonality, so that its recurrences suggest a modest lowering of the eyes. Only when she becomes carried away, first with a sprightly description of her daily

Ex. 6.6

round (typical 'little woman' music, to be recalled in *Tosca*), then by her joy at the April sun (an expansive lyrical flowering), does she forget her own diffidence, and with it her initial motif. By this time the rondo has become dovetailed into a wider ternary design, its outer section the episode in which Mimì describes her pleasure in 'little things' (Ex. 6.7). Here the doubling of melody and orchestral bass, more insistent than in any previous context, increases the propulsive effect of the softly syncopated accompaniment. The reprise brings the aria to an end on a note of regret—that the flowers of Mimì's embroidery have no perfume. So important is this melody to her portrayal that its opening strain (*x*) will furnish her with a subsidiary *Leitmotif* in the acts that follow.

Fearful of having bored her listener, Mimì subsides into a subdued babble of recitative, a far cry from the cadential flourish of the traditional prima donna. But then Mimì is an entirely new type of heroine, individualized as Manon is not. In an interlude of pure naturalism the voices of Rodolfo's companions are heard from outside ('Lumaca! . . . Poetuccio! . . . Accidenti al pigro!'). The musical content is reduced to a minimum: a fragment of Ex. 6.1a for the orchestra, a rudimentary ditty for the Bohemians ('Momus! Momus! Momus! zitti e discreti andiamocene via!'), who have grasped the implications of Rodolfo's 'Non son solo! Siamo in due')—and a wolf-whistle is not uncommon at this point. As Rodolfo turns from the window to see Mimì's figure bathed in a shaft of moonlight, the love-scene bursts into full bloom ('O soave fanciulla!') with the first phrase of Ex. 6.6 on a palette of woodwind, horns, harp, and shimmering strings rising and falling in waves over a pianissimo drum-roll. Here the tonal jump from G to A is entirely appropriate to Rodolfo's sudden sense of wonder; and how wise Puccini was not to have anticipated it elsewhere! In the mounting sequences

Ex. 6.7

generated by the love-motif we can sense the melodic experiments of the Prelude in A (1882) bearing fruit. An unusual feature is the climax in A major instead of the E to which the discourse has been tending. Why, then, do we experience it straightaway as the tonic? Partly from our memory of its opening assertion with an emphatic 6/4 chord, partly by the extra weight given by Mimì's entry in octave unison with the tenor. But there is also a remote precedent in the kiss motif from Verdi's *Otello*, whose climax likewise pulls back from an approach to dominant tonality. Here it launches an emotionally heightened reprise of the second half of Rodolfo's 'Talor del mio forziere', now a duet, but with the tenor in the lead.

As Mimì disengages herself from his embrace, a succession of sustained chords on full orchestra pianissimo moves chromatically in the direction of C major in a kind of cinematic wipe-dissolve. So to the musical *envoi*, composed, according to a note in the autograph, after the completion of Act II and finished at 2 A.M. on 5 June 1895 at Milan. The long dominant pedal supporting a *Meistersinger*-like fluidity of harmony has a double function. On the one hand it conveys the sly insinuation of the lovers' exchanges; on the other it prepares for a resumption of Ex. 6.5 to which they depart for the Café Momus ('Dammi il braccio, mia piccina'). The entire passage could be sensed as a perfect cadence of 21 bars' length—as fine a way as any of sealing off a whole act, and a convincing proof, if any were needed, of Puccini's sure sense of musical architecture. And who is to say that the melody of 'Che gelida manina' has not gained from being pitched half-a-tone lower than when we first heard it?

Act II, the 'Quartier Latin', is among the most intricately organized of all Puccini's acts, encompassing a wealth of simultaneous activity within a rapid lyrical continuum. A sense of bustle and excitement blazes forth from the Café Momu theme, now blatant on three trumpets (Ex. 6.8a). The foretaste of Stravinsky's *Petrushka*, often noted, is evident not only in the parallel triads but also in the rhythmic displacement at the sixth bar. For the scene is as confused as any Shrovetide Fair—street-vendors hawking their wares, clients of the café clamouring for attention, loving couples trying to thread their way through the crowd, not to mention Schaunard buying a horn with a false D from a second-hand dealer.

Ex. 6.8a

Ex. 6.8b

Puccini begins by laying out broad tonal areas: 63 bars of Ex. 6.8a in F punched home with cadential figures; then a plunge into A flat for a varied reprise which leads into one of those smooth, more periodic themes with which the composer habitually complements his brasher openings, the distinction pointed up with a different time-signature (Ex. 6.8b). Here the contrast provides a cut-away shot, focussing our attention on the soloists—Rodolfo and Mimì entering a milliner's shop to buy a bonnet, Colline recovering his famous overcoat, recently patched by a clothes-mender, Marcello making a half-hearted pass at one of the girls. Another theme, rhythmically derived from the third limb of its predecessor and sited in E major ('Ninnoli, spimelli! Datteri e cara-melle!') provides a centrepiece of 16-bar regularity. That it contains a sequential variation of Ex. 6.6 has no dramatic significance; for the conversation, distributed between soloists and chorus, is cheerfully matter-of-fact. It is here that Rodolfo makes his only mention of a millionaire uncle from whom he hopes to inherit. With this Puccini sets off a recapitulation of his ideas in reverse order, varying them to accord with the stage action. Ex. 6.8b dissolves into distortions of its antecedent as excitement mounts among the crowd, finally the theme itself (Ex. 6.8a) in its original form and key, the trumpet blaze enhanced by a roll on the cymbals.

Four episodes follow, each linked by some detail to what we have already heard. The first, confined to the soloists, sets Mimì and Rodolfo in relief by quoting at its climax Ex. 6.6, now unmistakeably a 'love motif' leading to a cadence of unclouded happiness ('Sei felice?' 'Sì, tanto!'). The distant voice of the toyseller Parpignol diverts the general attention, so allowing Rodolfo to present Mimì to his three companions in a small minor-major 'romanza' ('Questa è Mimì, gaia fioraia'). If the first strophe recalls the delicate texture of *Falstaff*, interwoven with an appropriate reference to Mimi's Ex. 6.7, the major-key complement, a paean to love and inspiration, is scored in Puccini's most expansive manner, provoking a gust of laughter from the Bohemians. However, they receive the newcomer with becoming gravity, only Marcello re-maining somewhat distant.

Parpignol, arriving with a crowd of urchins at his heels, provides another cut-away shot. The accompanying music is among Puccini's happiest *trouvailles*, a children's ditty as vivid as Respighi's for the first of his Roman fountains. Each statement is punctuated by a fragment of the Café Momus theme (Ex. 6.8a) on muted trumpets and xylophone with the added piquancy of a sharpened fourth, which will remain with it for the rest of the act. In a vigorous reply the mothers swoop down on their charges in an attempt to drag them away; but the whimpering of a small boy ('Vo' la tromba, il cavallin!'), cleverly counterpointed with the Bohemians' order of food ('E tu, Mimì. Che vuoi?' 'La crema'), melts their hearts; and a joyous reprise, with strings playing for several bars on the wood of their bows, sends the children trooping after Parpignol down an adjoining street.

The next episode is a late addition, designed to give the 'breathing space' that Puccini required for the middle of the act, and therefore absent from the autograph and early editions, where the voices of the children fading into the distance are followed by an imprecation from Marcello as he catches sight of Musetta approaching with her elderly escort. The insertion is for Mimì and the Bohemians alone, their subject

Ex. 6.9

Allegretto giocoso

her new bonnet. Here Puccini reverts to conversational lyricism with smooth melodic gradients that contrast effectively with the leaps and bounces of the episodes on either side. The opening strain ('Una cuffietta a pizzi tutta rosa ricamata') with its bar of 3/4 within the prevailing duple rhythm is typical of the music's loose periodic structure. Each recurrence is launched by the opening figure of Ex. 6.1, as though to underline the Bohemian presence, particularly emphatic where, at the final statement all rise to their feet for a toast—the perfect cue for Marcello's outburst ('Ch'io beva del tossico!').

With the arrival of Musetta and her protector the act enters on a new phase. The concern of composer and publisher to find a suitable soprano is understandable; for Musetta has no precedent in Italian opera. Half coquette, half termagant, she belongs strictly to the world of 'verismo'. Not for her the high-flown language of the Bohemians nor yet the sentimental naiveté of Mimì. Everything about her is capricious: first a preludizing figure that dances up and down across the interval of a seventh, then a more regular melody (Ex. 6.10), whose rhythmic detail constantly changes and whose first two bars will furnish Musetta with her personal *Leitmotif*. From the interplay of these two ideas composer and librettists distil a vein of rich comedy, Alcindoro grumbling, Musetta rudely ordering him about and making a scene in front of the waiter, much to everyone's amusement. The music settles to an interlude of general conversation in familiar lyrical style, during which Musetta does her best to attract Marcello's attention. Finally she plays what she hopes is her trump card, the waltz-song, 'Quando me'n vo' soletta per la via' (Ex. 6.11).

A typical Puccini melody, with stepwise descent, falling fifths, an unresolved seventh as point of repose, and a subdominant move to the central section, it originated in a *Piccolo valzer* written two years earlier for the launching of a battleship at Genoa. It is, of course, a 'stage item',

Ex. **6.10**

Ex. 6.11

Tempo di Valzer Lento

Musetta: Quan - do me'n vo',____ quan-do me'n vo' so - let-ta per la   via la gen-te sos-ta_e mi - re.

such as would have been sung even in a spoken play. So, by making it the basis of a *pezzo concertato* Puccini was able, as in Act III of *Manon Lescaut*, to avoid all sense of frozen time. The ternary structure of the song itself is reflected in the larger design of the ensemble, whose middle episode draws on previously heard motifs, all bent to the dramatic purpose in hand—Rodolfo's explanations to Mimì, Alcindoro's fretfulness, Colline's and Schaunard's amusement, Mimì's commiseration, and Musetta's gloating. In preparing the reprise of Ex. 6.11 within the concertato Puccini shows his skill in stretching the musical fabric so as to accommodate action and at the same time increase the emotional impact. The orchestral introduction to the song is expanded by a pause during which Musetta gives a cry of pain, complains that her feet are hurting, and displays a shapely ankle. As a result the waltz-song explodes with redoubled force. Now it is Marcello, completely vanquished, who sings the melody, while Musetta yells at Alcindoro to fetch her a new pair of shoes, and the remaining voices fill out the septet with appropriate comments. A peroration, thundered out on full orchestra, crowns the ensemble, as Alcindoro hurries away and Musetta falls into Marcello's arms, the general happiness marred only by the waiter's presentation of the bill. Then comes a daring stroke. The device of ending an act with a military band heard approaching from the distance is not new. It can be found in Mascagni's *L'amico Fritz* (1891). But only in *La bohème* does it obtrude on the foregoing music from an utterly remote key (B flat as against the orchestra's E major). If the opening of the 'Quartier Latin' points forward to Stravinsky, the concluding pages presage Charles Ives. The tattoo, played by four fifes, six trumpets, and as many side-drums, is described in the full score as a 'Fanfare from the age of Louis-Philippe'. Its source, however, remains obscure. Its effect is to bring the chorus back in full strength to watch the parade. While the side-drums continue to pound, the orchestra offers a montage of thematic reminiscences—Schaunard, the Café Momus, Musetta, Parpignol. Meanwhile Musetta solves the problem of the Bohemians' bill by planting it on Alcindoro's plate with an impudent note of her own which the Bohemians echo in unison. The soldiers come into view amid wild cheering. All present, the Bohemians included, follow them offstage in what was originally a much shorter exit with a few concluding bars of orchestra to bring down the curtain and no reappearance of Alcindoro. Later Puccini filled out the design with extra choral and orchestral participation and a re-statement of the tattoo theme between two recalls of the Bohemians' Ex. 6.1a Alcindoro now returns, but without the spoken curtain-line that Illica had suggested for him; he merely collapses in dismay on being presented with the bill.

Shortly before the première Illica, who would act as stage producer, wrote to Ricordi with an objection that had just occurred to him. In Act I the Bohemians had been complaining of the bitter cold in their garret; yet here they were dining in the open without even their overcoats. Ricordi dismissed this as of no consequence, nor has it ever worried an audience—simply because Puccini's music generates enough heat to make us unaware of it: a triumph of opera over dramatic realism.

Act III is prefaced by further quotations from Mürger describing the tempestuous love-life of Rodolfo and Mimì and the caprices of Musetta. Its setting is the Barrière d'Enfer just before dawn on a cold winter's day.

The initial two-note gesture on full orchestra may be an unconscious reminiscence of Amonasro's 'sortita' in *Aida*, for the key is the same, likewise the sudden air of menace. The descending parallel fifths on flute and harp (Ex. 6.12) have long been a *locus classicus* of tone-painting,

Ex. 6.12

suggestive of falling snowflakes; but they can also be heard as the obverse of the triads of Ex. 6.8a, combining with the tremolando open fifth of the cellos to evoke an atmosphere of bleak sadness where the former had exhaled a riotous gaiety. More direct images are conveyed by extra-musical means—the rattle of harness, the tinkling of horse bells, the clinking of glasses within the nearby tavern, whose sign is emblazoned with Marcello's 'Passage of the Red Sea' transformed into 'The Harbour at Marseille'. There are brief gleams of light: the distant chorus of revellers interspersed with a fragment of the waltz-song from Musetta; the cheerful exchanges of the peasant-women going about their business. But a pedal point of 114 bars produces a sense of enveloping stillness in contrast to the incessant movement of the preceding act, a difference reflected even in the verbal setting. Whereas in the 'Quartier Latin' the text, even at its most conversational, is borne on a tide of continuous lyricism, here the lyrical moments are confined to expressions of intense feeling. Mimì's entrance illustrates the difference. Introduced as in Act I by Ex. 6.4a on strings alone, her first words addressed to the Sergente ('Sa dirmi, scusi, qual'è l'osteria . . . dove un pittor lavora?') are declaimed in naturalistic recitative, part hurried, part hesitant, with the occasional 'lift' on an unaccented syllable ('*la*vora'), a characteristic of Italian speech likened by E. M. Forster to water flowing over a pebble. Athematic too is her request to the peasant woman to find Marcello—a weary declamation in speech rhythm over soft parallel discords. Not until after the painter's appearance (Ex. 6.1a backed by a peal of matin bells) does a melodic period take shape, as Mimì begins to unburden herself. Her duo with Marcello is compounded of two alternating ideas, both pervaded by the Puccinian falling fifth in the form of a broken triad, the first flexible and subject to manipulation, the second (Ex. 6.13) fixed and repeated in its entirety,

Ex. 6.13

conveying now Mimì's desperate cry for help, frequently breaking down into 'parlante', now Marcello's attempts to console her. Fragments of Ex. 6.1b, variously inflected, give warning of Rodolfo's imminent appearance. At this point the early scores have Marcello telling Mimì to hide behind a tree. Not until the definitive edition of 1898 does he bid her return home and avoid making a scene. Not only is this more reasonable, even if Mimì disobeys him; by expanding the original three bars to 14 Puccini was able to achieve a delicate combination of the love-motif (Ex. 6.6) with Rodolfo's Ex. 6.1b on flute.

The scene that follows is as much Rodolfo's as its predecessor had been Mimì's, Marcello acting as 'feed' for both. Again to Ex. 6.1b he comes straight to the point; he intends to separate from Mimì. From the devil-may-care manner of Schaunard, countered by accusations from Marcello (again in 'parlante' style, pointed up by sharp dissonances), he passes to ironic bitterness ('Mimì è una civetta che frascheggia con tutti'). But it soon becomes clear that the story of her flirtation with a 'moscardino di Viscontino' convinces neither him nor Marcello. To a more emphatic variant of the same melody Rodolfo prepares Marcello for the cause of his behaviour, which he is vainly trying to hide from himself. Mimì is desperately ailing, and he is unable to provide her with the comfort that she needs. Six bars of soft alternating chords moving in a subdominant-orientated sequence and ending with the knell of a plunging minor cadence encapsulate a world of understated tragedy (Ex. 6.14). To so powerful a moment—a turning point in the drama—the major-key sequel, slipping into a slow waltz rhythm reminiscent of the Prelude in A, may seem rather facile. Both ideas are restated, however, the first as a vocal trio, the second by orchestra alone, during which Mimì's presence is revealed, leading to a collage of motifs: Ex. 6.4a, vigorously harmonized, as Rodolfo tries to re-assure her; Ex. 6.4b as she shuns the suffocating atmosphere of the inn; Ex. 6.10 as a brazen laugh from Musetta that sends Marcello hurrying back inside.

Alone with Rodolfo, Mimì prepares to take a heartbroken farewell of her lover in an arioso ('Donde lieta uscì al tuo grido d'amore') interwoven with many a thematic reminiscence, mostly from her own music. The recurring valedictory theme which holds the structure together is an expansion of the phrase that ended her aria in Act I. Here

Ex. 6.14

Puccini's style is seen at its most flexible, comprising bars of different lengths from 2/4 to 5/4, yet never lapsing into incoherence.

So to the final quartet ('Addio dolce svegliare alla mattina') in which Mimì and Rodolfo, sunk in memories, finally agree to remain together until the spring, while Marcello and Musetta have a blazing row. The melody (Ex. 6.15) is that of *Sole e amore* (1888). The long, sinuous phrases, the pentatonic flavour of the second strain, the dwelling on a seventh inversion to set the conclusion in higher relief—all these are Puccinian traits, put to deeply expressive purpose by their new context. The key (G flat) together with the cabaletta-like repetitions suggests a recollection of the finale ultimo of *Aida* ('O terra addio'), while the prolonged tonal stasis serves to balance that of the act's beginning. However, to rank this with the great quartets of *Fidelio, I puritani*, or *Rigoletto* would be a mistake, for the interventions of Musetta and Marcello add nothing of significance to the musical fabric. They are made possible merely by the elasticity of Puccini's style, which allows him to extend

Ex. 6.15

his melodic interstices without detriment to the structure. But as a blend of idealism and 'verismo' it stands alone. Mimì and Rodolfo express themselves in terms of romantic poetry; Marcello and Musetta hurl vulgar abuse at one another (if the occasion of their quarrel seems trivial, be it remembered that in Mediterranean countries 'dancing' is often a euphemism). Two back-references may be noted: the opening of Ex. 6.1a spatchcocked into the third limb of the melody; and the two-note orchestral flourish that concludes the act as peremptorily as it began.

The quotations that preface Act IV are from chapter 22 of the novel ('Epilogue to the loves of Rodolphe and Mlle Mimi'), the events of which are re-arranged so as to provide a distorted mirror-image of Act I. Again the setting is the Bohemians' garret; and again the initial mood is carefree; but the gaiety is forced and shot through with nostalgic memories. Rodolfo and Marcello are both at work; but their thoughts keep straying to their absent sweethearts with appropriate motival references. Blaming respectively pen and paintbrush they give themselves up to regret for past happiness in a duettino ('O Mimì, tu più non torni'), prepared by the 'love-motif' (Ex. 6.6) with altered harmonies and launched by Rodolfo with a strain whose kinship with the central part of Musetta's waltz-song is merely a case of thematic economy within the *Bohème* style. The reprise joins both voices in unison as far as their different compasses will allow. The postlude for solo violin and cello two octaves apart is a later adjunct, not to be found in early editions.

Schaunard enters with Colline and a few meagre provisions; and for the next 36 bars the music is his (Ex. 6.3 with various consequents). Colline's Ex. 6.2 also returns, portentously extended as befits his claim to have an important appointment with the King and Prime Minister. Schaunard calls for a toast, but his attempts at a pompous exordium are cut short by his companions. Instead he proposes a dance (Ex. 6.1a for the last time). A medley of ballroom fragments—gavotte, fandango, quadrille—culminates in a lively rigaudon danced by Rodolfo and Marcello, while Schaunard and Colline, after an exchange of insults, engage in a mock-duel. Into the general roistering an unrelated tutti chord of E minor bursts like a thunderclap. The door flies open to admit Musetta supporting an exhausted Mimì.

From here on the score leans heavily on material already heard, beginning with Mimì's Ex. 6.4a protracted with Tristanesque harmonies in the manner of *Manon Lescaut*, and a sequential extension of the morbid Ex. 6.4b. Throughout the scene it is Musetta, now thoroughly chastened, who takes command, her voice never rising above a mezzoforte. Her account of how she found the sick girl alone and destitute is a 'parlante' beneath the principal section of Mimì's Ex. 6.7 from Act I. By the end Mimì herself has taken over the melody, now prolonged by a further lyrical expansion related to the 'love motif', as she experiences that false sense of recovery common in the last stages of consumption. Rodolfo, likewise hopeful, joins his voice to hers. But his companions are under no illusion. Paraphrasing Verdi's Dr Grenville, Schaunard murmurs, 'Fra mezz'ora è morta!'.

It is here too that Mimì, like Francine, expresses her wish for a muff. For each of her friends she has a kindly word, but especially for Musetta ('Marcello, date retta . . . è assai buona'), whose motif (Ex. 6.10) will from here on be clouded by a sharpened fourth in the second bar; and again it is she who insists to Marcello that they must fulfil what may be Mimì's last wish on earth—this to descending sevenths that echo Mimì's appeal in Act III to the peasant woman, followed by a repeated cadence no less poignant for having been lifted from the 'Quartier Latin'. But the biggest sacrifice falls to Colline, who must pawn his overcoat to pay for a doctor. His address to the garment that has done him so much service over the years ('Vecchia zimarra, senti') may raise faint echoes of Amonasro's 'Quest'assisa che vesto vi dica' with its dwelling on the dominant and the allusion may even be deliberate, since here too the subject is an article of clothing; but despite the minor tonality and the mournful resonance of the bass voice the tempo is 'allegretto moderato'; for Colline is cloaking his genuine emotion under

Ex. 6.16

a display of whimsy. Only the final orchestral comment strikes a note of grim fatality (Ex. 6.16).

He leaves with Schaunard, whose motif (Ex. 6.3), its pace slackened, its harmony enriched, dissolves into the music of 'O soave fanciulla' with its built-in repetitions of the 'love-motif'. But its point of arrival is an entirely new theme, like a darkened obverse of Mimì's Ex. 6.7, falling where its predecessor had risen, minor where it had been major. Common to both ideas is the doubling of the melody and bass with propulsive effect, though here the motion is weary (Ex. 6.17). The pathos is all the more moving for being subdued; for Mimì's immediate feeling is contentment at being left alone with her lover. Not until later in the discourse does a recall of Ex. 6.14 suggest a forewarning of her death. Together she and her lover relive their first meeting to music associated with it. Ex. 6.10 announces the return of Musetta with the muff—Rodolfo's gift to her, so Mimi thinks. Her gratitude finds expression in two widely spaced orchestral quotations from 'Che gelida manina', the scoring ever more attenuated. A chilling chord of B minor cuts short the final statement, signalling Mimì's demise to the audience. Musetta murmurs a prayer for her recovery, touched in with a reference to Ex. 6.7. The voices become quieter, subsiding into plain speech and so preparing for Rodolfo's unpitched outcry as the true situation dawns on him ('Che vuol dire quell'andare e venire . . . quel guardarmi così?'), a blast of realism far more heartrending than the customary lyrical effusion at such moments. It is left to the orchestra to bring down the curtain with an amalgam of Mimì's 'Son andati?' (Ex. 6.17) and Colline's Ex. 6.16, both ideas milked for their immediate emotional impact with-

Ex. 6.17

Andante calmo

Mimì: So - no_an-da - ti? Fin-ge-vo di dor-mi - re—— per-chè vol - li con te so-la re - sta - re.——

out reference to their previous context. There will be other such instances in the future.

Had Puccini written nothing else after *La bohème*, his permanent niche in the operatic repertory would have been assured. Here the composer's narrative technique is the more fluent for having dispensed with the quasi-symphonic apparatus to be found in much of *Manon Lescaut*. Some commentators speak of the opera's restraint in contrast to its predecessor. But it is surely just a more precise calculation of means to ends; for no opera of Puccini—not even *Madama Butterfly*—wrings the heartstrings more mercilessly than *La bohème*.

Nothing like it had been written before. How far can it be linked with the tradition of operatic 'verismo' inaugurated by *Cavalleria rusticana*? As noted earlier, the term 'verismo' can be applied to opera only in a relative sense, especially to the Italian variety, for which the verse-libretto remained *de rigueur* until Alfano's *Sakuntala* of 1921. What 'verismo' meant for an audience of the time was the converse of 'grand opera': a story of contemporary life among ordinary people who express themselves in homelier language and whose emotions were not curbed by the traditional forms of earlier *melodramma*. The fact that the immediate successors of *Cavalleria rusticana* dealt with 'life in the raw' among the poor and deprived has since led to an association of the term with violence and brutality. So it is that Carner sees Puccini's first encounter with 'verismo' in the torture scene in Act II of *Tosca*.[46]

Puccini's contemporaries would not have agreed. It was precisely the 'realism' of *La bohème* that repelled its severest critics, from Hanslick, who regretted its 'sensational break with the last romantic and artistic traditions of opera' to Fausto Torrefranca, who, in his celebrated attack of 1911, faulted the composer's imagination for its failure to rise above

[46] PCB, 288.

the most mundane details of the text. It was 'realism' that constituted the opera's chief virtue in the eyes of Camille Bellaigue, who, while conceding a certain lack of spiritual depth to the music, commended its attachment to 'concrete, palpable reality, . . . to its exterior and insignificant signs. . . . This surface reality . . . M. Puccini's music expresses marvellously, giving us its acute and constant sensation.'[47]

Indeed, realistic elements abound in *La bohème* as in no previous opera, whether of Puccini or anyone else: snatches of unsupported declamation that follow the inflections of everyday conversation with a fidelity never attempted by conventional recitative; spoken interventions, whose pitch, indicated in the autograph in the manner of 'Sprechgesang', would later be left to the individual executant; and, not least, the integration into the sound-picture of extraneous noises, as at the start of Act III. The intrusion of the tattoo in a key far distant from that of the ensemble on which it impinges is a touch of realism that will find an echo years later in the 'last post' of *Il tabarro*.

Mimì, it is true, is idealized throughout as a romantic heroine; and if the Bohemians' bombast is realistic by way of parody, many of her own expressions would sound odd on the lips of a *grisette*. However, there exists a bridge between romanticism and realism of which Puccini and the 'giovane scuola' (Mascagni alone excepted) were always ready to avail themselves. In their best-known works the central character is an artist, to whom a certain poetic effusion is natural. Giordano's Andrea Chénier is a poet, Cilea's Adriana Lecouvreur an actress, Leoncavallo's Zazà a singer, as indeed are Tosca and (by profession) Ciò-Ciò-San. *Pagliacci* is built round a travelling theatrical troupe. In *La bohème* everyone apart from Benoit and Alcindoro is in artist of a sort—even Mimì with her embroidery of artificial flowers. Consequently their oscillation between dream and reality avoids all sense of contrivance. No opera is more successful in reconciling these two aspects than Puccini's *La bohème*, certainly not Leoncavallo's treatment of the same subject, though initially received with greater acclaim. The most lettered of the 'giovane scuola', Leoncavallo keeps closer to the novelist than Illica and Giacosa. His range of characters extends to Schaunard's ill-treated mistress, Phémie, and that wealthy recruit to the Bohemian society, Barbemou-

---

[47] Groos and Parker, op. cit., 134–6.

che, said to be based on Baudelaire. His Mimì is Mürger's down to her last caprice; but this is less of a virtue than it might seem, since it precludes any real distinction between her music and Musetta's, apart from their respective voice-types. The idea of a 'courtyard' scene showing Mimì's elopement with the Viscount is realized at length; but its omission from Puccini's score, unlike that of the 'seductions' scene from *Manon Lescaut*, is not a matter for regret, since Mimì's character has already been fully defined and her departure prepared at the end of Act III. A defect that Leoncavallo's opera shares with *Manon Lescaut* is the concentration of all the gaiety in the first half and all the gloom in the second. Fortunately, by the time of his own setting of Mürger's subject Puccini had learnt his lesson, and his disposition of contrasting moods is masterly.

Throughout his opera Leoncavallo makes a parade of culture. Just as his printed libretto cites poems by Mürger and Alfred de Musset, so his score contains quotations from *Les Huguenots, Mefistofele*, and *Tristan und Isolde*, as well as a comic parody of Rossini. But this is no substitute for the consistency of Puccini's style, in which every phrase 'belongs', even when he takes in foreign material, as in the 'ritirata' of Act II. Particularly evident is Leoncavallo's failure (shared by many of his contemporaries) to find a system for the organization of an opera whose units are whole acts rather than individual scenes or musical numbers. A valid system had already been found by Puccini in *Manon Lescaut*. In *La bohème* it is fined down and loosened to reflect every twist of the drama together with the changing moods of each character. For an Italian opera in which the artificialities of the medium are so little felt there is but one precedent: *Le nozze di Figaro*.

CHAPTER 7

Tosca

A S PUCCINI STEPPED FROM THE TRAIN THAT BROUGHT HIM FROM
Palermo back to Milan, his first words to an unofficial committee
of welcome, as reported in Ricordi's *Gazzetta*, were, 'And now, my
friends, for *Tosca!*' Indeed at a banquet given in his honour in the Sicilian
capital he had already regaled the company with some of the musical ideas
for his new opera, of which he had so far received not a word of text. Evidently his mind was made up. It may be useful, therefore, to glance at the
drama which had haunted him intermittently over the past seven years
and which would occupy him during the next four.

Victorien Sardou (1831–1908) is one of those authors like August
Kotzebue whose oeuvre achieved an international circulation during
their lifetime, only to be forgotten 50 years after their death. A practitioner of the 'well-made play' in the tradition of Eugène Scribe, he
reached a pinnacle of glory with *La Tosca*, written for Sarah Bernhardt
and first performed by her at the Théâtre de la Porte St. Martin on 24
November 1887, from which she would carry it throughout Europe in
a blaze of publicity. In her castle at Craig-y-Nos Adelina Patti used to
delight her guests with a mimed representation in which, according to
the critic Hermann Klein, she displayed all the qualities of a great actress.
Only Bernard Shaw dismissed the play as 'an old-fashioned, shiftless,
clumsily constructed, empty-headed turnip ghost of a cheap shocker'.[1]

---

[1] *Shaw's Music*, ed. Dan H. Lawrence (London, 1981), i, 911.

Shaw was concerned, then as always, with dramas of ideas. *La Tosca* is a drama of happenings, a piece of clockwork mechanism lubricated by historical erudition, in which there is no pause for thought. The long speeches are all narrations, relating in detail the events that have led up to the moment at which they occur. From them we learn the background of each of the main characters: Mario Cavaradossi, a painter of liberal sympathies, born in Paris of a Roman father and a French mother, pupil of the Revolutionary artist Jacques-Louis David, called to Rome a year since to settle business regarding his deceased father's estate and detained there by his love for Tosca; Cesare Angelotti, consul of the short-lived Roman republic of 1798, recently escaped from the Castel Sant'Angelo, where he had been incarcerated at the instance of Emma, Lady Hamilton, whom he had 'protected' during her days as a prostitute at Vauxhall Gardens; Baron Vitellio Scarpia, chief of police, half religious bigot, half satyr, whose own life is in danger should he fail to recapture the fugitive; and finally Floria Tosca. Once a goatherd among the hills near Verona, she had been taken in and educated by Benedictine nuns. Cimarosa, visiting the convent, heard her voice in the choir and obtained the Pope's permission to have her trained as a singer, since when she has performed in the leading theatres throughout Italy. At present she is engaged at the Teatro Argentina, Rome. Fame, however, has in no way affected her peasant simplicity. 'Je ne lui sais même qu'un défait', Cavaradossi tells Angelotti; 'c'est une jalousie folle qui n'est pas sans troubler un peu notre bonheur. Il-y-a aussi sa dévotion qui est excessive; mais l'amour et la dévotion s'accomodent assez l'un de l'autre.' In a word, Tosca is all heart and no brain; and Sardou does not scruple to make fun of her. Presented by Cavaradossi with Rousseau's *La nouvelle Héloise*, she had shown it to her father-confessor, who had ordered her to burn it at once lest it burn her. And did she burn it, Cavaradossi wants to know? No, she even read it—'Et il ne me brûle pas du tout ce livre, mais là, pas du tout!' Much of the dramatic tension arises from her chance involvement in a cause which means nothing to her.

Puccini's description of the subject back in 1889 as 'not calling for a superabundance of music' is an understatement. At first sight it is difficult to envisage in it a place for music at all, apart from the rehearsal of Paisiello's cantata in Act II. This had no doubt occurred to Illica and was probably the reason why he steered Puccini away from the drama at their first meeting in 1891. More than three years later, having compressed Sardou's five acts into three for Franchetti (who, as noted, was only too happy to be rid of it), Illica was still unhappy with the result. 'The play is too intrusive and overpowers (*invade*) the libretto', he wrote to Ricordi.[2] The burden of his complaint is the endless chain of scenes 'a due'. Similar objections would in due course be heard from Giacosa, to whom Illica's libretto had been handed in the autumn of 1895 with the request that he set to work immediately on a monologue for Scarpia with which to open the second act. 'It seems to me', the poet replied, 'that to finish the first act with a monologue and begin the second with another by the same character is a bit monotonous—apart from the fact that to have this Scarpia waste time in describing himself is absurd. A Scarpia acts; he doesn't explain himself in words.'[3]

Nevertheless Giacosa would do his best to oblige. In July 1896, with a contract and Illica's draft in his hands, he became more specific. 'Believe me', he wrote to Ricordi, 'it is a terrible undertaking having to cut down to the right proportions an act as crammed full of facts as this first one. I'm working like a desperate wretch, but on the one hand the clarity must be respected, on the other the act must not exceed 300 lines. And that's already too many, and one can't omit a single fact or incident.'[4] He then submitted his Act I as far as the duet between Tosca and Cavaradossi, which Ricordi had copied and dispatched to Puccini; the remainder followed on 25 July. Having received it from the publisher, Puccini sent the manuscript to Illica, then the guest of Mascagni at Pesaro, where both were working on *Iris* ('Herewith the Buddhistic act. Read, scan, and help me. . . . Greetings to Pietro').[5] As on previous occasions Puccini had found the language too involved. Nevertheless, he was beginning the composition, possibly spurred on by favourable reports of progress on the other *Bohème* ('I understand from someone who has read Leoncavallo's libretto that it's a marvel! You'll see that if he puts a bit of trifling music in it and the opera just manages to stand

[2] CP 120, p. 113.

[3] CP 149, p. 136.

[4] CP 166, p. 149.

[5] CP 167, p. 149.

up, it will flood the foreign market, and it will be my fate to remain localized for the rest of my life!').[6] Hardly the case. But it was Leoncavallo's *Bohème* that first reached the Vienna State Opera, conducted by Gustav Mahler.

Meanwhile, stung by Ricordi's incessant prodding, 'the Buddha' was again offering to withdraw from the partnership. The gist of his long letter of 23 August was that *La Tosca* was totally unsuited to the medium of opera. There was no place in it for poetry or lyrical expansion. Like Illica, he complained of the abundance of duets, something that hardly mattered in a play written for a virtuoso actress but would only lead to monotony in a music drama. However, should his resignation not be accepted (and of course it was not) he promised to supply the second act by the beginning of September. In fact it did not reach Ricordi until 23 September. Various revisions and adjustments were necessary before Puccini felt able to return it to the publisher on 4 November. Of Act III there was still no sign. In his exasperation Ricordi fixed a deadline of 6 December for its receipt, imposing a fine of 50 lire per day thereafter. This time Giacosa did not fail him.

But the opera itself was still a long way in the future. So far Puccini's work on the score had been desultory, to say the least. Among his social and recreational activities, however, he found time to complete his setting of *Avanti Urania*, which he sent on 4 October 1896, to the Marchese Ginori-Lisci with a dedication to his wife. It is not a particularly attractive piece. Fucini's words are draped casually over a tune which seems to have occurred to the composer independently of them; and despite an effective final strain, its upward climb balancing the downward trend of the opening, it is commonplace Puccini. The Marchese was better recompensed with the dedication of *La bohème*.

Early in December Puccini returned from Torre del Lago to Milan. 'Prepare to put up with my company', he wrote to Illica, 'and arm yourself with patience for Toscan arguments. . . . Have ready for me emotions!'[7]—an indication that he was still finding Giacosa's language too literary and indirect. What resulted from their conference is un-

[6] CP 168, p. 150.
[7] CP 174, p. 154.

known; but by the beginning of January Ricordi felt able to wire to Sardou that the star of *Tosca* was beginning to shine.

As usual he was over-optimistic. The year 1897 was for Puccini largely one of attendances at *La bohème* at home and abroad, beginning with La Scala, Milan, now mercifully out of the hands of Sonzogno. Here the opera was given under Leopoldo Mugnone with a cast that included Angelica Pandolfini (Mimì), Fernando De Lucia (Rodolfo), and the original Musetta of Camilla Pasini. For 16 nights 'it emptied the tear-ducts of the audience', so Tito Ricordi told Illica. Long before the end of the run Puccini was back in Torre del Lago, thus avoiding several banquets in his honour. 'For the public' (Tito again) 'he is in Liverpool.'[8] And indeed an English première in that city had already been planned for February, to be given by the Carl Rosa Opera Company, Covent Garden having declined the option out of disappointment with *Manon Lescaut*. However, the schedule was changed, and the honour of planting *La bohème* on British soil fell to Manchester, whither Puccini journeyed in mid-April to supervise rehearsals. His impressions, whether of the town or the company, were not favourable. From the Queen's Hotel he wrote to Ramelde, 'I am alone in this horrible place' (not quite true; Tito Ricordi was with him). 'Smoke, rain, cold. . . . You should hear what dogs! . . . But here they like them.'[9] As always with the Carl Rosa company, the opera was performed in English as *The Bohemians*. Despite Puccini's misgivings the première on 22 April was a huge success. Hermann Klein, who accompanied him and Tito on the journey south, recalls a merry, smiling Puccini 'with a plentiful supply of Italian jokes, and radiant with the recollection of genuine Lancashire cheering'.[10]

His impressions of the journey home he recorded three years later in a letter to Caselli: London ('hardly a beautiful city, but a fascinating one'), Paris ('gayer, more beautiful but less busy . . . and with a character of its own'), where he enjoyed friendly contact with Zola, Sardou, and Alphonse Daudet ('who would have imagined this of the strolling

[8] BPP.

[9] PCE 213, p. 225.

[10] H. Klein: *The Golden Age of Opera* (London, 1933), 223.

organist of Mutigliano?'), and Brussels ('fine houses; palaces, monu-
ments, magnificent streets; yet rather provincial in comparison with
London and Paris').[11] His meeting with Sardou is described in an interview given to the journalist Eugenio Checchi. The playwright, it
seems, was only too happy to associate himself with the team of Illica
and Giacosa; but he objected to Illica's conclusion, in which Tosca,
confronted by her lover's dead body, brought down the curtain on a
'mad scene'. Puccini agreed; and he showed Sardou his copy of the
libretto on which he had scribbled over Illica's lines, 'This is the *paletot*
aria!', meaning that the audience, having foreseen the end, would be
rushing to the cloakroom to pick up their overcoats. Whereupon Sardou leapt to his feet, grasped Puccini by the hand and exclaimed, 'I see
that you are a man of the theatre!'[12] Further modifications were passed
on to Ricordi on Puccini's arrival in Milan.

By now Leoncavallo's *La bohème* had begun its run of performances
at the Teatro La Fenice, Venice, with Rosina Storchio as Mimì but
without the Schaunard of Victor Maurel, for whom the part had been
specially written. (It was not the first time that this most self-centred
of baritones had let down a composer to whom he had promised his
services; Isidore De Lara suffered the same experience with his opera
The Light of Asia in 1892.) Irritated by the barrage of publicity launched
by Sonzogno, Ricordi had decided to forestall the event by a revival
of Puccini's opera at the Teatro Rossini in the same city. It was not a
wise move. Press and public awarded the palm to Leoncavallo's work,
despite the obloquy already heaped on it by the opposing camp after a
mere glance at the vocal score. Not even the libretto was spared. '*Bohème* as I am Scandinavian', was Ricordi's verdict.[13] 'They talk like so
many Othellos, Iagos, Leers [*sic*], Macbeths', was Puccini's.[14] (In fact
the author's dialogue is most ingenious and reasonably true to Mürger's.)
Yet evidently their hostility was kept from Leoncavallo himself; otherwise Ricordi would hardly have sent him a copy of Act I of *Tosca* with

[11] CP 233, p. 201.
[12] E. Checchi: 'Giacomo Puccini', *Nuova antologia* (Dec. 1897), 470.
[13] BPP.
[14] Ibid.

all the latest revisions, 'as I was keen to have the opinion of so great a man!'[15] Leoncavallo, he told Illica, was duly impressed.

Back in Torre del Lago Puccini accepted an invitation from the journalist Parmenio Bettoli to write a piece for a 'numero unico' celebrating the centenary of Donizetti's birth ('only a few notes, since *Tosca* and a visit to Berlin will prevent me from devoting myself to other work').[16] Evidently he defaulted, for among the contributions of Boito, Mascagni, Massenet, and others those few notes are not to be found. The journey to Berlin, undertaken with the utmost reluctance, was for Germany's first taste of *La bohème* at the Kroll Theatre on 22 June. The cast was undistinguished, the performance in German, and Puccini's impression of it unrecorded. He returned to Torre del Lago to be laid low with the undignified complaint of a tapeworm. Hence, though he continued to bombard Illica with requests for adjustments to the libretto of *Tosca*, little if any work was done on the music. In August, however, he was cheered by the visit of a young tenor about to star as Livorno's first Rodolfo. At 24 Enrico Caruso had yet to gain even a national reputation (it would come to him in November of that year with the première of Cilea's *L'arlesiana*). 'Who sent you to me? God?' Such, according to Marotti, was Puccini's reaction on hearing him. But, though he would render signal service to *La bohème* throughout the world, not least at Covent Garden, where his performances with Nellie Melba in 1899 sufficed to place the opera firmly in the company's repertory, the public's future idol would not create a role in a Puccini opera until 1910, as the first Dick Johnson in *La fanciulla del West*.

Mid-September found Puccini in Vienna. Mahler, recently appointed chief conductor at the Vienna State Opera, had seen both *Bohèmes* performances at Venice. Of the two he had recommended Puccini's; but the previous incumbent had already settled for Leoncavallo's version; so the rival opera was relegated to the more modest venue of the Theater an der Wien. The production, first seen on 5 October, was chiefly memorable for the horde of children engaged for the 'Quartier Latin', who got in everybody's way. Mahler, present in a box, was

[15] RC.
[16] CP 176, p. 155.

moved to scornful laughter, which Puccini never forgot. Both *Bohèmes* came under the lash of Eduard Hanslick, but especially Puccini's, in which he could detect no principle of musical organization whatever— just a few sparks of melody (chiefly associated with Mimì) interspersed with 'dead spots' of mere noise. That the champion of Brahms should single out the parallel fifths and triads as examples of pure ugliness was surely predictable. These he ascribed to the deplorable influence of *Cavalleria rusticana*. As usual, Hanslick got everything wrong.

Tosca would suffer a further interruption at the end of November, when at Ricordi's insistence Puccini reluctantly consented to sit on a music committee held in Rome. But the visit was not unfruitful, for it brought him the acquaintance of the priest Don Pietro Panichelli, who would become a life-long friend, to be consulted on all matters ecclesiastical as they affected his operas. He it was who provided information about the exact pitch of the great bell of St. Peter's, which Puccini would introduce into the prelude to Act III of *Tosca*. This prelude he played out of his head to Eugenio Checchi, telling him in the interview mentioned above that he had so far written very little down: 'loose sheets, disconnected thoughts, quite a few cancellations. But I can't tell you how much time I shall still need. . . . It's a case of "He who goes slowly goes surely." '

One piece that he did manage to complete before the year was out is the *Inno a Diana*, a setting of verses by the Neapolitan poet Carlo Abeniscar, one of his hunting cronies at Torre del Lago. Dedicated to 'the Italian hunters', it preserves, for once, a four-bar regularity throughout: and, if no more distinguished than *Avanti Urania*, it has a certain melodic spontaneity, particularly in its opening flourish, treated throughout as a rondo theme. The harmonization, too, is characteristic.

By 1898 Puccini was a comparatively rich man. But years of indigence together with the difficulties of his domestic situation had left their mark. That he should baulk at the purchase of a three-wheeled motor car for 2000 lire is understandable. Less so is his refusal of a bridging loan to his brother-in-law, which he could quite well have afforded. Tax-collector for the commune of Pescia, Franceschini had recently suffered a disaster. One of his employees had absconded with a large sum of money, whose loss he was obliged to make good. This he could do by the sale of some of his property; but it would be a lengthy process. Ramelde at once applied to her brother for help in tiding them over, guaranteeing restitution at the earliest opportunity. Returned from a revival of *La bohème* at Parma, Puccini protested his inability to oblige on the grounds that all his available funds were tied up in a mortgage on a house in Milan. This was pure fiction. Never then nor at any other time did he consider buying property in that city. We may charitably suppose that it was Elvira who insisted on the excuse. She was never particularly well-disposed towards her future husband's family.

Now the composition of *Tosca* was beginning in earnest. In the autograph score the opening chords that make up the Scarpia motif are headed 'G. Puccini, January 98'. A draft of the libretto in the New York Public Library carries musical sketches scribbled in the margin together with a self-caricature with the date 'February 1, 1898' and the cryptic remark 'Tosca—the real one . . . But better return to it'.

Not, however, before another visit to Paris to make arrangements for the French première of *La bohème* scheduled for May at the Opéra Comique. At Ricordi's behest he again visited Sardou and played him the first act of *Tosca*. According to the *Gazzetta musicale di Milano* of 10 March 'the great French playwright was enthusiastic and especially struck by the way Puccini treated the passionate parts, and how he fleshed out the principal characters of the drama'. How much had been written down can only be guessed. But on his return to Milan Puccini could report to 'Arturetto' (Toscanini), '*Tosca* is going ahead well; remember that you must be her deflowerer!'[17] In the event it would be Leopoldo Mugnone.

After a month spent at Torre del Lago Puccini set out once more for Paris, now with Elvira and Fosca, to attend rehearsals at the Opéra Comique. The baptism of *La bohème* in its city of origin was an important event, and, again in the company of Tito Ricordi, Puccini was fêted by high society. This was not at all to his liking. The year before he had declared that he would gladly spend five months in the French capital. Now he could hardly wait to get back to his Tuscan retreat. 'I am sick of Paris', he wrote to Caselli in Lucca. 'I hate pavements! I hate palaces! I hate columns! I hate their capitals!', and more to the

[17] CP 181, p. 158.

same effect.[18] Above all, he disliked having to make public appearances in formal dress, as he bewailed to Giulio Ricordi, adding that rehearsals were proceeding at a snail's pace, though the cast were willing enough, apart from Isnardon (Leoncavallo's Schaunard) as Colline.

Bored as he may have been, Puccini was at least spared the disasters that were taking place in his own country. At the beginning of May a demonstration in Milan against the rising cost of living was fired upon by government troops with a death toll of 80. Numerous arrests followed. Eventually the ministry resigned, to be replaced by General Pelloux, whom the king invested with dictatorial powers. Though appalled at the loss of lives, Puccini was no democrat. Invited by his artist-friend Pagni to vote by post for Cesare Riccioni, mayor of Viareggio, as parliamentary candidate, he replied, 'I have plenty of admiration for our friend Riccioni, but I don't want to get mixed up in elections. I would abolish chamber and deputies, they're so dreary, those everlasting chatterboxes. If I were in charge I'd return willingly to "Carlo Dolovio", good soul.'[19] Carlo Ludovico, Grand Duke of Tuscany during the 1830s, may not have been a good ruler, but he was generous towards the arts.

The first night of La bohème was put back to 13 June, thereby depriving Puccini of a projected visit to London. The performance, however, satisfied him, particularly the Schaunard of Lucien Fugère. Illica, present for some of the rehearsals, was delighted by certain details in Albert Carré's production: the drunkard helped home by his wife at the beginning of Act III, Marcello throwing down his brushes after his quarrel with Musetta (no wonder they functioned badly at the start of Act IV!). Though cool, as in Italy, towards the 'Quartier Latin', the public was enthusiastic, the critics less so. Henri Malherbe found only 'melodic banality' in the score; to Adolphe Jullien of the Moniteur universel the opera amounted to second-rate Massenet combined with excessive Verdian sonority. Ernest Reyer in the Journal des debats was more flattering, even praising the parallel fifths of Act III as a legitimate harmonic innovation. But his was a lone voice. The 'giovane scuola' were not looked on with much favour by the French press.

[18] CP 185, p. 160.

[19] CP 182, p. 159.

Ever since April Puccini had been casting about for a permanent residence, whether by the Lake of Massaciuccoli or up in the hills where he could work at *Tosca*. So far nothing had been concluded; and after three weeks at Torre del Lago he accepted the hospitality of the Marchese Raffaello Manzi at his villa at Monsagrati in Pescaglia, ten kilometres north-west of Lucca. His immediate problem was to find a suitable chant for the crowd to murmur before the start of the *Te Deum* in the finale of Act I. First he applied to Guido Vandini in Lucca for a copy of the *Ecce sacerdos*. As this proved too emphatic, he turned once more to Don Pietro Panichelli, who obliged with a few lines which Puccini found 'very beautiful but lacking in the phonic accents needed to penetrate the sound of the organ and church bells'.[20] He wrote again to Vandini with an urgency that overrode elementary punctuation. 'Tell the bishop that I need something and he must invent it, if not I'll write to the Pope and make him pay a fine like a stupid employee. . . . Find me some little verse, if not I'll turn Protestant, tell that to the deacon.'[21] But no little verse was forthcoming; and it was Puccini himself who made do with the words 'Adjutorum [*sic!*] nostrum in nomine Domini qui fecit coelum et terram'.

To Ricordi he wrote asking him to obtain from Illica or Giacosa some new lines for the love-duet of Act I. It was Giacosa who supplied them, albeit with a bad grace. But one of his observations merits attention. 'I think I have done well in not making Tosca persist with her suspicions. . . . It seems to me that all she has said before and will say afterwards ('Ma falle gli occhi neri!') are more than sufficient. It seems to me . . . natural that she should allow herself to be overcome by Mario's erotic ardour.'[22] He had indeed done well. By refusing to dwell on his heroine's jealousy he helped to make her a far more credible character than her counterpart in the play.

Significant, too, are Puccini's interventions on the libretto of Acts II and III, on which he had already begun work in July. Thus in the second act: ' "How you hate me!" is effective and "Do you hate me?" doesn't work. Why have you taken out the last line "And before him

[20] P. Panichelli: *Il 'pretino' di Giacomo Puccini racconta*, 58.
[21] PLI 46, p. 79.
[22] CP 196, pp. 169–70.

all Rome trembled!"'? I put it in and it works well for me.' And in Act III: 'I hope to be able to do without the final triumphal "Latin hymn". I believe I will finish the duet with the words "I will speak to you a thousand words of love", and "I will close your eyes with a thousand kisses" '—thereby creating a bone of contention between himself and his collaborators which would remain to plague them for some time. At the same time he authorized certain changes to the wording of the torture scene suggested by Sardou, since these would not affect the music.[23]

Puccini left Monsagrati with his family on 22 September, but not before he had paid a visit to the hamlet of Chiatri high in the hills commanding a distant view of the Lake of Massaciuccoli. Here he had purchased some land on which to build a villa. In those days it was accessible only by mule-track; the construction was therefore long and arduous, and two years would pass before he was able to take up occasional residence.

Meantime he continued his work on *Tosca* at Torre del Lago, interrupting it only to travel to Rome for the première of Mascagni's *Iris* on 22 November. His impressions of it were given in a letter to Mascagni's friend Alberto Crecchi written after a revival at La Scala early in the New Year:

> *Iris* went off as you know and those *pigs* of the press were extraordinarily cruel, especially the *Corriere*. For me this opera, which contains so many fine things and is so brilliantly and colourfully scored, suffers from its fault of origin: the action is uninteresting and melts away and languishes over three acts. The result is that if the Lord God himself had set such a libretto to music He would not have done more than Pietro has done. You, who are his true friend, tell him to return to the passion, the living human sentiment with which he began his career so brilliantly. What I said to you about the libretto is strictly *inter nos*, you understand?[24]

Obviously he did not want it to get back to Illica. It did, however, reach Mascagni himself, who, after the cool reception given to Act II of *Tosca* in Rome, was heard to exclaim 'I the victim of a bad libretto,

---

[23] CP 193, p. 167.

[24] CP 201, p. 173.

he the victim of too good a one!'—a *boutade* which he reported to Illica.[25]

The rest of the year found Puccini 'working like a dog' at his opera, first at Torre del Lago, then at Milan, saddened only by a fortieth birthday, which meant a farewell to his youth. His low spirits found expression in a diatribe against his fellow-Luccans, probably addressed to Ramelde. Early in 1899 he made another trip to Paris—a brief holiday, as he confessed to Franceschini, for which a revival of *La bohème* at the Opéra Comique provided an excuse. There was talk of his being awarded the Légion d'Honneur, a possibility enshrined in a drawing by the Italian cartoonist Campiello, showing a Puccini grown distinctly plump (his weight at the time was 95 kilos). There were further meetings with Sardou ('a fine type, all liveliness and fire and full of historico-topico-geographical inexactitudes'[26]). For the last act the playwright had set his heart on a backcloth showing St. Peter's and the Castel Sant'Angelo with the Tiber flowing between them, quite undeterred by the fact that both buildings are on the same side of the river. On one point, however, he had his way. Tosca herself would die.

By 19 January 1899 Puccini had returned to Milan, having been cleaned out of 500 lire at Monte Carlo *en route*. Soon he was back in Torre del Lago, where on 23 February he began the scoring of Act II of *Tosca*. A month later Tito Ricordi was able to report that, thanks to the intervention of the French minister Camille Barrère, Puccini's nomination to the Légion d'Honneur had become a reality. A further bonus was the departure of Venanzio for America, so allowing the composer to purchase the modest dwelling at Torre del Lago, which, enlarged and extended by Bastiani, the architect of Chiatri, would become the present Villa Puccini. The problem now was the availability of the librettists. Illica was about to be married; Giacosa was his usual dilatory self. It was now Ricordi who took over the reins, altering words and placing the stage directions. Having received the complete Act II on 19 July, he wrote expressing the highest hopes for the final act. 'The dramatic situations are splendid, sublime, moving in the highest degree. So press on, Sor Giacomo! Make thousands and thousands of people

[25] P. Mascagni: *Epistolario*, ed. R. Iovino, M. Morini, and A. Paloscia, i (Lucca, 1996), 227.
[26] CP 200, p. 172.

shed tears, myself (alas!) included!!'[27] But Ricordi's tears, if shed, would at first be those of disappointment.

Two of the summer months Puccini spent at Boscolungo in the mountains north of Lucca. Here he could work in peace and comfort, while Elvira convalesced after a miscarriage. But it was at Torre del Lago that he felt able to write on the final page of his autograph 'End of the opera . . . 29 September 1899, 4.15 a.m.' Even then it was not quite complete. The prelude to Act III had yet to be written down. The main obstacle here had been the mingled chime that heralded the breaking of the Roman dawn. More than one manufacturing firm was approached; and the ensuing correspondence involved even the conductor Leopoldo Mugnone. Then, too, Puccini wanted a poem in Romanesque dialect for the shepherd boy to sing as he led his flocks to pasture. It was Don Pietro Panichelli who found him the poet Luigi Zanazzo, whose verses Puccini received at the end of October and accepted with minor modifications. In the meantime he dispatched to Ricordi the remainder of the act, beginning with Cavaradossi's 'E lucevan le stelle'.

Sad to say, the publisher was far from happy with it. In a letter of 10 October he set out his objections in detail. He liked Cavaradossi's aria and Tosca's entrance; he liked the novelty of the execution.

> But dear Holy God! What is the luminous centre of this act? The duet for Tosca and Cavaradossi. What do I find? A duet of little pieces traced in small lines which diminish the characters. I find one of the finest passages of poetry, that of 'the hands' simply underlined by a melody that is both fragmentary and modest, and, to cap it all, a piece *exactly the same* as one in *Edgar*! Wonderful if . . . sung by a Tyrolean peasant, but out of place on the lips of a Tosca or a Cavaradossi. In sum, what should have been a kind of hymn, whether or not a Latin one, at least a hymn of love, I find reduced to a few bars! So the heart of the piece is made up of three fragments that follow one another with interruptions that rob them of all effectiveness! Now really, where is that Puccini of noble, warm, vigorous imagination? . . . What? At one of the most terrible moments of the drama, did his imagination have to resort to another opera? What will people say about this way of getting out of a difficult situation?

[27] RC.

He would give the world to be proved wrong, but after 36 years his instinct had never yet failed him. Giacosa shared his opinion in full.

Puccini, however, stuck to his guns. No-one, he replied, knew better than Ricordi how scrupulous he was in interpreting words and situations and weighing them up before jotting down a note of music. The quotation from *Edgar*—and from an act which had long since been abolished—seemed to him to express perfectly the poetry of the text, as Ricordi would surely realize if he saw it performed on stage. As for the fragmentary quality, that was entirely deliberate:

> It can't be a tranquil, unchanging situation as with other amorous chit-chats. Tosca's worries about Mario's pretended fall and his behaviour in front of the firing-squad keep returning. As for the end of the duet, the so-called 'Latin hymn' . . . , I too have had my doubts. The poets haven't managed to give me anything good, or, above all, truthful: forever academic stuff and the usual amorous slobbering. I've had to get by as best I could to come to the end without boring the listeners with empty rhetoric.

Nonetheless, though several of his friends had approved the act as it stood, including Mugnone, who had declared it to be superior to Act III of *La bohème*, Puccini was prepared to come to Milan and either patch up the end of the duet (but would there be time?) or, preferably, convince his publisher that his judgment had been wrong.[28]

Ricordi was duly shaken but not wholly convinced. Nor would he hear a word against the poets, who, he insisted, 'have tried not a hundred but a thousand ways of hitting the mark as regards what should have been the "Latin hymn" and which is now reduced to a few lyrical snatches'.[29] Of these snatches, for which Giacosa would supply the definitive text in November, only a few lines were set by Puccini, beginning 'Trionfal di nova speme l'anima freme'.

By the time he received the Act III prelude ('absolutely stupendous!'), Ricordi's views had softened. Anticipated at the outset by a blast of four horns, 'Trionfal' now seemed to him to make complete sense. Even so, for 'O dolci mani, mansuete e pure' he would have expected something different—but that was a trifling cavil.

[28] CP 208–9, pp. 176–80.
[29] R.C.

By November Puccini's part in the proceedings was effectively over. He was now free to devote himself to hunting and in the intervals to the contemplation of future projects. The Neapolitan playwright Roberto Bracco had offered him through Carlo Clausetti his 'veristic' one-acter *Don Pietro Caruso*, which Puccini declined as dwelling exclusively on human misery without a touch of poetry or grandeur. Illica proposed Dostoievsky's *From the House of the Dead*, which he would consider, provided the poet could work into it some kind of plot. 'You ask me whether I like the setting. Yes, if it contains the heart of the matter. All settings are fine with me. I've no preferences or preconceptions.'[30] However, he turned down another Russian subject put forward by Illica, partly because of the 'Fedoric' costumes (he was referring to Giordano's *Fedora*, first performed in Milan the previous year). His own suggestions included Jean Richepin's latest hit, *La Glu*, Maeterlinck's *Pelléas et Mélisande*, as yet uncompleted by Debussy and, once again, Zola's *La faute de l'Abbé Mouret*—still promised elsewhere, but after the success of *La bohème* in Paris and, if all went well, *Tosca*, who knew whether the author might not change his mind? Then there was Alphonse Daudet's *Tartarin de Tarascon*, Balzac's *Les Chouans*, Pierre Louÿs's *Aphrodite*, or an unnamed but probably French *Jugurtha*. None of these would come to fruition, though *Tartarin* would haunt the composer for some time to come.

Before concluding the year 1899 mention should be made of two minor compositions which Puccini managed to turn out during the throes of his work on *Tosca*. From May to September the city of Como mounted an exhibition to celebrate the centenary of the discovery of the electric battery by its most famous citizen, Alessandro Volta (he of the eponymous 'volt'). The occasion was marked by the issue of a magazine, *I telegrafisti a Volta*, featuring a number of distinguished names including that of Giacomo Puccini, whose contribution consisted of a 'marcia brillante' for piano, later arranged for wind band and entitled *Scossa elettrica*—an amiable piece of light music cast in the traditional mould with sharply pointed rhythms in the principal section and a lyrical trio, both with repeated subdivisions. Revived with some success

---

[30] CP 215, pp. 182–3.

in 1910, it would hardly merit performance today. The mantle of Johann Strauss II sat uneasily on Puccini's shoulders.

Of more consequence is the lullaby *E l'uccellino*—to words by Renato Fucini. Dedicated to 'Il bambino Memmo Lippi', the son born posthumously to an old friend from Lucca, it remains the only song by Puccini ever to have found a place in the recital repertory: a personal miniature, finished in every detail. The melody lies mostly in the bass line, doubled by the voice at the octave above. Only in the second phrase does it separate from the pianist's left hand to yield a simple design of tenths like a caress. A recurring 'cheep' high up in the accompaniment indicates the 'little bird' of the title. 'Sleep peacefully', runs the poem. But the last sleep of Memmo Lippi would be in a German concentration camp in 1944.

The turn of the century found *Tosca* already in rehearsal at the Teatro Costanzi, Rome. It was an obvious venue, given the subject, even if it meant the loss of Toscanini, who was fully occupied at La Scala. But Mugnone, still in Puccini's good graces (though he would later fall out of them) promised to be a worthy substitute. The name-part was given to the Romanian soprano Ericlea Darclée, former heroine of Catalani's *La Wally* and Mascagni's *Iris*—an artist of high distinction, if a little lacking in temperament, so Catalani had thought. The Scarpia was Eugenio Giraldoni, son of Leone, Verdi's first Conte di Luna (*Il trovatore*) and Renato (*Un ballo in maschera*). Caruso, engaged at Rome for the same season, had hoped for the part of Cavaradossi; but it was entrusted to the more experienced Emilio De Marchi, probably at the publisher's insistence.

For since November Ricordi had taken the reins firmly into his own hands, excluding even the librettists from his confidence, much to their mortification. Illica had been further affronted by the publication in the *Gazzetta musicale di Milano* of the 'sonetto' ('Amaro sol per te') with an attribution to Giacosa alone. Nor had he been invited to assist with the staging, Tito Ricordi being in sole charge. Again it was Giulio who saw to the printing of the libretto with all Puccini's modifications save for a few unset lines of what remained of the 'Latin hymn'. Even this concession failed to mollify Illica, who poured out his grievances in a long letter to Ricordi shortly after the first performance. What the public was being offered, he wrote, was 'a mere shadow of the libretto that had once moved Giulio Ricordi to enthusiasm'. And why had the description of the Roman dawn been suppressed? Surely it would have been more helpful to the audience than all that campanological exactitude over which Ricordi had expended so much time and money. The abolition of the original finale (presumably his 'mad scene' for Tosca) had been an act of 'bestiality'. As for the music of *Tosca*, what little Illica had heard of it had all been re-cycled from *La lupa*.[31] But this last claim need not be taken at face value. Illica had obviously worked himself into a temper.

Puccini himself had high hopes of the outcome. 'I think the opera will have a success *hors ligne*',[32] he told Don Panichelli, who had supplied him with 'figurini' for the Pope's Swiss Guard. By 1900 a Puccini première had become a national event. The first night of *Tosca* on 14 January was attended not only by colleagues such as Mascagni, Cilea, Franchetti, Sgambati, and Marchetti, but also by General Pelloux and Queen Margherita, who arrived in time for the second act. The atmosphere was tense, for echoes of the unrest of 1898 still lingered. The police had received warnings of a bomb-scare; accordingly they instructed Mugnone to strike up the national anthem should any such threat materialize. And indeed a growing hubbub in the stalls caused him to interrupt the opening bars of the opera; but it was no more than a cry of protest at the admission of late-comers. Thereafter the performance proceeded smoothly enough.

But it was not the success that Puccini had foreseen. True, the tenor's 'Recondita armonia' and the Act I finale were both encored; so was Tosca's 'Vissi d'arte' but the curtain fell tepidly on Act II. In Act III there was applause for the dawn prelude and a cry of 'Fuori maestro!' 'E lucevan le stelle' and the subsequent duet were both repeated. At the end there were seven curtain calls, three of them for Puccini. Hardly a *furore*, therefore.

The critics, while paying tribute to Puccini's originality, had many reservations about the opera as a whole. Mostly, like Giacosa, they found the subject resistant to musical treatment. The most interesting review came from Ippolito Valletta in the *Nuova antologia*, clearly an informed musician, if, as he himself admitted, one whose tastes were old-fashioned. Hence his demurring at certain 'harmonic patterns and orchestral embroidery that modernism allows, nay demands'. He instanced

> certain ways of harmonizing the scale, many successions of fourths, huge delays in the resolution of dissonances (no question of their being prepared) rapid transitions through curious modulations, contrasts of rhythm, frequent syncopations, strong accents on the weak beats of the bar—such is the mobile, kaleidoscopic background in which Puccini takes pleasure in *La bohème* and in which he revels in *Tosca*. . . . Given this system, however, few avail themselves of it with the ease and cleverness of Puccini. He finds in his palette all colours, all shades; in his hands the instrumental texture becomes completely supple; the gradations of sonority are innumerable, the blend unfailingly grateful to the ear.

Above all, he left no doubt as to the opera's imaginative vigour and dramatic force.

The public, doubtful at first, quickly came round to this view. Twenty performances followed, given to packed houses. Before the end of the year *Tosca* had travelled to London, Buenos Aires, and New York. Nor, for once, did Puccini see fit to make any substantial changes in the published score.

With *Tosca* Puccini confronts for the first time an opera of action. Therefore the pace is swifter, the recurring motifs shorter, sharper and more numerous than in his previous works; nor do they always function as fixed signposts; their association with elements in the drama is sometimes looser than in *La bohème*, so forestalling the chameleon-like quality that will characterize certain motifs in the later operas. No time is wasted in the evocation of an ambience (the Church of Sant'Andrea della Valle). The springboard is a rapid pantomime under the shadow of evil. Angelotti is in desperate flight from the forces of authority headed by Baron Scarpia, whose unseen presence is established proleptically by a frightening musical image (Ex. 7.1). As an ideogram of villainy, traditionally indicated in Italian opera by unison flourishes (see Iago's 'Credo'), this is as original as it is masterly. To call it a whole-

Ex. 7.1

tone motif, as some have done, is surely wrong. The top line moves by semitones and each of the progressions is a major common chord. Only the bass can be said to carry hexatonic implications, later exploited in the kindred motif that will denote the well in the garden of Cavaradossi's villa (Ex. 7.10). What gives the motif a sinister force is the unexpected plunge into a remote key, like the slipping of a mask.

The flurry that brings in Angelotti (Ex. 7.2)—syncopated G minor on full orchestra dissolving into a chromatic slither on woodwind—will function both as a personal motif and a generic one of 'pursuit'. Here it is extended with various figures that illustrate Angelotti's frantic search for the key of the Attavanti chapel in which he intends to hide. His finding of the key is marked by Ex. 7.1, now quieter, its final chord pianissimo in high woodwind over cellos and basses—the shadow of

Ex. 7.2

Ex. 7.3

Allegretto grazioso

the police chief receding into the distance. Shortened restatements of Ex. 7.2 follow Angelotti into the chapel.

The tripping theme that introduces the Sacristan is one of pure comedy (Ex. 7.3). But, though it will be his throughout the act, it in no way delineates his character. Unlike Sardou's good-natured rogue of a Père Eusèbe he is a grumbling bigot with a hearty dislike of the painter, which he conceals under a show of respect. The smile in the music (at one point marked 'scherzoso') is entirely Puccini's. Among the thematic consequents that follow him as he goes fussily about his business a countermelody is adumbrated that will be associated with Cavaradossi's painting of the Magdalen and therefore assume great importance in the score. Once again Puccini has conferred memorability on a commonplace idea by an unexpected note—the F sharp that gives the tonality a momentary G minor inflection (Ex. 7.4).

At the sound of the Angelus bell (14 bars of repeated Fs over shifting harmonies, recalling the midnight vigil of Verdi's Falstaff) the Sacristan falls to his knees. It is thus that Cavaradossi finds him, having entered unobtrusively. He mounts the scaffold and unveils his painting, so launching Ex. 7.4 worked into a sequence and concluding with a richly scored anticipation of what will be the love duet (Ex. 7.9b). Here its meaning is evident. Tosca is ultimately the painter's inspiration. But that is not how the Sacristan sees it. He recognizes in the Magdalen's features those of a noblewoman whom he has often observed at prayer. Cavaradossi admits to having used her partly as a

Ex. 7.4

model, though without her knowledge, having been struck by her beauty and air of rapt devotion ('Get thee behind me, Satan!' from the Sacristan).

Cavaradossi sets to work, pausing now and again to survey the general effect. He then produces a medallion of Tosca and marvels at his success at reconciling two such contrasted beauties. His aria, 'Recondita armonia', interspersed with savage mutterings from the Sacristan, is therefore in part an action piece and its ternary plan modified accordingly. Three separate ideas, distributed between voice and orchestra are repeated in order with slight variation. The first is purely instrumental and descriptive, the parallel fourths on flutes over typical soft dissonances indicating the painter's rapid brush-strokes. The second ('Recondita armonia di bellezze diverse') forms the aria's main period, with the third (Ex. 7.5) as its central episode, carrying a mention of the 'unknown beauty' that will suffice to link it in future with the Attavanti herself. But although it has the last word as an orchestral postlude there is no question here of divided loyalties. The concluding bars of the vocal melody leave no doubt that Cavaradossi's heart belongs to Tosca. The Sacristan prepares to leave, not without a hopeful glance at Cavaradossi's basket of provisions, as yet untouched; for if there is one vice that he shares with Sardou's Eusèbe it is greed. Ex. 7.3 sees him off the premises, its repetition clouded with an embroidery of parallel fourths indicating the painter still at work.

To a blast of Ex. 7.2 Angelotti reappears, to be recognized after a moment's incredulity by Cavaradossi. For the tense exchanges that follow Puccini weaves two new motifs into the discourse: the first a chromatic rise and fall that will signify anything from agitation to jealousy, the second (Ex. 7.6) associated with Angelotti's escape from prison, reaching full definition at its second statement. Almost at once Tosca's voice sounds from without (again an orchestral foretaste of Ex. 7.9b).

Ex. 7.5

Cavaradossi: e   te bel-ta-de i-gno——— ta,——— cin-ta di chio-me bion - de

Ex. 7.6

A tumbling rhythm conveys Angelotti's faintness as Cavaradossi bundles him into hiding, handing him the basket of provisions coveted by the Sacristan (Ex. 7.3).

Tosca is directed to enter 'with a kind of violence, looking about her suspiciously'; but it is the devotional Tosca that the music paints with a theme which is all poise and serenity: flute and solo cello at two octaves' distance over pizzicato string triplets and sustaining wind (Ex. 7.7). There is no essential contradiction. Tosca is an actress with all the surface volatility of her kind. Her jealousy is largely a matter of habit and one which her lover does not take too seriously. She has come to lay flowers at the feet of the Madonna, and her underlying tranquillity is only briefly disturbed by a musical back-reference, where she mentions the sound of footsteps and the rustle of garments. A kiss from Cavaradossi is sufficient to calm her, eliciting a mild reproof ('Ah! Innanzi alla Madonna!'). The cadential phrase that concludes her devotions (Ex. 7.8a) will recur in a more casual, even flippant variant (Ex. 7.8b).

Tosca descends to practicalities. She is required for a concert that evening, but it will be a short one. They can then go together to his villa outside the city. 'Stasera!' Cavaradossi exclaims; and a snatch of Angelotti's Ex. 7.2 voices his unspoken thoughts. Tosca notices his abstraction. 'Non sei contento?' 'Tanto!' 'Tornalo a dir!' 'Tanto!' 'Lo dici male, lo dici male.' These are the words of an actress reproaching a

Ex. 7.7

Ex. 7.8a

Ex. 7.8b

a colleague for giving a bad performance. Puccini's Tosca, unlike her counterpart in the play, is an experienced woman of the theatre.

She now assumes an intimate, wheedling tone ('Non la sospiri nostra casetta'), no longer the dignified prima donna of Ex. 7.7, but the Puccinian 'little woman', eager and winsome. The 50-bar movement, like 'Recondita armonia', has a double structure, part ternary with a reprise, part rondo with variants of Ex. 7.8 as its refrain. Only a climactic intervention from Cavaradossi prevents it from qualifying as an aria.

Sequences of Ex. 7.8b, increasingly chromatic, and a bar of Ex. 7.2 accompany Tosca's reluctant preparations for departure. Suddenly she notices the figure in the painting, recognizing her as the Marchesa Attavanti. Her suspicions flare up to the same harmonic gesture that had signalled the Bohemians' dismay at the arrival of Benoit. So that was the meaning of the footsteps and the rustle of clothing! Throughout her tantrums Cavaradossi remains perfectly cool, and she ends by accepting his explanations. But she continues to feel the eyes of the portrait (blue, where hers are brown) taunting her; and a slow descent of whole-tone chords passing from woodwind to strings conveys her sense of being mesmerized. Cavaradossi's consoling reply (Ex. 7.9a) takes its cue from Tosca's Ex. 7.7, now set out in a flowing 9/8 and worked into a regular period of 16 bars that falls like balm on the preceding unrest. Tosca is immediately won over. The plain 3/4 of her rejoinder ('Oh come la sai bene l'arte di farti amare!') is couched in a

Ex. 7.9a

Cavaradossi:
Qual' oc-chio_al mon - do puo star— di pa - ro al-l'ar-den - te dell'oc - chio— tuo ne - ro?

Ex. 7.9b

Cavaradossi: Tosca: Si, lo sen - to— ti tor - men - to sen - za po - sa.
[ge]- lo - sa

subdominant of relaxed nerves; but she breaks off with a sly admonition ('Ma falle gli occhi neri!') marked 'maliziosamente'. In the play, it is spoken in all seriousness; for Sardou's Tosca is entirely lacking in humour. Puccini's hero can afford to tease her ('O mia gelosa!'), so launching the love duet, for whose opening (Ex. 7.9b) the composer has taken good care to prepare us in advance.

Since the mutual love of Tosca and Cavaradossi forms the heart of his drama, Puccini does not scruple to state the melody four times, variously distributed between the two voices. Voluptuous side-slipping sequences convey Tosca's delight ('Dilla ancora, la parola che consola') and lead to the third statement entrusted to Cavaradossi alone in the higher key of F, which not only permits him to exploit a top B flat but recalls to the listener his declaration of love in 'Recondita armonia'. The music relapses into E for the final reprise, a dialogue pianissimo and diaphanously scored. After repeating her admonition, again 'mischievously' but with a hint of underlying melancholy, Tosca hurries away leaving the first three notes of the duet suspended over a tonic bass. Unorthodox for the time, no doubt. But nothing conveys more strongly a sense of residual longing than a 'frozen sixth' by way of melodic conclusion. The same device will end the love-duet in *Madama Butterfly*.

The problem of 'rounding' a heroine at her first appearance is nowhere more triumphantly solved than here. Tosca is not a type, like

Mimì, whose characteristics can be summed up in her own self-description; she is very much an individual. Yet all of her is in her first scene with Cavaradossi—her poise, her piety (largely a matter of outward observance), her disposition to jealousy, her loving nature, her gleams of humour, and a certain theatrical worldliness. Here the opera scores heavily over the play, whose heroine remains purely one-dimensional. No wonder that Sardou himself came to prefer the opera.

With the re-appearance of Angelotti action takes over once more. Here the density of Puccini's motivic technique sets him far apart from his contemporaries of the 'giovane scuola.' A fragment of Ex. 7.2 merges into the three-note figure (*x*) of Ex. 7.9b ('É buona la mia Tosca, ma credente al confessor nulla tiene celato'). Sequences of the music associated with Angelotti's search for the key accompany the discussion of his plan to escape in women's clothing left for him by his sister, the Marchesa Attavanti. For Cavaradossi's description of her at prayer an extended statement of Ex. 7.4 leads back through Ex. 7.2 to repetitions of Scarpia's Ex. 7.1, the last a fortissimo comment on Cavaradossi's 'Fa il confessore e il boia!' But there is no time to be lost; Angelotti must hasten to Cavaradossi's villa (Ex. 7.8b in diminishing fragments interspersed with Ex. 7.2 and a single reference to the Marchesa's Ex. 7.5 when he takes up the bundle of clothes); then to the motif of the well in Cavaradossi's garden where he hopes to be safe (Ex. 7.10). Its relation to Scarpia's motif is patent: diatonic common chords over a whole-tone bass, here continuous. But there is nothing illogical in this; for the well will prove a false place of refuge.

A cannon-shot is heard from the Castel Sant'Angelo, a signal that

Ex. 7.10

Angelotti's escape has been discovered. But that is not the only piece of news. Even as Cavaradossi prepares to conduct the fugitive to his villa, the Sacristan's Ex. 7.3 is heard gradually mounting to an exultant climax with trumpets and horns blaring out the descending thirds over a tonic pedal. The Sacristan enters just in time to miss the two men. What a pity that he was unable to taunt the unbelieving painter with the latest victory of the Holy Cause! The church fills with an excited throng of clerics, acolytes, and choristers who surround the bearer of good news; hence an exultant figure tossed from one instrumental block to another, switching from key to key the rhythm varying from 9/8 to 6/8. The tempo relaxes for a dance-like consequent faintly recalling the apprentices of *Die Meistersinger*, as all look forward to a victory cele-bration. The jubilation reaches its height amid peals of laughter and cries of 'Viva il Re! Gloria! Te Deum!', to be suddenly quelled by Scarpia's Ex. 7.1, its final chord preceded by an upward sweep of flutes, piccolo, and violins that seems to catapult the police chief into their midst with Spoletta and a number of police agents at his heels.

Such a *coup de théâtre* is a commonplace of grand opera from *Le prophète* to *La Gioconda*; but nowhere is it as starkly impressive as here. It is Scarpia the bigot who first speaks ('Un tal baccano in chiesa! Bel rispetto!'), reducing the Sacristan to a state of gibbering terror ('Eccel-lenza . . . il gran giubilo . . . '). Distortions of his Ex. 7.3 persist beneath subdued reiterations of Scarpia's Ex. 7.1, as the crowd melts away. From now on the motifs become more widely spaced so as to accommodate important information. A prisoner has escaped from the Castel Sant'Angelo and may be hiding in this very church. Where is the At-tavanti chapel? The Sacristan indicates the door and is amazed to find it unlocked. Three statements of Ex. 7.6, each more emphatically scored than the last, tell us that the hunt for the fugitive is on and that Scarpia is getting increasingly 'warm'. He emerges from the Attavanti chapel carrying a fan with the Attavanti crest—surely a vital clue. He looks up at the portrait on the easel and recognizes the Marchesa's features; and here Ex. 7.5 proves especially useful, since its dotted triplet will furnish some 'unmotivic' connecting tissue in what follows. It is the Sacristan who names the painter, identified in the music by the first notes of the love-duet; 'L'amante di Tosca, un uom sospetto, un vol-terrian!' In the meantime a police agent has discovered in the chapel the basket of provisions—now empty. Astonishment once more of Sacristan. Cavaradossi had disclaimed any appetite, nor did he have a key to the Attavanti chapel. The dialogue is too detailed to allow a rich cushioning of motifs; these are therefore confined to snatches of Ex. 7.3, the last low on bassoon, helped out by contra-bassoon—a fitting comment on the Sacristan's comic abjection.

So far the action has followed that of the play fairly closely. Now the libretto takes a leap forward, anticipating a development that Sardou reserves for the next day, placing it in the Farnese palace where Tosca is about to perform. While she waits for the signal to begin Paisiello's cantata under the composer's direction, Scarpia proceeds to inflame her jealousy by means of the Attavanti fan, provoking her to one childish outburst after another. First she wants to seek out the Marchesa among the present company and smash the fan in her face. Told that she has left for Frascati, Tosca thinks she knows better; she herself will leave at once for Cavaradossi's villa where she will catch the lovers *in flagrante*. Let the Queen be told that she is ill and cannot sing. But this Scarpia forbids her under pain of arrest. Tosca takes out her frustration on Paisiello ('Charmante . . . elle a des nerfs', the composer confides apologetically to Scarpia). No sooner have the instruments struck up than there is a further interruption. Queen Caroline has just received a dispatch from the battlefield of Marengo and insists on reading it aloud. Beginning with the utmost confidence, her voice falters as she realizes that she is reporting not a victory but an ignominious defeat. She faints; the concert is cancelled and Tosca free to hurry to the villa, pursued at a distance by Scarpia and his men.

All this is wonderful theatre; but it has no place in the opera. Instead Scarpia's ploy is brought forward to the scene in the church, whither Tosca now returns (Ex. 7.9b). Dismayed at not finding her lover still at work, she calls his name; but it is Scarpia who steps forward. For the first time in the opera bells play an important part in the musical structure. Four 'campane medie' set up an ostinato which will persist for 32 bars, relieved only by a closely related episode. Here Puccini employs a technique similar to that pioneered by Glinka in *Kamarinskaia*, whereby a single phrase is re-iterated with different harmony and scoring—the perfect background to Scarpia's falsely pious insinuations. Beginning with flattery he passes to the subject of loose women who come to pray in church, and he glances pointedly at the portrait of the Magdalen. Tosca reacts with a violence ('Le prove! . . . le prove!') which sets off a fragment of Ex. 7.6 twisted into a whole-tone pattern on cellos and basses beneath tremolando upper strings. Scarpia produces the fan (Ex. 7.5—soft but tense). So Tosca's suspicions had been right all along! Yet her immediate reaction is one of grief rather than anger ('Ed io venivo a lui tutta dogliosa'); therefore a minor key, downward melodic gradient, and a double-subdominant sequence—all expressive of heartfelt misery.

Scarpia returns to his sly 'ostinato', but Tosca pays him no attention. Where can the lovers be, she wonders? Ex. 7.6, again hexatonic, increasing in volume and intensity with each repetition, seems to point her to Cavaradossi's villa. There she will go at once and break up their rendezvous (Ex. 7.2 in fortissimo bursts, now a simple motif of pursuit). To the strains of Ex. 7.9b, now a richly scored elegy for past happiness, Scarpia escorts her from the church. Throughout this scene Puccini's Tosca cuts a far more dignified figure than Sardou's.

Appropriately it is Ex. 7.2 (*energico e con tutta forza*) that brings back Scarpia to give orders for Tosca's pursuit ('Tre sbirri . . . una carrozza'), As he speaks, the finale begins, a huge crescendo based once more on a pattern set by the bells, this time a Puccinian see-saw of two notes. The action is minimal—a gradual filling of the church with a crowd of clerics, choristers, and congregation, who proceed from spoken responses to the singing of a 'Te Deum'. What keeps the passing moment before our ears is music that is in a constant state of dominant preparation. The melodic material is firmly diatonic, smooth in motion and contour. All the while Scarpia gloats over the prospect of a double victory—the capture of Angelotti and the possession of Tosca. The movement reaches its climax with the unison chant ('Te æternum Patrem omnis terra veneratur!'), which, by ending on B flat allows Scarpia to unmask with his motif *tutta forza* in its original key. But in the end it too must gravitate to the E flat established by the movement's opening. Extended over 94 slow bars, fortified by organ, bells, and periodic cannon-shots, this is the most powerful of Puccini's harmonic oscillations so far, not to be equalled until the Act I finale of *Turandot*.

Act II begins after one of those gaps in the action so common in opera. We have last seen Tosca hurrying to Cavaradossi's villa. In the

Ex. 7.11

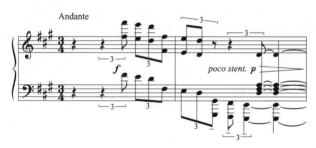

play we witness her arrival there, to be placated by the painter, who for the first time tells her about Angelotti. Scarpia and his men burst in soon afterwards and put Cavaradossi to the torture. In the opera the pursuit is delegated to Spoletta. Scarpia himself returns to his headquarters in an upper room of the Palazzo Farnese, to which the action now moves. We must take the lovers' reconciliation for granted, as indeed does Scarpia—so much is clear from the motivic cluster that accompanies his reflection as he sits dining alone. Quite new is the opening gesture (Ex. 7.11), which grabs the attention with a switch of key across a tritone (the *diabolus in musica*) before settling on a typical Puccinian dominant substitute, one sufficiently bland not to call for immediate resolution.

Above the sustained low E horns and violas recall Ex. 7.6 (Angelotti's escape); violins begin Ex. 7.9b giving way to Cavaradossi's consolatory Ex. 7.9a traced by solo clarinet (both motifs from the love scene). Ex. 7.11, its tonality straightened out by the dominant pedal, seals off the group. Tosca is a good hawk, Scarpia muses; her love for her Mario will set his bloodhounds on the scent of their prey, and the next day should see Angelotti and Cavaradossi dangling from a noose (Ex. 7.1). He summons his henchman Sciarrone. Has Tosca arrived at the palace, he wants to know? Not yet; they are waiting for her, so that the victory cantata can begin. Again Ex. 7.1 sounds, interrupted as Sciarrone opens a window, letting in the strains of a gavotte. Scored for flute, viola, and harp behind the scenes, it is not particularly distinguished; nor is it Puccini's own, having been lifted from a piece by his brother Michele.[33]

---

[33] D. Schickling: 'Giacomos kleiner Bruder'. SGP; 83

But its treatment is masterly, indeed impressionistic, the phrases reaching us fitfully, now sooner, now later than we expect, as though borne in on the breeze. Meanwhile Scarpia instructs Sciarrone to bring Tosca to him as soon as the cantata has finished. The thematic nucleus of Ex. 7.11 then takes up from where it had left off, Scarpia's words confirming what the music has already told us: that it is the possession of Tosca that is uppermost in his mind (Ex. 7.1 quietly malignant).

In a lyrical andante ('Ha più forte sapore la conquista violenta che il mellifluo consenso') Scarpia outlines his erotic philosophy. Not for him the flower-strewn paths of courtship, the twanging of guitars, the cooing of turtle-doves. Sight your prey, give chase, capture, then cast aside—that is his way. There is more concentrated villainy in Scarpia's orchestral motif than in anything he has to sing; and his opening period with its off-beat pulsations and velvety scoring has little to distinguish it from many a baritone meditation; but soon his excitement spills over into declamatory vehemence, horns and cellos punching home the words 'perseguo . . . me ne sazio', and the design is powerfully wound up by a final 'strepitoso' re-statement of Ex. 7.11, the tritone leap functioning as a massive swing of the pendulum in the direction of a cadence.

But the cadence never arrives, blocked as before by the motif's final chord. Meanwhile Scarpia has something else to distract him: the arrival of Spoletta from the villa. Terrified, the lieutenant tries to spin out his story as long as possible; but its upshot is—of Angelotti not a trace. They did, however, find Cavaradossi, whose insolent attitude suggested that he knew quite well where the fugitive was hiding. They therefore arrested him and brought him to the palace. Mention of the painter prompts a recall of Ex. 7.4 (the portrait), extended by downward sequences and coming to rest on a baleful motif that will recur from time to time as his interrogation proceeds. Rarely can a low flute have sounded to more sinister effect (Ex. 7.12).

By now the cantata has begun. A hymn to the Lord God of Victories, it follows a ternary plan (A minor–C–A minor) in mock-Renaissance style with the occasional imitation point. But what will strike the attentive listener is the element of bitonality in relation to what he hears from stage and pit. For if A minor is the key of the cantata, the recurrences of Ex. 7.12 fall invariably in E minor. True, there is no direct

Ex. 7.12

clash, since F sharp (x), on which the motif insists, has a place in the ascending scales of both keys; but the double perspective is subtly calculated to reflect the situation: piety behind the scenes, brutality before our eyes.

Before the cantata ends the interrogation of Cavaradossi has begun. At Scarpia's imperious 'Ov'è Angelotti?', strings tremolando sustain the baritone's E, from which clarinets, bassoons, and contra-bassoon trace a whole-tone descent to B flat resulting in the most brutal of tritones. It is again the orchestra that supplies the answer which Cavaradossi withholds: 'In the well in the garden' (Ex. 7.10), a logical consequent, since, as noted, it carries hexatonic implications of its own.

Adopting a milder, almost fatherly approach, Scarpia advises the young man to make a full confession and spare himself much agony. Muted trumpets stress the significance of his final words, while a tiny motif, an ideogram of suffering, hints at what is otherwise in store for him. (Ex. 7.13). The natural plangency of the cello in its upper register is thrown into stronger relief by the underlying palette of wind; and the augmented second interval (x) is like a stab of pain, all the sharper for having been used so sparingly in previous bouts of chromaticism. Scarpia repeats his question, to meet with the same rebuttal from Cavaradossi, contradicted, as before by the orchestra with Ex. 7.10, still louder and more emphatic. Tosca enters and hastens to her lover to a recall of a strain from the love duet over the same chord as when we heard it last. Cavaradossi has just time to tell her to say nothing before Scarpia announces that the Procurator wants him as a witness. Straightway Ex. 7.12 peals out on bunched brass, its menace now palpable. An interlude of 19 bars follows to allow the preparations for Cavar-

Ex. 7.13

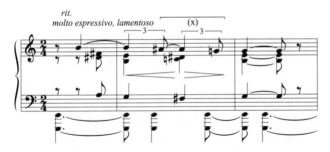

adossi's torture in an adjoining room. Its basis is Ex. 7.13 progressively softened and smoothed out into a 6/8 lilt which will dominate the police chief's questioning of Tosca. He begins by donning the velvet glove ('Ed or fra noi parliam da buoni amici'). Soon, however, a torture motif begins its inexorable thrust in a Dorian D minor—a 'sviolinata' edged by cor anglais and muted trombone, the tension sharpened by busy violas divisi: (Ex. 7.14). Not until its second statement—now on wind with fierce gestures in the strings and the traditional 'death-raps' on timpani—does Scarpia spell out what is happening to Cavaradossi. From here on there is a double torture: for the painter, whose pain is reflected in Ex. 7.13, and for Tosca, whose line abounds in terrified leaps. Allowed a sight of her lover momentarily released and still defiant, she becomes bolder, countering Scarpia's peremptory questions with a cadential finality ('Non so nulla!'), doggedly repeated in one key after another. In a sudden access of ferocity (a chromatic surge on full or-

Ex. 7.14

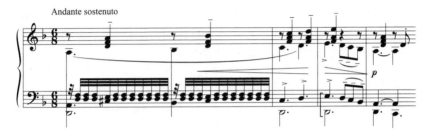

Ex. 7.15

Tosca: Ah!_____ ces - sa-te_il mar - tir!_____ è trop - po sof - frir!_____

chestra) Scarpia orders the door to be flung open so that Tosca can hear the prisoner's cries; and here Ex. 7.15 unfurls its full length over a span of two octaves accompanied by rising sequences of anguish from Tosca which culminate in a desperate lyrical appeal.

A long ebb balances the flow of Ex. 7.14, its sense of exhaustion intensified by Neapolitan depressions. Tosca begs Cavaradossi to let her speak, but he brushes her aside ('Stolta, che sai? . . . che puoi dir?'). 'Ma fatelo tacere!' from Scarpia, afraid that his words may encourage Tosca to hold out. But she has already collapsed on the divan, murmuring helplessly ('Che v'ho fatto in vita mia?'), while Spoletta, no less overcome, mutters lines from the 'Dies irae'. Scarpia gives the sign for the torture to recommence. A cry from Cavaradossi, and Tosca reaches the end of her tether: 'Nel pozzo . . . nel giardino', forestalled by the orchestra with Ex. 7.10 fortissimo. Cavaradossi is carried in unconscious. Ex. 7.12 at its most funereal, with violas and bassoons on the melody, is dovetailed into the painful Ex. 7.13, over which Ex. 7.9a pours its balm as Tosca tries to revive her lover with kisses. But the oasis is brief. Questioned by Cavaradossi, Tosca assures him that she has given nothing away; but Scarpia and Ex. 7.10 proclaim the truth. Cavaradossi curses Tosca for her betrayal.

Now the opera takes another of its short cuts. Sardou's Act III ends with Cavaradossi and Tosca, still at odds, being marched off to the Castel Sant'Angelo. But there will be time for a reconciliation in the remaining two acts. Not so in the opera. For while the painter is inveighing against his beloved, there is an unexpected diversion. Sciarrone returns with the news of Napoleon's victory at Marengo. At once Cavaradossi's mood changes to one of exaltation. If ever a new theme was needed it is here. Instead Puccini resorts to Ex. 7.4 (the picture), heroically proclaimed by trombones, bassoons, cellos, and basses beneath tremolando upper strings and rapping woodwind triplets—relevant only by the freest of associations. But worse is to follow: a terzetto ('L'alba vindice appar') in the old concertato manner during which Tosca pleads for forgiveness, Cavaradossi exults, and Scarpia threatens. Here the melody is indeed new, but it is not Puccini's. Once again he has borrowed from his brother Michele,[34] and here it shows: a patch of mechanical commonplace on an otherwise highly individual score. Nor is it convincing psychologically. Cavaradossi is not the man to forget his friend's betrayal in an access of enthusiasm for the cause he represents. Puccini's operas are based on the relationships of individuals to one another. Political idealism may have been Verdi's field; it was certainly not his.

Cavaradossi is dragged off to await execution. Tosca attempts to follow him (Ex. 7.15 shrilly scored and tormented by rubato) but the police agents thrust her back. The music subsides into a reprise of the motivic cluster that opened the act. Alone with the prima donna, Scarpia resumes the 6/8 blandishments of his earlier appeal. She alone, he says, can save her lover. Only a musical setting (a bleak 'declamato' beneath tremolando violins) can convey the deadly scorn of Tosca's 'Quanto? . . . Il prezzo!' It is the orchestra that supplies the answer, unfolding a motif that will symbolize Scarpia's lust (Ex. 7.16). The operative figure here is the upward leaping triplet, variously extended in the course of repetition. Over harmonies ever more rich and voluptuous Scarpia proceeds to a cantabile ('Già mi struggea l'amor della diva'), akin to his earlier 'Ha più forte sapore la conquista violenta', but with a wider melodic range befitting his new sense of power. A climactic effusion of Ex. 7.16 meets with the repulse of Tosca's Ex. 7.15 as Scarpia advances on her with open arms. Guessing her intention of seeking the Queen's intercession, he tells her that she would only reprieve a lifeless corpse: and here Puccini sends a message to the audience

Ex. 7.16

Allegro vivace

f

---

[34] See n. 33.

with a recall of Ex. 7.1 ending with a minor chord. For a corpse there will certainly be before the end of Act II, but it will not be Cavaradossi's. Their battle of wills is interrupted by a distant side-drum tattoo, while a Phrygian 'marche au supplice' on pizzicato cellos and basses sounds beneath pulsating seconds on clarinets, then bassoons (a legacy from *Edgar*), bringing home the imminence of Cavaradossi's fate. The seconds relax into thirds; the thirds become inverted parallel triads as Tosca begins her famous aria ('Vissi d'arte, vissi d'amore'), its drooping phrases expressive of helpless bewilderment. Puccini is said to have considered abolishing this aria on the grounds that it holds up the action unrealistically. But Scarpia is in no hurry; and surely at this supreme crisis it is plausible that the singer's past should unroll before her in an expanded moment: a life devoted to art, love, and religious observance. So much is epitomized in a major-key consequent: Ex. 7.7 (her entrance theme) amplified by a central episode and prolonged by the desperate Ex. 7.15. A chromatic shadow of Scarpia's motif accompanies his 'Risolvi!'; but it robs neither the cadence of its finality nor the singer of her applause.

Tosca makes one last plea ('Vedi . . . le man giunte io stendo a te!') rendered the more eloquent by the Puccinian thumb-print of the falling fifth grafted on to the melody of the earlier death tattoo, now Dorianized. Scarpia's reply is predictable: surges of Ex. 7.16 ('Sei troppo bella, Tosca!'). Again she puts up a resistance. But just then Spoletta enters with the news that Angelotti has been found dead by his own hand (Ex. 7.12). Very well! Let his body be hanged from the gallows. And the Cavaliere? All is ready. Tosca can no longer put off her decision. Tantalizing fragments of Ex. 7.1 convey the unbearable suspense. At length the final note, no longer a chord but a soft unison, closes the door. Two bars from the world of *Tristan* scored for string quartet with viola on the top line indicate Tosca's broken-hearted consent to the bargain, giving way to a fierce gesture of two notes which, as Carner observes, will connote 'deceit', and by the simplest of means: proceeding from dominant to flattened leading-note they contradict the prevailing tonality, as one who should say 'Not so!'

This same gesture will persist as a cohesive agent throughout the dialogue that follows, twice punctuated by an extended version of the 'well' motif—a suitable adjunct, since it too has to do with an illusory escape. Cavaradossi, Scarpia tells his lieutenant, will not be hanged but placed before a firing squad armed with blank cartridges, 'as we did with Count Palmieri'. Spoletta, having grasped his chief's meaning, departs. Scarpia is now ready to receive his reward. But Tosca has a further condition: a safe-conduct for herself and her lover. Scarpia consents 'con galanteria'—again the lilting 6/8. As he sits to write out the document. Tosca's eye falls on the knife on his table and a monstrous thought takes shape in her mind (Ex. 7.17). The theme has already run more than half its course before she acts, seizing the knife and hiding it behind her back; so that when Scarpia moves to embrace her (Ex. 7.16) she can plunge it into his heart. Amid the turmoil of dissonances and whole-tone chords, disposed so as to underline every moment of Scarpia's death agony and Tosca's triumph, the two-note 'deception' motif rings out like a taunt. The deed accomplished, the heroine's rage evaporates ('Or gli perdono'). During the pantomime that follows (strictly as in the play) Ex. 7.17 takes charge, now an elegiac 'sviolinata' coloured by low woodwind and horns. Tosca wipes the blood from her hands, takes the safe-conduct from the dead man's clenched fingers and is about to leave with her famous curtain-line ('E avanti a lui tremava tutta Roma!'), when her religious upbringing gets the better of her. Returning to Scarpia's body, she places lighted candles on either side of his head and a crucifix on his breast—all this to recalls of his libidinous Ex. 7.16 in a minor key over muted trombones and a solitary reminiscence of Ex. 7.9a on solo clarinet. The final comment is, of course, left to Ex. 7.1 pianissimo, its baleful glow extinguished once more by a minor ending. As in Act I (and later in *Turandot*) the repeated concluding motif is driven home by a shift to an earlier key to bring down the curtain.

Ex. 7.17

Ex. 7.18

The flourish that begins the final act (Ex. 7.18) is an anticipation of what remained of the 'Latin hymn'. Proclaimed by four horns in unison, like the opening of Verdi's four act *Don Carlos* it serves here as a call to attention (Ex. 7.18). What follows is a tone-picture of dawn on the Roman Campagna. There is a certain kinship with the Barrière d'Enfer (*La bohème*) in the descending line of triads in the Lydian mode over an oscillating bass; and here too the scoring—bright, delicate and diaphanous with piccolos, violins, and the occasional trumpet chord— shows the hand of a master painter. At times the music is stalked by the ghost of Scarpia (Ex. 7.1), whose spirit still walks abroad. Above softly thudding timpani a shepherd boy can be heard singing as he drives his flocks to pasture. Like the lamplighter's song from *Manon Lescaut*, this is invented folk-music, whose Lydian mode allows Puccini to integrate it into what has gone before. Sheep-bells, fading into the distance, give way to a gathering consort of chimes from nearby steeples, during which the musical substance is confined to strings. Over 40 bars violins trace a meandering, almost improvisatory melody abounding in falling fifths. Meanwhile there is a pantomime on stage to engage the visual attention, as the gaoler makes preparations to receive the latest

Ex. 7.19

prisoner. When at length Cavaradossi arrives escorted by a picket the musical commentary is an orchestral statement of the opera's most celebrated aria, 'E lucevan le stelle' (Ex. 7.19). A full anticipation quite so close to the aria itself is unusual for Puccini and must surely have a dramatic purpose. From his first appearance on the platform Cavaradossi is under the shadow of death—a state which for Puccini carries no posthumous glory but only blackness and annihilation. Ex. 7.19 prepares us for his most concentrated expression of 'mestizia toscana'. The melody's only two bars in the major key are poised on unresolved dissonances, any hint of consolation firmly negated by a turn into the mediant minor and a cadential figure echoed inexorably in the original key. A 'sviolinata' pitched as low as this inevitably favours the mournful tones of the cellos, while soft trombone triads and the intermittent strokes of the great bell of St. Peter's deepen the sense of an elegy.

As Cavaradossi asks for pen and paper to write a last letter to his beloved, Ex. 7.9b sounds on four solo cellos, a combination familiar from the love duet of Verdi's *Otello*, and one that adds special poignancy to the harmonic suspensions. The same motif accompanies his beginning of the letter, extended into that of Tosca's distress (Ex. 7.15). Overcome by memories he breaks off, and Ex. 7.19 steals in on solo clarinet, beneath which the tenor declaims the first words of his aria. Here there is a distant tribute to Massenet, who uses the same instrument to set the no less mournful tone of Chimène's lament for her father ('Pleurez, pleurez, mes yeux') in *Le Cid*, performed to great acclaim at La Scala in 1890. 'A sorrow's crown of sorrow is remembering happier things', Tennyson wrote, paraphrasing famous lines by Dante; so the initial contrast between the text, recalling a scene of sensual delight, and the spirit of the music is quite in order. The key words (inserted at Puccini's request) are 'Muoio disperato!', which define the mood of the entire aria. The melodic contours and insistent accents call for a 'veristic' delivery in the manner of 'Vesti la giubba' (*Pagliacci*). Freed, however, from the structural constraints imposed by Leoncavallo's strict verse metre, Puccini succeeds in welding a succession of irregular rhapsodic phrases into a perfectly rounded statement.

Tosca is brought in to a further recall of Ex. 7.9b, its half-close prolonged by that traditional ploy of post-Rossinian opera, the dominant pedal of joyous reunion. The sight of Scarpia's signature (Ex. 7.1) on the safe-conduct brings Cavaradossi up short. Here a comparison with Sardou's play is instructive:

Mario: Malheureuse! De quel prix as-tu payé mon salut?
Floria: D'un coup de couteau.
Mario: Tu l'as tué?
Floria: Ah! si je l'ai tué! (*avec une joie sauvage*), 'Oh, ça, oui je l'ai bien tué!'

For Puccini's Tosca there is no such outburst. She is content to quell Cavaradossi's suspicions with a snatch of repartee:

Cavaradossi: Scarpia che cede? La prima sua grazia è questa.
Tosca: E l'ultima!

Only when she relives the events of the previous act does emotion break through. It is one of those rare cases in which opera can afford a greater degree of realism than spoken drama. For Sardou's Tosca to recount to her lover what the audience has seen would be intolerably pleonastic. Post-Wagnerian opera, on the other hand, with its armoury of recurring motifs, thrives on narration, so that Tosca can hold our interest with musical allusions loosely strung together in a swiftly moving discourse: her vain appeal to the Madonna and the saints (Ex. 7.9a); the side-drum tattoo; Scarpia's attempt to embrace her (Ex. 7.16); the idea of murder prompted by the sight of the knife (Ex. 7.17); the final accomplishment (an arpeggio to and from a C *in altissimo*).

To Sardou's Mario it was a deed worthy of an ancient Roman. Puccini's hero reacts more sentimentally. That those delicate hands, made for the bestowal of kindness, should be capable of such a deed! Ricordi had wanted something more substantial here than Cavaradossi's brief arpeggiated melody ('O dolci mani mansuete e pure'); but by juxtaposing its reprise with the motif of the murder (Ex. 7.17) Puccini's lyrical paragraph makes its point with apt economy. There is no full cadence, for Tosca hastens to explain the plan of the mock-execution. This is the practical 'little woman' whom we heard giving Cavaradossi instructions about their rendezvous after her concert at the Palazzo Farnese. So plain harmonies and a restricted compass for 'L'ora è vicina; io già raccolsi oro e gioielli . . . una vettura è pronta'. But each return to the tonic is undermined by the two-note 'deception' figure. As Tosca mentions the boat that will carry them to safety ('Liberi . . . Via pel mar'), the music assumes a rocking motion, then proceeds to the lyrical heart of the duet ('Amaro sol per te era il morire'), a vastly improved version of an idea from the discarded fourth act of Edgar, for which (*pace* Ricordi) no apology is needed (see Ex. 4.11). Particularly affecting is the dying fall that follows the concluding repeat of the opening strain. Again the frozen sixth within the final chords conveys a sense of longing.

Ever mindful of the passing moment, Tosca resumes her instructions. Cavaradossi must fall on the instant, taking care not to hurt himself. If only *she* were required to do it! 'Colla scenica scienza / Io saprei la movenza'. It is the experienced actress trying to teach a novice. Nothing is more harrowing than Tosca's illusion that she is in control of the situation. But Cavaradossi's assent is marked 'tristemente', suggesting that he is well aware of what is afoot. He prefers to listen to her voice as they both indulge in a dream of future happiness. So to Ex. 7.18 ('Trionfal'), now a flight of rhetoric sung by both voices in unison, but without Illica's reference to the spirit of Ancient Rome that they will carry in their hearts. Instead, Puccini ends on a note of mutual tenderness, the last chord once more sweetened by the 'frozen sixth'.

The clock strikes, and Tosca repeats her admonitions, like an anxious mother. The firing squad arrive to a slow march mostly in three-part harmony with a widely stepping bass. There is something almost inhuman about its emotional neutrality, as it wanders freely into related keys with a relentless tread and an increasing sonority. The soldiers raise their rifles; whereupon the two-note 'deception' motif rings out on trombones, low woodwind, and the entire body of strings. Cavaradossi falls so naturally that Tosca is truly impressed ('Ecco un artista!'). After the squad has retired, her discovery that he is indeed dead is marked by a plain minor triad fortissimo, such as had announced Mimì's death to Rodolfo. From here on music takes second place to action. Distant cries indicate that Scarpia's body has been found. Spoletta and his men burst in to arrest Tosca. But she has already fled to the top of the battlements, from which, with a cry of 'O Scarpia, avanti a Dio!', she hurls herself below, while the full orchestra thunders forth the theme of 'E lucevan le stelle' (Ex. 7.19).

As a peroration this has been severely criticized on the grounds that the melody is associated exclusively with Cavaradossi, and Tosca has never even heard him sing it. Yet it is no more irrelevent than the comment that concludes *La bohème*, compounded of Mimì's 'Sono andati?' and the orchestral epilogue to Colline's 'Vecchia zimarra'. The truth is that Puccini was already evolving his own way with recurring motifs. The cases of Ex. 7.2 (Angelotti and 'pursuit') and Ex. 7.4 (the picture, the Attavanti, the cause of liberty) have been noted. In Act III Tosca's Ex. 7.15 is woven into Cavaradossi's memories of his beloved, though she has never sung it in his presence. Even the gaoler's acceptance of his ring as recompense for the permission to write a letter is marked by a barely gracious snatch of Ex. 7.8b, not heard since Act I. That Puccini should choose the blackest theme of the opera to sum up the final tragedy is therefore perfectly logical.

Tosca is an opera of happenings; therein lie both its strength and its limitations. The constantly changing situation precludes those pages of sustained growth to be found in *Manon Lescaut* and *La bohème*. To the dense packing of motifs the term 'kaleidoscopic' is particularly apt. At the same time sensational events require a more than usual amount of 'effects' music (Carner's term): isolated gestures of brutality, tonal wrenches, orchestral cascades over dissonant harmony which at times strain the musical coherence, while never allowing the tension to relax. Yet within the unrelenting pace room is found for some of Puccini's most delightful lyrical inspirations: 'Recondita armonia', 'Vissi d'arte', 'E lucevan le stelle', each perfectly matched to the character and situation. Of all Puccini's heroines Tosca is the most complex: hence the opportunities she offers to a great stage actress, such as Maria Callas.

No-one would claim *Tosca* as its composer's masterpiece. The emotions it generates are mainly on the surface. But as a triumph of pure theatre it will remain unequalled until *La fanciulla del West*, another opera of action, by which time the composer's technique will have undergone a certain modification.

CHAPTER 8

Madama Butterfly

W ITH THE PREMIÈRE OF *TOSCA* BEHIND HIM PUCCINI WAS
free to devote himself to the completion of his new residence
at Torre del Lago. Venanzio's shack was being transformed out of recognition, only the base of the tower (the 'turris eburnea') remaining
intact. Interior decoration was entrusted to the painters Luigi De Servi,
Plinio Nomellini, and Puccini's old friend Ferruccio Pagni. From the
Marchese Ginori-Lisci he obtained permission to fill in part of the lake
that bordered on the property so as to accommodate a garden and a
driveway flanked by trees. Converted after his death into a Puccini
Museum, the house became a tourist attraction, while the hamlet expanded into a village, complete with piazza, shops, restaurants, and,
more recently, an open-air theatre. Yet the villa itself retains the charm
of one of those gabled Victorian houses that adorn the shores of many
a Cumbrian lake, commanding a wide view across the Lago di Massaciuccoli to the Apuan Alps. By the beginning of April 1900 Puccini
was able to move in with his family to what would be his home for
the next 20 years.

In the meantime he resumed his practice of attending important
revivals of his latest work. The first of these was at the Teatro Regio,
Turin, on 22 February, where the original cast was conducted by Alessandro Pomè. 'The vile opera went well,' he reported to Pagni,[1] evi-

[1] CP 222, p. 194.

dently still smarting from the reactions of the Roman press. Still harsher verdicts awaited him at Milan, where *Tosca* was at last performed under Toscanini on 17 March, again with Darclée in the title-role and Giraldoni as Scarpia, but with a new tenor, Giuseppe Borgatti, soon to make his name in Wagnerian parts. The performance was unreservedly praised; not so the opera. The most withering comments came from Luigi Torchi, Italian translator of Wagner's *Oper und Drama*, now a contributor to the recently founded *Rivista musicale italiana*, who regularly attacked the 'giovane scuola' for failing to understand the principles laid down by the Master of Bayreuth. 'What is certain', he declared, 'is that with *Tosca* Puccini has not composed an original opera. He has had recourse to a kaleidoscopic manipulation of styles spanning the gamut from Wagner to Massenet.' Less controversial revivals followed at Verona and Genoa in the late spring.

Not all Puccini's train journeys can be thus accounted for. While *Tosca* was in rehearsal at Turin, a young woman entered his life, in which she would create a certain havoc over the next three years. Of her background we know nothing: merely that she was a law student and that her Christian name, real or assumed, was Corinna. At first their meetings were furtive, since both Elvira and Fosca had accompanied Puccini to the city. However, subsequent trips to Milan and elsewhere provided the occasion for many a rendezvous. Nor did the liaison remain a secret for long. In June an acquaintance caught sight of the lovers at the station buffet at Pisa and informed Nitteti, who at once wrote to her brother reproaching him for not coming to visit her. The letter fell into Elvira's hands with consequences that can well be imagined. Later she would accuse Giacomo of using Pagni as a post-office for correspondence with his new mistress. In vain he protested his innocence and begged Elvira to be less of a policeman. His peccadilloes were not easily kept from her.

For the present Puccini's operatic plans were at a standstill. Even his relations with Illica had become temporarily strained. Hence, no doubt, a meeting with Gabriele D'Annunzio, which occurred towards the end of February. It was not the first time that a collaboration between them had been mooted. In 1894 the initiative seems to have come from the poet by way of Carlo Clausetti; but, though Puccini professed himself delighted by the prospect of 'something sweetly original from Italy's greatest genius',[2] the project foundered on D'Annunzio's excessive financial demands—but only for the time being. Over the next 20 years it would re-surface sporadically without ever leading to concrete results.

Among the subjects proposed to Illica the previous November only one was beginning to take shape in the composer's mind: Alphonse Daudet's *Tartarin de Tarascon*, the comic adventures of a middle-aged Provençal fantasist. Illica was agreeable, merely pointing out the dangers of too close a resemblance to Verdi's *Falstaff*. He drafted out a scenario for a prologue and first act, which he submitted to Ricordi for his approval. Puccini's enthusiasm received a check when he found that the project had been leaked to the newspapers. This was premature; would it not be wiser to turn in the meantime to something else: perhaps Goldoni's *La locandiera* with its Florentine setting, or a subject taken from the fashionable Belgian writer Charles Paul de Kock? But Illica and Ricordi held out for *Tartarin*, and soon Puccini's imagination was running riot over its visual possibilities (' . . . a huge square with trees in bloom, oleanders of various hues, white terrain as in Palermo or Malta, the sky a dark cobalt blue, a large practicable bridge over the Rhone in the background').[3] All this on the eve of his departure for London, where he would see a play that would steer his thoughts in a very different direction.

The occasion of his second English visit was the Covent Garden première of *Tosca* on 12 July with Milka Ternina, Fernando De Lucia, and Antonio Scotti as Scarpia, a role that he was to make particularly his own. The conductor was Luigi Mancinelli. 'A complete triumph!', Puccini reported to Ramelde,[4] as indeed it was. George Maxwell, Ricordi's representative in New York, at once negotiated a performance at the Metropolitan Opera House, which took place the following year with the same conductor and cast apart from De Lucia, whose place was taken by Giuseppe Cremonini, creator of Des Grieux.

Puccini's stay in London lasted six weeks. It included a visit to the slums of the East End, which interested him very much, so he wrote

[2] CP 107, pp. 103–4.
[3] CP 232, pp. 200–1.
[4] PCE 240, p. 248.

to Elvira. He also mentioned a party given by the Rothschilds and a dinner with some friends at a fashionable restaurant 'where there were plenty of *cocottes*. What elegance and what beauties! But afterwards we went home very quietly like good little boys.'[5] Clearly he had not lost his habit of tormenting his life's companion.

More fruitful was a visit to the Duke of York's Theatre, where a double-bill of one-acters was playing: Jerome K. Jerome's *Miss Hobbs* and David Belasco's *Madam Butterfly*. Years later Belasco recalled how at the end of the performance Puccini rushed to his dressing-room and urgently begged him for the operatic rights to his play. 'I agreed at once and told him that he could . . . make any sort of contract, because it was impossible to discuss arrangements with an impulsive Italian who has tears in his eyes and both arms round your neck.'[6] An exaggeration? Perhaps, since Puccini described the play to a friend as 'very beautiful but not for Italy'.[7] However, that may have been no more than a ruse to quash untimely publicity. The fact remains that on his return to Milan he at once asked Ricordi to put out feelers in the appropriate quarter.

For the present it was merely one possibility amongst many. Over *Tartarin* there were legal difficulties with the author's executors, which would not be resolved until 1906. While in Paris on the way home he enquired whether the rights to Zola's *La faute de l'Abbé Mouret* had been granted to Leoncavallo, as so many newspapers had stated. No, came the answer, it was still committed to Massenet.

The upshot was that Puccini returned to Torre del Lago at the beginning of August 'un operaio disoccupato',[8] having heard nothing from Illica or Giacosa. As early as 1897 Illica had proposed an opera about Marie Antoinette to which the composer had given sympathetic consideration. Now he thought of returning to it, deterred only by the 'hackneyed colour' of the Revolution. Over the next three months he was occupied by revivals of *Tosca* at Lucca, Bologna, and Brussels, to say nothing of brief trips to Milan and Turin, whose purpose can all too easily be guessed. However, from Brussels he wrote to Illica, send-

[5] MP, 194.

[6] Cited in PCB, 135.

[7] QP, i, p. 98.

[8] PLI 40, p. 98.

ing him an 'opuscolo' regarding the French queen and urging him to include, by way of contrast to the 'regal tipo', a 'rivoluzionaria', whom he would make a contralto (shades of the baleful Zia Principessa in *Suor Angelica*?). And what about the scene in which the head of the Princesse de Lamballes is paraded before the queen on a pike?[9] There for the present the matter rested, though neither librettist nor composer had by any means done with it.

On his return from Bologna, where Caruso had sung Cavaradossi 'divinely', Puccini passed in review a number of subjects that had been proposed to him, including *Les misérables*, Benjamin Constant's *Adolphe* and Rostand's *Cyrano de Bergerac*. None of them would do. Meanwhile, had there been any news from America? 'The more I think of *Butterfly* the more irresistibly am I attracted. Oh, if only I had it here, I might set to work on it! I think that instead of one act I could make two quite long ones: the first in North America, the second in Japan. . . . I cannot understand how Mr Maxwell has *still* not answered.'[10]

Throughout these fallow months Puccini's domestic troubles had pursued him even abroad. From London he replied to an aggrieved letter from Elvira complaining of their isolation in country retreats such as Torre del Lago and, especially, Chiatri. Why could they not live in Milan, where at least there was life? Puccini retorted that for him the countryside was a necessity: nor could he understand why she and Fosca continually opposed his wishes in the matter. In Brussels, where he heard Richard Strauss conduct *Don Quixote* and *Ein Heldenleben* and wrote him a letter of congratulation, he received further reproaches from Elvira, to which he replied with a countercharge. How could they resume their old intimacy if she kept inviting her friends and relations to stay with them? There was another problem. Fosca was now of marriageable age and being courted by two suitors: the tenor Leonardi and an impoverished cellist for whom Puccini had secured a contract out of pity. That he should aspire to Fosca's hand—that was too much. 'It isn't just arrogance on my part. It is a justifiable aversion that I have to a man who is not worth anything and who is going to take away a being whom I have seen develop into someone sweet and beloved. . . .

[9] CP 237, p. 203.
[10] GPE 69, pp. 142–4.

I liked the idea of Leonardi; it is true he is a tenor, but at least it seems he has enough stuff in him to become a man.'[11] It was Leonardi whom Fosca married, though not with the happiest of results.

On 29 July 1900 King Umberto was assassinated by an anarchist out of revenge for the government's strong-arm tactics of two years earlier. The aged Verdi's intention to set a memorial prayer written by the royal widow never proceeded further than a few sketches. On the apolitical Puccini the sad event seems to have left no impression. One that did, however, was the death of Verdi himself on 27 January 1901. At the request of the mayor, Cesare Riccioni, Puccini agreed to represent the township of Viareggio at the funeral ('With Him, alas, the purest, most luminous glory of Italy is extinguished. For the glory of our country let us hope that his virtues as man and artist will be imitated and continued').[12]

By the end of March word had arrived from America that *Madam Butterfly* was at his disposal; and though the contract with Belasco would not be signed until September, the composer was able to entrust Illica with the drawing up of a scenario. The author who was destined to play so vital a part in Puccini's search for novelty was born in San Francisco in 1853 of Portuguese-Jewish parents. Brought up in a Catholic monastery (in token of which he wore a clerical collar), he joined a theatrical troupe at the age of 18, quickly making his mark as actor, dramatist, and producer. His plays, many of them based on foreign models, are as forgotten today as those of Sardou; but his importance in the history of American stage direction has been compared to that of Max Reinhardt in Germany. His speciality was the creation of striking pictorial effects by ingenious variation of stage lighting. Among these his own favourite—and evidently the public's too, since he owed to it the soubriquet 'wizard of the stage'—occurs in *Madam Butterfly*: a 14-minute transition from dusk to dawn, during which not a word is spoken. Puccini knew no English, and, had he done so, he might well have been defeated by the pidgin variety in which so much of the dialogue is couched. But a visual stimulus was always important to him;

[11] MP, 193.

[12] PLI 74, p. 100.

and there was enough in Belasco's naturalistic production to engage his interest through the eye alone.

The play is based on a story by John Luther Long, a lawyer from Philadelphia, which had appeared in the periodical *Century Magazine* in 1897. A lieutenant in the United States navy, whose ship has put in at Nagasaki, marries a young geisha according to Japanese law, then leaves her, promising to return 'when the robins build their nests again'. But when he does so, it is in the company of an American wife, in order to claim the child that has been born to him in the interval. The geisha attempts *hara-kiri*; but her maid binds up her wounds, and the lieutenant arrives to find their former home deserted. So much Long claimed to have taken from real life; but, like Leoncavallo's *Pagliacci*, the story owes at least as much to contemporary literature. Its immediate forebear is Pierre Loti's *Madame Chrysanthème* (1887), as is evident from its title, its locale (Nagasaki), and the profession of its male protagonist. Both stories are a sign of the times. Western interest in all things oriental had been steadily booming since the mid-nineteenth century. Of the Asiatic nations Japan was the last to be discovered by the European traveller, on whom the cleanliness of its towns, the courtesy of its people, and the simple, if exotic, perfection of its visual arts left a lasting impression. At Paris's Exposition Universelle of 1867 Japanese art obtained its first showcase in Europe. From then on its motifs began to infiltrate French painting (see Monet's portrait of Zola). A Japanese exhibition held in London inspired Sullivan's *The Mikado* (1885), to be followed by Sidney Jones's *The Geisha* (1894) and *San Toy* (1899). By this time a genuine knowledge of the nation's culture had been disseminated by the writings of Lefcadio Hearn, himself a naturalized citizen of the country. But it was *Madame Chrysanthème* which would fix the popular image of Japan for years to come. It is an autobiographical novel based on a diary that Loti kept during his service as a French naval officer. He too marries a native 'wife' for the duration of his stay in port, the marriage dissoluble after a month's desertion by either party. Captivated by the beauty of the country and the quaintness of its ceremonies, he casts a beady eye on its inhabitants. For him they are a race of monkeys, insects even, their minds impenetrable by a westerner. Chrysanthème herself is no different. The writer likens her to a pet cat. Her conversation bores him to distraction. Returning to their house to bid her a last farewell, he is relieved to find her hammering the coins he has left her to make sure that they are genuine.

Needless to say, the novel caused much offence not only to the Japanese themselves but to their more sympathetic visitors, among them Félix Régamey, who in 1894 published a novelette, *Le cahier rose de Madame Chrysanthème*, that is, her secret diary. Here Loti's plot is re-interpreted in such a way as to make his narrator appear stupid, insensitive, and cowardly. Significantly, for their *opéra comique, Madame Chrysanthème* (1897), André Messager and his librettists thought it advisable to add an epilogue in which the lieutenant receives a pathetic letter from the forsaken geisha and is duly remorseful.

Long's story can also be seen as a counterblast to Loti. His narration too begins with Lieutenant Benjamin Franklin Pinkerton being advised by a subaltern, not without cynicism, to take a temporary wife while in port. It then passes to a brief account of the wedding ceremony arranged with the family's complete approval until Pinkerton decides to ban them from the house; whereupon they solemnly cast the girl off. Forbidden by Pinkerton even her religion, Butterfly ('Cho-Cho-San' in Japanese) pays a secret visit to the Christian mission, returning happily 'not to adopt his religion but to hold it in reserve if her relatives should remain obdurate'. The story resumes several months after Pinkerton's departure, by which time Butterfly has borne him a son: and it traces her gradual disillusionment with the aid of the marriage-broker, her maid (both derived from Loti), a noble Japanese suitor, the American consul, and finally Pinkerton's American wife, Kate. Unlike Chrysanthème, Butterfly is a creature of flesh and blood. But she shares with her predecessor a 'bébété', conveyed by a primitive, phonetically rendered jargon that bears no relation to English as pronounced by the Japanese. But it would be retained together with much of Long's dialogue in Belasco's play.

This begins with Butterfly already abandoned and the mother of a child (female, where in Long it had been male). From then on events proceed as in the story, with only two differences. Long had placed the encounter between Butterfly and Kate Pinkerton at the American consulate. Belasco keeps the action at Butterfly's house throughout; and his heroine succeeds in her suicide attempt. Her last words are 'Too bad those robins didn't nes' again!'

Puccini's suggestion of a first act set in North America shows that he was as yet unfamiliar with Long's story. Early in March he had received a copy, which he sent to Illica with instructions to pass on his impressions of it to Ricordi. The publisher had been doubtful about the project from the start, and Illica did his best to convince him otherwise. Even the secondary characters were beginning to fire his imagination: the marriage-broker, who should wear a European suit; the consul, 'frank, genial, kindly, and at bottom a mine of philosophy due to his having lived in different countries; contemptuous of all customs and usages, appreciative only of good people, be they English or Boer, American or Japanese.'[13] The sequel to Pinkerton's departure he proposed dividing into three scenes, the second set in the American consulate, a villa situated in the European Concession and furnished accordingly. Indeed he thought that the story alone would provide the necessary material; but Puccini insisted that he see a copy of the play, in which 'the Japanese gentleman who tempts the forsaken "wife" is changed into a debauched American millionaire, greatly to the advantage of the so-called European element, which we need.'[14] Clearly at this stage he, like Illica, envisaged the drama as based on a culture-clash between East and West; but he was wrong about Belasco's Yamadori. Though he lives in New York, the Prince is as Japanese as Butterfly herself.

Even before receiving the play Illica had drafted a detailed scenario of his first act, which is preserved in the archives of the Casa Ricordi. In filling out Long's bare outlines it leans heavily on Loti for general atmosphere. Sir Francis Blummy Pinkerton (*sic!*) is Loti's narrator Pierre writ large with a brand of arrogance all his own. A sexual adventurer, he carries America in his heart. His marriage with Butterfly is a purely business arangement; there is no question of his taking her seriously as a woman, still less as a wife ('Che donna?!! . . . No! né moglie . . . Oibò!'). Sharpless, the consul, far from deploring his attitude, approves

[13] CP 249, pp. 209–10.
[14] CP 247, p. 248.

it entirely. His 'Quel diavolo d'un Pinkerton!' is spoken with a tolerant chuckle. In the opera it will take on a very different meaning.

Illica's Japanese are as ridiculous as Loti's. Butterfly's mother is a congenital glutton ('We shall make her drunk!' Pinkerton declares); her cousin quite unable to control her child, Riso, having borne him too young. Of her two uncles Bonze is a preacher who holds the family in subjection, Yakuside a tipsy buffoon, who disturbs the wedding ceremony by fighting with Riso over a sweet. To Pinkerton the festivities are a huge joke. Only when he mocks the figures of Butterfly's ancestors does Sharpless utter a word of reproof. So much is reasonably consonant with Long's narrative. But there are two departures from it. Butterfly's adoption of her lover's religion is wholehearted; and it is the Bonze who orders her family to cast her off. The love-duet is merely adumbrated; but Illica was confident of giving it 'a poetic quality almost greater than that of the scene between Rodolfo and Mimì'.[15] Nor had he any doubt that in the opera's final scenes Pinkerton, however antipathetic, would emerge 'a real tenor as regards character, modernity, everything. . . . Believe me, . . . *Butterfly* is the strongest thing that Puccini has ever had, strong and new, but not easy' (this to Ricordi).[16]

The draft was submitted to Giacosa with the composer's approval. But since the poet had not finished with it before September, Puccini remained inactive during the intervening months. In May he went in the company of Giordano to buy his first car, a De Dion Bouton. He spent a summer holiday with Elvira in Cutigliano, a village in the hills above Pistoia. It was not a happy time for either. By now the affair with Corinna had become common knowledge among Puccini's family and friends, Ricordi included. To Ramelde he protested that he was well on the way to a cure; but in this he deceived himself. The liaison would drag on for two more years and be broken only with difficulty.

Fortunately, despite Ricordi's fears to the contrary, his work remained unaffected. With Giacosa's first act finally in his hands he set about the composition and was soon communicating to Illica his ideas for an intermezzo to correspond with Belasco's lighting stunt ('We must

[15] See n. 13.
[16] CP 252, p. 211.

find something good. Mysterious voices humming, for instance').[17] And so it would be.

To this period belongs a song, *Terra e mare*, published in Edoardo De Fonseca's annual *Novissima*. A setting of three stanzas by the poet and music critic Enrico Panzacchi (an early champion of Wagner), it sounds a characteristic note of 'mestizia toscana', though the subject is merely the singer's half-waking impressions of poplars roaring in the wind and the distant murmur of breaking surf. The minor-key melody, recalled many years later in *Suor Angelica*, where two novices acknowledge the Mistress's reproof, is variously distributed throughout the texture in Puccini's mature manner, the harmonies filled out with parallel chords. The first and last of its three stanzas are anchored to a tonic pedal, real or implied, while the second modulates boldly over a pattern of alternating bass notes. A brief major-key postlude concludes the piece in a mood of tranquillity. Here was a vein far more suited to Puccini's temperament than the routine triumphalism of *Avanti Urania* or the *Inno a Diana*.

Throughout 1902 Puccini worked slowly and steadily on his opera without renouncing his habitual diversions of hunting in the locality and attending revivals of his previous works, among them *La bohème* at Monte Carlo in February with Melba and Caruso, *Tosca* at Dresden in October, and what was almost a Puccini Festival at Rome in December. His main pre-occupation was the search for Japanese folk music as a source of local colour. There were hints to be found in Sullivan's *The Mikado*, a copy of which exists in his library at Torre del Lago; but further research was obviously needed.

Illica suggested that he interview the Japanese actress Sada Yacco, performing with her company in Milan during April. However, by then Puccini claimed to have found 'plenty of material of the yellow race'.[18] Nonetheless in June he began a correspondence with the Belgian musicologist Gustav Knosp about Japanese melody and rhythm. Later he would contact the wife of the country's ambassador, who gave him information about nomenclature and sang him Japanese folksongs, of which she promised to send him a volume.

[17] CP 263, p. 215.
[18] CP 277, p. 221.

In the meantime Puccini kept his publisher posted as to his progress. On 23 April 'I am laying stone upon stone and doing my best to make F. B. Pinkerton sing as much like an American as possible'. On 3 May 'I have composed the passage for the entry of Butterfly and am pleased with it. Apart from the fact that they are slightly Italian in character, both the music and the scene of this entry are very effective.'[19] By the end of June the libretto was complete, and the authors imagined their work to be finished. Little did they know!

Throughout the summer Puccini remained at Torre del Lago working on his opera in an atmosphere rendered all the more tense by the absence of Fosca, now married and living in Milan ('You have left a great emptiness behind you', Puccini wrote to her, 'and the life that we lead, Elvira and I, is simply terrible.'[20] Nonetheless by 4 September he had finished the first act in short score and was proceeding with the second, when he suddenly decided on a radical change of plan. The original act division can be deduced from a letter of Giacosa written on 20 May. Act II was to have contained two scenes, the first laid at Butterfly's house, the second at the American consulate. Act III would revert to the house. At Giacosa's suggestion the scene at the consulate was postponed until after the second interval. Puccini now told Illica that he wanted it eliminated altogether, so that the opera would be in two acts only, 'the first yours, the second Belasco's with all its details. . . . No entr'acte and arrive at the end keeping the public nailed to their seats for an hour and a half. It's huge, but it's the life of the opera.'[21]

Illica was agreeable, merely advising an interval to give the audience a breathing-space; but Puccini thought it unwise to lower and then raise the curtain on the same scene (though after the first performance he would do just that). The two men spent a week in conference at Torre del Lago, after which Puccini could assure his publisher that the operation had been carried out to the satisfaction of both parties and that he was now busy with the scoring of his first act. Ricordi's only demur was that the opera might now turn out too short, and that a *Pagliacci* would be needed to complete the evening, but he allowed

[19] GPE 73, p. 146.
[20] CP 281, p. 223.
[21] CP 287, p. 225.

himself to be persuaded by Illica. Not so Giacosa, who considered his artistic integrity compromised by the cut. True, there was no consulate scene in the play, but that was in one act only. 'If we, who had the sound idea of adding a first act extraneous to the action, now fail to give that action sufficient development we shall upset the balance of the act and aggravate the defects of the play to the point of rendering them intolerable. . . . I am convinced that your alteration would do away with many exquisite poetic details.'[22] Far better to recast the entire libretto so as to conform to Belasco's drama. But with the first act already composed this was hardly realistic. In the end Giacosa, as usual, bowed to the wishes of his collaborators.

A glance at Illica's draft for the consulate scene may help to explain Giacosa's objection to its removal and Puccini's insistence upon it. Essentially it belongs to Sharpless who is present throughout. His first visitor is the marriage-broker Goro, who has brought with him four candidates for temporary marriage with members of the American ship's crew. After some discussion Sharpless manages to get rid of them. Enter Pinkerton in great agitation to pour out his feelings of remorse in a long solo. Unwilling to face his former bride, he hands over a sum of money for Sharpless to give her. Alone, the consul reflects on the distasteful nature of his duties in the grumbling manner of Hans Sachs. Butterfly arrives, having not yet abandoned all hope. Sharpless starts to break the sad news to her, but is interrupted by the appearance of Kate Pinkerton. In vain he tries to keep the two women apart. As in the play Kate addresses her rival as a 'pretty little plaything' (gingillo) and offers to kiss her; but Butterfly shrinks back in horror. She refuses the money and leaves with the line 'I go now to have a long, long sleep' (also from Belasco, where it is spoken to Suzuki).

In all this the pace and variety are nicely balanced, the characters of Sharpless and Pinkerton are further rounded, and there is ample room for the lieutenant to confirm his status as tenor lead and to regain some of the audience's sympathy (a point to which Giacosa would return the following year). Here too was an opportunity of highlighting the contrast between East and West by which the authors had originally set such store.

[22] Cited in PCB, 140–1.

On the other hand the scene would undoubtedly have slackened the momentum of a drama which Puccini felt should press on relentlessly to its tragic dénouement. In its present form *Madama Butterfly* sets the pattern for a number of his future operas: an assortment of episodes leading to a concentration on the central dramatic issue—here the desertion and death of the heroine. To have elevated Sharpless in the manner described would have been an irrelevance. He is not a catalyst but a mere bystander—a Colonel Pickering to Pinkerton's Henry Higgins. As for the East–West conflict, this had already been compromised by the finale to Act I. A love-duet inevitably requires that both parties speak the same musical language.

The first few weeks of 1903 found the opera firmly on course. Then on 25 February during his return with Elvira and Tonio from a dinner with Alfredo Caselli in Lucca, Puccini's De Dion Bouton left the road at a sharp bend, plunged down an embankment and overturned. Fortunately a doctor who lived nearby heard the crash and took the injured into his house—the chauffeur Barsuglia with a fractured thigh, Puccini with a broken shinbone and multiple contusions, Elvira and Tonio in a state of shock but otherwise unhurt. Next day Barsuglia was rushed to a hospital in Lucca, while his passengers were transported by coach and motor boat to Torre del Lago, where Puccini was laid up for the next four months, tended by Elvira, her sister Ida Razzi, and the widowed Nitteti. Unable during the first few weeks to move without pain, his only solace was a host of telegrams from friends and well-wishers, including the young King of Italy.

Not everyone viewed the accident as an unmitigated evil. To Suor Giulia Enrichetta (formerly Igenia Puccini) it was a warning to her brother from on high to mend his ways. 'Jesus has not dealt him this blow in vain', she confided to Tomaide. 'I believe that he loves Giacomo and doesn't want to lose him.'[23] In the longest letter he ever wrote to his protégé Giulio Ricordi expressed himself more forcibly, suspecting that Puccini's slow recovery—in fact due, as was later diagnosed, to a mild form of diabetes—had a more sinister cause traceable to Corinna. 'Is it at all possible', he thundered, 'that a man like Puccini, an artist who moves millions to tears by the spell and potency of his

[23] PCE 270, p. 265.

creations, can become an ugly, ridiculous toy in the meretricious hands of a vulgar and contemptible woman . . . , one who gets him into her clutches and like a foul vampire sucks his mind, blood, and life?' And he concluded, 'I say to this letter: go, penetrate his heart and convince him in God's name of the great, true, and loyal affection which has dictated you; and with a like affection I embrace you.'[24]

No stranger to his publisher's sermons, Puccini found this latest 'bill of indictment' singularly ill-informed and 'not very generous towards a certain person.'[25] Certainly Corinna was not as black as Ricordi painted her, probably not even the adventuress that she has seemed to Puccini's biographers, but a young woman genuinely in love with the composer and unwilling to give him up without a struggle. Be that as it may, she had placed his letters to her in the hands of a lawyer, and it was not until December that he managed to obtain their return.

For in the meantime fate had been active in another quarter. On the day after the motor accident Elvira's husband had died aged 46. The way was now open for Puccini to regularize his union with her. No-one was more zealous in this cause than Ramelde, who even sounded out Illica on the possibility of Elvira's foregoing the statutory ten months of widowhood before re-marriage. But here, Illica assured her, the King himself would be unable to help. Clearly the period of waiting would be a difficult time for both parties with Corinna hovering in the wings. 'But then', Illica admitted, 'I won't hide from you that Elvira gets on my nerves. If Giacomo behaves as he does it just means that Elvira hasn't been able to inspire in him greater respect. People get the governments they deserve, and so does Elvira!'[26]

Throughout the spring Puccini built up his strength with five meals a day, smoked a good deal, and read the tales of Maxim Gorki as well as Maeterlinck's play *Monna Vanna*. For composition he was dependent on his piano, at which he was unable to sit with his leg in plaster until it occurred to him to exchange his upright model for a grand. In May he was told that his leg would require three months to heal. Even after that he would for a time need two sticks as a walking-aid. Chiatri was

[24] PCB, 143. For the full text see C. Sartori: *Puccini*, 62–8.
[25] CP 315, p. 240.
[26] PCE 271, p. 271.

therefore out of the question as a summer retreat. Instead he and Elvira took a villa at Boscolungo near Abetone, from where at the end of August he felt able to send Ricordi an optimistic report both on his health and his progress on the opera. He had completed the 'famous' intermezzo of Butterfly's night vigil and was pleased with it. The remainder would not amount to much. The première could be fixed at La Scala for the Lenten season of 1904.

In September Puccini left with Elvira for Paris to attend rehearsals for *Tosca* at the Opéra Comique, undergoing daily massage in his spare time. Sardou was there to lend a hand with the production ('He gets worked up and is truly extraordinary; full of life and really youthful— more so than we!').[27] The first performance was given on 13 October under André Messager before a packed house—'a *veritable* triumph in the Italian manner with shouts and encores, despite the snobbishness of the critics').[28] This last was foreseeable. Ever since the appearance of *Cavalleria rusticana* in 1892 opposition to the 'giovane scuola' had been building up in French musical circles. Among his countrymen, however, Puccini was treated less harshly than most. Writing in *Le Figaro*, Gabriel Fauré recognized in him 'a true man of the theatre' and in *Tosca* 'a powerful, terrifying drama' supported by music that was 'ardent, impassioned, and commanding', but with disconcerting lapses into vulgarity. For Paul Dukas music could only blunt the impact of Sardou's play. Some of Puccini's ideas, he admitted, were quite good, others merely cheap. 'Puccini possesses more cleverness than genuine personality. His gifts sometimes seem rather artificial and limited to the use of bizarre harmonies that have no connection with the natural expression of the sentiments they accompany.' 'Not without talent, but could do better', seems to have been the general verdict among the French establishment.

Back in Torre del Lago Puccini's spirits alternately soared and plunged. Buoyed up by his Parisian triumph, he bought his first motor boat. But he declined an invitation to attend the long-awaited première of *La bohème* at the Vienna State Opera, then changed his mind and

[27] CP 325, p. 245.
[28] CP 327, p. 246.

journeyed north in time to catch the second performance. Why this *volte-face*? Probably to gain a respite from a domestic situation rendered intolerable by Corinna's obduracy. 'My life is a sea of misery', he wrote to Illica, 'and I'm stuck fast in it. It seems that I'm loved by nobody, you understand, nobody—and to think that so many people say that I'm to be envied!' He begged the poet for a visit, as did Elvira in a separate letter. 'I jot down a few notes because I have to, and I pass the time in the blackest of atmospheres.'[29] Nevertheless, by 27 December those few notes had brought *Madama Butterfly* to its conclusion; while on 4 January 1904 Giacomo and Elvira were finally wed, and an unsettling episode safely relegated to the past.

During those days a brief dispute flared up between Giacosa and Ricordi over certain lines for the returned Pinkerton which had remained unset. Puccini, the poet maintained, should have given his tenor lead more to sing at this point; and he cited in his support Cavaradossi's 'O dolci mani'. Ricordi retorted that Pinkerton was no tender-hearted lover but 'a mean American leech who is afraid of Butterfly and dreads her meeting with his wife and so beats a retreat.'[30] Anything like a 'romanza' would be ridiculous in the circumstances. But Giacosa was right, as Puccini himself realized after the first performance. For the present Ricordi yielded to the poet's wishes to the extent of printing his text in full in the libretto.

Rehearsals began on 7 January and proceeded in an atmosphere of total secrecy. None of the singers were allowed to take their parts home with them. At the end of the month Puccini sent Ramelde a proof copy of the libretto with strict instructions to show it to nobody apart from Otilia and Tomaide. The principals had been hand-picked: Rosina Storchio (Cio-Cio-San), Giovanni Zenatello (Pinkerton), Giuseppe De Luca (Sharpless); the conductor was Cleofonte Campanini. Within a fortnight of the première the theatre was sold out. All were fully confident of a triumph, not least Puccini himself. A note conveyed by him to Rosina Storchio a few hours before curtain-rise ran 'My good wishes are pointless! Your great art is so true, delicate, and compelling that the

[29] CP 332, p. 248.
[30] PCB, 147.

public will certainly be enthralled by it . . . Till this evening, then, with a confident heart and all my affection.'[31]

What actually happened on the night of 17 February has been told many times: glum silence during the first act until Butterfly's entrance, where a resemblance to a phrase from the aria 'Mi chiamono Mimì' provoked shouts of '*Bohème!*'; and when a draught from backstage caused Storchio's skirt to billow 'Butterfly is pregnant!'; laughter and cries of '*bis!*' when she presented her child to the consul; a pandemonium of animal and bird noises at Tito Ricordi's ill-judged simulation of a dawn chorus in the intermezzo; total apathy during the remainder; whistles and boos after the final curtain.

'A real lynching'—so Puccini described it to the banker Camillo Bondi. Yet his faith in the opera was no more shaken than Verdi's in *La traviata* after its initial reception. 'My *Butterfly*', he went on, 'remains what it is: the most heartfelt and evocative opera I have ever conceived.'[32] And to his nephew Carlo Del Carlo, 'I know that I have written a genuine, living opera and that it will certainly rise again.'[33] Ramelde was less sanguine. Reporting the events to her husband, she insinuated that Mascagni and Giordano, both present, had been overjoyed at the outcome. This was totally unjust. Gatti-Casazza recalls seeing Mascagni in tears before the curtain, upbraiding the audience for their behaviour (Ramelde had left before the end). The author of *Cavalleria rusticana* may have been much given to theatrical gesture, but he was never insincere.

The press was no more encouraging. Critic after critic accused Puccini of self-repetition—a fantastic charge. Only Giovanni Pozza of *Il corriere della sera* and Achille Tedeschi of *L'illustrazione italiana* predicted that with a little trimming the opera might be vindicated.

Puccini himself was in no doubt that the hostility had been organized in advance—but by whom? An educated guess points the finger at the rival publisher Edoardo Sonzogno. His two-year management of La Scala, during which all operas published by Ricordi were banned from the stage, had resulted in a massive deficit and the theatre's closure

[31] CP 349, p. 256.

[32] PCE 292, p. 295.

[33] CP 350, p. 260.

throughout 1898. A new committee of management chaired by Duke Guido Visconti di Modrone appointed Gatti-Casazza as impresario and Toscanini as chief conductor. Now it was Sonzogno's turn to feel the pinch. Over the next few years his only opera to be staged there was Mascagni's *Le maschere* (1901) in what was intended to be one of seven simultaneous premières given throughout the peninsula—a typical Sonzogno publicity stunt that failed outright. Two years later the delay to the production of *Madama Butterfly* consequent on Puccini's accident and slow recovery enabled Sonzogno to move in with Giordano's *Siberia*. A well-crafted work with a judicious sprinkling of Russian folk-song, it obtained at least a *succès d'estime*. All the more important, therefore, that it should not be eclipsed by Puccini's latest offering, which followed on its heels. In those days the resident claque had the power to make or mar an opera's reception. That Sonzogno, known for his unscrupulous tactics, should have availed himself of its services with a discreet bribe is more than likely. Max Beerbohm has observed that, though you cannot make a man from a flock of sheep, you can easily make a sheep from a crowd of men. Once the tone of the evening had been set by the claque, the rest of the public could be guaranteed to follow suit. Highly significant is a paragraph that appeared in *Il secolo* after *Madama Butterfly* had been withdrawn and replaced by Gounod's *Faust*. After applauding the management's decision the writer continued, 'A second performance would have provoked a scandal among the Milanese, who do not relish being made fun of. The opera is not one of those like *Il barbiere di Siviglia* that carry within them the seeds of resurrection. It shows that Maestro Puccini was in a hurry. Importuned as he was to bring out the work this season, sick as he was, he failed to find original inspiration and had recourse to melodies from his previous operas and even helped himself to melodies by other composers. . . . The opera is dead.'

The proprietor of *Il secolo* was Edoardo Sonzogno.

A revival in Rome under Luigi Mancinelli was immediately cancelled. Bologna and Turin were briefly considered; but it was Tito Ricordi who chose the Teatro Grande, Brescia, for the opera's reclamation. In the meantime the Milanese verdict had not gone unchallenged. Letters to the press complained of the public's disgraceful conduct. Puccini was particularly touched by a poem sent to him on a postcard from the poet Giovanni Pascoli urging the wounded insect to take flight once more. Yet, as he worked with Illica on modifications, his mood remained distrustful. He saw enemies everywhere, even among his intimates. A few flippant remarks that reached him from the Luccan critic Carlo Paladini caused a breach in their friendship that lasted for ten years. Even Clausetti and Mascagni came under suspicion, though the latter had recently conducted 'La tregenda' (*Le Villi*) in Rome. However, a return to Torre del Lago seems to have revived his spirits, since he was soon corresponding with Illica about future projects. In the event his hopes for the revised opera proved amply justified. On 28 May the Brescians showed themselves as enthusiastic as the Milanese had been hostile. Yet cast and conductor were identical, save for the replacement of Rosina Storchio (called away to Buenos Aires) by Salomea Krusceniski ('excellent as to voice and fully up to the mark in charm and sentiment', the composer reported).[34] The second performance was attended by the Queen of Italy, to whom Puccini had dedicated the score. Such changes as it had undergone, though significant, were certainly not enough to account for the altered reception. The theory of a malign conspiracy must therefore stand.

Madama Butterfly was never seen again at La Scala during Puccini's lifetime; but it quickly made its way round the world, beginning with Buenos Aires in July, where it was conducted by Toscanini with Rosina Storchio restored to the part she had created. But Puccini's revisions had by no means ended. A third edition with further cuts is based on the London première, which took place on 10 July 1905 under Campanini with Emmy Destinn, Enrico Caruso, and Antonio Scotti. This was printed the following year together with an English translation prepared for an American touring company. But it is the fourth edition, resulting from the Paris première on 26 December 1906, that presents the opera as we know it today. Albert Carré, manager of the Opéra Comique, who had seen the London production, insisted on further modifications. Ricordi, then engaged on the printing of a full score, demurred; but Puccini bowed to Carré's wishes. The French edition for voice and piano was followed in 1907 by what has become the standard Italian version, from which it differs hardly at all. However,

[34] GPE 87, p. 156.

that is not the end of the story. A vocal score used for a revival at the Teatro Carcano, Milan, in 1921 contains three manuscript inserts, all taken from the opera's first printed edition together with a note that their re-instatement was authorized by the composer himself. It is therefore impossible to speak of a 'definitive' *Madama Butterfly*. Since the autograph corresponds to the Brescia performance, the original edition cannot be revived without some discreet re-orchestration. The successive alterations will be briefly touched upon in context, so as to measure the distance traversed by the opera from its earliest conception to its current format.

Madama Butterfly is neither a succession of independent tableaux strung on a narrative thread like *Manon Lescaut* and *La bohème*, nor a fast-moving drama of shock and sensation like *Tosca*. It presents an action that evolves steadily, centering the interest on the protagonist from her first appearance onward, even during the rare moments when she is absent from the stage. There are no gaps to be filled by the spectator's imagination, such as the seduction of Manon by Geronte, the recon-ciliations of Tosca and Cavaradossi, or Mimì's desertion of Rodolfo for the Visconte Paolo. The three-year interval between Acts I and II in no way breaks the psychological continuity of the heroine as she pro-ceeds from happiness through steadfast hope to disillusion and death. This allows Puccini to develop his ideas on a larger scale than before and at the same time to further his technique of free association with regard to motifs. The Japanese folk-element adds a fresh colour to the Puccinian spectrum. Be it noted, however, that the native melodies are heard strictly through Western ears and their expressive possibilities ex-ploited accordingly. The character of their original texts bears no rela-tion to the use Puccini makes of them.[35] In this way they become fully integrated into the language of the score instead of remaining extra-neous patches on it.

The scene is a Japanese house with a terrace and gardens overlooking the port of Nagasaki. Goro, the marriage-broker, is explaining and demonstrating to Pinkerton the various appurtenances with a mixture of obsequiousness and self-importance. To convey the sense of bustle

[35] GGP, 216 ff.

Ex. 8.1

Puccini for the first time since *Manon Lescaut* resorts to fugue—a four-part exposition based on a subject whose opening figure (Ex. 8.1) will recur throughout the act, always with Japanese associations. For this is the Lilliputian world of Loti, evoking from Pinkerton nothing but amused contempt—therefore a rapid 2/4 pulse and a prevalence of small intervals. A subsidiary dance-like motif detaches itself from the contrapuntal web, touched in by percussion and eventually terminating in a repeated downward leap on to an unresolved seventh—Goro's incessant bowing, perhaps, with the added hint of a donkey's bray.

Goro's presentation of the three servants (Suzuki and two males) provides the usual smooth Puccinian complement, the slower triple pulse linked to the foregoing by semiquaver fidgets on flute. Pinkerton's offensive comments on their names ('Nomi di scherzo e scherno. Io li chiamerò musi! Muso primo, secondo e muso terzo') were removed from Paris onwards—easily enough, since they were set as unsupported declamation. A return of the fugue subject lets loose a spate of volubility from Suzuki. Since the saying she attributes to the wise Ocunama ('Dei crucci la trama smaglia un sorriso') is adapted from Ugo Foscolo's translation of Lawrence Sterne's *A Sentimental Journey*, Pinkerton's remark ('A chiacchiere costei mi par cosmopolita') is not inappropriate. Mention of the wedding party, expected at any moment, introduces a periodic melody which serves here to give a formal stiffening to a flux of heterogeneous ideas. A theme of chuckling comedy, only one instrument will do to announce it: the bassoon (Ex. 8.2).

While Goro lists the geisha's relations and archly alludes to her future progeny (Pinkerton's responsibility) the orchestra prepares for the arrival of Sharpless, laboriously climbing the hill to a plain marching rhythm. Like Colline's in *La bohème*, his is a casual entrance, the motif associated with him (Ex. 8.3) occurring as a consequent of the phrase that precedes

Ex. 8.2

it. Note the arpeggiated pattern (*x*) characteristic of many of the 'Western' themes in the opera.

The 'bustle' music dwindles to a pause, and a trumpet supported by brass and woodwind proclaims the first line of 'The Star-Spangled Banner' shorn of its upbeat, a recurring motif which will frame Pinkerton's Credo ('Dovunque al mondo'). This is a ternary aria in which an orchestral and a vocal theme dispute the primacy, the first (Ex. 8.4a) treated sequentially, the second (Ex. 8.4b) remaining constant, like a repeated statement of intent. Gone are the hard-boiled commercial expressions of Illica's first draft, while Sharpless's interventions, mostly to Ex. 8.4a, are no longer tolerant but carry a note of reproof ('È un facile vangelo'). But the anthem returns to seal the aria on a note of fellowship ('America for ever!'). However, Sharpless wants to know more. To the medley of motivic recalls that accompany Goro's effusive description of the girl's beauty (cheap at the price, too) Puccini adds a foretaste of Butterfly's naive charm—a simple descending phrase that will recur where she tells the Americans of her family history. Here it prompts the consul to ask his friend if he is really in love. Pinkerton attempts to describe his infatuation in a fleet melody ('Amore o grillo'), dwelling here and there on repeated notes as he searches for the right words. To a broad, widely arched complement in 3/4 time Sharpless recalls hearing Butterfly's voice when she called recently at the consulate and being struck by its sincerity. He concludes with a warning which Pinkerton will not heed until it is too late (Ex. 8.5).

Ex. 8.3

Ex. 8.4a

Ex. 8.4b

Cabaletta-like, the whole period is stated three times with minor variations; and by a cruel irony it is to Ex. 8.5 that the lieutenant looks forward to the day when he will bring home an American wife. From West to East, as Butterfly and her friends are heard approaching. Here Puccini draws on the first of his Japanese folk-tunes. 'The Lion of Echigo' (Ex. 8.6a), a dance theme from the Kabuki theatre featuring the peculiar intervals of the Japanese pentatonic *In*-scale. A second idea (Ex. 8.6b) derived from the same source will be exploited for its emotional charge later on.

Having applied the label 'Made in Japan', Puccini reverts to a cosmopolitan style for the entry of Butterfly and her companions—an

Ex. 8.5

Ex. 8.6a

Ex. 8.6b

outpouring of sustained lyricism without parallel in his previous operas. A two-bar pattern (Ex. 8.7a) worked into rising sequences generates a long-breathed melody carried by Butterfly herself (Ex. 8.8a). Both ideas were modified after the première (see Ex. 8.7b and 8.8b). The first now has a smoother line, while the second takes up a decoration of one of the previous sequences, bringing to it a sense of logical fulfilment.

Ex. 8.7a

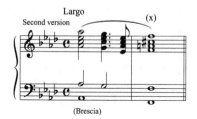

Ex. 8.7b

Ex. 8.8a

Ex. 8.8b

Clearly the audience's cries of '*Bohème!*' had rendered the composer a real service.

In making Butterfly heard before she is seen Puccini was doing nothing new. But by allowing her voice to emerge from what is essentially a tone-picture he achieved a perfect fusion of 'Ausdruck der Empfindung' with 'Malerei'. Ex. 8.7a, diaphanously scored, conjures up the vast expanse of sea and sky on which the female chorus exclaim ('Quanto cielo! quanto mar!'), the augmented fifth (*x*) with its cluster of whole tones adding to the suggestion of infinity, while all the loving warmth of Butterfly's disposition is in Ex. 8.8a. Dovetailed into its final cadence is a postlude (Ex. 8.9) adapted from a Japanese song to the spring. Based on the familiar 'black note' pentatonic scale, common to folksongs the world over, it seals the blend of East and West that informs

Ex. 8.9

the whole paragraph from Ex. 8.6a onward. If flutes, piccolo, bells, and harp with octave grace-notes give the melody an exotic flavour, the harmonies together with the expressive C flat (x) are strictly European. No theme will depict more movingly Butterfly's attempt to reach out into the world of her lover. It comes to rest on a cadence of Puccini's own coining (anticipated in *Tosca*), in whose last chord the dominant note is replaced by the 'frozen sixth', suggesting, as Carner aptly observes, a faint question mark.

The exposition proceeds in alternating stretches of leisurely dialogue and rapid ensemble. In a plain discourse compounded of previous motifs and fragments of folk-melody Butterfly tells her life story to the two Americans. Her claim to noble birth (universal amongst her people, she admits) is underlined by Ex. 8.6a, the storms that overturn the stoutest oak by Ex. 8.6b, now sorrowful. So she was forced to earn her living as a geisha. And her father? 'Dead.' To hint at what will later be explained Puccini again resorts to an authentic Japanese model, a 'Spring Song' which he invests with a sense of sinister finality (Ex. 8.10).

The first three editions offer a diversion in which the subject moves to Butterfly's two uncles: the Bonze—'a monster of wisdom', say her companions, though a jaunty, Japanese-comic quotation of Ex. 8.9 suggests that they do not take him very seriously; and the disreputable Yakusidé, who rates a motif of his own. But since it is neither memorable nor characteristic its subsequent removal is not a matter for regret. The definitive version passes directly to Sharpless, who asks Butterfly her age. Her artless prevarication is conducted over a light pattern of soft dissonances—seventh inversions for the consul's guesses, whole-tone chords for Butterfly's 'Quindici anni netti! . . . Sono vecchia diggià!' A burst of dancing semiquavers reacts to the childish quip with a ripple of laughter.

Once again the editions diverge. Another 38 bars were removed for

Ex. 8.10

Paris where Pinkerton called for the 'three mugs' ('musi') to bring in the comestibles—spiders, candied flies, birds' nests in syrup, all of which he finds disgusting. Nothing was lost here musically except a permutation of previous material.

Goro next announces the Imperial Commissioner, the Marriage Registrar, and Butterfly's abundant family. The Commissioner is tagged by the second phrase of the Japanese national anthem (Ex. 8.11a) harmonized in the Western manner, the Registrar to a unison fragment from the folksong 'The High Mountain' (Ex. 8.11b), which will be put to very different use in Act II. Under the sardonic gaze of Pinkerton ('Che burletta!') the relatives pour in to the comic strains of Ex. 8.2, each beat picked out by glinting woodwind grace-notes. Three ensembles of chatter build up amid Goro's vain attempts to impose silence. The first two are dominated by Ex. 8.2 treated in canon at a bar's distance; to this the second adds a pseudo-Japanese motif of festive character later appropriated by Goro; the third is enveloped by a broad melody initiated by Sharpless ('Amico fortunato!'), whose smooth rhythm, wide intervals, and rising arpeggio mark it as an American theme in marked contrast to the Japanese patter. Order is restored by Butterfly herself, as she bids the company to make obeisance to the two Americans ('Un . . . due . . . tre . . . , e tutti giù!').

From here on the scene was subjected to successive cuts, which may be indicated as follows:

Milan (50 bars): Goro brings forward the two officials and hands them their fees to a variant of 'The Star-Spangled Banner'. A ceremony of bowing

Ex. 8.11a

Ex. 8.11b

follows that threatens to become endless until Pinkerton protests his inability to continue. Much of the music is unharmonized and exotically coloured by the Lydian raised fourth.

Milan, Brescia, London (48 bars): Butterfly presents to Pinkerton her mother, her cousin, and the cousin's child ('Ec-cel-len-za', unpitched from the child at Milan, from the mother at Brescia and London). Next it is Yakusidé's turn to be introduced together with his motif. He echoes Pinkerton's mocking laughter, taking it for a compliment, and breaks into a profusion of absurd courtesies, a fidget in the bass suggesting that he is not quite steady on his feet. 'God, how stupid they are!' Pinkerton exclaims, while Ex. 8.3 indicates that his remark is addressed to Sharpless.

Milan, Brescia (42 bars): The guests make a dash for the tables and fall on the refreshments with eager cries. Sharpless presents the Commissioner and Registrar to 'Sir Francis Blummy Pinkerton' ('Benjamin Franklin Pinkerton' at Brescia). 'The Star-Spangled Banner', beginning in rudimentary canon, is answered by the Registrar's Ex. 8.11b. Sharpless then retires with Goro and the two officials to prepare the documents—this to six bars of 'consul' music that were retained for London.

All these passages were removed from the Paris edition, which proceeds straight to where Pinkerton and his bride are left alone with Goro lurking in the vicinity. Ex. 8.7a, softly and translucently scored, indicates that the lieutenant has turned his full attention to Butterfly. In the first three editions he offers her sweetmeats, which with some embarrassment she declines. In the final version he leads her towards the house to the same music as before, and asks her whether she likes it ('Vi piace la casetta?'), so eliminating a pointless piece of business. Her 'Signor F. B. Pinkerton . . . ' (the order of initials uncorrected except in the American edition) is spoken from a full heart beneath a wide melodic sweep from the clarinet. She then proceeds to unload the contents of her long sleeves.

In the 'andantino', during which Butterfly displays her 'tiny objects' one by one, Puccini adumbrates a technique adopted in his last operas, whereby large stretches are built from spaced out repetitions of a single motif, here two bars of Puccinian *japonnerie* (Ex 8.12). A genuine folk-song, 'The Cherry Blossom', is integrated into the design as an episode (Ex. 8.13). As she produces a long, narrow sheath the orchestra sends

Ex. 8.12

up a danger signal: two plunging descents across an augmented fourth, unmistakeably the 'diabolus in musica'. Butterfly disappears into the house with the offending object, and it is Goro who whispers to Pinkerton the explanation. The sheath contains a present to her father from the Mikado 'with the invitation . . . ' and he draws his hand upwards across his stomach. 'And her father?' 'He obeyed.' Ex. 8.10 resumed on pizzicato strings beneath a sustained wind unison tells the rest. Having returned, Butterfly displays the last of her possessions, the images of her ancestors. She then confides to Pinkerton her secret visit to the Christian mission over a pattern of unrelated chord-inversions that carry a sense of loneliness and pathos to be recalled in Act II (Ex. 8.14). This is her language at its most touching.

What follows was drastically curtailed after the première. Originally there were two full statements of Ex. 8.9, here making its most significant appearance in the opera as a noble declaration of faith. From the second edition onward the statements were reduced to one ('Io seguo il mio destino') and the preceding text cut except for the all-important 'Lo zio Bonzo nol sa, ne i miei lo sanno'—in Milan a 'parlante' within the first statement of Ex. 8.9, thereafter three bars of timorous declamation preceding its opening strain. For Paris there were further changes to the text. Where Butterfly had promised to live economically,

Ex. 8.13

Ex. 8.14

she now declares that she will pray in the same church as Pinkerton and to the same God. So much is an improvement. More questionable is the substitution of 'Amore mio!' for the original 'E questi via!', where she had thrown away the images, so provoking the savage outburst of Ex. 8.10. Now she merely lets them drop while the theme is already sounding.

The routine solemnity of the wedding ceremony is enlivened, Puccini-fashion, by a tiny gesture on Japanese bells echoed by flute and harp and repeated at intervals. At Milan and Brescia the proceedings were interrupted by ten bars of comedy in which Yakusidé and the child are noticed helping themselves to sweets, to the shocked dismay of all present and the mother's anger. From the third edition onward this episode vanished.

The contract signed, friends of the bride offer their felicitations to 'Madama Butterfly', which she coyly corrects to 'Madama F. B. Pin-kerton', never more Japanese than when she imagines herself American; hence another native folksong, 'The Nihon Bridge at Oedo' (Ex. 8.15). Sharpless signs off with the music that first introduced him. The two officials likewise take their leave, the Registrar with a polite augury for the young couple's posterity (Ex. 811a); and a recollection of Ex. 8.11b gives an edge to the consul's final warning—'Giudizio!'

Ex. 8.15

Milan, Brescia, London (60 bars): The 6/8 material of the previous interruption is expanded as Pinkerton proceeds to enjoy himself at his new family's expense. He gives a bottle of whisky to Yakusidé, who quickly gets drunk on its contents, watched by his relatives with mingled amusement and repulsion. The lieutenant then proposes mixing a drink for his mother-in-law, but Butterfly restrains him. He offers refreshment to some of the women. Yakusidé tries to forestall them, only to be driven back with cries of 'Il beone!' ('the drunkard!'), while Goro warns their host not to encourage him. After showering more sweets on the Awful Child, Pinkerton raises his glass with a 'Ip! ip!'

The editions converge for the toast ('O Kami! o Kami!), a smooth chant repeated in different keys and distributed between Pinkerton and his guests. For Paris, however, ten new bars were added to allow the lieutenant to cut a more respectable figure. Accordingly, his 'Sbrighiamoci al più presto in modo onesto' is no longer spoken in ironic parentheses but addressed to all with apparent good humour.

Milan (48 bars): Butterfly, embarrassed by the entire proceedings, timidly reminds her consort that the hour is late; but Pinkerton has not yet had his fill of entertainment. He asks for a song from the drunken Yakusidé, who is only too ready to oblige. 'All'ombra d'un Keki' celebrates the pretty girls of Nanki-Nunko-Yama; but the singer is in no fit state to sustain the melody, which is therefore entrusted to the orchestra. Much diverted, Pinkerton calls for and is granted a repeat; but this time Yakusidé breaks off before the end, having noticed the cousin's child making off with the whisky bottle. General laughter, frozen by the sound of the Zio Bonzo's distant voice ('Cio-Cio-San . . . Cio-Cio-San . . . Abbominazione!').

In subsequent editions the third statement of 'O Kami! o Kami!' terminates on a tremolando of violins and violas. At the Bonze's cry, each 'Cio-Cio-San!' followed by a stroke of the gong, the guests gather into a frightened huddle. Only Goro protests angrily before beating a prudent retreat. At length the Bonze appears (alone in the first three editions, with a small retinue in the last) and confronts Butterfly menacingly. What was she doing at the Mission? 'She has dishonoured us all and our ancient cult!' Friends and relatives shrink away from her with howls of horror. Among the brutal orchestral gestures one (Ex.

Ex. 8.16

8.16) stands out as a 'rejection' motif. Whole-tone harmony was by no means new to Puccini. But so far it had been little more than an impressionistic blurring of the musical contours. Here, situated within a minor-key context, its capacity to express negative emotion is for the first time fully exploited. Ordered off the premises by their host the family disperses towards the harbour to a thunderous explosion of the baleful Ex. 8.10—a proleptic death-sentence, their imprecations (Ex. 8.16) persisting like the waves of a receding tide.

Comforted by Pinkerton, Butterfly dries her tears ('Non piango più. E quasi del ripudio non mi duole per vostre parole'), and the strings match her words, soothing the cruel outlines of Ex. 8.10 with suave harmonies. Within the house Suzuki can be heard murmuring prayers to her ancestral gods, while quiet recollections of the opera's opening music re-establish a happier atmosphere.

As in *La bohème*, Puccini divides his first act into two areas: the first 'kinetic' with a wealth of incident and an array of characters, the second a 'static' scene confined to two principals. The ensuing love-duet is rightly regarded as Puccini's finest. As with its counterpart in Verdi's *Otello*, an inspired succession of lyrical ideas is governed by a firm underlying structure, interwoven, as Verdi's is not, with motivic recalls, Of its four sections I and II present variants of ternary design, III a large-scale *Bogenform*, and IV a climactic reprise of the music associated with Butterfly's first appearance.

Section I, laid out as A–A1–B–A2, finds Butterfly at her evening toilet, assisted by Suzuki and watched by the enraptured Pinkerton. The main period, 'Viene la sera' (A), is a three-limbed melody (another point of contact with the mature Verdi) entrusted to the orchestra, on which the two singers engage in hushed 'parlanti melodici'. But the

Ex. 8.17

Westernized pentatonic contour of the long third phrase with its hem-iola rhythm (Ex. 8.17) assign it spiritually to Butterfly in her role as Pinkerton's wife. In B with its ebb and flow of syncopations a snatch of Ex. 8.1 on oboe brings a touch of nocturnal mystery, like the distant cry of a night-bird; while in A2 a momentary recollection of the family's curse (Ex. 8.16) is answered by a serene cadence in the major key—a neat illustration of Butterfly's 'rinnegata . . . e felice!'.

The principal theme of Section II ('Bimba dagli occhi pieni di malìa') belongs unequivocally to Pinkerton, an expression of ardour sited in the most grateful register of the tenor voice and moving mainly by step. Here the design (A–B–A1) is more fluid, A merging into B without an intervening full close, B wandering through distant keys until recalled to the tonic with renewed urgency by A1. Butterfly, it seems, is trying to delay the moment of total surrender, afraid to offer words of love lest they bring death. 'Foolish fear!' Pinkerton retorts; 'love brings life, not death.' Here a new theme in 6/8 opens Section III on a note of warm re-assurance. And how clear-sighted of Puccini to have altered Ex. 8.7a(x) so that it now looks forward to the apex of the present idea (Ex. 8.18)!

Pinkerton is about to caress Butterfly's cheek when, to his surprise, she shrinks back. But why, since her next words are 'Adesso voi siete per me l'occhio del firmamento'? For answer we must turn to the duet in its pre-Parisian form, where Butterfly is struck by the sudden mem-ory of her aversion to marrying an American—'a barbarian, a wasp!' A twisting line over an ostinato of alternating chords, recalled in the intermezzo of Act II (see Ex. 8.26), gives way to 'The Star-Spangled

Ex. 8.18

Banner'. 'And then?' from Pinkerton. The rising arpeggiated figure that accompanies her change of heart can here be heard as an ennobled transformation of the American anthem's opening strain. In the standard version the connection is lost, and the word 'Adesso' makes no sense. Carner is not alone in regretting the elimination of those 37 bars, which breaks both the musical and textual continuity. In authorizing their reinstatement for the Teatro Carcano Puccini might well have been swayed by artistic considerations.

The music mounts to a climax that dissolves into the hexatonic Ex. 8.16 as Butterfly seems to hear once more the curses of her family; but she quickly recovers and resumes her adulation of Pinkerton ('Siete alto, forte. Ridete con modi si palesi'). Her melody will not recur in the course of the duet, but its final phrase with its suggestion of wistful longing will figure prominently in the second act (Ex. 8.19).

So to the still heart of the duet ('Vogliatemi bene, un bene piccolino'), comparable to the central 'cantabile' of the post-Rossinian age. Its theme, many times repeated, is first announced by a solo violin accompanied by muted upper strings—a symbol of the mite of affection that Butterfly craves from her spouse (Ex. 8.20). 'My Butterfly', Pinkerton exclaims, 'how rightly they have named you!' But surely, Butterfly objects, in the West butterflies are often impaled by a pin; and here the association of the rising arpeggio figure and Ex. 8.16 has a new meaning. Pinkerton's reassuring reply proceeds to a reprise of the 6/8

Ex. 8.19

Ex. 8.20

melody that opened the section, which in turn ushers in the culminating sequence of Exx. 8.7–8.9, precisely as at Butterfly's entrance. The first is assigned to Butterfly herself as she contemplates the stars; the second is sung by both voices mostly in an ecstatic unison, the last is an orchestral postlude dying away to a languorous close, as the two singers move slowly towards the house. But the hidden question mark remains.

Act II is set inside Butterfly's house after an interval of three years. A brief prelude points up the contrast between the decently appointed dwelling of Act I, where all is bustle and liveliness, and the threadbare state to which it is now reduced. Again there is the suggestion of a fugal exposition, beginning with the same three notes: but the texture is discontinuous, the scoring thin, and the counterpoint non-existent. Memories of the 'rejection' (Ex. 8.16) fade into fragments of Ex. 8.19, the motif of Butterfly's longing. To the Registrar's folk-tune 'The High Mountain' (Ex. 8.11b), here extended and harmonized over a minor-key ostinato, Suzuki is intoning prayers to her gods, now and then ringing a hand-bell to attract their attention. Butterfly attempts to put a brave face on their plight; but her anguish continually breaks through in an orchestral gesture that dominates their dialogue (Ex. 8.21). In between its recurrences, whose emphasis is progressively stepped up by rhythmic diminution, there is room for other recollections: the opera's

Ex. 8.21

Ex. 8.22

initial Ex. 8.1 as Suzuki replaces the money-box with its meagre contents; the consul's Ex. 8.3 where Butterfly alludes to his regular payment
of their rent; a blossoming of Ex. 8.7a to which she dwells on Pinkerton's concern for their safety. Finally she reminds her maid how on the
eve of his departure he had promised to return in the season of roses,
when the robins build their nests—a promise that merits a motif of
hope and tenderness (Ex. 8.22).

While flute, oboe, and pizzicati violins chirrup in seconds Butterfly
orders Suzuki to repeat her 'tornerà'. Suzuki does so, only to burst into
tears. Her maid's lack of faith elicits from Butterfly the opera's most
celebrated number, 'Un bel dì vedremo', in which she pictures Pinkerton's return, from the plume of smoke sighted on the horizon to
the moment when he takes her in his arms. Throughout the ternary
plan the sense of progression is maintained. The opening strain is an
archetypal Puccinian cantilena with its protracted descent in the manner
of Manon's 'In quelle trine morbide'; but here the doubling of the outer
parts combined with the rarefied scoring gives the effect of a melody
suspended in mid-air like a distant vision. Within the discourse Puccini
accommodates two recalls: the 'promise' (Ex. 8.22) and the motif of
longing (Ex. 8.19), here approached from a major key with the additional qualities of hope and of a 'madrigalism' portraying Pinkerton's
ascent of the hill. Its conclusion will be echoed fortissimo in a brief
codetta; and her longing finds imaginary fulfilment in an orchestral
peroration with the opening strain a triumphant 'sviolinata' doubled by
woodwind, trumpets, and horns over a tonic pedal.

Reality returns with Sharpless's visiting-card (Ex. 8.3); and a handful
of motifs associated with Goro and the wedding-party indicate that the
marriage-broker is also in attendance. The consul knocks and enters.
Butterfly corrects his salutation as she had corrected those of her friends
('Madama Pinkerton') and to the same folk-tune (Ex. 8.15). Their

Ex. 8.23

exchange of small talk while she does the honours brings in several new themes, one of which, adapted from the Japanese song 'My Prince', deserves particular attention (Ex. 8.23). There is a certain similarity here to the opening bars of Sullivan's *The Mikado*. Both ideas are 'black note pentatonic', and both to Western ears imply comic ceremony. Butterfly is convinced that she is playing the American hostess; yet she enquires after Sharpless's ancestors and offers him a pipe. Twenty bars later she will sing the same melody in joyful response to the news that Sharpless has received a letter from Pinkerton ('Io sono la donna più lieta di Giappone!'). After that the motif will be assigned to Prince Yamadori, who shares her pretensions to Western culture.

The civilities over, Butterfly comes to the point with her first question: how often in America do the robins build their nests? To the 'promise' motif (Ex. 8.22) framed by orchestral twitterings she gives her reason for asking. Sharpless replies evasively, the orchestra falling silent to allow Butterfly's difficulty with the word 'ornitologia' to emerge. She goes on to describe the offers of marriage she has received ever since Pinkerton's departure, mostly at Goro's suggestion; and here Goro himself intervenes alluding to the misery to which she has been reduced (Ex. 8.21 linked to recollections of Ex. 8.16). But before that Ex. 8.23 has already prepared the entrance of Yamadori, who arrives in state, parading the same theme majestically beneath tremolando violins and woodwind arpeggios with offbeats marked by a stroke on the cymbals. Butterfly, now in the highest of spirits, greets him to grandiose, almost Wagnerian gestures (clearly this is not his first visit). Surely he has never lacked for wives. 'I married them all', he replies with dignity, 'but now divorce has set me free.' 'The Lion of Echigo' from Act I (Ex. 8.6a) on muted trumpet taunts him with its *japonnerie*, while its consequent (Ex. 8.6b) reflects the consul's despair of being able to go through with his unpleasant task. Butterfly explains in detail how in *her* country (i.e., the United States) any man wishing to divorce his wife is hauled before a magistrate and sent to prison. (The naiveté of this passage was too much for Carré, who wanted it expunged. Puccini was inclined to agree—after all it amounts musically to no more than a few two- and three-chord ostinati and a hint of the American anthem—but Ricordi persuaded him to retain it.)

While Butterfly and Suzuki attend to the tea for their visitors, Goro, Yamadori, and Sharpless confer in whispers to a waltz-like theme that shades off into whole-tone harmony. Pinkerton's ship has been signalled; but he has no intention of returning to his former bride; and Sharpless has come to break the news to her as gently as possible. Butterfly offers the tea to her guests, making it clear, however, that she wishes to see the last of Goro and Yamadori ('Che persone moleste!'). The Prince takes his leave with Ex. 8.23, now a sentimental Andante elaborately harmonized in a parody of the Western manner. A reprise of Butterfly's ceremonious bow fades into the consul's Ex. 8.3; and to music that, by a cruel irony, recalls Pinkerton's words of comfort spoken during the love-duet, Sharpless tries to prepare her for the ordeal ahead. If his reading of the letter, constantly interrupted by an eager and impatient Butterfly, is one of the most moving moments in the opera, the reason lies in the radiant simplicity of the melodic thread drawn by solo bassoon beneath an arpeggiated rise and fall of pizzicato strings, a pathetic emblem of faith in a prospect that the audience knows to be illusory. A typical Puccinian anticipation, it will be expanded to form the famous 'humming chorus' that precedes Butterfly's all-night vigil.

Sharpless soon realizes the uselessness of continuing, and his 'Quel diavolo d'un Pinkerton!' here means precisely what it says. He decides to cut the knot with a direct question. What would Butterfly do if Pinkerton should never return? A unison thud on strings and timpani is sufficient to convey the deadly import of his words. Butterfly remains motionless while clarinets and bassoons set up an ostinato pattern jerking to and from a baleful D minor chord. She could do two things: go back to her life as a geisha or die. Helplessly, Sharpless advises her to accept Yamadori's offer. Butterfly's first reaction is to show him the door; but she quickly thinks better of it and accepts his excuses—only he had hurt her so very deeply. In all this the music in no way reflects the twists and turns of the dialogue; rather it depicts the growing an-

Ex. 8.24

guish that engulfs Butterfly like a tidal wave (note the persistence of a tonic pedal as in the torture scene in *Tosca*). But, she declares, it will soon pass, like clouds over the sea, though hexatonic triads rising and falling over a dominant seventh seem to give her the lie.

Then she has a sudden thought. She runs from the room and returns with a small child—Pinkerton's. Here a variant of Ex. 8.7a generates a new theme of authentic Japanese derivation, to be associated from now on with the infant (Ex. 8.24). Variously intertwined with other reminiscences, sometimes breaking into excited triplets, it illumines Butterfly's proud display of her offspring. Pinkerton must be given news of him; that will surely bring him back. Then she turns to the boy. 'Do you know what this gentleman has suggested? That your mother should carry you round the city in wind and rain while she entertains a heedless public with her singing.' This is hardly fair, since Sharpless had suggested nothing of the sort; but it prompts one of the finest pages of the score: a ternary aria ('Che tua madre') in which for the first time there are intimations of high tragedy. Pentatonic in contour, it takes in not only a quotation of the infant's theme but another genuine folk-tune, entitled 'Pathetic Melody', which will conclude the opera like a death-blow (Ex. 8.25). In the first three versions Butterfly imagines an encounter between her child and the Mikado, who takes him to his palace to be raised as the handsomest prince in the land (all this from Long, where it is spoken to Suzuki in rapturous pidgin-English). But the music with its prevailing minor-key orientation seems to tell a very different story—one of ever-deepening sorrow. Whether or not at Carré's in-

Ex. 8.25

stance, the text was changed for the final edition. Butterfly now dwells on the misery of a geisha's life and declares that she would rather die.

Before departing (Ex. 8.3), the consul asks the child's name. 'Dolore', his mother replies, but when Pinkerton returns it will be 'Gioia'; and the melody of 'Un bel dì', blazing triumphantly on four horns, tells us that she has no doubts on the matter.

No sooner has Sharpless left than a furious Suzuki bursts in dragging Goro ('Vespa! . . . Rospo maledetto!'). He has been telling everyone that nobody knows who is the father of Butterfly's child. Butterfly pounces on him and hurls him to the ground, drawing a knife and threatening to kill him; but Suzuki intervenes and he takes to his heels. The incident is dispatched over insistent patterns of Ex. 8.16 combined with a stabbing figure of three notes. A chain of accelerating sequences is cut short by the sound of gunfire. 'The harbour cannon!' Suzuki exclaims. The melody of 'Un bel dì' steals in pianissimo on flute, first violins, and violas over a shimmering tremolando, gathering strength and volume as everything seems to be happening just as Butterfly had foretold. With the aid of a telescope she makes out the name of the approaching ship—'Abraham Lincoln' ('Connecticut' in Belasco). The American anthem, merging into rising sequences of Ex. 8.6a winds up the paragraph on a note of triumph.

Butterfly's immediate thought is to deck the house with flowers. The so-called 'flower duet' is a lyrical fantasia, wide ranging in its tonality, each melodic idea springing spontaneously from the last. From a prefatory period in common time ('Scuoti quella fronda di ciliegio') the music proceeds through 3/4 to 6/8 for the main discourse, in which, as in 'Dovunque al mondo', two themes vie in importance. Rising, ever-tightening sequences culminate in a serene epilogue ('Gettiamo a mani piene mammole e tuberose') in which Puccini for the first and only time resorts to the age-old Italian device of linking two female voices in melting thirds.

For the London performance the design was tautened by two cuts, both of them beneficial. For Paris it was then expanded by 18 bars of orchestra for purely scenic reasons. Suzuki had been bidden to 'strip the garden'; but her numerous interventions had prevented her from proceeding further than the terrace, so that her 'Spoglio è l'orto' made no sense. Accordingly Puccini added 18 bars of orchestra to give her plausible time to carry out her orders.

About to attend to her toilet, Butterfly asks for the child to be brought to her (not in the Milan version, however, since he is already there). She looks into her mirror. How grief has changed her! In the first two editions a burst of hysteria ('Suzuki, fammi bella, fammi bella, fammi bella!') is answered by the maid with a soothing 'Gioia, riposo accrescono beltà'—an exchange eliminated from London onward. As Suzuki sets to work her mistress's spirits rise. What will all her relations think (Ex. 8.16)—and Prince Yamadori (Ex. 8.23)? (This passage too was curtailed for London with the loss of two further motivic references to Goro and the wedding festivities.) She calls for her bridal dress to the music of 'Viene la sera'. In the first two editions the melody is broken off for Butterfly to sing the child a nursery song ('È Roje un bimbo biondo'), then resumed a semitone above. In the third edition it proceeds, as now, uninterrupted, beginning in the higher key. A slow orchestral transition follows as Butterfly bores three holes in the *shosi*, through which she, Suzuki, and the child will watch 'like little mice' for Pinkerton's arrival. The mood is curiously desolate, as though filled with memories of past misery (Ex. 8.16 and a particularly poignant utterance of Ex. 8.21); but it eventually settles into the tranquillity of the 'humming chorus', a 50-bar cantilena sung without interruption amid the failing light by wordless voices behind the scenes with the lightest of orchestral accompaniments. Here is Butterfly, steadfast in her illusion. The curtain falls on total darkness.

Or so it does today, and has done ever since the Brescia revival. In the Milan edition the chorus is seven bars shorter, the last upbeat leading into 'The Lion of Echigo' (Ex. 8.6a) followed, as before, by Ex. 8.6b, at which point Suzuki wakes from a brief sleep, goes to light a few lanterns, and returns to keep watch beside her mistress.

The revision cuts straight to Ex. 8.6b, now a fortissimo flourish by way of opening to an intermezzo played for most of its length before a lowered curtain. The piece falls into two parts, one reflective, the other pictorial. The first begins and ends with coiling sequences of the 'repulsion' motif that Puccini excised from the love-duet (Ex. 8.26). If this has any relevance in the first three editions it has none in the last. The main burden, however, is carried by a new idea set out in Puccini's

Ex. 8.26

favourite waltz rhythm with a characteristic 'lift' towards the end of the first phrase. This is worked up into a rhetorical climax in the standard post-Wagnerian manner, interwoven with recollections of the past deployed so as to suggest the confusion of a waking dream. The pictorial phase opens with the cries of sailors rising from the harbour—an effect more probably derived from Act I of *Tristan und Isolde*, rather than *Pelléas et Mélisande*, which Puccini had not yet seen. From Brescia onwards this passage too was modified and a snatch of Yamadori's Ex. 8.23 discarded. Ten hushed bars of transition end with the eternally pregnant Ex. 8.19—longing, wonderment, a question mark? The listener is free to choose.

By now the curtain has risen, revealing Butterfly still gazing out to sea, while Suzuki and the child have fallen asleep. For the sunrise that follows Puccini availed himself of what amounts to a 'topos': an arpeggio figure with ancillary notes from the pentatonic scale (compare the 'Inno del sole' from Mascagni's *Iris* and 'Morning' from Grieg's *Peer Gynt* music). But the busy two-note figure (Ex. 8.27 (*x*)) reveals this as a Japanese sun, presiding over a wealth of bustling activity. The stage lights up gradually as the theme is propelled from key to key in a long crescendo, interspersed with Ex. 8.9, transformed into a jaunty background to the twittering of birds. For Brescia the sequences were pro-

Ex. 8.27

gressively shortened and a 17-bar coda added to round off what had become a separate piece. The two-note figure from Ex. 8.27 provides an orchestral gesture, its harmonies heavy with fatigue, during which the characters stir to life. Butterfly sings the child a lullaby ('Dormi, amor mio') evolved from Ex. 8.24 and ending with a cadential tag from Suzuki ('Povera Butterfly!'). After the first performance this too was abbreviated and the melody distributed to better effect between voice and orchestra. Butterfly leaves the room with the child in her arms.

Over the scene that follows Puccini spins a sad-sweet commentary of purely Western cut. Pinkerton and Sharpless enter on tiptoe. In a subdued conversation Suzuki tells them of Butterfly's all-night vigil, her anxious scanning of the horizon over the past three years; and she points to the flowers strewn about the room. 'Did I not tell you?', from Sharpless to Pinkerton. Fragments of the 'flower duet' falter, and then give way to agitated string pulsations as Suzuki notices a woman in the garden. It is Sharpless who reveals to her the bitter truth ('È sua moglie'). He explains that they had called early (Ex. 8.27) to enlist her help in preparing Butterfly for the blow. 'Che giova?', she repeats dully over a bleak minor triad of horns. There follows a vocal terzetto in the old concertato style, each singer being assigned a different text. Sharpless leads off with the melody that opened the scene, declaring that, while there can be no consolation for Butterfly, they must secure a future for the infant; Pinkerton gazes around him with feelings of remorse and nostalgia; Suzuki dwells on the cruelty of depriving a mother of her child.

The sequel was radically altered in the Brescia revision. In the first edition the agitated pulsations associated with Suzuki's alarm return for Pinkerton to tell Sharpless how the situation has brought him to tears, which he does not easily shed. All he can do is to give the consul some money to keep Butterfly from poverty; he himself dares not approach her. Two precipitate scales mark his retreat, hand on forehead, to the words 'Sono stordito! addio, mi passerà'. A distortion of 'The Star-Spangled Banner' comments on what must be the least dignified exit of a leading tenor in all opera. The remedy, undertaken for Brescia, gave the composer considerable trouble. Giacosa's revised text failed to satisfy him; and, as so often in the past, it was Illica who provided the lines for the new romanza ('Addio fiorito asil') in a metre specified by Puccini. Now more composed, Pinkerton hands the money to Sharpless over a string tremolando with brief recalls of his Ex. 8.6b on woodwind and horns to indicate his distress. Sharpless replies with a reprise of his solo in the duet 'Amor o grillo', here worded retrospectively and ending as before with his admonitory Ex. 8.11. Again Pinkerton expresses his contrition, which he now declares will *not* pass. Before leaving he delivers his footlight romanza, interlaced with a quotation from the 'flower duet' and a vestige of the distorted American anthem, Sharpless meanwhile nudging him with constant reminders. If 'Addio fiorito asil' adds nothing to the drama, its air of sincerity does something to rehabilitate the singer's character.

As before the music comes to rest on a cloudy dissonance of piled-up thirds over a tonic bass tramp, as Suzuki comes in from the garden with Kate Pinkerton. Words now take precedence over music, reducing the score to illustrative gestures touched in with minute thematic recollections. While Kate promises to care for the child as for one of her own and Suzuki consents to broach the subject with his mother we hear reiterations of the almost forgotten Ex. 8.1 and a solitary reference to Ex. 8.8a. Butterfly's voice is heard calling for her maid. Ignoring Suzuki's attempts to restrain her, she hurries down the stairs to search the room for Pinkerton. But there is no sign of him—only the consul and an unknown woman at whom she gazes with fear and foreboding. Harsh trumpet triads fade into shreds of the 'rejection' motif (Ex. 8.16). 'Who are you? . . . How beautiful she is!' (Milan); 'Who are you? . . . Why have you come?' (Brescia and London); 'That lady! . . . What does she want of me?' (Paris).

The encounter between the two women had caused Puccini concern from the beginning. From a letter written to Giacosa it seems that he wanted Butterfly let down as lightly as possible; and it was not until the Paris production that he arrived at the definitive text through a progressive reduction of Kate Pinkerton's role. First, however, seeing Sharpless about to break the silence, Butterfly begs him to spare her the truth, lest she fall dead on the instant. To a chord-sequence recalling the 'lonely' Ex. 8.14 she turns to Suzuki 'with affectionate and child-like kindness'. Is Pinkerton alive? Yes. But he will not return? A burst of anger at Suzuki's silence stirs the score into activity. Then comes the answer: he will not. But he has arrived? Yes.

Here the editions begin once more to diverge. Butterfly asks who is the blonde woman ('blonde' cut for Paris) who causes her so much fear. In the first three versions it is Kate herself who replies that she is the cause of her rival's misfortune. She approaches Butterfly, who shrinks from her touch. And how long has she been married to Pinkerton? A year. 'And will you let me do nothing for the child?' Kate asks (Ex. 8.24, suave on strings); 'I would tend him with loving care' (Pinkerton's Ex. 8.4a on cor anglais, its American flavour now bittersweet). 'It is very sad, but it is for his own good' (the despairing Ex. 8.21 merging into Ex. 8.16). 'Who knows?' Butterfly murmurs. 'All is now over.' To Kate's plea for forgiveness she replies (and still does), 'No woman beneath the vault of heaven is happier than you; be happy always and do not grieve for me. I would like you to tell [your husband] that I shall find peace.' Kate holds out her hand, but Butterfly refuses to take it. She would, however, give up her son if Pinkerton would come himself to claim him; let him come up the hill in half an hour (Ex. 8.19 in the bass, a 'madrigalism' as in 'Un bel dì vedremo', but now beneath a minor chord).

In the versions for Milan and Brescia Suzuki escorts Kate to the door, leaving Sharpless behind to hand over Pinkerton's money, which Butterfly gently refuses. To his question would he see her again she gives the same reply that she had given to Kate: and to the same motif. In London this passage was eliminated, so that Kate and Sharpless leave together and there is no talk of money.

For Paris the text was radically revised and some of the music cut. Now it is Sharpless who describes Kate as the innocent cause of Butterfly's suffering and begs forgiveness on her behalf. In place of 'Do not touch me!' Butterfly exclaims to the same notes 'Ah, she is his wife!' She no longer asks how long Kate and Pinkerton have been married, but merely murmurs that for her all is dead and finished, while Sharpless bids her take courage. To the infant's Ex. 8.24, scored and harmonized as before, she laments that they will take everything from her—even her child. Kate's 'Io lo terrei con cura affettuosa' becomes Sharpless's 'Fatelo pel suo bene il sacrifizio' and her 'È triste cosa . . . ma fatelo pel suo meglio' Butterfly's 'Ah triste madre . . . Abbandonar mio figlio!', followed by 'E sia! . . . A lui devo obbedir', instead of 'Chissa! Tutto è compiuto ormai!' Kate's first words are 'Potete perdonarmi, Butterfly?' In this way her encounter with the heroine is handled far more delicately than before without rendering the succession of motifs any less appposite. A cut of six bars eliminates her offer of her hand to Butterfly and Butterfly's refusal of it.

Alone with Suzuki Butterfly falls to the floor in a fit of desperate weeping. Here beneath pounding syncopations Ex. 8.19, hexatonically harmonized, takes on yet another significance, illustrating Suzuki's comparison of her mistress's beating heart to a trapped bird—aptly, since from a succession of whole-tone chords there is no obvious way out. Butterfly complains that there is too much light (Ex. 8.27, softly dissonant over a tonic pedal). 'Where is the child?' she asks, to two bars of Ex. 8.24. 'Playing', Suzuki replies. Should she call him? No, let her go and keep him company; but Suzuki refuses to leave her mistress.

In the first three editions this is to a passionate re-assertion of Ex. 8.19, again hexatonic. At Milan and Brescia it was answered by a device that Puccini would put to more effective use in the definitive version of *Suor Angelica*: an ironic back-reference to Suzuki's words where she had quelled Butterfly's fit of hysteria ('Gioia e riposo accrescono beltà'). For the third edition Puccini suppressed the repartee, possibly because the quotation was insufficiently exact to make the point ('Gioia' could obviously have no place in the present context). The sequence was therefore resumed where Butterfly sings what purports to be an old song ('Ei venne alle sue porte' in Milan, 'Varco le chiuse porte' in Brescia and London).

For Paris all this went, with no great loss. A coincidence of key allows the music to jump from Butterfly's 'Va a fargli compagnia' to a solo for timpani, pounding rapidly in fifths (for a more powerful use of this same effect see the 'poker scene' in *La fanciulla del West*). Butterfly kneels before the image of the Buddha, while cellos, playing in the G string, trace a tortured lament over the timpani semiquavers, which passes through the 'rejection' motif (Ex. 8.16) to the abrupt gesture that launched Ex. 8.10, as the fatal resolution takes hold of Butterfly's mind. Before she can carry it out, the child runs in propelled by Suzuki. With the 'hurry' music of his entrance Puccini establishes the key of B minor on which the opera will remain centred until the end. Butterfly's fare-well culminates in a bloom of sad Puccinian lyricism ('O a me sceso dal trono'), concentrated for Brescia into a mere ten bars with the con-tour of its opening strain altered into a longer, less repetitive line.

From here to the catastrophe all is slow 'action' music. Having told the child to play, Butterfly puts in his hand a doll and a small American flag and bandages his eyes, before going behind the screen to take her own life. A steady tramp of timpani, bass drum, and gong together with syncopated pulsations on low trumpet, cor anglais, and cellos begins a long drawn-out chromatic descent ending in convulsive gestures that recall the death of Carmen. During a pause the knife is heard to fall on the floor. A rush of climbing semiquavers on violins and violas portrays the wounded Butterfly as she struggles towards her child. From outside comes the sound of Pinkerton's voice crying 'Butterfly!', while beneath an F sharp swelling and diminishing over three bars trumpets and trom-bones blare forth Ex. 8.19, here encapsulating all its previous conno-tations—longing, wonder, entrapment, and even the ascent of the hill. Pinkerton and Sharpless burst into the room to find Butterfly on the point of death. It is left to the 'Pathetic Melody' (Ex. 8.25) to bring down the curtain. The boldest stroke of all is reserved for the final chord—not the simple B minor that the ear expects but one in which the dominant note is replaced by the sixth above, so creating a G major inversion. Why does it sound no less conclusive? Chiefly by an analogy with the final bar of Act I where the same procedure is applied to a major-key ending. Then, too, much play has been made with the sharp-ened sixth of the ascending minor scale in its melodic form (see Exx.8.6b and 8.19). Here it is firmly, even brutally negated, like a door slammed in the listener's face, and thus a perfectly logical full stop.

With Giulio Ricordi *Madama Butterfly* was never a favourite; rather it was a facile tear-jerker scarcely worthy of his protégé's genius. How strange that he should have overlooked the huge advance that it rep-resents in orchestral technique, harmonic range, and, not least, in the delineation of its protagonist! Mimì, though all of a piece in the way that Manon is not, remains in one groove throughout. Tosca exhibits different facets of a more complex personality. Only Butterfly *develops*. At first child-like in her naiveté, she becomes ennobled by suffering and disillusion. Nor is she a passive victim. Manon dies from hunger and exhaustion, Mimì from tuberculosis. Tosca, by hurling herself from the battlements, anticipates a fate that would have befallen her anyway. Butterfly does not have to die at all; she could have resumed her profession as a geisha unencumbered by her infant. Instead she chooses to take her life into her own hands for the sake of honour. With her Puccini gives us for the first time a heroine in every sense of the word.

Such a transformation would have been impossible without the new wealth of harmonic colouring to which the score bears witness. Here Japanese folk-material plays a vital part. Sometimes Puccini isolates it as a bare unison: at others he anchors it to a pedal note or open fifth; more often he inflects it with harmonies of his own that vary with the expressive demands of the context. There are even moments where he fuses East and West, fleshing out a pentatonic melody with auxiliary notes and orthodox progressions. Nor are the overtly American themes (in general, the least distinguished in the score) always free of 'black-note' contours. If this lessens the culture-clash that Puccini and Illica had at first envisaged, the gain in musical coherence is ample compensation.

Another source of enrichment is Puccini's exploitation of whole-tone harmony. By the turn of the century this was by no means a novelty in European music. Its earliest affirmation is in Glinka's *Russlan and Ludmilla* (1842), as a portrayal of supernatural evil in the person of the magician Chernamor. It figures also in the experimental piano pieces composed by the aged Liszt; and by 1904 it had become an abiding feature of Debussy's idiom. Puccini had already broached it at odd moments in *Tosca*. Not, however, until *Madama Butterfly* does it become the distinguishing property of a motif (Ex. 8.16). Nor does Puccini confine the device to moments of negative emotion. It will serve equally well for the whispered exchanges between Goro, Sharpless, and Yamadori and for Butterfly's shy admission of her age. A whole-tone chord may convey a sense of enchantment when arrived at by mere chromatic alteration, as at Butterfly's entrance in Act I. Likewise the epilogue of the 'flower duet' dwells dreamily on a similar progression before drifting to its cadence. In this way the whole-tone scale, far from being an intrusion, becomes integrated in varying degrees as a normal ingredient of Puccini's lyrical discourse—a process made all the easier by his habit of avoiding semitonal clashes. All this is a long way from the hexatonic flirtations that open Mascagni's *L'amico Fritz* (1891)—a pointless display of 'modernity' which the hero of *Cavalleria rusticana* doubtless felt to be expected of him. At the other end of the spectrum is Puccini's non-functional use of plain diatonic harmony for expressive purposes, of which Ex. 8.14 provides a clear example, each chord isolated from its neighbours.

Finally there is the evolution of Puccini's motival technique. 'When I choose a word', Humpty Dumpty told Lewis Carroll's Alice, 'it means what I want it to mean—neither more nor less.' 'The question is', said Alice, 'whether you can make words mean different things.' Puccini certainly could with his recurring themes. Rarely are they confined to a single image, person, or idea. Unlike Wagner's, they will often take time to disclose their full potential. The second fragment of 'The Lion of Echigo' (Ex. 8.6b) first appears as mere descriptive *japonnerie*. Only when harmonized unequivocally in the minor key does it carry Butterfly's regret at life's tempests and the consul's despair at her credulity. A feature that it shares with the multivalent Ex. 8.19 is the raised sixth of the melodic minor scale. Had Puccini continued it upward it would not have caught the attention: but in both cases it falls back. By bringing Ex. 8.19 to rest on the dominant he loaded it with ambiguity. It could be called an extension of the 'extraneous note' principle, whereby Puccini was able to stamp an otherwise unremarkable idea in the listener's memory. Nowhere is it put to more expressive use than here.

In a word, the motif of Puccini's maturity is like a prism, giving out a different colour according to the way in which it is tilted. In a style of opera which precluded the long Wagnerian rumination, this was of enormous benefit to the musical economy. That Puccini alone was able to exploit it goes some way to explaining why both as musician and stage artist he towers above his Italian contemporaries.

While *Madama Butterfly* remains with *La bohème* and *Tosca* one of the chief pillars of the operatic repertory, there has been some recent controversy as to the ideal version in which it should be given. Some maintain that in his successive revisions Puccini compromised his original conception in order to render the plot more palatable to a society that believed in colonialism. Recently the Milan version of 1904 has been tried out in Italy and abroad, pioneered by the Welsh National Opera in an edition by Julian Smith. Most listeners, however, would agree that in general the cuts amount to an improvement. Butterfly moves us more if she does not burst into tears as she contemplates her altered appearance; nor do we need to see her refusing Pinkerton's money, which we know she will not need. As for the comic scenes in Act I, all inspired by Loti, these are far more offensive to the Japanese than to Pinkerton. One can only conclude that Cio-Cio-San is well rid of so ridiculous an entourage.

To this rule, however, two exceptions could be made. There is something to be said for abolishing the second interval and restoring the transition between the two parts of Act II where the action remains suspended and the psychology shifts from the peace of the 'humming chorus' to the tumultuous recollections of the intermezzo. There is an even stronger case for re-instating the 37 bars cut from the love-duet, so as to improve the musical and dramatic continuity and to make sense of a later thematic recall. Otherwise let us be content with Puccini's sixth opera as he left it.

CHAPTER 9

La fanciulla del West

BETWEEN THE FIASCO OF *MADAMA BUTTERFLY* AND ITS VINDI-cation at Brescia Puccini was able to settle a piece of unfinished business. In January 1903 he had approached Alfred Michaelis of the Gramophone and Typewriter Company with a request for records of Japanese folk music such as the Russian choruses which he had supplied for Giordano's *Siberia*. In return Michaelis asked Puccini for a song 'written expressly for the Gramophone', to be published together with others commissioned from Franchetti, Giordano, Leoncavallo, and Mascagni. Puccini, who had no high opinion of Edison's invention, was reluctant to contribute. Nevertheless, on 16 April he allowed himself to be contracted for a 'song for solo voice' in exchange for 1000 discs of his own choice. For the poet he turned to Illica with a request for 'short verses, bold, or languid (two in all)', adding that the poet need not give himself too much trouble for someone who paid so badly. Illica sent two specimens, which evidently failed to meet the case; for in June Puccini asked him for a third, 'a *couplet*-style canzonetta, so that even Sor Giūlio will see it as a bit of a joke, the public also'. Records of Japanese music arrived in the autumn, probably too late to be of any use to the composer, who had yet to fulfil his part of the bargain. Not until the following year did he remind Illica that the Gramophone was still clamouring for its tribute. 'Send me two or three rhythmic verses with a concept that finishes at the end of each line. But please, no "dawn". Both Franchetti and Leoncavallo sing more or less darkly about the rising sun. So send me a poetic, impassioned thought, perhaps a lunar one, for tenor (for Caruso).'[1] The result was *Canto d'anime*, a salute to man's unconquerable soul amid trials and disappointments. It has little to recommend it beyond a stately march of ascending chords that anticipates Rinuccio's 'stornello' in *Gianni Schicchi*. Indeed, at one point Puccini considered delegating its composition to the singer Enrico Berriel under a pledge of secrecy. The chief beneficiary of Michaelis's enterprise was Leoncavallo, whose *Mattinata* still survives in the recital repertory; its chief victim was Michaelis himself, dismissed from the company for his over-ambitious schemes. A contract offered to Puccini empowering him to arrange and direct recordings of his own and other people's music thus remained a dead letter.

With the triumph of Brescia behind him Puccini could devote more attention to his health; hence a fortnight spent at the mud-baths of Acqui Terme north of Genoa for his leg ('How boring it all is. . . . All the women over 60!').[2] The high summer he passed with his family at Boscolungo. Visiting friends, among them Illica and Tito Ricordi, were treated to trips among the mountains in his new De Dion, Puccini himself at the wheel. After a further cure at Montecatini early in September he returned for a few weeks to Milan before setting out with Elvira for London. The occasion was not a specially important one: a brief season of Italian opera at Covent Garden under Cleofonte Campanini that included the first *Manon Lescaut* since 1894 with Ada Giachetti and Caruso and *Tosca* with the same soprano. But it would bring Puccini one of the most valuable friendships of his life.

Sybil Seligman, née Beddington, came of a musical family, her mother having been a concert pianist. Married to the banker David Seligman, to whom she had borne two sons, she belonged to that cultivated Jewish society that had recently come to the fore in Edwardian England. A lover of all things Italian, she numbered the poets D'Annunzio and Pascoli among her correspondents. Under the tutelage of Paolo Tosti she developed a fine contralto voice; and it was at Tosti's home, then as always an open house for distinguished Italian visitors, that she met the Puccinis. The nature of her relationship with Giacomo

---

[1] M. Kaye: *The Unknown Puccini*, 95–7.

[2] CP 385, p. 276.

has long been the subject of debate. Sybil's sister Violet Schiff assured Mosco Carner that it began as a torrid love-affair, and she, one would think, should have known. Sybil's son Vincent, on the other hand, used to declare that his mother's aversion to sex was such that he himself wondered how he had been conceived; and indeed her husband had to look elsewhere for his diversions. If Puccini was captivated by her at first, as some of his early letters to her seem to imply, it is more than likely that she kept him, quite kindly, at arm's length. Most significantly of all, Elvira, all too aware of her husband's susceptibilities, was never jealous of Sybil. Apart from a brief period, to be noted later, when she suspected her of siding with Giacomo against herself, she welcomed the Englishwoman as a family friend. Indeed Sybil was destined to play a role in Puccini's life second only to that of Giulio Ricordi. If the publisher was the father that he had barely known, she would become, in Schickling's words, his mother-confessor. To her he confided his problems, domestic or creative. She in turn offered him subjects for his operas, smoothed his path with English managements, and in general provided him with a shoulder to cry on, if mostly at a distance. 'You are the person', he wrote to her, 'who has come nearest to understanding my nature.'[3]

In mid-November the vindication of *Madama Butterfly* was further sealed at Genoa under Arturo Panizza, again with Salomea Krusceniski in the title-role. Puccini was present and lavishly fêted. A local bookseller was moved to have his newly born daughter christened 'Butterfly'. However subject to future modifications the opera's place in the repertory was now assured.

Not so Puccini's next choice of subject. Never was his search for novelty more assiduous than during this time, venturing as far afield as the Bible and the ancient chronicles of Lucca. Of Illica's proposals only Victor Hugo's *Notre Dame de Paris* struck a momentary spark. Already in February Puccini had expressed an interest in the medieval—'a Middle Ages of beauty, very poetic, and very terrible, . . . understood as it really was',[4] stripped of the false glamour applied to it by history. His own *Notre Dame* would be cast in the mould of *Mefistofele*: a prologue

[3] PAF, 64.

[4] CP 361, p. 265.

followed by seven or eight short scenes, each lasting no more than 15 minutes and each ending with a 'sensation'. The prologue would be a vast frontispiece: no action, merely the interior of the cathedral with the congregation on their knees, a chime of bells (chords, not single notes), organ, choirs of mixed and boys' voices, a Bach-style fugue, Gothic counterpoint, dim coloured lights here and there, the whole suggesting 'a fantastic vision'.[5]

But scarcely had Illica put pen to paper than Puccini's doubts began. 'Your prologue has great qualities, but it's too grand and lengthy a construction. I would have liked something lasting six or seven minutes in all.' Three weeks later came the ominous sentence, 'In case *Notre Dame* should run aground, couldn't you find me something else?'[6] By the beginning of October it was 'Damn this *Notre Dame!*'[7] For in the meantime something else had indeed been found, if not for long: a trilogy of one-act operas based on the short stories of Gorki which had engrossed Puccini during his convalescence of the previous year. Both Illica and Giacosa were agreeable; and the items chosen were certainly strong meat. *The Khan and His Son* tells of the dispute between both parties over a concubine. Having reflected that women bring nothing but sorrow and discord to their menfolk, father and son hurl the object of their desire over a cliff. The Khan, with nothing left to live for, follows her to his death, leaving his son to ascend the throne. *Twenty-six Men and a Girl* offers a picture of sweated labour in a biscuit factory. The inmates, all infirm, some syphilitic, derive their only solace from the visits of a 16-year-old girl, whose beauty and innocence they worship. Yet when an ex-soldier, newly employed by the firm, boasts of his amorous conquests, their foreman cannot resist daring him to attempt the virtue of their idol. He does so, and not in vain; whereupon they drive her away with foul-mouthed insults. For the third item Illica suggested *The Raft*, another low-life vignette, this time set on the Volga and showing a father carrying on with the buxom wench whom he has forced his son to marry (shades of *La lupa!*). Puccini approved, but, in case there should be any scenic difficulties, put forward as an alter-

[5] CP 384, p. 276.
[6] CP 388–9, pp. 278–9.
[7] CP 399, pp. 283–4.

native *Makar Chudria*, the tale of a proud, domineering gypsy girl, who enslaves the man she loves, only to be stabbed mortally by him and avenged in like manner by her father. But composer and librettists had reckoned without Giulio Ricordi, to whom a triple-bill meant a box-office risk.

Meanwhile Puccini had another iron in the fire. Unbeknown to Illica, he had been treating with the Tuscan playwright Valentino Soldani for a libretto based on his one-act 'mistero' *Margherita da Cortona*, written as a showpiece for the actress Gemma Caimmi. Its heroine is a thirteenth-century saint who, before entering a religious order, had lived for nine years as the mistress of a nobleman, to whom she had borne a son. The opening scene presents her carousing in the arms of her lover Alberto during a drunken orgy held at his villa while a thunderstorm rages outside. Her conversion to sanctity comes from an itinerant friar, bearing a soaked parchment from which he reads to the assembled company a poem about the crucifixion by Jacopo da Todi (alleged author of the *Stabat mater*). Mocked by one of the guests, defended by the host, his intervention results in a brawl, during which Alberto is killed. Margherita's first thought is to avenge her lover; then, rebuked by the friar, she strips off her finery and returns it to the bereaved family, to devote herself henceforth to good works. For two years the subject haunted Puccini's imagination, glowing and vanishing like a will-o'-the-wisp. He even paid Soldani's expenses for a trip to Cortona to absorb the local atmosphere. His letters to the playwright are of interest as setting forth his Credo to one who was a tyro in matters operatic (in this they recall Verdi's correspondence with Antonio Somma over *Un ballo in maschera* and the abortive *Re Lear*). 'You must poeticize, lyricize as much as possible. . . . Make the most of little situations which in music becomes great and which in the spoken theatre might pass as insignificant.'[8] Like Verdi, he insisted on verbal economy. 'Logic', 'line' (i.e., dramatic thread'), 'poetry'—the words recur like a refrain. The visual element was constantly stressed. As in *Notre Dame*, Puccini wanted a simple, 'sober' spectacle reflecting the architecture of the period; and above all 'a fine delineation of character'. But Soldani

---

[8] CP 387, pp. 277–8.

1   Church of San Michele, Lucca.
Photograph by Franco Bellato.

2   Albina Magi Puccini (1831–84).
Courtesy of Simonetta Puccini.

3   Giacomo Puccini, aged 17.
Courtesy of Simonetta Puccini.

4   Elvira Puccini (née Bonturi) (1860–1930).

5   A musical consultation.

6   Puccini, Giacosa, Illica.

7 Giulio Ricordi (1840–1912)

8 Victorien Sardou (1831–1908).
Photograph by Cautin and Berger, Paris.

9 A rehearsal at the Metropolitan Opera House.
Caricature by Enrico Caruso. Coutesy of the Metropolitan Opera Archives.

10   Sybil Seligman (1868–1935).

11   Rovescelli's sketch for *Il tabarro*.

12   Fragment of a letter from Puccini to Elvira written during rehearsals for *La bohème*. Courtesy of the Museo Casa Natale Giacomo Puccini, Lucca.

13   Puccini in his last year.

TORRE del LAGO. — La Bufatina.

14   Torre del Lago.

15   Puccini at the piano.

was no Illica. 'You've made it too much of a spoken drama', was the composer's final verdict.[9]

27 January 1905 saw the commemoration of the fourth anniversary of Verdi's death, planned to coincide with the opening of a new concert-hall in the Milan conservatory which had come to bear his name. The main event of the day was the celebration of a Mass in the chapel of the Casa di Riposo per Musicisti which he himself had founded. The service ended with a six-minute *Requiem* for soprano, tenor, bass chorus, viola solo, and harmonium composed by the Master's 'successor', Giacomo Puccini. Performed by choristers from La Scala, it was 'received with a silent admiration that was worth more to the composer than the most thunderous applause'—so the correspondent of Ricordi's monthly *Musica e musicisti* reported. The *Requiem per Giuseppe Verdi* was never revived during Puccini's lifetime, nor did he ever refer to it in his known correspodence. Doubtless it was intended as a historical gesture, no more. But a recent performance based on the autograph in La Scala museum and conducted by Herbert Handt has shown it to be not unworthy of its composer. Puccinian fingerprints are everywhere in evidence: here a falling fifth, there a sequence moving to the double-subdominant, throughout a modal colouring. Choral passages, imitative or homophonic, alternate with a viola motif, an ideogram of elegiac sadness that becomes shorter with each repetition—a case of *multum in parvo*.

February and March saw Puccini at work on the final revisions to *Edgar*, due for performance at Buenos Aires in July; but he remained on the look-out for fresh subjects. To both Illica and Giacosa, he wrote asking for 'a comedy in the true sense . . . without tears or satire—something to make the world split its sides'.[10] But the flicker of interest aroused by the news that *Tartarin sur les Alpes* was at last free quickly died; and the composer's thoughts returned to Gorki and the brooding imagery of *The Raft* ('the sea, the Volga, the seagulls as a background, the incest, the misery on earth combined with thoughts of heaven. . . . I'm dying to do it and I can't see how'). The chief obstacle was, of

[9] CP 460, p. 316.
[10] PCB, 159.

course, 'Signor Giulio', whose objections, he admitted, were 'not to be overlooked'.[11] But is there not a hint here of the *Tabarro* to come?

It was at this point that Illica began re-asserting the claims of *Maria Antonietta*. Faced with Puccini's refusal of it in 1901, he had offered it to Mascagni, who, since being unceremoniously dropped by Sonzogno after the failure of *Le maschere*, had become available to the Casa Ricordi. But Mascagni, disillusioned with Italian publishers in general, had preferred to treat with the French firm of Choudens for his next opera, *Amica*, composed to a libretto by Paul Berel and now running at Monte Carlo. Accordingly, in May 1905 a reluctant Ricordi summoned his protégé to Milan for Illica to read to them both his revised text. In the meantime Puccini had sent the author a copy of Octave Mirbeau's *Les mauvais bergers*, an ultra-left-wing play about armed strike-breaking in an iron foundry. Illica, a man of the far right, was appalled. It was, as he put it, '*Avanti*' (the communist newspaper) 'on the stage', the 'bad shepherds' of the title being not the capitalists but the liberal deputies who betrayed the cause they pretended to espouse. So wherein lay the attraction for the apolitical Puccini? A glance at the fourth act supplies the answer. In a forest outside the city the enraged workers, on the verge of starvation, threaten to lynch the strike-leader, but are dissuaded by the eloquent pleading of his sweetheart. Years later this scene, transferred to another context, would bear magnificent fruit.

The reading of *Maria Antonietta* over, Puccini declared himself impressed. 'But, alas', he wrote to the poet, 'the scale of the opera seemed to me frighteningly huge and in my opinion beyond all possibility of success. . . . it's very, very long, and it would be impossible to reduce to normal proportions even with cuts.'[12]

Illica's reaction may be gauged from Puccini's reply. 'Jove in a tantrum! But what about? If *Maria Antonietta* is to come alive again we must have a serious talk about it.'[13] Time, however, was short; for in a few days Puccini and his wife were due to embark for Buenos Aires, where they had been invited as guests of honour by the newspaper *La Prensa*, all expenses paid together with an additional fee of 50,000 lire.

[11] CP 412, pp. 290–1.
[12] CP 400, p. 294.
[13] CP 423, pp. 295–6.

For the present he accepted Ricordi's suggestion that he try his hand at something less arduous, that perhaps he could throw off during the voyage: a three-act operetta, whose text Illica had ready. Indeed he was all enthusiasm. 'An operetta is a matter of twenty little pieces', he wrote to the poet, 'and for abroad (London) it would be good business. . . . Anyway, if you feel that those three acts are for me, come along and out with them!'[14] But evidently Illica was still sulking, for the three acts never came.

In any case, the voyage to Argentina proved unconducive to composition. The weather was so bad that when the ship put in at Las Palmas in the Canaries Elvira threatened to disembark and go no further. Fortunately their reception in Buenos Aires left nothing to be desired. Housed in a luxurious apartment in the Palazzo Prensa, they were treated to a continual round of festivities. Nor did his hosts forget Puccini's favourite pastime; and an ostrich-hunt was duly laid on in the pampas. He had arrived to find the season of his operas already under way. *Edgar* came last with only two performances. Though the Act I finale and the prelude to Act III were both encored, the opera cut a poor figure beside its sisters. Puccini was not surprised. He and Elvira returned by way of Montevideo, whose music conservatory made him an honorary member. By September he was back in Italy and ready in theory to grapple with *Maria Antonietta*, at present in the hands of Illica and Giacosa. Soon, however, he was again called abroad, this time to England.

The London première of *Madama Butterfly* had taken place in July, with Cleofonte Campanini as conductor, Destinn and Caruso in the leading roles. What Puccini attended, and indeed supervised, was a revival on 24 October under Mugnone with Giachetti, Zenatello, and Sammarco, in itself a clear indication of the opera's earlier success. Nor was the public disappointed at a re-hearing. 'The charm of Puccini's music', wrote the critic of the *Morning Post*, 'lies in the fact that, while being essentially modern, it is always tuneful. . . . For this reason his music will live.' And the *Pall Mall Gazette*: 'In *Madama Butterfly* he reveals his mastery of the orchestra. . . . Puccini's music pursues the ideals of the great Verdi and has at its basis a deep and secure understanding

[14] CP 418, p. 293.

of dramatic feeling.' But the chief benefit for Puccini was the strengthening of his friendship with Sybil Seligman, who now began to interest herself in his search for new subjects. Her suggestions of *Anna Karenina*, Bulwer Lytton's *The Last Days of Pompeii*, and an unspecified work by Prosper Merimée he turned down at once. He gave sympathetic consideration to Tennyson's *Enoch Arden*, but found the material 'too slender for an opera', as well he might; for the story of a man who, believed lost at sea, returns after many years to find his wife re-married, yet gallantly preserves his incognito, offers no possibility of dramatic confrontation. Still more inept was Sybil's proposal of Rudyard Kipling's novel *The Light that Failed*, then running as a play with the great actor-manager, Johnston Forbes-Robertson as the war-correspondent-turned-painter who, afflicted with progressive blindness, dies a heroic death in the Sahara Desert. After Puccini had read the novel in a French translation, it was '*Kipling's* no good. . . . There are certain passages in it which I love, but taking it altogether it's too small and too much in one key. . . . Then that wretched blindness is not only at the end of the work but is the very kernel of the story—besides, the end of the novel with the death of a blind man on a camel in Africa isn't possible on the stage—at least, not on the Italian stage.'[15] And surely the strain of misogyny that runs through the novel would have ruled it out for the composer of *Tosca* and *Madama Butterfly*.

From London Puccini made a quick dash to Bologna in time to catch a *Butterfly* under Toscanini, with whose help he put the finishing touches to what would be the opera's third edition. The rest of the year he spent mostly at Torre del Lago, with a single excursion to a hunting-ground in the Tuscan Maremma as the guest of Count Gherardesca. Since *Maria Antonietta* was temporarily blocked by the illness of Giacosa, Ricordi and Illica suggested Pierre Loti's *Ramuncho*, an unhappy love-story set in the Basque country, in which the smuggler hero returns from three years' military service to find that his beloved has taken the veil. Again Puccini read and admired the novel; it was the ending that he found intractable—'too much based on silences and the inner drama of the characters for an opera', he told Illica.[16] He was not wrong. The

[15] PAF, 68–71.
[16] CP 437, p. 302.

subject was set by the Sicilian Stefano Donaudy in 1921 and failed miserably.

By December Giacosa had recovered sufficiently to bring alive once more the project of *Maria Antonietta*. Puccini was ready with suggestions as never before. 'We must abandon the idea of a strict chronicle and move straight to the fully-fledged Revolution, where the sorrows and misfortunes of Maria Antonietta begin.' No Trianon, therefore, with false shepherdesses, but the plot hatched at the Café du Caveau to attack Versailles, the attempted escape of the King and Queen, their arrest by night at Varennes (and here the etchings of Fortuny would be of help), the imprisonment and trial, during which the Queen is accused of corrupting her son, and a final scene at the place of execution. 'In this way the opera, shorn of rhetoric and empty virtuosity and things of no interest, would take on a quality of liveliness and rapidity that would leave no time for the audience to notice the lack of a true tenor or baritone. The protagonist is the crowd together with the great Revolution at the height of its grandeur or barbarity, whichever way you look at it.'[17] This from the man who would one day write the opening scene of *Turandot*. But by January 1906 the flame of enthusiasm was already guttering. The crowd scenes were all too alike—'the same cries, the same chants, the same musical impressions, the same distance from the audience'. Even the scene at Varennes no longer seemed to function, while the lack of a principal tenor he now considered a serious fault. After all, *Butterfly* was essentially an opera for prima donna alone; it would be unwise to repeat the recipe. The upshot was, '*Maria Antonietta* must be laid aside.'[18] It would, he knew, be a cruel blow to the poet, who had worked so long and hard at it. In fact Illica took the matter philosophically; presumably his piece might do for someone else, but what a pity, he told Ricordi, that Puccini had let such a powerful libretto slip through his fingers!

Alternatives were not lacking. It was at this time that Puccini resumed contact with D'Annunzio, whom he visited at the poet's villa outside Florence. A cordial exchange of letters followed that lasted into the late summer, each addressing the other with 'tu'. All seemed set fair

[17] CP 496, p. 307.
[18] CP 456, pp. 312–13.

for their partnership. 'His ideas about opera coincide with mine', Puccini reported to Carlo Clausetti[19] and indeed in a subsequent letter to the composer D'Annunzio had promised to curb his riotous imagination in favour of a simple, robust design, to be communicated to Puccini as soon as he had done the necessary research. In his turn Puccini offered to lower his terms in order to meet the poet's financial demands. A contract extremely favourable to D'Annunzio was duly signed on 16 April, requiring him to provide a sketch by 31 May and, if that proved acceptable, a three-act drama within six months. So there was plenty of time.

In March 1906 Giacomo and Elvira travelled to Nice for a performance in French of *Manon Lescaut*. Here they were joined by the Seligman family, for whom the French Riviera was a regular winter resort. It was from that occasion that the ten-year-old Vincent dated his first impressions of the composer, noting his various mannerisms—his habit of clicking his fingers when searching for a word, his chain-smoking, the jaunty angle of his hat. 'But more clearly than anything else do I remember the look of indulgent affection in his large brown eyes and the rare sweetness of his frank smile—and yet even when he was in his happiest and jolliest mood there always seemed to lurk at the corner of his mouth a hint of melancholy, the look that one sometimes sees on the faces of the blind. . . . Quite apart from his music', Seligman concludes, 'there was something extraordinarily lovable about Giacomo himself. He was, if I may be permitted a well-worn cliché, the type of man to whom children and dogs take instinctively.'[20] Cliché or not, it describes an endearing trait.

In May there was another diversion: a trip to Budapest at the invitation of Ervin Lendvai, a young composer whose music Puccini admired sufficiently to provide him with a testimonial. *La bohème*, *Tosca*, and *Madama Butterfly*, all given in Hungarian, more than repaid his expectations. A further attraction was Lendvai's sister Blanke, with whom Puccini seems to have enjoyed at least a flirtation, as Elvira would soon find out. He returned by way of Graz in time to catch a performance of Richard Strauss's *Salome*—'the most extraordinary, ter-

[19] CP 465, pp. 317–18.
[20] PAF, 73–4.

ribly cacophonous thing', he reported to Lendvai; 'there are some very beautiful orchestral sounds, but it ends by tiring one out. It is a most gripping spectacle.'[21] Whatever his reservations, Puccini never missed an opportunty of revisiting it in the future. And who can say whether it was Strauss's first operatic masterpiece that for a while turned his thoughts firmly in the direction of a truly 'decadent' subject?

A few months earlier he had asked Ricordi to procure the rights of Pierre Louÿs's novel *La Femme et le pantin*. The woman in the case, half-Salome (she is a young virgin), half-Carmen (she works in a cigarette factory), continually tempts a middle-aged roué, withdrawing her favours at the last minute—even simulating in his presence a sexual act with a young man behind an iron grille—until, provoked beyond endurance, he gives her a sound thrashing; whereupon she succumbs with delight. For the librettist Puccini first thought of Soldani, doubtless in order to compensate him for the time wasted on *Margherita da Cortona*. Then, summoned to Paris in July to discuss with Albert Carré the modifications to *Madama Butterfly*, he turned instead to Maurice Vaucaire, librettist of Louis Ganne's operetta *Hans, joueur de flûte* (once briefly considered for a French version of *Tartarin sur les Alpes*) and asked him to draw up a libretto to be revised and elaborated by Illica. To expedite the project Vaucaire was invited to Boscolungo in August, where Puccini was treating the Seligmans to jaunts among the mountains in his latest car. In between times the composer visited D'Annunzio at Pietrasanta, but their consultations proved fruitless. Puccini rejected both *Parisina* (later set by Mascagni) and *La rosa del Cipro* (a version of the Melusine legend), defeated by the poet's highly charged language and fantastical conceits. By the end of the summer the two had parted with expressions of mutual esteem and the hope of collaboration at some future date.

On 2 September Giacosa died after a long struggle with asthma. Puccini offered a brief but affectionate tribute in the columns of *La lettura*, of which the poet had been editor; then returned with growing commitment to *La femme et le pantin*, now to be entitled *Conchita*. To Carlo Clausetti he had already given a glowing account of Vaucaire's scheme:

[21] PLI 124, p. 130.

Scene 1: the tobacco factory: a noisy scene full of colour and episodes; the meeting of Mateo and Conchita.

2: Her home in the attic with her mother, a somewhat comic character.

3: The Baile, a café-concert in the poorer quarters of Seville; Conchita dancing almost naked before the Englishmen. . . . Then a scene to round it off, strong and tender.

4: The Patio Grille. Terrible!

5: Lastly, Mateo's home; a tragic scene with blows ending in an erotic duet, terrible, the two rolling on the ground.[22]

And yet a week before signing the contract with the Casa Ricordi Puccini was expressing his doubts to Sybil ('what frightens me is *her* character and the plot of the play—and then all the characters seem to me unlovable, and that's a very bad thing on the stage').[23] With the D'Annunzio project at an end, he wanted a second string to his bow. He asked her to send him Oscar Wilde's dramatic fragment *A Florentine Tragedy*, which she had read to him at Boscolungo. The manuscript, obtained from Wilde's executor, Robert Ross, reached him early in November in Paris, where he had arrived with Elvira to supervise the rehearsals for *Madama Butterfly*. 'It is only in one act', he wrote to Giulio Ricordi, 'but beautiful, inspired, strong and tragic: three principals, so-prano, tenor and baritone; three first-class roles. Epoch 1300; it would be a rival to *Salome*, but more human, more truthful, more in tune with the feelings of all of us.'[24]

Like *Salome*, and indeed Louÿs's novel, it deals in feminine perversity. An elderly merchant of Florence returns home to find his wife on the brink of an affair with a young nobleman. With every show of courtesy and an apparent interest only in the sale of his goods he manoeuvres the young man into fighting a duel and kills him. His wife, who had hoped for a very different outcome, now, without a glance at her lover's corpse, embraces her husband, saying, 'Why did you not tell me that you were so strong?' To which he replies, 'Why did you not tell me you were so beautiful?' Puccini commissioned a French translation and sent it to Illica, who was all the readier to co-operate in that both

[22] CP 487, pp. 328–9.
[23] PAF, 88.
[24] CP 492, pp. 331–2.

Vaucaire and Louys had found serious fault with his draft of *Conchita*. All this prompted a sarcastic outburst from Giulio Ricordi, who now foresaw endless delays to the completion of a work for which his protégé had been firmly and very favourably contracted. Puccini, he insisted, was costing his firm too much; perhaps when he himself had been incarcerated for debt the composer might take him a few trips round the prison walls in his latest high-powered car. As for the 'Florentine stupidity', Ricordi advised him to throw it into the fire. So for the present there was stalemate.

The indisposition and outside commitments of the prima donna, Mme Carré ('Madame Pomme-de-terre', as Puccini called her), put back the first night of *Madama Butterfly* until 28 December. The slow progress of rehearsals took its toll of Puccini's spirits; and he wrote to Sybil asking her to procure for him some medicine that would raise the morale ('Such a medicine must exist in London, and you, who know everything, will find it for me, won't you?').[25] What she sent him was veronal, of which she advised him to make sparing use—ironically, since, according to her family, she herself would eventually become dependent on narcotics.

Of the operas Puccini saw in Paris during this time the only one to interest him was Debussy's *Pelléas et Mélisande*. 'It has extraordinary harmonic qualities and diaphanous instrumental sounds', he wrote to Giulio Ricordi; 'it's truly interesting, but it doesn't transport you. . . . The colour is uniformly "sombre", like a Franciscan's habit.'[26] He would learn from it, however.

Despite Puccini's gloomy prognostications the French première of his latest opera, conducted by the German Ullmann turned out an unqualified success. Illica, who had arrived in Paris shortly before, found the production 'logical, practical, and poetic', Mme Carré, though technically hard-driven, genuinely moving in her interpretation, and Puccini restored to his old self—so he assured the still disgruntled publisher.[27]

For the problem of the new libretto was still unsolved when on 9

[25] PAF, 93.
[26] CP 495, pp. 333–4.
[27] CP 497, pp. 335–7.

January, 1907 Puccini and his wife embarked for a two-month visit to New York at the invitation of Heinrich Conried, manager of the Metropolitan Opera House, for a season of his operas from *Manon Lescaut* (then new to America) to *Madama Butterfly*. With the first he professed himself more than satisfied. 'Caruso, as usual, an extraordinary Des Grieux, Scotti very good.'[28] Rehearsals for *Madama Butterfly* boded less well. Geraldine Farrar had too small a voice for the size of the theatre and her pitch was uncertain. Even Caruso's Pinkerton came in for censure: 'As for your *God*', Sybil was told, 'I make you a present of him— he won't learn anything, he's lazy, and he's too pleased with himself. All the same', Puccini admitted, 'his voice is magnificent.'[29] Happily, the first night was a huge success with critics and public alike.

Scarcely had Puccini stepped ashore than he gave a hostage to fortune by announcing to journalists that he was thinking of writing an opera about the Wild West and intended to get in touch with David Belasco. This he confirmed the following day, adding that something 'stunning' could be made out of the '40s period'. The reference to *The Girl of the Golden West* could hardly be clearer. Belasco's play had been recommended to him earlier by his friend the Marchese Antinori; and while in New York he had certainly seen it performed on Broadway, as he told reporters before leaving, and had found the heroine 'fresh' and 'adorable'. To this he added a tribute to American women in general, whose charms he had praised in grosser terms to his sister Ramelde.

But from a letter to Tito Ricordi it seems that his plans were far from settled. 'I like the ambience of the West, but in all the "pièces" I've seen I've found only one or two scenes here and there. Never a simple thread, always a muddle, and now and then bad taste and old hat.' There were one or two hints in Belasco, but nothing solid or complete. He did not dispair, however. John Luther Long, whom he had met in Philadelphia, had promised him a new subject. He was going to see another Belasco play, *The Music Master*, and one by Gerhard Hauptmann, which he had heard highly spoken of. By now he was heartily sick of '*Bohème, Butt.* and Company.'[30] Novelty was of the

[28] CP 499, p. 339.

[29] PAF, 119.

[30] CP 500, pp. 339–41.

essence. But the main object of his letter, it seems, was to prepare the Casa Ricordi for his decision to abandon *Conchita* on the grounds that the special qualities of the novel would be lost in a stage adaptation.

On his return to Torre del Lago he continued to cast his net elsewhere. Suggestions, he told Ricordi, were pouring in from all sides. D'Annunzio had written to him that his nightingale had awakened with the spring and was ready to sing for Puccini once more. From his refuge in Switzerland Ferdinando Fontana, silent since the days of *Edgar*, offered a version of Wilde's early play *The Duchess of Padua*. Arturo Colautti, librettist of Cilea's *Adriana Lecouvreur* and *Gloria* (then running at La Scala) proposed a 'solitaire' of his own (it would be a preliminary act for *A Florentine Tragedy*). 'All junk! My God, what a poor theatrical world it is, Italian or foreign!' was Puccini's comment.[31]

Ricordi was unsympathetic, and with good reason. Both Vaucaire and Louÿs were threatening to sue for damages if *Conchita* were dropped. Replying to an irate letter from his publisher, Puccini amplified his previous objections to it. It was not that he feared the Anglo-Saxon prudery that had reacted so violently against the New York première of *Salome* (which he himself had witnessed). He was swayed purely by practical considerations, including the similarity of colour and ambience to *Carmen*, on which Illica had remarked when the subject was first suggested to him. Nonetheless he agreed to a meeting with Giulio in Milan, at which they would examine the libretto afresh, in case something could be made of it. In the event Puccini prevailed, and he could report to Sybil that he was at last free of 'the Spanish slut'.[32] Four years later, however, that same slut would establish the reputation of the young Riccardo Zandonai, as well as providing him with a wife in the person of the prima donna.

Now it was the turn of *Maria Antonietta* to re-surface in a still more concentrated form. Illica's scenes were reduced to three—'Prison', 'Trial', and 'Execution'; no tenor; merely the Queen, the crowd, divided into two opposing factions, and a host of secondary parts; the opera to last no more than two hours and to bear the title *L'austriaca*. However, during a correspondence with Illica that lasted throughout

[31] CP 502, p. 342.
[32] PAF, 125.

May the scheme put forth fresh shoots. A tenor principal was found in the person of one Toulan, a royalist, who plots the Queen's escape under the noses of the guards. Following a poem by Carducci, Louis XVI was to be seen praying for forgiveness for the Massacre of St. Bartholomew's Eve. There was also to be a part for the Dauphin sufficiently ample to engage the audience's sympathy. Illica supplied a song from the Revolutionary period which Puccini found highly serviceable ('a great feeling of sadness mixed with a feeling of folk-like gaiety'). It seems likely that he was already sketching the composition.

For the second act he was full of daring ideas. 'I feel within me the terrible accusation, Maria Antonietta's silence in the face of the jury's violent demand, to which they command her to reply; and then her famous appeal to the women present, to mothers throughout the world. I see the women fainting, the "frissons" of the crowd, the dismay of the judges, the guards trying under orders to calm the tumult, tears, ironic laughter, invective, defence, etc.'[33] At the same time Puccini was concerned to broaden the issue from the sufferings of one woman to the French Revolution considered, despite its cruelties, as the purification and renewal of a world grown stale through the abuse of power (again the inspiration here is Carducci). *L'austriaca* was in no sense to be a 'reactionary opera'. Here Puccini would indeed have broken fresh ground. All operas that deal with the French Revolution could be dubbed 'reactionary' in that they invariably campaign against its excesses. Be it remembered that Beethoven's Pizarro originated not as a symbol of the *ancien régime* but, like Mascagni's L'Orco (*Il piccolo Marat*), as an evil type of Jacobin.

An urgent commitment to supply a libretto for Ettore Panizza prevented Illica from proceeding further than the first act of *L'austriaca*. In the meantime the seed sown in America was slowly but firmly taking root. Soon after his return Puccini had written to Belasco from Paris, 'I have been thinking so much of your play, *The Girl of the Golden West*, and I can't help thinking that with certain modifications it might easily be adapted to the operatic stage. Would you please be good enough to send me a copy of the play to Torre del Lago, Pisa, Italy? I could then have it translated, study it more carefully and write to you my further

---

[33] CP 514, p. 349.

impressions.'[34] Now, at the beginning of June, he and Elvira paid a lightning visit to London, where Sybil pressed the claims of Belasco's play and undertook to procure a translation. On their way home the couple stopped again at Paris, where Puccini saw and disliked Dukas's *Ariane et Barbe-Bleu* ('Better a *Tosca* at Covent Garden', he wrote to Sybil,[35] intending no compliment to London's opera house), talked with Tito Ricordi about French Revolutionary songs, which he found in abundance, and signed an agreement with an American, so far unidentified, for the rights to Belasco's drama.

Puccini now had two subjects on hand and fully intended to compose both, The only problem was, which to tackle first. Illica's prior engagements made the choice for him. At the suggestion of Tito Ricordi the young Bolognese poet and journalist Carlo Zangarini was contracted for the libretto. True, he was as yet without experience in the operatic field (later he would collaborate with Wolf-Ferrari on *I gioielli della Madonna* and Zandonai on *Conchita*); but that he had an American mother may have been a deciding factor.

The Girl of the Golden West was written as a vehicle for Blanche Bates, the original Madam Butterfly, and first performed in New York in 1905. Like its predecessor it made use of spectacular scenic effects, beginning with a cinematic projection of the forests and mountains of California before the curtain rises. The action is set at the time of the Gold Rush. The heroine Minnie—identified throughout the text simply as 'Girl'— runs the Polka Saloon among a mining community. Belasco describes her as 'rather complex. Her utter frankness takes away all suggestion of vice—showing her to be unsmirched; happy, careless, untouched by the life around her. Yet she has a thorough knowledge of what the men of her world generally want. She is used to flattery—knows exactly how to deal with men—is very shrewd—but quite capable of being a good friend to the camp boys.' The young hoyden who holds her own in a male society is not new to Italian opera (see Donizetti's Marie and Verdi's Preziosilla). What distinguishes Minnie is her authority. A country girl born and bred, she speaks the miners' language and is never at a loss for the quick put-down. But she is better educated than they and

---

[34] H. Greenfeld: *Puccini*, 181.

[35] PAF, 135.

able to act as their 'schoolmarm'. None of them would dream of taking advantage of her, though several cherish hopes of a more or less honourable nature—less in that they already have encumbrances at home. The most insistent of her suitors is the sheriff Jack Rance, a man of strong passions, 'the cool, waxen, deliberate gambler' (Belasco again); but even he has to take 'Nope!' for an answer. One man, however, has already made a breach in her heart—a stranger whom she has met on the road to Monterey and who re-appears at the Polka Saloon, ostensibly a *bona fide* traveller in need of refreshment. The stage directions describe 'a young man of about 30—smooth-faced, tall—the one man in the place who has the air of a gentleman. At first acquaintance he bears himself easily but modestly, yet at certain moments there is a devil-may-care recklessness about him.' He gives his name as Johnson of Sacramento. No-one guesses him to be a notorious 'road agent' (i.e. bandit), who goes under the name of Ramerrez, and that he intends to rob the saloon, until the attractions of Minnie and his growing admiration for her cause him to change his mind. Later, however, he is identified and traced to the neighbourhood of Minnie's cabin, where she is entertaining him with due observance of the proprieties. Having learned who he really is, she orders him out into a raging blizzard; but when he falls back against the door wounded she takes him in and hides him in the loft, When drops of blood falling from the ceiling reveal his presence to the Sheriff, Minnie appeals to the gambler in Rance, proposing a game of poker, she to be his if he wins, Johnson/Ramerrez to go free if he loses. Rance accepts the challenge; they play, and she, by cheating, wins. Thence the drama winds down to a rather tame conclusion. There is an 'Academy', during which Minnie's uneasy conscience can be sensed undermining her ability to keep order among her pupils. Unknown to her, Johnson is recaptured by the men of the Wells Fargo Agency and led away to execution; but his plea for a last meeting with Minnie is granted. Their tearful farewell is overheard by the miners, who are so moved by it that they prevail on Rance to release their prisoner. The last act is no more than a brief epilogue showing the lovers awakening to a new dawn (doubtless a spectacular one).

Certainly the drama gains in interest from the fact that very few of the participants are without a streak of decency. Rance not only honours his bargain with Minnie but rises in the end to genuine, if reluctant magnanimity. Johnson's career as a road agent is of recent date, the inheritance of a criminal father 'who left me with a rancho, a band of thieves and nothing else'; and he always stopped short of killing. Faced with death himself, his only concern is for the Girl. Let her believe that he has escaped to lead a better life elsewhere. Among the subsidiary characters Nick the barman stands out as the one member of the community sympathetic to the lovers' cause from the start; and it is he more than anyone who helps to bring about the happy ending. Even the miners, rough and quarrelsome though they be, conceal tender hearts—witness their early 'whip-round' to enable a desperate fellow-worker to return home. Contumely is reserved for the outsiders: the dishonest Australian card-dealer known as 'the Sidney Duck' ('fat, greasy, unctuous and cowardly'); José Castro, a member of Ramerrez's gang, who creates a diversion in order to facilitate the robbery that never takes place ('an oily, greasy, unwashed Mexican greaser of a low type'); Billy Jackrabbit ('a full-blooded Indian, lazy, shifty, beady-eyed'). He and his squaw Wowkle, parents of an illegitimate child, are both comically stupid. Political correctness was never a consideration for Belasco.

A translation commissioned by Sybil Seligman in Puccini's name arrived at Torre del Lago in mid-July. Puccini's sharp eye to theatrical effect at once discerned the weakness of the dénouement. 'I don't much care for the third act', he wrote to her

> but I think it would be possible to re-arrange it if one takes three things into account: the scene where [Johnson] is brought on, bound—I should make the scene of his sentence and of the sheriff's insults take place then—*no school episode*—then *she* arrives, surprised, and there is a big scene in which she pleads for his freedom—everybody being against her except Dick [he meant, of course, Nick]. Finally the cow-boys [*sic!*] are stirred to pity, and she bids a moving farewell to all—there is a great love-duet as they move slowly away, and a scene of grief and desolation among the cow-boys, who remain on stage in different attitudes of misery, depression, etc. But the scene must take place outside the *Polka* in a big wood, and in the background to the right there are paths leading to the mountains—the lovers go off and are lost from sight, then they are seen again in the distance

embracing one another, and finally disappear—how does that strike you? In this way I mix the third and fourth act together.[36]

In the event there would be no final love-duet; the school episode would not be abolished but transferred to the first act with its character radically altered; otherwise Puccini's scheme would be followed to the letter. Much of it is, of course, Act IV of *Les mauvais bergers* moved from France to California.

In August Puccini was joined by the Seligmans, who found him entirely taken up with *The Girl* and unable to talk of anything else. When they had left he went to his hide-out in Chiatri, where he had invited Zangarini for a conference. 'The *Girl* promises to become a second *Bohème*', he wrote to Giulio Ricordi, 'but stronger, bolder, and more spacious.'[37] Small wonder, then, that *L'austriaca* sickened and died.

While he waited for Zangarini's libretto to arrive, revivals of *Madama Butterfly* claimed his attention: at Lucca in September, in Vienna at the Hofoper on 31 October under Francesco Spetrino (Mahler having handed in his resignation) with Selma Kurz in the name part, and in Genoa in November; then a week's shooting in Sardinia.

A *cache* of his letters to the poet has recently come to light, awaiting publication; meanwhile we must rely on the composer's reports to Sybil for information as to the opera's progress. As usual, it was an affair of switchbacks. 15 October: 'the Poet is here and at work—he has already completed the first act. But he won't let me read anything until he's finished it.' 5 November: 'The first act is finished now, but it will be necessary to return to it later, as it needs to be made clearer and to be smartened up. The second act is nearly finished, and, as for the third act, I'm going to create that magnificent scene in the great Californian forest of which I spoke to you at Abetone.' 8 November: 'I think the third act is going to be simply marvellous—if only the poet will understand me; but I'm going to make every effort so as to be certain of getting exactly what I want.' But by 8 January 1908: 'That Zangarini is beginning to annoy me—we've given him an ultimatum which expires on the 15th, and if by that date everything isn't ready . . . we'll get another librettist.' 11 January: 'I've still had nothing from that *pig*

[36] PAF, 139.

[37] CP 521, p. 353.

of a Zangarini.' 30 January: 'At last *The Girl* has arrived! I've had so much work to do with Tito and Zangarini these last days! The result is a really beautiful libretto—it is not fully built, but the foundations have been laid.'[38]

Most of February 1908 was taken up with a trip to Egypt with Elvira, partly to be present at a *Butterfly* in Alexandria with Salomea Krusceniski, partly to visit the various tourist attractions. They set sail from Naples, where Puccini had another opportunity of seeing *Salome* conducted by its composer. He was no more convinced by it than he had been at Budapest (indeed in a later interview he compared it unfavourably with Debussy's *Pelléas*), but he enjoyed Strauss's directions to the orchestra during rehearsals: 'Gentlemen, here we are not dealing with music; this has to be a *zoological garden; so blow hard* into your instruments!'[39]

From a densely packed tour, which found Elvira more than usually *souffrante*, Puccini returned to Torre del Lago, where he waited in vain for Act III of *The Girl*. He now determined that Zangarini should have a collaborator. Again there was a delay while he went to Rome for a *Butterfly* on 25 March under Leopoldo Mugnone, with whose interpretation he now began to find serious fault, though he had nothing but good to say of the cast. The International Society of Artists laid on a banquet in his honour attended by more than 200 guests, including all the notables of the city except for the Pope, since, so Puccini remarked, the ex-Patriarch of Venice was without a gondola for his conveyance.

By now his relations with Zangarini had reached crisis point. 'I'm at daggers drawn with that wretch of a poet', he informed Sybil early in April, 'because he doesn't want to have a collaborator: but tomorrow the matter will be decided with the aid of a lawyer.'[40] And so it was. Zangarini was forced to give way; and again it was Tito Ricordi who found the new incumbent—Guelfo Civinini, a young poet and journalist from Livorno. It would be his only foray into the field of opera (later he would achieve distinction as a war correspondent). No sooner

[38] PAF, 147–52.
[39] CP 538, pp. 363–4.
[40] PAF, 153.

was the contract signed than Puccini summoned him to Torre del Lago to work on the first two acts. Evidently the visit was a success, for soon the composer felt able to begin the composition, the earliest sketches for what he still called *The Girl* bearing the date 24 May 1908. Thereafter he retreated to the isolation of Chiatri from which he sent progress reports to Sybil and the Casa Ricordi. Throughout June the opera was 'taking small steps, but it is going ahead'.[41] This to Clausetti; and to Sybil, 'undoubtedly *The Girl* is more difficult than I thought—it's because of the distinctive and characteristic features with which I wish to endow the opera that for the time being I've lost my way and don't go straight ahead as I should like, . . . But how difficult it is to write an opera at the present day!'[42] By July he was becoming fretful. 'These librettists are a disaster', he wrote to Giulio Ricordi. 'One has disappeared and the other doesn't even reply to my letters. . . . This first act is long and full of details that are of minor interest. . . . I'm discouraged because I want to cut, but neatly and with coherence, and I can't do it by myself.'[43] In August the heat drove him to Boscolungo, where he received Civinini's third act ('good in many parts and in others it will need modifying. There are too many solos for the men of the chorus. I would have liked groups of seven or eight, angry and impetuous. But that we shall need to discuss.'[44] Again it was the weather—now cold and rainy—that decided the Puccinis to return to Torre del Lago after only a fortnight. There they were visited by Civinini, who worked with Giacomo on the libretto throughout September. At last *The Girl* seemed set firmly on course. The title, however, still remained vague. 'I'm going to call the opera either *La figlia del West* or *L'occidente d'oro*', Puccini informed Sybil. 'Which of the two titles do you prefer?'[45] She preferred neither; instead she proposed the one by which the opera is known today: *La fanciulla del West*.

On 29 November Puccini was invited by Edoardo De Fonseca, ed-

[41] CP 546, p. 368.

[42] PAF, 155.

[43] CP 548, p. 368.

[44] GPE 105, p. 179.

[45] PAF, 157.

itor of the periodical that had published his *Terra e mare* of 1902, to complete a questionnaire entitled 'Le tre case di Giacomo Puccini: Torre del Lago—Chiatri—Abetone (Boscolungo)', and to add a line of music to the Italian adage 'Casa mia, per piccina che tu sia, tu mi sembri una Badia'—the equivalent of 'There's no place like home'. From the composer's replies to his 23 questions De Fonseca concocted an article which he printed the following month in his magazine *La casa*, together with a facsimile of the musical manuscript. About this last Puccini was needlessly apologetic, recommending it for the waste-paper basket. True, it is no more than an epigram based on an ostinato of alternating chords with two tiny episodes: but only he could have written it.

Yet in the timing of its composition there was a cruel irony. For ever since October Puccini's home life had been far from blissful. The clouds were gathering for a storm of unprecedented violence. Doria Manfredi, the daughter of a widowed mother, had taken service with the Puccinis at the time of Giacomo's car accident in 1903, being then aged 16. Servants rarely stayed long with Elvira; but Doria was an exception. Totally devoted to the Master, she helped to nurse him through his convalescence and remained to become a domestic 'treasure'. Suddenly Elvira began to accuse her of an affair with her husband. Not only did she give her notice; she reviled her in public and threatened 'as surely as there is a Christ and a Madonna' to drown her in the lake. She tried to persuade the girl's family of her guilt; and they, naturally, threw the blame on her employer. Rodolfo, Doria's brother, wrote to Puccini that he would gladly kill his sister's seducer. Unwisely, since Elvira was spying on his every move (on one occasion dressed in his own clothes), Puccini met Doria in secret to offer comfort. He also wrote to her mother protesting the innocence of them both; but to no avail. Elvira claimed to have caught the two of them *in flagrante;* and many, including her own relations and even Tonio, believed her.

By the New Year 1909 matters had reached a crisis. Puccini fled to Rome for a temporary respite. The day after his departure Doria took poison. Every attempt was made to save her life; but she died five days later. An autopsy, conducted coincidentally by a doctor who had stood as witness to the belated marriage of Giacomo and Elvira, revealed her to have died *virgo intacta*. Puccini was thus vindicated and all rumours of an abortion quashed. Fortunately for her, Elvira had already left for Milan.

Apprised of the tragedy, Puccini's first thought was for a legal separation from his wife. A more pressing concern was to prevent a court case. But Doria's family were determined on retribution. On 1 February 1909 they filed a case against Elvira for defamation of character leading to suicide. All attempts to bribe them into withdrawing the charge proved fruitless. By now the affair had become common knowledge world-wide. Helpful suggestions poured in from Puccini's friends. Ervin Lendvai invited him to Berlin where he would be warmly welcomed and able to work in peace. Illica advised him to take ship to New York, the ideal ambience in which to complete an American opera. But it was to Torre del Lago that Puccini returned at the end of the month, where he persuaded one of his sisters (probably the widowed Nitteti) to keep house for him in Elvira's absence. His state of mind can be gauged from a letter to Sybil. 'I can't work any more! I feel so discouraged! My nights are horrible. . . . Always I have before my eyes the vision of that poor victim, I can't get her out of my mind—it's a continual torment. The fate of that child was too cruel; she killed herself because she could no longer bear the unceasing flow of calumny. . . . If Elvira has the slightest heart she should feel remorse.'[46]

But at the time Elvira felt nothing of the sort. In a long letter she heaped abuse on her husband's head, accusing him of selfish, heartless, and cowardly behaviour; of having always trampled on her devotion to him; of destroying his own family. But God would soon call him to account. He was no longer young nor in perfect health; he would end his life abandoned by everyone and it would serve him right. 'Not even your son', she went on, 'when he thinks of the suffering you have caused his mother, will be able to forgive you.'[47]

Indeed Puccini's relations with Tonio were then none of the easiest. They had been together earlier in Milan, where Puccini had gone to supervise rehearsals for *Manon Lescaut* at La Scala; and Tonio had painted a desolating picture of his mother's condition. Puccini still favoured a

[46] PAF, 174.
[47] PCE 359, p. 365.

separation, if only a temporary one, since perhaps Elvira was less to blame than her gossiping friends and relatives. He returned to Milan early in April for the Italian première of Strauss's *Elektra* ('*Salome* can get by; *Elektra* no!' was his verdict),[48] only to find that Tonio had left his employment with a motor-manufacturing firm and gone 'for a holiday' to Munich, where Elvira had joined him. Worse still, he was thinking of emigrating to Africa. Puccini sent him long, reproachful letters. Was he to lose his son as well as his wife? Fortunately, he managed to dissuade the young man from taking so drastic a step.

In her turn Elvira wrote to their mutual friend and confidant Alfredo Caselli hinting that she might be prepared to return to their home in Torre del Lago, provided certain people were kept away from it. 'It seems impossible', she observed, 'that my charming husband feels comfortable only with his enemies and mine.'[49] Among the latter, sad to say, she included Sybil Seligman, to whom she returned a present together with a cutting note about false friendships. Yet all Puccini's efforts to reach an understanding with his wife, whether by letter or personal meeting, resulted in an *impasse*. Elvira continued to insist that the blame was entirely his; nothing but an admission of guilt would satisfy her.

On the advice of her lawyers—surely misguided—Elvira stayed away from the trial, pleading illness. The prosecution held all the cards, among them a note scribbled by Doria shortly before her death protesting her innocence. Her persecutor was sentenced to five months and five days imprisonment, a fine of 700 lire to be paid to the Manfredi family by way of damages, and the defrayment of all legal costs. An appeal was lodged; and at the same time Puccini resumed negotiations with the plaintiffs for an out-of-court settlement. Eventually they agreed to withdraw the charge for the price of 12,000 lire—a very considerable sum; but Puccini could well afford it.

At first defiant, Elvira soon crumbled. She declared that she no longer wanted a confession from her husband and that she was willing to resume their life together. The end of July found father, mother, and son reunited at the spa town of Bagni di Lucca. 'Elvira seems to have changed a great deal as a result of the hardships of the separation which

[48] PAF, 177.
[49] H. Greenfeld: *Puccini*, 198.

she has endured', Puccini wrote to Sybil, 'and so I hope to have a little peace and to be able to get on with my work.'[50] A purgatory of ten months had come to an end.

It is difficult to believe that all the faults were on one side. Something more than mere suspicion aggravated by change of life is needed to account for the violence of Elvira's reactions. Dante del Fiorentino mentions an incident, apparently harmless, in which Elvira surprised Giacomo and Doria about to take a midnight stroll in the garden. But this may well have been relayed to him in a bowdlerized form. So, while there is no reason to doubt the doctor's findings (Puccini, be it remembered, was a diabetic), 'inappropriate contact' cannot be altogether ruled out. There, however, we must leave it.

A further casualty of this disastrous interlude was, of course, La fanciulla: yet for all Puccini's protestations of inability to work, his dallying with thoughts of suicide, it is evident that the mills of creation were continuing to grind, if with painful slowness. Now the pace quickened. Zangarini and Carignani, that trusty arranger of the vocal scores, both came to Bagni di Lucca, where Puccini remained throughout August, having decided to sell his villa at Boscolungo. The opera was beginning to take on life and strength, so Sybil was told; and by the end of September the second act was nearly finished in short score. In October Puccini felt able to spare the time for a fortnight's visit to Brussels for the Belgian première of Madama Butterfly. Back in Torre del Lago he reached the end of Act III by mid-November. A week later he began the scoring of Act I, which occupied him until 21 January 1910. Evidently the wounds of the past year were slow to heal; for his New Year greeting to Sybil ended with the words 'For the time being I have Minnie—the rest is emptiness. But at least my health is good (touch wood!).'[51]

The paucity of correspondence during the early months of 1910 bears witness to Puccini's total absorption in his new opera. However, a few notes to Ramelde seem to indicate that the black mood was still upon him. A telephone call to Elvira, then detained in Milan by the illness of her daughter Fosca (by now estranged from her husband)

[50] PAF, 181.
[51] PAF, 188.

elicited a conciliatory, if faintly tart reply ('You perhaps miss me for your home comforts. I miss you in quite another way'—and she signed herself with 'your Topisia', that endearment of bygone days).[52] The scoring of Act II was finished '24 minutes before midnight, April 7–8', after which Puccini resumed writing to Sybil. As usual, he painted a gloomy picture. 'I'm living like a hermit, *without emotions and without anything else.* I've still got the whole of the third act to do, and I'm beginning to be a little fed up with Minnie and her friends. Let's hope that the third act will satisfy me as much as the other two.'[53] He proposed dedicating the opera to Queen Alexandra.

June brought a necessary interruption. Gatti-Casazza, who had succeeded Heinrich Conried as managing director of the Metropolitan Opera House, New York, had decided to inaugurate his régime with a visit of the entire company to Paris for a season of Italian opera at the Théâtre du Châtelet with Toscanini as conductor and Caruso as chief star. It was in part a declaration of intent, namely to reverse the German bias of his predecessor. The novelty for Paris was Puccini's *Manon Lescaut*, hitherto withheld from the Opéra Comique, where it would have been given in French, for fear of unfavourable comparison with Massenet's masterpiece. A performance in Italian would be less dangerous; and in the event, thanks to Toscanini's conducting and Caruso's Des Grieux, always one of his outstanding roles, the opera carried the day with the public. Only the critics were merciless. 'If Massenet ever dreamed of being dethroned', remarked the correspondent of *Le courier musical*, 'he should sleep soundly now.' Puccini, however, was used to such treatment from the French press and could afford to ignore it. Indeed, so delighted was he with Toscanini's interpretation that he entrusted him, not for the last time, with various 'lightenings' of the full score which Ricordi proposed to bring out in print. At the same time Acts I and II of *La fanciulla del West* were dispatched to Ettore Panizza in London, whose task it would be to make a reduced orchestration of an opera that calls for larger forces than the average provincial theatre could muster. Before leaving Paris Puccini signed a contract with Gatti-Casazza for the première to take place at the Metropolitan Opera

[52] MP, 103.
[53] PAF, 189.

House in December. It was not a sudden decision. It had long been planned that his American opera should receive its baptism on American soil.

After another spell in the fastness of Chiatri Puccini completed the scoring of *La fanciulla* on 6 August ('Hosanna! Hosanna! Hosanna!' from Giulio Ricordi). Family and friends were bidden to a rented house to celebrate the event. Among them was Toscanini, with whom Puccini went through the score establishing the tempi. '*The Girl* has come out, in my opinion, the best opera I have written', Puccini informed Sybil.[54] Toscanini appears to have agreed with him.

A trip to Switzerland with Elvira and Tonio followed by way of relaxation. Travelling in yet another new car, they stopped at the Simplon Pass to witness the first attempt of the Peruvian aviator Jorge Chavez to cross the Alps, an event described by Puccini in graphic detail to Ramelde. Yet, as so often after the completion of an opera, he was already in pursuit of new subjects. He wrote to Sybil asking for news of Maeterlinck's *L'oiseau bleu*, then running in English at the Haymarket Theatre, London, 'since the book interests me very much'. It is difficult to see why. A fairy-tale heavily impregnated with symbolism, it proceeds by a series of complex transformation scenes and calls for a multitude of characters representing animals, trees, and inanimate objects, vaguely forecasting Ravel's *L'enfant et les sortilèges*. The two principals are children; and here, perhaps, lay the attraction. The idea of an opera about children with no love interest would occur to Puccini more than once in the future. Sybil's countersuggestions of Guinera's *Terra baja* and *Las fioras* by the Quintero brothers Puccini dismissed. True, he would welcome a Spanish subject that would be poetic and original. 'I would like to put an end to *blood*—but that's going to be difficult in Spain.'[55]

Early in November Puccini embarked for America. A passage for two had been booked on the luxury liner 'George Washington' by the management of the Metropolitan Opera, clearly with Elvira in mind. But doubtless recalling the discomfort she had suffered on their previous voyage Puccini decided to leave her at home and take Tonio instead.

[54] PAF, 192.
[55] PAF, 193.

They were accompanied by Tito Ricordi, to whose father Puccini waxed eloquent over their princely accommodation. In New York he was more than ever the cynosure of moneyed society, the press, and the autograph hunters (it is said that a signed extract from Musetta's waltz-song procured him the price of a motor-boat!). The festive atmosphere was marred for him only by plaintive letters from Elvira ('You have deprived me of the satisfaction of participating in your triumph. . . . The only thing that consoles me is the thought that at least you are happy without me. . . . Now you are a great man, and compared to you I am nothing but a pigmy', and more to the same effect.[56]

Meanwhile rehearsals made good progress. Belasco was there to help with the production, his chief concern being to make the multi-national cast look and behave like Americans. Grimaces and gesticulations were out; for the miners hands in pockets were the order of the day. 'The opera is coming out splendidly', Puccini wrote to Elvira, 'the first act a little long, but the second act magnificent, and the third grandiose. . . . Toscanini the *zenith—good, kind, adorable*—in short I'm happy with my work and hope for the best.'[57] The dress rehearsal was attended by Blanche Bates, creator of Minnie on Broadway, who is said to have left at the end in tears.

The première on 10 December 1910 with Emmy Destinn (Minnie), Caruso (Dick Johnson), and Pasquale Amato (Jack Rance) proved one of the most spectacular events in the annals of the theatre. The house was packed with notables of every variety—diplomats, generals, leaders of high society, and such artists of eminence as happened to be in the city, among them the pianist Josef Hoffmann and the composer Humperdinck. *The Sun* summed up the occasion with the banner headline, 'GOLDEN WEST IN OPERA DRAWS GOLD FROM EAST'. The performance itself had every appearance of an uncontested triumph: 47 curtain calls and a silver wreath presented to the composer by Gatti-Casazza amid loud cheers. Next day a banquet in Puccini's honour offered by the Vanderbilts.

But the critics had more than their usual reservations. Some were downright hostile. In *The Musical Courier* we read: 'The music is with-

[56] MP, 236.
[57] MP, 239.

out any appeal beyond that of emphasising the meretricious elements of the libretto. Puccini's harmonic scheme is extremely limited and consists of intervals studiously made unconventional and tonal successions arbitrarily distorted to titillate the senses.' To the critic of *The Nation* the composer's adoption here and there of a Californian folk idiom was due to the drying up of his own melodic invention. Many dwelt on the music's indebtedness to Debussy, an influence to which Puccini had been unwise enough to admit in an interview. The most balanced judgment came from Richard Aldrich of the *New York Times*. He recognized and indeed welcomed the advance in Puccini's harmonic language, and he repudiated the notion of him as an imitator of Debussy; on the contrary, the style remained personal throughout, even if it was not precisely that of *La bohème, Tosca*, and *Madama Butterfly*. But in undertaking a plot of such complexity, such rapidity of action, Puccini had set himself an extraordinarily difficult task. Had he succeeded? Time alone would tell.

In the short term Aldrich's implied doubts were confirmed. After apparently well received premières in London, Rome, Budapest, and Paris, the opera was for the most part laid quietly aside. Even in Italy it failed to enter the central repertory. For this various reasons have been adduced: the trauma of the Affaire Doria, which is thought to have weakened Puccini's inspiration (Marek); a plot that is over-complex and about as credible as *Snow-White and the Seven Dwarfs* (Siciliani); a happy ending which prevented the composer from playing from strength (Seligman). None of these is valid. The tragic events of 1908–9 did no more than hold up the work's completion; the drama is articulated with perfect clarity and rendered wholly believable by the music, while by cutting off Belasco's Act IV Puccini contrived a dénouement in which nostalgia prevails over happiness. True, the score is unusually large with quadruple woodwinds and an infinite variety of percussion, including a wind-machine; but for the smaller theatres a reduced orchestration had been available from the start. The real obstacle to the opera's circulation was the unexpected tartness of the harmonic language and a style of vocal writing that often approximates to the early Baroque 'recitar cantando', with a consequent diminution of the lyrical element. In other words, Puccini had outstripped the popular taste of his day. Now at last time has caught up with him and accorded *La fanciulla del West* the place in the Puccini canon that it deserves.

For the first time since *Le Villi* Puccini opens with a self-contained prelude, an equivalent to Belasco's cinematic projection of the Californian forest in all its majesty; but it is also a statement of musical intent, The initial idea welds whole-tone and diatonic harmony, notably in its second phrase (Ex. 9.1a) as naturally as the first six bars of *Pelléas et Mélisande*. Nor is this the only lesson learnt from Debussy: with it comes a greater emancipation of the discord from its 'functional' role, a logical continuity of unrelated dissonances softened by subtleties of texture, and a rapid flow of dialogue punctuated by orchestral gestures. In its present context the motif yields a consequent (Ex. 9.1b) that treads more familiar Puccinian territory: a downward swaying phrase built up into rising sequences. Both are cardinal themes in the opera; and if in the prelude their effect is pictorial, evoking a measureless landscape with branches of giant trees tossing in the wind, each carries an emotional charge which will be exploited to very different purpose elsewhere.

Ex. 9.1

Ex. 9.2

The three-note droop (*x*) in Ex. 9.1a will convey feelings that vary from compassion to regret, while the rhetoric inherent in Ex. 9.1b will find its place in scenes of high tension. An alternation of both themes drives the prelude to a C major climax together with the introduction of a third idea proclaimed by brass, one of the few whose associations remain constant throughout the opera (Ex. 9.2). This is the motif of Ramerrez the bandit, to which the 'cakewalk' syncopations underlined by an assortment of percussion give a Latin American flavour appropriate to one who is believed, however falsely, to be Mexican.

In Belasco's play the curtain rises on the Polka Saloon in full activity. The opera shows it waking to life as the miners return in successive groups from their day's work; hence a much clearer dramatic exposition. The theme (Ex. 9.3), gently oscillating over a tonic pedal, would seem to take its cue from the inscription above one of the windows—'A real home for the boys'. Wide intervals and an upward coiling line add a fresh colour to the Puccinian melodic spectrum.

At present the only occupants are Sheriff Rance, whose cigar can be seen glowing in the dusk (not for him the traditional 'entrance' to which most principals consider themselves entitled), Larkens, the unsuccessful miner, about to post a sad letter to his family, and Nick the

Ex. 9.3

bartender quietly going about his business in preparation for the men's return. The music traces a ternary pattern touched in with whole-tone elements and sprinkled with dissonances soothingly scored (note the parallel fourths reminiscent of Cavaradossi's brush-strokes at the reprise). The surface is ruffled only by cheerful cries from without ('Hello! Hello!') and a typical anticipation of what will become one of the key-themes of the opera (see Ex. 9.6), here sung by a nameless baritone ('Là lontano, là lontano piangerà').

With the first arrivals, among them Joe, Harry, Happy, Bello (Handsome), and Sid (the Sidney Duck), key, rhythm, and tempo change abruptly. The leaping 2/4 characteristic of the American reel takes over. The initial idea (Ex. 9.4a), a direct quotation of George Cohan's song, 'Belle of the Barber's Ball', yields two smoother consequents (9.4 and 9.4c). 'Dooda dooda day', sung rather oddly to Ex. 9.4b, is, of course, a reference to 'The Camptown Races', a different melody altogether, which is heard in full from behind the scenes at the start of Belasco's play.

At the invitation of Sid several of the miners settle to a game of faro. The entry of a fresh contingent headed by Sonora and Trin introduces

Ex. 9.4a

Ex. 9.4b

Ex. 9.4c

Ex. 9.5

a new theme which is rhythmically akin to Ramerrez's Ex. 9.2, but whose pointed articulation and heavy descending bass line proclaim it robustly American. The game proceeds to workings of Ex. 9.4a, in the course of which the prelude's opening theme, functioning as an augmented continuation of Ex. 9.4b, diverts the attention to Larkens, lost in nostalgia for his home in Cornwall; and here the droop (x) of Ex. 9.1a sprouts a gesture that prolongs the sense of yearning, piquant seconds replacing orthodox thirds in the harmony (Ex. 9.5).

The action focuses once more on the card-table, where the atmosphere is becoming heated. Fragments of Ex. 9.4a are superimposed on a wandering bass, whose dotted rhythm recalls the gambling scene in Massenet's *Manon*. The pace slackens as Nick interrupts the game with an invitation to the adjoining dance hall. Several of the miners accept, but not Trin and Sonora, who have no wish to dance with men. Each in turn enquires of Nick in confidence of his chances with Minnie; and each is given reassurance. Their exchanges form a neat musical pattern—a bouncing melody for the two miners, a chain of descending dominant ninths for the barman's diplomatic replies. The music subsides into a protracted plagal cadence that will launch the 'key melody' referred to above: the song of Jake Wallace, the camp minstrel, to which distance lends enchantment (Ex. 9.6).

Here the recent researches of Allan W. Atlas dispose of a legend.[58] According to most accounts the melody is that of the traditional American song 'Old Dog Tray'. Certainly it has nothing to do with Stephen Foster's song of that name, though there is evidence that this was what Belasco originally intended to use in his play. But by the time Puccini saw a performance the piece chosen was 'Echoes from Home', a similarly nostalgic melody in the course of which Old Dog Tray is mentioned. Puccini used a different melody altogether, taken from the

---

[58] A.W. Atlas: 'Belasco and Puccini: "Old Dog Tray" and the Zuni Indians'.

Ex. 9.6

recently published 'Festive Sun Dance of the Zuni Indians' arranged by Carlos Troyer. As with the folksongs of *Madama Butterfly*, he bent the music to his own purposes without reference to its original character.

Jake enters and leads the company in a free 'pezzo concertato', nowhere sung at full voice, its sense of nostalgia accented by a Puccinian subdominant bias. A happy detail is the propulsive fidget that occurs three times in the interstices of the melody like a 'vamp', arresting the attention with its rhythmic ambiguity, whereby the accent which seems naturally to belong to the third semiquaver in fact falls on the second. It is all too much for Larkens, who bursts into convulsive sobbing. To a long diminuendo the men offer what they can to send him home. An extended cadential phrase worthy of a negro spiritual hummed softly by the miners in unison and richly harmonized brings the episode to a conclusion.

The game resumes to varied workings of Ex. 9.4a,b, and c. Suddenly Bello catches Sid in the act of cheating. The miners immediately call for him to be strung up. The tumult is calmed by Rance, who proposes a more condign punishment ('What is death? A kick into the dark, and then good night!'). He pins to Sid's jacket a card for him to wear 'like a flower'—a sign to all the camps in the neighbourhood that he must never touch cards again. If he attempts to remove it he will be put to death. So much is free declamation with the minimum of orchestral support save for an opening hexatonic gesture expressive of scorn (Ex. 9.7).

About to join the miners in a game of poker, Rance is hailed by a new arrival: Ashby, agent of the Wells Fargo Travelling Company— again a 'cakewalk' motif with the added distinction of a raised Lydian fourth degree. He tells the company that he is on the track of Ramerrez and his gang of Mexicans. At this point, evidently as an afterthought,

Ex. 9.7

Puccini added an ostinato of 14 bars in bolero rhythm (*allegro moderato alla spagnola*) during which a tiny figure is heard on violas and clarinets—an ideogram of danger (Ex. 9.8).

Nick offers drinks on the house, by courtesy of Minnie. All raise their glasses to the Girl—'soon to be Mrs Rance', adds the sheriff, so sparking off a fierce quarrel with Sonora, now well into his cups. The music builds up in harsh, jagged sequences. Sonora threatens Rance with his revolver, but Trin grabs his arm and the shot rings out harmlessly just as Minnie herself appears in a blaze of glory radiating from full orchestra (Ex. 9.9). This theme is one of the main pillars of the score, being associated exclusively with the heroine, whose authority over the men is considerably greater than that of Rance. It is very much the 'new' Puccini: short phrases with wide intervals, each concluding with a dissonance that remains unresolved until its successor brings a change of harmony. Only the final chord is baulked of its resolution by a fresh idea. Behind the tonal shifts a clear C major is felt as a point of departure and arrival. And indeed a pedal note of C persists throughout the following bars as the tension relaxes and the texture thins out into a delicate filigree of strings and woodwind. One by one Joe, Harry, and Sonora offer Minnie their modest tokens. She salutes Rance to a smoothed-out Ex. 9.8, here suggestive of cool indifference. Sonora hands over to her his earnings for safekeeping; whereupon Ashby mut-

Ex. 9.8

Ex. 9.9

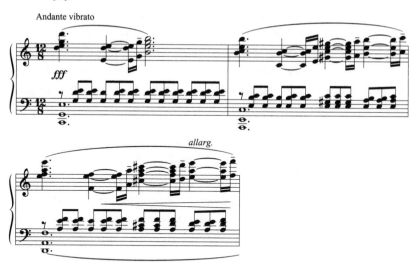

ters darkly about the folly of holding such sums on the premises (once more the bolero rhythm and the warning of Ex. 9.8).

Peace restored, Minnie opens her 'Academy'—a self-contained episode with an instrumental refrain that foreshadows the crystalline sonority of Aaron Copland's *Appalachian Spring* (Ex. 9.10). Her text is taken from the Psalms of David. 'And who was David?' she asks Harry. His reply, a sing-song of alternating sevenths, confuses David with Samson (a 'hee-haw' from the orchestra illustrates 'the jawbone of an ass'). Laughter from Minnie and comic by-play from Trin and Joe. She then proceeds to her reading. 'Purge me with hyssop and I shall be clean.'

Ex. 9.10

'What is hyssop', Trin wants to know? 'A plant that grows in the East', she replies. 'Not here?' (from Joe). 'Yes, even here'—a sign that there is no sinner in the world who is beyond redemption. For this Ex. 9.1a is drawn upon, its wide, hexatonic curve conveying the world's immensity and the three-note droop (x) suggesting compassion; and by way of a postscript Jake Wallace's Ex. 9.6, re-harmonized so as to give a sense of reassurance. Here is Puccini's 'prismatic' use of motifs at its most deft.

By shifting the 'Academy' from Belasco's Act III to his own Act I Puccini altered its dramatic significance not a little. In the play Minnie's discourse on redemption is prompted by her uneasiness over her own lapse of honesty in her card game with Rance. Nor has it anything to do with the book from which she intends to teach—not the Bible but *Old Joe Miller's Jokes*. In the opera she enjoins the Christian virtues out of sheer goodness of heart; hence the men's respect for her.

Originally there followed an exchange with Billy Jackrabbit, whose hexatonic motif (see Ex. 9.16) was heard for the first time. Minnie had noticed him licking the glasses left by the miners. She now bade him count up to 20. Arrived at 'seven', he proceeded to 'jack, queen, king' to general laughter (a detail, this, from the play, where the figure of fun is a dim-witted newcomer, Bucking Billy). Minnie took a number of filched cigars from the Indian's pocket and sent him packing with a reminder to marry his squaw. Puccini wisely omitted this tasteless episode from his definitive edition.

The arrival of the post provides another panel for the fresco of Act I, establishing a mood of cheerful excitement. A dispatch for Ashby informs him that Ramerrez's movements have been betrayed by a certain Nina Micheltorena—and here an impudent syncopated figure like a wink insinuates itself; for Minnie knows all about the pseudo-Spanish cutie from Cachuca who ogles all the men. The sheriff doubts whether such a woman could be trusted; Ashby insists that 'Hell hath no fury. . . .'

The miners disappear into the dance hall, leaving Minnie alone with Rance. Nick enters to tell them of a stranger who is asking for whisky with water, a request unheard of at the Polka ('We'll curl his hair for him!' is Minnie's reaction). Nick leaves, and the peaceful Ex. 9.3 of the Polka Saloon, all fourths and fifths, yields to Rance's Ex. 9.7, its harsh-

ness softened by the prevailing 6/8 lilt; for the sheriff is about to bare
his heart to the woman whom in his own way he loves. Muted strings
launch a long, elegiac melody to which he pleads his cause in dialogue
with Minnie. As it proceeds the pentatonic contours combine with
organum-like progressions to recall the kind of music that Vaughan
Williams was writing at the time (Ex. 9.11).

In his only solo ('Minnie dalla mia casa son partito') he tells her that
no-one ever cared for him; that gambling alone gave him pleasure, since
gold never let him down. Yet he would sacrifice a fortune for a kiss
from her lips—all this to a brief, concentrated arioso held together by
a recurring dip of a sixth, an equivalent in miniature to the figure that
permeates King Marke's monologue ('Tristan, dies' zu mir!'), which
may well have been its inspiration.

Minnie replies with an arioso of her own ('Laggiù nel Soledad ero
piccina'), freer in form than Rance's, more lightly scored and harmonized, and punctuated by tiny, dancing figures including a reference to
Ex. 9.4a on solo violin. Her memories of childhood are delivered in
intimate declamation in a parlante register. Only when she recalls her
parents' love for one another does she rise to four bars of exalted lyricism ('S'amavan tanto!'). Certainly this was not the sort of aria that
audiences expected of Puccini; nor does it come to a full close. But it
has a remote ancestor in Fra Melitone's sermon in Verdi's *La forza del
destino*.

In sum, Minnie will only marry the man she really loves. 'Perhaps
you have found that pearl already', Rance sneers. But it is the orchestra,
not Minnie, who gives the answer with a blast of the Ramerrez motif
(Ex. 9.2) on full orchestra, here a genuine 'carte de visite'; for the man
who now enters, haughtily demanding who wants to curl his hair, is
indeed Ramerrez, strictly incognito. Both he and Minnie suppress a

Ex. **9.11**

motion of surprise, for they have met before. A rising orchestral line betrays the warmth of feeling that invades each, beneath which the syncopated Ramerrez rhythm persists, as Minnie tells Nick, much to his and Rance's surprise, that the stranger may take his whisky as he pleases. By now the tempo has relaxed into a leisurely 6/8 with the Ramerrez motif floating harmlessly over simple pulsations. But Rance is far from satisfied. In the exchanges that follow two motifs are brought into play, the first (Ex. 9.12a) expressive of Rance's ill-concealed hostility, the second (Ex. 9.12b) the easy friendliness of Minnie and the stranger. But where the latter gives his reason for stopping at the Polka—the need for rest and perhaps a game of baccarat—Ex. 9.8 on three clarinets twice sends up a danger signal.

The stranger gives his name as Johnson of Sacramento; then, when Rance has left in a rage, he and Minnie recall their encounter on the road to Monterey. Here Ex. 9.12b dominates a beguiling conversation piece, its last recurrence cut short by the return of Rance, bellicose as ever (Ex. 9.7, now peremptory). He knocks the glass out of Johnson's hand and calls to the miners that there is a stranger in the camp who refuses to state his business. Here occurs the most ironic of Puccini's

Ex. 9.12a

Ex. 9.12b

anticipations; for Rance's words are sung unaccompanied to the strains of what will become the love-duet of the second act (see Ex. 9.17). The men come out of the dance hall ready to do battle; but Minnie calms them with an assurance of Johnson's *bona fides*. Now they are all cordiality towards the stranger. Sonora's 'Buona sera, Mister Johnson' echoes Rance's proclamation in gentler vein; while the playful 2/4 motif that follows suggests a parody of Rance's Ex. 9.7 for the miners are far from displeased at the sheriff's discomfiture. Harry invites the young couple to dance—no matter if Minnie, by her own confession, has never danced before. Obediently the orchestra sets up 32 bars of neutral waltz music. To a cry of 'Hip! Hurrah!' from the miners she and Johnson take the floor, passing slowly into the dance hall. The melody, sung by the men in a soft unison as they clap their hands and stamp their feet in time to the rhythm, shows that Puccini had not lost his faculty for turning out a simple, popular tune (Ex. 9.13).

The waltz has barely touched on an episode when shouts of 'Al laccio!' are heard from outside. Harmonically the music remains frozen in its tracks, working up in a crescendo that explodes into an 'allegro feroce' of rapping quavers, a tramping bass, and a busy inner line, as a group of men headed by Ashby burst in with a captive, the 'greaser' Castro—one of Ramerrez's men, they assume; but Castro protests that he hates the bandit and is only ready to set them on his trail, indeed would gladly deliver the death-blow himself. The miners bind him hand and foot, then go to saddle their horses. In the meantime Johnson returns from the dance hall, passing near enough to Castro for the greaser to whisper to him that several of his men are lying in wait nearby and that a whistle will give the signal for the robbery to take place. The posse, having made ready, set off with Rance in command, taking Castro with them.

Action music, therefore, enlivened by woodwind sweeps up and

Ex. 9.13

Tempo di Valzer Moderato

down, lightning flashes, and gusts from a wind-machine (for a storm is threatening)—but by no means amorphous. The initial theme is extended by subdominant-tending sequences, while Castro's protests are underpinned by chord-alternations played by strings *sul ponticello* and a combination of sustaining wind. Even the four-note 'whistle' on piccolo has its place in the general design. It has already been heard 'con sgarbo' on woodwind, horn, and strings, where Castro declares his wish to stab Ramerrez in the back, and again, more heavily scored, where he calls for brandy in order to remove Nick from earshot.

As the men depart with their prisoner the persistent tremolando dies away in a succession of whole-tone chords which transform themselves into Ex. 9.1a, over which Nick wishes them good luck. Then to the waltz strains of Ex. 9.13, its harmonies sweetened by suspensions and appoggiaturas, Minnie re-enters from the dance hall. Like the first acts of *La bohème* and *Madama Butterfly*, that of *La fanciulla* rises to a plateau of serenity, where it remains until the end with only the occasional brief disturbance. The comparison with *La bohème* is particularly apt, since both operas deal with the burgeoning of romantic love in the course of growing intimacy. The difference is that, whereas Mimì and Rodolfo both give an account of their lives, here, for obvious reasons, the self-revelation is all on Minnie's part. Again the writing is new for Puccini, a compound of vocal and orchestral melody virtually independent of one another. A phrase of the latter, tinged with minor-key melancholy, will be associated with Minnie's sense of solitude, dwelt on with mingled pride and regret (Ex. 9.14). The concluding figure (*x*) will recur with the persistence of an *idée fixe* in the act that follows.

Ex. 9.14

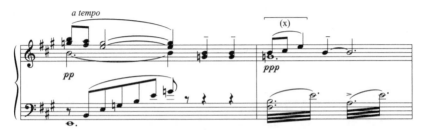

Lyrical expansion is curbed until Johnson takes over the reprise of Ex. 9.13 with heart-warming effect. A postlude merges into the Polka motif (Ex. 9.3), as Minnie confesses to mingled feelings of joy and fear, suddenly breaking off at the sight of Nick re-entering anxiously; he has just noticed another greaser lurking near the camp. Amid the flurry of orchestral agitation violas and clarinets signal danger (Ex. 9.8) followed by the four-note whistle, now from human lips. Minnie is alarmed. The barrel containing the miners' savings is guarded each night by a member of the camp; but since they are all away hunting the bandit it will fall to her to keep watch until they return. Anyone who intends a robbery will have to kill her first (Ex. 9.14, richly scored). In a sombre arioso ('Povera gente!'), shortened by 38 bars in the definitive edition, Minnie paints a desolating picture of the men's situation, forced to work themselves to the bone to provide for their impoverished families. Falling fifths in the vocal line and chromatic slithers of muted trumpets add to the sense of poignancy. At once Johnson's mind is made up. His resolution is conveyed in a noble 'sviolinata' of compassion, fortified by full wind, that melts into whole-tone harmony and is thus able to merge with material from the prelude, which in turn takes on the same emotional connotations (Ex. 9.15).

Before leaving (presumably to call off the robbery) Johnson begs Minnie's permission to visit her in her cabin later that night. A drawn-out reprise of her Ex. 9.9, ethereally scored, brings the music to rest on a soft C major chord, which the listener will easily recognize as forestalling the act's ultimate point of arrival. As the couple take a protracted

Ex. 9.15

leave of one another, Minnie self-deprecating and tearful, Johnson consolatory, Ex. 9.15 takes command, swaying slowly between the chords of C and B flat. The last word is spoken by Ex. 9.9, twice stated pianissimo at full length and backed in the definitive version by a chorus of 15 tenors softly humming. Alone, Minnie reflects on Johnson's parting compliment. 'He said . . . What did he say? . . . The face of an angel.' In the opera her words are followed by an unpitched 'Ah!' English translations, however, usually preserve Belasco's 'Oh hell!' The final chord of a major seventh, sustained by a gradually decreasing body of strings and the faint, lingering tones of the 'fonica' (a modern equivalent of the Aeolian harp) remains firmly unresolved.

Act II, set in Minnie's cabin, opens with a comic scene for Billy Jackrabbit and his squaw, Wowkle, who is rocking their baby to sleep to a monotonous chant said to derive from an Indian source ('Il mio bimbo è grande e piccino'). They converse in the kind of pidgin Italian—all infinitives—that Italians themselves frequently employ towards the ignorant foreigner. Billy reports Minnie's order that they get married the next day, which leads to a desultory discussion about the dowry. But they agree to go to the Mission for the ceremony. Belasco's Wowkle has no desire to stay married for longer than six months. Puccini's Indians, for all their impassivity, are a reasonably settled couple, however crude their appetite for whisky and jewels. All this Puccini sets as a light-hearted scherzo, delicately scored with many an inventive grouping of instruments. The music veers between the diatonic and whole-tone systems, always piquant, sometimes astringent—nowhere a simple triad until the singers join in the recollection of a hymn ('Come fil d'erba è il giorno che al uomo diè il Signor'). The idiom is defined in the opening bars, during which the Indian motif (Ex. 9.16) is heard for the first time in the definitive edition.

Not precisely an idyll, therefore; yet Puccini's Indians, unlike Belasco's, are not without a certain charm. They separate hastily as Minnie enters in a state of mild excitement. She dismisses Billy with a reminder of his wedding and tells Wowkle that there will be two for supper. A snatch of Ex. 9.14(x) like a raised eyebrow indicates Wowkle's surprise ('Altro venire? Ugh! Mai prima')—a piece of tactlessness that provokes a snappy reply from her mistress ('Zitta! pulisci!'). However amid her preoccupations Minnie spares a thought for the baby—a ribbon which

Ex. 9.16

Allegretto moderato

she throws to Wowkle, having received confirmation of her marriage plans. She prepares to receive her guest in such modest finery as she possesses ('Voglio vestirmi tutta come in un giorno di festa'). The light 6/8 gives way to a broad, rising orchestral theme related to Ex. 9.1b from the prelude, culminating, however in Ex. 9.14(x); for even amid her complacent preening Minnie's sense of solitude is never far away. Gloves, perfume—is she perhaps overdoing it? At that moment Johnson's knock at the door ('Hello! Hello!') produces a quick diminuendo. He enters, amazed to see her so smartly dressed. Is she going out? Minnie's confused 'Si . . . No . . . Non so' is corrected by the orchestra with a full statement of Ex. 9.14. She repulses Johnson's attempt to embrace her ('Come siete graziosa!'); hence embarrassment, hesitant syncopations, inchoate figures, and at one point a rocket of flutes in seconds. Peace restored, cellos resume the waltz melody from Act I, now expanded as Minnie recalls Johnson's visit to the Polka, oboes giving a touch of malice to her words (was he perhaps on his way to Nina Micheltorena?).

Johnson turns the conversation to their present surroundings. What a strange life she must lead, alone in the mountains! Minnie's reply corresponds to one of the longer speeches of the play, an evocation of the Californian landscape in all its varied beauty. Puccini's solution is apt and original: a musical triptych, each panel based on a pedal note: mediant in the first with a glittering orchestration, beneath which the voice rises and falls in cascades of near-coloratura, dominant in the second, where the orchestra carries the discourse up to the dizzy heights from which Minnie longs to touch the gates of Heaven. The third panel too has a dominant pedal, but one that becomes dislodged as she passes to the subject of her 'Academy'. Here Ex. 9.1a takes over, prolonged by Ex. 9.5, which now serves as a lever for the theme of the love-duet,

Ex. 9.17

Andante calmo

already casually anticipated after Puccini's fashion in the first act (Ex. 9.17).

Typically, too, it is the orchestra that lights the spark of love in advance, for as yet the couple are engaged in small talk. From the biscuits laid before them they pass to books, especially love stories. The librettists have wisely filleted Belasco's preposterous dialogue with its references to 'Dant' and Beatrice. For Minnie true love is for ever. When Johnson counters that there are men who would give their lives for an hour of love, she wonders how many times he has given his. But her irony becomes submerged by an ostinato of leaping and plunging octaves deriving from the Polka motif (Ex. 9.3), here expressive of Johnson's growing ardour, soon to transform itself into his demand for a kiss—another instance of Puccini's thematic economy.

But Minnie is not yet ready to yield ('Mister Johnson, si chiede spesso la man per aver il braccio'). He can stay for an hour or two; but first Wowkle must be sent home. She opens the door on a blizzard ('Ugh . . . Neve!')—the snowflakes of *La bohème* now storm-tossed by full strings, woodwind, cymbals, rolling timpani, and wind-machine. For Wowkle it must be the hay loft. Alone with Minnie Johnson waxes ever more insistent ('Un bacio, un bacio almen!'); and the ubiquitous fragment (Ex. 9.14x) signals her consent. The door flies open (shades of *Die Walküre!*) as the lovers embrace to an explosion of Ex. 9.1b hexatonically harmonized, then reverting to its normal diatonic area as the door swings shut and the tumult subsides, but with no lowering of the emotional voltage. The orchestra remains in full charge, expressing the feelings that Minnie experiences all too keenly but which Johnson, tormented by conscience, believes it his duty to suppress ('Ah, non mi guardare, non m'ascoltare! Minnie, è sogno vano!'). Despite her protestations, he makes to leave; but four bars of orchestral blizzard and the sound of distant shots put this out of the question. Perhaps Ramerrez is in the vicinity (Ex. 9.2 fortissimo on muted brass within a sustaining tutti). It remains for Johnson to swear eternal fidelity to Minnie and so launch the love-duet ('Io non ti lascio più') to Ex. 9.17. Here at last is the expansive lyrical bloom for which the audience has been waiting, the voices in total command of the melody whether in alternation or ecstatic octave unison. By general consent Puccini was unwise to have extended it by 16 bars for a revival in Rome in 1922, taking both singers up to a sustained high C with full cadence and (hopefully) a bout of clapping. It adds nothing of value, is exceptionally tiring for the singers and consequently omitted today. No applause, therefore, but a dreamy, long drawn out epilogue compounded of material from the waltz and the Polka derivative. Minnie will sleep before the fire wrapped in a bearskin rug, leaving Johnson to occupy her bed alone. The swaying Polka intervals now take on the quality of a lullaby, only once disturbed by a stealthy, hexatonic tread of flutes, clarinets, and harp over a cushion of strings, during which faraway shouts are faintly discernible, to Johnson's alarm. Merely the wind in the branches, Minnie assures him. Drowsily she asks him his Christian name. 'Dick', he replies. Has he ever known Nina Michelterona? 'Never.' And so 'Good night' (the Polka derivative, voluptuously protracted).

But it was not the wind. 'Hello's' from Nick and Sonora bring Johnson with a bound to the door, revolver at the ready. Minnie hustles him back to the bed and draws the surrounding curtains; for she has no choice but to admit her visitors. Enter Nick, Rance, Ashby and Sonora, relieved to find her unharmed. Sid had seen Ramerrez making in the direction of the hut. Not for the first time the orchestra hints at what is to come. Over rolling timpani and tremolando cellos and basses, fragments of Ramerrez' Ex. 9.2 in discordant bitonality are followed by Minnie's Ex. 9.14(x) of solitude, here like a cry of pain, so anticipating her reaction to Rance's revelation after 36 bars of brisk exchanges and busy orchestral figuration that Johnson and Ramerrez are one and the same (Ex. 9.2 in full panoply). To her passionate denials Ex. 9.14(x) adds repeated protests of its own; while from it arises a new theme to which the men proceed to press their point (Ex. 9.18).

The alternating chords and pedal bass are familiar Puccinian territory; but the melodic line with its widely disjunct intervals, extended

Ex. 9.18

over 18 bars in a variety of twists and turns, belongs strictly to the en-larged vocabulary of the present opera. It ends in a cluster of motivic recalls, among them the minatory Ex. 9.8 sounding in the nether regions as Nick's observant eye falls on a half-smoked cigar. Benign as ever, he tries to draw his companions off the scent ('Forse ho sbagliato . . . Quel Sid è una linguaccia!'). But Minnie insists on knowing the name of Rance's informant. 'Nina Micheltorena' is the answer which the sheriff is only too pleased to communicate; and he produces the photograph of Johnson which she had given him. Minnie's laughter at the sight of it is belied by her 'solitude' motif, fierce and discordant on upper woodwind. From here until the men leave (Minnie hav-ing refused Nick's offer to remain) it will dominate the parting ex-changes.

Her 'Vieni fuori!', three times hurled over a solitary drum roll, is answered by a fully scored Ex. 9.1b hexatonic and staggering from beat to beat as Johnson emerges 'defeated, dishevelled'. The music of Min-nie's recriminations, vainly interrupted by her lover, is lean and ener-getic with plenty of movement in the bass as though to compensate for the abundance of pedal notes in the preceding scene. At last Johnson succeeds in gaining her attention. For his *apologia pro vita sua* Puccini takes the easy option of re-running past material, however irrelevant to the present text: his visit to the Polka with the Ramerrez rhythm rising from bass to treble; his passage of arms with Rance in tramping 6/8 (Ex. 9.12a), the danger motif (Ex. 9.8). All this has nothing to do with his father's death and his inheritance of a band of robbers. Only when he mentions his first meeting with Minnie and his resolve to lead a better life with her do the motifs (Exx. 9.12b, 9.1b, 9.17) fall neatly into place. Minnie is moved, but she cannot forget that this is the man who took her first kiss under what she regards as false pretences. 'È finita . . . Finita!', she murmurs mechanically, closing the door behind him. But at least she is spared the indignity of her counterpart in the play ('I'll be like the rest of the women I've seen. I'll give that Nina Micheltorena cards and spades [*wiping her nose*]! There'll be another huzzy round here!').

Now the drama takes on a darker hue, reflected in music of an almost unrelieved minor tonality, while the previous interplay of motifs gives way to larger blocks hewn from the same material. A pistol shot from without launches a succession of thuds pianissimo on massed instruments from cor anglais downward, in the course of which a figure of three descending chords takes shape that will in various guises monopolize the 'scène d'action' in which Johnson falls wounded at the door and is dragged inside protesting by Minnie. An altercation of over 50 bars culminates in a heartfelt declaration wrung from Minnie ('Io t'amo, resta . . . resta . . . Ah! Sei l'uomo che baciai la prima volta. Non puoi morir!'). The orchestral theme which answers it is perhaps the most powerful in the opera (Ex. 9.19).

The rising sixth from dominant to mediant with following re-entrant has been a 'topos' for the avowal of love from Mozart to Richard Strauss. Where the sixth is minor, as in *Tristan und Isolde*, the sense is troubled; and so it is here. The foreign chord (*x*)—the furthest from

Ex. 9.19

the original tonality—increases the feeling of torment, as does Puccini's weighting of the sonority towards the bass with the help of timpani, bass drum, and tam-tam. Minnie lets down a ladder from a trapdoor in the ceiling and helps the enfeebled Johnson to mount it (and here the upward harp glissando serves as a 'madrigalism' for the effortful ascent). She has just time to draw the ladder out of sight, when Rance enters, this time alone. The pentatonic theme (Ex. 9.11) that had launched his first dialogue with Minnie in Act I here takes on a sinister quality on bass clarinet, muted horn, and violas as he advances, pistol in hand, his eyes searching every corner of the room. The musical discourse, solemn and periodic, shifts from key to key, punctuated by a cadential figure that stresses the authority of Rance the sheriff. Finding no trace of the fugitive, he imagines himself mistaken, though he could have sworn that he saw him enter. There is a residual pathos in his plea for Minnie's assurance that she is not in love with Johnson (note the falling sixth of 'Minnie, dalla mia casa' from Act I). 'Siete pazzo!' (Minnie). 'Lo vedi! Son pazzo di te!' (Rance)—and amid a burst of orchestral turmoil he embraces her; but she breaks free, snatches a bottle, and threatens to strike him with it. Rance regains control of himself; but Minnie's behaviour has given him the answer he hoped not to hear. The phrase to which he faces the bitter truth ('Sei fiera! L'ami! Vuoi serbarti a lui!') is taken up by trumpets and horns as an angry challenge that will echo persistently while the tell-tale drops of blood fall on Rance's hand, until broken off by his exultant 'È là! è là!'; thence to a tug of war between him and Minnie to volleys of bunched chords over a pounding bass.

But of course she is the loser. 'Mister Johnson, scendete!' Rance commands, while Ex. 9.19, carried by strings tremolando, dissolves into quaver patterns marked by effortful appoggiaturas as Minnie helps her lover down the ladder and desperately plays for time. The tonality freezes on an A minor chord for Rance to offer his victim the choice of the pistol or the rope. But Johnson has fainted. Minnie takes her momentous decision, her words condensed from Belasco's text: 'He doesn't hear you. . . . But me—me—I hear you—I ain't out of it. [. . .] We're gamblers—we're all gamblers! You asked me to-night if my answer to you was final. Now's your chance! I'll play you a game—straight poker. It's two out of three for me. . . . If you're lucky you git him an' me; but if you lose, this man settin' between is mine to do

with as I please—an' you shut up an' lose like a gentleman.' It falls to
the orchestra to convey the sense of urgency with climbing appoggiaturas; but at the mention of 'una partita a poker' it subsides into plaintive re-iterations of Ex. 9.19 carried by solo oboe over hollow
harmonies lightly scored. 'Come l'ami!' Rance mutters to whole-tone
progressions of profound bitterness. But he accepts Minnie's challenge.
The orchestral theme that will preside over the game of poker (Ex.
9.20) has been compared unfavourably with that which presages Tosca's
murder of Scarpia (Ex. 7.17). But this is surely to miss the point. Even
if Rance's words ('Son tutto della sete di te arso e distrutto') bring him
close to the Roman police chief, Minnie has no intention of killing
him. Just as the emotional clue to Cavaradossi's 'E lucevan le stelle' is
given by his final 'E muoio disperato', so the key to Ex. 9.20 lies in a
later remark of Minnie's not to be found in the play ('È una cosa ter-
ribile pensar che una partita decide d'una vita'). Hence the marking
triste and the elaborated Neapolitan depression (*x*) at the end of the
third bar.

For the first hand, won by Minnie, double basses *divisi* set up a re-
iteration of bichordal semiquavers just above the level of audibility. At
the second, won by Rance, Ex. 9.20 falls away, leaving the basses to
patter and the voices to declaim in rapid alternation. As the cards are
shuffled and cut for the third time, Minnie starts nervously to wheedle
her opponent ('Rance, mi duole delle amare parole. . . . Ho sempre
pensato bene di voi, Jack Rance . . . e sempre penserò'), but to no purpose. Rance throws down what appears to be a winning hand;
whereupon Minnie pretends to feel faint, timpani and cellos joining in
the semiquavers of the basses. Rance, full of genuine concern, goes to

Ex. 9.20

fetch water and a glass, so enabling Minnie to exchange her cards on the table for others which she has concealed in her stocking. Rance returns to find her in a state of collapse—'because you have lost', he surmises in triumph. 'No, because I have won!'—and she displays her three aces and a pair. With an icy 'Buona notte' Rance takes his leave. For the sensational happenings of the last few minutes a handful of shrill orchestral signals suffices. But no sooner is Minnie alone than Ex. 9.19 peals forth in a magnificent peroration, enhanced by her cries of 'È mio!' amid bursts of hysterical laughter. Puccini was never at a loss for a strong curtain.

By the start of Act III a week has passed. The scene is a clearing in the Californian forest with logs scattered here and there and in their midst a fire burning. In the background several men are sleeping, among them Ashby, lying beside his horse. Huge pine trees form a colonnade, above which snow-clad summits are visible. It is a winter's night, shortly before the break of dawn. Puccini, normally so adept at conjuring up a specific ambience, makes no attempt to do so here. The slow bass ostinati, the isolated chordal figures disposed on different instrumental groups evoke the silent brooding of Rance and Nick as they sit facing one another across the fire. Their dialogue is abbreviated fom the play, where it takes place in the Polka. Rance's bitterness finds expression in a distorted recall of Ex. 9.11. The thought of Minnie enjoying her lover's caresses while he and his men were freezing in the blizzard was enough to make him blurt out the truth of his bargain to the whole camp. But he did not do so, Nick reminds him; his behaviour was entirely chivalrous ('Rance, you're my "'deal of a real gent'" '). But the compliment brings no comfort to the sheriff, who can only wonder what Minnie sees in 'that dummy' ('Sacramento shrimp' in the play). To Nick it is just the love that sooner or later comes to all of us, whether from heaven or hell—and a traditional death-figure on violins suggests that the latter is more probable. It has come to Minnie (Ex. 9.9 delicately scored for flute, horn, and a handful of strings).

From here to the end the dramatic scheme is strictly Puccini's. Clearly his aim was to recover the choral dimension of Act I in the manner conceived for *L'austriaca*, the vocal distribution varying between massed forces, small groups, and solo interventions. What results is a broad canvas dominated by a driving 6/4 rhythm, whose switchback motion is generated by the persisting two-note bass ostinato. To sustain the excitement a detailed action is devised. At the sound of distant shouts all present leap to their feet; Ashby saddles his horse with a 'Urrah, ragazzi! . . . Sceriffo, avete udito? . . . N'ero certo! Han trovato il bandito!' Men begin to pour onto the stage. Ashby orders them to lay down their arms, since he intends to take Johnson alive. He departs with the men, leaving Rance to gloat over the prospect of Minnie's misery to a swaying theme that spills over into Ex. 9.11, now instinct with savage glee. But another group of miners headed by Joe, Harry, and Bello burst in from the opposite direction with the news that Johnson has escaped. The chorus, evidently with a clear view of the action from backstage, describe Johnson's flight in graphic terms and are about to join in the pursuit when Sonora arrives to tell them of the bandit's recapture. The general rejoicing is conveyed, surprisingly but not altogether inappropriately, by the melody of the love-duet (Ex. 9.17). The 'allegro selvaggio' which follows is an expended reprise of Ex. 9.4b and c, which here takes on the quality of a war dance. For a few bars the 'Urrah's' cease, allowing us to hear Nick bribing Billy Jackrabbit, hitherto sitting apart unnoticed, to delay tying the noose for Johnson's hanging; after which he slips away, clearly to fetch Minnie. At last Ashby rides in followed by a horseman with a much battered Johnson tied to his saddle. The sway of hexatonic chords that opened the tumult now breaks out again in full force, all present crying out for the 'Spaniard's' blood. Ashby consigns the prisoner to Rance, who receives him with ironical courtesy.

A kind of trial begins, as Bello, Trin, Happy, and Harry lay their various charges against the helpless defendant in the manner of Lucrezia Borgia's accusers in Donizetti's opera. Here Puccini achieves a transition of rare subtlety. Amid the cries of anger, the recalls of the minatory Ex. 9.8, and the extensions of Ex. 9.4b, no longer wholly negative, a pattern of common chords takes shape virtually identical with those that had accompanied Edgar's renunciation of his life with Tigrana. This is Johnson facing death, proud and composed ('Risparmiate lo scherno. . . . Della morte non mi metto pensiero'). Even the miners are temporarily abashed and can only mutter angrily when he asks permission to say a word about the woman he loves. Sonora defends his right to speak; whereupon he pleads that Minnie should never be told the manner of his death; that she should believe him to have escaped to lead a better life far away.

So to the one detachable aria of the opera, and to many its gem ('Ch'ella mi creda libero e lontano'). To give it the quality of a prayer Puccini directs the melodic instruments to play with an organ-like legato; while for the first and only time he adds double basses to the vocal line. There are two strophes only, the second varied with elements of 'parlante'; but what lends it particular distinction is the manner in which Puccini with Verdian skill has united the third and fourth limbs into a single flight of lyricism built on rising sequences: It may be noticed that, unlike in Cavaradossi's 'E lucevan le stelle', the words do not always contribute to the thrust of the melody, but are often distributed over it in notes of lesser value in accordance with the more naturalistic style of *La fanciulla*. The story that during World War I this aria served as an equivalent to the British 'Tipperary' might be thought apocryphal were it not that Vincent Seligman actually heard it sung 'in perfect unison' by an Italian detachment on its way to Salonica to relieve British troops in 1917. 'It was,' he remarks, 'a moment I shall never forget.'[59]

Here, however, it proves too much for Rance, who punches the singer in the face. A rudimentary 'marche au supplice', similar to that which prepared Cavaradossi for the firing-squad, but much fiercer, accompanies the arrangements for Johnson's hanging.

All is in position when to galloping violas and cellos Minnie rides in at full tilt with two 'Ah's', later increased to four. Originally, too, she was followed by Nick, whose temporary absence from the scene was thus explained; but, of course, she makes a far more effective entrance alone.

At once operations are suspended. There follows a fierce altercation between her and Rance, shortened and tightened in the definitive edition. A few of the miners make a move to carry out the sheriff's orders, only to face Minnie's revolver. In vain Rance calls on the men to overpower her ('Nessun di voi ha sangue nelle vene? Una gonna vi fa sbiancare il viso?'); but a prolonged blaze of Ex. 9.9 holds them back. Again it is Sonora who restores order, allowing full rein to Minnie's eloquence. Taking up the miners' shouts of 'Basta!' she asks whether

[59] PAF, 198n.

any of them had cried 'Enough!' when she devoted her youthful years to their service. Here her motif fades into a suaver 3/4 melody that peters out in two motivic recalls: Ex. 9.14(x) where she assures them that the former bandit died days ago beneath her roof, the pleading Ex. 9.5 conveying here both her entreaty not to have him killed and Sonora's sorrow that Johnson has robbed them of something more precious than gold—Minnie's heart. The result is a foregone conclusion. One by one Minnie appeals to the men with memories of the past, while the chorus, at first resistant, are gradually won over. From all this Puccini builds a spacious concertato, whose initial phrase ('E anche tu lo vorrai, Joe') derives from Ex. 9.3 of the Polka Saloon, 'a real home for the boys'. As the music wanders from key to key earlier motifs are woven into the fabric, all sustaining the prevailing mood and confirming the cyclic quality of the score. For the definitive version Puccini thickened the choral texture and doubled some of the solo entries, as he had done in the man-hunt. At the climax of capitulation what had been a solo line for Minnie is now backed by full chorus and soloists, Rance and Billy Jackrabbit alone excepted. There is one further improvement. In the first edition the miners' chorus continue to mutter their opposition to Johnson's reprieve, indicating their final surrender by a silent nod of the head. In the second they end by confessing 'Resister non possiam'.

By now Puccini has established the radiant E major in which the opera will end. The lovers begin slowly to move away with words of farewell to their beloved California. In various attitudes of grief the miners respond with that epitome of nostalgia, Jake Wallace's Ex. 9.6, once in the original version, twice in the revision, the second time joined by Nick who has reappeared, to be embraced by the two principals. Between each statement Minnie and Johnson interject a snatch of their love-duet (Ex. 9.17), both voices rising to a B above the stave before fading into the distance.

A happy ending, therefore? Certainly, insofar as for the first time in a Puccini opera the lovers gain their hearts' desire. Musically, however, the closing bars remain drenched in melancholy, the words 'Mai più!' echoing in the listener's ears. English opera-goers may see a parallel with Vaughan Williams's *Hugh the Drover*, in which Mary, the darling of a Cotswold village, escapes to a new life with a stranger whom the villagers have treated quite as badly as the miners have treated Johnson. There too it is the grief of those left behind that leaves a far stronger impression than the happiness of the lovers. What strikes us above all is the pity of it.

Like *Tosca, La fanciulla del West* is an opera of action, but built on a far larger scale, richer in incident and faster moving. Here the use of 'prismatic' recurring themes together with others of fixed connotation is of particular benefit in enabling Puccini to make a musical organism from Belasco's sprawling drama. Important too is the modification that can be observed in Puccini's vocal technique, especially as it affects some of the lyrical moments of the score. In 'Recondita armonia' and 'E lucevan le stelle' words and melody are inseparable, the second appearing to spring from the first. In Rance's 'Minnie, dalla mia casa' and Johnson's 'Ch'ella mi creda' the text is often spread over the melody in notes of lesser value, thus displacing much of the expressive burden to the orchestra, which consequently achieves a greater degree of autonomy than in the previous operas. Relevant here is the increasing tendency to build large blocks from spaced-out repetitions of a single motif. At the same time the steady widening of Puccini's musical vocabulary, already noticeable in *Madama Butterfly*, is still more in evidence here. In addition to the soft dissonances of piled-up thirds widely spaced, *La fanciulla* takes in sharper clashes of seconds, major and minor, a wealth of tritones, and of discords resolved late or not at all. Even the hexatonic chords, far more abundant than ever before, will sometimes be underpinned by a foreign bass note that gives them a harshness exceeding anything to be found in the anathema of the Zio Bonzo. The melodic writing, too, takes in an unaccustomed 'angularity' of contour. All this permits a new variety and depth of characterization. To a simple, sweet disposition Minnie adds a strain of toughness and authority perfectly reflected in the music. As the antagonist, Rance has the advantage of Scarpia in being portrayed in depth. Unpleasant he may be; but he is at least human. Of the principals Johnson is the most feebly drawn, his confession to Minnie in Act II no more convincing in the opera than in the play. Not until Act III does his stoical behaviour in the face of death command our sympathy.

As with the mature Verdi the expanding harmonic range is matched by a growing inventiveness of scoring, even if there is evidence that some of the ultimate refinements are attributable to Toscanini.[60] Here the lessons of Strauss's *Salome*, revisited by Puccini on every possible occasion, bear ample fruit. *La fanciulla* impresses not only by the novelty of its instrumental groupings but also by the subtlety of their dynamic gradation.

The last word can safely be left to Anton Webern, who, after hearing a performance of the opera in Vienna in 1919, described it in a letter to his teacher Arnold Schoenberg as 'a score with an *original* sound throughout, splendid, every bar a surprise. . . . Not a trace of *Kitsch*. . . . I must say I enjoyed it very much. . . . Am I wrong?'[61] No, he was not.

---

[60] See G. Dotto: 'Opera, Four Hands: Collaborative Alterations in Puccini's *Fanciulla*', *JAMS*, xlii (1989), 604–24.

[61] Cited in SGP 312.

CHAPTER 10

La rondine

O N 26 DECEMBER, LADEN WITH EXPENSIVE GIFTS FOR HIS family, Puccini set sail for Europe with Tonio, Tito Ricordi remaining behind to supervise revivals of *La fanciulla del West* in Chicago and Boston. To Carla Toscanini, the conductor's wife, he sent a long letter of gratitude for help and hospitality during his American sojourn, recalling in particular the happy atmosphere that prevailed in her household. Here we may discern a sub-text: 'If only my own wife were as understanding as you!' For whatever Toscanini's private virtues, marital fidelity was not one of them. Written at 3 A.M. on board the 'Lusitania,' the letter is an all-too-characteristic outpouring of small-hours depression ('completely alone in the world . . . always longing for something and never finding it . . . always misunderstood . . . too far on in years'),[1] which need not be taken too seriously.

After two days in London, where he was honoured by a dinner invitation from the great Marconi, Puccini was back in Milan on 7 January 1911, from then on to pass the year in his usual activities: the search for new subjects, visits to cities at home and abroad to attend local premières of his latest opera, and outdoor recreations, to which must now be added sea-trips, first on his motor-boat 'Ricochet', after August in the more luxurious yacht 'Cio-Cio-San', ordered soon after his return from America. No summer retreat in the mountains,

---

[1] CP 572, p. 383.

therefore, but merely a week motoring with Elvira in South Tyrol. Most of May he spent supervising rehearsals for *La fanciulla* at Covent Garden under Cleofonte Campanini with Emmy Destinn in the name-part. Hard on its heels followed the Roman première (12 June) with Toscanini in charge and a cast that included Amato, the original Rance, Eugenia Burzio, and Amedeo Bassi replacing the indisposed Caruso. The applause was unstinted; but the critics were distinctly guarded in their attitude to Puccini's 'new manner'; and indeed the editor of *Il messaggero* went so far as to write personally to the composer expressing his doubts. Puccini sent the letter on to Clausetti, begging him to draft a tactful reply to the effect that all composers from Verdi to Mascagni had evolved their style over the years, that he himself was being constantly reproached for self-repetition and that the melodic substance of *La fanciulla* was still very much his own. It was a question of 'self-renewal or die'.[2] He could, however, take comfort from a personal letter of congratulation from the opera's dedicatee, Queen Alexandra, together with the gift of a diamond and a ruby pin.

After a revival of Brescia on 23 August with Carmen Melis and the young Giovanni Martinelli as the two lovers it was the turn of Puccini's native Lucca, which mounted a performance during the traditional September season, doubtless from the version for reduced orchestra. This was certainly the form in which it was given in English at Liverpool on 6 October. Puccini paid a lightning visit to England for the occasion, and might have stayed longer had not Sybil been abroad at the time. 'How sad is the Northern sun!' he wrote to her, 'and without Sybil England isn't worth very much.'[3] The last revival of the year took place at the San Carlo Theatre, Naples, under Leopoldo Mugnone, whose direction Puccini now found feeble and flabby. But the theatre remained gratifyingly packed for several nights.

Meanwhile the search for new subjects proceeded at a leisurely pace. Again Sybil's help was enlisted. Puccini's suggestion of Hall Caine's *The Prodigal Son* (a wide-ranging odyssey that begins and ends in Iceland) she countered with Sudermann's play *Johannisfeuer;* but Puccini found in it 'no fluttering of the spirit behind the words, that something which

[2] CP 583, p. 392.
[3] PAF, 210.

evokes music, the divine art which begins, or ought to begin, where the words end'.[4] More to his taste was the novel *Two Little Wooden Shoes* by the Anglo-Belgian writer Louise de la Ramée, pseudonym Ouida, published in Italian as *I due zoccoletti*. Here was the traditional Puccinian heroine—deceived (but not seduced) by a dissolute French painter. Shunned by the villagers, who had hitherto idolized her, she makes her way alone to her lover's house in Paris, where a glimpse through the window reveals him carousing in low female company. Broken-hearted she returns home to drown herself in the river. As collaborator he had in mind the Neapolitan playwright Roberto Bracco, whose *La piccola fonte* he had briefly considered in 1906. Clausetti was asked to make the necessary approaches. If Bracco demurred, why not something new from his pen? 'He is original, bizarre, a human poet, full of heart and feeling, and he has a sense of theatre.'[5] But Bracco failed to rise to the bait; so there the matter rested.

Another counsellor now entered the lists: Riccardo Schnabl-Rossi, a wealthy musical amateur, probably of Austrian-Jewish provenance, with whom Puccini had been in desultory correspondence since 1899, and who would soon become a close confidant. His was the suggestion of Gerhardt Hauptmann's play *Hanneles Himmelfahrt*, which tells the story of a poor orphan girl who, mortally ill, is taken in by a kindly village family. During her last sleep she has a dream in which the people who have figured in her life are transformed into supernatural beings who lead her to the gates of Paradise. There seems little here for Puccini other than an appeal to that Dickensian preoccupation with the death of children that would haunt his imagination from time to time. At first, therefore, his response was negative. But a month later he decided that with a little more variety it might pass as a modest three-acter. He begged Schnabl to approach Hauptmann with the suggestion that he take an Italian collaborator to work on the libretto, allowing the girl a few moments of cheerfulness and leaving gaps for 'sinfonismo rappresentato' (presumably descriptive interludes). Hauptmann declared himself willing on principle; but there was the difficulty that the rights had been granted to the French composer Camille Erlanger, who would

[4] PAF, 206.

[5] CP 584, pp. 392–3.

eventually set the subject, though his opera never reached the stage. However, by the time he had returned from Liverpool Puccini's enthusiasm had cooled. It was all too sad and monotonous—not the meat for 'our Tripolitanian temperament'[6] (a sly reference to the recent Libyan campaign, opposed only by a small group of socialists and republicans, among them one Benito Mussolini, who was thrown into prison for having tried to organize a general strike by way of protest).

Sybil returned to the attack with *Samurun*, a wordless play drawn from *The Arabian Nights* that had been running at the London Coliseum under the direction of Max Reinhardt. Having received a copy of the scenario, Puccini undertook to have it translated, 'though the *East* doesn't interest me very much'. He wondered about Italian translations of the novels of R. D. Blackmore, in particular *Lorna Doone*, surely a subject attuned to the composer's latest manner, with its wild, moorland ambience and undercurrent of violence. Nothing came of it, however. Instead Puccini's thoughts turned once more to comedy. 'Do you know of any grotesque novel, or story, or play full of humour and buffoonery?' he wrote to Sybil. 'I have a desire to laugh and to make other people laugh.'[7]

But it was Giulio Ricordi who put forward what at first seemed a likely subject: *Anima allegra* by the brothers Joaquin and Serafin Alvarez Quintero. The 'Cheerful Soul' of the title is a young girl who comes to stay with a family of straitlaced, snobbish relatives, sorts out their problems, and presides over a gypsy wedding in the locality. The piece had been playing since 1909 in an Italian translation at Milan, where it had made little impression on the composer. Now he felt that, given a librettist who could fill out the action with extra characters and episodes, it might succeed as an opera. It was here that Ricordi rendered his last and by no means least valuable service to his protégé in the person of Giuseppe Adami, a 33-year-old journalist and playwright already at work on the text (never to be completed) of an operetta, *Tappeto rosa*. Puccini was willing to accept him, provided that he took a collaborator—Illica, perhaps, Flavio Testi (author of a comedy about Rossini), his own nephew Carlo Marsili (Nitteti's son), or, better still,

---

[6] PRS 10–13, pp. 32–7.

[7] PAF, 210–12.

Zangarini—and he went so far as to append a scheme of three acts, the second portraying the gypsy wedding, the third a scene of general rejoicing, the merriest of all being the stiff-necked matriarch whose shadow had hitherto blighted the household. The meeting with Adami took place in April 1912, after which the usual doubts began. Spain (not for the first time) evoked the ghost of Bizet. Adami proposed moving the action to Flanders, but to no avail. By August Puccini could inform Sybil, 'Anyone who likes can do the *Anima allegra*, not I—it was a great mistake and I've thought better of it as I did of *Conchita* (and that time I wasn't wrong).'[8] But for both partners the experience had not been unfruitful: Adami's libretto would be set by the composer Franco Vittadini in 1921; while on his part Puccini had found in the poet a resourceful and biddable collaborator for the future and a sympathetic, if not always reliable biographer, the first to publish a selection of his letters.

Indeed 1912 was far from being a cheerful year for the composer. Already the previous autumn Ramelde was showing symptoms of the illness that would carry her off in April. Two months later Giulio Ricordi died, to the composer's inexpressible grief. True, by this time he had less need of the publisher's guiding hand; but from then on his relations with the firm would never be the same. Although he continued to correspond cordially with the new director, Tito, he never trusted him as he had trusted his father, especially since he appeared to be giving his chief backing to a younger rival, Riccardo Zandonai—'who does not lack talent', Puccini admitted to Sybil, having seen a performance of *Conchita*, 'but who at present hasn't got that little something that is needed for the theatre'.[9]

This, too, was the year in which the critic Fausto Torrefranca launched his famous broadside, *Puccini e l'opera internazionale*. A booklet of some 130 pages, its author was the chief spokesman for what has become known as the 'generazione dell'ottanta', a group of composers born in the 1880s comprising Alfredo Casella, Gian Francesco Malipiero, and Ildebrando Pizzetti, who set out to recover the glories of Italy's instrumental past and who regarded the 'giovane scuola' as a millstone

[8] PAF, 223.
[9] PAF, 220.

around the nation's neck. For Torrefranca opera was by its nature inferior to symphony and sonata, a false trail blazed by Monteverdi. The sin was later compounded by Paisiello and Cimarosa, who gave up writing instrumental music altogether. From then on Italy plunged ever deeper into the mire of mediocrity, reaching its nadir in the works of Puccini, which typify the cynical commercialism of modern bourgeois society. He does not deny the author of *La bohème* a certain vitality; but it is that of an essentially uncultivated musician. Take away the words, and the notes are meaningless. Not that the texts are less than contemptible (so much for Giacosa!); but even if they had merit that would not compensate for the composer's total inability to organize his material. Only those who had proved themselves in the symphonic field were justified in writing operas; and here Puccini had shown himself utterly wanting. Above all, by his absorption of foreign influences he had betrayed his national heritage. In a few years he would be forgotten.

Obviously such reasoning would exclude Verdi from the ranks of the great; nor were Torrefranca's heroes averse from doing so. Casella published an attack on Italy's Grand Old Man, which he lived to repudiate. Pizzetti associated himself with Torrefranca in condemning Puccini's commercialism; but he too would modify his opinion in later years. As for the original author, he would eventually describe his defamatory pamphlet as a 'sin of youth', but one which had the merit of forcing Puccini to consider his art more carefully. In fact there is no evidence that Puccini took much notice of it. After all, he could afford to 'cry all the way to the bank'.

Much of this year, like the last, was spent in travelling: first to Budapest for the Hungarian première of *La fanciulla del West;* then to London to see Beerbohm Tree's stage adaptation of George du Maurier's *Trilby*, recommended to him by Alfredo Angeli, one of Sybil's circle (she herself was absent at the time and would hardly have approved of a subject with such a heavily anti-Semitic slant). At all events, results were negative; and Puccini returned home, to set out with Elvira a few weeks afterwards for Monte Carlo for another 'prima' of his latest opera, which a local critic described as 'véritablement triomphale'. The same company conducted by the young Tullio Serafin and reinforced by such principals as Carmen Melis, Caruso, and Titta Ruffo gave *La fanciulla* as part of their guest season at the Paris Opéra, an event which drew the Puccini family, including Fosca, to the French capital for most of May. While there Puccini resumed contact with D'Annunzio, probably saw Stravinsky's *Petrushka* and almost certainly happened upon Didier Gold's apache drama, *La Houppelande*, then playing at the Théâtre Marigny—an experience which would take time to bear fruit. Meanwhile, the public flocked to the Palais Garnier, 'but my fellow-composers and the journalists are real enemies' (to Sybil).[10] He prepared to leave Paris 'rather unwell and in a black humour. . . . I feel my years . . . and then I've another secret reason which I'll tell you of by word of mouth' (to Ramelde's daughter, Albina).[11]

The 'secret reason' that now emerges from the shadows can be identified as the Baroness Josephine von Stengel, the most serious and long-lasting *innamorata* of Puccini's later years. Born in Augsburg in 1886 of a military family, at 20 she had married an officer in the German army to whom she bore two daughters. According to Marotti her acquaintance with Puccini began abroad (in Paris?), after which, probably at the composer's suggestion, she decided on a summer holiday at Viareggio, now his favourite base for boating trips during the hot weather (fortunately, Elvira hated the sea). Nevertheless, their trysts would be beset with danger; hence a series of unexplained excursions on Puccini's part, of alibis requested from friends who were in the secret. Mid-June found him in Munich—'for theatrical reasons', he told D'Annunzio unconvincingly, at the same time begging him for another operatic subject ('By now you know what I need. . . . Great sorrow in little souls').[12] Clearly Josephine's company was not distracting him from his eternal quest. A 'cure' at Carlsbad followed in August, Angeli providing a suitable cover for what was another lovers' meeting. Nor is there any doubt that Josephine accompanied the composer to the Bayreuth Festival that same month, where *Parsifal* brought him 'three days of pure enchantment'.[13] By an unlucky chance he was recognized by a fellow-enthusiast, Carlo Placci, who pointed him out to Cosima Wagner. She at once sent Placci to invite him and his companion to her box. This

[10] PAF, 216.

[11] PCE 412, p. 410.

[12] CP 597, p. 399.

[13] CP 597, p. 401n.

was, of course, out of the question, and Placci had to return pretending that he had been mistaken.

With *Anima allegra* running aground, Puccini reverted to *A Florentine Tragedy*, all the more readily since Giulio Ricordi was no longer there to object to it. He wrote to Sybil asking her to find out whether it was still free. Robert Ross, Wilde's executor, confirmed that it was and recommended that Puccini make use of a preliminary act written by the Irish poet, T. Sturge Moore. Puccini, however, had other ideas, which he outlined to Illica. The elderly husband is set upon by a hostile throng who rain down on him various objects from their windows. A young nobleman comes to his rescue, having caught an imploring glance from his wife. The old man notices the growing sympathy between them and pretends to leave on a journey, then unexpectedly returns, 'and we're at the second act, Wilde's'. He insisted that the first should be full of variety, of stage pictures large and small, of episodes which would allow his music to expand and develop in different 'attitudes'. The lovers should not meet like Faust and Marguerite; they should already be known to one another.[14]

As usual, the prescription was too vague to be of much use to the poet. Moreover, Tito Ricordi was no more friendly to the subject than his father had been; so *A Florentine Tragedy* joined *L'austriaca* on the Illican scrap-heap. Nonetheless Puccini went on urging his old collaborator to cudgel his brains to find the 'quid' that matched his own sense of theatre; and he raised the subject of modern productions, such as those of Max Reinhardt, as a fertilizing source.[15]

With D'Annunzio events seemed to be taking a more hopeful turn. Again from Carlsbad Puccini poured out a rhapsody of sounds and images. 'Not a grand structure. Find me two or (better) three acts, varied, theatrical, enlivened by all the emotional strings—little acts—of sweet little things and people. Leave much room for the visual part; have as many characters as you like; put in three or four women. Women's voices are so beautiful in small groups; put in children, flowers, loves, sorrows.'[16] A performance of *La fanciulla del West* at Marseille

[14] CP 599, p. 400.
[15] CP 636, p. 404.
[16] CP 601, pp. 401–2.

provided the excuse for a trip to France and a meeting with D'Annunzio at his residence at Arachon near Bordeaux. The outcome was a project that seemed to promise well: a tragedy based on the historic Children's Crusade, surely an answer to Puccini's incessant demand for novelty. D'Annunzio was also let into the secret of Josephine, and therefore hardly surprised to receive letters from Munich on Puccini's way home ('I've arrived here for a little happiness that does me so much good. . . . How much better I feel for having completely opened my heart to you!'). Again he vented his enthusiasm in a sound-fantasy: 'I've made out a list, but it has the difficulty of being a kind of orchestra *dans la coulisse*. Harmonium, muted trumpets, muted horns, voices heard through a kind of comb-and-paper, high and low flutes, violas, ocarinas, organ of bells, glassware lightly brushed by hand, . . . and so much else that I can't define, but which I feel.' He urged the poet again to be sparing of words and to give full scope to the loves of two young crusaders.[17] On his part D'Annunzio felt sufficiently confident to write to Tito Ricordi, 'The subject, *La crociata degli innocenti*, is quite unique, full of intense pathos, of impassioned conflicts, dreams, and purity. It is a real, genuine *Mystery*.'[18] But when his draft reached Puccini in January 1913, the first act fully versified, the remaining three merely sketched, it was the old story. 'D'Annunzio has given birth to a small, shapeless monster, unable to walk or to live', Sybil was told.[19] A glance at the poet's 'canovaccio' published the following year as the basis for a film, more than bears out Puccini's withering description. From a scene-setting designed for 'the poet of the woods and the marshes' (Puccini's self-description) it descends into a farrago of mysticism and 'decadentismo'—a leper woman miraculously cured and turned saint, an infant murdered and no less miraculously restored to life, a voyage into the unknown to the strains of a heavenly chorus and much else. The mystery is that D'Annunzio should ever have thought it meat for Puccini.

Yet the year 1912 had not been entirely barren. In November Puccini had turned out a lullaby entitled *Sogno d'or* to words by his nephew

[17] CP 628–9, p. 413 (re-dated SGP, 275).
[18] CP 610, pp. 405–6.
[19] PAF, 216.

Ex. 10.1

Andantino mosso

Bim - bo, mio bim - bo d'a - mor, men - tre tu dor - mi co - sì——— un an-giol

ppp

Carlo Marsili, whom he had briefly considered grooming as his librettist. Published in the Christmas-New Year number of the periodical *Noi e il mondo*, it is a delightful miniature, its simple harmonies coloured by added seconds. Nor would Puccini let it go to waste, as will be seen (Ex. 10.1).

Over the New Year 1913 his attention was claimed by the première of *La fanciulla del West* at La Scala with Tullio Serafin as conductor and Martinelli as Dick Johnson. March took him to Berlin for a performance of the same opera in German at the recently opened opera house in the Charlottenburg Bismarckstrasse. The company was evidently second-rate and the prospects of success doubtful. The turmoil of Puccini's feelings is reflected in his letters to Elvira: first a brusque rebuttal of her complaints at not having been asked to accompany him ('You do not understand that when a man has work to do a woman is a hindrance').[20] Then a cry from the depths ('I am not very well, . . . The prima donna is a nincompoop. The conductor is a mischief-maker. They don't understand a word of Italian or French, . . . I'm invited out but I refuse because that's not for me. Therefore I estrange people, and perhaps arouse more antipathy than sympathy. Yet that is my destiny, always and with everybody. Even you don't seem to care about my worries, . . . Nevertheless . . . I have only found you to whom I can write. . . . I wish that my life were finished . . . '). But after the first

[20] MP, 95.

night, 'I assure you that I have never been present at a success like it. The interpretation was really very fine and the staging marvellous. . . . Everybody loves me, everybody feasts me, and the women—don't be jealous—they don't touch me!'[21]

One of them seems to have done so, however: Margit Veszi, a Hungarian painter and journalist from Budapest, with whom he attended a performance of *Der Rosenkavalier* at the Hofoper, and to whom he wrote what can only be called a love-letter after his return to Milan. A mere flirtation, perhaps, since their correspondence was continued in more sober terms over the next year. Nor did the episode affect his relations with Josephine von Stengel, who in April obtained a divorce from her husband.

In the meantime he had come to a firm decision, namely to secure the rights to Didier Gold's *La Houppelande*. 'It is an "apache" subject in every sense of the word', he wrote to Illica on 9 February, 'almost, and not just almost Grand Guignol. But no matter. I like it, and it seems to me highly effective. But we must counterbalance this splash of red with something absolutely different; that's what I'm looking for.'[22] Here, then, was the first step along the road towards the composition of a triple bill, so long opposed by Giulio Ricordi. The rest of the story, beginning with the search for suitable companion pieces, may usefully be deferred until the next chapter.

Not that he had ceased to cast his lines elsewhere. He still had his eyes on Ouida's *Two Little Wooden Shoes*. Later in the year he would acquire the rights (via Sybil) to Anthony Wharton's comedy *In the Barn* which he had seen performed in Milan in Italian under the title of *Mollie*. Nor was he averse to Adami's suggestion of a subject (unspecified) from Dickens, whose novels were among his favourite reading. He continued to harp on the difficulty of writing an opera in the modern world—witness the silence of Debussy after *Pelléas et Mélisande* and the (in his opinion) unsuccessful experiments of Richard Strauss after *Salome*. He was intrigued, however, by Stravinsky's ballet *Le sacre du printemps,* which he saw in Paris that summer with Elvira ('Ridiculous

[21] MP, 247–8.

[22] CP 619, p. 410.

choreography, the music an absolute cacophony, but strange not without a certain talent. But all in all it's the work of a madman').[23]

In October he set out on another of his promotional travels for *La
fanciulla del West*, first to Hamburg, then Leipzig, and finally Vienna,
where it was given at the Hofoper with Maria Jeritsa and Alfred Piccaver as Minnie and Johnson, respectively. Here he made the acquaintance of the city's leading music critic, Julius Korngold, and his
precocious, gifted son, Erich Wolfgang, soon to achieve fame with *Die
tote Stadt*. He also struck up a lasting friendship with Franz Lehár, whose
operetta *Die ideale Gattin* he saw and admired. It was Lehár who introduced him to Siegmund Eibenschütz, director of the Karltheater, and
Emil Berté, a publisher of operetta. From them came the invitation to
compose a piece for Vienna to a book by Alfred Maria Willner, author
of Lehár's highly successful *Der Graf von Luxemburg*, for the sum of
200,000 kronen. Immediately on his return home he opened negotiations with the Karltheater using his Viennese contact, Angelo Eisner,
as a go-between.

It was the first time that he had proceeded without reference to the
Casa Ricordi. Ever since the previous December, when Tito had
wanted him to sign a contract for *La crociata degli innocenti* before he
had even committed himself to composing it, their relations had become strained. Though they continued to correspond with apparent
cordiality, the words 'My publisher is now my enemy' recur like a
refrain in letters to Sybil and Elvira. The new head of the firm appeared
to be devoting too much time to Zandonai at the older composer's
expense. Worse still, he had failed to send a telegram after the Viennese
première of *La fanciulla*, as his father would certainly have done. During
the next year Puccini seriously thought of taking his custom elsewhere.

But, as usual, he moved cautiously on all fronts. Before signing a
contract with the theatre's management he would need to be fully convinced of the subject on offer. Any intention he had of composing an
operetta with spoken dialogue evaporated on receipt of Willner's sketch.
'It's the usual slipshod, banal operetta', he told Eisner, 'the usual contrast
between East and West, ballroom festivities and opportunities for danc-

[23] GPE 159, p. 239.

ing, with no study of character and in short no dramatic interest (most serious of all). And so? An operetta is something I shall never do; a comic opera, yes, see *Rosenkavalier*, only more entertaining and more organic.'[24]

This letter clearly disposes of Adami's account, whereby Puccini started to compose an operetta and then gave up after writing the first two numbers. True, he had toyed with the idea as early as 1907; and in the meantime the genre had made considerable headway in Italy. Leoncavallo had scored a minor triumph with *La reginetta delle rose* in 1912, which may have played its part in deterring Puccini from a similar purpose. Never, he told his niece Albina, would he descend to Leoncavallo's level. It would seem therefore that, as far as he was concerned, the Viennese commission was to have been a through-composed opera from the start.

By April 1914 Willner, assisted by Heinz Reichert, had submitted a plot more to Puccini's taste. *Die Schwalbe* (*The Swallow* in English, *La rondine* in Italian) has been compared to *La traviata;* but it is a *traviata* from which all the larger issues have been banished. The heroine, Magda, is merely a 'kept woman' attempting to live out an impossible dream. Gone is the mortal illness that plunges Violetta into a hectic pursuit of pleasure; gone, too, the iron pressure of bourgeois morality in the person of Germont *père*, which bars her from a lasting union with the man she loves. Here the 'antagonist' is her protector, Rambaldo, who holds the purse strings. There is no death in a state of moral redemption, merely renunciation, operetta's nearest approach to a tragic dénouement. Ruggero, the naïf young provincial for whom Magda falls, has an operatic forerunner in Jean, the *jeune premier* of Massenet's *Sapho*. The rest belongs strictly to the lighter genre. The subsidiary pair of comic lovers, Lisette and Prunier, are a cliché of operetta (see Camille and Valencienne in *Die lustige Witwe*). The maid who dresses up in her mistress's clothes is an obvious borrowing from *Die Fledermaus*. Nor is it the only one. The 'brindisi' had long been a commonplace of the lyric stage. In Italian opera it is traditionally a lively number with choral refrain, a paean to the joys of the moment. For a slow brindisi, a celebration of 'togetherness' worked up into a concertato in the manner

[24] CP 638, p. 417.

of Puccini's 'Bevo al tuo fresco sorriso' there is only one precedent: 'Brüderlein und Schwesterlein' from Johann Strauss's masterpiece. Fortunately, Puccini had the right melody to hand (see Ex. 10.1).

In May he set up a meeting in Milan with Willner and Adami, who would write the Italian text, Tito Ricordi being unwisely excluded. By July he could inform Sybil, 'I am writing some rather pretty music for *La rondine*—light, but I think interesting—and as clear as spring water'. And in September: 'It's a light sentimental opera with touches of comedy—but it's agreeable, limpid, easy to sing with a little waltz music and lively and fetching tunes. . . . It's a sort of reaction against the repulsive music of today.'[25]

This sounds confident enough; however, the correspondence with Adami attests a difficult gestation with frequent changes of mind. Willner's scenario has not survived, but some of its features can be deduced from Puccini's comments together with a letter from the author written years later, in which he reproaches the composer for his deviations from it. The dénouement was to have been sparked off by an anonymous telegram informing Ruggero of his lover's past; hence a fierce quarrel while a thunderstorm raged without, and Magda's abrupt departure from the love-nest. At first Puccini approved. 'It should turn out grand, compelling, moving. It should be the theatrical *lynch-pin* [*chiodo*] in which all the forces should find an outlet.'[26] But soon he found it absurd. 'Where did he [Ruggero] find Magda, in a convent, perhaps? So this great love of his collapses the moment he finds out who she is? Whoever sees and hears this drama won't be convinced by it and will find the ending almost illogical.'[27] Adami's solution was to substitute for the anonymous telegram a letter from Ruggero's mother, giving her blessing to their marriage. It is now Magda who takes the lead in the final duet, insisting to the broken-hearted Ruggero the necessity of leaving him.

Meanwhile on 30 July World War I had broken out amidst an orgy of flag-waving and euphoria among the parties involved. War fever was in the air. This disagreeable phenomenon, already apparent in the

[25] PAF, 251–8.
[26] GPE 112, p. 188.
[27] GPE 121, p. 194.

Franco-Prussian conflict of 1870, is happily a thing of the past, though war, alas, is not; nor were musicians always immune from it. Wagner had hoped to see the French capital razed to the ground. In 1914 the conductor Hans Richter returned all his English decorations. A year later Leoncavallo would do likewise with those he had received from the Kaiser after *Roland von Berlin* (1904). Puccini's attitude was un-equivocal from the start. 'War is too horrible a thing, whatever the results', he wrote to Sybil, 'for whether it be victory or defeat human lives are sacrificed.'[28] There is no reason to doubt his sincerity.

Although at the time Italy was still neutral, indeed officially tied to the Central Powers by the Triple Alliance of 1882, there was a strong current of feeling in favour of the Allies, particularly among artists and intellectuals who hoped for an end to Austrian rule in South Tyrol. Puccini, with an Austrian contract on his hands, was an obvious target for suspicion on the part of militant patriots. A fierce argument between him and Toscanini that summer resulted in a mutual estrangement that lasted for several years. More embarrassment was to follow. In November the English novelist Hall Caine canvassed Europe's most celebrated names for contributions to his *King Albert's Book*, a tribute to the Belgian monarch forced to flee his capital by the German invasion of his neutral territory. Among musicians Debussy, Messager, Saint-Saëns, Paderewski, Elgar, Leoncavallo all obliged. Puccini at first played for time, giving out through his wife that he was away for a few days and would attend to the matter on his return. He consulted hurriedly with Carlo Clausetti and Tito Ricordi about a suitable reply; for neither he nor they were in favour of a step that might lead to the banning of his works in Austria and Germany. The letter that he eventually sent could hardly have pleased its recipient:

You ask me for something that my spirit would willingly do, for I too have been moved by the sad fate of Belgium and have admired the heroic defence of that people, led by the courageous King Albert.

But I have already received requests to join in other tributes and protests from other parties. I have answered all of them that I wish to stand aside,

[28] PAF, 259.

and because of this did not want my name to appear in public. I tell you this, asking you to forgive my reserve.[29]

One such protest concerning the German bombardment of Rheims has already been issued by the International Society of Artists held in Rome in September. Puccini had indeed held aloof. But this did not prevent a German theatrical correspondent from naming him as one of the signatories; and there was an immediate call for the boycott of his operas. Puccini replied with an open letter to the offending source: 'I have just learned from my publisher, Signor Ricordi, that you count me among those who have taken up a position against Germany. I am pleased to declare to you that I have always abstained from any mani-festation against your country.'[30] True, the 'I am pleased' caused him some uneasiness; and it certainly served to fuel the campaign that was being waged against his operas in France with Léon Daudet, Alphonse's son, at its head. Even some of his own countrymen, among them Illica, were reproachful. No doubt self-interest played a part in Puccini's con-duct. But an avowed anti-German stance might well have incurred the wrath of his publisher, as happened to Leoncavallo, whose name ap-peared on the Rome manifesto, and who later issued a feeble disclaimer to the effect that he had not been present at the Association's meeting (which was true) and that he had no intention of insulting the German nation. His operas remained on the German index, nonetheless.

Then, too, there was Puccini's liaison with Josephine von Stengel. In March her husband met his death on the Western front. Entrusting her two children to the care of her in-laws, she left Germany hoping to settle in a villa in Viareggio, the site of which had been bought for her by Puccini. From this period date three love-letters addressed to the composer at a *poste-restante*. Among their embarrassing endearments one sentence stands out: 'My good Kaiser wants to do well by every-body; but the world is ungrateful.'[31] Puccini would be wary of disagreeing.

Did he really intend separating permanently from Elvira and setting

[29] C. Sartori: *Puccini*, 291–2.

[30] H. Greenfeld: *Puccini*, 234.

[31] PCE 430, p. 424.

up a *ménage* with Josephine? She clearly thought that he did. But their idyll was interrupted when on 30 May Italy entered the war on the side of the Allies. Austria had tried to ensure the country's continuing neutrality with the offer of territorial concessions; but the government, supported by D'Annunzio and that erstwhile pacifist Mussolini, was determined that Italy should take the disputed lands by her own, unaided efforts. At first the auguries were good. The Italian army advanced north to establish a front on the river Isonzo, which would hold out for two years. Tonio enrolled as a volunteer motor-cyclist, later transferring to the Medical Corps, to become a lieutenant in a military hospital. Even Puccini himself took an optimistic view of events, confident of a speedy end to the conflict. Now was the moment for a gesture to appease the French. He therefore ceded his rights to *Tosca* at the Opéra Comique for a whole year to a fund for the nation's wounded. But Tito Ricordi's suggestion that he write a piece similar to Leoncavallo's *Hymn to France* he turned down flat. He had no aptitude for 'occasional' music; nor had he any wish to come second to 'Leonbestia, that *pig*, who, to Italy's shame, is called "maestro" '.[32] There remained, however, the Viennese contract, of which he was determined, if possible, to rid himself. This, he assured Tito, would not be difficult since only a few of Willner's and Reichert's scenes remained in Adami's libretto. Accordingly he arranged a meeting with Berté on neutral territory in Zürich, which proved inconclusive, since Berté's partners had to be consulted. The upshot was that the Austrians retained their rights to the first performance of *Die Schwalbe* but that they would defer it until after the war. All that Puccini had gained from his trip to Switzerland was a few days spent in the company of Josephine, banished from Italy as an enemy alien. 'I am not seeing that person', he wrote untruthfully to Elvira, 'The long war has put barriers and impediments in our way. . . . Let time and circumstances do their work. You alone are my wife.'[33]

La rondine was not completed until April 1916. The problem now was to find an Italian publisher. Tito Ricordi wanted no part in it on the grounds that the Austrian terms were too onerous. Possibly, as Puc-

---

[32] C. Sartori: *Puccini* 294.

[33] MP, 92.

cini heard tell (though Adami assured him otherwise), he considered the music 'bad Lehár'. More probably he had objected to being presented with a *fait accompli* and wished to teach the firm's oldest protégé a lesson. Despite his resentment Puccini subsequently signed an agreement for the publication of all his future operas by the Casa Ricordi.

Fortunately, help for *La rondine* was at hand. The Casa Sonzogno, once the cradle of operatic 'verismo', had fallen on evil days since the retirement of Edoardo, leaving the management in the hands of two quarrelling nephews, Lorenzo and Riccardo. A series of unlucky speculations led to the dismissal of the former, who retaliated by setting up a publishing house of his own, to which Mascagni, Leoncavallo, and Giordano at once transferred their allegiance, and with good reason, for under the indolent Riccardo the original firm was heading for bankruptcy. Riccardo's sudden death in 1915 enabled Lorenzo to repair the breach and assume sole command of the company, to which he now added his own Christian name. Having already invested in the works of Richard Strauss, Humperdinck, and Rimsky-Korsakov, the Casa Lorenzo Sonzogno seized the opportunity of acquiring an opera by Italy's foremost living composer. Not only that; he purchased from the Viennese publisher the right to give the first performance outside Austria. The venue agreed upon was the opera house of Monte Carlo, which under the enterprising direction of Raoul Gunsburg could boast two Massenet premières and the first staging of Berlioz's *La damnation de Faust*. Though nominally independent, Monaco lay under the protection of France; so Léon Daudet felt justified in launching another vitriolic attack on Puccini and promoting the prosecution of Gunsburg for mounting an opera which belonged to the enemy. The impresario was absolved, while Puccini defended himself with a dignified letter to the leading French newspapers describing the origins of the Viennese commission, his own attempts to have it annulled after the outbreak of war, and Lorenzo Sonzogno's success in achieving the opera's liberation. He concluded: 'So M. Daudet's accusation amounts to this: I withdrew from our enemies something which was their property and I gave my opera to an Italian publisher. If this is my crime, I have reason to be proud of it.'[34]

[34] FGP, 160–2.

This was not the whole story. The Austrians still had a claim on the first Viennese performance in German, though this would not take place until three years later and at the Volksoper, not the Karltheater. But for all practical purposes *La rondine* was indeed free and Puccini's conduct in the matter entirely blameless. Indeed during the last two years of the war he was unsparing of public-spirited gestures. As an adjunct to a performance of *La bohème* given in Turin for the benefit of the wounded he contributed an untitled piano piece of 16 bars—admittedly of no great distinction—that was published by the Associazione Stampa Subalpina Torino. In the same city he devoted to a similar fund the proceeds from the twenty-fifth anniversary revival of *Manon Lescaut*. To a volume issued by Ricordi to the Italian Red Cross containing pieces by Boito, Franchetti, Giordano, Leoncavallo, and Mascagni he added a song, *Morire?* The verses by Adami are a reflection on the meaning of life, a question to be answered only by those who had passed beyond it. Puccini's melody, much of it poised over a tonic pedal, has a certain languorous charm enhanced by a characteristic falling sequence in the second quatrain. An unusual feature is the free, cadenza-like conclusion where the singer addresses the spirits of the departed. The same melody would reappear as a 'romanza' for Ruggero in the Viennese version of *La rondine*, the 'cadenza' occurring at the point where the singer turns from a footlight soliloquy to address the company with a specific question. There it makes far better sense; hence a suspicion, confirmed by Adami's early placing of an undated letter referring to a tenor 'romanza', that it might have been intended for the opera's original version and then discarded. But there is no proof either way.

The première of *La rondine* took place on 27 March 1917, the cast headed by the young Gilda Dalla Rizza as Magda, partnered by Tito Schipa as Ruggero. The conductor was Gino Marinuzzi. Its reception was all that Puccini could have hoped for. The press, local and foreign, was unanimous in praising the new genre, half opera, half musical comedy, and predicting a long and glorious flight for the swallow.

Yet no sooner had the bird alighted on Italian soil than the prospect altered. The first performance at Bologna, conducted by Ettore Panizza with Aureliano Pertile as Ruggero and Toti Dal Monte as the maid Lisette, was much applauded by the public and approved by Puccini himself; but the critics were captious, complaining that the opera fell between two stools. At the Teatro Dal Verme, Milan, the audience remained benign, but the critics condemned still more severely the hybrid nature of the work. Puccini blamed the singers ('Dogs, double dogs, triple dogs!') and especially the 'left-handed' conductor, Mugnone, for failing to strike the right note of gaiety and charm.[35] *La rondine* continued to circulate; but by the following spring Puccini had decided on substantial revisions: Prunier to be lowered from tenor to baritone, Ruggero given a 'romanza' to the music of *Morire?;* Lisetta's tessitura raised here and there; the brindisi-concertato in Act II slimmed down to a quartet of principals. In Act III Prunier and Lisette, instead of quarrelling, as in the original version, would unite in trying to persuade Magda to return to her protector. Ruggero would duly return with his mother's letter but leave before Magda could protest at its contents. The final duet would replace him with Prunier, who would lead the sorrowing Magda away.

The new version was tried out at the Teatro Massimo, Palermo, under Vittorio Gui on 20 April 1920. Although absent for the occasion. Puccini felt able to report to Schnabl that it had gone well. He did, however, help with the preparation of the long-awaited Viennese première, which took place at the Volksoper on 7 October. In the absence of Felix Weingartner, then touring in the United States, the opera was conducted by Pietro Starnich, the male lead being taken by Miguel Fleta, who alone sang his part in Italian. The press, while benevolent towards the composer, found fault both with the libretto and the staging. But there was general agreement that *Die Schwalbe* was an improvement on Mascagni's *Lodoletta* ('Little Lark') given at the same theatre earlier in the season. The producer, Ludwig Dreher, was less sure. In the face of falling box-office receipts, he exclaimed to the sub-director, 'Bring me another of those damned birds and I'll shut up shop.'[36]

Puccini too was less than enchanted. '*La rondine* went well', he reported to Sybil, 'but I wasn't happy with the performance or the *mise-en-scène*.' A few days later, 'I am going to re-write *La rondine* for the third time! . . . Adami has been here and has come to an agreement

[35] PCE 446, p. 443.

[36] M. Pravy: 'Mascagni a Vienna', *Studi su Pietro Mascagni* (Milan, 1967), 21.

with the publishers and the Viennese librettists.'[37] Acts I and II would revert to the first edition with a few retouchings of no great significance. Act III, on the other hand, would be radically overhauled and brought into line with Willner's original scheme, but without the thunderstorm. Although Puccini continued for some time to urge this final edition on singers and managements, it was never performed during his lifetime. Indeed in the years following its première *La rondine* had fared badly abroad. Despite Puccini's assurance to Sybil that it was 'just the thing for a London theatre',[38] no manager could be found to take it on. Lorenzo Sonzogno had died in 1920, and the new directors evidently saw little point in giving themselves trouble over an opera for which there was so little demand. Therefore the third edition was never put into circulation. Both autograph and orchestral material remained in the firm's archives, which were bombarded during World War II. Only a vocal score survives containing six pages of new music. As with the fourth act of *Edgar* it is impossible to revive this version as Puccini originally wrote it. Many have assumed that Puccini himself authorized a return to the Monte Carlo edition; but for this there is no documentary evidence. More probably, with *Turandot* on the stocks, he simply lost interest in the matter. By 1922 from 'an opera full of life and melody'[39] *La rondine* had become 'this pig of an opera'.[40] The listener must judge for himself.

' . . . see *Rosenkavalier*, only more entertaining and more organic' (Puccini to Eisler). In one respect he did indeed follow his German contemporary, namely in the updating of his dance-music. If Strauss has no compunction in planting Romantic waltzes in the Vienna of Maria Theresa, neither has Puccini in suffusing his portrait of Second Empire Paris with the ballroom rhythms of his own day. His opening theme (Ex. 10.2a) has the character of a quick-step, launching a compact variant of a familiar pattern: a bouncy motif complemented by a smoothly flowing antithesis (Ex. 10.2b) suggestive of sentimental languour. A

[37] PAF, 319–20.
[38] PAF, 303.
[39] PAF, 269.
[40] PRS III, p. 195.

Ex. 10.2a

Ex. 10.2b

variety of percussion, pitched and unpitched, combine with full or-chestra to create a palette of sophisticated brilliance. Among the guests at Magda de Cuivry's salon the conversation has turned to the eternal theme of love. It is the poet Prunier who holds the floor. In Paris, he tells his incredulous hearers, romance is all the rage. As he warms to his subject a sinuous, conversational melody passes through touches of tango rhythm to dissolve into dreamy whole-tone inflections before being brought down to earth by the maid Lisette. A French Zerbinetta, she defends the permissive society ('Mi vuoi?' 'Ti voglio.' 'É fatto!'). The impudent cadential figure (Ex. 10.3), a musical equivalent of 'So there!', will pepper the score at various points with or without the 'extraneous' note (x).

The poet resumes his discourse, now answered by Magda's friends, Yvette, Bianca, and Suzy, in various attitudes of ironical yearning (Ex. 10.2b with triplet inflections on divided strings). The badinage contin-ues, floated on a distribution of themes already heard, until the poet mentions his latest heroine, Doretta, herself a victim of the fashionable disease. Cue for song. Prunier seats himself at the piano and preludises in lavishly spread chords. 'Chi il bel sogno di Doretta potè indovinar' tells of a girl who refused a king's bribe for her favours, believing that

Ex. 10.3

gold does not bring happiness. But why? Magda, taking Prunier's place at the piano, supplies the answer from her own experience. A student's kiss has revealed to Doretta the whole of life's sweet mystery. The musical design—two strophes with repeated refrain connected by a snatch of 'mélodrame'—owes much to operetta; but it is operetta with a new sophistication. The verse has all the rhythmic flexibility of the mature Puccini, enhanced by moments of organum-like harmony, the refrain (Ex. 10.4) forming the natural point of arrival. At first entrusted to muted violin solo coloured by harp and celeste above murmured comments by Prunier ('Ah creatura! . . . Dolce incanto!'), it later becomes an ecstatic cantilena for Magda, to whom the story means far more than it does to its inventor; hence a richer orchestration throughout. The conclusion debouches into Ex. 10.2b, rendered more voluptuous than ever with up-and-down sweeps on harp and a countertheme on cellos, clarinets, and bassoons, as Prunier takes a rose from a vase and scatters the petals at Magda's feet ('Ai vostri piedi tutte le grazie della Primavera!').

By now Rambaldo with three friends has joined the group at the piano. All express their admiration. Rambaldo, however, has a prophy-

Ex. 10.4

Ex. 10.5

lactic against the prevailing bug of romantic love: a pearl necklace which he hands to Magda. The accompanying theme with its academic harmonies over a tonic pedal (Ex. 10.5) has a down-to-earth gravity that will serve from time to time as a subliminal recall from the world of dreams. Magda's retort ('Ho una sola risposta; non cambio d'opinione') brings the first of the opera's waltz themes with its characteristic hemiola (Ex. 10.6).

There is a brief interruption as Lisette hurries in, takes Rambaldo aside, and whispers to him that he has a visitor who refuses to leave. Seven bars of rapid quavers *martellati*, expressive of her breathless incoherence, momentarily obscure the tonality in a manner unheard of for operetta; but the dialogue quickly settles down into a plain diatonic melody in the rhythm of a fast waltz, punctuated by variants of Lisette's pert Ex. 10.3. Amid the subsequent conversation a new waltz-theme makes its appearance (Ex. 10.7)—of no dramatic significance, but sufficiently memorable for Puccini to recall it at the start of Act III; while

Ex. 10.6

Ex. 10.7

the succession of hemiolas into which it dissolves allows a natural transition into Ex. 10.2b in its enriched form for Magda's revulsion at the power of wealth.

Since Prunier has joined the men, who have retired to the terrace for a smoke, Magda now has an exclusively female audience to whom she can recount an adventure of long ago. One night she escaped from the custody of an elderly aunt to spend an evening at the Café Bullier. There she met a student. It was the *coup de foudre*. To this day she remembers every detail of their encounter: how, when they tired of dancing he ordered two glasses of beer and tipped the waiter lavishly; how at his request she traced her name on the table-top, then fled; for through her new-found happiness a distant voice seemed to warn her of the dangers of total surrender (' "Fanciulla, è sbocciato l'amore" '). Here lies the kernel of the narrative—a plain waltz theme rendered distinctive by the initial distribution of bass notes (Ex. 10.8).

Yet even as she declares that the memory still haunts here, Ex. 10.5, again in the now remote key of E flat, makes clear that she has returned to the present. Rejoined by Prunier, her three friends twit him for having missed a fascinating story; and they dance round him to the vapid strains of Ex. 10.6. The texture is reduced to the lightest of threads so that the badinage can emerge in all its fatuity. Not for Prunier a casual conquest; rather a *grande dame*, refined, elegant, even perverse: a Galatea, Berenice, Francesca, Salome! (and the clarinet quotes a gesture from Richard Strauss's opera, pointed up more emphatically in the second version to make sure that the Viennese should not miss the joke). His hearers are impressed. But Magda, now practical (Ex. 10.5), would like to know how the poet can be certain that the woman will be worthy of him. Her destiny, Prunier replies, will be written in her hand. So to a display of palmistry. He calls for the screen to serve as a fortune-teller's booth. The music—all hollow fourths and fifths over a pizzicato

Ex. 10.8

string bass—has a mechanical, marionette-like quality, suggesting nothing more serious than an intriguing game. A variant of Lisette's Ex. 10.3 prompts a 'cut-away' shot to her own reappearance with a visiting card on a tray. Enter Ruggero Lestocq, shy and embarrassed, with a letter of introduction. Magda, concealed by the screen, cannot have seen him. But Puccini, in true Wagnerian fashion, allows the orchestra to tell us something as yet hidden from the characters it concerns: a dreamily scored restatement of the 'warning' (Ex. 10.8), foretelling the ill-fated romance that will blossom in the next act. Meanwhile, as Prunier reads Magda's hand, the ostinato-based pattern gives way to a motif of solemn chords over a pregnant doninant pedal (Ex. 10.9). One day, the poet predicts, Magda will take flight like the swallow towards a sunlit land far beyond the sea, where love awaits her . . . and then . . . who can tell?

We return to Rambaldo and his guest. Is this his first visit to Paris? Here in the second, Viennese edition Ruggero interpolates his 'romanza' ('Parigi! É la città de' desideri'). An old-fashioned 'footlights' soliloquy, it merely holds up an action that has hitherto moved forward at the speed of a spoken play. Only the last three lines are addressed to present company, in this case Lisette, Rambaldo, and his friends, since the rest are still attending to Prunier behind the screen.

Ex. 10.9

So where should Ruggero spend his first evening in Paris? Rambaldo calls upon Prunier to give advice. 'In bed!' is the poet's response. The glory of Paris is nothing but a myth (this to a snatch of the *Marseillaise*, mockingly echoed by three trumpets). There is a shrill protest from Lisette ('No! No! Mille volte no!'), whose torrent of words the poet tries in vain to silence. The music settles to a graceful polka, as the guests put forward their various suggestions. It is, of course, Lisette who carries the day, insisting on the Bar Bullier.

The return of Ex. 10.2a indicates that the party is at an end. Magda, who so far has taken no notice of the new arrival, begs the company not to pester the poor boy ('No . . . povero figliolo! . . . Un poco di pietà . . . ') But it is clear that mention of the Bar Bullier has awakened memories. She twirls her new necklace, then throws it on the table. To Ex. 10.5 the guests bid her good night, leaving her musing to the waltz strains of Ex. 10.6, diaphanously scored with rippling harp and violins. She orders her carriage from Lisette, who, before retiring, reminds her mistress that this is her night off (Ex. 10.3).

Alone, Magda recalls Prunier's prophecy, the final chord lingering over eight bars like a thought that refuses to be dispelled. Then she too retires. Everything points to a hushed curtain. But Puccini has not yet finished. For Prunier has returned for an assignation with the maid, who reappears dressed in an outfit belonging to her mistress. Their dialogue, compounded of reproaches and endearments, betrays an intimacy of long standing. The entire *scène-à-deux* provides a fine instance of Puccini's new 'block' construction. Its basis is a theme of four bars, variously approached and scored, and perfectly calculated to express a

Ex. 10.10

sly affection (Ex. 10.10) It is love in the manner of Heine rather than D'Annunzio. Magda has not yet left in her carriage. She re-enters dressed as a *grisette*, now speaking, now singing, to bring down the curtain on a cluster of thematic recalls: the 'warning' and Doretta's dream moulded into slow waltz rhythm. Purely orchestral at Monte Carlo, Ex. 10.4 was sung in Vienna to a paraphrase of the original text. But Magda's 'Ma sì, ci mi riconoscerebbe?' spoken over a pause makes a far better conclusion.

Act II, Chez Bullier, presents a busy choral tableau recalling that of the Café Momus. Again there are two contrasted ideas: a driving theme (Ex. 10.11a) whose rhythm recalls the gambling scene of Massenet's *Manon* and a smooth complement (Ex. 10.11b) which supervenes at the point where a number of girls make advances to a young man seated at a table alone—Ruggero, of course! Note here the typically 'extraneous' E natural in an otherwise straightforward melody. But it soon yields to brilliant variants of its predecessor as they try and fail to draw him out. Magda's appearance at the head of the stairs leading to the street is signalled by a gesture sufficiently akin to Ex. 10.2b to fuse with elements from the opera's opening.

Several students approach her; then, observing her glance at Ruggero returned by him with interest, they lead her tactfully to his table and leave them to a *tête-à-tête*. Magda's opening gambit, faltering and embarrassed ('Scusatemi . . . scusate . . . Ma fu per liberarmi di loro'), is set to a prosaic harmonization of Prunier's prophecy, to which Ruggero replies with unexpected warmth. Their growing sympathy is traced with the lightest of touches through a sequence of ideas that merge into the waltz in which they decide to join, Magda, like Minnie, protesting

Ex. 10.11a

Ex. 10.11b

her inexperience. Two thematic anticipations (Ex. 10.12a and b), both within the initial 4/4 pulse, exploit a technique of transition last noted in the Act I love-duet of *Manon Lescaut*.

As Magda and Ruggero disappear into the dancing throng, the first theme becomes a fully fledged choral waltz with Ex. 10.6 from Act I as a pendant. Ex. 10.12a is then whipped up into a vigorous Viennese flourish. To a recall of Ex. 10.12b, now swaying gently in triple rhythm, the voices of Magda and Ruggero float in from the veranda in a languorous unison ('Ebbrezza! Incanto! Sogno!').

The chorus resumes with a lightened texture where a number of girls symbolizing Spring enter dancing in couples to a new melody (Ex. 10.13), which combines neatly with Ex. 10.12a in its waltz guise. A brusque unison gesture alerts us to the two latest arrivals—Prunier and Lisette. Here the world of dreams is invaded by real-life comedy, the poet continually urging his companion to 'act refined', while she herself chatters impatiently. They disappear into the crowd. Magda and Ruggero return to their table, hot and exhausted; and, following the rules of Puccinian economy, the unison gesture that had introduced the maid

Ex. 10.12a

Ex. 10.12b

and her *beau* serves equally well for Ruggero to call for 'due bocks', just like the student of long ago.

As history repeats itself, so does the music; for we are now back with Magda in her memories; and from here on material from her narration of Act I seeps ever more insistently into the musical fabric. The discourse settles into a slow fox-trot ('Perché mai cercate di saper ch'io sia?'), during which Ruggero's growing urgency sweeps Magda off her feet. To a recall of Ex. 10.12b the couple unite in a long kiss, watched with admiration by a number of bystanders. The atmosphere is abruptly shattered by a cry from Lisette, who has recognized her mistress ('Dio!

Ex. 10.13

Lei! Guardala!'). Prunier hastens to convince his companion that she is mistaken. Introductions are effected, Prunier retaining his poet's poise, Lisette's excitement persisting until her pert cadence (Ex. 10.3) falters into silence. Her lively anapaests resume, however, as she confides to Magda her habit of borrowing her mistress's clothes without her knowledge ('É Salome, Berenice?' from Magda to Prunier, who is duly abashed).

But the time has come for a toast ('Bevo al tuo fresco sorriso'), a grand concertato with chorus launched by Ruggero. Here the original lullaby (Ex. 10.1) is expanded into a cantilena of Bellinian length, variously embellished with such devices as imitation, countertheme, and descant and continually putting forth fresh shoots. Musically this is the high point of the opera; and Puccini did it no service by diminishing it for Vienna.

So to the second shock of the evening: the appearance of Rambaldo. Prompt action is called for. As before, Prunier takes the initiative. He tells Ruggero to escort Lisette out of sight while he himself remains to shield Magda. Rambaldo brushes his greetings aside and asks his mistress for an explanation. Magda stands her ground. She has no intention of returning with him, now that she has found happiness in a new love. Rambaldo makes no protest; he merely hopes that she will not live to regret her decision. All this Puccini encompasses within repetitions of a brisk woodwind melody. Then the hall empties, leaving Magda alone with her thoughts. The music dwindles to a syncopated pulsation of string chords in a static G flat major punctuated at wide intervals by a cadential figure on solo bassoon. From outside comes the voice of a soprano doubled by offstage piccolo with a haunting pentatonic melody, the words a poetic variant of the warning that had sounded through Magda's previous adventure. It would not be the last time that Puccini used a distant voice to establish an atmosphere (see *Il tabarro*).

Never was his habit of laying out broad tonal areas towards the end of an act put to surer psychological purpose than here. It is as though Magda remains frozen by the enormity of her decision and unable to still the voice of conscience. Only when Ruggero returns is the spell exorcized by a melting modulation to E major for an extended reprise of the brindisi theme transformed into an avowal of love, steadily mounting to an ecstatic climax with both voices in unison. An orchestration both sumptuous and translucent, including two glockenspiels of different range, closes the act on a note of rapt enchantment.

Act III opens with Magda and Ruggero taking tea on the terrace of a hotel garden on the Côte d'Azur. The music depicts them still enveloped in a waltz by appropriate melodies from the previous two acts re-deployed in accordance with their mood of calm contentment. Nor is the brindisi theme forgotten. From it Puccini spins a huge paragraph during which Ruggero confides a secret: he has written to his parents asking not only for money but for their consent to his marriage with Magda. Undeterred by her alarm, he looks forward to their future in a brief solo ('Dimmi che vuoi seguirmi alla mia casa'). More arioso than aria, its opening strain, set out in simple, two-part harmony, conveys all the young man's earnest naiveté (Ex. 10.14). As he warms to his subject, the progressions gain in richness and intensity with many a Puccinian parallel seventh and ninth before returning to the gravity of Ex. 10.14 for his crowning vision—a child of their own, who knows? A musical as well as a verbal question, it is answered by the 'warning' from Act I (Ex. 10.8), now imbued with a caressing sweetness, as Ruggero kisses Magda and leaves for the post-office. Magda's consternation ('Che più dirgli? Che fare?') finds expression in two reiterated gestures, the first recalling Johnson's self-justification to Minnie, the second (Ex. 10.15) a pattern of hollow ninths like a muted echo of Cio-Cio-San's despair.

She retires to the nearby summer-house as the voices of Prunier and Lisette are heard approaching. The poet has been attempting to groom Lisette for a stage career. The maid-turned-actress is another borrowing

Ex. 10.14

Andante sostenuto
con molta dolcezza

Ruggero: Dim - mi che vuoi   se - guir-mi_al-la mia ca - sa

Ex. 10.15

from *Die Fledermaus*. But, of course, Adele's talents were not put to the test. Lisette's were, and with disastrous results. For this she holds Prunier entirely to blame, while he can only protest at her ingratitude. Their quarrel is dispatched in a nimble Allegro 2/4, a kaleidoscope of motivic recalls, all variously manipulated so as to point up the text. The only new material of note is a two-bar tag answered in the dominant by way of repartee (Ex. 10.16).

Having announced their presence to the butler, Prunier again rounds on Lisette, to receive her cadence (Ex. 10.3) like a slap in the face ('M'insulti? . . . Ti sprezzo!')—a gesture worthy of Musetta. But no sooner has Magda entered than her anger subsides, leaving her 'motto' to take its place as a gentle ostinato. To the waltz strains of Ex. 10.7 Prunier tells his former hostess that a life in the country is not for her; but Magda cuts him short. What of himself and Lisette? She is told of her maid's disastrous début in Nice and the end of her theatrical ambitions. So much is mere declamation over punctuating chords; but no sooner has Magda consented to take Lisette once more into her service

Ex. 10.16

Ex. 10.17

than Prunier's Ex. 10.10 steals in on horns, violas, and bassoons; for though he is merely telling Magda that, should she change her mind, there is someone in Paris willing to welcome her back, his thoughts are clearly elsewhere; hence his parting question whispered to Lisette; at what time will she come off duty?

Lisette goes happily about her business, her 'motto' giving out lyrical offshoots with little or no orchestral accompaniment. But with Ruggero's return seriousness breaks in. To sequences of the swaying Ex. 10.2b he hands Magda the letter that he has received from his mother giving her blessing to their marriage and bids her read it aloud. This she does in a long arioso dominated by a recurring phrase whose rising intervals are a favourite Romantic 'topos' of piety (Ex. 10.17). The mother signs off with a kiss for her prospective daughter-in-law; whereupon Ex. 10.2b returns with a new urgency expressive of Magda's agitation. She is unworthy of Ruggero, she came to him 'contaminated': for her to become his wife would bring him to social ruin. The same motif is transformed by jagged rhythms that screw up the tension, finally giving place to the frantic gestures of Magda's earlier soliloquy. Ruggero protests that her past means nothing to him; that his only concern is that she should not go out of his life. Their duet culminates in a sad, sweet melody, he pleading, she resisting (Ex. 10.18). Here

Ex. 10.18

Puccini reverts to the cabaletta principle with repetitions of the same music, the final reprise being entrusted to the orchestra with the voices 'parlanti'. Throughout, distant chimes sound the death-knell of the lovers' idyll. Ruggero breaks down in tears. Magda leaves supported by Lisette, her last note a high A flat ('Ah!') heard from afar amid Ruggero's sobs.

Such is the opera as we generally hear it today. Of the two successive editions the Viennese can be quickly disposed of. Its objective seems to have been twofold: to avoid any resemblance to *Die Fledermaus* and to meet Willner's criticism of the dénouement ('Whenever did a man behave so wretchedly in real life, let alone on the stage, where he has to hold the attention?'[41]). Hence the attenuation of the brindisi, already noted and deplored. Still less of an improvement is the alteration of the key-sequence in the act's final pages, which robs us of the exquisite modulation that marks the reappearance of Ruggero and Magda's return to her dream world.

In converting the quarrel between Prunier and Lisette in Act III into a terzetto for both parties with Magda, Puccini retained much of the original music with consequent blunting of its cut-and-thrust. But as Prunier begins to apply pressure the harmonies become less pungent, the rhythm smoother and the original thematic reminiscences are replaced by others drawn from the love scene in Act II, including an ironic reference to the passage where Ruggero likened Magda to the simple girls from his native Montauban. The piece ends with a simple lyrical period recalling the idyllic opening of *Edgar*, in which the two visitors bid their friend awake from her dream.

Out goes all mention of Lisette's fiasco in Nice and her happiness at being taken again into service. Instead, she and Prunier are hastily packed out of sight as Ruggero returns with his mother's letter (Ex. 10.2b as before). The music that carried Magda's protests of her own unworthiness becomes an effusion of endearments from Ruggero. He kisses her and retires, leaving her to tormented recollections of her earlier soliloquy. Meanwhile Prunier has re-entered unobtrusively; and it is he who initiates the final duet. Over the concluding reprise he leads Magda to a table and has her write a note of farewell. To this she

---

[41] Cited in GGP, 360–1.

adds a ring which Ruggero had given her as he left for the post-office. Exeunt and curtain.

Not all the alterations to Act I and II can be faulted. The raising here and there of Lisette's line adds a certain piquancy, and an extra prominence given to Rambaldo lays the dramatic issues more clearly before us. But the elimination of all comedy from Act III, with Prunier transformed into a wise baritone counsellor, weakens the interest. Nor does the new text always sit easily on the old music. Not surprisingly, the Viennese version has yet to be revived.

There is more to be said for the third edition. Here the first two acts revert in all essentials to those of 1917. In Act III, however, the changes are far-reaching. The first part of the opening love-duet is re-worked as an orchestral prelude, while the concluding waltz, by compensation, is extended with a further repetition sung by both voices in unison. Three *vendeuses*, Fleury, Mariette, and Rorò, display their wares to Magda to the same strains of the brindisi motif that had accompanied Ruggero's preamble to the confession of his 'secret'. Now he comes more quickly to the point, with no mention of his financial problems (he had merely told Magda to send the girls away). Prunier's quarrel with Lisette remains as in the first edition. But when both have left the stage Magda has another visitor—Rambaldo. His music—five pages of vocal score, most of it new—is all tenderness and manly concern: a leisurely, climbing theme in 6/8, then an apt reference to Ex. 10.5, the motif of worldly reality ('Il vostro cuore ancora non capisce'), another to the frivolous waltz (Ex. 10.5) with which Magda's friends had greeted her story of the student ('La vita è dura, piccola creatura'), and finally an Andantino ('Son di moda a Parigi dei piccoli ornamenti') with a faintly martial strut to it. Here Rambaldo produces a purse filled with gold and emblazoned with the image of a white swallow on a black background—a symbol of his comprehension and the 'placid affection' he is prepared to offer if she should come back to him. Before she can react, ten bars of 'hurry' music announce Ruggero's return. She sends Rambaldo away, then plunges into the final scene with an 'Amore mio!' But Ruggero has brought not a letter from his mother but the anonymous telegram envisaged by Willner, which he reads aloud in unsupported recitative: 'La donna che tu credi degna della tua vita è l'amante di Rambaldo'. His 'Ah, chi sei? Che hai fatto?' are now charged with fury. It is he who accuses Magda of having come to him 'contaminated'. In vain she protests that she feels herself redeemed by his love. The ominous gestures of her soliloquy now mark the point where Ruggero catches sight of the purse—the ultimate proof, he thinks, of her perfidy. In the concluding 'cabaletta' (Ex. 10.18) his interventions are kept to a minimum, since the music is hardly suited to invective. Before the final reprise of the melody he has already stormed out, leaving the last exchanges to Magda and Lisette, who has meanwhile crept in to comfort her mistress. Otherwise the ending remains unchanged.

The earliest attempt to mount this third version of the opera was made at the Teatro Comunale, Bologna, in 1987 under the guidance of the scholar Alfredo Mandelli, who solved the problem of the missing orchestral material by having the music played on the piano from an adjoining room in the hotel, on the analogy of the nocturne performed behind the scenes by the *soi-disant* nephew of Chopin in Giordano's *Fedora*. For a revival at the Teatro Regio, Turin, in 1994 the composer Lorenzo Ferrero orchestrated the five pages of vocal score; and in this form the opera has occasionally been given elsewhere, notably by Britain's Opera North that same year. Certainly it makes for a stronger dénouement in purely dramatic terms; but it needs to be matched by stronger music. Then, too, if Ruggero appears less craven than in the first version, Magda is fatally diminished. Far better that the decision to leave should be hers.

For its first two acts *La rondine* can rank with any of Puccini's mature operas. Here his melodic fertility is seen to flower with renewed vitality without renouncing the harmonic conquests of the earlier opera, while his mastery of orchestral colour is never shown to better advantage. But the third act, in whatever version, falls short. The absence of a strong dramatic current prevents Puccini's cyclical method from bearing fruit. His thematic reminiscences gain nothing from their new context. Ruggero himself remains the least interesting of Puccini's tenor leads. Nor does the Magda of Act III engage our sympathy as do her operatic sisters, whose idyll is likewise shattered. Both Violetta and Mimì know that their days are numbered. Magda enjoys perfect health; all she lacks is money of her own to keep her and her lover afloat. How long did she imagine her dream would last without it? In a word, just what did she think she was about?

To link the plot of an opera with its composer's private circumstances is always a dubious proceeding. Nonetheless it is tempting to see in *La rondine* a reflection of Puccini's relationship with Josephine von Stengel, which proved as fragile as that of Magda and Ruggero. After Italy's declaration of war she moved with her daughters to Lugano in Switzerland, where Puccini was able to pay her surreptitious visits while wintering in Milan—until the Italian consul, possibly prompted by a note from Elvira, withdrew his visa. The love-nest which he intended to build for Josephine in Viareggio was indeed completed after the war; but it would serve for Puccini himself and his family. Instead he installed his mistress and her daughters in a hotel in Casalecchio del Reno near Bologna, passing himself off as a friend of her late husband. News that she had formed a liaison with an Italian officer put an end to their affair. In 1921 Josephine moved to Bologna, from where she wrote to Puccini asking for a loan of 10,000 lire with which to open a hotel. At first Puccini was inclined to refuse. Later he told Dante Del Fiorentino, now his parish priest, 'When I think of the beautiful moments she gave me, it seems to me that I have no right to be deaf to her plea. . . . She asks for a loan, but I don't believe in such things, and anyway it is highly unlikely that her hotel will succeed. So I shall lose the investment. . . . I think the best thing is to send her five thousand lire as a gift.'[42] And so he did. It was a gesture worthy of Rambaldo.

[42] D. Del Fiorentino: *Immortal Bohemian*, 170–1.

CHAPTER 11

Il trittico

PUCCINI'S LETTER TO ILLICA OF 9 FEBRUARY 1913 RECOM-
mending *La Houppelande*[1] marks the end of their correspondence
about future projects. Thereafter only one letter survives, in which Puccini reproaches his old comrade-in-arms for having criticized his failure
to sign the manifesto against the bombing of Rheims. There is no
record of Illica's reply. He himself was an ardent 'interventionist', and
would volunteer for service in the Italian army, though well over the
age limit. Possibly he had taken offence at Puccini's suggestion, relayed
to him by Tito Ricordi, that he collaborate with the young playwright
and future librettist Renato Simoni, Giacosa's successor as editor of *La
lettura*. When Illica died in 1919, Puccini expressed his regret to Adami,
but he did not bother to attend the funeral.

In the meantime, a more likely collaborator had appeared: Giovacchino Forzano, playwright, critic, and librettist, later to make his name
as producer on stage and screen. Five years younger than Adami, his
career had run curiously parallel to that of Antonio Ghislanzoni, poet
of Verdi's *Aida*. Trained in medicine and the law, he first came before
the public as a baritone before devoting himself to literary composition
and journalism (he was for many years editor of Florence's newspaper
La nazione). According to his memoirs he was approached by Puccini
with a request to translate into Italian a French libretto of *La Houppe-*

---

[1] See chapter 10 n.22.

lande made by Maurice Vaucaire. He declined, however, on the grounds that he preferred to work on an original subject (oddly, since at the time he was already adapting Ouida's *Two Little Wooden Shoes* for Mascagni). Instead, he suggested Ferdinando Martini, one time governor of Eritrea. Together he and Puccini visited the old man, then living in retirement at Monsummato near Montecatini. But such verses as he eventually supplied, though beautifully turned, hardly lent themselves to a musical setting, nor were they remotely attuned to the nature of the subject. So he too was obliged to withdraw, leaving the ball to fall into Adami's court.

La Houppelande is indeed Grand Guignol, with a setting that could be said to recall Gorki's *The Raft*. Michel, captain of a barge on the River Seine, is secretly cuckolded by his young wife Georgette with Louis, a stevedore in his employ. On discovering the adulterer he stabs him mortally and wraps the body in a cloak, whose contents he then displays to his wife in a particularly brutal fashion. At the same time another stevedore, Goujon, driven to drink by his own wife's infidelities, emerges from a quayside inn brandishing the knife with which he has finally dispatched her (a crowning horror which would be omitted from the libretto).

Puccini made his vision of the piece very clear to Adami:

> What I'm concerned for is that the Lady Seine [*La Signora Senna*] should be the true protagonist of the drama. This life-style of the boatmen and stevedores dragging out their wretched existence in the traffic of the river, resigned to their lot, is in complete contrast to the longing that throbs in Giorgetta's breast—a yearning for dry land, regret for the noisy clamour of the suburbs, for the lights of Paris. Love snatched at for the odd quarter of an hour is not enough for her. Her dream is to escape, to tread the pavements, to leave the cabin on the water where her child died. . . . These are gleams and shadows that must give the crime a sharp and delicate flavour, like an etching.

Adami grasped his meaning at once. Within a week, he tells us, he had completed and versified the entire libretto.

> I gave Luigi . . . , Giorgetta's lover a revolutionary slant against the miserable slavery that bent his back and shoulders beneath the weight of sacks. For

Giorgetta a feverish desire for a life of freedom, obsessed by memories of Belleville, of old friendships, of Sunday trips to the Bois de Boulogne in merry parties. For Michele, the skipper, the melancholy of old age and a restrained sorrow mingled with the suspicion that he can no longer charm his young dreamer of a companion. I enriched the quayside with eminently Puccinian episodes. I even introduced a ballad singer who distributes loose sheets of paper with a song of Mimì amongst the *midinettes*, and who accompanies himself on an out-of-tune barrel organ.[2]

He sent off the result to Puccini, who wired back his enthusiastic approval. The foundations of *Il tabarro* were thus firmly laid.

So far Puccini had envisaged two operas to make up the evening, one tragic, the other comic. Now he reverted to the idea of a triad of one-acters steeply contrasted from one another. Therefore a piece elevated in tone, possibly mystical or religious, was needed to complete the spectrum. For the last time Puccini sought out Gabriele D'Annunzio, but the poet evaded all attempts to contact him. Valentino Soldani once again offered his services with an abridged *Margherita da Cortona* only to have it rejected, although the subject was not far distant from one that Puccini eventually chose.

For a while the Viennese commission put an end to the search; and his attention switched to Ouida's *Two Little Wooden Shoes*, hitherto no more than a tempting possibility, but now rendered all the more desirable by the news that Mascagni was after it as well. But although Puccini went to great lengths to try to secure the rights to the novel, even to the extent of making an advance payment to the Pretore of Viareggio, it seems that he had no intention of standing in Mascagni's way. Rather he was concerned to prevent his rival's publisher, Lorenzo Sonzogno, from excluding himself. He was on the best of terms with Mascagni's librettist, Forzano, who would be involved as 'literary consultant' in the auction of Ouida's effects which took place in March 1915. To Tito Ricordi, who was now acting for him, Puccini wrote, 'I have shown a certain coolness over the matter of exclusive rights.'[3] So evidently the prospect of 'Four Little Wooden Shoes' did not worry him. The rights to the novel were duly obtained for him by his publisher. That he

[2] ARP, 218–29.
[3] CP 663, pp. 429–30.

intended sooner or later to proceed with it appears from a subsequent letter written to Adami, in which he sketched ideas for the scene of Bébée's death among the water lilies—a backward glance, surely, at that project long cherished but never set: Zola's *La faute de l'Abbé Mouret*!

In October 1915 Adami was summoned to Torre del Lago to put the finishing touches to *La rondine*, to work on the conclusion of *I due zoccoletti*, and to 'go over' the libretto of *La Houppelande*, which Puccini hoped to finish 'in a few weeks'. In the event it would take him just over a year with the usual interruptions. After a hunting expedition in the Maremma he wrote to Adami for more lines for Michele's apostrophe to the Seine ('Scorri, fiume eterno!'), which he would replace in the definitive edition; then for a passionate intervention from Giorgetta at the point where Michele pleads with her to return to his side—a subject which he would raise again the following June in his concern to avoid a near-monologue for the baritone. The duet for Giorgetta and Luigi would need stronger lines for its conclusion ('I beseech you therefore *with feet and hands clasped* to put some warmth into them and give me a winged ending or if you can't find wings at least make it effective as an end should be').[4] What he did not tell Adami is that he had written to Tito Ricordi asking him to contact the playwright Dario Niccodemi, then resident in Paris, from whom he hoped for an Italian equivalent of Didier Gold's Parisian argot. Fortunately, the matter went no further.

He continued to belabour Adami for fresh subjects with which to fill out the evening. Gold himself offered a two-act drama, of which nothing is known save that it failed to meet the case. By the time *Il tabarro* was finished in November 1916 it was still on its own. Puccini's idea of presenting it at Rome or, possibly, Turin in tandem with *Le Villi* foundered on the unavailability of suitable singers during a time of war, even though the baritone Titta Ruffo, an ideal Michele, had hoped to obtain leave from the armed services for the occasion. Eventually it was Forzano who came to the rescue with two pieces of his own invention. The first, *Suor Angelica*, originally intended as a spoken play, concerns a nun of aristocratic lineage who, forced by her family to take the veil for having borne an illegitimate child, takes poison after

[4] GPE 139, p. 214.

hearing from an unforgiving relative that her child has died. But her mortal sin is pardoned by the Virgin Mary who appears to her during her death agony, leading her little son by the hand. 'Puccini', Forzano recalls, 'liked the subject very much. . . . He told me to start writing the verses and rushed off to Milan to tell his publisher Tito Ricordi about it.'[5] In the absence of precise dates, so much can safely be assigned to the early weeks of 1917. With *La rondine* complete and ready for performance Puccini set to work on the 'new nun'. Once again he turned to his friend Don Pietro Panichelli for a liturgical text to be sung by the angels heralding the appearance of the Madonna. 'So no *prega per noi*. Instead we need a *Nostra Regina* or *Santa delle Sante;* but something that can also be repeated in Latin. . . . Then at the moment of the miracle I would like a *Royal March of the Madonna*.'[6] Panichelli was as helpful as he had been over *Tosca;* and it is to him that Puccini owed the definitive text from 'O gloriosa virginum' to 'Coeli recludis cardines'.

But he also had a source of 'copy' nearer to hand: the Convent of Borgopelago, of which his sister Igenia was now Mother Superior. Although hers was strictly speaking an enclosed order, she obtained from the bishop permission for her brother to visit the premises, where he was able to try out passages from his new opera before the assembled company, many of them moved to tears. No documents exist to chart the progress on *Suor Angelica*, since throughout its genesis Forzano remained within easy reach at Viareggio. But from the poet's letters to Tito Ricordi it is clear that the going was smooth. In March, 'I am happy to tell you that the first scene is already ahead musically and that the Maestro has found accents so simple, so noble, so clearly . . . Franciscan that the work could not have a happier beginning'. And to Carlo Clausetti, '*Suor Angelica* threatens to become the Grand Mother Superior of operas!'[7] Evidently in Forzano Puccini had found a kindred spirit.

There remained the trilogy's comic component. Puccini's researches had taken him as far afield as Bernard Shaw, Sacha Guitry, and the then

[5] G. Forzano, *Come li ho conosciuti*, 14.

[6] CP 707, p. 452.

[7] CP 709–10, pp. 454–5.

fashionable team of Flers and Caillevet. Again it was Forzano who came up with the solution. Taking his cue from a few lines in the 30th canto of Dante's *Inferno* amplified by a contemporary commentary first published in 1866, he built his plot round the Florentine rogue Gianni Schicchi, who cheated the Donati family out of an inheritance by impersonating the deceased and dictating a new will in his own favour—but in Forzano's version with the laudable intention of uniting two loving hearts.

At first, it seems, Puccini was less than enchanted. 'I'm afraid that ancient Florence doesn't suit me', he wrote to Adami; 'nor is it a subject that will appeal much to the general public', and he urged Adami to think of a better idea.[8] However, as Forzano developed his theme the composer's imagination took fire—witness two snatches of doggerel sent to the poet indicating that he had already plunged into *Gianni Schicchi* while still at grips with *Suor Angelica*. Nonetheless it was the 'opera claustrale' that was finished first on 14 September 1917. *Gianni Schicchi* was not ready until 20 April the following year. Meantime the collective title had already been arrived at, so Marotti tells us, during a game of cards among Puccini and his intimates including Forzano. *Treno* (Puccini), in case it should prove a fiasco? *Tripodio*? Too funereal. Marotti himself claimed the credit for *Trittico*.[9] Various objections were raised, but Tito Ricordi liked it, and it stuck.

But these were dark days both for Italy and Puccini himself. The rout at Caporetto in October 1917 had thrown the Italian front 150 kilometres back from the Isonzo to the Piave; nor would the situation improve until the recapture of Vittorio Veneto the following year, by which time the epidemic of 'Spanish flu' was making heavy inroads on the population, claiming 80 victims in Torre del Lago alone. Tragedy struck Puccini's family when his sister Tomaide died in August. Elvira's discovery of the consul's letter from Lugano withholding her husband's visa was the occasion for further outbursts of jealousy. The following summer Tonio, caught up in an unhappy love affair, attempted suicide from an overdose of laudanum. Fortunately, he survived to return to his posting at Lake Garda. 'Every day life becomes more difficult' (Puc-

[8] GPE 141, p. 215.
[9] MPI, 175–7.

cini to Sybil). But, as usual, with a completed work behind him, he was soon on the look-out for new plots. To Sybil again, 'I have in mind a subject, full of emotion, in which the leading parts are those of two boys (they would be women in the opera)—a subject which I regard as being suited to the taste of every country, but particularly that of the British public.'[10] No further details are forthcoming, but an educated guess might point to a celebrated Victorian 'weepie' which had run into more than 20 editions since it appeared in 1874—*Misunderstood* by Florence Montgomery, the title referring to the elder of two brothers, both children, who dies after saving the other from drowning. Long forgotten in England, it has twice been turned into an Italian film.

There remained the problem of placing the première of *Il trittico*. A suggestion that it be given at Buenos Aires Puccini turned down flat on the grounds that he would never allow so complex a work to be performed without having seen it mounted in Italy. Surprisingly, however, he agreed to its being launched at the Metropolitan Opera House, New York, even though at the time there seemed to be no possibility of his attendance. As usual, he gave much thought to the staging. He was particularly concerned that *Il tabarro* should not be played too far forward even in theatres (by that time very few) that retained the large proscenium. The action should take place on the barge throughout, apart from a few quayside episodes which should come from the back of the stage.[11] All this, he declared, would be new and highly original. Nor was it a mere experiment, but an integral part of the opera's conception—a restrained 'verismo' far distant from the noisy rhetoric usually associated with the term.

The première took place on 14 December 1918—in Puccini's absence, since, although the armistice was a month old, there was still danger from unexploded mines in the Atlantic. The conductor Roberto Moranzoni had already received the composer's instructions in September. All that remained was a last-minute extension to Suor Angelica's aria 'Senza mamma', which Puccini sent off post-haste in October ('since with this piece the part takes on greater importance and besides

[10] PAF, 276–8.
[11] CP 724, pp. 463–4.

it isn't difficult to perform').[12] Of the principals only Giulio Crimi doubled as Luigi in *Il tabarro* and Rinuccio in *Gianni Schicchi*. Claudia Muzio played Giorgetta, Geraldine Farrar Suor Angelica. Giuseppe De Luca distinguished himself in the title role of the comedy. The impresario Gatti-Casazza cabled an enthusiastic report on the first night's success; but in fact the reviews were mixed. By general consent the triumph belonged to *Gianni Schicchi*, which was felt to be destined for the repertory—'so uproariously funny . . . so full of life, humor and ingenious devices' (Henry Krehbiel in *The New York Herald Tribune*), 'gaiety . . . irresistible . . . as frothy and exhilarating as champagne' (James Gibbons Huneker in the *New York Times*); 'full of Composer's Old Time Inspiration' (*The North American* of Philadelphia). John H. Raferty of *The Morning Telegraph* was alone in finding *Il tabarro* the best of the three pieces. Others rated it below *Cavalleria rusticana* and *Pagliacci*. For *Suor Angelica* there was scarcely a good word: 'an obvious failure . . . the music far too lacking in refinement . . . excessive repetition' (*The Dial*); 'a false Maeterlinck' (Huneker, referring to the Belgian poet's *Soeur Béatrice*, which likewise ends with a miracle), 'the appearance of the Virgin merely an illuminated Christmas card'. Nevertheless, *Il trittico* survived intact for two seasons before being subjected to dismemberment. *Suor Angelica*, as might be expected, was the first to go.

More important to Puccini was the Italian première, given at the Teatro Costanzi, Rome, on 11 January 1919 under Gino Marinuzzi. Among the hand-picked cast Carlo Galeffi doubled as Michele and Schicchi, Edoardo De Giovanni (the American tenor Edward Johnson) as Luigi and Rinuccio, Gilda Dalla Rizza as Angelica and Lauretta. Maria Labia would remain his favourite Giorgetta, even though, by her own account, she had criticized his writing for soprano to his face.

As in New York, critical opinion pronounced in favour of *Gianni Schicchi*. *Suor Angelica* was kindly treated—'the poetic opera of the triptych' (Matteo Incagliati in *Il giornale d'Italia*). But there were serious reservations over the ruthless 'verismo' of *Il tabarro*, a genre which was felt in Italy to have had its day. Among the audience was Toscanini.

[12] CP 753, pp. 468.

Several years earlier he had read the libretto and pronounced it utter trash, Grand Guignol of the worst sort. Now he ostentatiously left the theatre as the first curtain fell, making no attempt to hide his disgust and so, for a while, joining the ranks of Puccinian 'pigs'.

That he should be engaged for the London première of *Il trittico* planned for the season of 1920 was therefore out of the question, though such had been Tito Ricordi's intention. 'I won't have this *God*', Puccini stormed to Sybil. 'If he comes to London *I shan't come*, which would be a great disappointment to me.'[13] He would have been happy with Sir Thomas Beecham, so he said, but whether because that most capricious of conductors declined, the honour passed to Gaetano Bavagnoli with a cast that included Gilda Dalla Rizza as Suor Angelica and Tom Burke, then known as 'the Lancashire Caruso', as Luigi and Rinuccio. The first night, 18 June, was attended by King George V and Queen Mary, who called Puccini to their box to give him their congratulations. The audience received him with boundless enthusiasm but, as more than one critic hinted, more as the composer of *La bohème, Tosca,* and *Madama Butterfly* than of the latest *Trittico*. Here the dismemberment followed quickly. First *Suor Angelica* was dropped, then *Il tabarro,* leaving *Gianni Schicchi* to accompany Diaghilev's Ballets Russes. From Italy Puccini protested in vain, particularly aggrieved at the exclusion of his 'opera claustrale', which he firmly maintained to be the best of the three. But it would not return to Covent Garden until nearly 20 years after World War II. It would fare better at Vienna, where the entire *Trittico* was given in German at the State Opera in October 1920 with Maria Jeritza as Giorgetta, Alfred Piccaver as Luigi and an outstanding Angelica in Lotte Lehmann. After a revival at Bologna in 1921 Puccini, having shortened Michele's 'Scorri, fiume eterno!' by 18 bars, decided to replace it altogether. He outlined his ideas in a letter to Adami of 1 November: 'I want something direct, moving, new, deeply felt, not long. That monologue is really too academic and damages the end of the drama. We need a piece that allows for a variety of movement. And finish with a *muoio disperato* rhymed and in rhythm and above all suited to a musical flight which I hope to find with the

---

[13] PAF, 293.

guidance of your words.'[14] The result was the infinitely more powerful 'Nulla! Silenzio!' to be heard today.

The last revival of importance took place at La Scala on 29 January 1922. By now the first and third panels of the triptych had reached their definitive form. There remained, however, a significant change to *Suor Angelica* for which no documentation has so far come to light. In the original score Angelica's aria 'Senza mamma' had been followed by another, listing the flowers from which she intends to brew a deadly potion. This 'aria dei fiori' is one of Puccini's boldest harmonic ventures, in which tonality is virtually suspended. Most sopranos omitted it from early on, including Gilda Dalla Rizza, despite Puccini's pleas to the contrary. Yet in the definitive edition it no longer appears. Its place is taken by an ironic back-reference to an earlier episode, woven into the preceding intermezzo.

The idea of a triple-bill whose components complement one another by contrast was strictly Puccini's own; nor are there any precedents for it. Contrast, however, would not have been enough; and it may well have been Forzano who, given *Il tabarro* as a starting point, found the necessary linking thread in death, treated brutally in the first piece, sentimentally in the second, and with cheerful cynicism in the third. There remains the problem of length—'as long as a transatlantic cable', Puccini wrote during the rehearsals at Bologna in 1921.[15] But he continued to insist that his triptych be given in its entirety.

Of the three operas *Il tabarro* represents the most remarkable step forward in the direction of objectivity. In 1894 Puccini had given as his reason for rejecting Verga's *La lupa* the lack of 'a single *luminous* and appealing figure'. But is this any less true of Gold's *La Houppelande*? Georgette no more commands our sympathy than Leoncavallo's Nedda. Her requited passion for Louis is merely biological, a case of youth calling to youth (their respective ages, 25 and 20, are given in the cast lists of both play and opera). At 50 Michele is a quiescent volcano, as terrifying in his final eruption as Scarpia or Rance. Yet, unlike Gold, Puccini endows his characters with touches of humanity that raise them

[14] GPE 195, p. 271.
[15] Ibid.

above the level of items in a crime report. Here, then, is a new 'verismo' in which the emotional rhetoric typical of the movement's earliest
musical products is allowed only occasionally to break through the surface of observed phenomena.

For once the curtain rises on a silent picture which the orchestra proceeds to fill out in terms of sound. For his vision of life on the water
Puccini elaborates a navigational 'topos' that reaches as far back as Handel's time: an andante in compound rhythm over a pattern of pizzicato
basses (Ex. 11.1a). The rise and fall of the melodic line is calculated to
suggest the irregular swirl of a busy waterway, while the widely spaced
quavers of the double basses, reaching down to the bottom of their
compass, convey a sense of depth, within the hollow, Debussyan dissonances. The lack of tonal definition—G, part major, part modal with
an inclination to E minor—permits the assimilation of naturalistic unpitched sounds: the siren of a tugboat, the horn of a distant motor, both
anticipating by several years the typewriters of Hindemith and Satie.

Ex. 11.1a

Ex. 11.1b

All this is musical impressionism of a high order, comparable to a painting by Monet of Dieppe harbour. Of two further ideas generated by the opening theme the first (Ex. 11.1b), during which the stevedores emerge sack-laden onto the deck, is both a 'madrigalism' of ascent and an expression of toil and weariness, emphasized by the heavy appoggiatura at its highest point (*x*). Thirty-two bars pass before a word is spoken. Giorgetta, uneasy, wonders how long her husband will stand gazing afar off. He turns the conversation to the men at work. The bass quavers break almost imperceptibly into a soft, swaying tramp as the stevedores are heard alternating shouts with snatches of a sea-shanty (compare the English 'Blow the man down', quoted in Milhaud's *Le pauvre matelot*). Interlaced with varied extensions of Ex. 11.1b, it forms a background to a troubled dialogue between Michele and his wife. He moves to embrace her, but she coldly offers her cheek, preferring, as he leaves her, to direct her attention to Luigi, who has just appeared from the hold. A sharper harmonization and scoring gives a new tilt to the prism of Ex. 11.1b, as she gazes at him with meaning before retiring to fetch wine and glasses for the men. His fellow-workers, Talpa and Tinca, have now arrived, protesting their fatigue. But at Giorgetta's return the mood lightens. The key turns to unequivocal C major, the rhythm to a robust 3/4 with only a slight quickening of the pulse (Ex. 11.2). A Puccinian cadential figure of consecutive sevenths rounds off the period.

Areas of tonal stability are now firmly, almost insistently established with the aid of pedal notes. Giorgetta invites the entire company to partake. Ex. 11.2 is taken up in different keys first by Talpa, then Tinca (Gold's Goujon) with a touch of bravado; for wine alone consoles him for his wife's promiscuity. Luigi invites a passing organ-grinder to give them a tune. Only dance music appeals to Giorgetta— so she says with a significant look at Luigi, intending, surely, a *double*

Ex. 11.2

Allegretto con vivacità
ben ritmato

Luigi: Ec - co - la la pas - sa - ta!   Ra - gaz - zi,   si   be - ve!

Ex. 11.3

entendre. Appropriately, with typical Puccinian prescience, pizzicato strings give out a dark, self-perpetuating motif that will assume crucial importance later (Ex. 11.3). For instruments that play out of tune, each note of the melody rendered discordant by a major seventh below, there is a precedent in Leoncavallo's *Zazà* (1900). But Puccini's model has long been recognized as a passage from Stravinsky's *Petrushka* (1911), which he is known to have admired. Just as the Russian availed himself of Josef Lanner's *Hofballtänze*, so Puccini drew on two popular French melodies identified by Carner as 'Georgette' and 'La Petite Tonkinoise'.[16] But Girardi is surely right in detecting the presence of Chopin's Valse in A flat, Op. 34, No. 1, from whose coda there is a literal quotation.[17]

It is not Luigi but Tinca, flushed with wine, who takes Giorgetta in his arms, causing general hilarity by his failure to keep in step with her. As Luigi pushes him aside and takes his place, a chromatically rising fidget beginning on muted violins suggests a tingling of the blood. Michele's re-appearance puts an end to the dance; Luigi throws the organ-grinder a coin and retires with Tinca and Talpa, leaving husband and wife once more alone together. Waltz strains persist, restless and inconclusive, while Giorgetta questions Michele with feigned casualness about the plans for next day. Will they move on? Will they take Tinca, Talpa—and Luigi? Her husband's replies are brief and unsatisfactory (yes, they will take Luigi if only to save him from starving). The triple pulse merges into the gentle sway of Ex. 11.1b, into which Puccini splices the voice of an approaching ballad singer. His 'Primavera', sung before a group of admiring *midinettes* who take it up in thirds, is a musical epigram akin to Puccini's 'Casa mia' and has as its punch-line a quotation of Mimì's motif (Ex. 6.4a) from *La bohème* on muted string

[16] PCB, 484n.

[17] GGP, 391.

quartet. But the Mimì of the song is one who has been deserted by her lover in the hour of her death; and the poem contains the fateful line 'Chi ha vissuto per amore per amore si morì'. The sparse accompaniment with harp on stage allows us to hear Giorgetta nagging at her husband. No, he has never made scenes; she would rather that he had beaten her; but Michele continues to stonewall.

As the girls' voices trail away into the distance, La Frugola, Talpa's wife, crosses the gangplank onto the barge. Possibly it is the unconscious irony of her greeting ('O eterni innamorati, buona sera') that sends Michele into the cabin. The old woman, a scavenger by occupation, chatters to Giorgetta about her pickings. A restless motif faintly recalling Schubert's *Die Forelle* generates a wealth of kindred material illustrating her fussy gestures as she displays the contents of her sack. She caps her list with a set piece ('Se tu sapessi'), a modal melody, Aeolian in the vocal line, Dorian in the accompaniment of parallel common chords and saved from monotony by a side-slip into and out of a remote key before the concluding phrase—the music, in fact, of an amiable freak (Ex. 11.4).

An episode brings up the subject of her cat, Caporale, also mentioned in Gold's play, but only as one who leaves around 'ses petites ordures'. It took Adami and Puccini to elevate him into a philosopher, whose

Ex. 11.4

purr tells us 'Better to be master in a hovel than slave in a palace'. From this La Frugola draws her own moral: 'Better feed on two slices of an animal's heart than eat out your own for love'. Eight bars of D minor chords rendered pungent by the touch of an underlying C sharp drive home the message.

Seine music again takes over for the exchanges that follow the men's re-emergence from the hold, their day's work done. Why is Tinca in such a hurry to leave? To drown his sorrows in drink, of course, La Frugola observes reproachfully. Tinca retorts with a defiant assertion of Ex. 11.2, its cadential phrase prolonged amid shouts of laughter. He is answered by Luigi with an arioso ('Hai ben ragione') railing at the lot of the working man in the rhetorical manner of Mascagni. Its pivot is a broad orchestral statement of Ex. 11.1b in A minor. Before it the progressions keep returning to E major with a sense of bitter irony; after it the magnetic pole remains C minor up to the end, reached by a distorted parody of Tinca's cadential figure ('Piegare il capo ed in-curvar la schiena!').

La Frugola, more equable, looks forward to the day when she and her husband can retire to a cottage in the country—an idea quite for-eign to Gold's La Furette, but close to Puccini's own heart. Over a subtly shaded tramp of strings, harp, and solo woodwind the voice declaims softly and rapidly ('Ho sognato una casetta'), rarely departing from the D that persists throughout the bass line—a perfect illustration of Giorgetta's remark 'È la tua fissazione, la campagna!' Her own dream is very different ('È ben altro il mio sogno!'). A soaring melody takes us back to the romantic Paris of *La bohème* (Ex. 11.5). Here is Puccini's

Ex. 11.5

nearest approach to a formal number in the old style: a melodic period stated three times with an episode before the final reprise. But the structure is looser-limbed, the voice part frequently proceeding alongside the melody in naturalistic declamation à la Fanciulla, as Giorgetta recalls the pleasures of her native Belleville with interventions from Luigi and La Frugola. The sympathy that prompts Luigi to join her concluding statement gives it more than a hint of the cabaletta of a love-duet, its significance fortunately lost on Talpa and his wife, who depart to the strains of La Frugola's 'cottage' soliloquy whispered over a busier accompaniment.

After this brief shaft of sunlight, the melancholy atmosphere of the Seine descends once more with Ex. 11.1a topped first by a 'sopranino', then a 'tenorino' singing wordlessly behind the scenes, and at the end a prolonged siren note from far off.

The use of an offstage voice to prepare for a vital turning-point of the drama has been pioneered in Act II of La rondine, where in the deserted Bar Bullier Magda reflects before deciding to burn her boats. Here it marks off the long exposition from the moment at which the action begins to move towards its tragic dénouement. Like Magda, Luigi and Giorgetta remain frozen in thought. Then muted strings tremolando set up an electric tension, beneath which stalks the 'intrigue' motif (Ex. 11.3), as Luigi steps towards his beloved, to be halted by her with a warning of Michele's imminent return. Originally in C minor, the key in which the motif was first heard, the pitch was later raised by a semitone, so that the preceding chord now takes on the quality of a dominant preparation for the new tonality, in which feelings that had been brewing beneath the surface find their outlet. Ex. 11.3 is treated here like the four-note ostinato that accompanied Scarpia's insinuations regarding the Marchesa Attavanti in Tosca, namely repeated with varied scoring and embroidery, but concentrated within the same tonality like a relentless obsession. Michele does indeed return, surprised to find Luigi still present. In a passage of neutral declamation the young man asks to be put ashore at Rouen; but Michele dissuades him; he would find no work there. When he has left Giorgetta's alarm breaks forth in a graphic gesture—nothing more than an ascending harmonic minor scale, but, like so many of Puccini's motival fragments, intensely gripping (Ex. 11.6).

Ex. 11.6

Why did Luigi propose to leave at Rouen? In Gold's play it is from a sense of guilt. In the opera it is because he cannot bear to share Giorgetta with another. And yet, though both long to elope, they have no plans to do so. Indeed the kisses snatched in secret add piquancy to their love affair. Pressure of emotion forces their music out of the prevailing triple rhythm, until a sudden awareness of Michele's proximity restores a stealthy pounding of Ex. 11.3 as the lovers rehearse their regular plan for a tryst. As a signal for Luigi to step aboard Giorgetta will light a match (high piccolo over unison cellos and basses and a roll on the bass drum). A figure of three soft discords adds an air of tantalizing mystery, soon to be charged with a more sinister meaning (see Ex. 11.8 (*x*)).

Two bars later the ascending Ex. 11.6 is transformed by richer scoring and an appoggiature at its peak into a motif of passionate desire. Luigi's paroxism unleashes the full orchestra, Ex. 11.3 resuming its iron grip fortissimo on trombones. There is a long Wagnerian subsidence as Luigi hurries across the gangplank propelled by an agitated Giorgetta. The orchestra falls silent, leaving her to murmur helplessly, 'How difficult it is to be happy!' Certainly, if one wants it all ways, as Giorgetta appears to do.

The music moves without a break or even a change of pulse onto an entirely new plain. Michele comes out of the cabin for a long duo with his wife in which he vainly tries to re-awaken her affection for him. The dominating motif (Ex. 11.7) has the insistent regularity of Ex. 11.3 but is soft and caressing where the latter had been sharp and minatory. An intervening oscillation of narrow intervals suggests the singer's difficulty in broaching the subject he has to heart.

At first they converse desultorily about the crew. For the present Michele only needs two workers; so why, Giorgetta asks, does he not

Ex. 11.7

dismiss Tinca, who is always drunk. He drinks, Michele replies, to keep himself from murdering his unfaithful wife. Giorgetta's start does not go unnoticed by her husband ('Che hai?'), nor by the orchestra, which throws up a reminiscence of the three mysterious chords of the 'tryst'. Michele asks her why she has ceased to love him. Her denial, cool and unconvincing ('Ti sbagli; t'amo. . . . Tu sei buono e onesto') leads him to recall their past happiness, when she would rock their baby to sleep in her arms—and here Ex. 11.7 over rippling harp takes on the character of a lullaby. So to his first mention of the cloak with which he used to envelop them in a loving embrace. But the orchestral motif that it prompts (Ex. 11.8) is far from loving. Isolated from the rest of the discourse by rhythm, tonality, and scoring, it offers the audience a glimpse of the horror to come.

Now that their child is no longer with them, his own grey hairs seem an insult to Giorgetta's youth—this to a lyrical flight of great intensity, the harmonies enriched by major seconds (Ex. 11.9). Giorgetta joins her voice to his in an attempt to calm him ('Ah, ti supplico,

Ex. 11.8

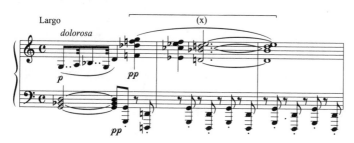

EX. 11.9

Michele, non dir niente, ah no!'). The climax is marked by a sharp dissonance and a burst of orchestral figuration. Giorgetta, desperate to put an end to the conversation, protests a mortal weariness. But Michele knows that she cannot, or will not, sleep; and he begs her to remain by his side ('Resta vicino a me!). By now a decrescendo has brought the music to rest on a tranquil plateau of E flat. Detached fragments of Ex. 11.9 are floated over a 12/8 pattern of hollow fourths and fifths, partly bringing to mind the ever-present 'Signora Senna', partly illustrating the emptiness of Michele's longing. Only when he makes his final appeal ('Ah! Ritorna, ritorna come allora, ritorna ancora mia!') does the harmony thicken for two bars. But Giorgetta is impervious. She reminds him that age has changed them both; and with a 'Buona notte, Michele. . . . Casco dal sonno' she moves away into the cabin, as a distant bell chimes the hour. Michele promises to join her; but no sooner has she left than he pronounces, almost tonelessly, the word 'Sgualdrina!' ('Whore!'). A jump to the furthest possible key of A minor, low woodwind, strings, and brass bunched in a baleful common chord, shifts the drama into its final phase.

Once again Puccini marks a cardinal moment by an interlude of stasis with voices heard offstage. Here it is a kind of Aristotelian 'anagnorisis'—Michele's 'recognition' of his wife's infidelity, though not yet of the adulterer. The distant voices are those of two lovers alternating strains of sweet melancholy; and instead of the tugboat siren a bugle-call from a nearby barracks, its B flat tonality clashing with the pedal A that has persisted throughout the interlude (compare the military band in *La bohème*).

The original version of Michele's monologue ('Scorri, fiume eterno') corresponds to his speech in the play, where, with no thought of revenging himself on his wife's lover he apostrophizes the river, in whose depths he hopes to find eternal rest. Ex. 11.8 is extended into a period of ten bars like a funeral march, its sense of foreboding heightened by a harmonic side-slip towards the end. The design is unusually formal: a symmetrical repetition of the opening period, an episode in the major, where Michele reflects with compassion on the many suicide victims claimed by the river, and finally, as he foresees a similar fate for himself, a full-blooded reprise with rushing chromatic scales on strings and a two-bar epilogue—Ex. 11.8 again taking him up to a high G answered orchestrally by the three descending chords (*x*) at their most strident. It is impressive, certainly; but the vocal line, melodic throughout, and always moving at the same pace, does not avoid a feeling of monotony.

In re-writing the monologue to a new text ('Nulla! . . . Silenzio! . . . È là!') Puccini retained the outer bastions of his original structure, but without repeating the opening period. In a new, more varied episode Michele passes in review the possible adulterers. Talpa? Too old. Tinca? He merely drinks. What about Luigi? No, that very evening he had asked to be put ashore the next day; but Ex. 11.3 beneath the orchestral figuration reminds us of the truth. As Michele's murderous intentions take shape, a turmoil of Ex. 11.8, variously fragmented, leads to the earlier reprise, which to the new text, in which he determines to join his own fate with that of the culprit, takes on a terrifying force. Falling back exhausted, Michele proceeds to light his pipe. Luigi, waiting on the wharf, mistakes the flame for the signal agreed with Giorgetta. The action scene that follows is again dominated by Ex. 11.8, first pattered by lower strings as Luigi hurries across the gangplank, then spaced out with frantic, cascading gestures, as Michele seizes him by the throat, forces him to confess, and strangles him. Hearing his wife's voice at the

cabin door, Michele wraps the body in his cloak. After a brief dialogue—she timid, he menacing—Michele opens the cloak and presses
her face against that of her dead lover. Sequences of Ex. 11.8(x) high
on woodwind over tremolando cellos and basses finally give way to a
full statement of the motif together with the harmonic side-slip of
Michele's monologue, from which, as in *Madama Butterfly*, Puccini con-
trives a final cadence of rare originality: A minor to C minor!

In *Il tabarro* Puccini's structural technique achieves the transformation
pre-figured in parts of *Madama Butterfly* and *La fanciulla del West*,
whereby an interplay of contrasted motifs is replaced by large homogeneous blocks, usually based on a single motif variously extended and
modified. Of the recurring themes only one bears a fixed connotation,
namely Ex. 11.3, which stands throughout for the furtive intrigue of
Luigi and Giorgetta. The 'Seine' motifs of Ex. 11.1a are part pictorial,
part expressive in the manner of Ex. 9.1 in *La fanciulla*. A more interesting case is Ex. 11.8. Usually described as the 'tabarro' motif since its
earliest appearance coincides with the first mention of the cloak, its
immediate recurrences have no apparent connection with the garment
in question. Rather they embody Michele's growing determination to
exact a bloody vengeance on his wife's seducer, in which the cloak will
merely figure as a last-minute expedient. Yet, viewed from a different
perspective the motif can still be seen as the 'tabarro' casting an ever-
deepening proleptic shadow over the events on stage, obliterating the
triple smooth rhythms that have so far prevailed throughout the score.
To this end it undergoes modifications both in pace and physiognomy,
its full flowering reserved for the moment of murder.

With its one-act format, low-life setting, and undercurrent of violence *Il tabarro* allies itself to the genre initiated by *Cavalleria rusticana*,
which, short-lived as it was, left an enduring mark on the style and
musical language of the entire 'giovane scuola' and led to the grouping
of their operas under the title 'verismo'. But if there is any opera to
which the term can logically be applied, it is surely the first panel of *Il
trittico*. By bringing 'la Signora Senna' into the foreground Puccini is
able to take the rhetorical weight off his characters and to view them
with a detachment that brings them nearer to the literary world of Verga
and Capuana from which the movement takes its name. Here are no
poets or artists, given to lyrical effusion at the drop of a hat, but ordinary

men and women, poor and hardworking, neither more nor less articulate than their counterparts in everyday life. Outbursts of violent emotion, flights of song-like melody are kept strictly in their place. Certainly it is not a pretty story; but in Puccini's hands it is a very human one.

Among the reservations that greeted the opera's appearance at home and abroad, one review stands out as wholly perceptive. '*Il tabarro*', wrote Giorgio Barini of *L'epoca*, 'is one of those works which contain far more than is evident from a first impression; the more one hears it, the more one grasps its inner strength; the more one savours the various, well-harmonized elements that make up its tissue; the more one appreciates its organic power, its real importance.' That is exact.

As a one-act opera for female voices *Suor Angelica* is indeed a novelty, though it can claim a near precedent in Massenet's all-male *Le jongleur de Notre Dame* (1902), which likewise ends with a miracle. Giordano's one-act *Mese Mariano* (1910, revised 1913) offers a further crossbearing. Here, as in *Suor Angelica*, the nub of the drama is a child born out of wedlock who has since died.

All three operas share a religious ambience; but whereas in those of Massenet and Giordano the secular world obtrudes, *Suor Angelica* is enveloped throughout by the atmosphere of a convent. Nowhere, however, does Puccini attempt to convey this in Massenet's manner by an elegant pastiche of liturgical counterpoint. A simple bell-chime of four bars is taken up by muted strings and celeste in a pattern of soft dissonances created by the added second below. To this an 'Ave Maria' sung by the nuns from within the chapel forms a descant. A snatch of birdsong on offstage piccolo completes the picture of a fine spring evening outside a place of worship (Ex. 11.10). As the 'Ave Maria' continues to the same regular phrases, the scoring subtly varied and enhanced by organ participation, two lay-sisters cross the stage and enter the chapel followed by Sister Angelica, who kneels to kiss the threshold, after which, in the way of Puccini heroines, she is first heard singing out of sight. The service ended, the nuns issue in pairs from the chapel, to be blessed by the Abbess. A prolonged full cadence rounds off what is in effect a descriptive prelude.

There follows a dramatic exposition of a type already familiar: a succession of unrelated episodes which turn out to have a bearing on

Ex. 11.10

the final outcome. Among the devout even the mildest of sins must be atoned for; the Monitress therefore proceeds to hand out punishments to defaulters: to the lay-sisters who failed to kiss the chapel threshold, and must therefore pray 20 times for the poor and sinful; to Suor Lucilla who is bidden to work in silence for having caused laughter during the service: and to Suor Osmina for having hidden in her sleeve a couple of red roses. So much could appear almost comically banal, were it not for Puccini's tactful handling of the musical dialogue. Small intervals and a restricted compass prevail. The Monitress's admonitions are backed by the lightest of woodwind consonances, broken only by two stinging false relations at the mention of poverty and mortal sin. A lay-sister expresses her penitence in a modal line of parallel 6/4 chords supported by two clarinets only. She and her companion then join in an unaccompanied prayer in naive two-part harmony ('Cristo Signore, Sposo d'Amore'). Strings are reserved for the prosaic comments of the Mistress of the Novices and the rebelliousness of Suor Osmina, sharpened by a dotted rhythm and breaking off at an insistent unresolved seventh. A brief woodwind gesture of parallel triads frames a motif sung by six nuns to the accompaniment of muted trumpets (Ex. 11.11). This will serve as a kind of 'icon' of the Virgin Mary, recurring wherever her presence is either felt or specifically mentioned.

Ex. 11.11

Re-gi - na Vir - gi-num, o - ra pro - ea

The orchestral palette now fills out in long sustained chords as the
Monitress announces the hour of recreation; and the tonality, hitherto
confined to F and B flat, moves into the bright key of A major with a
slow cantilena for muted horn, two violas, and cellos, whose embroidery reaches into a solo for Suor Genovieffa ('O sorelle, sorelle'). A
kindly soul akin to Massenet's Father Boniface, she points to the rays
of the setting sun that are about to light up the nearby fountain—a
'miracle' that occurs only three evenings in May. The conversation that
follows is conducted to a characteristic motif (Ex. 11.12) variously modified in contour and harmony, sometimes combined with the 'Ave Maria' descant, and finally, where the nuns recall the death of one of their
number, superimposed on whole-tone progressions. Here is Puccini's
'block' construction at its most skilful, reflecting every nuance of the
dialogue together with the melancholy that gradually descends on the
company.

A moment of silence follows while strings, tremolando 'sulla tastiera',
intone a sorrowful derivative of this same motif, each of the parallel
chords underpinned by a second below the fundamental note. Again it
is Suor Genovieffa in a rise and fall of sad-sweet melody who proposes
laying a wreath of flowers on the grave of their departed sister. The
nuns murmur their assent, since that is what she herself would have

Ex. 11.12

desired. Mention of 'desire' prompts the first substantial intervention from Suor Angelica ('I desideri son i fiori dei vivi'), whose long periodic phrases, enriched by a counter-melody in contrary motion proclaim her the aristocrat in their midst. Desires, she tells them, are the flowers only of the living; the dead have no part in them. The flower metaphor is in character, since Angelica is the gardener of the convent. Her final assertion ('O sorella, la morte è vita bella') for the first time unleashes the full orchestra with a burst of rhetoric that far exceeds the limits of the vocal line—an indication of feelings that the singer can barely control and a statement of faith that will soon be put to a cruel test (Ex. 11.13).

The Monitress interrupts her thoughts declaring that desires are forbidden even to the living order. But Suor Genovieffa begs to differ. She herself was once a shepherdess, and still she sometimes longs to

Ex. 11.13

hold a lamb in her arms; surely the Lamb of God would be the first to understand and forgive (casuistry at its most naïf, certainly: but it will not be lost on Suor Angelica). Pitched in G minor in the first edition, in E flat minor in the second—the widest of all Puccini's transpositions—Genovieffa's arietta ('Soave Signor mio') is in the composer's most wistful vein, its accompaniment a tracery of softly bleating woodwind linked to what has gone before by rhythmic recalls of Ex. 11.12 and an intermediate cadence based on the gesture that framed Ex. 11.11.

There is a moment of light relief. Suor Dolcina (the name is self-explanatory) also has a desire; but it is hardly a secret one, since everyone knows her for a glutton; and a jaunty, dancing figure indicates their mockery. And Suor Angelica—has she a desire? Her 'Io? . . . no, sorella' sparks off an excited murmuring from her companions. May Jesus forgive her for having told a lie! For the last seven years she has been longing for news of her family. Subdued chatter gives way to a long cantilena of parallel sevenths divided between two groups of nuns, each retailing what little they have heard of her past—that she is of noble birth and has been forced to take the veil as a punishment, but for what? Who can say? And the melody dwindles into silence.

There follows the episode of the wasp, originally intended by Puccini as an optional cut and still so marked in the definitive edition, although, as will be seen, there it has a special relevance. The Nursing Sister arrives in a state of panic. While trimming a rose bush, Suor Chiara has disturbed a wasps' nest and been stung. Now she is lying in her cell in agony. Suor Angelica has a remedy to hand in the garden she so lovingly tends.

There is little here of musical interest apart from a sharp 'sting' from pizzicato strings, staccato woodwind, and harp. One phrase, however, stands out with sufficient prominence to lodge in the memory. As Angelica plucks the remedial herbs, the Nurse observes that she never fails to find among her plants a cure for every ailment (Ex. 11.14). In the opera's definitive version words and music will take on a new significance in retrospect.

Again the mood lightens for the entrance of two tourières with a donkey-cart full of provisions. Carefree diatonic harmonies and tripping rhythms prevail, with a couple of orchestral 'hee-haws' to set the scene.

Ex. 11.14

Clearly their haul has been a good one; and the sisters cluster eagerly round the cart as the various items are unloaded, Suor Dolcina and her motif being much in evidence. A brief strain of good cheer ('Buona cerca stasera, Signora Dispensiera') sums up the general satisfaction, after which the music proceeds to one of the most riveting transitions ever effected by Puccini. As the sisters busy themselves with the comestibles, the harmonic movement slows to a halt beneath fussy gestures from flute, oboe, and solo violin. The point of arrival is a piquant dissonance, widely spaced, lightly scored, yet pregnant with a sense of expectation strangely at variance with the casual dialogue. One of the *tourières* has noticed a richly caparisoned coach standing outside the convent gates. A surge of chromatic harmony between the horn pedal note and the persistent G quavers high above indicates Angelica's barely suppressed agitation. She begs for a detailed description, which the *tourière* is unable to give. By now the dissonance has resolved into a sustained, richly textured melody that signals the start of the drama proper, gliding into relentless motion with a speed that outstrips the text. This, the longest single melody that Puccini ever wrote, is essentially orchestral, though doubled here and there by voices. Here it is spun out over incessant semiquaver pulsations to more than 70 bars across a trajectory that passes from F major to A minor in three phases, the first (Ex. 11.15a) grave, 'conventual' almost but with an undercurrent of excitement; the second (Ex. 11.15b) an expression of Angelica's desperate anxiety; the third (Ex. 11.15c) a codicil for orchestra alone, full of a resigned foreboding.

Ex. 11.15a

Andante mosso

Ex. 11.15b

Ex. 11.15c

The design is expanded by wondering comments from the sisters and by the clanging of the convent bell, announcing the arrival of a visitor—but for whom? Genovieffa echoes Angelica's Ex. 11.15b over still more poignant harmonies, as she expresses the general hope that the visit will be for their noble sister. During Ex. 11.15c pantomime predominates. The Abbess appears and calls Suor Angelica's name. The sisters retire after filling a watering-can from the fountain, now 'miraculously' turned to gold by the setting sun. Angelica begs the Abbess to tell her more. For seven years she has offered her all to the Virgin by way of expiation—and here a recollection of Ex. 11.15b is woven into the orchestral pulsations, which slowly die away for the Abbess's frigid response. From the nearby graveyard come the voices of the nuns chanting a 'Requiem' to the strains of Ex. 11.12, its peaceful major tonality helping Angelica compose her thoughts. This accomplished, the Abbess comes to the point. Angelica's visitor is her aunt, the Princess, in whose presence she must show herself humble and submissive; the Blessed Virgin will hear her every word. These admonitions are punctuated by a motif totally different from any heard in the opera so far: a sinuous, ascending line rising higher with each repetition and coming to rest on an unrelated minor triad on muted horns (Ex. 11.16).

Ex. 11.16

That this motif is a thumbnail portrait of the Princess is not in doubt, even if it anticipates her entrance by more than 20 slow bars. All her glacial austerity is in the unharmonized climb; while the horn chord suggests the heart of stone. During the course of the scene that follows the motif will be variously modified, sometimes transformed into a bass tramp prolonged beneath baleful chromatic chord-clusters that exploit its implications of bitonality. The Princess offers her hand to her niece to kiss and proceeds to the purpose of her visit. Angelica's parents, dead these 20 years, had divided their bequest evenly between their two daughters, but giving the Princess power to alter the terms of the will should circumstances so demand. Angelica is now required to sign a parchment surrendering all claim to her part of the inheritance. All this her aunt delivers in cold, business-like tones above widely spaced variants of her motif. Angelica's reply, over a slow march of harp and pizzicato cellos *divisi*, is both touching and dignified. Seven years have passed since last they met. Can her aunt remain unmoved by the peace of the convent (Ex. 11.11 on muted trumpets)? Indeed she can and does. Her younger niece, Anna Viola, is about to be married—and here strings evoke the tender memories of her sister that steal over Angelica. Oboes and bassoons in a distant subdominant region recall the young girl who has now become a woman. But whom is she to marry? 'One whose love is strong enough to ignore the stain that you have left upon the family's escutcheon.' The solemn, almost hieratic pronouncement ignites a rebellious protest from Angelica. To hear her own mother's sister speak to her so! The Princess is no less angry. How dare Angelica invoke her mother's name against her! Discordant strands of counterpoint over a pedal bass match her fury. Her composure re-

Ex. 11.17

Princess: Nel si - len - zio di quei rac - co - gli - men - ti

gained, she describes her nightly communion with her dead sister's soul. Note the Aeolian church mode and the religious 'topos' of rising fourths, as the Princess for the first time parades the extension of her contralto voice (Ex. 11.17).

One thought remains to her: expiation. Her niece must offer all she holds most dear to the Madonna. In submissive tones Angelica protests that she has already done so—save for one thing (Ex. 11.11, sketched lightly by flutes, oboes, and bassoons): the memory of the son she has seen but once. Surely the sweetest of all mothers would not grudge her that (a reasoning worthy of Suor Genovieffa!). She importunes her aunt with questions about him to a desperate, self-perpetuating motif of one bar, heavily chromatic in line and harmony (Ex. 11.18).

A novelty here is the variation of pace to which the motif is subjected, from Allegro moderato ma agitato to Andante sostenuto, reflecting the turmoil of Angelica's spirits. Eventually it fades into incoherent fragments in the face of the Princess's stony silence. Whole-tone harmony takes over as Angelica, near to hysteria, presses her aunt for a reply in the name of the Madonna (again Ex. 11.11 now hexatonically inflected). Impassively the Princess tells how two years ago the boy fell mortally ill. Everything was done to save his life. 'He is dead?'

Ex. 11.18

Allegro moderato ma agitato

from Angelica. Her aunt inclines her head, she herself falls to the ground with a shriek. The Princess summons with her stick a sister, who returns with the Abbess bearing a small table with writing materials and a lamp, for by now darkness has fallen. Angelica drags herself to the table, signs the document, and shrinking from her aunt's departing salutation bursts into a fit of passionate weeping.

All this is handled by Puccini with a subtle technique of musical transformation. Angelica's 'Ah!' releases a chaos of plunging sevenths rendered cacophonous by the addition of an extraneous note below the bass, then returning to the preceding hexatonic freeze. A three-note ostinato serves as the fulcrum for the restoration of diatonic harmony, over which the presence of the Princess broods like a miasma. The sanctimonious chords of Ex. 11.17 descend into spaced out reiterations of Angelica's beseeching Ex. 11.18, to which there is no answer but the thudding of a low pizzicato pattern. Again it is the chords of Ex. 11.17, now fraught with an overwhelming sense of desolation, that launches the heroine's only set-piece ('Senza mamma, o bimbo, tu sei morto!'), preserving the Aeolian mode throughout.

In its original form, at 24 bars only, this aria encapsulated a world of grief, its pain sharpened by two unexpected progressions—a turn to the mediant minor at the start of the third phrase and two unrelated major ninths in the course of its approach to the final cadence. By enlarging the design with the whole of Ex. 11.15, now a single uninterrupted period, Puccini allowed a note of consolation to creep in, which For-zano's verses confirm. Now that her child has become an angel, An-gelica can feel his presence about her. Surely he might give her a sign as to when she might join him in Heaven? Even the brooding Ex. 11.15c is modified so as to cast a faint gleam of hope.

A sign is indeed vouchsafed, if a false one. There is a move to the tonic major, like the clearing of a sky, as Suor Genovieffa returns from the graveyard with her companions. Knowing nothing of what has passed, they assure Angelica that her prayer has been heard. In a state of 'mystical exaltation, but without emphasis' she proclaims the descent of divine grace (Ex. 11.19). The majestic parade of parallel common chords, the line rising in sequences, the marching regularity of the phrases all contribute to a sense of high aspiration; but the melody itself lacks the distinction that it will soon be required to carry. As it swells

Ex. 11.19

Moderato con moto

Suor Angelica:
La gra-zia_è di-sce-sa dal cie - lo, già tut - ta, già tut - ta m'ac - cen - de,

to a climax the nuns, retiring to their cells at the sound of the evening bell, fill out the texture in three-part harmony, and the music comes to rest in an elaborated plagal cadence. The stage is now bare and lit only by the moon rising above the cypresses. The intermezzo that follows is a further reprise of Ex. 11.15, partly an epilogue to the foregoing tragedy, partly the backcloth for a scene of silent action.

Here the opera's two versions diverge radically. In the original, 34 bars pass before Angelica emerges from her cell with an earthenware jar, which she fills with water from the fountain. She then gathers twigs with which to light a fire. At last she makes her intentions plain in a monologue of 84 slow bars in duple rhythm—the so-called 'Aria dei fiori' (Ex. 11.20) in which she lists the ingredients of the deadly potion she is about to brew.

That Puccini should have been under pressure to cut this aria is understandable. Not only does it hold up the action; it is also very difficult for the singer to pitch. Yet its tonal blurring, its wealth of dissonances softened by the utmost refinement of scoring, its pedal bass constantly at variance with the modal melody can all be justified as representing Angelica's furthest flight from reality. Not until the end does the music settle into Romantic harmony, where she blesses the flowers that will bring her eternal peace. At first Puccini agreed to a handful of 'nicks' in the orchestral interstices, balanced by a shortening of the verbal text. Not until a revival in 1920 did he arrive with Forzano's help at the definitive edition, whereby the stage business

Ex. 11.20

was brought forward by 20 bars into the preceding intermezzo. At the start of Ex. 11.15c Angelica quotes the Nursing Sister's line ('Suor Angelica ha sempre una ricetta buona fatta coi fiori') just as in the early versions of *Madama Butterfly* Cio-Cio-San, likewise determined on suicide, had thrown back at Suzuki her counsel of peace and tranquillity as a cure for a troubled heart. As in the original monologue, Angelica addresses the flowers as her friends, adding that with their drops of poison they will repay her for all the loving care she has lavished upon them.

By rendering the 'Aria dei fiori' superfluous the change has meant the sacrifice of a splendid piece of music. But it brings one dramatic advantage. The episode of the wasp is drawn into the central action; and there can no longer be any question of cutting it. One is reminded of a dictum of Verdi referring to Filippo Marchetti's *Don Giovanni d'Austria*, that it is sometimes necessary to have the courage to sacrifice good things in the interests of theatre.

Before taking the potion Angelica bids a touching farewell to the sisters who have treated her so kindly and to the chapel where she has so often prayed. Fourteen bars of luminous 12/8 over a dominant pedal, harmonized in the second-encrusted language of the opera's opening, merge into the march of Ex. 11.19, sealed orchestrally with the rhetorical flourish that had concluded Angelica's first solo (Ex. 11.13).

No sooner has she drunk the potion than reality breaks in. Angelica has committed a mortal sin, for which she will be eternally damned. Here Ex. 11.18 is pressed into service, pounding with the inexorability of a death sentence between Angelica's frantic cries for forgiveness. But its power is overcome by a distant chanting of Ex. 11.11 ('Regina Virginum, Salve, Maria!') accompanied by piano and muted trumpets offstage. In short, the miracle is about to take place. Ex. 11.19 duly supervenes worked into a grand crescendo, with the help of full mixed choir, organ, and two pianos rippling at the top of the keyboard; while internal recurrences of Ex. 11.11 leave no doubt as to who is being celebrated. Soon Angelica can be heard above the heavenly throng, her voice rising to C above the stave. At this point the Madonna makes her appearance leading the infant by the hand towards Angelica, who with a final cry falls dead. The music fades to a hushed close over the same elaborated plagal cadence as before.

To Puccini himself Suor Angelica remained the best of the trilogy; and its rejection, above all in Britain, occasioned the one faint note of asperity in his correspondence with Sybil. 'As to what you say about the religiosity of the subject . . . which cannot appeal to the English', he wrote to her, 'I will permit myself to say that I am not of your opinion. The fact is, and I've said it already, that the opera didn't have time to make its way into the public's ears—because the story is really one of passion, and it's only the environment which is religious. And besides, why was Max Reinhardt's Miracle at Olympia such a success? There you have Madonnas and churches etc. to your heart's content.'[18] True; but in no other opera is the Madonna so constantly invoked; and in a country where 'Mariolatry' could still cause a frown this was hardly a recommendation.

The qualities that so endeared the opera to Puccini are easy to un-

[18] PAF, 324.

derstand. For many years he had dreamed of a peaceful setting amid flowers, trees, and the song of birds; and it is surely significant that sketches for Ouida's *Two Little Wooden Shoes* found their way into the early scenes of *Suor Angelica*. In the first printed libretto Forzano lays out the plot as a 'Via crucis' in seven stages. The listener is more likely to experience it as a variant of the two-part structure habitual to Puccini's dramaturgy since *Madama Butterfly*: an exposition of contrasted episodes and a relentlessly sustained action. What is remarkable here is the precision with which each of the vignettes is mirrored in the tragic consequent: the punishments of the nuns by the far greater punishment meted out to Angelica; Genovieffa's longing for her lamb by Angelica's yearning for her child; while the flowers that cure the pain of Suor Chiara will cure Angelica of a more deep-seated agony. Even the 'miracle' of the fountain that turns to gold can be seen as presaging the final miracle of the opera. The moment at which the drama moves into action is the more electrifying for its lack of immediate emphasis. With Ex. 11.15 Puccini transforms the restrained idiom of the convent into a cantilena of sustained lyrical intensity; nor need we follow Carner in ascribing its three-fold repetition to creative fatigue, since at each occurrence it takes on a different dramatic colouring.

The scene between Angelica and the Princess is unique in Puccini's oeuvre. As with the best of Verdi's dramatic dialogues, its effect is obtained by one party maintaining a fixed attitude while the other passes through extremes of varied emotion. The Princess may not have a great deal to say; but within her allotted space she is as sharply etched as Scarpia or Rance.

There remains the problem of the final miracle—'pasteboard religiosity' according to Carner, and most listeners would be inclined to agree. Not so, however, Girardi, who maintains that it was never intended as a supernatural event, but rather as a figment of Angelica's disordered imagination and that therefore the vision itself could be dispensed with. Certainly Puccini's flippant description of Ex. 11.19 as 'the Royal March of the Madonna' might suggest that he did not believe in it either. The main objection to this view is that it takes away the force of Angelica's sudden realization of the mortal sin she has committed. Here, surely, she returns to reality with a vengeance. According to her beliefs nothing short of a miracle can save her. That such a miracle should be seen to happen allows her to die with dignity. What is missing is the note of transfiguration that the event requires. The exalted regions open to Verdi and Wagner were closed to Puccini.

With *Gianni Schicchi* the composer fulfilled at long last his desire 'to laugh and make others laugh'. That he possessed an aptitude for comedy was evident as early as *La bohème*. But his comic scenes were never more than incidental to the drama, flashes of light that set the darker moments in stronger relief. Laughter beneath a cloudless sky was something new for him. Forzano's Dante-derived plot belongs to the tradition of Ben Jonson's *Volpone*, its subject the greed and final frustration of a family who hope to benefit from the death of a rich relative (for modern equivalents see Guy de Maupassant's *En famille* (1885) and Stanley Houghton's Lancashire comedy *The Dear Departed* (1908)). The dramatic climate is reflected in a musical language quite distinct from that of *Il tabarro* or *Suor Angelica*: diatonic with no trace of modality, sparing of chromatic inflection, quick-paced, and rhythmically vigorous. Violent dissonance is not altogether avoided, but it is never of the searing, anguished variety. The composer's chuckle is never far away, while his 'prismatic' use of motif results in a rare economy of material.

The opening flourish, as uninhibitedly cheerful as a comic mask, generates a theme (Ex. 11.21a) which will supply much of the opera's narrative thread. Unremarkable except for its offbeat appoggiature it lends itself readily to sequential prolongation, fast or slow according to

Ex. 11.21a

Ex. 11.21b

context, suggesting first the anxious bustle of a household, then settling into a minor-key threnody with the aid of a funereal side-drum tattoo. Now and again, however, it will be topped by a tiny figure (Ex. 11.21b) whose pointed rhythm and disjunct intervals imply a sly wink from the composer. Later it will be appropriated by Schicchi himself.

Nine members of the Donati family are kneeling before the four-poster bed whose curtains conceal the dead body of their relative, Buoso. As in *Il tabarro*, the age of each is specified: from Simone (70) and Zita, known as 'La vecchia' (60), down to her nephew Rinuccio (24), and the boy Gherardino (7). Only the deceased's brother-in-law, Betto di Signa, a poor relation, is denied a precise number of years. Clearly the others look down on him; and when Gherardino disturbs the general sighs and lamentations by upsetting a chair it is on Betto that they all turn with a loud 'Shush!' But the boy needs to 'be excused'; and Zita, as head of the household, snaps at his father to take him out— a piece of humorous by-play that deflates the solemnity of the scene without affecting the musical flow. The relatives resume their mourning in ever more extravagant language. All their lives they will weep for Buoso; but a brief telescoping of Ex. 11.21a and an increasing predominance of Ex. 11.21b, whole or in fragments, indicates that their thoughts are beginning to wander. For Betto has heard some disturbing news. At Signa they are saying that Buoso has left everything to a monastery. For this Puccini develops the first motif into suave, lyrical phrases, almost as though Betto is not wholly displeased at upsetting his wealthier relations. There is a moment of shocked silence before the prevailing motif resumes in darker mood. All turn to Simone for advice; for he is the oldest and once was mayor of Fucecchio. To ten bars of pompous harmony he declares that if the will is in the hands of a lawyer they must remain in ignorance of its terms; but if it can be found in the house then there is still hope for them. At once all scramble to their feet to begin the search. Ex. 11.21a, now an Allegro vivo lightly scored and brilliantly embroidered, illustrates the frantic hunt, halted from time to time by a false alarm ('No! Non v'è!'). It is Rinuccio who happens upon the document and brandishes it aloft to a theme that will henceforth connote his love for Lauretta, daughter of Gianni Schicchi (Ex. 11.22). Harmonized with voluptuous warmth, it has to wait 14 bars for its completion, while Rinuccio rapidly explains to his aunt his marriage

Ex. 11.22

plans; only then does it receive its typically Puccinian seal of an expanded bar. Zita's reply is simple and benign. If the will is in their
favour Rinuccio can marry whom he chooses, even though she be a
she-devil ('versiera').

As the family cluster excitedly round 'La vecchia' who now holds
the document, her nephew bribes Gherardino with a few coins to fetch
Gianni Schicchi and his daughter. The old woman reads aloud the first
words of the testament, which seem to augur well: 'To my cousins,
Zita and Simone. . . .' At once all compose themselves in attitudes of
conventional grief (Ex. 11.21a spelt out in fragments over a pedal note),
but thoughts of Buoso's most valuable legacy—the mule, the house in
Florence, and the mills at Signa—rise bubbling to the surface (Ex.
11.21b above whispered chatter).

Zita opens the parchment for all to read, her gesture marked by a
ceremonious C major theme that suggests a recollection of Wagner's
Mastersingers (Ex. 11.23). Tremolando strings sustain the tension over
18 bars while the motif is repeated in different keys each time re-

Ex. 11.23

turning firmly to its original tonality. Gradually the expectant smiles fade; while interventions from Ex. 11.21b, chromatically altered, turn the screw of disappointment in rising sequences. All look at each other aghast. Simone solemnly marches to the bed and blows out the candles; whereupon the family give vent to their feelings, working themselves up to a pitch of discordant frenzy as they picture the monks gloating over their discomfiture. Yet amid the turmoil of thematic fragments, each a 'counter' of rage, the elegance of a Paisiello or Cimarosa is not wholly forgotten (Ex. 11.24). Again they appeal to Simone; but he too is defeated. It is again Rinuccio who suggests a possible saviour: Gianni Schicchi. The family are outraged; Schicchi is a nobody, not even a true Florentine. But it is too late, for Schicchi is already on his way to the house. Rinuccio's defence of his intended father-in-law takes in two gestures, the first (Ex. 11.25a) standing for Schicchi's nimble resource, the second (Ex. 11.25b), a crow of triumph, for his invariable success.

Thence to a celebration of Florence ('Firenze è come un albero fiorito'), a city which owes so many of its glories to outsiders (Ex. 11.26). This is the Puccini of *Canto d'anime* (1904), now genuinely heroic, the form strictly tailored to the subject: ternary as regards tonality, but with

Ex. 11.24

Ex. 11.25a

Ex. 11.25b

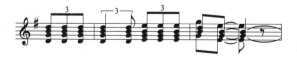

no conventional melodic reprise, since every line lists a different feature of the city and its surroundings. The first of two cadences that take the singer up to high B flat prompts an orchestral motif that will serve more than one purpose: arpeggio-born, spanning an octave and a half, it is here an expansive gesture indicating all that makes Florence what it is, not least its newest inhabitants. So there is every reason why it should reappear shortened in the bass to launch Rinuccio's final 'Viva la gente nuova e Gianni Schicchi!' (Ex. 11.27).

During a marching peroration there is a knock at the door. Enter the man himself together with his daughter (Ex. 11.27 surmounted by an appropriate twinkle of Ex. 11.21b, prolonged in a wide arc, then

Ex. 11.26

Ex. 11.27

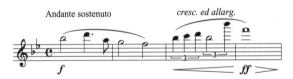

moved through different keys). The lovers exchange tender greetings. Schicchi, observing the doleful faces around him, concludes that Buoso must be recovering. But no, the candles signify a death (Ex. 11.21a). So he offers ironical comfort. At least there's an inheritance to come. 'Yes, for the monks!' Zita's wrathful response is carried by two elements from the ensemble of fury and crowned by a reference to the will (Ex. 11.23). Father and daughter can take themselves off, since she will never allow her nephew to marry without receiving a dowry. Schicchi's 'Brava la Vecchia, brava!' sparks off a riotous concertato, Schicchi heaping insults on Zita, she endeavouring to drag Rinuccio away from Lauretta. There is a brief flowering of Ex. 11.22, expanded into 4/4 time, as the lovers see their hopes of marriage receding ('Addio, speranza bella'). By now the other relatives are piling in with pleas for the parties to stop quarrelling and turn their attention to the will. But Schicchi has had enough and peremptorily orders his daughter to come away with him ('Vien! vien! vien!'). Rinuccio appeals alternately to Zita and Schicchi, but in vain. It is left to Lauretta to carry the day with the opera's one detachable number ('O mio babbino caro'). Here Ex. 11.27 receives its final definition, the wide intervals now those of supplication. The rippling accompaniment, the strict regularity of the phrase lengths (highly unusual in the mature Puccini), the simple yet melting harmonies all evoke the drawing-room song of some 20 years earlier. No harm in that. Lauretta is an *ingénue* and nothing more. It is by appealing to Schicchi as 'daddy's little girl' that she is able to move him. 'O mio babbino caro' remains a perfectly fashioned miniature. By planting her opening strain well in advance Puccini made sure that the piece 'belongs'.

Reluctantly Schicchi gives way ('Datemi il testamento!'). Bassoon, then horn accompany him with a variant of Ex. 11.21b, determined and business-like, as he paces up and down with the will. Twice he halts with a trumpet-backed 'Niente da fare!' to which Lauretta and Rinuccio respond in unison with a lamenting Ex. 11.22. The second time, however, interrupted by his sudden 'Però!' they conclude the melody at a faster tempo—perhaps they may be able to marry after all. Thus by a mere alteration of speed Puccini is able to reverse the emotional content of a theme.

Before answering the family's eager 'Ebbene?' Schicchi sends Lauretta out to the terrace to feed the birds (Ex. 11.21a and b embellished by a sporadic twitter from flute and violin harmonics). Assured that Buoso's death is unknown outside the house, he gives orders for the body and candelabra to be removed into an adjoining room—just in time. For a knock at the door announces Spinelloccio, the doctor. Schicchi slips into the bed and draws the curtains, warning the family to keep their visitor at a distance. An import from the *commedia dell'arte*, Spinelloccio speaks with a Bolognese accent. The relatives tell him that his patient has much improved—a fact confirmed by Schicchi with a perfect imitation of the dead man's voice. All he needs now is to sleep; so would the doctor please call again in the evening. The muffled ostinato tramp of harp, lower strings, and side-drum that had marked time during the previous pantomime is transformed into a drowsy succession of parallel inverted thirteenths. Spinelloccio takes his leave marvelling at the progress of medical science, for which all credit must be given to the Bologna school (Ex. 11.23).

His mimicry judged faultless, Schicchi's triumph is proclaimed by the orchestra with Ex. 11.25b. He then unfolds his plan. Someone (it will be Rinuccio) must fetch a lawyer and a couple of witnesses, in whose presence he himself, invisible behind the bed-curtains, will dictate a new will in the family's favour. Here Puccini reverts to modernized Paisiello ('Si corre dal notaio'), incorporating a fragment of commonplace soon to be put to ceremonious use (Ex. 11.28). Elements of Exx. 11.23 and 11.21 are drawn upon, eventually settling into a periodic melody with the slink of the modern ballroom ('In testa la cappellina!' (Ex. 11.29)). All Schicchi's cunning is in this, the opera's only melody confined to a minor key, with its stealthy chromatics and ambiguous glances towards the subdominant area, culminating in an outburst of self-glorification that already hints at the fate to which Dante will con-

Ex. 11.28

sign the singer ('O gente! Questa matta bizzarria che mi zampilla nella fantasia è tale da sfidar l'eternità!').

But the Donati are not in the least shocked. In a frenzy of joy they crowd round their saviour, kissing his hands and his garments, calling his name and even embracing one another in an access of family feeling ('Come è bello l'amore fra i parenti!'). During the hubbub a figure of three notes, rising and falling, begins to take shape, not to receive its full definition until individual members, following the example of Simone, stake their claim to the portion of the inheritance which they consider their due. The harmonic sophistication (two combined hexatonic patterns within an open fifth) is in marked contrast to the childish sing-song of the melody (Ex. 11.30). Tossed between different registers and instrumental groups this motif will function as an insistent 'Give me . . . ', a symbol of mindless greed.

So far there is general agreement as to the distribution, until they reach the three items coveted by all: the mule, the house in Florence, and the mills at Signa. At once the atmosphere becomes charged with suspense, broken when Simone blandly assumes that as the oldest member and a former mayor of Fucecchio they should go to him. The protest, led by Zita, puts a swift end to family feeling. A turmoil of angry seconds dissolves into reiterations of Ex. 11.30, brought to a sudden halt by the tolling of a bell. Has news of Buoso's death got about? If so Schicchi's plans are set at nought. Happily it was a false alarm.

Ex. 11.29

Ex. 11.30

The bell was for the death of a neighbour's servant. Never were the words 'Requiescat in pace!' sung more gleefully.

Returning to the disputed items, Simone, suave and dignified as ever, proposes that their allocation be left to Schicchi's sense of fairness. Motion carried—without, however preventing individual members, as they help Schicchi into Buoso's night-clothes, from promising him lavish gifts should he decide for them. Ex. 11.29 provides the backcloth for their furtive whisperings and Schicchi's assent to each.

A lyrical interlude follows for Zita, Ciesca, and Nella, gazing with admiration at their hero. Half-waltz, half-lullaby, it winds its way characteristically to the subdominant. Here Puccini parodies the Romantic manner as adroitly as Verdi in the second scene of *Falstaff*, not least in the eloquent 'O Gianni Schicchi, nostro salvatore!' Mostly the material is new; but the strain that first defines the end-key of the movement ('E il Buon Gianni . . . cambia panni . . . per poterci servir!') turns out to be a transformation of the winkling Ex. 11.21b, now a musical caress descending in sequences.

As the relatives hustle him towards the bed Schicchi stops them with a gesture. Tonality and texture darken once more as he warns them of the penalty for falsifying a will: amputation of the right hand and exile. As a mnemonic, he bids the relatives repeat after him a chant of farewell: a single strain stated three times with a final elaboration (Ex. 11.31). For what is essentially a 'stage item' Puccini draws for the only time on Tuscan folk idiom, the melisma (*x*) being characteristic of many a traditional 'stornello'. But, as usual, he has left his own stamp on it: the Lydian C sharp subsequently contradicted and a warning from muted trumpets over the final bar of each statement.

Ex. 11.31

There is a brief flurry of activity as the relatives set the scene for the newcomers, who duly arrive escorted by Rinuccio ('Ecco il notaro!'). From here to the end Puccini relies entirely on previous material redeployed and varied so as to point up each turn of the drama. Lawyer and witnesses enter to a measured statement of the solemn Ex. 11.23, to which Ex. 11.28 now forms a pendant, conveying their salutations ('Messer Buono, buon giorno!'). Schicchi replies to them over Ex. 11.21a. Ex. 11.25b, now distorted and crestfallen, matches the grief of Pinellino, the cobbler, at finding a valued customer reduced to so pitiable a state. For the drawing-up of the will Ex. 11.23 is variously extended with light contrapuntal trimmings and the model of *Die Meistersinger* not far behind. An overlay of Ex. 11.21b in sequences accompanies the discussion of the funeral—a modest one, Schicchi insists. A mention of the monks recalls the first ensemble of fury: but it turns to relief when Schicchi bequeaths them five lire. The money is to be equally divided among the family (Ex. 11.30). Allocating the properties already agreed upon, Schicchi employs the suave manner of Simone over unclouded harmonies. Tremolando strings set up a breathless tension as he passes to 'the mule, the house, and the mills'. But Schicchi takes his time. First, the mule 'which costs three hundred florins and is the best mule in Tuscany' (three notes of Ex. 11.21b on woodwind and horns) 'I leave to my devoted friend, Gianni Schicchi!' (Ex. 11.21b prolonged in a downward plunge). Sensation! Simone, with a show of reason, asks what use would the mule be to Gianni Schicchi. Throwing the same music back at him, the false Buoso retorts that he himself knows what is of use to Gianni Schicchi (a snatch of repartee borrowed from the anonymous commentator on Dante's text): and Ex. 11.25b above the smoothly flowing quavers cocks an appropriate snook. The house in Florence, similarly bequeathed, detonates an explosion of wrath to the pattern of major common chords with which the opera had opened, the comic grin now turned to a grimace. As it subsides into a mutter, Schicchi can be heard intoning Ex. 11.31. There remain the mills at Signa. Here Schicchi's dictation is accompanied by pounding dissonances (two conflicting chords of the seventh recognized by Stravinsky as a recollection of his own tuba solo from *Petrushka*) while his voice alternates between declamation and the chanting of Ex. 11.31, prolonged inconsequentially so as to stifle the family's cries of protest. Zita is ordered to pay the lawyer and the witnesses, who take their leave with many a bow of thanks (Ex. 11.30) several times repeated.

Amid cries of abuse the relatives set about pillaging what they can lay hands on, while Schicchi leaps from the bed and drives them away with Buoso's stick. Sequences of 'hurry' music give way to reiterations of Ex. 11.30 as they break into unpitched shouting that fades into the distance, allowing Ex. 11.22 to come into its own as a miniature duet for the two lovers. It remains for Schicchi to close the proceedings with a spoken *envoi*. Indicating the lovers, he ask whether Buoso's wealth could have finished in better hands. His trickery may have consigned him to everlasting perdition; but, with due respect to Father Dante, he hopes that, if they have enjoyed themselves, the audience may grant him mitigation. A single phrase from Rinuccio's 'stornello' in praise of Florence underlines his plea; and Ex. 11.25b fortissimo on full orchestra epitomizes his triumph.

Gianni Schicchi remains the last Italian lyrical comedy of universal appeal, irresistible even to those antipathetic to Puccini's music in general. Like Rossini's *Il barbiere*, it can be seen as a descendant of the *commedia dell'arte* with Schicchi as its Arlecchino (though not a servant). Hence a certain flatness in the general characterization. Lauretta, Rinuccio, Zita, and Simone are no more than 'types'. Nowhere does Puccini delve below the surface in the manner of Mozart, Wagner, or Verdi. But for comic verve *Gianni Schicchi* can stand comparison with any opera in the repertoire. Credit, too, must be given to Forzano, who so often uses rhyme (a cheap commodity in Italian verse) to point up the important word, so that musical and verbal wit are perfectly matched.

★   ★   ★

A question still hangs over the concept of *Il trittico*. Many commentators see it in terms of a progress from darkness to light, each item a preparation for its successor. Nothing in Puccini's correspondence supports such a view. His avowed aim was to fill out an evening with a trilogy of contrasted colours—no more. Carner's comparison with the three parts of Dante's *Divina commedia* is especially difficult to sustain. The joys of *Gianni Schicchi* are those of *Schadenfreude* rather than of Paradise. It crowns the triptych more in the spirit of the satirical plays (now, alas, lost) that used to follow the tragedies of Ancient Greece. If performances of *Il trittico* in its entirety have been comparatively rare, it is because each panel forms a complete, self-sufficient statement, and their combination in a single evening can strain an audience's digestion. Hence the practice of pairing each with a short opera by a different composer. Only *Suor Angelica* with its special casting requirements and weak dénouement tends to remain a wallflower. But as a manifestation of creative self-renewal over a wide area *Il trittico* is indeed outstanding and goes far to justify the composer's entitlement to the soubriquet 'Verdi's successor'.

CHAPTER 12

Turandot

AT THE BEGINNING OF FEBRUARY 1919, NEWLY DECORATED AS 'Grand'Ufficiale della Corona d'Italia', Puccini returned to Torre del Lago to put the finishing touches to the second edition of his three one-act operas, now to be issued separately. He also had a far from congenial task to fulfil.

In April of the previous year the city fathers of Rome had commissioned the poet Fausto Salvatori to write an ode in celebration of the recent Italian victories which had reversed the disaster of Caporetto. The music was to have been by Mascagni. Salvatori duly obliged with a set of Sapphic verses, every third a refrain ending with the lines: 'Tu non vedrai nessuna cosa al mondo/Maggior di ROMA.' His own view was that the honour of setting them should be competed for, the winner receiving a gold medal. No further action was taken, however, until at a banquet given for Puccini after the Roman première of *Il trittico* the mayor, Prospero di Colonna, invited him as the man of the moment to undertake the assignment. Puccini accepted without enthusiasm. He disliked Salvatori's verses, and the thought of having to confine himself to a popular style and a melodic range suited to children's voices dismayed him. 'This Hymn to Rome is driving me crazy', he wrote to his friend Guido Vandini[1]; and to Elvira on 26 March, 'I've finished the Hymn to Rome, a right load of rubbish [*una bella porch-*

[1] PLI 220, p. 184.

eria].'² The première was planned for 21 April, the date on which Rome was supposed to have been founded. It was to be a double event: in the afternoon an open-air concert in the grounds of the Villa Umberto, the music arranged for municipal band fortified by military brass and sung by a chorus some 4,000 strong, mostly from the state schools but with a stiffening of 500 soldiers (Puccini's suggestion); in the evening a performance at the Teatro Costanzi preceded by a revival of *Madama Butterfly* with Rosina Storchio in the title role. A cloudburst put an end to the first, scattering the spectators, who included the King and Queen of Italy; a lightning strike put paid to the second with the consequent closure of the theatre, besieged by an angry crowd of ticket-holders demanding their money back. The *Inno a Roma* had to wait until 1 June, when it was performed at the National Stadium on the occasion of the Royal Gymnastic Competition, again amid the trappings of a 'concert monstre'. This time all went well; the public was enthusiastic, and both Salvatori and Puccini (who was absent) received gold watches for their pains.

Puccini was surely right in thinking poorly of his composition. In form and character it follows the pattern laid down by Sousa and followed by Elgar in his *Pomp and Circumstance* marches: ternary, with a quiet episode that is thundered out in full panoply by way of coda. The difference here is that there is no reprise of the original idea. The episode, first heard in the dominant, is immediately repeated fortissimo in the home key. For this a memorable tune is essential; and that is precisely what Puccini fails to provide. The melody hangs pointlessly about the fifth degree of the scale, and no amount of trumpet flourishes can give it any significance. Of all Puccini's non-theatrical compositions the *Inno a Roma* is the most inept.

Nevertheless its martial character combined with the composer's name kept it in circulation during the Fascist era. It was published by the Casa Sonzogno in 1923, Ricordi having understandably turned it down. Gigli recorded it in 1937; and in 1942, its text translated into German, it entered the corpus of Nazi war-time propaganda—a fate it richly deserved.

For all the celebrations of peace and victory the country was in a

² CP 751, p. 483.

bad way. Alone of the Allies Italy seemed to have lost the war. The 'sacro egoismo' proclaimed by the government in 1915 had yielded no profits, for the rewards promised by the Treaty of London were not forthcoming, since President Wilson refused to recognize its validity. While mandates and protectorates were doled out to Britain and France ('Albion has once again known how to look after herself', Puccini wrote bitterly to Sybil)[3] Italy received only South Tyrol, Trieste, and its surroundings—territories to which she had long laid claim. Unemployment was rife; strikes and lock-outs would persist over the next three years, while the threat of communism haunted the impoverished bourgeoisie. In such a climate, Puccini, whose bank balance was healthier than ever, was regarded by many of his neighbours as a war profiteer. Dante Del Fiorentino recalls an occasion on the Lago di Massaciuccoli when a passing fisherman called out to Puccini, 'It's yours now; soon it will be our turn!'[4] Then, too, the construction of a peat factory was disturbing the peace of the 'turris eburnea', so that Puccini spent more and more time at nearby Viareggio, where he founded the 'Gianni Schicchi Club', successor to the 'Bohème' of pre-war years, with himself as founder, Forzano as vice-president, and many of his cronies, old and new, as members. Among the latter were the Luccan critic Carlo Paladini, whose strictures on *Butterfly* were now forgiven and Angelo Magrini, a wealthy industrialist, who would be of great service to the composer in his final years and would even be present at his death-bed in Brussels.

Meanwhile, the plot of land that he had bought for Josephine von Stengel in 1915 would now be the site of a new villa for Puccini himself and his family, to be their permanent home. More than two years would pass, however, before they were able to move in. Situated at a crossroads near the shore with a large pine-girt garden, it was designed by the architect Plonio as a spacious red-brick building with a touch of the Orient about it. Visitors would be impressed by the number of new-fangled gadgets: the aerial for radio reception, the automatic sprinklers that operated from the trees, several of which were hung with Chinese lanterns, the entrance door opened by remote control. Although it was

---

[3] PAE, 291.

[4] D. Del Fiorentino: *Immortal Bohemian*, 194.

two-storeyed, Puccini always referred to the house, rather oddly, as his 'Californian bungalow'.

He also had his eye on a winter retreat: the ancient fort of Torre della Tagliata in a remote part of the Tuscan Maremma ('10 metres from the sea, . . . plenty of hunting and fishing, . . . climate: Montecarlo, because it's sheltered by the hill of Ansedonia, . . . altogether a real delight.'[5] By October 1919 he had completed the purchase and was able to move in after Christmas. But his delight was of short duration. Within a year he was inveighing against the desolation, the stink of the marshes, and, above all, the debilitating 'scirocco'. In 1922 he put the property up for sale.

Death continued to take its toll of those about him. A month after his return from Rome it came to his brother-in-law, Massimo Del Carlo, who as mayor of Lucca had done much to further Puccini's interests in his native city. Five days later it was the turn of Carignani, a friend since their schooldays together and the arranger for voice and piano of his operas from *Edgar* onwards. With his abiding fear of mortality Puccini generally avoided funerals. He made an exception, however, for Leoncavallo who had died on 9 August of that year. He even joined Mascagni as one of the pall-bearers, which seems odd, since all references to his former rival in his letters remain hostile to the end. On the other hand, Del Fiorentino speaks of frequent visits by Leoncavallo to Torre del Lago and of Puccini's later description of him as having 'the head of a lion, the body of a horse and the honest heart of a boy'.[6] If this was meant seriously, it erred on the side of charity. The most that can be said for Leoncavallo's 'honesty' is that he sincerely believed his own lies.

In June Puccini resumed his solitary travels, first to London to sound out plans for the Covent Garden première of *Il trittico*, due to be given the following year. He himself had every intention of being present, provided that 'that *pig* of a Toscanini'[7] was not engaged to conduct. The Seligmans found him little changed. 'His hair had begun to turn white', Vincent noted, 'but it was abundant as ever; his movements were per-

[5] CP 752, p. 483.

[6] D. Del Fiorentino: *Immortal Bohemian*, 203.

[7] PAF, 292.

haps a little slower and more measured; but the coming of old age over which he continually laments in his letters was with him a very gradual and almost imperceptible process, and no-one would have guessed that he had turned sixty; and he looked, as he always did until a few months before his death, the very picture of health.'[8] His boyish enthusiasm for the shops and sights of London was undiminished. Bond Street provided him with presents for Elvira as well as the opportunity for restocking his own wardrobe. His purchases included ties to which he was not strictly entitled; and Vincent urged him not to wear them until he arrived home. Nonetheless it was an Old Etonian Puccini who would attend one of the rehearsals for *Il trittico*.

As usual, he frequented the London theatres—Covent Garden, however, only with reluctance, since it had made a poor post-war start with inferior productions of *La bohème* and *Tosca*, the first with a 60-year-old Melba as Mimì. He saw Frederick Norton's musical comedy *Chu-Chin-Chow*, a smash-hit since 1916; also the melodrama *Mr Wu* by H. M. Vernon and H. Owen, which would later provide the basis of an opera by Eugen d'Albert. That either pointed him in the direction of an oriental subject seems unlikely, since at the time he had a very different project in mind: Forzano's *Cristoforo Sly*, expanded from the prologue to Shakespeare's *The Taming of the Shrew*. Sly, a hard-drinking, disreputable tinker, is discovered by a noble lord in a tavern, sleeping off his potations. As a prank the lord has him transported to his palace, where he wakes surrounded by servants, who assure him that his past life has been a hallucination induced by an illness of which he is now cured. It is in his honour that the play is performed. Forzano follows the jest through to its cruel dénouement. Disabused of his new-found status, Sly is thrown into prison as an impostor. In the meantime, however, the lord's ex-mistress Dolly (an addition of Forzano) has fallen in love with him. She comes to see him in prison, only to find that he has cut his veins. Sir Thomas Beecham, then musical director of Covent Garden, promised to supply Puccini with appropriate specimens of Elizabethan popular song, but in the event did nothing (he had not taken to Puccini the man, however much he admired his music; and the feeling was mutual). In any case it would have been wasted labour. A

[8] PAF, 300–2.

year later it was, 'Sly is no good. Forzano is unhappy about it, and so am I—for his sake.'[9] The tragic ending had seemed to Puccini out of key with the rest of the drama. However, Forzano's work had not been in vain. His *Sly* enjoyed great success in Italy as a prose play and as such even travelled to England. In 1927 it was set as an opera by Wolf-Ferrari under the title *Sly—la leggenda del dormiente svegliato*.

On his way home Puccini stopped at Paris to visit Tito Ricordi, lately ousted from the family firm for much the same reason as Lorenzo Sonzogno, namely unprofitable speculation. Unlike his rival publisher Tito was unable to bounce back. Having settled in the French capital with a view to making a career in the cinema, he ended his life in reduced circumstances. With his successors Carlo Clausetti and Renzo Valcarenghi Puccini had always been on the best of terms. Nevertheless the departure of Tito, son of his old counsellor, friend, and benefactor, represented a sad break with the past.

August found Puccini at work with Adami on the revisions to *La rondine* for Vienna. Evidently it was in the poet's company that he renewed an acquaintance which went back to 1904. Renato Simoni, born in Verona in 1875, was, like Forzano, a literary jack-of-all-trades. Giacosa's successor as editor of *La lettura*, Puccini, as already mentioned, had considered pairing him with Illica on the libretto of *Il tabarro*. Since then he had proved his theatrical flair with his adaptation for Giordano of Sardou's *Madame Sans-Gêne* (1915). More significantly, he was the author of a biography of Carlo Gozzi written at the age of 28. He it was who would put forward the subject of Puccini's last opera.

But in the autumn of 1919 that was still to come. Not that Puccini was exclusively committed to *Sly*. He had already sounded Forzano about 'a little subject, perhaps a fairy-tale set in the hills around Lucca'.[10] And to Adami and Simoni, 'Create something for me that will set the world weeping. They say that sentiment is a sign of weakness, but I like being weak! To the strong, so-called, I leave the triumphs that fade'[11] (a reference, perhaps, to D'Annunzio's swashbuckling capture of Rijeka). Adami mentions a libretto based on Dickens's *Oliver*

[9] PAF, 312.

[10] PGP 1, p. 117.

[11] GPE 173, pp. 255–6.

Twist. Entitled *Fanny*, it probably centred on Bill Sykes's ill-fated mistress Nancy. But by the time Adami had finished it the wind had changed once more.

In October Puccini paid a brief visit to Vienna, again to pick up old threads and, more specifically, to arrange for next year's première of *Il trittico*, to be given in German at the Staatsoper. While there he saw Lehár's operetta *Wo die Lerche singt*, which he praised highly in a letter to the composer, at the same time regretting that he was unable to do anything for Lehár's cousin, still held as a prisoner of war in Italy.

About this time a rumour had reached Puccini's ears about the possible nomination of an Italian composer as Senator of the Realm, and he charged Paladini to find out more. Was it to be Mascagni? Was he himself excluded because of a 'defeatist' attitude during the war? He volunteered to give Paladini an interview that would set the record straight. It was true that Forzano, who had friends in high places, regularly spoke ill of Mascagni, but was he sincere? As one who had settled in Livorno, might he not wish to support a candidate from that city? Not that Puccini himself set much store by the honour. 'If the affair goes up in smoke, don't think that I shall be all that sorry—but I'd mind if it went to the other chap.'[12] For the moment it went to neither.

New Year's Day 1920 was the occasion of a house-warming party at Torre della Tagliata, to which all friends were bidden who could make the journey, access to the tower being far from easy. Toscanini, as might be guessed, was not among them. Earlier, in accordance with a custom that still prevails in Italy, Puccini had sent him a 'panettone', or Christmas cake, as a season's greeting, following it with a telegram: 'Panettone sent by mistake'. Back came the reply: 'Panettone eaten by mistake'.

It was during a meeting with Puccini and Adami in a Milan restaurant, probably about mid-March, that Simoni dropped the magic word 'Turandot'. He gave Puccini a copy of Gozzi's play to take with him to Rome, where *Il trittico* was enjoying a successful revival. From there Puccini wrote to him:

I've read *Turandot* and I don't think we should abandon this subject. Yesterday I was speaking to a foreign lady who told me that this work had

[12] PGP II, pp. 129–30.

been given in Germany with a mise-en-scène by Max Reinhardt in a very curious and original manner. She is going to write for a photograph of this mise-en-scène, so that we can see what it amounted to [as always, a visual stimulus was important to Puccini]. But for my part I would advise sticking to this subject. Simplify it as regards the number of acts so as to make it run smoothly and effectively; and above all heighten the amorous passion of Turandot which she has smothered so long beneath the ashes of her pride. . . . All in all, I consider *Turandot* the most normal and human of all Gozzi's works. In short, a *Turandot* filtered through a modern brain—yours, Adami's and mine.[13]

How ironical that the feature of Gozzi's drama that attracted him most was the one that lay beyond his capacity to realize in music!

The age-old fable of the Princess whose hand can only be won by the solution of three riddles, failure costing the suitor his head, had entered European literature by way of *Les mille et un jours* (1710–12), a collection of Arabian folktales translated by François Pétis de la Croix. From there it passed to Carlo Gozzi for the fourth of his 'fiabe teatrali', all produced in Venice during the 1760s. A patrician of 'La Serenissima', Gozzi intended his stage works as a counterblast to Goldoni's comedy of manners, which he regarded as socially disruptive. He harnessed to his purpose the stock characters of the *commedia dell'arte* with their improvisatory skills; so that while his principals, all noble, express themselves in high-flown verse, his Brighellas, Tartaglias, and Truffaldinos speak prose, now Italian, now Venetian, many of their speeches extemporized from stage instructions. With his exotic settings and magical contrivances Gozzi was clearly harking back to the Baroque 'theatre of wonders'. Paradoxically it was these that awoke a response in the nascent spirit of German Romanticism. It was Gozzi's *La donna serpente* that launched Wagner on his stage career with *Die Feen*.

Alone among the 'fiabe' *Turandot* dispenses entirely with magic; hence, no doubt, Puccini's description of it as the most 'normal' and 'human' of Gozzi's works. What chiefly kept it alive during the nineteenth century was an adaptation made by Schiller for the Weimar court theatre in 1802, couched in blank verse throughout. The intrigues that

[13] CP 766, p. 490.

follow Prince Calaf's offer of a counter-riddle to which the answer is his own and his father's name pursue their labyrinthine course as in Gozzi. Chief among the secondary characters are the Emperor Altoum, Calaf's father Timur, Barack, their family retainer empressed into the Emperor's service and the captive princess Adelma, Turandot's favourite slave and confidante, who, having designs of her own on Calaf, tricks him into revealing the two names and passes them on to her mistress— too late, for Turandot's heart has already melted. For a revival at Stuttgart in 1809 incidental music was provided by Weber, who took his principal theme from Rousseau's *Dictionnaire de musique*. Familiar to us to-day from Hindemith's *Symphonic Metamorphosis of Themes by Weber* it is among the first instances of melodic 'chinoiserie' in Western music to have come down to us. Whether or not Puccini knew it can only be guessed.

Two Italians had preceded him in setting the subject to music. In 1867 his teacher Antonio Bazzini had launched a *Turanda* at La Scala, Milan. The libretto by Antonio Gazzoletti eliminates several of Gozzi's characters, including the Venetian masks. The action is shifted from China to Persia; yet there is no trace of the exotic in the music that survives. 'A stupid, totally uninteresting libretto, an absolute lack of melody of any kind, no form, new or old, . . . an opera that will live for just a few days.' Thus the young Giulio Ricordi in a letter to the conductor Franco Faccio.[14] His prophecy was duly fulfilled. That Bazzini showed the score to his pupil or even mentioned it to him is in the highest degree unlikely. No doubt *Turanda* was an experience that he preferred to forget.

Of far greater importance is Busoni's *Turandot*, which occupied the composer over a period of some 16 years. Originally a suite of five movements designed to serve as incidental music for the Gozzi play, Busoni reworked it into a two-act opera to a German libretto written by himself. As such it was first performed in tandem with his *Arlecchino* at Zürich in 1917. In 1921 a new finale ultimo (*Nachtrag zu Turandot*) was added, uniting the whole cast.

Puccini was always keen to keep abreast of contemporary music; but Busoni seems never to have crossed his path. Although he too was

[14] K.-M. Lo: *"Turandot" auf der Opernbühne*, 307.

Tuscan-born, his preferred country of residence was Germany. His professed model for *Turandot* was *Die Zauberflöte*, which doubtless accounts for the prominence given to a Sarastro-like Emperor Altoum. Much as he admired the later Puccini, his own aesthetic could hardly be more different. While Puccini aimed at a 'human' drama, Busoni was concerned to create a world of artifice, a never-never land of fairy-tale grotesques, viewed with ironic detachment. Elements of folksong are not lacking; but they are not confined to China. The second act opens with a 'Lied mit Chor' to the melody of 'Greensleeves'.

Puccini's *Turandot*, therefore, owes nothing to his Italian predecessors, being conceived entirely *ex novo*. Three undated letters to Adami, clearly to be assigned to late March 1920, indicate the direction of his first thoughts: local colour to be obtained from Chinese folk melodies and the use of Chinese instruments on stage; the addition of 'another figure', not in Gozzi, to give the story a touch of charm (it would be the slave-girl Liù, who would in effect replace Adelma); the Venetian masks, if not eliminated, to be kept marginal to the action, merely providing an oasis of Italian common sense amid so much Chinese mannerism.

By mid-May Adami had supplied a scheme for the first act ending with the scene of the riddles. Puccini professed himself satisfied in broad outline; but all further discussion was cut short by his trip with Forzano to London to supervise the British première of *Il trittico*. Here Puccini was all the rage, with *Manon Lescaut, La bohème, Tosca,* and *Madama Butterfly* playing at Covent Garden concurrently with English performances of the last three at the Lyceum. The Daily Express dubbed him 'the King of Melody'—a description that was gleefully relayed to friends at home. 'What would Covent Garden be without Puccini?' asked the *Times* critic. However, not even he could save Beecham's company from financial collapse before the year was out. Puccini himself was not displeased. 'How glad I am about Pill!' (a reference to the source of Beecham's wealth). 'And so that pig has gone bankrupt; well, peace be to his soul.'[15]

Back at home—a sad anticlimax, he told Sybil, after the order he had seen prevailing in London—he received schemes for Acts II and

[15] Sotheby's *Fine Music and Continental Manuscripts* (1999)

III of *Turandot*. This time his reservations were stronger. 'In the third [act] I had imagined a different dénouement. I had thought that [Turandot's] capitulation would be more *prenante* and I would like her to burst into expressions of love *coram populo*—but excessively, violently, shamelessly, like a bomb exploding.'[16] In August there was a meeting with both librettists at Bagni di Lucca. It was here that the 'other figure' began to take shape ('Have you given thought to the little woman?', he wrote to Simoni afterwards).[17] He also took the opportunity of visiting Baron Fassini Camossi, a former diplomat in China, who possessed a musical box that played Chinese melodies of which Puccini would use three in his opera, including the Imperial Hymn. Four others he would take from von Aalst's *Chinese Music* (1884), sent to him by Carlo Clausetti in June of the following year.

A proposed trip with Schnabl to Munich to catch up on contemporary German music—notably Richard Strauss's *Die Frau ohne Schatten* and Pfitzner's *Palestrina*—came to nothing. But he had an opportunity of seeing the former (which impressed him not at all) during his visit with Elvira and Tonio to Vienna in October for *La rondine* at the Volksoper and *Il trittico* at the principal theatre. His reception in the Austrian capital was as cordial as it had been in London. Festivities included a 'Puccini Abend' at the Konzerthaus; and there was a happy reunion with Lehár, who presented his colleague with a photograph inscribed 'To Puccini from his most loyal supporter'. During a performance of *Tosca* Jeritza, accidentally stumbling, found herself singing 'Vissi d'arte' prone, and would do so ever after with Puccini's entire approval.

No sooner had the family returned to Torre del Lago than reaction set in. Puccini poured out his heart to Adami. 'So you think that . . . I am happy after the welcome I received in Vienna? On all my travels I have carried about with me a large bundle of melancholy. I have no reason for it, but that is the way I am made. . . . I'm afraid that *Turandot* will never be finished. . . . When the fever abates it ends by disappearing, and without fever there is no creation; because emotional art is a kind of malady, an abnormal state of mind, over-excitement of every fibre and every atom of one's being.' Then to practicalities. 'I am going

[16] GPE 181, p. 261.

[17] CP 774, p. 495.

to the Maremma . . . towards the end of the month. Will you come there or would you rather come here first? It depends on you and how much work you've done. What about Simoni? . . . Is he still on his high horse? Because as far as I'm concerned the libretto is not something to be trifled with. It isn't a question of finishing it. It's a question of giving lasting life to something which must be alive before it is born'[18] (a libretto is, after all, essentially pre-natal).

Adami made the journey to Torre della Tagliata with the first act complete. 'In general I liked it', Puccini reported to Simoni, 'but to tell the truth I have to say that the act needs shortening at all costs in many places—and above all we must devise a more effective curtain.' He had expected a swifter action and a language more evocative and less literary. True, the verses were beautifully turned, 'but you know that in an opera one must be more succinct than in a spoken play. So you must trim, trim, and give more pace and effectiveness to the individual scenes'.[19] From which it would seem that Adami was to be the Illica and Simoni the Giacosa of the partnership.

Meanwhile Puccini found time to recommend to Carlo Clausetti an opera, *Petronio*, by a fellow-Luccan, Gustavo Giovanetti (based on Sinckiewic's novel *Quo Vadis*, it would be given at the Teatro Costanzi, Rome, in 1923.) By this time the first act of the Gozzi libretto as it then stood was ready for the press. A copy of the proof, held in the Library of the Milan Conservatory, reveals the action and distribution of the characters roughly as we know them today. Timur is present from the start attended by Liù. The Masks, wholly Chinese, are reduced from four to three and function as a group, though as yet with no scene to themselves. Calaf's 'Non piangere, Liù' precedes instead of following Liù's first aria, which here refers to the Prince's smile in the courtyard that first won her heart. The curtain falls after Calaf's offer of a counter-riddle to Turandot.

'Fine the general lay-out', Schnabl was told, 'but too many words, too much literature.'[20] But by January 1921, Puccini was more hopeful ('It will be a fine libretto and above all highly original, full of colours,

[18] GPE 184, pp. 263–4.

[19] CP 783, p. 499.

[20] PRS 67, p. 112.

surprises, and emotion.'[21] In March there was a brief interlude in Monte Carlo to attend the local première of *Il trittico*, whose total success, together with the presence of Sybil, doubtless offset the loss of 12,000 lire at the casino, while a flirtatious motor trip to Ventimiglia with Gilda Dalla Rizza (the Angelica and Lauretta) together with three of her companions soothed, so he said, the feelings of encroaching old age.

April saw him finally at work on the first act in alternating moods of enthusiasm and despondency. To Sybil on 21 April, 'I don't seem to have any more faith in myself; my work terrifies me, and I find nothing good anywhere. I feel as though from now on I'm finished—and it may well be that that is so.'[22] But to Adami nine days later it was, '*Turandot* is going well; I feel that I'm on the high road. I'm at the masks and in a little while I shall come to the riddles!'[23] Evidently he was not composing the score in order; for not until 22 May could he report to Simoni, 'I've finished the terrible song of the executioner— I'm starting the moon chorus and the funeral march for the Persian prince. The opera is taking on huge proportions'. On June 7: 'I'm at the Ghosts! I'll merely say that I've already done Non piangere, Liù, and Per quel sorriso' (the original first words of Liù's first aria).[24] The première of Mascagni's *Il piccolo Marat* on 2 May had left him pleasurably disappointed ('After what I've heard in Rome I feel more in the mood . . . ').[25]

During June he wrestled with the riddles, his spirits only mildly ruffled by the news that his rival had been nominated 'Grand'Ufficiale dell'Ordine Maurizio' as 'the most noble creator of Italian music'. He then worked backwards to the march which precedes the Emperor's entrance, asking for more lines for the chorus.

August was cheered by a visit of Sybil and Vincent Seligman, to whom Puccini played the music he had so far written. It was to be their last sight of him together, and it left on the whole a happy impression. 'The vague feeling of tension', Vincent recalls, 'of which in

[21] PRS 70 p. 116.

[22] PAF, 328.

[23] GPE 189, pp. 365–6.

[24] CP 506–7, pp. 797–9.

[25] Lo, op. cit., 373.

the old days I was always conscious when Giacomo and Elvira were together had completely disappeared. Elvira was still a confirmed pessimist and complained—for hers was a complaining nature—of the high price of food, of the weather, of the strikes—of everything, in fact, except her husband and her family. Yet age, which had destroyed her looks, had given her a new sweetness and a new serenity. As for Giacomo, he was the same as ever: tender, gentle, affectionate, gay—and yet always with that touch of sadness that lurked at the corners of his mouth even when he was smiling.'[26] Meanwhile Adami had arrived with the second act, of which Puccini approved sufficiently to set in motion the contract with the Casa Ricordi.

Then in September came a *volte-face* which threatened to bring proceedings to a halt. Puccini now wanted *Turandot* in two acts only. This is not entirely surprising. His first reaction on receiving Adami's sketch for Act I had been to wonder whether, once the tangle of intrigues following the solution of the riddles had been thinned out, there would be enough incident to fill two further acts. 'In short', he wrote to Adami, 'I don't think we should delay much after the riddles. Delay here means weakening the opera.' For Simoni he set out a detailed scheme which he summarized impressionistically for Adami:

> Enter Turandot nervous after the ordeal of the riddles. Little scene ending with the threat: Let no-one sleep in Pekin. Romanza for tenor. No banquet after that, but a scene in which the three masks take the lead. Offers, drink, and women, beseeching Calaf to speak. He no: I lose Turandot. Urgent proposals to have him escape. He no: I lose Turandot. Then threats to his life with daggers. Appeal of dignitaries, then some rapid little plotting and attack. Turandot appears; they flee. Duet, shorter—then torture, this too quicker, etc., up to I've lost her. Exit Turandot, face aflame, heart wildly beating. Liù remains to speak with Turandot. Black-out—change of scene. Room in yellow and pink—scene for Turandot and slaves—rich mantle. Pangs of jealousy. Black-out, then final scene, grandiose, in white and pink: Love![27]

[26] PAF, 330–1.

[27] GPE 192–3, pp. 268–70.

He stressed the visual advantages of the two-act format, beginning with sunset and ending with sunrise. To Simoni he raised the possibility of arriving at the conclusion by way of a transformation scene modelled on the third act of Parsifal ('the Chinese holy grail').[28]

Further ideas poured in from Bologna, where Puccini was supervising *Il trittico*:

> Calaf must kiss Turandot and show how much he loves her. After he has kissed her with a kiss that lasts some long seconds, he must say, 'Nothing matters now; I am even ready to die,' and he speaks his name to her lips. Here you could have a scene which should be the pendant to the gloomy opening of the act with its Let no-one sleep in Pekin. The masks and perhaps the dignitaries and slaves lurking nearby have heard the name and shout it aloud. The shout is repeated and taken up and Turandot is compromised. Then in the third act [an obvious slip of the pen] when all is prepared with the executioner etc. As in the first act, she says: his name I do not know, to everyone's surprise.[29]

To this barrage of suggestions it was some time before the librettists could bring themselves to reply. Puccini turned once more to Sybil for a possible alternative. '*Turandot* languishes. I haven't yet got the second act as I want it, and I don't feel myself capable any more of composing music; if I had a charming, light, sentimental subject, a little sad and with a touch of burlesque in it, I think I could still do something good; but with a serious subject, a really serious subject, no.' Evidently he was in earnest, for in November he wrote to her again, '*Turandot* will end by going to the wall because the libretto of the second act is no good—and I have done the first act! I'm looking for something else with Forzano with an eye to London.' Forzano himself added a postscript: 'We're hoping to find something else worthy of the Great Man! We're going to use all the brains we've got!'

The resultant draft was sent to Sybil for her opinion, which was apparently favourable. 'I'm glad that Forzano's Chinese Play met with your approval', Puccini replied. 'I too liked it in many places—but I've

[28] CP 816, pp. 514–15.
[29] GPE 196, p. 272.

got *Turandot* and I can't change now. You say I should use the music already written, but it's not possible—you know how I fit the words exactly to the music.'[30] Since this last remark was manifestly untrue, the real reason for Puccini's change of heart must be sought elsewhere—almost certainly in a meeting with the librettists early in December, at which it was decided to split the first act into two. So much was briefly reported to Schnabl. Now at least it was possible to reduce the remaining act to reasonable proportions and to move to the dénouement with the dispatch that Puccini wanted. By compensation Acts I and II would need to be enlarged. Therefore to Adami and Simoni: 'With regard to the new Act I, if you find you can expand it in certain directions, do so. This to make it less rapid. And for the first scene of Act II, consider the daughter of heaven high up beside the Emperor's throne, beseeching and praying that she be not thrown into the stranger's arms.' Then to Adami alone: 'If only you could bring down the curtain after the masks have done their pleading and almost exhausted their powers of persistence! The two—the old father and the slave girl—must complete the ensemble together with the three masks and we should finish after Calaf's hymns (phrased as in the trio of *Faust*) with the striking of the great gong.'[31] And so it would be, apart from Gounod's three-fold pattern of rising phrases, which would find a more effective place elsewhere, as will be seen.

The year 1922 brought its share of distractions, not all of them pleasurable. At La Scala *Il trittico*, cordially received by the public, prompted a stinging notice in *Il secolo* from the composer Giacomo Orefice ('poor impotent creature fed on bile and envy!').[32] Moreover, word had reached Puccini of a foxtrot based on the humming chorus from *Madama Butterfly*, which had been published by Ricordi's New York branch. His first thought was to bring an action against the firm he had served so well and which was now profiting from the 'disfigurement' of his music. Nor was that all. Instead of promoting his interests, the Casa Ricordi was showering publicity on Zandonai, and *Giulietta e*

[30] PAF, 334–7.

[31] GPE 200–1, pp. 276–7.

[32] PRS 93, p. 162.

Romeo was about to go into production at the Teatro Costanzi. Called to Rome in February for a meeting of the Commissione Permanente per l'Arte Musicale, Puccini went to hear Zandonai's opera for himself, and disliked it intensely. Since his contract with the Casa Ricordi was still unsigned, he considered offering *Turandot* directly to the Società Autori ed Editori, but as usual, took no further action.

A consolation, however, was the presence of the German soprano Rose Ader, in a revival of *Il trittico* in the same theatre. Thirty-two years his junior, she had sung Angelica at Hamburg in February 1921. Schnabl, who produced, found her insufficiently dramatic for the role. Puccini, who attended at least one performance, formed a more positive opinion, though he would later admit that the final scenes were too heavy for her. Photographs were exchanged, and by the spring a love affair had blossomed. Of his many letters to her, known to exist in private hands, only one, dating from May of that year, has found its way into print—an extravagant outpouring of infatuation ('the only woman I love in the world etc').[33] Yet, as with Wagner and Judith Gauthier, one suspects that the affair was more in the mind than in the flesh. There is no record of secret trysts, of carefully laid plans to elude Elvira's detection. But it would seem that his feelings for her clouded his judgment. The singing coach Luigi Ricci gave a devastating account of Rose Ader's Mimì ('her top C like the whistle of a train').[34] When Puccini recommended her to Gatti-Casazza for the New York Metropolitan he was told that singers of her calibre could easily be recruited locally.

In the meantime an important decision had been reached. Act II would open with a trio for the masks, variously referred to by Puccini as a 'fuori scena' or a 'chitarrata'. Returned from Rome in March, he began the scoring of Act I, which he completed up to the final ensemble in June. But his fears for the opera's future were by no means over. Like Verdi at the same age he was feeling out of tune with the times; hence a tirade against contemporary music addressed to Simoni, from whom he still awaited the third act:

[33] G. Magri: *L'uomo Puccini*, 205–6.

[34] L. Ricci: 'Fleta e le note filate, presente Puccini', *Rivista Musicale Curci*, xxx (April 1977), 22–4.

Perhaps you think I'm working to no purpose—and you may well be right—for by now the public's taste for new music is no longer in order—it likes, or it puts up with, senseless, illogical music—nobody writes melody any more—or if they do it's vulgar—they think that 'symphonism' should hold sway, whereas I think that would be the end of opera—in Italy they used to sing; now they don't any more—blows, discords, false expression, transparency—opalescence—lymphaticism—all Celtic diseases, a real ultra-montane pox.[35]

Again his thoughts turned to an alternative subject. He proposed to Adami 'something original—that comes entirely from your youthful brain—something delicate and moving; not too much psychology but an exploration of souls in grief or else a note of gaiety, freshness'.[36] But he still harped on the need for the complete libretto of *Turandot*.

This arrived towards the end of June; and Puccini's spirits rose accordingly. It was at this time that he coyly suggested to Sybil that, given the popularity of his music in England, might he not be considered for an English decoration? A passing thought, he hastened to add, and one to which she need pay no attention. Nor did she. A knighthood, such as had been granted to his friend Paolo Tosti, would have been available only to someone resident in the United Kingdom.

Puccini now felt able to sign the contract for *Turandot* with the Casa Ricordi, the more readily since the 'foxtrot affair' was in process of being settled out of court. A substantial advance led him to double the allowance paid to his widowed sister Nitteti. Needless to say he wanted further adjustments to the opera's text: a grand aria for Turandot in Act II and in Act III a telescoping of the action towards the final curtain, with the duet dovetailed into the concluding ensemble—'a moment of loving intimacy before finding themselves coram populo—and the two of them joined in a loving embrace, moving with loving steps towards the father's throne amid the astonished crowd. . . . she says, "I do not know his name"; and he: "Love has conquered" . . . and finish in ecstasy, in rejoicing, in glorious sunlight'.[37] A splendid idea, never, alas, to be brought to fruition.

[35] CP 831, p. 524.
[36] GPE 202, p. 278.
[37] GPE 203, p. 279.

Since July Puccini had promised himself a long holiday abroad to re-charge his batteries. Norway had occurred to him; but in the event he opted for a motor trip through Austria, Germany, and Holland, return-ing through the Black Forest and Switzerland. Setting out with Tonio on 20 August, he was joined at Cutigliano by Magrini and four mem-bers of his family. At Oberammergau they were fortunate enough to catch a performance of the ten-yearly Passion play, which, however, left Puccini cold. But he was so impressed by the Holbein portraits at the Hague that he bought a reproduction of one of them to hang in his studio. At Ingolstadt near Munich there occurred an event of evil augury. During supper a bone lodged in Puccini's throat, needing the services of a doctor to extract it. Whether or not this gave rise to the tumour that brought about his death two years later can only be guessed. The Puccini family, as already noted, had a disposition towards cancer. But the incident may well have determined its point of attack.

Back in Viareggio he was in no hurry to return to *Turandot*. His years lay heavily upon him; and in the following months he would dally with the idea of undergoing the rejuvenating surgery advertised by the Austrian physiologist Eugen Steiner. The death of his sister Igenia at Vicepelago on 1 October was a further reminder of mortality. His only work during that month was the extension to the love duet in Act II of *La fanciulla del West* (see p. 321). Earlier the playwright Luigi Motta had sent him the scheme of a libretto based on the adventures of Casanova. Puccini found it good, except for the last act. For the present he had no intention of setting it, but he would keep it in mind; and it is perhaps significant that the 'light, sentimental' subject that he would continue to urge on Adami would from now on become 'Venetian'.

October 1922 saw the Fascist march on Rome and the formation of a coalition government with Mussolini in effective, if not yet absolute control. Puccini was at first sceptical. 'Here, as you will know, the Fascists want to gain power', he wrote to Schnabl. 'We'll see whether they succeed in restoring this great and beautiful country of ours to order; but I have my doubts.'[38] Later, however, to Adami: 'What about Mussolini? Let's hope he's what we need. A welcome to him if he can

[38] PRS 113, p. 201.

rejuvenate our country and calm it down a bit.'[39] This tells us all. That Fascist ideology meant nothing to Puccini is clear from the fact that, when invited to become an honorary member of the party, his first instinct was to refuse. True, he was prevailed upon to accept, if only so as not to prejudice his chances of being nominated Senator of the Realm, an honour that was duly granted to him. But an audience with Mussolini the following year, described by Marotti in what purports to be Puccini's own words, failed in its object. Puccini wanted to interest the dictator in two projects: the formation of a National Opera House in Rome and the financing of an Italian opera season at Covent Garden. He got as far as the first of these before being interrupted by brusque reiterations of 'There isn't the money!' Puccini's protest that a more modest scheme than the one proposed might be feasible was cut short with 'Either a grandiose project worthy of Rome or nothing!' 'From these words', Puccini allegedly remarked, 'I felt his commanding authority [imperio] and I thought that Italy had at last found her man.'[40] But Marotti was writing in the first flush of the ventennio. Puccini's reference to the episode in his letters to Sybil suggests no such enthusiasm ('I don't think Mussolini is giving a thought to Italian opera at Covent Garden', and 'I saw Mussolini but only for a few minutes, and I wasn't able to talk much').[41] Not for Puccini, therefore, the passionate loyalty to the Duce shown by Mascagni. Certainly he approved of the man who put an end to chaos in Italy, unaware that much of it was of the Fascists' own making: and, as with all those who profess indifference to politics, he invariably gravitated towards the right.

After a visit to Paris for the French première of *Gianni Schicchi*, given at the Opéra Comique on its own, Puccini once more addressed himself to *Turandot*. He was now at work on the concluding ensemble of Act I, he told Adami, and merely needed a few extra lines for the singers. But his next letter struck a chilling note. 'I'm so miserable! And I've even lost faith in myself. *Turandot* is there with the first act done, and with no light on the rest, which is dim and perhaps eternal, impenetrable darkness. I'm thinking that I may have to leave this work on one

[39] GPE 204, p. 280.
[40] MPI, 172.
[41] PAF, 351.

side.' Astoundingly, he proposed returning to the two-act format (fortunately, a passing whim). He dwelt further on the final transformation scene. Then came a fateful decision. 'I think that Liù will have to be sacrificed to grief, but don't see how this could be developed—unless we have her die under torture. And why not? Her death might be a powerful factor in melting the Princess's heart.'[42] Perhaps; but it would also ensure that all sympathy would be diverted towards the victim and so render the opera's dénouement doubly problematic. Mid-December found his invention still in the doldrums. He could find no way of beginning the second act. If only he had the nice little subject that he had so long been looking for, it would now be ready for production. He was sick to death of China, and half minded to restore the Casa Ricordi's advance and free himself from the contract.

Soon, however, his morale would receive a powerful boost. A revival of *Manon Lescaut* had been planned to open La Scala's carnival season of 1922–3 on 26 December with Toscanini as conductor. Relations between the two men had already taken a turn for the better. Puccini had given a glowing account to Schnabl of Toscanini's *Rigoletto* in January; while a photograph of both together with Toscanini's wife and daughter Wally taken at Viareggio in June shows that they were once more on visiting terms. The performance, with Juanita Caracciolo, Aureliano Pertile, and Ernesto Badini in the leading roles, surpassed Puccini's expectations. Throughout the run the hall was packed. More than one critic suspected the composer of having revised the opera for the occasion—a supposition that Puccini was only too happy to refute in an open letter to the *Corriere della sera*! Puccini's gratitude to his favourite conductor (see p. 108) was sufficient to weather another hitch in their relations. For a revival of *La bohème* at La Scala in June, he had hoped for a similar miracle from Toscanini's baton. But the conductor, capricious as ever, delegated the performance to an assistant, Franco Ghione. An urgent telegram from the composer remained unanswered. This time Puccini's annoyance went no further than sarcastic references to the 'divinity' (*divo*) without whose help his operas were perfectly capable of making their own way.

The candle of *Turandot* still guttered, however. 'No! no! no! *Turandot*

[42] GPE 206, pp. 281–2.

no!' was his heartfelt cry to Adami. 'I've part of the third act. It doesn't work. Perhaps, and even with no perhaps, it's I who don't work any longer! I don't want to say, "I die despairing" (*muoio disperato*), but it's not far off. . . . I curse *Turandot*.' Fortunately a comforting telegram from Adami steadied the flame. 'Now I'm tackling Ping and Co. But I'm not yet on the right track.'[43] The death of his sister Otilia was another setback. 'My morale is black, black', he wrote to Sybil. 'This infamous *Turandot* terrifies me and I shan't finish it; or if I do finish it it will be a fiasco. . . . I live from day to day like a lost soul.'[44]

Yet still he pressed on. By mid-April his mood had lightened. To Adami he wrote:

> Turandot's aria is almost finished, but what a work! However, I shall need a few changes to the lines. I think that high up, on the head of the staircase, this aria shouldn't do too badly. The Trio of the masks too is coming on quite nicely. This piece too is very difficult and it's of the greatest importance, being a morceau with no scenic element and therefore almost an academic piece. . . . In short, amid the usual discouragements and the usual small, brief joys of composition *Turandot* advances by little steps, but it does advance.[45]

In May Puccini was called to Vienna, where *Manon Lescaut* was due for its première at the Staatsoper. Before setting out with Tonio and Angelo Magrini he had arranged a meeting with his two librettists at Viareggio, at which the third act was drawn up more or less to his satisfaction. With a heavy weight thus lifted off his shoulders Puccini was able to enjoy what amounted to a holiday in the city where he felt most appreciated. True, it was no longer the rich imperial capital of former times. Inflation was rampant and the living hard for all except the wealthy. But the musical life was as abundant as ever, and standards of performance had never been higher, even though Puccini grumbled about much of what he saw and heard—a 'colourless' *Walküre* conducted by Clemens Krauss in which Jeritza's Sieglinde alone stood out; a disastrous *Butterfly* with the ageing Selma Kurz. No praise, however,

[43] GPE 209–11, pp. 284–5.

[44] PAF, 346.

[45] GPE 213, p. 286.

was too high for Jeritza's Tosca; and if Strauss's *Elektra* pleased him no better than before, the 'naked Evas' in the composer's *Josephlegende*, he declared, were such as to turn the brain of St. Francis. He went with Lehár to a performance of *Die gelbe Jacke* (later revised as *Das Land des Lächelns*). Both composers were wildly cheered by the spectators. Rehearsals for *Manon Lescaut* were held up by the indisposition of Lotte Lehmann; and the première would have to be deferred until the autumn. Puccini, however, was happy to stay on for a while, to be fêted by a society that treated him, so he told Adami, 'like the Kaiser or the Crown Prince'.

Back in Viareggio work began on Act III of *Turandot*. For the tenor romanza 'Nessun dorma' Puccini predicted the popularity of 'E lucevan le stelle'; nor was he mistaken. A much quoted letter to Adami comparing himself and Elvira to two ancient family portraits tickled now and then by cobwebs at least suggests a domestic tranquillity all too rare in the past.[46] Yet composition proceeded slowly and 'without fever'. By September he had arrived at the death of Liù. The music of her final aria he had already written; all he needed was the text. He sent to Adami two specimen quatrains, which the poet saw no need to change apart from the odd word. 'Tu che di gel sei cinta' therefore remains entirely Puccini's, both words and music.

In October he returned with Elvira to Vienna for the long-awaited performance of *Manon Lescaut*. The conductor Franz Schalk, in whom he had placed high hopes, turned out a disappointment, but Lotte Lehmann he declared the finest Manon of his experience. The visit to Dr Steiner's clinic, contemplated the previous year, never took place; but before leaving Puccini spent some days in a cottage hospital in the suburb of Währing undergoing the newly discovered insulin treatment for diabetes. With Elvira immobilized by an attack of lumbago, he took the opportunity of seeing *Parsifal* at the Staatsoper ('five hours of the utmost bliss, out of this world!')[47] before making the long journey home.

For the rest of 1923, with intervals for shooting at Torre del Lago and another visit to Rome for the afore-mentioned Commissione and

[46] GPE 216–17, p. 288.

[47] MPI, 162.

the interview with Mussolini, Puccini remained at Viareggio, working 'very sparingly' on *Turandot*. The sticking point was the grand duet of Act III. On 18 September he sent Adami's latest version to Simoni for 'poeticizing'. 'Poor Liù is dead', he added, 'and I think that the funereal accompaniment has come out well and movingly.'[48] But the following month it was to Adami that he turned for yet another version of the duet—his fourth, so he told Schnabl. Of particular interest is his request that the final chorus of rejoicing should be in the metre of the tenor romanza—an indication, surely, that the concluding melodic reprise of 'Nessun dorma' that we hear today in Alfano's completion was intended by Puccini from the start. This certainly accords with his usual practice.

While he waited for the duet Puccini worked steadily at the scoring of Act II and as much as he had written of Act III. By this time his optimism had returned. 'All the music I've written up to now seems to me a joke', he told Adami, 'and I don't like it any more. Is this a good sign? I think it is.'[49] Suggestions for the missing duet continued to pour from his pen: an offstage chorus spying on the two lovers, to be set with 'imitative harmony of a Chinese flavour'; a powerful conflation of the various texts already supplied. Indeed, when Simoni's revision of the last arrived in mid-February 1924 Puccini declared that they were not yet home and dry. But in the meantime plans were going ahead for the production. The première was to take place at La Scala with Toscanini to conduct. With it was to be linked a performance at the New York Metropolitan in Puccini's presence. For the scenery he had in mind Galileo Chini, who had spent four years in China and whose designs for *Gianni Schicchi* he had particularly admired. A collaboration between him and Umberto Brunelleschi, a Tuscan painter resident in Paris, would produce 'a mis-en-scène both artistic and, above all, powerful and original'.[50] His ideal Liù would be Gilda Dalla Rizza, and he wrote to tell her so. In the printed score the whole of the finale to Act I was to be lowered by a semitone.

An event that Puccini was determined not to miss was the first per-

[48] Lo, op. cit., 407.
[49] GPE 228, p. 294.
[50] CP 882, pp. 547–8.

formance of Schoenberg's *Pierrot Lunaire* in Florence on 1 April under the master's direction. Through the composer Alfredo Casella, who accompanied the tournée, he obtained an introduction to Schoenberg himself, who received him cordially and provided him with a score with which to follow the performance. His reactions are reported by Marotti, also present on the occasion: 'To arrive at a conception of such a musical world one must have gone beyond a normal sense of harmony, that's to say one must possess a nature quite different from what one has at present. Who can say whether Schoenberg may not be a point of departure for a goal in the distant future. Just now—unless I understand nothing—we are as far from a concrete realization of it as Mars is from Earth.'[51] To Schoenberg Puccini was simply 'a great man', superior to Verdi at least in technique.

An event of more national acclaim was the première of Boito's *Nerone*, to be given at La Scala, Milan, under Toscanini's direction. The subject had occupied Boito for most of his life; and his delay in bringing it to fruition had become proverbial. As early as 1901 he had published the text of five acts, of which he claimed to have composed approximately four; and it was Giulio Ricordi who, shortly before his death in 1912, persuaded him that his drama was complete without the final act. But that was not the end of the matter. When Boito died in 1918 he left an autograph so full of erasures, corrections, and alternatives that six years would pass before with the help of Vittorio Tommasini a viable score could be produced. The outcome was eagerly awaited on all sides, not least by members of the 'giovane scuola', who had grown up beneath the composer's shadow. Toscanini, however, excluded them all from the dress rehearsal on 29 April, thereby causing considerable umbrage, though only Mascagni went so far as to write to Mussolini in protest. Puccini, who had travelled to Milan specially for the occasion, took the ban as a personal affront. But a total breach with the only possible conductor of *Turandot* was not to be thought of. Hence a long letter of remonstrance, in which Puccini ascribed his exclusion to false rumours that he had spoken ill of the work itself. In fact, however, he had written to Schnabl that he expected *Nerone* to turn out a complete

[51] MPI, 165–6.

'bluff'—a view which Schnabl is unlikely to have kept to himself. Toscanini's reply has not survived; but cordial relations with the composer were quickly resumed.

Meanwhile work on the final duet of *Turandot* ground slowly forward, but under a steadily darkening cloud. Ever since March a sore throat combined with a dry cough had begun to reveal itself as more than a seasonal ailment. For a while Puccini did nothing about it. But it was to the spa town of Salsomaggiore, where he had gone in May with false hopes of a recovery, that the librettists were instructed to send their fifth version of the duet, having preserved the original metres so as to accommodate the music already sketched. Puccini continued to ask for textual adjustments to the first act, which he inserted in the finished score. Otherwise the summer passed without further progress. A visit from Sybil Seligman in August raised his morale sufficiently for him to resume composition for a while. However, it was she who first suspected the real nature of Puccini's malady. Four throat specialists had been consulted, all of whom made different diagnoses and recommended different treatments, so Schnabl was told. The general consensus was that the pain was essentially rheumatic; and so for the time being Puccini continued to believe. The première of *Turandot* was now planned for April 1925 with the young Beniamino Gigli as Calaf, to whom Puccini wrote personally. To Toscanini he played what he had written so far, much to the conductor's approval. But even he agreed that the text of the final duet was not quite right. 'An elephant's head', was how Puccini described the piece to Adami, 'of which we must rid ourselves as soon as possible.'[52] September brought the long-awaited nomination of 'Senatore del Regno' ('Suonatore', as Puccini liked to term it). The final good news was the arrival early in October of the duet as versified by Simoni to the composer's entire satisfaction.

But his throat was giving him no peace. Once more a specialist in Florence was consulted. To Puccini himself he gave a reassuring verdict. The pain was caused by a slight swelling under the epiglottis which could be rendered harmless either by radium or by an operation. To Tonio he told a different story: that his father was suffering from an inoperable cancer. Tonio took care to conceal the truth from both his

[52] GPE 233, p. 297.

parents; but the Puccini who attended the celebrations at Celle com-
memorating his ancestor, the first of his dynasty, was obviously a sick
man. A final vignette of the composer in those dark days is offered by
Marotti. A few chords touched on the piano had turned the conversation to *Tristan*. Puccini played through the Prelude, then suddenly
threw down the score. 'Enough of this music!' he burst out. 'We are
mandolin-players, amateurs. Heaven help us if we get caught up in it!
This terrible music annihilates us and makes us unable to achieve
anything!'[53]

Clutching at straws, Tonio arranged for a last consultation with another specialist, Professor Toti, on 28 October. He at least offered a ray
of hope. The new developments in radium treatment at Professor Le-
doux's clinic at Brussels had rescued many a patient from the jaws of
death. Accordingly, Puccini set out for Belgium on 4 November in
reasonably good spirits, taking his musical sketches with him. He was
accompanied by Tonio. Elvira, being unwell, was unable to make the
journey.

The rest of the story has been told often enough and need only be
summarized here. The treatment proceeded in two stages. At first radium was applied externally by means of a steel collar, which allowed
the patient to move about freely, if in considerable discomfort, and even
to attend a performance of *Madama Butterfly* at the Théâtre de la Mon-
naie. Various friends came to visit him, including Carla Toscanini, Riccardo Schnabl, and Sybil Seligman, who brought him a pillow. On 24
November a surgical operation took place which lasted over three
hours, given under a local anasthetic due to Puccini's diabetic condition.
By now Tonio had sent for Fosca and Angelo Magrini to cheer his
father's bedside. Unable to speak, nourished by means of a nasal tube,
Puccini was nonetheless declared on the road to recovery. Optimistic
bulletins were sent out to Elvira, Carlo Clausetti, even to Lehár—all
to no purpose. At 11.30, on 29 November Puccini's heart finally gave
out. The operation had been successful; but the patient had died.

A funeral service was conducted two days later at the Church of
Sainte-Marie, Brussels, by the Papal Nuncio, after which the coffin was
taken by train to Milan for the official ceremony. This took place on

[53] MPI 205–6.

3 December at the Cathedral, now decked out with symbols of mourning appropriate to a death in the royal family. The Cardinal Archbishop of Milan pronounced the liturgy; Toscanini directed the orchestra of La Scala in the 'Requiem' from *Edgar*. Amid pouring rain a vast procession accompanied the transport to the city's main cemetery: friends, family, singers, librettists, conductors, fellow-composers whom Puccini hardly knew, to say nothing of the local notables, who included the consuls of Belgium, Germany, Austria, Switzerland, Japan, and the United States. Only Elvira remained, shattered by grief and illness, in Viareggio.

The body was laid provisionally in the family tomb of the Toscaninis. Two years would pass before it was taken at Elvira's suggestion to a tiny mausoleum at Torre del Lago, in which she too now lies buried. There a memorial service took place on the second anniversary of Puccini's death. Simoni and Mascagni delivered suitable orations; Gaetano Bavignoli conducted a choir of 100 and a 60-piece orchestra in a selection of motets by Palestrina and Mendelssohn, Puccini's own *Crisantemi*, 'L'abbandono' (*Le Villi*), Jake Wallace's ballad (*La fanciulla del West*), and Liù's funeral cortége.

Meantime the problem of *Turandot* had remained to be addressed. Within days of the composer's death Tito Ricordi from his home in Paris suggested to Riccardo Schnabl that the opera be completed from the existing sketches by Franco Vittadini, a 40-year-old composer and conductor who in 1921 had set the libretto of *Anima allegra* that Puccini had turned down. Toscanini on the other hand was in favour of Zandonai; but his proposal was allegedly blocked by Tonio. Eventually the choice fell on Franco Alfano, whose Tolstoy-based *Risurrezione* of 1904 had established him as a competent practitioner of the 'giovane scuola', while his *Sakuntala* (1921) had demonstrated his skill in treating an oriental subject. To him, therefore, were entrusted the 23 pages of Puccini's sketches. The completed score was delivered by the end of January 1926 and passed to Toscanini, who at once found fault with it. There was too much of Alfano's own invention, so he thought; and he forced the composer, much to his annoyance, to reduce his score from 377 bars to 268. Meanwhile, however, the Casa Ricordi had already printed the original version in their first vocal score. The abbreviation had to wait until the second edition, published at the end of the year.

The première, planned for the end of April 1926, was threatened by a political contretemps. Mussolini, who in 1924 had broken the news of Puccini's death in the Italian parliament, making much of the composer's recent adherence to the Fascist party, now declared that he would honour the first night of *Turandot* with his presence, provided that it was preceded by a performance of 'Giovinezza', the Fascist equivalent of the Nazis' 'Horst Wessel Lied'. This was a particularly sore point with Toscanini. Originally, like so many of his countrymen, a supporter of the future dictator, he had turned violently against him once he had assumed supreme power; and when in 1923 a crowd of blackshirts invaded La Scala commanding him to perform their theme song he refused outright. If on the present occasion the management insisted that it be played, they would have to find another conductor. Since this was out of the question, Mussolini prudently backed down, giving out that he had no wish to distract the public's attention, which should be devoted wholly to Puccini. It was the musical, not the political dictator, who won the day.

The performance took place on 25 April amid a blaze of world-wide publicity, but without the principals of Puccini's choice: as Calaf not Beniamino Gigli but Miguel Fleta; as Liù not Gilda Dalla Rizza but Maria Zamboni; while the name part to which only Maria Jeritza could have done full justice, both visually and musically, was entrusted to the Polish soprano Rosa Raisa. As Liù's funeral cortège melted into the distance, Toscanini laid down his baton, turned to the audience, and announced in words that vary from one account to another that at this point Puccini left his opera unfinished. Amid the hush that accompanied the slow descent of the curtain, a voice rang out 'Viva Puccini!' The cry was taken up throughout the hall. Tears were shed in abundance, so Lehár recalled; nor is there any reason to doubt his testimony.

As to what happened on subsequent nights, reports differ. According to some Alfano's original completion was performed so long as Toscanini remained in charge, the abbreviation being introduced when Ettore Panizza took over the direction the following autumn. Given Toscanini's temperament this seems in the highest degree improbable (as if he would perform a version of which he disapproved!). The shortened ending has remained in force until recent times, when a revival of the opera in concert form at the Barbican Centre, London, under the management of Alan Sievewright and the direction of Owain Arwel Hughes presented Alfano's original score to considerable acclaim. Since then it has been taken up and staged in various cities, including Salzburg during the Festival of 1994. The arguments for and against it will be touched on later.

In 1889, smarting from the semi-fiasco of *Edgar*, Puccini had made clear his desire to escape from the incubus of 'grand opera' which had dominated the Italian stage for the last two decades. With *Turandot* he returned to it, not as a prisoner but as a conqueror. 'Grandeur' stole upon the opera gradually during its four-year gestation with the slowing-down and simplification of the action, the filling out of musical details and above all by the central placing of the riddles as a scene of high ceremony, its design governed by the 'rule of three' (compare the trial of Radames in Verdi's *Aida*). The expanded sense of scale is reflected in the forces employed. The orchestra of *La fanciulla del West* is amplified not merely by a multitude of percussion, pitched and unpitched, but also by a stage band of trumpets, trombones, two alto saxophones, organ, and extra battery. As in *Manon Lescaut*, the dramatic exposition is laid out in successive 'phases', each sited within a tonal area, and thus likened by certain scholars to a symphonic movement. But there is nothing symphonic about their articulation, which proceeds according to Puccini's latest manner by blocks hewn from the same material. Nor is his past wholly forgotten. The start of Act I presents a spaced-out variant of his favourite opening gambit: a sharp-edged, driving theme of wide intervals balanced by one of more lyrical contour. That the initial gesture (Ex. 12.1a) owes something to the Credo of Verdi's Iago is likely enough, the tritone (x) adding an extra touch of brutality. An immediate echo in diminution half a tone lower over the sustained bass chord of arrival sets up a clash of adjacent tonalities that persists throughout the Mandarin's proclamation of Turandot's edict, the Persian prince's failure to solve the riddles, and his imminent execution. Savage bitonal barks, the lower notes sustained like a persistent growl, settle into a two-bar ostinato of alternating pitches, punctuated here and there by strokes of a Chinese gong, lurid flashes of Ex. 12.1a on upper wood-wind and a typical Puccinian 'fidget' on xylophone suggestive of the executioner's block. An outburst of excitement from the chorus winds up the various elements into a fortissimo climax. Only then, as the

Ex. 12.1a

Ex. 12.1b

guards thrust back the populace, causing panic and confusion, does the lyrical consequent arrive with its characteristic cluster of semiquavers and falling fifth (Ex. 12.1b).

That an elegiac theme redolent of the world of *Manon Lescaut* should form a natural complement to material so uncompromisingly modern may seem baffling. The truth is, however, that, for all its bitonal dissonance, the opening complex keeps the original tonality firmly in view. Turn the F naturals of the Mandarin's proclamation enharmonically into E sharps and none of the notes will be found to exceed the key of F-sharp minor. Indeed, the chord itself is formed by Puccini's long established practice of piling up thirds, the resulting dissonance being resolved into the euphony of Ex. 12.1b.

The focus has now shifted to the main characters: Liù is calling for someone to help her blind master, who has fallen during the mêlée; Calaf runs to her aid, recognizing his long-lost father. But the reunion is not a joyful one. It remains enveloped by the mournful shroud of Ex. 12.1b propelled from key to key with a characteristic subdominant

Ex. 12.2

bias, the sense of poignancy increasing with every shift. To the sound of funeral drums and a low, subdued scoring, Timur tells of his defeat in battle and flight into exile with only Liù to guide him ('Perduta la battaglia'). The reason for her devotion? Merely that Calaf had once smiled at her in the courtyard of their palace. The pentatonic outline of her answer proclaims her of Chinese origin. The arrival of men bearing the whetstone for the executioner's sword rouses the populace to a crescendo of bloodlust ('Gira la cote!'). So to the next 'block' ('Ungi, arrota!'), based on a barbaric theme (Ex. 12.2) that hurtles forward with a subtly varied insistence recalling the Stravinsky of *Petrushka*.

Announced quietly by 12 basses with offstage trumpets and trombones giving a sinister edge to the prevailing string texture, it provokes frenzied participation from the crowd with orchestral interjections of Ex. 12.1a and—a wholly original touch—a climbing figure in more measured tempo like the effortful cranking of an engine, each time discharging a fresh burst of energy. A final, towering affirmation of F-sharp minor is sealed by Ex. 12.1a 'con tutta forza'; whereupon the music moves to a calm plateau of D major, as the people gaze up at the darkening sky and await the rising of the moon, the signal for the Persian prince's execution. This is Puccini's nearest approach to D'Annunzian 'decadence' (indeed the meeting of Paolo and Francesca da Rimini in Zandonai's opera, set in the same key, is not far away). The choral fragments slowly coalesce into a motif that rises by disjunct intervals (Ex. 12.3).

Though smeared with chromatic filigree in a variety of delicate shadings the musical core remains firmly diatonic. Amid voluptuous dominant ninths and seventh inversions the discourse mounts by semitonal shifts to F major, to be pulled sharply backward to E flat as the full moon appears. The crowd calls for the executioner, Pu-Tin-Pao, in a

Ex. 12.3

succession of 'rat-a-tats' (the death-figure of operatic tradition), underpinned by an ostinato of alternating chords, the second based on the
flattened leading note and creating a species of plagal cadence (Ex. 12.4).
By an inspired piece of riveting this same D flat in alternate bars is
extended throughout the idea that follows: the Chinese folk-melody
'Mo-li-hua' ('The Jasmine Flower'), sung by a troupe of boys approaching from the distance, their line doubled by two saxophones, the
accompanying chords by chorus 'à bouche fermée' (Ex. 12.5). This, the
first authentic folk-tune taken from Baron Fassini's musical box, will
stand throughout the opera for the Princess. Here it is a hymn celebrating her mysterious beauty. No matter that the recurring D flat chord
jars with the pentatonic idiom. It is the harmonic equivalent of the
unexpected, sometimes alien note with which Puccini stamps some of
his simplest motifs on the memory. Not only that: it allows for juxta-
positions of the melody with subtly elaborated recurrences of Ex. 12.4,
not, as here, a preparation but more often as a menacing consequent.

Having faded into the distance, the hymn gives way to a long threnody for the cortège accompanying the Persian prince to the scaffold in

Ex. 12.4

Ex. 12.5

view of a populace suddenly moved to pity (Ex. 12.6). The melodic idiom too has changed from Chinese pentatonic to minor mode with that commonplace of Near-Eastern exoticism, the interval of an augmented second between third and fourth degrees. Note, however, a chromatic deviation that throws into relief the third phrase, whose recurrences are mainly reserved for Calaf, the most urgent of the onlookers. A long-drawn-out cadential preparation leads to a burst of 'Mo-li-hua' on orchestra and stage band as Turandot appears on a balcony of the palace, her face illumined by the moon's rays. With an imperious gesture she confirms the death sentence and retires—a reversal of Puccini's practice of having his heroines heard before they are seen. Here it makes perfect dramatic sense. Whereas in Gozzi—and Busoni—Calaf, like Mozart's Tamino, falls in love with a portrait, in Puccini it is the sight of Turandot herself that first entrances him; and the impression is all the stronger if she appears as a silent vision. As the procession resumes, the music that had carried Calaf's pleading serves equally well to convey his sudden conversion ('O divina bellezza, o

Ex. 12.6

meraviglia!'). The crowd disperses, the procession passes on escorted by the 'white priests', who bring the movement to a hushed conclusion with a prayer to Confucius to receive the dead man's soul ('O gran Koungtze!'). Appropriately, their four-note motif is taken from the 'Hymn to Confucius' in the publication by van Aalst.

The silence is broken by Timur in an attempt to recall his son to a sense of reality ('Figlio, che fai?'). Calaf's replies invest Turandot's motif with a wistful yearning, extending it through chords that bring to mind the desolation of Cio-Cio-San. His father's insistence grows in a pattern of rising sequences, only to be countered by Calaf's cries of 'Turandot!', the last of which, taking him up to a high B flat, releases another fortissimo affirmation of the same motif on horns and trumpets, sliding abruptly into a heavy bitonal 'rat-a-tat' for the execution of the Persian prince, whose echoing 'Turandot!' launches a brutal recall of the opera's opening gesture. The Princess is thus presented in all her beauty and cruelty to our ears alone—and all within the space of eight bars.

Undaunted, Calaf waxes ever more enthusiastic ('Vincere, padre, nella sua bellezza!'). He rushes towards the gong to proclaim his challenge; but his way is barred by three Masks, Ping, Pong, and Pang, a baritone and two tenors. Although allotted different functions in the cast list, they operate throughout as a team, only the baritone, Ping, being allowed a certain prominence. They announce themselves in unison ('Fermo! Che fai?') with the longest of the folk-tunes from Baron Fassini's musical box (Ex. 12.7a), its pauses between phrases contracted into bars of 3/4 within the duple rhythm. The term 'scherzo' is not inapt, since both music and text speak a language of grotesque comedy. From 'chinoiserie' Pong and Pang descend to Western common sense over a suave orchestral theme (Ex. 12.7b), bidding Calaf escape death while he can ('O scappi, o il funeral per te s'appressa!'). As usual, Puccini's adroit harmonization avoids all sense of incongruity between the two melodic strands, dissonant interjections conveying both the Prince's obstinacy and the mocking laughter of the Masks.

Their appeal to him is cut short by a group of young girls who appear on the battlements and enjoin silence: the Princess's slumbers must not be disturbed. The bright, unvarying A flat gives way to a shaded F-sharp minor, conjuring up for Calaf a vision of his beloved as she lies asleep. A murmur of *divisi* cellos, softly throbbing percussion, and a

Ex. 12.7a

Fer - mo! che fai? T'ar-re - sta! Chi sei, che fai, che vuoi? Va' vi - a!

Ex. 12.7b

Pong [O] scap-pi,_o il fu-ne-ral per - te s'ap - pres - sa!
Pang

sinuous, floating line doubled by female voices and touched in with bitonality from faint chords on flute, celeste, and harp create an atmosphere of unearthly mystery. The Masks mutter angrily ('Via di là, femmine ciarliere!'), only too aware of the effect that this is having on the Prince. The maidens retire, leaving him transfixed with wonder ('Si profuma di lei l'oscurità!'), while the Masks look on in dismay ('Guardalo, Pong! . . . Guardalo, Ping! . . . '). During another eloquent silence they gather round him and try again, one by one. The enigmas are insoluble, harder than iron, bronze, or rock—this to a mock-Chinese fragment endlessly repeated over minor-key harmonies, its brittle scoring varied in the Russian manner of Glinka's *Kamarinskaia*. But again Calaf refuses to listen; and his resolution is strengthened by the appearance high on the ramparts of the ghosts of Turandot's former suitors, longing for a sight of their beloved. There are no ghosts in Gozzi, or indeed in any previous opera on the subject. It is therefore just possible that the idea came to Puccini and his librettists by way of Pfitzner's *Palestrina*, where the spirits of the composer's predecessors also play a part in moving him to action. True, Puccini did not see the opera before Adami and Simoni had submitted their first draft of Act I of *Turandot*, in which the ghosts are already present. Yet *Palestrina* was by then four years old and its plot could well have been known to the parties concerned.

Musically, however, the link is with the moment in *Gianni Schicchi* where the false Buoso, invisible behind the bed-curtains, reassures the doctor about his health. Again there is a slow procession of muffled parallel chords in triple time based on dominant seventh inversions but with an accretion of semitonal dissonances so widely spaced as to lose their acerbity. All sense of tonality would be suspended were it not for the ghostly voices—four contraltos and four tenors singing behind the scenes with hands cupped over their mouths—who keep throughout to an A minor. The march of muted strings and harp, the cheeps on piccolo, the taps on bass drum and Chinese gong all contribute to the eeriness of the scene.

Calaf's cry that Turandot is for him alone ('No, no, io solo l'amo!') provokes another mocking outburst from the Masks to fragments of Ex. 12.1a. Now they try a different tack. Turandot does not exist. She is an illusion, like the phantoms he has just seen. Ping elaborates this argument to the strains of Ex. 12.7b; but not even the appearance on the battlements of Pu-Tin-Pau holding aloft the Prince of Persia's severed head to shouts from the Masks ('Stolto! Ecco l'amore!') and a cascade of Ex. 12.1a on upper woodwind, celeste, and glockenspiel can deflect Calaf from his purpose.

Now it is Timur's turn. His eight-bar solo ('O figlio, vuoi dunque ch'io solo trascini pel mondo la mia torturata vecchiezza?') breathes an infinite weariness, evident in the dark, low-pitched scoring and the characteristic falling fifths in the melody.

From here to the end of the act all grotesquerie is banished; the music speaks only from the heart. Liù's aria ('Signore, ascolta!'), in Chinese-pentatonic throughout, is an exquisite miniature. Built from supple, irregular phrases, it falls into two periods, the second longer and more widely ranging than the first—an appeal stated plainly, then enlarged upon, each time returning to a tiny repeated refrain that encapsulates the singer's entreaty (Ex. 12.8). Calaf's reply ('Non piangere,

Ex. 12.8

Adagio

Liù!') is a minor-key aria in ternary form that again harks back to the Puccini of the 1890s, its sadness heightened by an insistence on the dominant note and a long delay to the resolution of the final cadence that seems to stress the Prince's inability to return the slave-girl's love for him.

So without a break to the concertato finale, melodically interwoven with the preceding aria and impregnated with the same melancholy. Never has Puccini put his favourite device of an ostinato of alternating chords to more impressive use. Set within a slowly swaying triple metre it embodies the tug-of-war between Calaf and the bystanders, progressively reinforced by the band and chorus behind the scenes. With three cries of 'Turandot!' Calaf wrenches the minor tonality to the major key half a tone lower. He strikes the gong, which reverberates like a Wagnerian thunderclap. 'Mo-li-hua' peals forth with full choral backing. A return to the original key focusses the attention on the despair of Liù and Timur.

The 'chitarrata' (Puccini's term) that opens Act II owes nothing to Gozzi. The function of Puccini's Masks is to set the monstrous events of the drama in perspective by their down-to-earth views. If the urgency of the previous act has inclined them to the grotesque, here they are allowed a more human face. A short proemium touched with bitonality sets the pace, as Ping calls to his companions and all three take their seats on the balcony. Pong and Pang will prepare for either eventuality—a wedding or an execution. So they declare to a jaunty Chinese folksong from van Aalst's collection on the familiar theme of a young girl in search of a husband. But the minor-key framework suggests the resignation of men who are trying to keep up their spirits in ungrateful circumstances. Ping, more soulful, leads them towards remoter keys with chromatic and whole-tone encrustations, regretting the passing of China's once peaceful existence, now given over to senseless butchery. Ex. 12.7b is pressed into service, as the ministers reckon up the tally of Turandot's victims with the stranger prince as No.13 in the Year of the Tiger. They themselves are now ministers of the executioner (Ex. 12.2), as will become frighteningly clear in Act III. Again it is Ping whose thoughts wander back to his house in the country by a lakeside ('Ho una casa nell' Honan'). A single gesture (Ex. 12.9) suffices to convey a dreamy nostalgia, and by the simplest means: a lingering on the dom-

Ex. 12.9

inant in both melody and bass; an accidental that seems vainly to reach towards a new key; and the rise and fall of the vocal line.

The music takes 25 bars to reach a tonic anchorage, where Pong and Pang expatiate on their own longings; thence after further meanderings to a philosophical reflection on the madness of lovers ('O mondo, pieno di pazzi innamorati!'). Memory goes back to the fate of individual suitors for the Princess's hand. Marionette music, all open fifths over a static bass, allows a recurrence of Ex. 12.2 fortified by offstage chorus, as the image of Turandot's cruelty rises to the surface. In a unison lament ('Addio amore, addio razza'), pentatonic yet wholly Puccinian, the Masks rise to a genuine nobility of utterance, its cadential phrase (Ex. 12.10), several times repeated, has already been foreshadowed by Liù's self-introduction in Act I.

Nonetheless the Masks permit themselves to hope. Perhaps there will be a wedding after all. Hence another quotation from van Aalst, the so-called 'Guiding March' associated with Imperial court ceremony, here dreamily harmonized (Ex. 12.11). A light-hearted ditty in Pucci-

Ex. 12.10

Ex. 12.11

nian mock-Chinese ('Non v'è in China per nostra fortuna'), tricked out with brilliant yet delicate scoring and a bout of wordless humming from the two tenors, rounds off the 'chitarrata'—a 'stretta', some say, to balance the 'cantabile' of 'Ho una casa nell'Honan'.

Distant brass and side-drum recall them to the present. The musical transformation scene is, of course, a Wagnerian legacy, familiar to Puccini from *Parsifal*. The transition which now follows is nearer to that in the last act of Rimsky-Korsakov's *Le coq d'or*, though more elaborate and sophisticated. A pattern of marching inverted sevenths from stage trumpets and trombones based on the key of G flat obtrudes on the Masks' G major cadence. The thread then passes to the pit, stage trumpets twice interjecting a *Petrushka*-like flourish. The texture grows fuller and busier. The harmonies take on a hexatonal thickening: wisps of melody on high woodwind debouch into a plain processional theme given out by stage brass for the entry of the eight wise men bearing the scrolls that contain the answers to Turandot's riddles. Taking up the strain with hushed reverence, the crowd salute them; then, as the initial rhythmic pattern resumes, the 'Imperial Hymn' from Baron Fassini's musical box begins to take shape on horns and clarinets, first in mounting sequences of its opening phrase (Ex. 12.12a), finally broadening into a massive period of 36 bars, the chorus joining in with a burst of acclamation ('Diecimila anni al nostro Imperatore!') on the one strain that departs from the pentatonic mode (Ex. 12.12b) and again on the concluding phrase ('Gloria a te!'), which is Puccini's own, designed to bring the hymn to a Western-style tonic cadence (Ex. 12.12c) punched home by a varied recall of Ex. 12.4.

By now the clouds of incense have dispersed to reveal the Emperor

Ex. 12.12a

Ex. 12.12b

Ex. 12.12c

Altoum seated on his throne surmounting a vast stairway. Ten bars of trumpet fanfare set the scene. Three times the Emperor tries to dissuade the Prince from his undertaking. Three times Calaf returns the same answer ('Figlio del cielo, io chiedo d'affrontar la prova!'), echoed by an instrumental unison, the last one set out more emphatically in triplet rhythm. Up to this point in the opera unsupported declamation has been avoided. Its occurrence here raises the dialogue to a new plane of significance. Here, too, is Puccini's nearest approach to authentic 'chinoiserie', though without the help of an actual folk-tune. The Emperor finishes regularly on a supertonic note, the Prince on a submediant—both features characteristic of the Chinese idiom. It is left to the orchestra to interject a minatory C (the Western tonic) in the bass register, not as part of the melodic design but rather as a reminder of the inexorable law that threatens the Prince's life.

The challenge sadly accepted, three reminiscences prepare for the appearance of the Princess: the Imperial Hymn (Ex. 12.12b), now soft and mellifluous as young girls scatter flowers on the great stairway; the Mandarin's brutal proclamation complete with xylophone 'fidget'; and 'Mo-li-hua' again sung by boys behind the scenes and doubled by the humming of the crowd. The Princess takes up the final chord of 'Mo-li-

Ex. 12.13

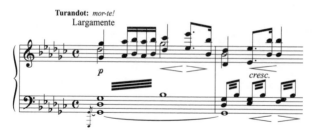

hua', now glacial on flutes and muted horn, and begins the aria ('In questa reggia'). Alone among Turandots from Gozzi to Busoni she has a precise motive for her decree: the desire to avenge her ancestress, Princess Lo-u-Ling, tortured and murdered by an invading host. With the mention of her name the freely ranging, declamatory opening settles into a steady narration in F-sharp minor (the executioner's key!) that proceeds in stages, each marked off by a shift of tonality and rhythmic articulation in such a way as to give the illusion of a gradual ascent. An emphatic cadence opens out into a broadly arched pentatonic melody in the major mode, expressive of the Princess's resolution to remain forever chaste (Ex. 12.13).

From here on the model of Gounod's 'Anges purs, anges radieux' (*Faust*) with its triple rise is evident, though the working-out is more concentrated and the gradient far steeper, proceeding by major thirds, the melodic burden carried by the orchestra. Only the third statement is taken by Turandot in its entirety ('No, no! Mai nessun m'avrà! Ah, rinasce in me l'orgoglio di tanta purità!'). On a dominant F sharp she warns the Prince not to try his fortune, then swings down to E flat—a *reculer pour mieux sauter*—for her concluding aphorism: 'Gli enigmi sono tre, la morte è una!' (Ex. 12.14). Here too the threefold ascent applies;

Ex. 12.14

but the range is sufficiently narrow for a vocal delivery of each statement. The Prince retorts 'Gli enigmi sono tre, una è la vita!' Finally
both join in unison, each with their own variant of the text, rising to
a C above the stave, the highest note in their respective compasses. So
the summit is reached after a haul of 56 slow bars.

The chorus provide an epilogue with Ex. 12.13 ('Al principe stran-
iero'), which dissolves into a transition to the posing of the riddles.
These have no great significance in themselves, and their answers
vary from one version of the story to another ('The Sun', 'The Year',
'The Lion of the Adriatic' in Gozzi; 'The Year', 'The Eye', The
Plough' in Schiller; 'Human Intellect', 'Fashion', 'Art' in Busoni).
Adami and Simoni provide three of their own, no less arbitrary.
What counts is the solemn, hieratic manner of their delivery. Three
tantalizing chords encircling the tonic and a minatory bass thud (Ex.
12.15) sets the tone for each question. For the first of them orchestral
participation is confined to fragmentary gestures instinct with tension.
Across a span of 24 bars every phrase ends with an upward interrog-
ative inflection, tonic and dominant figuring merely as notes of
passage.

Calaf replies with Turandot's opening strain, now fully harmonized
and decorated with flourishes on clarinets, violins, and cellos, as one
fully confident of knowing the answer: 'Hope' ('La speranza')—and he
proclaims it with a dominant-to-tonic plunge that settles the matter, so
letting loose an orchestral cataclysm of distorted scales in contrary motion like the crumbling of a bastion. Amid the reverberation the Wise
Men murmur approvingly 'La speranza', prompting Turandot to a bout

Ex. 12.15

of savage repartee ('Sì! La speranza che delude sempre!'); and her anger continues to resonate over four bars of diminishing orchestra.

The second riddle follows the basic format of the first, but is backed continuously by a gossamer-like instrumental texture illustrating the substance that darts and flickers like a flame, but is no flame. At this point Puccini gives a new twist to the dramatic pacing. In Gozzi and Busoni it is the third enigma that causes the Prince to hesitate, over-whelmed by Turandot's sudden unveiling—logically, because this is the first time that he has seen her face as distinct from its portrait. Not so Puccini's Calaf. By making him hesitate after the second enigma the composer can recall us to the grimness of the situation with the opera's initial gesture (Ex. 12.1a) and at the same time allow the bystanders, including the Emperor, to show that they are rooting for the Prince. Even Liù offers a mite of encouragement ('É per l'amore!'), her only contribution to the entire act. But in tones no less confident than before and to the same music Calaf comes up with the answer: 'Blood' ('Il sangue!'). Again the orchestral tumult and the murmured confirmation by the Wise Men. Encouragement from the crowd enrages Turandot still further; and she orders the guards to drive them back. For the third riddle she descends the steps to face Calaf directly; and he duly falls on his knees. Her question is now pitched half a tone higher with an accompaniment that reflects the contrast within the proposition—'the ice that turns to fire'. But Calaf is equal to that one too: 'Turandot!' This time the orchestra's downward sweep is unopposed by contrary motion in the bass. The Princess's defences are razed to the ground. The Wise Men's echo of 'Turandot! . . . Turandot!' is taken up by the courtiers over a huge crescendo leading to a triumphant reprise of 'Mo-li-hua' as all present hail the conquering hero ('Gloria, gloria O vinc-itor!'). To this Ex. 12.12b forms a lyrical consequent, softly sung and harmonically elaborated with moving inner parts and a moment of so-prano descant. Before it can finish Turandot takes up the melody with a desperate plea to be released from her bargain. But her father stands firm. Her line twists and turns with chromatic and whole-tone inflec-tions as she perseveres—all to no purpose. Everyone is on Calaf's side. Again to 'Mo-li-hua', now in the Emperor's key of C major, more grandiloquent than ever in harmony and scoring, all echo his reminder of the binding oath. The prince offers his counter-proposal with the

Ex. 12.16

same motif that served for the three riddles, but after eight bars a warm, lyrical theme steals in on violins anticipating what Puccini knew would prove the 'hit-number' of his score (Ex. 12.16). He ends it on two bars of subdominant harmony, to be expanded in the following act for the aria's beginning. Here they give way to another, longer quotation of van Aalst's 'Guiding March' (Ex. 12.11) played by the stage band with percussive stresses precisely as in the original source, while the Emperor expresses his hope that the next day will see Calaf his son. The Imperial Hymn, proclaimed by massed forces, including the stage organ, brings down the curtain with the cadence of Ex. 12.4 as its final word.

Act III opens with the Prince alone in the palace gardens. It is still night, evoked by Puccini with a marvel of atmospheric tone-painting. But the basic orchestral motif (Ex. 12.17) is not entirely new. It is evolved from the Mandarin's proclamation of Act I, the chords now disposed by full orchestra without flutes and piccolo in a swaying rhythm.

Again there is a triple design. Three times distant heralds proclaim Turandot's decree that no-one may sleep in Pekin; that failure to discover the Prince's name by morning will mean death. Three times an unseen chorus take up the vital words ('Nessun dorma!'), their falling line amplified expressively by an orchestral comment, whose final statement is balanced by the ascending figure that prepares the Prince's aria. Eight bars of rapt G major, linked to Ex. 12.17 by the same ostinato of unrelated fifths in the accompaniment, form a subdominant springboard to the aria's principal melodic idea (Ex. 12.16)—a scheme that allows the Prince to wind up the aria quite logically with a prolonged plagal cadence. An orchestral peroration is broken off as the Masks emerge from the bushes followed by a gathering throng. All are in fear for their lives should the Prince's name remain unknown. First the Ministers push forward a bevy of odalisques. As they surround the Prince with

Ex. 12.17

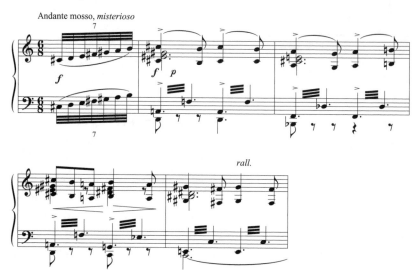

merry laughter, the dark, mysterious colouring gives way to an instrumental chatter based on four notes both vertically combined and horizontally repeated at different speeds and pitches—an instance of Far-Eastern 'heterophony' traced by Carner to a Siamese source (Ex. 12.18). This in turn generates the final quotation from van Aalst (Ex. 12.19), which will dominate the 'scene of the temptations' from now on.

Finding the Prince deaf to their entreaties, the Ministers and bystanders threaten him with their daggers to a final reprise of Ex. 12.19 dissolving into savage triplets. The arrival of a company of soldiers dragging in Timur and Liù puts an end to the dispute. Across the abrupt key-switch from C to E flat the triplet rhythm is maintained as the basis for the flurry of action that follows. The Prince rushes forward protesting that his name is unknown to the couple; but the soldiers continue to hold them fast. Ping and his fellow-ministers have seen them in conversation with Calaf. They and the crowd call for Turandot, whose appearance dispels the semitonal dissonances of the action-music with 'Mo-li-hua' fortified by stage brass. All fall prostrate, only Ping advancing humbly to tell her the good news. The spectacle of Liù and

Ex. 12.18

Timur at the mercy of a hostile throng brings back the mournful Ex. 12.1b. As its coils unfold, the dialogue pursues a course of its own. Turandot and the Prince exchange taunts. Neither of the captives, Calaf declares, knows who he is. Turandot does not believe this for a moment; she commands Timur to speak. Liù at once interposes, insisting that the Prince's name is known to her alone. The crowd breathe a sigh of relief ('La vita è salva . . . l'incubo svanì!') until Liù's determination to remain silent provokes a crescendo of angry cries ('Sia legata, sia straziata . . . perché parli, perché muoia!'). The tumult subsides over a drooping pattern of six notes which will serve as an emblem of Liù's resistance. Anticipated by a furious Calaf ('Sconterete i suoi tormenti!'), repeated by the orchestra behind Turandot's order to have him bound, it reveals its full significance harmonized softly but emphatically in parallel common chords to Liù's 'Signor, non parlerò!' It surfaces again on solo viola, then solo cello as a riposte to Turandot's 'Mo-li-hua'. Nor can it be silenced by the soldiers' rough treatment of their victim, causing her to cry out in pain.

Even Turandot is impressed; she demands to know the reason for

Ex. 12.19

Ex. 12.20

such heroic endurance. Liù's answer is simple ('Principessa, l'amore!'). This she elaborates in the second of her 'romanze' ('Tanto amore segreto'). Like 'Signore, ascolta!' it is compounded of irregular phrases with a refrain, here inconclusive (Ex. 12.20). The 'sapore cinese' that Puccini mentioned to Adami has been identified as deriving from the passage from one pentatonic mode to another by way of 'exchange notes'.[54] What will probably strike the listener are harmonies that recall 'L'abbandono' in *Le Villi* of 40 years earlier—yet another instance of the organic growth of Puccini's idiom.

All Liù's eloquence is lost on the Princess. Despite Calaf's protests she commands that the girl be further tortured, urged on by Ping and the crowd, who call for the executioner (Ex. 12.2 with a hexatonic twist). Soft descending dissonances, widely spaced, indicate the victim's ebbing strength. Yet she rallies for one last appeal to the ice-cold Princess ('Tu che di gel sei cinta'), the words Puccini's own (Ex. 12.21).

Note the threefold repetition of what might be called the minor-key 6/4 of desolation, arrived at as in Mimì's 'Sono andati?' by a doubling of the outer lines and here set in relief by the C that follows as though to indicate a striving towards the dominant key, only to be forced back to an inexorable tonic. This same tendency is amplified in a longer consequent (' . . . l'amerai anche tu!') in which the higher key is constantly negated by a C flat; hence a perfect balance between the two ideas which accounts for the entire ensemble that builds up from Liù's solo. The kinship with the embarcation scene from *Manon Lescaut*

---

[54] PCB; see W. Ashbrook and H.S. Powers: *Puccini's 'Turandot': the End of the Great Tradition*, 98–9.

Ex. 12.21

is too obvious to need stressing. But it took all the harmonic and orchestral resources of the mature Puccini to extend such limited material into a large-scale structure that matches the action at every point.
The familiar piling up of soft dissonances reaches its climax where
amid unpitched shouts from the crowd ('Parla! . . . Parla!') Liù stabs
herself. Calaf cries out in despair ('Ah! Tu sei morta, o mia piccola
Liù!') and in the terrified silence only Timur is heard calling on the
girl to awake. Told by Ping that she is dead, he breaks out in an agony
of grief harmonized in the manner of Chopin's 'marche funèbre'.
There is a hushed choral epilogue ('Non farci del male!') as Liù's body
is slowly borne away. Ex. 12.21 resumes as a threnody uttered
throughout by Timur ('Liù! bontà! . . . Liù! dolcezza!') while he accompanies the cortège, taking the dead girl's hand in his own. His
words are echoed by the departing crowd, the sopranos (as always the
soft-hearted element) adding their own prayer for her forgiveness. So
ends a musical monument worthy of the one character who throughout the act has behaved honourably.

The two final scenes present an insoluble problem. No matter how
continuous the sketches for an unfinished work, their fleshing out by
another hand can only yield a hypothetical result. Shortly before his

departure for Brussels Puccini is reported to have played the remainder of his opera to Toscanini, the scenographer Galileo Chini, and his son. But the material that he took with him—three smallish continuity drafts in short score with occasional instrumental markings and a number of jottings, some of them alternatives—fall a long way short of a fully articulated discourse. Therefore Alfano's task required a good deal of independent composition. By 1924 Alfano had arrived from Mascagnian beginnings to a sophisticated style of his own, evident in every page of his most highly regarded work, *La leggenda di Sakuntala*—a language of rich, impressionistic harmony, somewhat in the manner of Szymanowski, combined with a tense, 'veristic' *vocalità*. The mysterious East is ever present; but it is not Puccini's. Where Alfano's invention is obliged to depart from his predecessor's, it achieves a logic of its own which the cuts imposed by Toscanini quite often damage. A detailed examination of the two versions in relation to Puccini's sketches has been undertaken by Jürgen Maehder.[55] Here it will suffice to touch on the main points of divergence.

For the start of the duet Puccini left a continuity draft that offers no difficulties of realization. Taking up the rhythm of the funeral cortège at a tritone's distance, Calaf upbraids the Princess for her cruelty ('Principessa di morte! . . . Principessa di gelo!') to a harsh tutti of unisons and open fifths (Ex. 12.22). His tirade over, he tears the Princess's veil from her face. A downward coiling figure several times repeated at different pitches accompanies her anger ('Che mai osi, straniero!'). Her veil may be his, but her soul lies well out of his reach; to which he retorts that though her soul may remain on high her body is beside him—this to a caressing movement in 9/8 vaguely reminiscent of the act prelude, but without its bitonal dissonances and with a particularly happy modulation on the word 'vicino'. It is, of course, logical that the Princess's resistence should find expression in a recall, verbal and musical, of Ex. 12.13 ('No! Mai nessun m'avrà!'), and not inappropriate that Calaf should counter with Ex. 12.14, to the words 'Il bacio tuo mi dà l'eternità'. But precisely how to proceed from there to the kiss and away from it afterwards was something about which Puccini had yet to

[55] J. Maehder: 'Studien zum Fragmentcharacter von Puccinis "Turandot"', *AnM*, xxii, (1984), 297–379.

Ex. 12.22

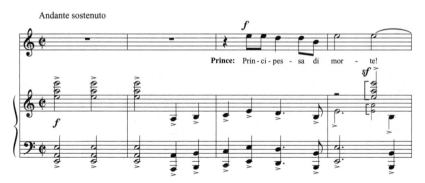

make up his mind. The indications in his sketches are confusing. Clearly, however, he had intended to draw on Ex. 12.14 for the culminating moment, probably laid out as a grand 'sviolinata' in D-flat major. Given his ability to make the same motif take on different meanings according to context, this might have worked, though it could hardly have reached the height of transcendance that the situation ideally requires. Alfano, however, went his own way. In his original score Calaf's Ex. 12.14 is poised over a dissonant pedal on the leading note. It dissolves into a tumult of athematic figuration from which Turandot's Ex. 12.13 emerges on central wind instruments with trombones prominent, for the first and only time in a minor mode! Certainly this could serve as the ultimate negation of her pride. But a kiss that transforms her entire nature needs something more impressive. In his second version Calaf's proclamation is allowed plain euphonious harmony, while the music that accompanies the kiss is reduced from nine bars to three, ending with a double hammer blow in the bass register, not so much an osculation as a slap in the face.

Puccini resumes with a tenderly insistent motif based on a recurring inverted seventh, as the Prince dwells poetically on Turandot's charms ('Oh! Mio fiore mattutino!'), beneath the delicate embroidery of an unseen women's chorus, while she herself can only reflect disconsolately on her defeat. A recall of 'Mo-li-hua' sung by boys and tenors behind the stage signals the approach of dawn ('L'alba, luce e vita!'); but the clearing of the harmonies brings no comfort to the Princess.

Ex. 12.23

The draft breaks off at her words 'La mia gloria è finita!' For Calaf's triumphant retort ('Miracolo! La tua gloria risplende nell'incanto del primo bacio') Alfano chose a simple, unclouded motif noted down by Puccini for a later context. Here, carried over a dominant pedal by high woodwind and violins in octaves with an altered rhythmic articulation (Ex. 12.23), it falls neatly into place, dying away in diminishing sequences in preparation for the next stage of the duet, Turandot's confession ('Dal primo pianto'), whose opening bars were supplied by Puccini himself with his favourite ostinato of alternating soft discords (Ex. 12.24). Ever since Calaf had appeared before her she had felt a premonition of disaster. Her previous suitors she had despised; only he inspired her with fear, for in his eyes was the light of heroism (Ex. 12.23, as originally planned by Puccini). Again the rhythmic disposition is Alfano's, and the sequences now rise triumphantly towards Turandot's avowal that for the torment he had caused her she both loved and hated Calaf. Appropriately, the word 'amato' that marks the climax is given a bitter harmonic tang; after which the piece subsides into a pattern of restless progressions similar to those with which it had opened.

All this Toscanini's scissors reduced from 79 bars to 51, thereby doing it no service whatever. The original structure is ample, allowing full scope for the expression of the Princess's torment even at the cost of verbal repetition. Not only is the revision more perfunctory; it results in the occasional *non sequitur* in the scoring together with phrases that lead nowhere. But more radical alterations were to follow. Turandot

Ex. 12.24

concludes by telling the Prince to leave, his name still unknown. But Calaf has no such intention. At the risk of his life he reveals his identity, so allowing Turandot to regain the initiative. A transformation scene brings us to the Emperor's court, where to her father and the assembled multitudes she announces that she knows the Stranger Prince's name: it is 'Love'. General rejoicing, and curtain.

In both versions Turandot's plea to Calaf ('Più grande vittoria non voler!') is sung softly to a widely spaced orchestration of Ex. 12.23. The first takes her up to C above the stave with a few bars of declamation over sustained chords to follow ('Di tanta gloria altero, va, parti, straniero col tuo mister!'). At 'mister' Alfano introduces a motif of his own (Ex. 12.25). Calaf takes up the all-important word ('Il mio mister? . . . Non ne ho più!') and proceeds through a crescendo of exaltation to the disclosure of his name: 'Io son Calaf, figlio di Timur!' At once Turandot's former pride is rekindled. She knows his name! His fate is now in her hands, and she no longer feels humbled in his presence. Over 32 bars of restless figuration, taking in distortions of Ex. 12.23, their dialogue continues in an atmosphere of mounting tension, Turandot exultant, Calaf both defiant and resigned. The point of arrival occurs with his line 'La mia gloria è il tuo amplesso!' sung to the riddle motif (Ex. 12.15) sequentially prolonged with voices rising ever higher, while offstage trumpets and trombones announce the trial to come.

In the second version text and music are drastically shortened. Tos-

Ex. 12.25

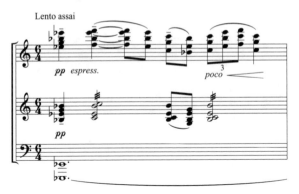

canini evidently objected to Ex. 12.25 as beyond its composer's remit. So for Calaf's 'Il mio mister? . . . Non ne ho più' Alfano had recourse to a jotting of Puccini's for the same passage—a reach-me-down pattern of four notes developed into a rising sequence which brings the Prince more speedily to his revelation. What he did not use in either version is Puccini's sketch of a D major melody to accompany the Princess's words 'So il tuo nome! Arbitra son del tuo destino' with the cryptic annotation 'Poi Tristano' (probably meaning no more than 'a long love-duet'). In the second Turandot is merely allowed to declaim twice 'So il tuo nome!', after which music and text jump to Calaf's Ex. 12.15 and the dialogue proceeds as before.

For the interlude that accompanies the scene-change Puccini left a motivic fragment together with various indications for the scoring, from which it is clear that he had in mind a tapestry of exotic timbres cor-responding to the transition in Act II. Alfano took the motif but de-veloped it quite differently with a brass-heavy orchestration from which all 'chinoiserie' is banished. In his original version the interlude runs to 32 bars and includes an offstage women's chorus ('Nella luce mattutina') of Alfano's own devising; and very charming it is. But, needless to say, Toscanini would have none of it. So the interlude, too, is heavily curtailed.

With the Imperial Hymn on massed forces the two scores converge.

In both the Princess's declaration 'Il suo nome è Amor!' prompts a blast of Ex. 12.13 on horns and trumpets, showing that it can operate as a 'love theme' after all. In accordance with Puccini's intention the concluding lines are sung to the melody of Calaf's 'Ma il mio mistero è chiuso in me' (Ex. 12.16). But in Alfano's first setting its approach to the final cadence is given a new prolongation, evidently suggested by the transition from the original aria to the intervention of Ping. The idea is reasonable enough and might well have occurred to Puccini. Far from happy, however, is a note in the harmonization, which gives a minor shading completely at variance with the radiance of the melody itself. Toscanini was right to veto it.

Since its revival Alfano's original version has found a number of advocates. Certainly it is more consistently paced than the revision, and its ampler proportions allow more scope to the feelings of the participants ('Dal primo pianto' gains particularly in this respect). Alfano's Ex. 12.25 gives musical interest to an important twist of the plot, and the female chorus provides a welcome oasis of calm amid the brassy tumult of the interlude. On the other hand, the moments of what might be called exasperated *vocalità* (Turandot's tritonal melisma on her cry of 'Ah!', her upward portamento across a wide interval during her phrase 'col tuo mister', and the Prince's hectic approach to the revelation of his name) put a heavy strain on the performers of two extremely demanding roles. There is something to be said for proceeding swiftly to the final scene after Calaf has told Turandot his name, without dwelling unduly on her menacing hints, since it is unlikely that even such a ruthless virago, having confessed her attraction to the Prince, would have him decapitated. Also, as Maehder has observed, the scoring and vocal distribution in the passages that precede the kiss are improved in the revision, while the ending, if more perfunctory than in the original version, is truer to the spirit of Puccini's music.

Neither version, however, succeeds in crossing the opera's chief hurdle, namely, the transformation of its heroine by the power of love. But would Puccini himself have been any more successful? Every decision that he took during the opera's gestation rendered his task more difficult. He had originally described *Turandot* as the most 'human' of Gozzi's *fiabe*. Yet in his hands it became progressively more inhuman.

Gozzi's princess wavers from the start; Puccini's remains iron-clad up to the moment of the kiss. In the play she is content that her discovery of the Prince's name should release her from the statutory bargain and leave him free to depart unharmed. In the opera it gives her the right to have him executed. What is more, failure in the search threatens the entire population of Pekin; hence the behaviour of the crowd, non-existent in Gozzi, an important presence in Puccini.

In Act III it is the Prince who appears inhuman. True, he protests angrily at the torture of Liù, as does Ponchielli's Enzo (another unsympathetic *jeune premier*) at the crowd's hounding of La Cieca; but words cost little. Nothing in the text of the final duet suggests that Calaf's love for Turandot amounts to anything more than a physical obsession: nor can the ingenuities of Simoni and Adami's text for 'Del primo pianto' convince us that the Princess's submission is any less hormonal, a case of nature re-asserting itself after years of repression. How very different is the selfless devotion of Liù, who commands our sympathy throughout, while Puccini's decision to have her die under torture, leaving the Princess totally unmoved, made sure that it remains with her. Only a miracle of musical transcendence could redeem the two principals; and that is something that lay outside Puccini's range. As a self-confessed master of 'great sorrows in little souls', his heart—to adapt the words of Shakespeare's Mark Antony—was in the coffin there with Liù. Which is why the opera that represents the summit of Puccini's achievement both as musician and music-dramatist was never brought to a satisfactory conclusion.

With *Turandot* a tradition of Italian opera that had obtained for more than three centuries came to an end. If the flame had sometimes burned low, it had always been rekindled by some pioneering spirit—an Alessandro Scarlatti, Rossini, or Mascagni—who brought the tradition up to date without renouncing its past. The result was a common denominator of audience expectation that kept even minor exponents of the genre afloat. After World War I all this would change. By the mid-1920s Puccini's contemporaries of the 'giovane scuola' were effectively played out. Ermanno Wolf-Ferrari, who at the beginning of the century had inaugurated a personal genre of light Goldonian comedy had declined into self-repetition. Of the younger generation—Casella, Malipiero, Pizzetti—each went his own way independently of his fellows, as Italian composers have done ever since. Puccini alone succeeded in pulling the age-old communal tradition of Italian opera into the post-war world, due to that power of self-renewal that he shared with Verdi. But alas, there was no-one to follow him. Gian Carlo Menotti's attempts to fan the embers into life have proved a failure. *Turandot* remains unique and unrivalled.

Puccini as Man and Artist

'THE MAN WHO HAS RECENTLY LEFT US WAS ONE OF THE
most likeable [*simpatiche*] figures in the world of music.'[1] So
the composer Alfredo Casella began a brief notice of Puccini's death
for the German periodical *Anbruch*. For him Puccini typified the Tuscan
artist of all ages: balanced, practical, aware of his own limitations; and,
above all, modest. From a leading representative of the so-called 'generazione dell'80', whose artistic ideals were far removed from his own,
this was a judgment both generous and acute. Born into a family of
musicians on both sides, Puccini never felt that his calling set him apart.
Entirely without 'side', he made friends from every walk of life—shop-
keepers, priests, wealthy landowners as well as fellow-artists—and with
few exceptions kept them to the end. No composer received more
affectionate posthumous tributes than he. Affable, well-mannered, gifted
with a broad sense of fun (reflected in his doggerel verses and Tuscan
love of word-play), he rarely failed to charm all who met him. Only
public functions found him ill-at-ease and longing to return to the circle
of his intimates and his beloved Torre del Lago. Like most Italians he
was very much a family man. He remained in close contact with his
sisters for as long as they lived, providing a monthly allowance for the
widowed Nitteti and even considering grooming her son Carlo as a
librettist. When his favourite Ramelde died, he continued their cor-

[1] A. Casella: *21 + 26* (Rome, 1931), 147–9.

respondence with her daughter Albina. Even his amorous escapades never seriously threatened the stability of his marriage. When it came to the crunch, Elvira came first. That 'Corinna' and Josephine von Stengel received a different impression may not be to his credit. But Puccini was neither the first nor the last wayward lover to err in this respect.

Outside his music he was not a forceful character. Certainly he lacked the combative instincts of a Mascagni. He rarely responded to personal attacks, and when he did so his replies were usually drafted by someone else. Faced by the tragedy of Doria and the ensuing scandal, his immediate reaction was flight. But in the end habit, strengthened by family feeling, prevailed. Habit too played its part in preventing a rupture with the Casa Ricordi, which under Tito's management he believed to be acting against his own interests. Puccini was a bad hater. His quarrels were infrequent and sooner or later patched up. The word 'pig' (*anglice*) that recurs in his letters to Sybil Seligman meant no more than (as her son put it) 'someone with whom I have a temporary disagreement'.[2] Even his animosity towards Leoncavallo that persisted after the *affaire Bohème* is confined to his correspondence. Puccini's detestation of Zandonai's *Giulietta e Romeo* did not prevent him from paying the composer a courtesy visit at the première. No-one could ever suspect him of intriguing.

In money matters people will often reveal unexpected sides of themselves. Puccini, though hospitable, free with presents to family and friends, was not particularly generous. He refused to Ramelde's husband a loan which he could have easily afforded; and, considering his vast wealth, he could have done far more for Nitteti than he did. Yet he spent freely enough on himself: six habitations, fourteen cars, and five motor launches including an expensive yacht, all over a span of 28 years. Works of public benefaction *à la* Verdi were not for him. Given the climate of the age, this is not surprising. 'L'Italietta' of the early twentieth century was not a land of great causes; and Puccini's lack of public spirit was in no way unusual. Politics meant nothing to him. All that he wanted was a system of government that would ensure him a comfortable existence and allow him to compose in peace and quiet. The

---

[2] PAF, 60.

idea of social reform never entered his head. The miseries of the poor would merely serve him as emotional fodder, a means of wringing the heart strings. In this, as in so much else, he showed an affinity with Charles Dickens.

How far an artist's work can be related to his character and personality is difficult to determine. The greatest creations of the human spirit arise from cognitions, which are seldom, if ever, reflected in the creator's everyday behaviour. Often, as in Wagner's case, a carapace of single-minded egotism is necessary for the protection of his genius. So much may seem obvious; but it has a bearing on Mosco Carner's theory that the limitations of Puccini's art are due to a fundamental flaw in his psyche, namely a 'mother-fixation', which views womanhood across an unbridgeable polarity between the madonna and the prostitute. Hence a projection of guilt on the woman who loves, such as can be expiated only by death.[3] The argument is shaky at both ends. The vast majority of nineteenth-century operatic heroines from Norma to Isolde and Aida die for love, often with a sense of guilt; yet no-one has ever accused their composers of a mother-fixation. Nor is there any evidence that Giacomo was abnormally attached to Albina. If he addressed her with the polite 'lei', so did the rest of her children. Nor is it true, as Carner maintains, that Puccini's temporary affairs were with women of a lower class—a description that fits neither 'Corinna' nor the German baroness. What is clear is that he, like his brother, had a strong sexual urge and a roving eye. In such cases the victory often goes to the partner with the strongest will-power; and this Elvira certainly possessed. If only it had been combined with sympathy and understanding (the parallel with Minna Wagner has often been remarked upon) their life together would have been spared a good deal of unhappiness. But theirs is a common enough story in the life of an artist and one which need have no bearing on the quality of his work. As well connect the torture scenes of Tosca and Turandot with what Puccini called his 'Neronic instincts' with regard to wild game. His love of this particular sport, contracted, it is said, at Lucca from his teacher Angeloni, was merely a hobby shared with thousands and of no more significance for his art than his fascination by mechanical gadgetry.

[3] PCB, 300ff.

Over the centuries Italian opera has always thrived on tradition, each composer building on the achievement of his predecessors. During the years of Puccini's artistic formation that tradition was at its weakest. Throughout the Peninsula foreign imports were the rage. Grand opera in Meyerbeer's manner was the most prestigious genre, yet one to which the average native composer was unable to measure up. Verdi summed up the situation when he wrote to a friend in 1875, 'The trouble is that all the operas of these young men are the product of fear. None of them writes with abandon. [Their] overriding concern is not to clash with the public and yet to enter into the good graces of the critics.'[4] Not until *Cavalleria rusticana* was a new, specifically Italian mode inaugurated which enabled a few secondary composers to produce at least one work of enduring vitality.

From his student days onward Puccini had determined to cut his own way through the various influences that impinged on Italian opera during its years of uncertainty, forging a language that is instantly recognizable through procedures on which, whether or not anticipated elsewhere, he put his own personal stamp. By the time of *Edgar* these procedures were all in place, so permitting the assimilation of contemporary elements into a sturdy, developing organism. *Manon Lescaut* shows the impact of *Tristan und Isolde* and, in much of the writing for tenor, *Cavalleria rusticana*. In the airier texture of *La bohème* can be sensed the experience of *Falstaff*. At the same time all three components of the popular trilogy (*La bohème, Tosca*, and *Madama Butterfly*) sit comfortably within the tradition of the 'giovane scuola', which, as he himself pointed out, Puccini had helped to found and which he eventually outgrew. In bringing his idiom up to date without renouncing the conquests of his youth he revealed a sure instinct for the 'modernisms' it permitted him to draw upon. His partiality for the 'soft dissonance' that avoids semitonal clashes reached easily into varieties of pentatonic and whole-tone progressions. From his use of added notes to colour a melodic line it is a short step to moments of non-functional harmony that point up an emotion in defiance of academic rules. Yet amid the boldest excursions of his later operas Puccini never loses contact with his roots. *Turandot*, his furthest venture into the contemporary scene, accom-

[4] A. Alberti: *Verdi intimo* (Verona, 1931), 182.

modates elements that reach back to the world of his youth; which is why, as Carner observes, with its perfect fusion of the heroic, exotic, grotesque, and sentimental, it represents, even in its unfinished state, the sum of its composer's creation.

From *Manon Lescaut* onward Puccini demonstrated an almost unique ability to match the musical and dramatic structure of an act. Here his personal way with recurring motifs plays an important part. Thematic recollection was common enough in nineteenth-century opera, sometimes in the form of a phrase first heard sung (e.g., 'Di quell'amor' from *La traviata*) sometimes as an orchestral label for a character or an idea (e.g., the 'fate' motif from *Carmen*). Mostly such recalls occur as isolated points of reference. It was left to Wagner to elevate the *Leitmotiv* into a principle of organization that governed the entire score, giving it a psychological dimension that was quite new for its time. Alone among his Italian contemporaries Puccini followed Wagner's example in bringing the motif into the forefront of his narrative, sometimes voicing the singer's unexpressed thoughts, sometimes sending out a signal to the audience of which the character is unaware. Yet even when it forms the kernel of a block of kindred material, as in the later operas, it is never varied and developed in Wagner's manner—a procedure that would threaten the supremacy of the voice, so essental to Italian opera. Indeed, few of the motifs would lend themselves to such a treatment; mostly short, incisive, stamped by an unexpected note, harmony, or rhythmic quirk, they arrest the attention as theatrical gestures, whose impact would be blunted if subjected to variation. However, if Puccini's use of the recurring motif remains schematic by comparison with Wagner's, his ability to endow each with a different significance according to context allows him to maintain the naturalistic pace that contemporary taste demanded without sacrificing formal unity.

Fundamental to Puccini's art is a feeling for the stage picture. To this his skill in musical description, aided by the ability to distil an infinite variety of shades from a vast orchestra, made a vital contribution. In both *Madama Butterfly* and *Il tabarro* a visual stimulus was his starting point; and it was their pictorial possibilities that drew him towards a number of subjects that he failed to pursue (notably *Tartarin*, *The Raft*, *Two Little Wooden Shoes*, and in all probablity *La faute de l'Abbé Mouret*). His letters, especially those regarding the later operas, team with instructions for their staging and in the case of *Turandot*, for the colours to be employed. His tone-painting is always vivid, never failing to evoke the feelings associated with the scene portrayed—which is, after all, music's special province.

'It should be said', Casella observes, 'that Puccini's greatest strength lies precisely in that wonderful, infallible sense of his own limitations. Never was Puccini seen to undertake a labour that lay outside his ca-pabilities.'[5] Well, hardly ever. There is no denying that the dénouements of *Suor Angelica* and *Turandot* call for a sublimity to which his creative imagination did not extend, possibly inhibited by a deep, underlying pessimism. Otherwise his sense of means to ends was indeed sure. His mastery of the lyric theatre never faltered. Not even Wagner was more successful at integrating word, note, and gesture in an evolving action.

No composer communicates more directly with an audience than Puccini. Indeed, for many years he has remained a victim of his own popularity; hence the resistance to his music in academic circles. Be it remembered, however, that Verdi's melodies were once dismissed as barrel-organ fodder. The truth is that music that appeals immediately to a public becomes subject to bad imitation, which can cast a murky shadow over the original. So long as counterfeit Puccinian melody dominated the world of sentimental operetta, many found it difficult to come to terms with the genuine article. Now that the current coin of light music has changed, the composer admired by Schoenberg, Ra-vel, and Stravinsky can be seen to emerge in his full stature.

[5] See n. 1.

Calendar

Year	Age	Life	Contemporary Musicians and Events
1858		Giacomo Antonio Domenico Michele Secondo Maria Puccini born 22 Dec., at Lucca, son of Michele Puccini, cathedral organist, and Albina Magi.	E. Smyth born, 22 Apr. Auber aged 76; Berlioz 55; Boito 16; Brahms 25; Bruckner 34; Catalani 4; Chabrier 17; Dvořák 17; Gounod 50; Halévy 59; Leoncavallo 1; Liszt 47; Marschner 63; Massenet 16; Mercadante 63; Meyerbeer 67; Offenbach 39; Pacini 62; Ponchielli 24; Rimsky-Korsakov 14; Rossini 66; Saint-Saëns 23; Smetana 34; J. Strauss (ii) 33; Tchaikovsky 18; Verdi, 45; Wagner, 45. Offenbach's *Orphée aux enfers* given, Paris, 21 Oct. Assassination attempt on Napoleon III, 14 Jan.
1859	1		L. Ricci (54) dies, 31 Dec.; Spohr (75) dies, 22 Oct. Austria invades Piedmont, 29 Apr. Battles of Magenta, 4 June, and Solferino, 23 June. Peace of Villafranca. Plebiscite unites Parma, Modena,

			Romagna, and Tuscany with Piedmont. Verdi's *Un ballo in maschera* given, Rome, 17 Feb. Gounod's *Faust* given, Paris, 19 Mar.
1860	2		Albéniz born, 25 May; Charpentier born, 25 June; Franchetti born, 18 Sept.; Mahler born, 7 July; Wolf born, 13 May. Garibaldi invades Kingdom of Two Sicilies, May. Cialdini marches into Eastern Papal States, Sept.
1861	3		Cavour dies, 6 June; Marschner (66) dies, 14 Dec. Première of Wagner's revised *Tannhäuser*, Paris, 13 Mar.
1862	4		Debussy born, 22 Aug.; Delius born, 29 Jan.; Halévy (63) dies, 17 Mar. Verdi's *La forza del destino* given, St. Petersburg, 10 Nov.
1863	5		Mascagni born, 7 Dec. Pio Nono issues Syllabus of Errors, Dec.
1864	6	Michele Puccini (50) dies, 23 Jan.	Meyerbeer (73) dies, 2 May; Richard Strauss born, 11 June. Florence becomes capital of Italy, 11 Dec.
1865	7	Attends seminary of San Michele.	Dukas born, 1 Oct.; Glazunov born, 29 July; Sibelius born, 8 Dec. Verdi's revised *Macbeth* given, Paris, 21 Apr. Meyerbeer's *L'Africaine* given, Paris, 28 Apr. Wagner's *Tristan und Isolde* given, Munich, 10 June. Local government offices moved from Lucca to Florence.
1866	8		Busoni born, 1 Apr.; Cilea born, 26 July; Satie born, 17 Mar. Italy declares war on Austria and is defeated at Custozza, 24 June, and Lissa, 20 July. Garibaldi captures Trentino with volunteer

army that includes Faccio,
Boito, and Giulio Ricordi.
Prussians defeat Austria at
Königgratz, 3 July. Austria
cedes Veneto to France, who
hands it over to Italy. Sme-
tana's *The Bartered Bride*
given, Prague, 30 May.

| 1867 | 9 | Enters cathedral seminary. |

Giordano born, 27 Aug.; Gra-
nados born, 24 July; Pacini
(71) dies, 6 Dec. Garibaldi
defeated at Mentana, arrested,
and kept under surveillance
at Caprera, aut. Verdi's *Don
Carlos* given, Paris, 11 Mar.

| 1868 | 10 | |

Rossini, (76) dies, 13 Nov.
Boito's *Mefistofele* given,
Milan. Bruckner's Symphony
no. 1, Linz, 9 May. Wagner's
Die Meistersinger von Nürnberg
given, Munich, 21 June.

| 1869 | 11 | |

Berlioz (66) dies, 8 Mar.; Dar-
gomizhsky (56) dies, 17 Jan.;
Pfitzner born, 5 May; Rous-
sel born, 5 May. Opening of
Suez Canal. Verdi's revised *La
forza del destino* given, Milan,
27 Feb.

| 1870 | 12 | |

Mercadante (75) dies, 17 Dec.;
Lehár born, 30 Apr. Pio
Nono proclaims papal infalli-
bility as official dogma. Outbreak of Franco-Prussian
War, Aug. French defeated at
Sedan. First siege of Paris begun. Reform of musical conservatories in Italy.

| 1871 | 13 | |

Auber (89) dies, 12 May. Skry-
abin born, 25 Dec. German
Empire proclaimed at Ver-
sailles, Jan. Paris capitulates.
Capital of Italy moved to
Rome. Commune and sec-
ond siege of Paris ends with
massacre of Communards,
May. Italian première of
Wagner's *Lohengrin*, Bologna,

		19 Nov. Verdi's *Aida* given, Cairo, 24 Dec.
1872	14	Vaughan Williams born, 12 Oct.
1873	15	Rakhmaninov born, 20 Mar.; Reger born, 19 Mar.
1874	16	Begins study with Angeloni at Istituto Pacini; active as organist and piano accompanist in neighbouring villages and holiday resorts; takes Carlo Della Nina as pupil.	Cornelius (50) dies, 26 Oct.; Schoenberg born, 20 Sept. Musorgsky's *Boris Godunov* given, St. Petersburg, 8 Feb.; Johann Strauss's *Die Fledermaus* given, Vienna, 5 Apr.; Verdi's *Requiem*, Milan, 22 May.
1875	17	Wins organ prize at Istituto; composes romanza *A te*.	Bizet (37) dies, 3 June; Montemezzi born, 31 May; Ravel born, 7 May. Bizet's *Carmen*, Paris, 1 Mar.; Boito's revised *Mefistofele*, Bologna, 4 Oct.
1876	18	Travels to Pisa on foot to hear Verdi's *Aida*; completes *Preludio a orchestra*, 8 Aug.	Alfano born, 8 Mar.; Falla born, 23 Nov.; Wolf-Ferrari born, 12 Jan. Bayreuth Festival inaugurated with Wagner's *Ring*, 13–17 Aug. Ponchielli's *La Gioconda*, Milan, 8 Apr.; Brahms's Symphony no. 1, Karlsruhe, 4 Nov.
1877	19	Motet, *Plaudite popoli* performed 29 Apr.; cantata *I figli d'Italia* entered for competition but rejected.	Dohnányi born, 27 July; Petrella (65) dies, 7 Apr; F. Ricci (68) dies, 10 Dec. Tchaikovsky's *Eugene Onegin*, Moscow, 29 Mar.
1878	20	Composes *Credo* for composite Mass by pupils of the Istituto and (probably) *Vexilla regis prodeunt*.	Vittorio Emanuele II dies, succeeded by Umberto I, Jan. Pio Nono dies, Feb. Italian première of Massenet's *Le roi de Lehore*, 13 Feb.
1879	21	Composes *Valzer* for town band (untraced).	Ireland born, 13 Aug.; Medtner born, 25 July; Respighi born, 7 July.
1880	22	*Messa a 4 voci* performed at church of S. Michele, 12 July. Admitted to Milan Conservatory, begins study with Bazzini, Oct.	Bloch born, 24 July; Offenbach (61) dies, 4 Oct.; Pizzetti born, 20 Sept.

1881	23	Composes String Quartet in D major for Bazzini.	Bartók born, 25 Mar.; Musorgsky (42) dies, 16 Mar. Offenbach's *Les contes d'Hoffmann*, Paris, 10 Feb.; Verdi's revised *Simon Boccanegra*, Milan, 24 Mar.; Italian première of Weber's *Der Freischütz*, Milan, 27 Feb.
1882	24	Ponchielli replaces Bazzini as P's teacher, Mar. *Preludio sinfonico* performed, July. Marriage of Ramelde Puccini to Raffaello Franceschini. Arrival of Mascagni as fellow-student, Dec.	Kodály born, 16 Dec.; Malipiero born, 16 Mar.; Stravinsky born, 5 June. Wagner's *Parsifal* at second Bayreuth Festival. Triple Alliance formed between Austria, Germany, and Italy.
1883	25	Sets four poems by Ghislanzoni and Romani's 'Mentia l'avviso'; *Capriccio sinfonico* composed as passing-out piece for conservatory. Enters Concorso Sonzogno for a one-act opera with *Le Villi* to libretto by Fontana.	Bax born, 6 Nov.; Casella born, 25 July; Szymanowski born, 21 Sept.; Wagner (69) dies, 14 Nov.; Webern born, 3 Dec.; Zandonai born, 18 May. Deaths of Hugo and Garibaldi.
1884	26	*Le Villi*, rejected by adjudicators, mounted at Teatro Dal Verme Milan, 31 May. bought by Giulio Ricordi, who commissions new opera from P. and Fontana and provides P. with monthly stipend. Death of Albina, 17 July. Publication of *3 Minuets* for string quartet, Dec. *Le Villi* revised into 2 acts, Teatro Regio, Turin, 26 Dec.	Smetana (60) dies, 12 May. Massenet's *Manon* given, Paris, 19 Jan.
1885	27	Composition of *Edgar* begun. Probable start of love affair with Elvira Gemignani.	Berg born, 7 Feb.
1886	28	Moves with Elvira and her daughter Fosca to Caprino Bergamasco. Tonio born, Monza, 22 Dec.	Liszt (75) dies, 11 July; Ponchielli (52) dies, 16 Jan.
1887	29	Moves between Milan, Lucca, and Caprino Bergamasco.	Borodin (53) dies, 16 Feb. Verdi's *Otello* given, Milan, 5 Feb.
1888	30	Composes *Sole e amore* for periodical *Paganini*, Mar. Visit with Fontana to Bayreuth	Italian première of *Tristan und Isolde* conducted by Martucci, Bologna, 2 June.

Festival, July. Completes *Edgar* at Vacallo, aut.

1889	31	Première of *Edgar*, La Scala, Milan, 21 Apr. Second visit to Bayreuth, July. Praga and Oliva contracted for libretto of *Manon Lescaut*. Works on revisions to *Edgar* in Vacallo and Milan.	Mahler's Symphony no. 1, Budapest, 20 Nov. Italian première of Wagner's *Die Meistersinger*, Milan, 26 Dec.
1890	32	*Crisantemi* published, Feb. Praga withdraws from *Manon Lescaut*, spr.; Leoncavallo co-opted unofficially on libretto, aut.	Franck (68) dies, 8 Nov. Mascagni's *Cavalleria rusticana*. Rome, 17 May.
1891	33	Completes Act I of *Manon Lescaut* in full score in Milan, Jan. Death of brother Michele in Brazil, May. Rents rooms in the tower-house of Venanzio Barsuglia at Torre del Lago, summer. *Edgar* in revised 4-act version given at Lucca, 5 Sept. Illica rescues *Manon Lescaut*, aut.	Bliss born, 2 Aug.; Delibes (55) dies, 16 Jan.; Faccio (51) dies, 23 July; Prokofiev born, 11 Apr. Wagner's *Die Walküre* in Italian, Turin, 22 Dec.
1892	34	Attends *Edgar* in 3-act version at Ferrara, 3 Feb., and Madrid, 19 Mar. Libretto of *Manon Lescaut* finally shaped, June, and music completed at Vacallo, late sum. and aut. At Hamburg for German première of *Le Villi* under Mahler, 29 Nov.	Honegger born, 20 Mar.; Lalo (69) dies, 22 Apr.; Milhaud born, 4 Sept. Leoncavallo's *Pagliacci* given, Milan, 21 Mar; Catalani's *La Wally*, given Milan, 20 Jan. Publication of Debussy's *L'après-midi d'un faune*.
1893	35	Première of *Manon Lescaut*, Teatro Regio, Turin, 1 Feb. Ricordi sets up partnership of Illica and Giacosa for libretto of *La bohème*. Quarrel with Leoncavallo over claim to the subject. At Hamburg for German première of *Manon Lescaut*, 7 Nov.	Catalani (39) dies, 7 Aug.; Gounod (75) dies, 18 Oct.; Tchaikovsky (53) dies, 25 Oct. Humperdinck's *Hänsel und Gretel*, Weimar, 23 Dec. Verdi's *Falstaff*, Milan, 9 Feb.
1894	36	Attends *Manon Lescaut* at Budapest, Apr.; travels to London for *Manon Lescaut* at Covent Garden, 14 May; then to Catania for consulta-	Chabrier (53) dies, 13 Sept.; A. Rubinstein dies, 8 Nov.

tion with Verga over *La lupa*,
June. Resumes work on *La
bohème*, July. Foundation of
'Club La Bohème' at Torre
del Lago.

1895	37	At Fiume (Rijeka) for *Manon Lescaut*, May. Rents villa at Castellaccio, near Pescia, June to Oct. Sees Sardou's *La Tosca* in Florence, Oct. *La bohème* completed, Nov.	Castelnuovo-Tedesco born, 3 Apr.; Hindemith born, 14 Nov.; Orff born, 10 July.
1896	38	Première of *La bohème*, Teatro Regio, Turin, 1 Feb; given at Rome, Naples, and Palermo, Feb. to Apr. Completes *Avanti Urania*, Oct.	Bruckner (72) dies, 11 Oct.; Thomas (85) dies, 12 Feb. Italian defeat at Battle of Adua, 1 Mar. Giordano's *Andrea Chénier*, Milan, 28 Mar.
1897	39	Travels to Manchester for English première of *La bohème* given by Carl Rosa Company, 22 Apr.; returns via Paris and Brussels; meets Sardou. To Vienna for Austrian première of *La bohème* at Theater an der Wien, 10 Oct. To Rome as member of music committee, Nov.; acquaintance with Don Pietro Panichelli. Composes *Inno a Diana*, Dec.	Brahms dies, 3 Apr.; Korngold born, 29 May. Leoncavallo's *La bohème*, Venice, 6 May.
1898	40	Begins composition of *Tosca*, Jan. Visits Paris, Mar. and Apr., remaining for *La bohème*, Opéra Comique, 13 June. Further consultations with Sardou. Works on *Tosca* at Monsagrati, Pescaglia, July to Sept. Buys land for villa at Chiatri.	Gershwin born, 26 Sept. Mascagni's *Iris*, Rome, 22 Nov. Riots in Milan put down by government troops. General Pelloux appointed President with dictatorial powers.
1899	41	To Paris for revival of *La bohème*, Jan. Awarded Légion d'Honneur, Mar. Composes *Scossa elettrica*, May, and *E l'uccellino*, autumn; completes *Tosca*, Oct.	Poulenc born, 7 Jan.; Johann Strauss II (74) dies, 3 June. Sibelius's Symphony no. 1, Berlin, 26 Apr. Outbreak of South African War.
1900	42	Première of *Tosca*, Teatro Costanzi, Rome, 14 Jan. Revival at Turin, 22 Feb. Liaison	Copland born, 14 Nov.; Krenek born, 23 Aug.; Weill born, 2 Mar. Umberto I

begun with 'Corinna'. First contact with D'Annunzio. Establishes permanent residence at Torre del Lago. To London for *Tosca* at Covent Garden, 12 July. Sees Belasco's *Madam Butterfly* at Duke of York's Theatre. To Brussels for *La bohème*, Oct.

assassinated, 29 July, succeeded by Vittorio Emanuele III.

1901 43 Death of Angeloni, 13 Jan. Acquires rights to Belasco's play. Buys first car, May. Summer at Cutigliano. Begins work on *Madama Butterfly*, Sept. Composes *Terra e mare*.

Egk born, 17 May; Verdi (87) dies, 27 Jan. Queen Victoria dies, succeeded by Edward VII.

1902 44 To Monte Carlo for *La bohème* with Melba and Caruso, Feb. Attends performance of Sada Yacco's troupe, Milan, Apr. Correspondence begun with Gustav Knosp on Japanese folk-music. Fosca married to Salvatore Leonardi. Summer at Torre del Lago. To Dresden for *Tosca*, Oct.

Walton born, 29 Mar. Cilea's *Adriana Lecouvreur*, Milan, 2 Nov. Debussy's *Pelléas et Mélisande*, Paris, 11 Jan.

1903 45 Car accident, 25 Feb. Death of Elvira's husband, 26 Feb. Long convalescence at Torre del Lago. Spends Aug. in newly bought villa at Boscolungo, Abetone. To Paris for rehearsals for *Tosca*, Opéra Comique, 13 Oct. Buys first motor-boat. To Vienna for *La bohème* at Hofoper, Nov. Completes *Madama Butterfly*, 27 Dec.

Khachaturian born, 6 June; Wolf (42) dies, 22 Feb.

1904 46 Marries Elvira, 4 Jan. Fiasco of *Madama Butterfly*, La Scala, Milan, 17 Feb. Successful revival of altered score, Brescia, 28 May. Composes *Canto d'anime* for Gramophone and Typewriter Company. Summer at Boscolungo between cures at Acqui Terme and

Dallapiccola born, 3 Feb.; Dvořák (53) dies, 1 May; Petrassi born, 16 July. Entente Cordiale between Britain and France.

Montecatini. To London for aut. season at Covent Garden; acquaintance with Sybil Seligman. Correspondence with Soldani about *Margherita da Cortona* and Illica about *Notre Dame de Paris* and Gorki trilogy (vetoed by Ricordi).

1905	47	*Requiem* for 4th anniversary of Verdi's death performed at Casa di Riposo, Milan, 27 Jan. Revises *Edgar*, Feb. to Mar., with Illica's *Maria Antonietta* in prospect. To Buenos Aires for première of definitive *Edgar*, 8 July. To London for revival of *Madama Butterfly*, Oct. Puts finishing touches to the opera's third version with Toscanini at Bologna.	Tippett born, 2 Jan. Lehár's *Die lustige Witwe*, Vienna, 30 Dec. R. Strauss's *Salome*, Dresden, 9 Dec.
1906	48	Abortive correspondence and discussions with D'Annunzio. To Budapest for Hungarian première of *Madama Butterfly*, 12 May. Summer with Seligmans at Boscolungo. Giacosa dies, 8 Sept. To Paris for French première of *Madama Butterfly* at Opéra Comique, in final version, 18 Dec. Interest in Louys's *La femme et le pantin*.	Arensky (64) dies, 25 Feb.; Lutyens born, 9 July; Shostakovich born, 25 Sept.
1907	49	First visit to New York for season of his operas at the Metropolitan Opera House, Jan. Sees Belasco's *The Girl of the Golden West* on Broadway. Returns via Paris, Mar. Receives translation of play, July. Works on scenario of *La fanciulla del West* at Chiatri with Zangarini, Aug. To Vienna for *Madama Butterfly* at Hofoper, 31 Oct. Resumes contact with Illica over *Maria Antonietta*, rechristened *L'austriaca*, but proceeds with Belasco subject.	Grieg (64) dies, 4 Sept.

1908	50	To Egypt for *Madama Butterfly* at Alexandria, Feb. Co-opts Civinini on libretto of *La fanciulla del West*. Begins composition of opera, 24 May. Works at Chiatri during summer. Composes *Casa mia*, Dec.	Elliot Carter born, 11 Sept.; Messiaen born, 10 Dec.; Rimsky-Korsakov (64) dies, 21 Jan.
1909	51	Suicide of Doria Manfredi, Jan. Family file suit against Elvira, Feb. Lucca tribunal sentences her to 5 months' imprisonment, but the case is settled out of court. Reconciliation with Elvira at Bagni di Lucca, Aug. To Brussels for *Madama Butterfly*, 29 Oct.	Albéniz (48) dies, 18 May. R. Strauss's *Elektra*, Dresden, 25 Jan.
1910	52	To Paris for French première of *Manon Lescaut* at Théâtre du Châtelet with New York Metropolitan company under Toscanini, 9 June. Completes *La fanciulla del West*, Aug. Holiday with Elvira and Tonio in Switzerland, Sept. Sets out for America via Paris and London, Nov. Première of *La fanciulla del West* at New York, 10 Dec.	Barber born 9 Mar.; Balakirev (73) dies 29 May; Schuman born, 4 Aug. King Edward VII dies, succeeded by George V.
1911	53	To London for *La fanciulla del West*, 29 May. Promotional visits to Rome, (June), Brescia (Aug), Liverpool and Turin, (Oct.), Naples, (Dec.) Interest in Ouida's *Two Little Wooden Shoes*, Hauptmann's *Hanneles Himmelfahrt*, and *Anima allegra* by the Quintero brothers.	Mahler (50) dies, 18 May; Menotti born, 7 July. R. Strauss's *Der Rosenkavalier,* Dresden, 26 Jan. Ravel's *L'heure espagnole*, Paris, 19 May. Stravinsky's *Petrushka*, Paris, 13 June. Italy declares war on Turkey.
1912	54	To Budapest for *La fanciulla del West*, 29 Feb. Ramelde dies, Apr. Attends French première of *La fanciulla* in Paris and probably sees Gold's *La Houppelande*, May. Giulio Ricordi dies, 6 June. Liaison begun with Josephine von	Cage born, 15 Sept.; Françaix born, 23 May; Massenet (70) dies, 19 Aug. Schoenberg's *Pierrot Lunaire*, Berlin, Oct.; R. Strauss's *Ariadne auf Naxos*, (first version), Stuttgart, 15 Oct. Italian conquest of Libya.

Stengel, with whom he travels to Munich and Bayreuth
for *Parsifal*, 8 Aug. Visits
London, Mar. and Oct.
Composes *Sogno d'or* for periodical *Noi e il mondo*, Dec.
Publication of Fausto Torrefranca's *Puccini e l'opera internazionale*. Interest in Wilde's
A Florentine Tragedy. Discus-
sions with D'Annunzio about
La crociata degli innocenti.

1913	55	Secures rights to Gold's drama, Feb. Search for companion pieces from Gold, Illica, D'Annunzio, and Soldani. To Berlin for *La fanciulla del West*, 18 Mar. Josephine von Stengel obtains divorce. First meeting with Adami. Sees Ballets Russes in Paris, June. Promotional tours to Hamburg, Leipzig, and Vienna, Oct. Accepts from the Karltheater directors, Eibenschütz and Berté, commission for an operetta. Acquaintance with Korngolds, father and son, and Lehár.	Britten born, 22 Nov.; Lutosławski born, 25 Jan. Mascagni's *Parisina*, Milan, 15 Dec. Montemezzi's *L'amore dei tre re*, Milan, 20 Apr. Stravinsky's *Le sacre du printemps*, Paris, 29 May.
1914	56	Rejects Viennese subject in favour of comic opera. Accepts Willner's new scenario, Apr. Works with Adami on *La rondine*. Outbreak of World War I, 4 Aug. Fails to sign manifesto against German bombardment of Rheims and refuses to contribute to Hall Caine's *King Albert's Book*.	Sgambati (73) dies, 14 Dec. Zandonai's *Francesca da Rimini*, Turin, 19 Feb.
1915	57	Acquires rights to *Two Little Wooden Shoes*, Mar. Meeting with Forzano. After her husband's death in battle, Josephine moves to Viareggio, wh ere P. has bought plot for her future residence. Italy enters the war, 23 May. Tonio	Goldmark (84) dies, 2 Jan.; Skryabin (43) dies, 27 Apr. Italian army establishes front on Isonzo river.

volunteers for military service. Josephine, banished from Italy as enemy alien, moves to Lugano, Switzerland. Meeting with Berté in Zürich fails to dissolve Viennese contract, Aug. Begins composition of *Il tabarro*, Oct.

1916	58	Completes *La rondine*, Apr. Lorenzo Sonzogno buys it and obtains rights to a première outside Austria. Composes short piano piece for benefit of wounded in Turin. Completes *Il tabarro*, 25 Nov.	Butterworth (31) dies, 5 Aug.; Granados (48) dies, 24 Mar.; Reger (43) dies, 13 May; Tosti (70) dies, 2 Dec. Battle of the Somme.
1917	59	Begins composition of *Suor Angelica*. Première of *La rondine*, Monte Carlo, 27 Mar. Attends Italian revivals during sum. and aut. Swiss passport withheld by consul. Completes *Suor Angelica*, Sept. Composes *Morire?* for Italian Red Cross.	Busoni's *Arlecchino* and *Turandot*, Zürich, 11 May. Mascagni's *Lodoletta*, Rome, 30 Apr. Pfitzner's *Palestrina*, Munich, 5 June. Russian revolution and abdication of Nicholas II. Italian defeat at Caporetto.
1918	60	Completes *Gianni Schicchi*, 20 Apr. Revises *La rondine* with Adami. Première of *Il trittico*, Metropolitan, New York, 14 Dec.	Bernstein born, 25 Aug.; Boito (76) dies, 10 June; Debussy (55) dies, 25 Mar.; Parry (70) dies, 7 Oct. Bartók's *Duke Bluebeard's Castle*, Budapest, 24 May. Italian victory at Vittorio Veneto. General armistice, 11 Nov.
1919	61	Italian première of *Il trittico*, Teatro Costarzi, Rome, 11 Jan. Composes *Inno a Roma*. Founds 'Gianni Schicchi Club' in Viareggio. Death of Carignani, 5 Mar. Tito Ricordi dismissed from family firm. To London to arrange for *Il trittico* at Covent Garden, June. With *Sly* in prospect, requests Elizabethan popular songs from Beecham. Completes revision of *La rondine*. Initiates construction of new villa at Viareggio.	Leoncavallo (61) dies, 9 Aug. R. Strauss's *Die Frau ohne Schatten*, Vienna, 10 Oct. Mussolini forms Fascist party. Treaty of St. Germain cedes Trentino, Alto Adige, and Istrian peninsula to Italy. D'Annunzio occupies Fiume (Rijeka) with a corps of volunteers.

Purchases Torre della Tagliata, Oct. Death of Illica,
16 Dec.

1920	62	*Turandot* proposed by Simoni. To London for *Il trittico* at Covent Garden, 18 June. Receives scenario of *Turandot* from Adami. To Vienna for *La rondine* (2nd version) at Volksoper, 9 Oct. Decides to make third version.	Bruch (82) dies, 2 Oct. Maderna born, 21 Apr.
1921	63	To Monte Carlo for *Il trittico*, 24 Mar. Begins composition of *Turandot*, Apr. Death of Caselli, 15 Aug. Visits Munich to hear German novelties. Suggests *Turandot* in two acts. To Bologna for *Il trittico*, 27 Oct.; composes new monologue for Michele. Returns to 3-act format of *Turandot* with original first act divided into two.	Malcolm Arnold born, 21 Oct. Caruso (48) dies, 2 Aug. Humperdinck (67) dies, 27 Sept.; Saint-Saëns (86) dies, 16 Sept. Janáček's *Katya Kabanova*, Brno, 23 Nov. Mascagni's *Il piccolo Marat*, Rome, 2 May. First post-war election in Italy. Growing support for Fascists.
1922	64	Moves to villa at Viareggio. Completes scoring of first act of *Turandot* except for new finale, July. Holiday trip through Germany and Holland, Aug to Sept. Death of sister Igenia, 2 Oct. To Paris for *Gianni Schicchi*, Opéra Comique, 6 Nov. Revival of *Manon Lescaut*, La Scala, Milan, under Toscanini, 26 Dec.	Xenakis born 29 May. Fascist march on Rome, Oct. King Umberto invites Mussolini to form coalition government.
1923	65	30th anniversary performance of *Manon Lescaut*, La Scala, under Toscanini with last revisions to the score, 1 Feb. Works on trio of Masks in *Turandot* Act II. and composes 'In questa reggia', Mar. To Vienna to supervise rehearsals for *Manon Lescaut* at Staatsoper, May. Returns there for première, 13 Oct. Composes 'Nessun dorma',	Ligeti born, 28 May. Law establishes Fascist majority in Parliament.

1924 66 Completes scoring of *Turandot*
Act II, Feb, and Act III up
to Liù's death, Mar. First
symptoms of final illness.
Hears Schoenberg's *Pierrot
Lunaire* at Florence, Apr. At
Salsomaggiore in hope of
cure, June. Consultation with
specialists in Florence, Aug.
Nominated Senator of the
Realm, Sept. P's condition
confided by specialist to
Tonio, Oct. Sets out for
Brussels with sketches for fi-
nal duet of *Turandot*, Opera-
tion was 24 Nov; death 29
Nov.

June. Interview with Mussolini, Dec.

Busoni (58) dies, 27 July;
Fauré (79) dies, 4 Nov;
Nono born, 29 Jan. Stanford
(71) dies, 29 Mar.

Alfano aged 49; Bartók 43;
Berg 39; Bernstein 6; Britten
11; Cage 12; Carter 16; Ca-
sella 41; Castelnuovo-Tedesco
29; Charpentier 64; Cilea 58;
Copland 24; Dallapiccola 20;
Dohnányi 47; Gershwin 26;
Giordano 57; Hindemith 29;
Kodály 42; Korngold 27; Le-
hár 54; Ligeti 1; Mascagni 61;
Medtner 44; Menotti 13;
Messiaen 16; Poulenc 25;
Prokofiev 33; Ravel 49; Re-
spighi 45; Schoenberg 50;
Shostakovich 18; Sibelius 59;
R. Strauss 60; Stravinsky 42;
Tippett 19; Walton 22; Wolf-
Ferrari 48; Zandonai 41.

Murder of Mateotti. Mussolini
assumes absolute power.

List of Works

I OPERAS

Le Villi, leggenda drammatica in 1 act, libretto by Ferdinando Fontana after short story *Les Willis* by Alphonse Karr, Teatro Dal Verme, Milan, 31 May 1884; revised as opera-ballo in 2 acts, Teatro Regio, Turin, 26 December 1884; definitive version pub. 1892

Edgar, dramma lirico in 4 acts, libretto by Ferdinando Fontana after closet drama *La coupe et les lèvres* by Alfred de Musset, Teatro alla Scala, Milan, 21 April 1889; revised in 3 acts, Teatro Comunale, Ferrara, 18 January 1892; definitive version, Teatro de la Opera, Buenos Aires, 8 July 1905

Manon Lescaut, dramma lirico in 4 acts, libretto by Luigi Illica and Domenico Oliva after *Histoire du Chevalier Des Grieux et de Manon Lescaut* by François-Antoine Prévost, Teatro Regio, Turin, 1 February 1893; revised Teatro San Carlo, Naples, 21 January 1894; definitive version, Teatro alla Scala, Milan, 26 December 1922

La bohème, scene liriche in 4 tableaux, libretto by Giuseppe Giacosa and Luigi Illica after *Scènes de la vie de Bohème* by Henry Mürger, Teatro Regio, Turin, 1 February 1896

Tosca, melodramma in 3 acts, libretto by Giuseppe Giacosa and Luigi Illica after the play *La Tosca* by Victorien Sardou, Teatro Costanzi, Rome, 14 January 1900

Madama Butterfly, tragedia giapponese in 2 acts, libretto by Giuseppe Giacosa and Luigi Illica after the play *Madam Butterfly* by David Belasco and a story of the same title by John Luther Long, Teatro alla Scala, Milan, 17 Feb 1904; 2nd version, Teatro Grande, Brescia, 28 May 1904; 3rd version, Covent Garden, London, 10 July 1905; final version, Opéra Comique, Paris, 28 December 1906; definitive edition pub. 1907

La fanciulla del West, opera in 3 acts, libretto by Guelfo Civinini and Carlo Zangarini after the play *The Girl of the Golden West* by David Belasco, Metropolitan Opera House, New York, 10 December 1910

La rondine, commedia lirica in 3 acts, libretto by Giuseppe Adami from a scenario by Alfred Maria Willner and Heinz Reichert, Théâtre de l'Opéra, Monte Carlo, 27 March 1917; 2nd version, Teatro Massimo, Palermo, 10 April 1920; 3rd version, Teatro Regio, Turin, 22 March 1994

Il trittico, Metropolitan Opera House, New York, 14 December 1918; definitive version pub. 1922

    Il tabarro, libretto by Giuseppe Adami after the play *La Houppelande* by Didier Gold

    Suor Angelica, libretto by Giovacchino Forzano

    Gianni Schicchi, libretto by Giovacchino Forzano from *Commento alla Divina Commedia d'Anonimo fiorentino del secolo xiv*

Turandot, dramma lirico in 3 acts completed by Franco Alfano, libretto by Giuseppe Adami and Renato Simoni after the 'fiaba' *Turandotte* by Carlo Gozzi; Teatro alla Scala, Milan, 25 April 1926

II CHORAL AND RELIGIOUS WORKS

Plaudite popoli, motet, baritone, mixed chorus, orchestra, (1877) (unpub.)

Credo, tenor and baritone soloists, chorus, orchestra (1878), later incorporated into *Messa a quattro voci*

Vexilla regis, 2 male voices, organ, text by Venantius Fortunatus (1878) (M. Kaye: *The Unknown Puccini*, Oxford, 1987, pp. 16–26).

Messa a quattro voci, tenor and baritone soloists, chorus, orchestra (1880) (Ricordi & Mills, NY, 1951 repr. 1984)

Requiem, 3-part chorus, viola, harmonium (1905) (Elkan & Vogel, NY, 1976)

Inno a Roma, unison massed choirs, instrumental accompaniment, poem by Fausto Salvatori (1919) (Kaye, 136–41)

III MUSIC FOR SOLO VOICE AND KEYBOARD

'A te', voice and piano, poem anonymous (c.1875) (Kaye, 5–11)

'Mentia l'avviso', recitative and aria, tenor and piano, text by Felice Romani (1883) (ibid., 37–44).

'Salve del ciel Regina', soprano and harmonium, poem by Antonio Ghislanzoni (1883) (ibid., 30–32)

'Ad una morta!' baritone and piano, poem by Antonio Ghislanzoni (1883) (fragment, ibid., 218–22)

'Storiella d'amore', soprano or tenor and piano, poem by Antonio Ghislanzoni (1883) (ibid., 50–54)

'Sole e amore', soprano or tenor and piano, poem anonymous (1888) (ibid., 56–9)

'Avanti Urania!', voice and piano, poem by Renato Fucini (1896) (ibid., 66–8)

'Inno a Diana', voice and piano, poem by Carlo Abeniacar, (1897) (ibid., 75–8)

'E l'uccellino', lullaby, voice and piano, poem by Renato Fucini (1899) (ibid., 82–4)

'Terra e mare', voice and piano, poem by Enrico Panzacchi (1901–2) (ibid., 88–9)

'Canto d'anime', voice and piano, poem by Luigi Illica (1904) (ibid., 107–9)

'Casa mia', voice and piano, words traditional (1908) (ibid., 117)

'Sogno d'or', lullaby, voice and piano, poem by Carlo Marsili (1912) (pub. in periodical *Noi e il mondo*, Jan. 1913)

'Morire?', voice and piano, poem by Giuseppe Adami (c.1917) (Kaye, 123–6)

IV INSTRUMENTAL MUSIC

Preludio a orchestra (1876), unpub.

Fugues in 4 parts (1880–3), unpub.

String Quartet in D, 1st movement (1881) (Boccacini & Spada, Rome, 1985)

Largo adagietto in F orchestra (c.1881), fragment, unpub.

Scherzo in A minor string quartet (1881) (Boccacini & Spada, Rome, 1985)

Scherzo in D minor string quartet (?1881), arr. for piano duet by Michele Puccini, unpub.

Adagio in A piano (c.1881), unpub.

Preludio sinfonico in A (1882) (Theodor Presser Co., Bryn Mawr, PA, 1977)

Capriccio sinfonico (1883) (Boccaccini & Spada, 1978)

Three Minuets, string quartet (1884) (Ricordi, Milan, 1987)

Crisantemi, elegy string quartet (1890) (Ricordi. Milan, 1987)

Piccolo valzer, piano (1894) (pub. in *Armi e arte*, Genoa, Sept. 1894)

Scossa elettrica, march, piano (1899), later scored for band (pub. in *I telegrafisti a Volta*, Como, 1899)

Calmo e molto lento, piano (1916) (Associazione della Stampa, Turin, 1916)

V MUSIC LOST

I figli d'Italia, cantata (1877)

Valzer, town band (1879)

'Ah, se potessi', tenor and piano (?1882)

'Melanconia', voice and piano (1883)

Personalia

Adami, Giuseppe (1878–1946), Italian playwright and journalist. He wrote the libretti of *La rondine, Il tabarro,* and (in partnership with Renato Simoni) *Turandot,* also the text of the song *Morire?*. He published the first collection of Puccini's letters (1928) and two biographies of both Puccini (1935 and 1942) and Giulio Ricordi (1933 and 1946).

Ader, Rose (1890–1955), a German light soprano. She made her début in 1915 at Hamburg, where she sang Angelica in the German première of *Il trittico* in 1921. Puccini urged her without success on Gatti-Casazza at the Metropolitan Opera House, New York. He sent her a copy of the first version of Liù's aria in Act I of *Turandot,* probably having her in mind for the première. Thereafter she made occasional appearances in the European capitals until Hitler's racial policy forced her as a Jewess to emigrate to America. In 1949 she settled in Buenos Aires as a teacher. 163 letters to her from Puccini (1921–3) are in private hands.

Angeloni, Carlo (1834–1901), Italian composer and music teacher. A pupil of the elder Michele Puccini, he succeeded Fortunato Magi as professor of composition and counterpoint at the Istituto Musicale Pacini, Lucca, so becoming Puccini's first teacher of importance and (it is said) the man who infected him with a passion for hunting. As a composer, he was sound but unremarkable. Puccini recommended his *Stabat mater* to Toscanini for performance at the Paris Exhibition of 1898.

Bazzini, Antonio (1818–97), Italian violinist, composer, and teacher. On the advice of Paganini he spent his early career touring Europe as a virtuoso, winning the esteem of Mendelssohn and Schumann, who described him as 'Italian in the best sense of the word'. Settling in Italy in 1863, he devoted himself to composition and the regeneration of Italy's instrumental tradition (he was the first Italian violinist to form his own quartet). Appointed professor of composition at the Milan Conservatory in 1873, he taught Puccini from 1880 until his assumption of the directorship the following year. Apart from the famous *Ronde des lutins* for violin and piano, his output includes six quartets of decent workmanship and some incidental music still occasionally to be heard. Among his favourite composers were Saint-Saëns and Gounod, whose influence can be discerned in the *Dies irae* that he contributed to the composite *Messa per Rossini* of 1869. His one opera, *Turanda* (1867), was a failure.

Belasco, David (1854–1931), American playwright. His productions were renowned for their naturalism and inventive use of stage pictures, exploited to particular effect in his one-act *Madam Butterfly* (1900). Among his many works his own favourite was *The Girl of the Golden West* (1905), written as a show-piece for the actress Blanche Bates (creator of Butterfly), which enabled him to draw on an ambience with which he had been familiar since childhood.

Berté, Emil (1855–1922), music publisher and co-director with Siegmund Eibenschütz of the Karltheater, Vienna. He negotiated the contract with Puccini that led to the composition of *La rondine*. He is not to be confused with his brother Heinrich, author of the Schubert-pasticcio *Das Dreimäderlhaus* (known in English as *Lilac Time*).

Carignani, Carlo (1857–1919), Italian composer, conductor, and singing teacher. A fellow-pupil of Puccini at the Istituto Musicale Pacini, Lucca, he remained a life-long friend of the composer, arranging the piano and vocal scores of all his operas except for *Le Villi* and *Turandot*. He conducted the first performance of *Edgar* in its 3-act version at Ferrara in 1892.

Carré, Albert (1852–1938), French impresario, director of the Opéra Comique, Paris, from 1898 to 1912. He mounted the premières of Charpentier's *Louise* (1900), Debussy's *Pelléas et Mélisande* (1902), and Massenet's *Cendrillon* (1899) and *Grisélidis* (1902), having persuaded the composer to write a new, powerful scene for the revival of his *Sapho* in 1898. It was at his instance that for the Parisian première of *Madama Butterfly* in 1906 Puccini made substantial changes to the score, all of which were incorporated in the standard version. In 1902 he married the soprano Marguerite Guiraud ('Mme Pomme-de-Terre', as Puccini called her), who from then on became his prima donna.

Caruso, Enrico (1873–1921), Italian tenor of legendary fame. He first made his name in operas by the 'giovane scuola', creating the tenor lead in Cilea's *L'arlesiana* (1897), Giordano's *Fedora* (1898), and Franchetti's *Germania* (1902). As Canio in Leoncavallo's *Pagliacci* he is credited with having appropriated the opera's concluding line ('La commedia è finita!') originally assigned to the clown Tonio. His performance with Melba of *La bohème* established the opera in the repertory of Covent Garden.

While under contract to the Metropolitan Opera House, New York, he created the part of Dick Johnson in *La fanciulla del West* in 1910. A clever caricaturist, he has left several amusing sketches of Puccini and the company with whom he worked.

Casella, Alfredo (1883–1947), Italian composer, pianist, teacher, and essayist, leading figure of the so-called 'generazione dell'ottanta'. Having studied in Paris under Fauré, he acquired a thoroughly cosmopolitan outlook and played a prominent part in the International Society for Contemporary Music after World War I. He introduced Puccini to Schoenberg at the performance of *Pierrot Lunaire* at Florence in 1924. *La donna serpente* (1932), the best of his three operas, is based, like Puccini's *Turandot*, on a 'fiaba' by Gozzi (the same that had served Wagner for *Die Feen*). He ended his career as a teacher at the Accademia Chigiana, Siena.

Caselli, Alfredo (1858–1921), proprietor of a grocery store and café in Lucca, which became a meeting-place for the artists and intellectuals of the neighbourhood, among them Giovannu Pascoli, who dedicated two of his poems to the owner. He remained a life-long friend of Puccini, who corresponded with him regularly. During the Doria Manfredi scandal, he was the confidant of both Giacomo and Elvira.

Catalani, Alfred (1854–93), Italian composer. Like Puccini, a native of Lucca, he studied first with Fortunato Magi, then spent half a year in Paris before passing to the Milan Conservatory. Of his five operas, all distinguished by a refined taste and delicate pictorial imagination, only the last, *La Wally* (1892), maintains a foothold in the repertory. Though he recognized Puccini's talent, he deeply resented the favouritism shown him by their publisher Giulio Ricordi. He died of consumption, an embittered man.

Cerù, Nicolao (1817–94), Italian doctor, first cousin to Albina Puccini. He did much to sustain the family during the years that followed the death of the elder Michele, and helped to provide for both Albina's sons during their studentship at Milan.

Civinini, Guelfo (1873–1954), Italian journalist, novelist, and poet. In 1908 Puccini co-opted him with Zangarini on the libretto of *La fanciulla del West*. After the opera's first performance he published an angry letter protesting against the composer's treatment of his verses. He later achieved fame as a foreign correspondent and travel writer.

Clausetti, Carlo (1869–1943), Italian composer and businessman. As manager of the Neapolitan branch of the Casa Ricordi, he did much to further Puccini's interests in southern Italy. Always ready to help the composer in his search for operatic subjects, he was the first to put him in contact with Gabriele D'Annunzio. In 1920 he assumed directorship of the firm jointly with Renzo Valcarenghi, a post he held until 1940.

Dalla Rizza, Gilda (1892–1975), Italian soprano. She made her début in Bologna in 1910 as Charlotte in Massenet's *Werther*. An artist of rare versatility, she created the role of Magda in *La rondine* (1917) and distinguished herself as Angelica and Lauretta in the Italian première of *Il trittico* (1919). Hearing her in *La fanciulla del West* in Monte Carlo (1921), Puccini pronounced her his ideal Minnie. During his last years he kept up a cordial, mildly flirtatious correspondence with her. She was his final choice for Liù in *Turandot*, though she took no part in the opera's posthumous première.

D'Annunzio, Gabriele (1863–1938), Italian poet and playwright. As the leading literary figure of his generation, he held a powerful attraction for Italian composers, several of whom (Mascagni, Franchetti, Pizzetti, Montemezzi) drew on his plays for their operas. His attempts to collaborate with Puccini foundered on the complexity of his dramatic ideas. After his year-long occupation of Fiume (Rijeka) in 1919 with a band of volunteers he proved an embarrassment to Mussolini, who saw to it that his final years were spent in isolated retirement.

Del Carlo, Otilia (née Puccini) (1851–1923), Puccini's eldest sister and the first to leave home. In 1872 she married the doctor Massimo Del Carlo, who for a time was mayor of Lucca and by whom she had one child, Carlo.

Del Fiorentino, Dante (*b* 1888), Italian priest. Born in Quiesa near Lucca, he made Puccini's acquaintance at the time of his motor accident in 1903. After World War I he was appointed curate at Torre del Lago. Later he emigrated to America, where he published an affectionate memoir of the composer (*Immortal Bohemian*, 1951). He was also responsible for the publication of Puccini's *Messa a quatto voci* under the misleading title *Messa di gloria*.

De Servi, Luigi (1863–1945), Italian painter. Born in Lucca, he remained a life-long friend of Puccini since childhood. After a spell in Argentina he lived for many years in Genoa. He was one of the artists who decorated Puccini's villa at Torre del Lago, and he painted several portraits of the composer.

Eisner-Eisenhof, Baron Angelo. Viennese nobleman. Puccini made his acquaintance during his return from Hamburg in 1892, where *Le Villi* had had its German première. From then on he became the composer's unofficial agent in the Austrian capital, acting as intermediary in the negotiations with Willner and the directors of the Karltheater that led to the composition of *La rondine*.

Faccio, Franco (1840–91), Italian conductor and composer. After the failure in 1865 of his second opera, *Amleto*, written to a libretto by Arrigo Boito, he devoted himself exclusively to the podium, becoming the leading Italian conductor of his generation. As musical director of La Scala from 1871, he conducted the premières of Ponchielli's *La Gioconda* (1876), the revised versions of *Simon Boccanegra* (1881) and *Don Carlos* (1884), and, most notably, *Otello* (1887). He played an important part in the early diffusion of Puccini's music, conducting his *Capriccio sinfonico* both at the conservatory (1883) and at a public concert of his Società Orchestrale (1884), *Le Villi* at La Scala (1885), and the first performance of *Edgar* (1889). That year he went with Puccini to Bayreuth to work out cuts for the forthcoming Italian première of Wagner's *Die Meistersinger* (Carnival season, 1889–90). He died in an asylum in Monza.

Filippi, Filippo (1830–87), Italian music critic, the most authoritative of his day. A man of wide sympathies, he did much to promote the music of Wagner in Italy. His appreciation of Puccini's talents, expressed in the columns of *La perseveranza*, made an important contribution to the young composer's success.

Fontana, Ferdinando (1850–1919), Italian poet, playwright, and librettist. Introduced by Ponchielli to Puccini, he provided the libretti of *Le Villi* and *Edgar*. A late adherent to the iconoclastic movement known as the 'scapigliatura', his dramatic theories are set forth in the pamphlet *In teatro* (1884). He wrote for Franchetti the libretti of *Asrael* (1888) and *Il signor di Pourceaugnac* (1897). For his part in the disturbances of 1898 he was exiled to Switzerland, from where he tried in 1907 to interest Puccini in Oscar Wilde's *The Duchess of Padua*. His output includes several plays in Milanese dialect, and Italian translations of Eugen D'Albert's *Tiefland* and Lehár's *Die lustige Witwe*.

Forzano, Giovacchino (1884–1970), Italian playwright, librettist, and producer. After an early career in journalism he found his true métier as a man of the theatre. As a librettist he was particularly resourceful, devising rather than adapting most of his plots. For Puccini he wrote *Suor Angelica* and *Gianni Schicchi*, for Mascagni *Lodoletta* (1917) and *Il piccolo Marat* (1921); for Giordano *Il re* (1929); for Franchetti *Notte di leggenda* (1915) and *Glauco* (1922). His *Sly, ovvero La leggenda del dormiente risvegliato*, intended for Puccini, was set by Wolf-Ferrari in 1927. He also provided the text for Leoncavallo's posthumous *Edipo re* (1920), whose music was compiled from the composer's earlier works. During the Fascist régime Forzano achieved fame as a director on stage and screen (he it was who produced the première of *Turandot* at La Scala in 1926). He was co-author with Mussolini of three propaganda plays.

Franceschini, Ramelde (née Puccini) (1859–1912), youngest and favourite sister of Giacomo. Her husband, Raffaello, was a tax-collector at Pescia, a hunting-companion of Puccini, and the butt of many of his jokes. She had three daughters by him, with the eldest of whom, Alba (Albina), the composer kept up an intimate correspondence after her mother's death.

Franchetti, Alberto (1860–1942), Italian composer and nobleman. Having studied in Venice under Fortunato Magi and in Munich under Rhein-berger, he was classed with the Italian 'giovane scuola' along with Puc-cini, Mascagni, Giordano, and Leoncavallo; but his style is more cosmopolitan and eclectic than theirs. His skill with the large *tableau*, evident in *Cristoforo Colombo* (1892) and *Germania* (1902), earned him the soubriquet of 'the Italian Meyerbeer'. Generous and accommodating towards his colleagues, he yielded the libretti of *Andrea Chénier* to Gior-dano and *Tosca* to Puccini.

Gatti-Casazza, Giulio (1869–1940), Italian impresario. From directorship of the Teatro Comunale, Ferrara, where the 3-act *Edgar* had its première in 1891, he passed to La Scala, which he managed from 1898 until 1908. The rest of his career until his retirement in 1935 was spent as director of the Metropolitan Opera, New York, where together with Toscanini he did much to correct the German bias shown by his predecessor, Heinrich Conried. A keen admirer of Puccini, he helped to secure for his theatre the world premières of *La fanciulla del West* and *Il trittico*.

Gemignani, Fosca (1880–1968), daughter of Narciso Gemignani and Elvira Puccini, she accompanied her mother in her elopement with Puccini and was brought up as the composer's stepdaughter. She was first married to the tenor Antonio Leonardi, to whom she bore three children. Her second husband was the industrialist Mario Crespi.

Gherardi, Tomaide (née Puccini) (1852–1917), second daughter of the elder Michele and Albina Puccini. Married to Enrico Gherardi, a widower with two children, she taught at a primary school.

Giacosa, Giuseppe (1847–1906), Italian poet and playwright. He was one of the outstanding literary figures of his time. Two of his plays—*Tristi amori* (1887) and *Come le foglie* (1900)—show the influence of Ibsen. His part-nership with Luigi Illica for Puccini's operas was set up by Giulio Ricordi in 1893. Illica's task was to draft the scenario, Giacosa's to put the text into polished verse. Although Giacosa found the work uncongenial, the collaboration resulted in three of the composer's most successful operas: *La boheme, Tosca*, and *Madama Butterfly*.

Ginori-Lisci, Marchese Carlo (1851–1905), Italian nobleman. Puccini's neigh-bour at Torre del Lago, he granted the composer hunting rights in his estate, putting a lodge at his disposal, and allowing him to extend the property surrounding his villa. Puccini dedicated to him *La bohème* and wrote the song *Avanti Urania!* to celebrate his purchase of a yacht.

Gold, Didier. French playwright, whose one-act drama *La Houppelande*, first given at the Théâtre Marigny, Paris, in 1910, provided the basis for *Il tabarro*. He offered Puccini another subject to fill out the evening, but the composer turned it down.

Gunsbourg, Raoul (1859–1955), Romanian-born impresario. Under his di-rection the theatre at Monte Carlo rose to a position of high prestige in the world of opera and ballet with the premières of Massenet's *Le jongleur de Notre Dame* (1902), *Thérèse* (1907), *Don Quichotte* (1910), *Roma* (1912), and the posthumous *Cléopatre* (1914) and *Amadis* (1922), Fauré's *Pénélope* (1913), and Ravel's *L'enfant et les sortilèges* (1925). He mounted the first performance of *La rondine* in 1917. Puccini later tried unsuccessfully to urge on him the third version of his opera. Between the wars Gunsbourg made his theatre the home of Diaghilev's ballet company, whose title became the Ballets Russes de Monte Carlo.

Illica, Luigi (1857–1919), Italian playwright and librettist. Having made his name as a writer of plays, mostly in Milanese dialect, he moved into the world of opera during the late 1880s to become the leading Italian librettist of his generation, commanding a wide variety of literary styles. His instinct for the striking stage picture, together with a strict attention to historical detail and local atmosphere enabled the 'giovane scuola' to produce some of their best work. His acquaintance with Puccini dates from 1891, when he was called in to salvage the libretto of *Manon Lescaut* As co-author with Giacosa of *La bohème, Tosca,* and *Madama Butterfly,* his main task was to devise the incident and set out the dialogue in prose; but he also was responsible for late alterations to Giacosa's verses made at Puccini's request. For all other operas he insisted on working alone. For Catalani he wrote *La Wally* (1892), for Franchetti *Cristoforo Colombo* (1892) and *Germania* (1902); for Mascagni *Iris* (1898), *Le maschere* (1901), and *Isabeau* (1911). After Giacosa's death in 1906 he remained in contact with Puccini, but none of their joint projects came to fruition. Among Illica's papers an operatic scenario has come to light entitled *2001*—a satirical sketch of a socialist Utopia. A nationalist of right-wing views, he volunteered for military service in 1915.

Jeritza, Maria (1887–1982), Austrian (Moravian) soprano. A member of the Vienna State Opera from 1911 until 1932, she created the title role of Strauss's *Ariadne auf Naxos* in both versions, the Empress in his *Die Frau ohne Schatten,* and Marietta in Korngold's *Die tote Stadt.* With her splendid voice, personal beauty, and acting skills she was an especially memorable Tosca, much admired by Puccini, who hoped for her as Turandot.

Lehár, Franz (1870–1948), Austrian composer. After studying at the Prague Conservatory he worked in various cities as a military band conductor before settling in Vienna, where his waltz *Gold und Silber* established him as waltz-king in succession to Johann Strauss II. With *Die lustige Witwe* (1906) he initiated a series of operettas which revived a genre that was already in decline. He and Puccini had the greatest admiration for each other's work. Puccini kept a signed photograph of Lehár on his piano at Torre del Lago.

Leoncavallo, Ruggero (1857–1919), Italian composer. The son of a Neapolitan magistrate, he studied at the Naples Conservatory, thereafter pursuing a chequered career in Potenza, Bologna, Egypt, and Paris, where he played the piano at cafés-chantants in the suburbs. His ambition, however, was to write words and music for a trilogy about the Italian Renaissance to stand comparison with Wagner's *Der Ring des Nibelungen*. The baritone Victor Maurel recommended him to Giulio Ricordi in Milan, where he arrived in 1889. While showing no interest in the trilogy, Ricordi enlisted his services the following year on the libretto of *Manon Lescaut* for Puccini. The two composers fell out, however, in 1893 over their respective claims to priority in the setting of Mürger's *Scènes de la vie de Bohème*; and, though they would remain on visiting terms, all Puccini's references to his former colleague in his letters are disparaging. Leoncavallo's output ranges from operetta to the grand historical pageantry of *I Medici* (1893) and *Roland von Berlin* (1904). His *La bohème* (1897) and *Zazà* (1900) are still occasionally to be heard; but only *Pagliacci* (1892) remains firmly in the repertory.

Magi, Fortunato (1839–82), Italian composer, conductor, and teacher. Puccini's uncle on his mother's side, he studied at the Istituto Musicale Pacini, Lucca, with Michele Puccini, after whose death he was nominated professor of counterpoint. Appointed director of the institute in 1872 he resigned after a dispute with the city council, moving successively to Sarzana, Ferrara, and La Spezia and finally settling in Venice as director of the Liceo Musicale 'Benedetto Marcello'. Although a sound teacher (his pupils included Catalani in Lucca and Franchetti in Venice), he was clearly a difficult character with little time for his idle nephew, to whom he taught the rudiments of music. His compositions, however, show a fine orchestral imagination, from which the young Puccini may well have learned.

Magrini, Angelo. Italian industrialist. A neighbour and close friend of Puccini's last years, he accompanied him with his family on a European tour in 1922 and went with him to Brussels for his final operation.

Mancinelli, Luigi (1848–1921), Italian composer and conductor. Having launched his career as a cellist in the orchestra of the Teatro della Pergola, Florence, he first took up the baton in Rome in 1875 for Verdi's *Aida*, becoming the most distinguished Italian conductor between Faccio and Toscanini. He was held in high regard by Wagner, who corresponded with him on the interpretation of his scores and hoped that he might conduct a revival of his youthful symphony in Venice in 1882 (unfortunately other commitments prevented him from complying). While Principal of the Liceo Musicale in Bologna he conducted *Le Villi* at the city's Teatro Comunale in 1885 and the first 3-act version of *Edgar* in Madrid in 1892. His compositions include three operas, in which Wagnerian influence can faintly be discerned, and a wealth of choral and instrumental music.

Marotti, Guido (1890–1988), Italian journalist. Puccini's neighbour at Torre del Lago, he wrote with the painter Ferruccio Pagni the earliest book of recollections of the composer (*Puccini intimo*, 1926).

Marsili, Nitteti (née Puccini) (1854–1928), the third surviving daughter of the elder Michele and Albina Puccini. She married the Pisan lawyer Alberto Marsili, to whom she bore two children, Carlo and Alba. Widowed after six years of marriage, Nitteti and her family were given a yearly stipend by Puccini. Following his car accident in 1903, Nitteti helped to nurse him back to health. Carlo provided the poem of *Sogno d'or* (1912); and for a while Puccini considered him as a possible librettist.

Mascagni, Pietro (1863–1945), Italian composer and conductor. After studying at the Istituto Cherubini in his native Livorno, he proceeded in 1882 to the Milan Conservatory, where for a while he shared lodgings with his fellow-student Puccini. He left the Conservatory without finishing his course to tour as conductor of more than one operetta company, before settling in Cerignola as municipal music master. From there he was rescued by the triumph in 1890 of his one-act opera *Cavalleria rusticana*, submitted for the Concorso Sonzogno. Of his subsequent operas, written on a wide variety of subjects, only *L'amico Fritz* (1891) and *Iris* (1898) have remained on the fringes of the repertory; but he attained a certain standing as a conductor (it was he who introduced Tchaikovsky's *Symphonie pathétique* to Italy). His friendship with Puccini endured, though it was occasionally clouded by suspicion and rivalry. The two composers regularly met in Rome as members of a jury appointed to decide on the merits of new operas submitted to them. During the Fascist era Mascagni saw himself as the champion of national music, sending glowing reports to the Duce of performances which he had conducted abroad; hence the coolness shown to the revival of his music after the last war, *Cavalleria* alone excepted.

Mugnone, Leopoldo (1858–1941), Italian conductor and composer. He directed the premières of *Cavalleria rusticana* (1890), *Tosca* (1900), and the definitive version of *Edgar* in Buenos Aires (1905). At first delighted with his interpretations, Puccini later found his direction flabby and lifeless. His operetta *Il birichino* (1892) achieved a certain success.

Oliva, Domenico (1860–1917), Italian poet and lawyer. In 1889 he was called upon by Marco Praga to collaborate on the libretto of *Manon Lescaut*, putting Praga's prose dialogue into verse. Although the result was drastically overhauled by Luigi Illica and published without an attribution, Oliva maintained in a letter to the press that the text of the final act was entirely his.

Pagni, Ferruccio (1866–1935), Italian landscape painter. A native of Livorno, he became a neighbour, close friend, and hunting-companion of Puccini. In 1904 he emigrated for a short while to Argentina, where he founded an academy of fine arts at Rosario. He was one of the decorators of Puccini's villa at Torre del Lago and joint author with Marotti of the book *Puccini intimo* (see above).

Paladini, Carlo (1861–1922), Italian music critic and teacher. A native of Lucca, in 1899 he was appointed professor of English Literature at the Istituto Galileo Galilei, Florence, a post he held until his death. In 1903 he published a biography of Puccini which appeared in instalments of Ricordi's *Ars et labor* (monthly successor to the *Gazzetta musicale di Milano*); but his derogatory comments on *Madama Butterfly* caused a breach between them that lasted 15 years. After their reconciliation Puccini suggested to Paladini that he write a new life of him in the first person; but Paladini died before this could be carried out. His son Giuseppe, however, republished the earlier biography in 1961, bringing it up to date and including valuable letters written by Puccini to his father from 1918 to 1922.

Panichelli, Don Pietro. Italian priest and teacher of literature. Born in Pietrasanta, he entered the Dominican order and settled in Rome. Puccini consulted him over liturgical texts required for *Tosca* and *Suor Angelica* and the exact pitch of the great bell of St. Peter's. Panichelli also found him the poet Luigi Zanazzi to write the verses in Romanesque dialect for the shepherd boy's song in Act III of *Tosca*. An honorary member of the 'Gianni Schicchi Club' in Viareggio, he published a book, *Il pretino di Giacomo Puccini racconta* (1940).

Ponchielli, Amilcare (1834–86). Italian composer, the most eminent among the generation that succeeded Verdi. After 16 years' drudgery as a bandmaster in northern Italy, he enjoyed a modest success with his revised opera *I promessi sposi* in Milan (1872), scoring a triumph with *La Gioconda* (1876, rev. 1880). Appointed professor of composition at the Milan Conservatory in 1880, he succeeded Bazzini as Puccini's teacher and found him in Fontana the librettist for his first operatic venture, *Le Villi*.

Praga, Marco (1862–1929), Italian playwright. Son of the 'scapigliato' poet Emilio Praga, he was the author of a successful play, *La moglie ideale*, written for Eleonora Duse. He was the first to be approached by Puccini for the libretto of *Manon Lescaut* in 1889, but soon withdrew from the project. Later he would act as D'Annunzio's unofficial agent in his abortive negotiations with Puccini.

Puccini, Albina (1830–84), wife of the elder Michele Puccini and mother of Giacomo. Widowed in 1864, she devoted the rest of her life to securing a future for her large family.

Puccini, Antonio (1885–1946), only child of Giacomo and Elvira. Educated in Milan, he studied engineering in Germany. During World War I he volunteered for service in the medical corps. He had one child, Simonetta.

Puccini, Elvira (née Bonturi) (1860–1930). First married to the merchant Narciso Gemignani, to whom she bore two children, she eloped with Giacomo in 1885, taking her daughter Fosca to live with them. Their son, Antonio, was born later that year. The death of Gemignani in 1903

enabled Elvira and Giacomo to legitimize their union, which would
survive many a tempestuous incident.

Puccini, Iginia (1856–1922), daughter of Albina and the elder Michele Puccini. She entered the order of Augustinian nuns, taking the title of Suor Giulia Enrichetta. Eventually she became Mother Superior of the convent at Vicepelago, near Lucca.

Puccini, Michele, the elder (1813–64), composer and organist. The fourth in a line of Luccan musicians, he studied at Bologna and Naples, returning to take up a teaching post at the local musical institute of which Pacini was the director. Later he was appointed organist of the cathedral of S. Martino. Widely respected as a composer of sacred music and, above all, as a teacher, with treatises on harmony and counterpoint to his credit, he remained the city's presiding musical genius until his death.

Puccini, Michele, the younger (1864–91), youngest child of Albina and Michele the elder, born three months after his father's death. Like Giacomo, he was trained as a musician, passing from the Istituto Musicale Pacini to the Milan Conservatory, which he left before completing his course to emigrate to South America. After a spell of teaching in Buenos Aires and Jujuy, an adulterous relationship forced him to take flight to Rio de Janeiro, where he died of yellow fever. Giacomo used two of his melodic ideas in *Tosca*.

Ricordi, Giulio (1840–1912), music publisher, son of the elder Tito (1811–88) and grandson of Giovanni (1785–1853), founder of the family firm. The most astute and enterprising of the dynasty, he brought about the collaboration of Verdi and Boito and launched the young Puccini on his operatic career, buying the rights to *Le Villi* and granting him a monthly stipend to be deducted from future royalties. A musician himself (he wrote operettas under the pseudonym of J. Burgmein) he took a hand in the shaping of *Manon Lescaut* and set up for Puccini the partnership of Giacosa and Illica for the three operas that followed. He never ceased to devote himself to Puccini's interests, suggesting new subjects and smoothing over his difficulties with librettists. His final gift to his protégé was to have found him Giuseppe Adami, librettist of *La rondine, Il tabarro*, and (with Renato Simoni) *Turandot*. All Puccini's operas except for *La rondine* were published by the Casa Ricordi.

Ricordi, Tito, the younger (1865–1933), music publisher and stage director, son of Giulio. He managed the family firm after his father's death until some ill-judged speculations resulted in his dismissal in 1920. He produced the premières of *Tosca, Madama Butterfly*, and—with Belasco's help—*La fanciulla del West*. Though their relations remained outwardly cordial, Puccini suspected him of favouring Zandonai over himself, and his refusal to publish *La rondine* was a further source of grievance. Nonetheless Puccini contracted with him for the publication of all his future works.

Sardou, Victorien (1831–1908), French playwright. The most successful practitioner of the 'well-made play' after Scribe, his works inspired Massenet's *Grisélidis* (1901) and Giordano's *Fedora* (1898) and *Madame Sans-Gêne* (1915). His best-known drama was *La Tosca*, written in 1887 for Sarah Bernhardt. He himself took a lively interest in its operatic adaptation, first for Franchetti, then for Puccini.

Schnabl-Rossi, Riccardo (1872–1955), Italian landowner of Austrian family. As a keen music lover he enjoyed Puccini's confidence on artistic matters, accompanying him on many of his trips and sometimes acting as his mediator in the German-speaking countries. Their correspondence, edited by Simonetta Puccini, reaches from 1899 to the composer's death.

Seligman, Sybil (1868–1935), English hostess, wife of the London banker David Seligman. A singing pupil of Paolo Tosti, she met Puccini in 1904 and remained his life-long friend and confidante. She suggested to him various operatic subjects and kept him informed about musical life in London. A selection of Puccini's letters to her was published by her son Vincent in his book *Puccini among Friends* (1938).

Simoni, Renato (1875–1952), theatre critic, playwright, and librettist. In 1906 he succeeded Giacosa as editor of the literary periodical *La lettura*. Librettist of Giordano's *Madame Sans-Gêne* (1915), it was he who suggested to Puccini the subject of Gozzi's *Turandot*, having himself written a play about the author. He collaborated with Adami on the resulting libretto. Later he made a reputation as a film director.

Soldani, Valentino (1874–1935), Tuscan journalist and playwright. Over a number of years Puccini corresponded with him about a possible adaptation of his medieval drama *Margherita da Cortona*.

Sonzogno, Edoardo (1830–1920), music publisher. He first brought the family firm into rivalry with the Casa Ricordi, set up the Concorso Sonzogno for one-act operas, and brought out the works of Mascagni, Leoncavallo, Cilea, and Giordano.

Sonzogno, Lorenzo (1877–1920), nephew of Edoardo. On his uncle's retirement he shared the direction of the firm with his cousin Riccardo. Dismissed for unfortunate speculations, he set up a publishing house of his own, until his cousin's death enabled him to assume sole directorship of the original firm. He published Puccini's *La rondine* and the *Inno a Roma*.

Storchio, Rosina (1876–1945), Italian soprano. She made her début in 1892 as Micaela in *Carmen* at the Teatro dal Verme, Milan. A lively and versatile actress, she was Ricordi's first choice for Musetta in *La bohéme*, and though unavailable for the première she triumphed in the opera's first revival in Rome. She created the title-role of *Madama Butterfly* at its disastrous first night in 1904.

Toscanini, Arturo (1867–1957), Italian conductor, the greatest of his generation. He directed the premières of *La bohème* (Turin, 1896), *La fanciulla* *del West* (New York, 1910), and *Turandot* (Milan, 1926). Puccini had the highest regard for his interpretations and accepted his modifications to the scores of *La fanciulla* and *Manon Lescaut*. His attitude towards Toscanini the man are summed up in the remarks reported by Del Fiorentino: 'Oh, he's a pig all right, but such a great pig! Yes, he's a god, and he knows it—that's the trouble. . . . With all his faults Toscanini is the greatest of all conductors.'

Tosti, Sir Francesco Paolo (1846–1916), Italian song-writer and singing teacher. He studied at the Naples Conservatory under Mercadante. His lyrical gifts and charm of manner soon procured him an *entrée* into fashionable society. In 1880 he was appointed singing teacher to members of the English royal family. Visiting Italian musicians were always welcome at his London home, none more so than Puccini, who owed him his acquaintance with Sybil Seligman. Although he claimed to speak hardly any English, he set to music English as well as Italian and French poems. He was knighted in 1908.

Valcarenghi, Renzo (1860–1947), employee of the Casa Ricordi. He assumed direction of the firm with Carlo Clausetti in 1920.

Vandini, Alfredo. Italian government official. A native of Lucca, he was a childhood friend of Puccini. Having settled in Rome, he became the composer's unofficial agent in the capital. Puccini kept up a steady correspondence both with him and his brother Guido, a music teacher in Lucca.

Willner, Alfred Maria (1859–1929), Austrian librettist and composer. Co-author with Heinz Reichert of the texts of several operettas by Lehár, notably *Der Graf von Luxemburg*, he drew up the scenario of *La rondine*. His complaints about Adami's treatment of it probably induced Puccini to make his third version of the opera.

Zandonai, Riccardo (1883–1944), Italian composer. Having studied with Mascagni at the Liceo Musicale at Pesaro, he made his name with *Conchita* (1911), based on a subject that Puccini had considered, then turned down. Hoping to groom him as Puccini's successor, Tito Ricordi helped to draw up the text of his one enduring success, *Francesca da Rimini* (1914), taken from D'Annunzio's tragedy of the same name. Puccini admired it, but detested the composer's *Giulietta e Romeo* (1921). Zandonai in his turn held his older rival in utter contempt. Of his later operas only *I cavalieri di Ekebù* (1925) is occasionally to be heard.

Zangarini, Carlo (1974–1943), Italian poet and librettist. The son of an American mother, he collaborated with Civinini on the libretto of *La fanciulla del West*. With Golisciani he wrote for Wolf-Ferrari the book of *I gioielli della Madonna* and for Zandonai that of *Conchita*, both first given in 1911. In 1924 he was appointed Professor of Drama and Poetry at the Liceo Musicale Martini, Bologna.

Select Bibliography

Abbreviations

AcM	*Acta Musicologica*
AnMc	*Analecta Musicologica*
BRG	G. Biagi Ravenni and C. Gianturco (eds.): *Giacomo Puccini: l'uomo, il musicista, il panorama europeo*, Atti del Convegno Internazionale di Studi su Giacomo Puccini nel 70° anniversario della morte (Lucca, 1997)
COJ	*Cambridge Opera Journal*
CrP	*Critica pucciniana* (Lucca, 1976)
ECL	J. Maehder (ed.): *Esotismo e colore locale nell'opera di Puccini*, Atti del Convegno Internazionale sull'opera di Puccini, Torre del Lago, 1983 (Pisa, 1985)
JAMS	*Journal of the American Musicological Society*
ML	*Music & Letters*
MO	*Musica d'oggi*
MQ	*Musical Quarterly*
NA	*Nuova Antologia*
NCM	*Nineteenth Century Music*
NRMI	*Nuova Rivista Musicale Italiana*
OQ	*Opera Quarterly*
PRMA	*Proceedings of the Royal Musical Association*
PW	S. Puccini and W. Weaver (eds.): *The Puccini Companion* (New York and London, 1994).
QP	*Quaderni Pucciniani*
RIM	*Rivista Italiana di Musicologia*
RMC	*Rivista Musicale Curci*
RMI	*Rivista Musicale Italiana*
SP	*Studi Pucciniani*
VBP	V. Bernardoni (ed.): *Puccini* (Bologna, 1996)

Letters and Documents

G. Adami: *Epistolario di Giacomo Puccini* (Milan, 1928); Eng. ed. trans. E. Makin as *Letters of Puccini* (London, 1931), rev. M. Carner (1974)

V. Seligman: *Puccini among Friends* (London, 1938)

L. Marchetti: *Puccini nelle immagini* (Milan, 1949)

——: 'Gabriele D'Annunzio: lettere a Puccini', *NA*, no. 447 (1949), 337–50

E. Gara (ed.): *Carteggi pucciniani* (Milan, 1958)

C. Paladini: *Giacomo Puccini* (Florence, 1961)

A. Marchetti: *Puccini com'era* (Milan, 1973)

G. Magri: *Puccini e le sue rime* (Milan, 1974)

G. Pintorno (ed.): *Puccini: 276 lettere inedite* (Montecatini, 1974)

P. Ross and D. Schwendimann Berra: 'Sette lettere di Puccini a Giulio Ricordi', *NRMI*, xiii (1979), 851–65

S. Puccini (ed.): *Giacomo Puccini: lettere a Riccardo Schnabl* (Milan, 1981)

P.M. Ferrando (ed.): *Tutti i libretti di Puccini* (Milan, 1984)

M. Busnelli (ed.): 'Carteggio Giacomo Puccini / Domenico Alaleona (1919–1924)', *QP*, ii, (1985), 217–30

S. Puccini (ed.): 'Lettere a Luigi de' Servi', *QP* ii (1985), 17–45

M. Beghelli: 'Quel "Lago di Massaciuccoli tanto . . . povero d'ispirazione!", D'Annunzio-Puccini: Lettere di un articolo mai nato', *NRMI*, xx (1986), 605–25

R. Cecchini (ed.): *Trenta lettere inedite di Giacomo Puccini* (Lucca, 1992)

R. Giazotto: *Puccini in casa Puccini* (Lucca, 1992)

S. Puccini and M. Elphinstone (eds.): 'Lettere di Ferdinando Fontana a Giacomo Puccini', *QP*, iv (1992)

R. Cecchini: *Giacomo Puccini: lettere inedite ad Alfredo Vandini* (Lucca, 1994)

M. Alinovi (ed.): 'Lettere di Giacomo Puccini', *QP*, v (1996), 187–274

G. Biagi Ravenni and D. Buonomini: ' "Caro Ferruccio . . .": trenta lettere di Giacomo Puccini a Ferruccio Giorgi (1906–1924)', *BRG*, 169–209

S. Puccini (ed.): Lettere di Giacomo Puccini ad Alfredo Caselli', *QP*, vi (1998)

Biography: Life and Works

A. Weissmann: *Giacomo Puccini* (Munich, 1922)

A. Fraccaroli: *La vita di Giacomo Puccini* (Milan, 1925)

G. Marotti and F. Pagni: *Giacomo Puccini intimo* (Florence, 1926, repr. 1942)

G. Adami: *Giulio Ricordi e i suoi musicisti italiani* (Milan, 1933)

——: *Puccini* (Milan, 1935)

K.G. Fellerer: *Giacomo Puccini* (Potsdam, 1937)

L. D'Ambra: *Puccini* (Rome, 1940)

G. Adami: *Il romanzo della vita di Giacomo Puccini* (Milan, 1944)

——: *Giulio Ricordi, l'amico dei musicisti italiani* (Milan, 1945)

P. Nardi: *Vita e tempo di Giuseppe Giacosa* (Milan, 1949)

P. Panichelli: *Il 'Pretino' di Giacomo Puccini racconta* (Pisa, 1949)

G.R. Marek: *Puccini c: a Biography* (New York, 1951; London, 1952)

D. Del Fiorentino: *Immortal Bohemian: an Intimate Memoir of Giacomo Puccini* (London, 1952)

G. Forzano: *Come li ho conosciuti* (Turin, 1957)

A. Fraccaroli: *Giacomo Puccini si confida e racconta* (Milan, 1957)

M. Carner: *Puccini: a Critical Biography* (London, 1958; rev. 1974; 3rd definitive ed. 1992)

E. Greenfield: *Puccini, Keeper of the Seal* (London, 1958)

C. Sartori: *Puccini* (Milan, 1958, repr. 1978)

V. Gui: 'Ricordando (Puccini)', *L'approdo musicale*, ii/6 (1959), 72–80

G. Marotti: 'Incontri e colloqui col maestro', ibid. 53–71

A. Gauthier: *Puccini* (Paris, 1961)

C. Paladini: *Giacomo Puccini* (Florence, 1961)

G. Gatti-Casazza: *Memories of the Opera* (New York, 1973)

L. Pinzauti: *Puccini: una vita* (Florence, 1974; repr. as *Giacomo Puccini*, Turin, 1975)

E. Siciliani: *Puccini* (Milan, 1976)

W. Weaver: *Puccini: the Man and his Music* (New York, 1977)

C. Casini: *Giacomo Puccini* (Turin, 1978)

H. Greenfeld: *Puccini: a Biography* (London, 1981)

A. Valleroni: *Puccini minimo* (Ivrea, 1983)

M. Girardi: *Puccini—la vita e l'opera* (Rome, 1989)

M. Sansone: 'Verga, Puccini and *La lupa*', *Italian Studies*, xiv (1989), 63–76

D. Schickling: *Giacomo Puccini: Biographie* (Stuttgart, 1989)

R. Giazotto: *Puccini in casa Puccini* (Lucca, 1992)

G. Magri: *L'uomo Puccini* (Milan, 1992)

G. Battelli: 'Giacomo Puccini all'Istituto Musicale "G. Pacini' ", *BRG*, 3–21

C. Wilson: *Giacomo Puccini* (London, 1997)

D. Schickling: 'Giacomo Puccinis bayerische Geliebte', *Literatur in Bayern*, no. 56 (June 1999), 14–26

Musical studies

F. Torrefranca: *Giacomo Puccini e l'opera internazionale* (Turin, 1912)

I. Pizzetti: 'Giacomo Puccini', *Musicisti contemporanei, saggi critici* (Milan, 1914), 48–106

M. Carner: *Of Men and Music* (London, 3rd ed. 1945)

L. Ricci: *Puccini interprete di se stesso* (Milan, 1954)

Giacomo Puccini nel centenario della nascita, ed. Comitato Nazionale per le Onoranze a Giacomo Puccini (Lucca, 1958)

S. Hughes: *Famous Puccini Operas* (London, 1959, repr. 1972)

R. Leibowitz: 'L'arte di Giacomo Puccini', *L'approdo musicale*, ii/6 (1959), 3–27

C. Sartori (ed.): *Giacomo Puccini-Symposium* (Milan, 1959)

D. Vaughan: 'Puccini's Orchestration', *PRMA*, lxxxvii (1960–1), 1–14

F. D'Amico: 'Naturalismo e decadentismo in Puccini', *I casi della musica* (Milan, 1962), 284–97

W. Ashbrook: *The Operas of Puccini* (New York and Oxford, 1968, repr. 1985)

G. Tarozzi: *Giacomo Puccini: la fine del bel canto* (Milan, 1972)

L. Pinzauti (ed.): 'Giacomo Puccini nelle testimonianze di Berio, Bussotti, Donatoni e Nono', *NRMI*, viii (1974), 356–65

L. Baldacci: 'Naturalezza di Puccini', *NRMI*, ix (1975), 42–9

J. Meyerowitz: 'Puccini: musica a doppio fondo', *NRMI*, x, (1976), 3–19

L. Gherardi: 'Appunti per una lettura delle varianti nelle opere di Giacomo Puccini', *Studi musicali*, vi (1977), 269–321

S. Martinotti: 'I travagliati Avant-Propos di Puccini', *Il melodramma italiano dell'ottocento: scritti in onore di Massimo Mila*, ed. G.Pestelli (Turin, 1977), 451–509

N. Christen: *Giacomo Puccini: analytische Untersuchungen der Melodik, Harmonik und Instrumentation* (Hamburg, 1978)

J.R. Nicolaisen: *Italian Opera in Transition, 1871–1893* (Ann Arbor, 1980)

C. Osborne: *The Complete Operas of Puccini* (London, 1981)

G. Musco: *Musica e teatro in Giacomo Puccini*, i (Cortona, 1989)

H.M. Greenwald: *Dramatic Exposition and Musical Structure in Puccini's Operas*, (diss., City University of New York, 1991)

R. Parker and A. Atlas: 'A Key for Chi? Tonal Areas in Puccini', *NCM*, xv (1991–2), 229–34

H. Greenwald: 'Recent Puccini Research', *AcM*, lxv, (1993), 23–50

L. Fairtile: *Giacomo Puccini's Operatic Revisions as Manifestations of his Compositional Priorities* (diss., New York University, 1995)

M. Girardi: *Giacomo Puccini: l'arte internazionale di un musicista italiano* (Venice, 1995): Eng. ed. trans. L. Basine as *Giacomo Puccini: His International Art* (Chicago and London, 2000)

S. Döhring: 'L'italianità di Puccini', *VBP*, 203–10

J. Maehder: 'Il processo creativo negli abbozzi per il libretto e la composizione', ibid., 287–328

J. Budden: 'La dissociazione del *Leitmotif* nelle opere di Puccini', *BRG*, 453–66

M. Conati: 'Puccini drammaturgo: strategie dell'emozione', ibid., 399–424

H.M. Greenwald: 'Character Distinction and Rhythmic Differentiation in Puccini's Operas', ibid., 494–515

A. Mandelli: 'Puccini e alcune proposte: dal vecchio Finale del primo atto della "Manon Lescaut" alla scomparsa dell'Aria dei fiori' in "Suor Angelica" ', ibid., 467–93

C. Orselli: 'Puccini e Strauss: la platea e il giardino', ibid., 529–45

G. Salvetti: 'Come Puccini si aprì un sentiero nell'aspra selva del wagnerismo italiano', ibid., 49–79

D. Schickling: 'Giacomo Puccini and Richard Wagner: a Little-known Chapter in Music History', ibid., 517–28

R. Vlad: 'Puccini, Schoenberg e Stravinsky', ibid., 547–80.

V. Bernardoni: 'La drammaturgia dell'aria nel primo Puccini', *SP*, i (1998), 43–56

J. Budden: 'Puccini's Transpositions', ibid., 7–17

D. Schickling: 'Giacomos kleiner Bruder: fremde Spuren im Katalog der Werke Puccinis', ibid., 83–94

Iconographical Studies

L. Marchetti: *Puccini nelle immagini* (Milan, 1949)

G. Arrighi and others (eds.): *Mostra pucciniana*, catalogue (Lucca, 1974)

S. Puccini and G. Pintorno, (eds.): *Puccini, 30 novembre 1974–11 gennaio 1975*, catalogue (Milan, 1974)

A. Ceresa and G. Marchesi: *Puccini a casa* (Udine, 1982)

S. Puccini (ed.): *Puccini e i pittori*, catalogue (Milan, 1982)

G. Biagi Ravenni (ed.): *Una tradizione, Lucca, la musica*, catalogue (Milan, 1993)

M. Viale Ferrero: 'Riflessioni sulle scenografie pucciniane', *SP*, i (1998), 19–42

Bibliographical Studies

C. Hopkinson: *A Bibliography of the Works of Giacomo Puccini (1858–1924)* (New York, 1968)

V. Bernardoni, G. Biagi Ravenni, M. Girardi, A. Groos, J. Maehder, P. Ross, D. Schickling (eds.): 'Bibliografia degli scritti su Giacomo Puccini', *SP*, i (1998), 127–211

Locative Studies

C. Sartori: *Giacomo Puccini a Monza* (Monza, 1958)

G. Magri: *Puccini a Torino* (Turin, 1983)

S. Puccini (ed.): *Puccini a Milano* (Milan, 1989)

Specialist Publications

Istituto di Studi Pucciniani, Milan

S. Puccini (ed.): *Giacomo Puccini: lettere a Riccardo Schnabl* (1981)

—— *Puccini e i pittori* (1982)

Quaderni pucciniani, i (1982), ii (1985), iii (1992), iv (1992), v (1996), vi (1999) [*QP*]

Centro Studi Giacomo Puccini, Lucca

Studi pucciniani, i (1998), ii (2000) [*SP*]

Periodical Numbers

L'approdo musicale, ii/6 (1959)
Opera Quarterly, ii/3 (1984)

Individual Works

Le Villi

M. Carner: ' "Le Villi" ', *QP*, ii (1985),15–29
J. Budden: 'The Genesis and Literary Source of Giacomo Puccini's First Opera', *COJ*, i/1
(1989), 79–85

Edgar

F. Cesari: 'Genesi di "Edgar" ', *Ottocento e oltre: scritti in onore di Raoul Meloncelli*, ed. F. Izzo
and J. Streicher (Rome, 1993), 451–69
——: 'Autoimprestito e riciclaggio in Puccini: il caso di "Edgar" ', *BRG*, 425–52

Manon Lescaut

*Disposizione scenica per l'opera "Manon Lescaut", dramma lirico in quattro atti di Giacomo Puccini,
compilata e regolata seconda la messa in scena al Teatro Regio, Torino, da Giulio Ricordi* (Milan,
1893)
C. Hiss: *Abbé Prevost's "Manon Lescaut" as Novel, Libretto and Opera* (diss., University of
Illinois, 1967)
C. Casini: 'Tre "Manon" ', *Chigiana*, xxvii (1973), 171–217
M. Morini: 'Nuovi documenti sulla nascita di *Manon Lescaut*', programme book, Teatro
Comunale dell'Opera, Genoa (1983), 89–98
M. Girardi: 'La rappresentazione musicale dell'atmosfera settecentesca nel second' atto di
"Manon Lescaut", *ECL*, 65–82
S. Scherr: 'Editing Puccini's Operas: the Case of "Manon Lescaut", *AcM*, lxii (1990), 62–81
D. Schickling: 'Giacomos kleiner Bruder: fremde Spuren im Katalog der Werke Puccinis',
SP, i (1998), 83
D. Schickling: ' "Manon Lescaut": Giacomo Puccini's Wagnerian Opera'
S. Scherr: 'The Chronology of Composition of Puccini's "Manon Lescaut" ', *BRG*, 81–109

La bohème

E. Hanslick: ' "Die Boheme" von Puccini', *Die moderne Oper*, viii (1899), 75–85
M. Morini: ' "La bohème": opera in quattro atti (cinque quadri): l'atto denominato "Il cortile
della casa di via Labruyère" di Illica e Giacosa', *La Scala*, ix/109 (1958), 35–49
P. Santi: "Ne' cieli bigi . . ." ', *NRMI*, ii (1968) 350–8
R. Leibowitz: 'Comment faut-il jouer "La bohème" ', *Le compositeur et son double: essai sur
l'interprétation musicale* (Paris, 1971), 156–77
N. John (ed.): *La bohème*, English National Opera Guide no.14 (London, 1982)
M. Kalmanoff: 'Aria from the "Missing Act" of "La Bohème" ', *OQ*, ii/2 (1984), 121–5

D. Goldin: 'Drammaturgia e linguaggio della "Bohème" di Puccini', *La vera fenice: libretti e librettisti tra Sette e Ottocento* (Turin, 1985), 335–74
A. Groos and R. Parker (eds.): *Giacomo Puccini: 'La bohème'* (Cambridge, 1986)
J. Maehder: 'Paris-Bilder: zur Transformation von Henry Mürger's Roman in den "Bohème"—Opern von Puccini und Leoncavallo', *Jahrbuch der Opernforschung*, ii (1986),109–76; It. trans. in *NRMI*, xxiv (1990), 403–56
W. Drabkin: 'Il linguaggio musicale de "La bohème" ', *VBP*, 97–120
L. Alberti: 'Puccini "regista": "La bohème", *BRG*, 369–98
A. Groos: 'TB, Mimì, and the Anxiety of Influence', *SP*, i (1998), 67–81
P. G. Gillio: 'La Barriera d'Enfer: documenti sulla gestazione letteraria del Quadro III de "La bohème" nell'archivio di Casa Giacosa', ibid., 95–123

Tosca

L. Torchi: ' "Tosca": Melodramma in tre atti di Giacomo Puccini', *RMI*, vii (1900), 78–114
R. Leibowitz: 'Un opéra contestataire: "Tosca", *Les fantômes de l'opéra* (Paris, 1972), 261–74
N. John (ed.): *Tosca*, English National Opera Guide no.16 (London, 1982)
G. Gavazzeni; 'La "Tosca" come campione esecutivo pucciniano', *QP*, i (1982), 77–88
S. Döhring: 'Musikalischer Realismus in Puccinis "Tosca", *AnMc*, xxii (1984), 249–96
M. Carner (ed.): *Giacomo Puccini: "Tosca"* (Cambridge, 1985)
G. Paduano: 'La scenica scienza di Tosca', *Strumenti critici*, ii, (1987), 357–70
A.W. Atlas: ' "Tosca": a New Point of View', *Studies in the History of Music*, iii (1992), 249–73
D. Burton: *An Analysis of Puccini's "Tosca": a Heuristic Approach to the Unknown Elements of the Opera* (diss., University of Michigan, 1995)
——: ' "Tristano", "Tosca" (e Torchi)', *BRG*, 127–45
M. Sansone: 'La dimensione decadente nel libretto di "Tosca" ', ibid., 111–25

Madama Butterfly

M. Bortolotto: 'La Signora Pinkerton: uno e due', *Chigiana*, xxxi (1976), 347–63
M. Carner: *"Madama Butterfly": a Guide to the Opera* (London, 1979)
J. Smith: 'A Metamorphic Tragedy', *PRMA*, cvi (1979–80), 105–14
C. Garboli: 'Sembra una figura di paravento: "Madama Butterfly" ', *QP*, i (1982), 91–102
M. Peretti: *"Madama Butterfly" i–iv tra variante e ricomposizione: appunti e rilievi per una realizzazione scenica e musicale* (diss. University of Venice, 1983)
N. John (ed.): *Madama Butterfly*, English National Opera Guide no.26 (London, 1984)
K.G.M. Berg: 'Das Liebesduett aus "Madama Butterfly": Überlegungen und Szenendramaturgie bei Giacomo Puccini', *Die Musikforschung*, xxxviii (1985), 183–94. It. trans., *VBP* 39–96
P. Ross: 'Elaborazione leitmotivica e colore esotico in "Madama Butterfly", *ECL*, 99–110
J. Smith: 'Musical Exoticism in "Madama Butterfly", ibid., 111–18.
A.Groos: 'Return of the Native: Japan in *Madama Butterfly/Madama Butterfly* in Japan', *COJ*, i/2, (1989), 167–94
A.W. Atlas: 'Crossed Stars and Crossed Tonal Areas in Puccini's "Madama Butterfly" ', *NCM*, xiv (1990–91), 186–96; It. trans., *VBP*, 183–202
A. Groos: ' "Madama Butterfly", the Story', *COJ*, iii/2 (1991), 125–58
——: 'Lieutenant F.B. Pinkerton: Problems in the Genesis of an Operatic Hero', *PW*, 161–92
——: 'Da Sada Yacco a Cio-Cio-San: il teatro musicale giapponese a "Madama Butterfly", *La Scala* (1995–6), no. 3, pp. 71–89.
——: ' "Madama Butterfly"; il perduto atto del consolato', *BRG*, 159–68
——: 'Luigi Illica's Libretto for "Madama Butterfly" ', *SP* ii, 190–204

D. Schickling: 'Puccini's 'Work in Progress': the So-Called Versions of "Madama Butterfly" ', *ML*, lxxix (1998), 528–37

La fanciulla del West

P. Levi: *Paesaggi e figure musicali* (Milan, 1913), 468–83
C. Zangarini: 'Puccini e la "Fanciulla del West" ', *Propaganda Musicale*, nos. 1–5 (1930), 197ff
G. Gavazzeni: 'Nella "Fanciulla del West" protagonista è l'orchestra', *MO*, i (1958), 545–52
A. Marchetti: 'La variante che Puccini non azzeccò', *RMC*, xxix/3 (1976)
G. Dotto: 'Four Hands: Collaborative Alterations in Puccini's "Fanciulla", *JAMS*, xlii (1989), 604–24
A.W. Atlas: 'Belasco and Puccini: "Old Dog Tray" and the Zuni Indians', *MQ*, lxxv (1991), 362–98
———: ' "Lontano-Tornare-Redenzione". Verbal Leitmotives and their Musical Resonance in Puccini's "La fanciulla del West" ', *Studi Musicali*, xxi (1992), 359–98
M. Girardi: 'Il finale de "La fanciulla del West" e alcuni problemi di codice', *Opera & Libretto*, ii (1993), 417–37
D. Schickling: 'Ferdinando Martino Librettista e collaboratore', *SP* ii, 205–19

La rondine

C. Sartori: ' "Rondine" o l'evasione della guerra', *MO*, i (1958), 484–8
A. Mandelli: 'Il caso "Rondine" ', *RMC*, xxiv/1 (1971), 13–20

Il trittico

R. Allorto:' "Il trittico" ', *La Scala* (1958–9), 409–13
J. Leukel: *Studien zu Puccini: "Il Trittico"* (Munich and Salzburg, 1983)
M. Bianchi: 'Il caso "Trittico": vitalità di morte e declino della vita', *BRG*, 215–29.

Il tabarro

R. Mariani: 'Fermenti e anticipazioni del "Tabarro" ', *MO*, ii (1959), 56–60
H. Greenwald: 'Puccini, "Il tabarro" and the Dilemma of Operatic Transposition', *JAMS*, li (1998), 521–58.

Suor Angelica

A. Damerini: ' "Suor Angelica" in una rara bozza di stampa', *Giacomo Puccini nel centenario della nascita* (Lucca, 1958), 84–8
R. Allorto: ' "Suor Angelica" nell'unità del "Trittico" ', *MO*, ii (1959), 409–13
J.C.G. Waterhouse: 'Ciò che Puccini deve a Casella', *RMC* xix/4 (1965), 8–13
F. D'Amico: 'Una ignorata pagina malipieriana di "Suor Angelica", *RMC*, xix/1 (1966), 7–13
H.M. Greenwald: 'Verdi's Patriarch and Puccini's Matriarch: Through the Looking-Glass and what Puccini Found there', *NCM*, xvii (1993), 220–36
A. Mandelli: 'Il ricupero dell Aria dei fiori' in "Suor Angelica" ', *QP*, v (1996), 161–72

Gianni Schicchi

G. Setaccioli: *Il contenuto musicale del "Gianni Schicchi" di Giacomo Puccini* (Rome, 1920)
M. Morini: 'Momento del "Gianni Schicchi", *MO*, ii (1959), 98–104

Turandot

M. Lessona: ' "Turandot" di Giacomo Puccini', *RMI*, xxiii (1926), 239–47

P. Revers: 'Analytische Betrachtungen in Puccinis "Turandot", *Österreichische Musikzeitschrift*, xxxiv (1979), 342–51

M. Girardi: ' "Turandot": il futuro interrotto del melodramma italiano', *RIM*, xvii (1982), 155–81

S. Bussotti and J. Maehder: *Turandot* (Pisa, 1983)

N. John (ed.): *Turandot*, English National Opera Guide no. 27 (London, 1984)

J. Maehder: 'Studien zum Fragmentcharakter von Giacomo Puccinis "Turandot" ', *AnMc*, xxii (1984), 297–379. It. trans. *QP* ii (1985), 79–163

G. Gavazzeni: ' "Turandot", organismo senza pace', *QP* ii (1985), 33–42

N. Grilli: 'Galileo Chini: le scene per "Turandot" ', *QP* ii (1985), 183–7

A. Pestalozza: 'I costumi di Caramba per la prima di "Turandot" alla Scala', *QP* ii (1985), 173–81

I. Stoianova: 'Remarquez sur l'actualité de "Turandot", *ECL* (1985), 199–210

W. Ashbrook & H.S. Powers: *Puccini's "Turandot". The End of a Great Tradition* (Princeton, NJ, 1991)

A.W. Atlas: 'Newly Discovered Sketches for Puccini's "Turandot" at the Pierpont Morgan Library, *COJ*, iii/2 (1991), 171–93

P. Korfmacher: *Exotismus in Giacomo Puccinis "Turandot"* (Cologne, 1993)

K.-M. Lo: *"Turandot" auf der Opernbühne* (Frankfurt-Bern-New York, 1994)

J. Maehder: ' "Turandot" and the Theatrical Aesthetics of the Twentieth Century', *PW* (1994), 254–67

K.-M. Lo: 'Giacomo Puccini's "Turandot" in Two Acts. the Draft of the First Version of the Libretto', *BRG* (1997), 239–58

J. Maehder: ' "Turandot" e "Sakuntala". La codificazione dell'orchestrazione negli appunti di Puccini e le partiture di Alfano', Ibid., 281–315

H.S. Powers: 'Dal padre alla principessa: roriorientamento tonale nel Finale primo della "Turandot" ', Ibid., 259–80

Orchestral Music

M. Elphinstone: 'Le prime musiche sinfoniche di Puccini: quanto ne sappiamo', *QP*, iii (1992), 115–62

Songs

M. Kaye: *The Unknown Puccini A Historical Perspective on the Songs (including little-known music from "Edgar" and "La rondine")* (New York-Oxford, 1987)

Juvenilia

A. Cavalli: 'Inediti giovanili di Giacomo Puccini', *Giacomo Puccini nel centenario della nascita* (Lucca, 1958), 105–11

'I frammenti pucciniani di Celle', *CrP* (1976), 16–34

Index

Aalst, J. van, 427, 454, 461, 462
Abeniscar, Carlo, 188
Adam, Adolphe, *Giselle*, 41
Adami, Giuseppe, 91, 95, 335–36, 345, 348,
    350, 370, 371, 373, 383, 422, 423, 427,
    430, 432, 440, 459, 472, 495, 496, 497
Ader, Rose, 433, 497
Albert, Eugen d', 421
Aldrich, Richard, 304
Alfano, Franco
    Risurrezione, 444
    Sakuntala, 178, 444
    Turandot completion and, 440, 445, 446,
        467–71, 496
Amato, Pasquale, 303, 333
Angeli, Alfredo, 337
Angeloni, Carlo, 6, 497
Anima allegra (Quintero), 335, 339, 444
Ashbrook, William, ix
Atlas, Allan W., 308
Auber, Daniel, *Manon Lescaut*, 90

Balfe, Michael, *Bohemian Girl, The*, 134
Barbican Centre (London), 445
Barini, Giorgio, 391
Barrère, Camille, 193
Barrière, Théodore, 135
Basevi, Abramo, 14
Bassi, Amedeo, 333
Bates, Blanche, 291, 303
Bavagnoli, Gaetano, 378, 444
Bayreuth Festival, 64, 88, 131, 338–39
Bazzini, Antonio, 15, 20, 22, 24–25, 26, 47,
    61, 113, 131, 497–98
    Turanda, 425
Beecham, Sir Thomas, 378, 421, 426
Belasco, David, 226, 228–29, 288, 290–91,
    293, 306, 307, 495, 498
Bellaigue, Camille, 179
Bellini, Vincenzo
    Linda di Chamounix, 70, 93
    Puritani, I, 69
    Sonnambula, La, 69, 93
Berel, Paul, 280
Berlioz, Hector, 30, 349
Bernhardt, Sarah, 87, 151–52, 181
Bettoli, Parmenio, 187

Biaggi, Girolamo, 39
Biagini, Carlo, 24
Bizet, Georges
    Carmen, 19, 39, 59, 70, 84, 90, 289, 478
    Pêcheurs de perles, Les, 71
Boccherini, Luigi, 2, 6, 47
Bohème, La (Leoncavello), 137, 179–80, 183–
    84, 186
Bohème, La (Puccini), 34, 65, 107, 131–80,
    185, 188, 193, 218, 221, 222, 238–39,
    316, 359, 382, 384, 389, 405, 426, 437,
    464, 495
Bohème Club, 147–48
Boito, Arrigo, 14, 21, 27, 40, 41, 43, 46, 48,
    133
    Mefistofele, 20, 24, 26, 95, 180, 276
    Nerone, 441–42
Bracco, Roberto, 334
Brunelleschi, Umberto, 440
Buonamici, Giuseppe, 142
Burke, Tom, 378
Burzio, Eugenia, 333
Busoni, Ferruccio, 20, 425–26, 459, 460
    Arlecchino, 425
    Turandot, 425, 450

Cahier rose de Madame Chrysanthème, Le
    (Régamey), 230
Caimmi, Gemma, 278
Callas, Maria, 222
Cameroni, Felice, 40, 58
Camossi, Baron Fassini, 427, 449, 451, 456
Campanini, Cleofonte, 239, 242, 275, 281,
    333
Capuana, Luigi, 39, 93, 390
Caracciolo, Juanita, 437
Carducci, Giosuè, 65, 290
Carignani, Carlo, 7, 9, 47, 66, 67, 147, 151,
    300, 420, 498
Carlo Rosa Opera Company, 185
Carner, Mosco, ix, 34, 55, 130, 178, 216,
    222, 249, 257, 276, 382, 404, 416, 462,
    478
Carré, Albert, 190, 242, 262–63, 285, 498
Caruso, Enrico, 187, 197, 227, 233, 242, 275,
    281, 288, 301, 303, 337, 498–99
Casa Lucca, 22, 38